Creating Emotionally Safe Schools

A Guide for Educators and Parents

Jane Bluestein, Ph.D.

Health Communications, Inc.
Deerfield Beach, Florida

www.bcibooks.com
www.janebluestein.com

Library of Congress Cataloging-in-Publication Data

Bluestein, Jane.
Creating emotionally safe schools : a guide for educators and parents / Jane Bluestein.
p. cm.
Includes bibliographical references (p.) and index.
ISBN-13: 978-1-55874-814-9 (trade paper)
ISBN-10: 1-55874-814-8 (trade paper)
1. Schools—United States—Safety measures. 2. School environment—United States—Psychological aspects. I. Title.

LB2864.5 .B58 2001
371'.001'9—dc21

2001039136

Publisher: Health Communications, Inc.
3201 S.W. 15th Street
Deerfield Beach, FL 33442-8190

R-10-05

Cover design by Lisa Camp
Inside book design by Dawn Grove

Contents

Acknowledgments

I am deeply indebted to a great number of people who had a hand in the creation of this book. Many of these individuals are doing remarkable work with kids and schools. I am a better person for knowing them. My sincerest thanks to:

Titus Alexander, for circulating my survey among his numerous connections and for his encouragement from too far away.

John Barnes, principal of Mountview Elementary, Taupo, New Zealand, for the tour of his school and the research by Louise Stoll.

Michele Borba—whose intelligence and academic thoroughness are always inspiring—for understanding the complexity of the topic, for the benefits of her books and research, and for being a reliable and honest sounding board.

Nathaniel Branden and Robert Reasoner, for their invaluable work in self-esteem research, and for their willingness to provide information, input and feedback.

Terry Burik, for her feedback and fact checking, and understanding of some of the more difficult concepts in this book, and the balance she added to body and soul.

Chiropractor Jennifer Burns and receptionist Ruth Hanckel, who literally and figuratively held me together when I was writing for far more hours per day than my back or neck could reasonably handle.

Sherri Davidman, who stood by me from day one, for her help with the initial outline (organizing over two hundred index cards, each with a different topic), her insights that helped me process where I was heading and what I wanted to say, for supporting me when I was most frazzled and frustrated.

Matthew Diener and Terry Burke, at Health Communications, Inc., who saw the potential for a new book on emotional safety in schools in a casual breakfast conversation about what was, at the time, my latest workshop topic.

Lisa Drucker, editor extraordinaire, whose encouragement, feedback and support kept me going through some of the most difficult parts of the writing process.

Josh Freedman, of *6 Seconds,* for a ton of resources and information on emotional intelligence.

Laura Gutman, for simply understanding the process of writing (and the phenomenon of writer's block), for listening and for helping me sort out my various computer dilemmas when they occurred.

Carla Hannaford, whose books and workshops filled in a number of large gaps in my understanding of body and brain, whose work provided me with a neurological context for behavioral and academic issues with which I had been working, and whose positivity and friendship helped me when my energy, faith and optimism would falter.

Jane Hersey, of the Feingold Association of the United States, who provided me with a wealth of information about food allergies and environmental sensitivities.

John Hoover, for the great work he's doing and for the information he sent on bullying.

Mark Ita, program developer at the Bureau of Education and Research, for sharing his wisdom, and a wealth of quotes and stories, with me.

Kathy Jenkins, for all those dinners early on, which helped me focus my efforts and stay on task, and for a great deal of additional information on emotional intelligence.

Eric Katz, for reading the first draft of this book and for his valuable feedback, and even more for his continual stream of encouraging correspondences that kept me going when this project most threatened to overwhelm.

Eileen Kupersmith, lifelong friend, for circulating my survey and sending me all those wonderful articles.

Tom Lagana, for circulating my survey in his newsletter.

Beth Langley, for her help during the International Montessori conference in Myrtle Beach, which allowed me to work on this book when I wasn't presenting.

Robert Low, for reading the story of *The Animal School* to me over the phone so I could make sure I had an accurate version to work from.

Anne Marshall, for her follow-up information on Project 81, and for being a part of my teaching world since my preservice days.

Marvin Martinez, for his insights and knowledge, which provided me with a great deal of background information on gangs.

Evelyn Mercur, for all the articles she sent and her nonstop encouragement throughout this project.

Jeff Michel, Dan Boyd and Susan Schrader, Clinton (Iowa) High

School, and the many other teachers worldwide who invited or allowed me into their classrooms.

D. Moritz, for the resources and articles she sent, and for circulating my survey among her students and colleagues.

Barbara Muller-Ackerman, for sharing the survey among her contacts in ASCA, and for all of the wonderful responses—and new friends—I encountered as a result of her efforts.

Erica Orloff, brilliant line editor, who always manages to find far more punctuation and usage errors than I would on my own, and whose technical expertise with the vagaries of the English language allowed me to focus on content, rather than on certain grammatical issues for which I may always be somewhat impaired.

Aili Pogust, for the materials she sent, for her wit, wisdom and vast conceptual knowledge, for fact checking, for reality checking and for helping me stay grounded and balanced, even more than she knows.

William Purkey, for his brilliant work in the area of invitational education, and for the materials he shared with me on this topic.

Jordan Riak, of Parents and Teachers Against Violence in Education, for an immense amount of information on corporal punishment.

Neža Rojko, my interpreter in Slovenia, for the survey responses from her students.

Linda Sorenson, for the cards and gifts and good cheer that kept me going during the most challenging parts of this project, and for the immense contribution she made to this book with her own experiences, the dozens of articles she forwarded to me and other contributors she sent my way, and for being the first to read and give feedback on what I was writing.

Karen Baker Stilson, for the information on health, nutrition and ADHD.

Debra Sugar, for sharing the benefits of her own research, experiences and explorations in the areas I explore in this book, and for her feedback and support on my ideas, my outlines and intentions as I was getting started, and throughout the time I was researching and writing.

Jerry Tereszkiewicz, best buddy and husband, for taking care of innumerable details for this book, for transcribing hours of interview tapes, for doing all the cooking and laundry while I was holed up with my laptop, and for tolerating, for months at a time, the immense clutter of printouts, index cards and piles of books throughout the house.

Clairr Waldeman, for her friendship, vision and support.

Mary Sue Williams and Sherry Shellenberger, occupational therapists, for everything I learned in their workshop, through their book and over lunch, about how different nervous systems "run."

Emily Wirth and Omar Durant at Albuquerque Public Schools Library Services, and Barbara Piper for their efforts to find a copy of *The Animal School* for me.

Additionally, I wish to thank:

The Rio Grande Library System, which saved me enormous amounts of time and effort with their on-line search and request processes. Also a special thanks to the various librarians who found specific information or resources I never would have been able to obtain on my own.

The English department at York Suburban High School, York, Pennsylvania, which, back in 1967 to 1969, taught me how to organize references and notes for research. With over a thousand resources for this book, I never would have made it past page one without the benefit of what I learned there.

The students I observed and interviewed, particularly those with whom I was privileged to work in various settings during the past two years.

The dozens of people who took up the cause and, in a true testament to the power of e-mail forwarding, passed copies of the original survey along to everyone in their database! I know the survey made the rounds throughout various state departments of education and organizations, and I thank all of those who were anonymously involved in this process.

In addition to the contributors mentioned above, the following individuals offered informaion, personal experiences and observations, all of which were tremendously helpful in shaping the text and direction of this book. Although I was not able to include the valuable input provided by each contributor, I am immensely grateful to each individual who took the time to talk with me, or send me letters or e-mails describing their experiences. (I have included the names of all whose initial contacts with me could be confirmed by mail or e-mail.) All contributors whose comments were used in this book have been mentioned in the text by name, unless they requested that this material be used anonymously.

Adam Adache
Andrea Adamko
Faizah Alkaff
Brad Allison
Rudenia S. Anderson-Howard
Duane Askew
Hamidah Bahashwan
Claude Beamish
Charles Beckman
Betty Begeal
Richard Biffle
Janet Bliss
Michele Borba
Nathaniel Branden
Roberta Braverman
Dee Brumley
Dave Bruno
June Buchanan
Joanna M. Carman
Christina Chapman
Linda Classen
Paul Clements
Lynn Collins
Peggy Corcovelos
Laurie A. Couture
Cheryl Cramer
Elizabeth Crary
Sherri Davidman
Beverly Davies
Verónica de Andrés
James R. Delisle
MaryAnn Dockstader
Mimi Doe
Gordon Dryden
Gail Dusa

Nadia M. El-Ockaili
Mary Faber
Vic Fantozzi
Cheryl Ficocello
Charles Fisher
Rich Forer
Pat Freeman
Erica Frenkel
Nancy Garner
Stephen L. Gessner
Tanya Gjerman
Bob Gritt
Laura Gutman
Carla Hannaford
Rachel Harnish
Stephen Haslam
Betty Hatch
Faye Hauwai
Dave Hinckley
Sandra Holgate
John Hoover
Barry Hopping
Victor Allan C. Ilagan
Mark Ita
Henry Jackson
Kathy Jenkins
Cori Jennings
Carol Nevius Jones
Eric Katz
Nicole Kauffman
Ron Kimmel
Nancy Knickerbocker
Hannah Kohl
MaryAnn Kohl
Marcia Kons
Olga Sraj Kristan
Jason Krueger
Rob Krueger
Krista Kuisma
Adam Kupersmith
Sandra LaRose
Joseph Lancaster
Beth K. Lefevre
Patti Lentz
Elaine Lesse
Ross Logan
Lynn Lowrance
J. D. Lucas
Ginny Luther
Loretta Maase
Anne K. Marshall
Marvin Marshall
Wendy Marshall
Christina Mattise
Linda McGinnis
Pat McIntosh
Rita Mercier
Braulio Montalvo
D. Moritz
Jenny Mosley
Barbara Muller-Ackerman
Sandy Murray
Gary Myrah
Anne Naylor
Barbara Nielsen
Wendy Paser
Aili Pogust
Jean Potter
Michael Powers
Patti Present
Stanka Prezlj
Susan Priest
William Purkey
Sione Quaass
Pam Quatse
Andy Quiñones
Rico Racosky
Robert Reasoner
Jordan Riak
LeAnn Risch
Michèle Robin
Jan Rogers
Frances Ryan
Annick Safken
Sumiati Said
Laurie Schmidt
Mike Selby
Betsy Sheets
Lindsay Shepheard
Mary Ellen Simmons
Linda Sorenson
Emily Stafford
Maria Stewart
Judy Stillwell
Bob Sugar
Debra Sugar
Sharon Tandy
Paul Tegg
Jerry Tereszkiewicz
Steve Tipps
Aaron Trummer
Kathryn Tyler
Kathi Foster Vlcek
Hazel Walker
Robin Warnes
Tonia Wechsler
Shayna Weitz
Marla West
Bonnie Wilde
Mary Sue Williams
Barbara Y. Wills
Elizabeth Wolfe
Barbara Yerby
Bobbie Yoakum

Introduction

School safety involves first and foremost an atmosphere of safety; a climate in which children feel comfortable and happy.

Carol Silverman Saunders[1]

Much like the air we breathe, school climate is ignored until it becomes foul.

H. Jerome Frieberg[2]

We must not, in trying to think about how we can make a big difference, ignore the small daily differences we can make.

Marion Wright Edelman

The person who removes a mountain begins by carrying away small stones.

Anonymous

I never set out to do a research-based book. When I agreed to write about improving the emotional climate in schools, I was thinking in terms of my previous work with discipline and motivation, places in which emotional safety is often compromised. But the more I played with the concept, the clearer it became that my original vision was limited at best. I decided I needed to step back a bit to get a better sense of how big this issue really is, and what it truly involves. I started with what seemed, at the time, a fairly simple question: *What affects emotional safety in schools?* The answers overwhelmed me. Once I started digging, I realized that just about *anything* can have an impact on school climate, and can affect how safe schools feel to the people who spend their days there, kids and adults alike. Every door I opened led to other doors, or down hallways I never expected to explore. Factors I hadn't counted on, things like the weather or the color of the classroom walls, begged consideration. After a few months, I had an outline with more than 140 topics, any of which could have become a book (or two) on its own.

The more I learned, the more I realized that, if nothing else, this book would have to reflect the enormity of the topic it intended to explore. This goal came, in part, because regardless of what we intend our schools to accomplish, the emotional climate is going to be an issue. The need for the "big picture" also emerged in response to the number of programs and reactions which targeted isolated parts of the problem with little or no regard for the context in which the problem occurred—a process not unlike trying to solve a puzzle with only a few of the pieces.

Yes, safety is about guns and violence, but this book isn't just about getting kids to and from school in one piece. School safety covers a much broader landscape than the violence that has served to get our attention. It's also about learning styles, social interactions, discipline policies and bathroom breaks. It's about the roles schools assume in our society and the demands of an economy our students will ultimately serve. It's about the brain, body and heart. It's about content and assessment, and it's about desirable-but-unmeasurable commodities like curiosity and creativity. It's about the discrepancy between the goals we express and hold in our hearts, and the priorities we actually honor with the behaviors we practice and the choices we make. It's about people and communities and values and politics, and the interesting dynamics that can happen when we overlay these factors on diverse academic imperatives.

Now, certain limitations are inherent in taking on a topic this big and multidimensional. For one thing, representing what is essentially holographic in its complexity according to the linear constraints of a book format led to certain decisions and necessary compromises. Painting a picture as broad and complete as possible required a fair amount of condensing, as well. This often resulted in a fairly superficial treatment of topics to which dozens of books could be—or indeed have been—devoted. In collecting data for this project, I found, learned and received far more information than I could share here. There were a number points I intended to mention but couldn't work in, mountains of notes and hundreds of facts and examples that never made their way into text, and details and dimensions of nearly every topic that simply went beyond the scope of this book. I beg that these decisions be considered within the context of this project, and with regard to my intention to present as many different factors affecting emotional safety as possible.

(I've included an enormous number of resources in the chapter notes, as well as a recommended resources section, to assist readers who may be interested in exploring specific topics in greater depth. I also have a growing number of links to relevant resources and information available on my Web site.)

I attempted to present a number of different viewpoints and occasionally used resources with which I disagreed (or which recommended approaches that would sacrifice safety in the name of some short-term outcome) simply because they offered a perspective or specific bit of information I found valuable. Some of the factors I address are rather controversial, with equally passionate advocates on either side of the issue. My own biases tend to coincide with the degree to which any practice supports emotional safety, and all of the topics I examine, including many of the traditions we have come to expect in education, are presented in terms of their impact in this regard. Many of the areas I explore suggest the need for a great deal more attention and study, particularly those policies and practices whose impact on emotional safety may never have been considered in the past. With regard to critical incidents that sometimes occur in a school, my position has always been one of prevention. While I certainly do not dismiss the need for crisis or situational response preparation, I do not address specific trainings or strategies here.

A few other things bear mentioning. Regarding references and citations: I sometimes list more than one reference for a particular fact or paragraph. I found a great deal of overlap in the data I researched and in many cases, the information cited appeared in a number of sources. I didn't want to overwhelm with a zillion footnotes, although I tried to make sure that specific ideas that were unique to a particular resource were represented appropriately. In addition to the more traditional citations, many of the notes contain anecdotal information that didn't fit in the regular text. In some cases, these notes offer additional details about the text, the process or related findings; in others, the notes provide some interesting tangents, observations or personal experiences.

When it came to referencing people—whether authors, interviewees or survey respondents—I chose to omit their titles or degrees, partly because I did not always know what they were. I did not wish to represent anyone inaccurately, either by mislabeling or by omission. Similarly, whenever I mentioned a resource by name, I attempted to identify the person by the nature of his or her work. In most cases I was limited to a word or two, such as "author," "school counselor" or "educator," for example. Unfortunately, these descriptions fail to do justice to the number of talents (or job titles) that many contributors possess. In some instances, I did not have much to go on, and extrapolated the reference from the text or bio of a written article, or from the content from an anonymous interview or conversation. I made every effort to represent individuals—and their positions at the time they recorded or reported the information—as accurately as possible. Any errors are unintentional.

While this book focuses on American schools, and its history, traditions and programs, I received and included feedback from teachers and students throughout the world. I did this for several reasons. For one thing, I have been fortunate to work in schools outside the United States and, for better or worse, have found that the problems and concerns I see at home are reflected, to varying degrees, wherever I work. Second, the basic need for emotional safety, and the various neurological, social, instructional, emotional and physical considerations involved, are similar, if not identical, throughout humanity. Kids in Malaysia have no less a need for safe learning environments than kids in Missouri, and I found the observations and experiences from overseas to be highly relevant to schools in the United States.

In referencing specific individuals, I typically omitted the name of the school, district or organization with which they are affiliated, unless the text would have lacked clarity had that information been left out. In all cases, I used the names of contributors (from survey responses or interviews) except for those instances in which the individual specifically requested anonymity, or in the case of comments from workshop participants whose names I never learned. Most often, these contributors are identified only as "one middle-school teacher" or "a counselor in one elementary school," for example. In other cases, particularly when their comments are used as quotes at the beginning of a chapter or section, I assigned a single first name. Likewise, I have not identified schools—or, for the most part, their locations—when reporting specific events or experiences. Whether positive or negative, I found that most of what I observed, read or heard about were things that one might expect to find in any number of school settings.

Despite the existence of strong, solid programs and enormously positive, dedicated and successful individuals within school systems throughout the world, a great deal of the statistics and stories I encountered were downright depressing. I included certain negative incidents, trends and traditions because it would have been impossible to write about the things that impact the emotional climate of a school and ignore their existence. They are certainly not meant to characterize all teachers or education in general nor suggest cause for despair. But our awareness of these "land mines," as well as their potential to compromise emotional safety (and thereby compromise learning and cooperation) is an important step in making the changes that will ensure a more positive school climate.

In the end, I would hope that what comes through is a sense of optimism, rooted in a firm belief in our ability to create the kind of school environments and relationships that will support learning, achievement and cognitive growth, as well as compassion, creativity, resiliency, commitment, productivity, self-understanding and self-actualization. For as bleak as the picture can sometimes appear, I believe that there has never been a better time to be involved in education. We have never known as much as we know now—about how people learn and think and interact, or the variety of factors that can affect these behaviors. This knowledge comes with a certain accountability, however, for where our predecessors may not have reckoned with the outcomes of the traditions they imposed or followed, we have come to know the cost of ignoring their potential impact. The world has changed and, in many cases, "business as usual" no longer serves. It is my hope that this book will help us get a better sense not only of where we are or how we got here, but also of the many promising paths that lie ahead.

Part I

Dimensions of a Very Big Picture

Teaching is the greatest act of optimism.

Colleen Wilcox[1]

The starting point for a better world is the belief that it is possible.

Norman Cousins[2]

Before the beginning of great brilliance, there must be Chaos.

I Ching[3]

There's this commercial that begins by showing us a couple standing on top of a medieval castle. As the camera pulls back, we see that the castle is actually a chess piece on a board between two people riding on a train. The camera pulls back again and we see the train through the window of a house—as part of a model railroad in a family's playroom. Each time we step back, we realize that each world-within a world, complete as each seemed to be, is simply a part of a much larger reality. The continual change in perspective is both breathtaking and brilliant, an important reminder about how an image or event can, in fact, simply be one small facet of a far bigger reality.

So it goes with safety in schools. Invariably, whenever somebody brings up the topic, the conversation seems to focus on one little piece of this reality—usually a headline-grabbing instance of violence or vandalism. However, if we apply the "big picture" perspective to this issue, we realize that the more extreme breaches of school safety are only a very small part of a much larger issue. Unfortunately, despite our efforts to place these events in a larger context, we can easily become fixated on the intensity of a terrible moment, and lose our sense of the multidimensional reality in which the events occurred. When our focus narrows to one little corner of the picture, we can neglect the millions of other details that are also a part of the scenery, much less how all these threads are woven together or how they impact one another. When our vision fails to go beyond the immediacy of the moment, our lack of perspective can have serious consequences, particularly with regard to how we respond to the event and the solutions we propose.

Certainly safety is an issue whenever violence occurs. But it's also an issue for the student who is terrified of being called on to give an oral presentation to the class, the kid anticipating being harassed or attacked on the playground, or the child who knows that the end of the school day leads back to an unstable or violent home. It's an issue for kids who don't test well, for kids who learn best by touching and moving, and for kids whose strengths lie in areas the schools neither assess nor value. It's an issue for the child nobody notices, the child nobody will play with, the child who camouflages inadequacy with a string of achievements. It's an issue for nonlinear thinkers and for students who look "different." It's an issue for parents, particularly when their kids are having—or causing—problems. And it's an issue for teachers who are faced with increasing demands and inadequate resources, who are held accountable for many things over which they have very little control, and whose work often fails to generate the respect and compensation it deserves.

For the most part, we haven't placed a very high premium on providing emotionally safe learning environments for kids or adults. Even when we acknowledge its importance, safety can easily become a casualty to traditions that make assessment more important than learning, or those that value subject matter over students. We sacrifice safety when we fail to notice a child in distress or ignore the hurtful behavior of one student to another, when we use tests or grades to punish, when we ignore academic needs in favor of curricular mandates. Emotional safety is undermined by sarcasm, impatience and contempt, by "gotcha" discipline policies, by pop quizzes, by teachers who yell or humiliate.

In fact, emotional safety is an issue in so many situations in school that any improvement effort worth its salt—as narrowly focused as that effort may need to be—will necessarily take the "whole" into account. Yet how often are policies implemented or programs adopted before their potential impact on the emotional climate of the school is taken into account? It's one thing to expect our schools to produce every type of outcome under the sun—from higher academic performance to good citizenship—and quite another to create the type of environment in which these reasonable expectations can actually unfold. In the absence of a safe learning environment, a great deal of energy is expended in an effort to *create* safety, self-protecting by any means necessary, and not always in the most constructive ways. Learning is undermined and teaching is far more difficult than it needs to be. So we deal with the symptoms and react to the events, but until we quit dancing around the core issues and the dynamics that keep feeding the beast, we will continue to be disappointed when quick-fix surface solutions fail, one after the other—or make the problems even worse.

So here's the deal: Let's look at the big picture and some of the factors that play into making a school climate what it is. And let's look at some of the ways that kids and adults need to feel safe before we zero in on one little corner of the room and imagine that if it's clean, the rest of the house will be just fine. Yes, it's big, but it's doable. Maybe all we need to do is step back and take in the immensity and complexity of it all, for therein lie potential and magnificence. And in the end, what could be more worthwhile?

1 What Safety Is

I have this recurring nightmare: I'm back in high school and I can't get out.

Ruthie

I was a slow reader and a slow answerer. My learning style didn't "work." I was terrified. I never understood anything right.

Sheryl

Of course I'm right-handed. I went through three years of school with my left hand tied to my desk.

Martin

Forty-five years later, there are two words that still strike an icy fear in my heart: gym class.

Ron

I was never afraid of my teachers, unless I didn't know something. Or forgot my book. Or came late. Or made a mistake.

Hallie

Excerpts from various survey and interview responses to questions about emotional safety in respondents' school experiences.

It's 1999, right before Thanksgiving, and I'm sitting down to breakfast with the Sunday paper. I reach for the comics and the color supplements, which is where I normally start, but I can't get past the headlines: *Deming Girl Dies.* A thirteen-year-old middle-school student in southern New Mexico is now dead at the hands of a classmate, shot in the back of the head in the lobby of the school. On page two, a story about a boy the same age in Palmdale, California, dead after a fistfight in which he hit his head on the sidewalk. On the following page are details of the Texas A&M University bonfire tragedy, which killed twelve and injured twenty-seven. I haven't even been at the table ten minutes, and I've gotten a very strong message over and over in the first three pages of our local newspaper:[1] Our schools are not safe.

We read and hear much about death and violence in schools, even though fewer than 1 percent of all violent deaths of children occur on school grounds.[2] In fact, assuming we can trust the numbers, schools are safer for children than their homes or communities.[3] And yet, what gets the greatest attention and the widest coverage? Even the U.S. Department of Education's Annual Report on School Safety, which affirms that "the vast majority of America's schools are safe places," focuses much of its reporting on crime, substance abuse and violence.[4] These statistics, and the stories we see in the papers and on the news, are important and valuable for bringing attention to the need for safety in schools. My concern is that these resources, understandably, perhaps even necessarily, work from a definition of safety that is deceptively narrow.

I don't think we can expect to see sensational media accounts any time soon of the student who is berated for a wrong answer or the child who is teased and humiliated by her peers, unless, of course, these events end in violence. And while no one would presume to compare the relative traumas of a scolding to a shooting, make no mistake about it, these and countless other interactions compromise and erode the emotional climate in schools on a daily basis. These incidents, and the hundreds of other situations, techniques and exchanges that do not support basic safety needs, may be harder to spot, document or measure, but they deserve our attention, and they deserve to be taken seriously, for they, too, leave scars. It's easy to get caught up in the extreme events we have witnessed, as well as the finger-pointing and hand-wringing that occur in their wake. But the headlines also point to a host of other serious, if grossly subtler, problems, and as far as emotional safety goes, we've got bigger fish to fry.

In a hierarchy of more than two dozen human needs compiled from the works of Abraham Maslow, Alice Miller, Andrew Weil and William Glasser, "safety" is number two, just above basic survival needs, like food and shelter.[5] The need for safety—and I want to stress that I am talking about emotional and psychological safety, as well as the absence of physical threat—is so basic and so important, that unless this need is met, all other higher-level needs, like the needs for belonging, success and purpose, to name a few, become extremely difficult to satisfy or achieve in healthy ways. Oh sure, most of us become masters of adaptation, and anyone who spends much time with kids with a history of not feeling safe can probably reel off a long list of behaviors and attitudes used to compensate. But this is hardly the same as learning, inquiring and relating, much less self-actualizing, and few parents or educators would suggest that we should be satisfied with compensation.

We react to tragedy wanting to know *why,* but I want us to start asking different questions before another tragic event occurs. For the moment, at least, I'm far more concerned with how schools *feel,* and if kids—and their teachers—are not looking forward to school each day as an exciting and enriching opportunity to meet their higher-level needs, I want to know what we can do to make it right. I want to know how kids and grownups are treated in school, and the degree to which all are (and feel) valued. I want to know what kinds of opportunities exist for *all* students, not just for learning, but for success, as well. I want to know how we're listening, and how we let kids know they're worth listening to. I want to know how we're supporting personal and social development, and teaching kids ways to deal with problems and hurt feelings without hurting themselves or anyone else. I want to know, if I walk into your classroom as a student, if I will be welcome there, regardless of my previous grades and test scores, my appearance, my personality, my learning preferences or how much I love your subject area. As counselor Barbara Wills reminds, "Emotional safety is in the eye of the beholder. A place can be very safe, but if the student perceives it not to be, it isn't."

The good news appears in the form of new research, new technologies and new programs, and the fact that schools throughout the world are starting to examine and address issues that go beyond the academic concerns that have grabbed the lion's share of our attention in years past, often to the exclusion of other, equally important dimensions of human growth and development. Much of the research I uncovered and many of the people I interviewed point to large numbers of individuals who are working very specifically on quests that will ultimately contribute to advances and improvements in emotional safety, whether or not that was their initial intention. And I have seen much evidence to suggest that as we strive to eliminate the emotional, psychological and even instructional injuries that children sustain in schools, we're going to see fewer and fewer headlines of horrifying violence, despite numerous other influences that could, indeed, lead children in that direction.

I pray that we never see another tragedy in school and would give anything if the ones that have occurred could somehow, magically, be reversed. However, if recent violence forces us to step back and see how much this issue of safety really involves, if it bring us closer to a willingness to look at all of the factors that impact a child's life and learning (including the factors we don't want to look at or don't believe we're equipped to handle), if it can somehow take us from blame and regret to prevention and solutions, then perhaps some greater purpose will have been served.

Defining Emotional Safety

> *Emotional safety means seeing a smile on my teacher's face the first day of school instead of a list of rules that is taller than my arm is long. It means being able to use the word "Neanderthal" instead of "caveman" and not be made fun of because my vocabulary is too big. It means being able to go through the lunch line without fear of somebody grabbing for my money or my cupcake. It means having a teacher who hands back papers privately instead of reading the grades out loud as I pick up my test. Emotional safety is unconditional acceptance of me. Emotional safety, first and foremost, allows me to wear my natural face instead of a fake one. . . .*
>
> James Delisle
> professor, Education Foundations

> *Emotional safety means being able to act, think and feel without fear. It means being able to try activities I'm not good at, express my ideas without censoring them, display my feelings and have them respected, question my teachers without fear of punishment. It means being able to take risks and expose what I don't know. It means being valued for who I am instead of how well I perform. It means that the teacher is interested in me, in my ideas and experiences. . . .*
>
> Debra Sugar
> school social worker

A 1992 districtwide survey of over sixty-five thousand students in Houston showed that 48 percent either "disagreed" or "strongly disagreed" with the following statement: "The school is a safe place." Another 12 percent did not know.[6] These are troubling statistics, and even without knowing the specifics of what the surveyors or students meant by the word "safe," we have to wonder about the climate, not to mention the amount of learning going on, in an environment in which a sense of safety is not a given for more than half of the student population. Yet what do these numbers really tell us?

The emotional climate in a school is the complex product of a huge number of factors. How a school feels on any given day can be influenced by, among other things, the condition and design of the physical structure itself, the community in which the school exists, the mental health of the adults in the building, the functionality of the families whose children attend, the political and economic climate of the area (and the world), the calendar, the weather and, perhaps, the position of the planets, as well. Local events can have a big impact: A community crisis, a mean-spirited editorial or even a winning football season can add a layer of energy to a school environment that hits you the second you walk in the door. Add to that the normal social hierarchies, power dynamics, agendas and unresolved personal issues that are present any time you have a group of people living or working together, and you've got a pretty volatile mix of factors, all of which have an impact on how people work, learn and interact in this environment.

In order for schools to be safe—and to *feel* safe to all concerned—a number of things have to happen, and, for the most part, they have to happen together. It's much like a recipe that requires a balance of certain ingredients, procedures, techniques and sanitary considerations, none of which can be ignored or left out without affecting the final product's appearance, taste or nutritional potential. The number of factors in this instance can be more than a bit overwhelming, to be sure, but if this book does nothing else, I want it to shine some light on just how much this issue entails by addressing as many of these factors as possible.

Author-educator Rita Mercier defines a safe school as one that "creates an environment for learning that allows all students, regardless of mental ability, language, culture, race, appearance, physical differences, economic status, emotional, social or physical challenges, learning styles, temperament, gender or any other diversity, to achieve their maximum potential—academically, personally and socially."[7] Or consider the definition by elementary-school counselor, Christina Mattise, created for her developmental guidance program in which emotional safety means, "I have the right to be myself and to have the freedom to learn, work and play without having my heart, my head or my body hurt."[8]

Both of these definitions say a lot more than it might seem at first glance, and encompass a large number of safety factors. Let's go a little deeper now, and look at what these specific factors include. For the purposes of this book, I use the term "emotional safety" to refer to a classroom or school environment in which students can experience *all* of the following:

- a sense of belonging, of being welcomed and valued; being treated with respect and dignity; acceptance
- the freedom to *not* be good at a particular skill, make mistakes, forget, or need additional practice and still be treated respectfully and with acceptance
- encouragement and success; recognition; instruction, guidance and resources according to need (developmental, cognitive, affective, modality) and *regardless* of need
- having one's own unique talents, skills and qualities valued, recognized and acknowledged
- understanding and clarity (about requirements and expectations); predictability (consistency of follow-through); freedom from arbitrary, indiscriminate and unexpected punishment and reactivity
- the freedom from harassment, intimidation (including labeling, name-calling, ridicule, teasing, criticism or contempt) and threat of physical harm from adults or peers
- the freedom to make choices and influence one's own learning, pursue personal interests and control various factors in the process of learning (such as content, presentation, media, location; social context; direction; specific assignments or approaches) based on personal needs and preferences
- the freedom from prejudice, judgment and discrimination based on physical characteristics and general appearance; religious, racial or cultural background; sexual orientation
- the freedom from prejudice, judgment and discrimination based on academic, athletic, creative or social capabilities; modality or learning-style preferences, temperament, hemispheric dominance or similar profiles
- the freedom to have (and express) one's own feelings and opinions without fear of recrimination

Clearly, "creating safe schools involves much more than preventing crimes on campus," as Mercier points out. In the absence of the full complement of the above safety factors, two important "saving graces" exist. One is having some place to connect—that is, having a person or a group who values and respects you, having some in-school relationship in which you can truly be yourself, or, as survey respondent Dee Brumley suggests, "having someone or a lot of someones there to support you when you fall or just need a shoulder to cry on."

The second is having some place to succeed. Many of the individuals who shared their experiences with me said that they created a sense of safety in school simply by doing well there. Others claimed that they never would have made it through school if they hadn't had one class or subject area—often music, art, theater or gym—that offered them a refuge from difficulties in other classes, mistreatment or rejection by their peers, or a miserable home life. Certainly other valuable support influences exist, in and out of the educational environment, and differences in personality and temperament will make some children far less vulnerable than others to unsafe conditions and interactions. But sadly, many children go through years of school without even these most minimal of benefits.

Safety for Adults in Schools

I've had to break up a number of cliques among my faculty. I want everyone to feel that they belong in our school community.

elementary-school principal

Nobody messes up with a kid in the classroom because they want to. But that's what we hear about. The lack of respect and constant criticism, from everyone from parents and upper administration to the media, make it hard to support one another if our morale is shot.

middle-school teacher

Emotional safety means I can live and work without being afraid of threats of abuse. It means parents have the right to know and participate in their child's education, but do not have the right to physically or verbally abuse the administration or staff in the school system. And it means administrators have the right to effectively manage, but not through fear, intimidation, bullying, anger or any other manner that would be construed as emotional intimidation or harassment.

Ross Logan
elementary-school counselor

If schools are going to be safe for kids, they're going to have to be safe for grownups as well. Teachers, counselors, administrators and other school staff whose energy is distracted by a need to self-protect for any reason just don't have as much to offer kids as adults who feel secure, supported and valued in their positions. Interestingly, the factors listed in the definition of emotional safety for children are quite similar to those required by educators, counselors, administrators and other adult staff, with the important addition of the ability to experience the following:

- respect for one's professional judgment and opinions
- respect for one's teaching or management style, special skills and preferences, especially when these can be matched and accommodated with appropriate grade level, subject area or administrative assignments, partner and schedule configurations, room and environmental configurations, resources and materials
- requests and respect for one's input, and a feeling of being included in decisions that have a direct impact on one's well-being and ability to perform effectively
- a sense of being valued and respected by the administration, policy makers and community
- a sense of being supported (backed up) by the administration, policy makers and community

Just imagine the climate in a school in which all of these safety factors were present! Indeed, there are currently many, many people committed to making sure that these conditions are in place in their own classrooms, schools and districts. The point is, once we agree that creating schools that are emotionally, socially, intellectually and psychologically safe—in addition to being physically safe—is a goal worth pursuing from a comprehensive and inclusive standpoint, we can start working to achieve the specifics described by the various safety factors above. The more of these factors that exist in any school setting, the more we increase the odds of schools not only being safe, but also feeling safe—all the time and for all students and adults. As we will see, establishing such a climate has enormous implications for student learning, success and behavior.

It's reassuring to know that kids are, in fact, safer in school than anywhere else, but it's well worth whatever commitment it will take to stack the odds in favor of an emotionally safe school climate, because statistics are, after all, just numbers. For even if there's only a billion-in-one chance of a house falling on you from out of the sky, if you are that "one," it can really ruin your day.

2

The Heart of the Matter: Feelings and School

We can no longer turn away from the emotional fabric of children's lives or assume that learning can take place isolated from their feelings.

Linda Lantieri and Janet Patti[1]

Consciousness and emotion are not at odds with each other. This is not a zero-sum game.

Bernard J. Baars[2]

In the whole process of my education, from elementary school to university, there was never any effort to take care of emotional security or spiritual development of students.

Olga Sraj Kristan
elementary-school gym teacher

Emotion is the chief source of consciousness. There is no change from darkness to light, or from inertia to movement without emotion.

C. G. Jung[3]

When the emotions and body were dissociated from cognition, rational behavior and learning were absent.

Carla Hannaford[4]

Educating the mind without educating the heart is no education at all.

Aristotle[5]

I remember a conversation between a young teacher and a twenty-year veteran, which occurred in the faculty lounge during my first year of teaching. The younger woman was relating a story about some playground incident the previous day, and how the anger and hurt feelings had trailed back into the classroom with the kids, disrupting anything she tried to do all afternoon. "Well, there's your problem," the veteran admonished. "I tell my students they have to check their feelings at the door when they walk into *my* room. We're there to learn!"

I'll never forget that expression: "Check their feelings at the door." How does *anyone* do that? I couldn't even model that for my students, much less demand it of them. And even if this goal was possible, was I really called to teaching simply to preside over a roomful of emotionless drones silently doing their lessons? Okay, so maybe during those first few weeks of my teaching career, "emotions" seemed to be the only thing happening in my room, and I was often reminded that my class was far behind the other fifth-grade classes in the school. But there had to be some middle ground, some way to make the emotions and intellect work together, a way to address emotional needs and still get some work done.

Throughout my preservice and subsequent training, I heard messages about appreciating and teaching to the whole child, and about valuing the affective dimensions of education. And while I have found that most teachers can agree that "we teach students, not subjects," I have also noticed that philosophical ideals clash with reality when the cognitive and the measurable become the defining elements of what schools are all about. Most often our effectiveness as a teacher is measured by our students' test scores or how quietly the kids can stay on task. Few teachers are evaluated for their ability to listen or support a child in crisis, and often efforts to accommodate emotional and other learning needs are seen as frivolous, "soft" or distractions from the "real" job of teaching content. While perhaps less true today than when I started teaching, in many settings, the emotional dimensions of education are either relegated to some separate, unintegrated, spare-time activity or ignored altogether—at least until some fairly severe event occurs.

In a 1999 article, University of Oregon professor Robert Sylwester writes, "John Dewey began this century with an eloquent plea for the education of the whole child. It would be good for us to get around to it by the end of the century."[6] Clearly, attention to affect is nothing new. Back in the 1950s, Abraham Maslow took a long look at what made successful and well-adjusted people tick, focusing on the ingredients of health and well-being, instead of the more traditional emphasis on illness and failure. Another important shift began in the next decade, when Carl Rogers's work "asked us to put the learner or client in focus," rather than the teacher or psychologist.[7]

In the early 1970s, terms like humanistic education, self-concept development and values clarification started popping up in teacher-education programs. In addition, new studies brought a growing awareness of right- and left-brain capabilities and how the hemispheres worked together. This was all part of a burst of new research and activity in the field of affective education, with contributions like George Brown's "confluent education," John Grinder and Richard Bandler's neurolinguistic psychology, Rita and Kenneth Dunn's work with individual styles of learning, and Lawrence Kohlberg's research in moral development.[8]

In the late 1970s and early 1980s, the aging counterculture met the recovery movement and as far as emotions went, all bets were off. Feelings became the by-word, self-disclosure the new social currency. Old wounds became public spectacles and emotional trauma became a connecting ground, in some cases the very foundation of relationships. Sadly, emerging affective priorities sometimes translated into classrooms that ended up being too unstructured, undisciplined or touchy-feely for their own good (not to mention the good of the students).[9] Perhaps the extremes we witnessed during this time were simply a backlash to a tradition of repression and marginalization of the emotional. For even as far back as ancient Greece, convention elevated the cognitive and rational over the emotional, with more recent proponents like Piaget, Freud and Kant urging the development of cognitive skills in isolation from emotional development.[10]

The end of the twentieth century saw us swing closer to center, supported by advances in brain research and the social sciences, evident in the works of individuals such as Daniel Goleman and Howard Gardner. Now more than ever, we are looking for balance. We know that we need something more diverse and multidimensional than a tradition which, according to author Anne Wilson Schaef, reflects the myth that "it is possible to be totally logical, rational and objective."[11] Sylwester maintains, "We know emotion is very important to the educative process because it drives attention, which drives learning and memory." In a school setting, however, emotions are more difficult to understand and regulate than the more rational aspects of learning. Too much or too little emotion is typically defined as misbehavior, although feelings may find acceptable outlets in the arts, PE, recess and extracurricular programs.[12]

Recent findings in a variety of fields suggest that logic, rationality and objectivity aren't all they're cracked up to be, at least not on their own. Researchers and observers are recognizing the influence of emotion, learning styles and modality preferences, feelings and relationships, and even intuition on a pupil's ability to learn and function. This is a good thing. In fact, we've all seen what happens when we try to pretend that these factors don't exist—or don't matter. Even when the results aren't worthy of a headline, the cost of separating emotion from logic is high. Sure, we simplify school management and evaluation when we attempt to eliminate the affective from our considerations, "but we've also separated two sides of one coin and lost something in the process."[13] Eric Jensen, an expert in brain-compatible teaching strategies, concurs: "Nearly every part of the brain is involved in almost every activity."[14] Ignoring one "part" or another is pointless and counterproductive, particularly in an instructional environment.

The experience of emotions is universal. Studies across various cultures have identified six primary emotions—joy (or pleasure), fear, sadness, surprise, disgust and anger—that are shared by people throughout the world. Feelings are a part of being alive, so much so that the English language contains over six hundred words relating to affective experiences![15] The fact is, the learning we so much want to happen in our classrooms cannot and will not happen without emotions. Author Diane Schilling suggests that we think of emotions as the ignition switch and fuel for learning.[16] Clinical professor and child psychiatrist, Stanley Greenspan, claims that what makes the mind grow are not cognitive experiences, but "types of subtle emotional exchanges . . . In fact, emotions, not cognitive stimulation, serve as the mind's primary architect."[17] To use the recipe metaphor again, our tradition of focusing on the development and use of the intellect to the exclusion of all other dimensions is like trying to make a stew with nothing but salt. And telling kids to "check their feelings at the door" makes about as much sense as telling them not to breathe while they are in class.

3

Safety: It's a Brain Thing

Unless we begin to build awareness of neurological and emotional development into the education programs, we will continue to fail to educate large numbers of children even after holding them for thousands of hours in the classroom.

Stanley Greenspan[1]

I remember being yelled at, teased and embarrassed in class and not hearing or remembering a thing afterwards. Even though I looked attentive, all my energy was tied up with replaying the event, rehearsing a response, feeling indignant, scared or hurt, or trying not to cry.

Juanita

People can survive, but while they are in a survival mode, they certainly cannot think about working toward bettering their lives.

Sandi Redenbach[2]

In January 1994, I was spending the night at a friend's house, up the hill from a busy freeway in southern California. In the middle of the night, my bed started to shake, hard enough to awaken me. I interpreted the motion in the context of my previous experience: "Boy, that's one big truck!" I thought. In the next second, I heard my friend shout with great urgency, "Get in the doorway *now!*" Only at that point did I realize that we were in the middle of what turned out to be the Northridge earthquake.

In that moment, I experienced a dramatic—and immediate—change in my body. My heart rate went through the roof, I was soaked with sweat, my stomach tightened into a ball and my legs felt like they were made of rubber. As long as I believed that the motion I felt was caused by freeway vehicles, I felt no threat and experienced none of the symptoms that emerged the second my brain perceived that my safety was threatened. Once the survival override kicked in, I was *in* the doorway. I didn't deliberate, nor did I consciously choose to go there. My body simply reacted, a "flight" response that didn't bother to check in with the rational part of my brain before simply getting my body where it thought it would have a better shot at staying safe. What an amazing process, and a clear example of how our brains are wired to ensure our survival. All higher-level functioning must pay homage to this service, and thinking and learning will always take a back seat to surviving. If we're going to talk about the emotional climate of a school and the impact it has on a student's capacity to learn, we need to take a look at the role of the brain, because this is where the perception of safety, as well as our reaction to threat, begins.

"In a very real sense," writes author Daniel Goleman, "we have two minds, one that thinks and one that feels."[3] He considers these to be two different ways of knowing, one more rational and analytical, the other more impulsive and emotional, even illogical at times. Nonetheless, the parts of the brain that comprise these "two minds" actually work together, along with the body, mind and emotions, in a linked system.[4] Although earlier research tended toward a more compartmentalized view of the brain parts and their functions, current findings make it clear that even basic survival functioning involves more of the brain than was previously imagined.[5]

The basic systems that make up the brain have evolved from the most simple to the most complex: the brain stem, the midbrain, the limbic system (which is typically included as a part of the midbrain or used to describe primary midbrain functions) and the cortex.[6] Although described separately, these different systems are interdependent, working together in all we do, with their primary purpose being to ensure our survival. The brain stem, sometimes referred to as the reptilian brain, controls basic and essential functions such as heart rate, respiration, body temperature and digestion. This area develops between conception and approximately fifteen months of age. This part of the brain also houses the perceptual register—technically, the reticular activation system or RAS—which screens incoming data picked up by our senses. The RAS filters impulses according to strength and significance, and regulates our attention and alertness to the outside world, allowing us to ignore thousands of bits of sensory information that are available in our environment, but not particularly important or meaningful. The brain stem influences behaviors geared to personal survival and to species preservation, such as social conformity and hierarchies, territoriality, bluffing and deceptive behavior, and ritualistic and instinctive attention-getting behaviors. Learning attitudes are tradition-bound and resist change, innovation and risk taking; formal reasoning does not occur at this level.[7]

The midbrain, sometimes called the early mammalian brain, develops between fifteen months and about four years of age and includes the amygdala, thalamus, hypothalamus, hippocampus and other related areas in the brain. This is the part of the brain most often equated with feelings and emotional responses to sensory stimuli. The midbrain regulates the immune and autonomic nervous system, appetite and sleep, and is critical to memory and learning. It is involved with our hormones, social bonding and relationships, our values and priorities, contextual memories and our sense of meaning, and is critical to the transfer from short- to long-term memory. In terms of learning, repetition appeals to the midbrain area, as does sensory-motor, visceral and emotionally charged input.[8] This part of the brain was thrust into the spotlight with Goleman's book, *Emotional Intelligence,* where its influence on our reactions—particularly those extreme reactions which bypass more rational centers in our brain when we are under severe threat or stress—was illustrated. It's also an important player when it comes to the impact of emotional safety, or its absence, on learning and behavior.

The cortex is a part of the cerebrum, or neo-mammalian or upper brain, which begins to develop around age four. The cortex covers the cerebral hemispheres in a wrinkled, gray layer about six cells deep, and may be referred to as the cerebral cortex, neocortex or gray matter. We often equate the cortex with intellect, although it also controls speech and language, creativity, problem solving, planning and muscular movement, as well. This is where rational thinking, intellectual and abstract thought, visualization, reflection, innovation and creativity take place, the part of the brain that craves novelty, challenges, change and new ideas.[9]

The cortex—the thinking part of our brain—is inextricably linked to the feeling part of our brain. It's the part of our brain that "allows us to have feelings about our feelings," where we gain insight into why we feel the way we do and determine what we're going to do about it.[10] The cortex is where we gain an understanding of what we perceive, although not all of our perceptions make it to the cortex before we act on them. Under threat, the midbrain simply reacts faster than the more analytical cortex, even though it may not be particularly well-informed. In fact, rational thought may not catch up to limbic responses until long after we have exhibited the behaviors the midbrain has inspired. Interestingly, a threat does not need to be real to trigger a fight-or-flight response—as long as it is perceived as real, the outcome will be the same. To illustrate, a few months after Northridge, I was staying in a motel in a small town in western Nebraska. At some point in the middle of the night, a train went by, close enough to cause the whole building to shake. Before I was completely awake, I found myself standing, trembling, in the doorway to the bathroom, at which point, the more rational part of my brain nudged my limbic system with a gentle reminder that this was, after all, Nebraska, and the rumbling had only been a train.

The biology behind this event starts with a signal, in this case the noise and motion of the train. The first step in the brain's initiation of an emotional response—for which my half-asleep leap to the bathroom door would certainly qualify—is the appraisal of the potential danger or benefit in a situation. The appraisal begins when incoming sensory information—from a perceived sight, sound or sensation—goes from our body's sense organs to the thalamus in the limbic system. The thalamus then signals the amygdala and sends a second signal to the neocortex. These reports are quick and factually limited, although the cortex will sift the information through several levels of brain circuits to get a better understanding of what's going on. The amygdala isn't bothered with these formalities. It is far more concerned with assigning an immediate emotional value to the incoming data. In the meantime, the hypothalamus lets the brain know what's happening inside the body and, when necessary, can initiate a fight-or-flight response, all before the cortex has a chance to say, "Hey, get a grip! This is Nebraska—that's just a train."[11]

Author Dianne Schilling assigns the amygdala and the neocortex to the roles of Sentry and Strategist, respectively. The Sentry is always scanning for trouble and reacts much more quickly than the more rational Strategist, often rushing to act without regard for consequences: "In an emotional emergency, the amygdala proclaims a crisis, recruiting the rest of the brain to its urgent agenda. . . . [This] occurs instantaneously, moments before the thinking brain has a chance to grasp what is occurring and decide on the best course of action."[12] There are times that this emotionally loaded response can be a real lifesaver, but too often the emotional charge can override a logical response that would be far more appropriate to the situation. This is what Goleman calls an emotional hijacking and it's the kind of thing we see over and over in the outbursts and explosive behavior that occur when people simply act, or react, without thinking—or before they've had a chance to determine whether the threat is, indeed, real.

The Strategist, or neocortex, is certainly capable of a more reasoned response, even in the presence of intense emotions. It can act as a damper switch and even suppress or ignore emergency signals from the limbic system when necessary (like when a parent runs into a burning building to save a child). But this process takes longer, involves more circuitry, and may be hampered by the fact that we have many more neural fibers going from the limbic system to the cortex than the reverse. Given these mechanisms, it's easy to see how an emotional hijacking can take place.[13] Nonetheless, when emotional outbursts occur in a school environment, they can seriously disrupt teaching and learning. Once during my first year of teaching, when my students were working fairly intently on an activity, one girl suddenly jumped out of her seat and over a table, pounding on one of the boys because "he looked at me." I've seen outbursts from kids in a similar settings, offense taken to seemingly inoffensive remarks, reactions that seemed excessive in the context of what was going on at the time. Here again, the limbic system holds sway.

The amygdala is "the storehouse of emotional memory," which allows us to recognize the personal significance of the signals we get from the environment. Depending on previous experience and other signals in the environment, different sensory input will elicit different appraisals in different people, and different appraisals elicit different actions and feelings.[14] A child who is afraid of dogs, for example, will behave quite differently in the presence of a large German shepherd than the child who has experienced dogs as friendly and cuddly. By the same token, I probably would not respond very strongly to a negative comment you make about my car, although I've seen people so outraged by insults about what they were driving that the exchange ended in an argument, street race or even a fight. Much as I like and appreciate the convenience and comfort it affords, my belief system doesn't tie much of my identity, worth or honor to my vehicle. Comments about its value or coolness have very little personal significance to me. (Mention my thighs, however, and it's a whole other ballgame.)

Authors Robin Karr-Morse and Meredith S. Wiley remind that "each of [the] parts of the brain is responsive to the environment, or use-dependent . . . and will be shaped by the individual's unique experience of his or her surroundings."[15] Put kids in a learning situation that is positive or neutral for them—meaning that they either love the subject, have had previous successes or have had no prior *negative* experiences—and their behavior will be quite different from the students who have a history of failure in that subject, particularly if that failure carries with it the pain of a teacher's impatience, ridicule or contempt. Even though the new placement might be appropriate, the new teacher caring and enthusiastic, and the new activities inviting, the emotional mind will make the association with anything that feels strikingly similar to previous experience, assuming the beliefs that were fashioned in the original setting will apply here, regardless of evidence to the contrary.[16] "Memory is not just a matter of rational or even verbal recall. We also have a nonverbal, essentially emotional memory, particularly for experiences, events and people that carry a strong emotional valence."[17]

And students' emotional memories can be pretty obvious at times. Anybody who's been in the teaching business long enough knows that you don't always need to look over students' cumulative records to know their history. Take, for example, the thirty-eight eighth-graders who sauntered reluctantly into my math class on the first day of school, eyeing me suspiciously, their arms folded defiantly across their chests. I hardly needed a stack of file folders to tell me that these kids had problems with math in the past (and didn't feel safe here). Their body language told me plenty.

4

Learning and the Brain

A thought can change brain chemistry, just as a physical event in the brain can change a thought.

Michael Gazzaniga[1]

Each neuron is alive and altered by its experiences and its environment. As you read these words, neurons are interacting with each other, reforming and dissolving storage sites, and establishing different electrical patterns that correspond to your new learning.

David A. Sousa[2]

Whenever we engage in new behavior, the brain remodels itself.

Michael Merzenich[3]

There is no thinking without feeling and no feeling without thinking.

Karen Stone McCown, Joshua Freedman, Anabel Jensen and Marsha Rideout[4]

Most of us begin life with the neural networks necessary for seeing, hearing, speaking and moving already in place. Along the way, we develop the networks we need to do things like read, add fractions, speak a second language, rebuild a carburetor or play the violin. How does this happen? Our brains contain about 100 billion nerve cells, or neurons. These neurons are specifically designed to send electrical messages throughout the body. They can transmit between 250 and 2,500 electrical impulses per second, sending them along an axon and across a synapse (the space between one neuron and another), to the thousands of dendrites (or branches) of a nearby cell. There are 1,000 trillion connect points between the neurons, with the number of potential pathways estimated to be more than 100 times the total number of atoms in the universe![5] This is truly a free-form network, "making all information within the brain available at any time from any point."[6]

While most of our neurons are with us at birth, neural organization is pretty limited in the beginning. But as educator Robert Valiant maintains, "It appears that learning consists of the growth of neural connections."[7] Growth in the brain, from one pound to three pounds over the first twenty-one or so years of life, occurs as the brain adds dendrites and glial (supporting) cells. From birth on, and throughout our lives, our interaction with the world offers stimulation to our brains through our senses and our movements. This stimulation causes new dendrites to grow and new connections to form, although there are many more connections in a child's brain than in an adult's. (Around puberty, the growth rate begins to slow and a process begins by which pathways most often used are secured while those no longer useful are eliminated.)[8]

As cells communicate with one another, neural pathways are formed and new connections are made. "When we first learn something, it is slow going, like beating a path through untraveled terrain," claims neurophysiologist and educator Carla Hannaford. However, continual use of these pathways strengthens them, turning them into "superhighways," and making certain patterns of thinking, knowing or behaving easier and more automatic. This process is aided by a layer of myelin, the fatty insulation along the axon, which builds up as neurons are used over and over, increasing the speed of nerve impulses across that cell. We see evidence of this process as we practice a particular skill: The more practice, the more myelin, and the more smooth and automatic the behavior. According to Hannaford, "The process of nerve cells connecting and networking is, in reality, learning and thought. As associations are made and information is synthesized, pathways become complex networks"; these networks are further altered by new experiences and stimulation.[9]

To some degree, the myelin "is laid down around the axons in genetically predetermined patterns."[10] However, different experiences create different patterns of myelination in different individuals, accounting for variances in talents and abilities between individuals. This is what makes our jobs as educators at the same time so interesting and challenging. As educational researcher Claude Beamish describes, "Since the brain is developing or myelinating over a period of so many years, teachers are dealing with students who have brains that have differing levels of development."[11] If we're only teaching to one type of pattern, what happens to the kids whose development and neural circuitry leave them out of this group?

Students will also vary in their sensitivities to sensory data—information in the environment that makes its way into perception and awareness. These sensitivities will be discussed in various places throughout this book, but for now, suffice it to say that in any learning situation, there is more than just the lesson being presented or the book being read that is getting through to the brain. There are sights and sounds, odors and physical sensations, background and foreground, that can distract or enhance concentration. In addition, many students are especially sensitive to the emotional energy in a classroom, particularly that which is subtly broadcast by the teacher's emotional state. These students can sense tension, impatience and hostility, or enthusiasm, delight or calm in others, and may be particularly adept if they come from a background of trauma or abuse, where this hypervigilance is a practiced survival skill. This element of the emotional climate in a classroom can have a strong impact on the degree to which factual information can be processed, retained and recalled.

With our senses picking up an estimated forty thousand bits of information per second (on average and over time), we'd never be able to focus on anything if our brains didn't have a built-in screening mechanism in the form of the perceptual register (the RAS or reticular activation system). This device "monitors the strength and nature of the sensory impulses and, in just milliseconds, uses the individual's experience to determine the data's degree of importance."[12] The less-important data gets blocked, as when we are able to sleep or read despite nearby highway noises. Our brains are constantly sifting data, bringing the more important elements into our consciousness for further processing, storage and recall. The more important data that gets through this filtering process goes on to what is actually another filtering system: short-term memory. One of two temporary memories, short-term memory operates subconsciously, holding information for about thirty seconds for additional evaluation. If personal experience deems the data significant, the information moves to the next level, working memory, for conscious processing. If unimportant, the incoming signal is dropped from the processing system and stays in the background, out of our conscious awareness and, because it has not been stored, is unavailable for later recall.[13]

Where educator David Sousa represents short-term memory with a clipboard, he uses an image of a work table to illustrate working memory, indicating a place where we can work with a limited amount of information for a limited amount of time, after which the data will either go into long-term storage or be dropped from memory.[14] Getting information into long-term storage for retention and later recall is one of the more important missions for most educators. And yet, for this to happen, the information has to not only make sense, but also has to have some personal relevance or meaning for the student in order to be integrated into understanding.[15] New information has to connect somewhere. Cognitive scientist Stephen Kosslyn states that data in working memory requires "an interplay between information that is stored temporarily and a larger body of stored knowledge," that is, long-term memory.[16] Decades ago, even certain proponents of expository teaching recognized the need for an "intellectual scaffolding," a place of previous personal knowledge and experience on which individuals can "hang" new information.[17] The process requires the help of the hippocampus, down in the limbic system, which converts "important short-term experiences into long-term declarative memories that are stored in the cortex."[18] If you remember, the hippocampus adjoins the amygdala, which, in this instance connects the emotional dimensions of a learning experience when new information is transferred into long-term storage. Therefore, even the most factual learning relies on the "emotional brain" for encoding and transfer to the "thinking brain." In fact, without the element of emotion, most new information will not remain in storage in the brain for long.

Memory and Emotion

What engages them emotionally takes their attention; the lesson becomes an afterthought.

Karin Frey[19]

My happiest memories are of the sheer wit employed in their teaching styles, certainly enough to keep me well awake and concentrating on the work in hand, and often provoking a roomful of laughter.

Murray White[20]

I took art and painting classes with a local artist when I was in high school. Throughout that time, painting was my refuge, a place to retreat and be safe. Although I haven't painted in years, I was in a store the other day where someone was demonstrating various art supplies. The second I got a whiff of the paint and linseed oil, the happy memory of every Saturday I spent in art class came flooding back to me.

Frieda

I learn more here, 'cause nobody yells.

Jeremy

When I was interviewing people for *Mentors, Masters and Mrs. MacGregor,* a book about teachers who'd had a positive impact on the lives of their students, I often started by simply asking, "Tell me about your favorite teacher." As contributors shared their experiences with me, I noticed something amazing. None of the stories was offered as a purely factual account. Every one was charged with emotion—feelings connected to the events and recalled, in some instances, decades later, with astonishing intensity. I saw grown men and women smile and giggle like the young selves they were describing, and quite a few became very emotional during the interview, breaking down in tears or, on a few occasions, becoming extremely agitated as they relived a more unpleasant event.

This phenomenon is an example of what brain scientist Joseph LeDoux describes as "flashbulb memory," that is, an event we recall with particular clarity and intensity because of its emotional implications.[21] We've all encountered this process any time we experience something that has a strong emotional impact on us. In fact, it is exactly this emotional impact that makes the memory so clear—and in many cases, so long-lasting. Researcher Gordon Bower describes studies in which students were given lists of adjectives to memorize. The subjects "recalled far more of the adjectives that had evoked more intense affective reactions." Interestingly, it didn't matter whether the reaction to the material was positive or negative. "Events associated with strong emotions tend to be well learned."[22]

The necessity for the emotional components of our memories is critical for nearly all forms of complex learning, including language development, abstract thinking, reading comprehension or simply gaining an understanding of "the complexities of life."[23] Greenspan notes that we use a kind of a "dual code" to interpret what our senses pick up in the environment. We label sensory perceptions by their physical properties, like bright, big, loud or smooth. But we also label these perceptions by the emotional qualities we connect with them, as we experience something as pleasing or soothing, or jarring or unpleasant. As we grow and learn, this double coding allows us to cross-reference our memories using perceptions like images and textures, and feelings as well.[24] LeDoux differentiates between emotional (or implicit) memories and the more factual (or explicit) memories of an emotional event. Explicit memories are our conscious remembrances of an event or experience, memories that can be recalled and described. While we are consciously aware of explicit memories, "implicit emotional memories may capture aspects of experiences that escape attention and awareness."[25] The interaction of these two types of memories helps create our knowledge base and belief systems, as well as the feelings we have about certain things.

Implicit memories are powerful. They can account for the feelings we get when we recall an event that had a strong emotional impact, feelings that can last long after the details of the experience have faded. In particular, our implicit memories, the feelings we have about past experiences, can be transferred to new situations—in many cases, the self-protective fear that was conditioned by previous negative events. This is the knot in the stomach we get when we drive past the restaurant in which we broke off an important relationship, when we have to interact with an angry boss who recently threatened to fire us, when we suit up for a gym class that has never afforded us much besides failure and humiliation. These memories can be particularly resilient and, in fact, without some intervention, "may represent an indelible form of learning."[26] David Sousa reminds us that "memories . . . are more than just information. They represent fluctuating patterns of associations and connections across the brain from which the individual extracts order and meaning."[27] Many of our memories are contextual or episodic, each with its own set of feelings, sensations and highly personal, experiential connections. In fact, it is exactly these things—the emotion, the sensory input and experiential dimension—that makes rich-context learning so much more effective than, say, simply memorizing content.

The context in which we learn has a significant impact on how, what and how well we recall what we learn and experience in the original situation. Go back to the context and guess what? The feelings and memories can recur with amazing intensity. Think of those times when a certain smell and taste, song, sound, color, expression or even the sensation of how the air felt transported you back to a particular moment in your life, even though the rest of your immediate environment in no way resembled the original occurrence. Or remember a time when someone asked you to recall something simple and factual—like where you were when Kennedy was assassinated or what you got for Christmas last year—and along with the cognitive data, you retrieved a host of images, feelings, sensations, stories and other information associated with that context. Little in the brain seems to be stored in isolation.

The associative properties of the brain account for the power of context as it applies to learning and remembering. Have you ever left your work area, for example, to go get something in another room, only to find that you've completely forgotten what you've gone to fetch (or even why you're in the other room in the first place)? When this happens to me, which is more often than I care to admit, I often find that I absolutely cannot recall what I needed until I go back to the place where I had the initial thought, at which point I remember, usually the moment I am in that original environment.

The impact of context—the situation or conditions present when something is learned—is sometimes referred to as "state-dependent learning." This phenomenon has been documented in studies in which students learning a list of words found that their memory for those words was better if they were tested in the same room in which they first learned the words. Additionally, "memory for words is also better if the learning and recall take place while the subject is in the same mood state."[28] The role of "state" in a student's learning is particularly evident for teachers working with adolescents returning from juvenile detention or treatment centers. These teachers have a special challenge. Many complain that although the students come back clean and sober, they also come back seemingly less intelligent than before they left. LeDoux explains, "Learning that takes place in one situation or state is generally remembered best when you are in the same situation or state." What students learn while under the influence may be better recalled when they are stoned than when they are straight![29] Many of these students need to go through a process of relearning, or regaining knowledge in their new, detoxified "state."

Obviously there's a lot more to learning and remembering than just storing facts and figures. And while recreating the appropriate "mood state" for each learner during testing may not be practical, just knowing that the students' feelings and moods can have such an enormous impact on their learning obliges us to pay serious attention to the emotional context in which new learning is presented. In fact, the climate in which students learn is so important that Gordon Dryden and Jeannette Vos recommend that we "establish the right state," that is, a climate and environment conducive to learning, as the first step for teaching anything more effectively.[30]

Fear, Stress and Learning

In a school carried on by sheer cruelty, whether it is presided over by a dunce or not, there is not much likely to be learnt. I believe our boys were, generally, as ignorant a set as any schoolboys in existence; they were much too troubled and knocked about to learn.

Charles Dickens[31]

Under conditions of extreme threat or rage, when the brain is flooded with stress hormones, the "fight or flight" human is not under the governance of the analytical cortex, the seat of rationality and wisdom.

Robin Karr-Morse and Meredith S. Wiley[32]

At a time when apparently there was such a thing as a stupid question and a leather strap across the hand for the wrong answer, school work suffered as I withdrew from active class participation.

Neil Blacklock[33]

It is difficult to pay attention to the teacher if you believe you may be assaulted in the classroom. It is difficult to concentrate if you know that you will be extorted on the way to lunch.

Chester L. Quarles[34]

Pilot, author and motivational speaker Rico Racosky frequently addresses groups of students around the country. He likes to use the analogy of the USS *Enterprise* from the *Star Trek* television series to illustrate how we deal with threats. To protect itself, the starship engages its shields, an energy field that minimizes damage from natural celestial hazards or enemy attack. There is a tradeoff, however: While these deflectors are in place, the ship may indeed be safer, but maintaining shields at 100 percent means diverting power from other ship functions, rendering certain other systems completely inoperable.[35]

Human beings are not much different. When under stress or attack, our brains have certain mechanisms that work to protect us. And like the *Enterprise,* when our "shields" are up, some of our other systems are down. As Racosky says, "A human being who lives day-to-day having to continuously 'energize his shields' for protection has little remaining energy to direct toward positive endeavors, such as schoolwork, meaningful classroom participation or healthy peer-adult interaction." We know that engaging children emotionally is an important part of the learning process, and that the emotional intensity of an event helps cement the details of that event into memory. However, not all emotional experiences in a classroom are necessarily productive ones.

The brain is pretty objective about events, comments and other stimuli in the environment. It is only our *interpretation* of this input that engages our emotional reaction. When the brain perceives an experience as positive, pleasantly exciting and fun, it releases certain chemicals that assist learning and recall. However, when input is experienced as negative or threatening, different chemicals are released, and in terms of learning and retention, these chemicals have the exact opposite effect.[36] High on educator Susan Kovalik's list of brain-compatible components of effective teaching and learning is the absence of threat,[37] and with good reason. Threat triggers survival-oriented emotions and behaviors which get in the way of learning. "Who would think of teaching mathematics to patients in a dentist's waiting room?" ask William Purkey and David Aspy.[38] Stress and anxiety block learning. Circuitry from the amygdala to the cortex create what Schilling calls "neural static, sabotaging the ability of the prefrontal lobes to maintain working memory. That's why we complain that we can't think straight when we are upset."[39]

And yet, absence of threat does not mean absence of emotional energy. Learning requires arousal, an attentional "state" that involves a sometimes tricky combination of appropriate challenge and low stress. Different tasks require different levels of arousal, and to make things more interesting, what's challenging and curiosity-provoking to one student can trigger paralyzing fear in another. Gazzaniga distinguishes between constructive and destructive stress, the former characterizing a situation perceived as challenging, and offering the potential for some personally meaningful benefit. Destructive stress, on the other hand, tends to focus on the potential for loss—whether the loss of dignity, physical safety, power, belonging, identity, respect, opportunity, success or some other meaningful entity.[40] The same goes for anxiety. At a certain level, the combination of alertness, anticipation, curiosity and fear that mix to create anxious feelings, can actually inspire "a search for new information and solutions."[41] We're talking about a value continuum, with benefit for learning on one end and interference on the other. However there are dangers here, and the fact that fear, stress and anxiety can indeed serve some useful purpose has perhaps allowed us to rationalize certain ineffective teaching behaviors or techniques as necessary, appropriate or "not really all that harmful."

Rather than quibble over "good stress" and "bad stress" and the murky territory in between, let's talk instead about a good and appropriate challenge, something that engages and encourages learners, a mix that creates an intellectual curiosity and hunger, as well. Because in the end, as Sylwester affirms, "emotionally stressful school environments are counterproductive. . . . They can reduce the students' ability to learn. . . . It's often difficult to identify the line that separates intellectual challenge from emotional stress, but we must be aware of that line when dealing with the emotional lives of students."[42] When we do cross that line, when something provokes an anxiety response in our students, they will experience physical reactions that might include sweating, dry mouth, shallow breathing, headache, pounding pulse, intestinal distress, weakness, incoordination, or "freezing" or "going blank." In addition, anxiety can provoke behavioral reactions such as panic, irritability, depression, agitation, worry, inattention, forgetfulness, distractibility,[43] not to mention disruptive and sometimes hurtful outbursts. None of these reactions enhances our students' understanding of the principles of convection, fractions or supply-and-demand, and no matter how dazzling our presentation and activities, fear and stress will block our most well-intended instructional objectives.

Here's what's happening neurologically when cognitive functioning is blocked, and why emotional safety is so important for learning. When students perceive that their safety is in some way at stake, a survival mechanism called "downshifting" occurs. If you recall, the brain's main job is sifting through and prioritizing incoming stimuli in the interest of our survival. Anything that suggests the possibility of danger, whether real or imagined, becomes a higher priority than anything else that is going on at that moment. This data is processed first, shifting our attention from cognitive processes down to the faster-acting limbic system, while more complex cerebral operations shut down. Additionally, stress hormones affect the hippocampus, inhibiting the growth of new dendrites (or actually causing dendritic branches to die off), leading to decreased memory and learning.[44] Downshifting can block our long- and short-term memories, as well as our ability to focus, "down to as low as 10 percent of our normal ability."[45] Under stress, blood flow and electrical activity in the brain changes. Jensen cautions, "You get more predictable, rote, knee-jerk reaction behaviors when the brain senses any threat that induces helplessness. Survival always overrides pattern-detection and problem solving. This fact has tremendous implications for learning."[46]

Stress shuts down the system. The culprit is a chemical called cortisol, a hormone released by the adrenal glands to protect us from danger. At one end of the value continuum, cortisol puts the mind and body on alert for danger and, at low levels, it can even produce euphoria.[47] However, Gazzaniga reminds that "stress starts to take its toll when cortisol levels shoot up constantly and remain high."[48] For at the other end of the continuum is what we see in the research on abused and neglected children in which cognitive and developmental delays correlated with a harmful imbalance of cortisol in the brain. Evidence suggests that excess cortisol leads to hippocampal damage, "causing memory lapses, anxiety and an inability to control emotional outbursts," as well as difficulty regulating attention in a classroom setting.[49] Long-term or chronically high levels of cortisol have a negative impact on blood pressure, protein metabolism and the immune system; however, even short-term elevation of cortisol in the brain can have a serious and negative effect.[50]

"Once emotions occur, they become powerful motivators of future behaviors," says LeDoux.[51] And feelings from an unpleasant event can reverberate long after the event itself. Bower explains: "A strong affective reaction after an event also causes the reactivation, rehearsal or 'mulling over' in working memory of the encoded version of that event." This pattern cements the emotional experience into memory and seems to be "especially prominent with negative, aversive events."[52] When the mind "dwells on feelings of anger, embarrassment and fear," even a great lesson is not likely to get through. To make matters worse, the inability to focus on and process content is likely to trigger or "intensify any learning problems that may be present."[53] Clearly, a stressful school environment interferes with its instructional objectives. Part of the problem is the sheer number of factors that can impact the emotional climate of a school. The list at the end of the chapter includes a wide variety of experiences students can encounter in a school environment, any one of which can interfere with their focus, commitment and memory. Understandably, students who experience a large number of these events, or who experience one or more with great frequency, are most at risk.

Stress and anxiety have behavioral, as well as instructional, ramifications. When children's ability to process information is compromised, it becomes difficult for them to attend to important environmental cues, encode and transform data and select an appropriate response.[54] Students under stress are less able to "hear" what is being said to them or asked of them, and are likely to misunderstand or distort the information they do receive.[55] The resulting downshifted, or survival, behaviors can result in additional anger, punishment, failure or alienation, a cycle of reactions that compounds the problem. (Negative reactions can come from adults or other students, depending upon the context in which the negative events—and survival responses—take place.) School becomes an increasingly difficult and unpleasant place to be. For many students, it's just easier to shut down and drop out. When we look at the potential for these avoidance behaviors alone, not to mention more serious or destructive responses, the need to minimize stress and threat in the classroom becomes rather imperative.

Stressful or Painful School Events, Experiences and Situations That Can Compromise Emotional Safety[56]

- Being assigned to complete educational material above actual ability level
- Unclear directions; directions not repeated or available if you didn't get them the first time
- Not being given enough help or assistance
- Not having resources, structure or guidelines, people or information needed to complete an assignment (before having to respond or explain)
- Not having enough time to complete work; unrealistic deadlines
- Not having enough time to think about a question or process new information
- Inability to speak the language
- Teacher's impatience, annoyance or disgust
- Overhearing teachers or other significant adults discussing you negatively within earshot (either deliberately or accidentally)
- Having a seemingly uncaring, uninvolved or weak principal
- Rarely (or never) being given any choices or input in decisions that affect you
- Not being taken seriously; being ignored or dismissed, laughed off
- Rigid application of rules and negative consequences (punishments)
- Spanking, paddling or whipping used as punishment
- Rough physical contact used deliberately or reactively to control or punish (pinching, grabbing, pushing, hitting)
- Witnessing classmates being shamed, spanked or punished
- Being punished for moving, squirming, wanting to touch things, doodling, swinging your leg, or other forms of "hyperactivity"
- Being routinely recognized or praised, threatened or punished with conditional approval from teacher or other adults
- Favoritism of some students over others
- Prejudice or discrimination (by adults or peers) based on race, ethnicity, religion or other cultural factors

- Prejudice or discrimination by adults or peers, including judgments, ridicule, rejection, devaluing, shaming, insulting, demeaning, exclusion or other negative reactions, whether verbal or nonverbal, based on body size, clothing (style, cost, value or where purchased), hairstyle, jewelry or other factors related to appearance
- Prejudice or discrimination (by adults or peers) based on abilities and interests, or on a lack of abilities or interest in a particular area
- Prejudice or discrimination (by adults or peers) based on sexual orientation, whether expressed or inferred
- Being left-handed and being pressured or required to use right hand
- Being punished long after an incident occurs
- Being wrongly accused or wrongly punished
- Being punished because of a teacher's mistakes or disorganization (lost papers, poor or inaccurate record keeping, for example)
- Inability to read or otherwise perform on grade level
- Unpredictable or inconsistent teacher behavior
- Teacher's reliance on someone else (principal, counselor, parents, for example) to handle or punish discipline problems
- "Gotcha" tests, pop quizzes, useless tests or evaluations used mainly to "catch" or punish you
- Unrealistic rules and expectations
- Demands that do not respect your developmental or ability level
- Ineffective professionals trying to help; adults who don't know how to help even if they want to (or who inadvertently make things worse)
- Not being positively recognized or acknowledged for positive behavior, achievement, effort, cooperation, etc.
- Little variety in day-to-day curriculum
- Little variety in day-to-day schedule
- Feeling little love in school in general
- Teachers' inability or unwillingness to help the slow learners or kids who need extra help
- A lack of understanding or difficulty communicating thoughts and feelings that is frequently interpreted as laziness
- Feelings of helplessness and lack of power to change an uncomfortable situation; inability to see a possible solution to a problem
- Teachers' hollering, explosive behavior
- Not being allowed to express problems openly and verbally to a teacher
- Not being allowed or able to express feelings without fear of negative reaction or consequence
- Being called names that suggest stupidity or incompetence

- Being told you're not applying yourself
- Being shamed or criticized for dropping something or knocking something over; being told you're clumsy
- Being shamed or criticized for not understanding something the first time it is explained
- Feeling afraid to share, speak up or say anything in class
- Feeling sad and lonely and not being able to share these feelings with anyone
- Feeling that no one really cares about you
- Being picked last for a game in recess or gym class
- Being bullied, harrassed or intimidated by other students
- Going to a new school, having to make new friends
- Not being supported or protected by teachers or other adults who witness other children hurting you (verbally or physically)
- Being punished, shamed or excluded from an activity because you did not respond quickly enough
- Speaking, reading or presenting in front of the class
- Being in the lowest reading group; knowing that your classmates think you are slow (not as smart as they are)
- Anticipating an activity or class you know you're not good in
- Having your grades (low or high) read in class; being seated in class according to grades
- Having to wait to go to the bathroom until the scheduled time; being denied access to the bathroom when needed
- Having to sit so long at your desk without a break that your mind and body become numb or restless
- Being shamed, ridiculed, humiliated or set up to fail in front of your peers
- Being sensitive to or intolerant of the noise, visual stimulation or movement in the classroom
- Not having any privacy
- Not being able to rest when you feel you need to
- Poor match of learning style to teaching style; learning styles and preferences not accommodated

5

Body and Mind

The body grows the brain.

Carla Hannaford[1]

If kids can't sit still and do their homework, they're held in from recess. What they need is to be going out to recess every fifteen minutes and then coming back in and having five minutes of math.

Patti Lentz
physical therapist

Although I've never been particularly athletic, it's always been hard for me to sit quietly. I would get fidgety or start to doodle on my book covers. Chewing gum helped, but of course that wasn't allowed. I was always in trouble in school.

Dale

Occupational therapist, Mary Sue Williams, plays with a small piece of putty as she addresses our class. She's telling us how movement gets sensory information into our brains. Handling the putty helps her anchor her thoughts as she speaks. As she talks, a number of teachers in the audience sit and listen, while others play with rubber bands, doodle on their papers, chew on plastic straws or unbend the coils of a paper clip, these items having been deliberately placed on our tables with instructions that they be used as needed. They're there to help the more tactile-oriented regulate our nervous systems in order to better attend to what the instructor is saying. In the meantime, I'm sitting off to the side taking notes. In between, I've brought my knitting, and as I'm listening, work on a scarf I plan to give as a Christmas present in a few weeks. Around 11:30, when attention and enthusiasm have begun to droop, Mary Sue and her co-presenter Sherry Shellenberger, pass around a bag with different types of gum. The majority jump at the treat and there is an immediate change in alterness around the room. There is a variety of attending and listening behaviors among the participants, but no question that everyone, in his or her own way, is taking in a great deal of information. How different this is from the classrooms most of us experienced as children! Despite the encouragement, many of us approach these "fidgets" cautiously at first. Even in this environment, in which their use has been encouraged, many await the *true* agenda to emerge in the inevitable command to "put that away and sit *still!*" The spectre hovers, old messages that confused movement with inattention. But the criticism and corrections never come, and eventually the message gets through: Movement in a classroom is not only acceptable, it's absolutely necessary.

Author Linda Verlee Williams notes, "Sensory and motor systems are part of both the brain and body, and their proper development is a prerequisite to successful cognitive functioning."[2] However, much like students' emotional needs, sensory-motor needs have taken a back seat to cognitive objectives in most classroom environments. Notable exceptions include the "legitimate" outlets available in physical education, art, music, shop or drama classes. But as with the affective component, attempting to ignore the demands of the body can have serious consequences in terms of a student's learning and behavior.

Long-standing tradition projects an image of a well-run classroom with teacher standing in front and a group of students, if not hunched over their papers, then sitting quietly, feet on the floor, hands folded, eyes front. Sadly, in many settings, this image is still held as the ideal, evidence of the teacher's competence and control. The upshot is another tradition, one in which movement is restricted or forbidden, supposedly in the name of learning and attending. But as we see in schools everywhere, in religious services, or in the car on long rides, children will move and fidget whether they're allowed to or not. This may explain many of the problems we see in school. "You cannot sit still and pay attention," says Mary Sue. "You can do one or the other, but you can't do both."

Movement and Learning

The sensory and motor systems form the foundations for later development of both verbal and abstract thought. Skills like reading and writing require complex coordination of these systems.

Linda Verlee Williams[3]

When we feel safe, we can play—and when we play, we can learn.

Carol Stock Kranowitz[4]

A really great teacher is somebody who lets us do other things like play cards, do sports or do arts and crafts.

Jason[5]

Our nervous systems are wired for movement. The brain makes use of the information that comes in through our senses, and this means *all* our senses. While we naturally think of our sight, hearing, taste, touch and smell as the channels through which sensory information makes its way into the brain, we also have proprioceptive senses as well. According to author, Carol Stock Kranowitz, proprioception refers to "sensory information telling us about our own movement or body position. It provides intake that helps integrate touch and movement sensations."[6]

The proprioceptive senses include the vestibular, kinesthetic and visceral systems. The vestibular system registers information such as movement, direction, speed and our body's position in space. Kinesthetic senses are related to our muscles and movement, and the visceral system takes in sensations from our internal organs. Ideally, all of these systems work together to create a multidimensional picture for the brain in any given situation.[7] Limit access to any of these sensory channels and our understanding and appreciation of an experience is likewise limited, much like trying to enjoy a delicious dessert when you're stuffed up from a cold (and can't smell) or numb from the dentist (and can't register touch, temperature or texture in certain parts of your mouth).

Movement is critical to learning and thinking. A study involving more than five hundred children in Canada showed that the children who spent an extra hour in gym class each day performed better on certain cognitive tasks than less active children.[8] Movement activates the frontal lobes of the cerebral cortex, a part of the brain involved in higher-level reasoning, planning future behaviors, problem solving, fine motor development, self-control, altruism, empathy and compassion.[9] Once again we see how parts of the brain are interrelated. In this case the cerebellum and basal ganglia, once associated exclusively with muscle movement, are tied to thinking and emotion through their connections with the frontal cortex and limbic systems.[10]

Movement helps us process and anchor our thoughts. Author Julia Cameron recommends regular, repetitive action, to "prime the well" and help us focus and unblock for future creative efforts.[11] Hannaford agrees: "Many of us have a distinct tendency to think better and more freely while engaged in a repetitive, low concentration physical task. I've heard people say they think best when they are swimming laps in a pool, taking a walk or while shaving."[12] Movement activates our mental processes and is likewise necessary for integrating new learning into our neural circuitry.[13] Movement also can help relieve or discharge stress which, as we saw in the previous chapter, interferes with learning. Many educators use simple games, jokes (laughter is movement), songs, stretching or breathing exercises, for example, to help relax and center kids before a test or new activity, when transitioning between activities (especially when the activities vary strongly in physical or emotional intensity) or after an incident or experience that has some significant emotional impact on the students. Georgi Lozanov, developer of *Superlearning,* used an integrated body-mind approach to "help dissolve fear, self-blame, cramped self-images and negative suggestions about limited abilities."[14] He found that intense left-brain learning can increase tremendously when "the body and right-brain abilities are in harmony, are lending their support, are playing in concert."[15] Specific directed movements, such as those found in Sunbeck's *Infinity Walk* or the Dennisons' *Brain Gym* exercises, not only have a positive impact on stress and anxiety, but also bring different parts of the brain into an integrated state for maximized learning efficiency.[16]

We all have ways of regulating the energy in our bodies, whether discharging excess energy, settling ourselves down or keeping ourselves awake when energy lags. These techniques allow us to regulate how fast or slow our "engines" (as Williams and Shellenberger refer to our bodies and nervous systems) are running. A certain level of arousal is necessary to detect, store and use sensory information, and for neural associations which are needed for learning, to form.[17] Different activities require different levels of arousal, or learning states. A big gap between the level of arousal necessary for a task and the actual level at which the student's "engine" is running can present a challenge. We see the effects of this "gap" when we try to put a wound-up kid down for a nap, for example, or attempt to spark an energetic response from a lethargic class on a gray, rainy day. Learning to regulate our level of alertness allows us "to attain, maintain and change arousal appropriately for a task or situation."[18]

In our class with Mary Sue and Sherry, we are asked to identify our own sensory-motor preferences and sensitivities, and to look at the kind of options we are willing to offer kids. I think of those years when I absolutely could not read a college text without a highlighting marker in one hand and a cigarette in the other. I remember a problem I could work through only after I had a chance to process it in longhand in my journal. I recall the drawings in the margins of my class notes, pens I chewed into oblivion, and my discomfort at having to sit and listen for long periods of time to even the most engaging speaker without some kind of crafts project to occupy my hands.

And I think back to my former students and evoke an image of Nicole sucking her thumb and twirling her hair, Damien counting holes in the ceiling tiles, Tyrone rocking back on his chair, DaNiece pulling fuzzballs off her sweater, Charles nodding his head in time to music only he could hear. Some part of me marvels at their creativity and resourcefulness, and I ache for the children whose efforts to self-regulate attract labels and punishment when adults do not understand.

Turn It Up, Turn It Down

When children are appropriately relaxed, the incoming and outgoing information travels through the system more completely, more accurately and more efficiently than when the body is tense and inflexible.

Clare Cherry, Douglas Godwin and Jesse Staples[19]

Breathing also affects emotions. We can calm ourselves with abdominal breathing or excite ourselves with rapid breathing.

Elaine DeBeaufort and Aura Sofia Diaz[20]

When children don't have appropriate outlets for their sensory-motor needs, or if their need for movement is restricted for a long time, it's not uncommon for them to act out in ways that can be pretty disruptive. Typically, the disruption is met with more restriction, when a few minutes of solid play, a trip to the water fountain or a chance to stretch or run a message down to the opposite end of the building can so often prevent things from getting out of hand in the first place. Physical therapist Patti Lentz advises, "We can shame kids into cooperative behavior, we can scare kids into cooperative behavior, or we can do it from the bottom up, feeding their nervous systems so that the higher brain functions are available to them."

Williams and Shellenberger suggest five categories of sensory input we can make available to help children turn their engines up or down according to the changing demands of the environment. They encourage us to help kids learn that if their engine is too low or too high, they can put something in their mouth, move, touch, look or listen to change the way their engine is running.[21] They remind us that most of us prefer one category over the others, with specific preferences within each category. (Modality preferences and learning styles will be explored in greater detail later in this book.) Options in the first category involve oral motor input—putting something in your mouth, chewing, crunching, biting, eating, drinking or sucking through a straw, for example. Another type of input is movement: vestibular or proprioceptive input, movements such as squirming, rocking back and forth, tapping your toe, stretching, bouncing or specific outlets such as riding a bike or dancing. Tactile input can include any kind of touch, like playing with your hair, fidgeting with your jewelry or desk supplies, jangling your keys or coins, petting a dog or cat (or blanket), or receiving touch (as in a massage or a shower). Visual input might involve watching fish in a tank or a sensitivity to a particular kind of light, and auditory input can include listening, singing or talking to yourself, or a sensitivity to certain noises in the environment.[22]

While many educators will acknowledge the importance of sensory-motor needs in a classroom, few are truly prepared to accommodate these needs in an instructional setting. "It's hard enough to get through the day when kids are quiet, attentive and sitting still," complained one teacher. The idea of *more* movement or expression can be unnerving at best, and rarely do teachers feel supported in their efforts. Teachers who fear that movement will compromise their ability to manage a class, or those with an extremely high sensitivity to visual distractions have the greatest difficulties when challenged to provide opportunities for kids to meet sensory needs. Those more flexible and comfortable with movement sometimes encounter resistance from other teachers, parents or administrators who can't understand why kids in their class are allowed to listen to music, chew gum or work sprawled out on the floor.[23]

There will be times when a few minutes of silliness and play will buy us *many* more minutes of attention and on-task behavior. Nonetheless, movement does not necessarily mean chaos, and part of this process involves teaching children to self-regulate without driving us, or anyone else, around the bend. There are, indeed, ways for kids to get auditory input without bothering students (or teachers) with weaker or more sensitive auditory channels, for kids to sit and fidget in parts of the room where they won't be directly in the line of sight of low-visual kids. However it's a good bet that we'll have to teach students not only which options are available, but also how to take care of their sensory-motor needs nondisruptively and make choices within a certain amount of time. We need clear boundaries and solid follow-through (discussed later in this book) regarding movement and noise with regard to the sensory inputs we are willing to allow. And we're going to need to know our own limits and tolerances if any of this is going to work, because nothing is more crazy-making than allowing something we really can't handle and suddenly going ballistic on kids who didn't think they were doing anything wrong. A little forethought and experimentation can go a long way, however, and our respect for students' sensory-motor needs, as conveyed in the options we make available for their expression, can ultimately create an environment in which these particular needs can indeed be satisfied without creating a problem for anyone else.

How We Look, What We See

Trying to learn something new can be like trying to walk through a door without opening it . . . a neurological pathway must be created before we can expect to retain or apply new learnings.

Deborah Sunbeck[24]

Intense physical activity or emotional engagement will "reset" the brain's normal rhythm patterns. This is critical because the brain is very poor at extended learning.

Eric Jensen[25]

The legacy of the "talk-and-chalk" teaching model has left us primed to overlook or misunderstand a number of behaviors kids adopt to compensate or self-protect. We have a picture of what "paying attention" looks like, often with little room to accommodate kids whose attending styles don't fit into this norm. I've often shared the story of the girl who was sent down to the counselor in her high school because she had been drawing a picture of a dragon during a history lecture instead of looking at the teacher or taking written notes while he talked. But for this girl, drawing took the place of note-taking, and as she tearfully demonstrated to the counselor, she could point to any part of the drawing and recite, almost word for word, what the teacher had been saying while she was drawing.[26] Imagine how negative, unsupportive and unsafe this classroom must have felt to this student.

One of the quickest ways to sabotage emotional safety for students is to make them wrong for the way they learn or listen. "The worst of all is being shamed for things in and around your mouth," says Mary Sue Williams. Our school culture has made this type of sensory input particularly unacceptable. I hear this from teachers throughout the world: "This one sucks her thumb." "He's always thirsty." "I'm constantly yelling at him to get rid of the toothpick." "I send three kids a day to the office for chewing gum." This can't be fun for anybody. (I could just imagine the reaction of my adult audiences if I suddenly started blasting them for chewing gum or drinking water in my workshops!) Imagine an alternative, where this belief gets turned on its head.

In various interviews, I hear about a boy who looks at the floor to concentrate on what the teacher is saying because there is visually so much going on in his class that he can't look at the teacher—and all the colors, shapes and movement around her—and keep his auditory channels open. I hear about the girl who is labeled lazy and learning disabled because she can't articulate how the noise from the class next door prevents her from thinking straight and doing her work. And Mary Sue tells of a child with certain tactile sensitivities that help explain why he goes off the deep end every time he has to fingerpaint.

Am I suggesting that we all become sensory-motor fanatics? Hardly. In fact, I'd be more concerned with someone interpreting this information as an excuse to put another set of labels on kids. What I'm asking is that, first of all, we pay attention to the fact that living organisms have certain sensory needs and that, as a part of our survival, we look for ways to get these needs met. Second, I'm entering my vote for increased sensitivity on our part to the diversity of students' learning, listening and regulating preferences (as well as our own), and that we find ways to bring as many of these options into our school environments as possible. And finally, I'm asking that we start looking at some of the behaviors we see in classrooms as clues to how kids learn instead of displays of defiance, disrespect or disability. For there's a very real chance that at least some of the moving, touching, humming and tapping might actually be signs of bodily-kinesthetic or musical-rhythmic intelligence, strengths to be channeled and developed, rather than punished, discouraged or medicated. And when we can see the potential in these signals, I suspect that these children will be treated differently—and feel far more safe—in school.

6

Monsters in the Closet: Where Children Are Coming From

While genetics do set broad parameters, actual matter in the brain is built—or not—by sound, sight, smell, touch and movement from the outside environment . . . After birth, development is an interactive process between the baby's physiology and his or her environment.

Robin Karr-Morse and Meredith Wiley[1]

There is a vital need for children to grow up in a loving, sustaining environment. The key pathways in the brain are laid down in those early years, and a warm, friendly, loving environment is critical, along with access to a safe and stimulating physical environment.

Gordon Dryden[2]

When a child's basic needs are frustrated, the result is acute pain. Often embedded in that pain is the feeling: Something is wrong with me. Somehow I am defective.

Nathaniel Branden[3]

In a perfect world, babies are carried to term by healthy mothers with little stress in their lives. Their arrival is anticipated with excitement and met with delight by family members who care, touch, stimulate, protect and nurture them. In the context of these loving relationships, newborns set about to master a set of skills they will need throughout their lifetimes. The first order of business, or what Greenspan calls "the real ABCs," involves developing the ability to regulate attention and self-comfort, to relate to others with warmth and trust, and to communicate, through gestures, symbols and sounds, eventually gaining an understanding of increasingly complex ideas and the connections among them.[4] All of these skills are learned through interactions with a loving caregiver, and if kids ever needed safety and nurturing in their lives, the need during these first few years is especially critical.

Our early relationships and interactions contribute to our developing belief system and sense of self. Verbal and nonverbal responses from caregivers shape ideas about wants, needs and feelings, and our understanding of the connections between them. Greenspan notes that this inner sense of self begins to emerge before adolescence: "After years of being dependent on what others think about them, children from about ages ten to twelve begin to develop a more consistent sense of who they are," with the beginnings of their own goals, internal values and pictures of the future being a part of this process.[5] Critical here is their earlier dependence, for if their caregivers have been nurturing and emotionally available, if they've operated with healthy boundaries, if they've been able to provide a positive sense of consistency and predictability, then a healthy sense of self can indeed emerge.

But few children grow up in a perfect world. For example, a quarter of preschool children live below the poverty rate. "The price these children pay for being poor is enormous," claims author Ron Renchler. He cites the increased likelihood of prenatal exposure to drugs and AIDS, poor nutrition, exposure to lead, low birth weight, poor nutrition, personal injuries and accidents, and abuse and neglect, each of which has the potential to be what he calls "educationally damaging."[6] Additionally, every minute, a baby is born to a teen mother.[7] While some teens do manage to navigate these waters successfully, according to a report by the Forum on Child and Family Statistics, children born to teen parents are at greater risk for a number of problems that can affect their children's behavior and performance in school and in life, including low birth weight and infant mortality. These children are also more likely than babies born to older mothers to be raised without adequate emotional support or cognitive stimulation.[8]

Imperfections in primary relationships can have an enormously detrimental impact on a child's growth. Psychotherapist Nathaniel Branden reminds, "Much of the drama of individuation and autonomy occurs and can only occur through encounters with other human beings." For children who experience terror and instability instead of safety and security, particularly in the early years, their sense of self is fractured before it is fully formed.[9] Those growing up with disapproval, shame or lack of acceptance suffer what Abraham Maslow calls a "secret psychic death," characterized by a "loss of self" and a gradual agreement with the adult's perception that the child is unacceptable.[10] When children venture out into the world with a belief system based on fear, inconsistency and negative messages about their basic value, we shouldn't be particularly surprised when they come up short, either as social beings or as learners.

While we have developed all of the basic brain cells we'll have in our lifetime by eighteen weeks in utero, the growth of the connecting structures (dendrites and synapses) doesn't take off until after birth, when we start interacting with our environment.[11] The number of neural connections increases dramatically in the first year, and while the process of building and losing neural pathways continues throughout a lifetime, the most important opportunities for learning occur during the first ten years of life.[12] Base patterns built by sensory and emotional input in the early years become a template for everything else we learn in the course of our lifetime.[13]

We are born with our brains wired for learning, and current findings indicate that infants are capable of thinking, reasoning and drawing conclusions even at birth.[14] The actual development of these skills depends on the babies' interaction with the environment; kids growing up in enriched, nurturing environments will have a developmental edge over children reared in impoverished, neglectful or abusive settings. The failure to develop cognitive and social skills is closely tied to the degree to which caregivers fail to meet the child's emotional needs at each stage of development.[15] Nurturing need not be particularly complicated: Some "interested adult attention, baby talk and an opportunity to explore" may be all most babies need to thrive and grow.[16] But how many children are denied even this most basic care?

Monsters in the Closet

I attended school from 1954 to 1967 in a small suburb of Detroit. I remember fearing tornadoes and atom bombs, but not my fellow students. . . .

Wendy Paser
prekindergarten teacher

Students dealing with the death of a family member aren't helped by increasing the amount of time spent in science class.

Reginald R. Mayo[17]

I was brought up on air force bases during my elementary-school years as my father was in the Canadian Armed Forces. Certainly my first few years in school were anxious, in part I suppose because we moved around a fair bit, but also because I didn't feel safe from corporal punishment and verbal abuse. Yelling at kids was common and seemingly acceptable, as was the use of sarcasm.

Susan Priest
certified education assistant

It was almost Halloween. I was thirteen years old, and my father was driving me home from school. I just handed him my first junior-high report card. The car skidded quickly to a halt, and I received a verbal beating of such intensity that to this day I feel sick when thinking about it. As usual, I did my courageous best: I sat there with tears running down my burning, red face, overwhelmed with fear, confusion and contempt for myself.

Mike Selby
author

I've come to believe that one of the worst things anyone ever could ever say to a child is some version of the following: *Cheer up, this is the best time of your life!* In addition to the fact that this sentence leaves few prospects for a happier future ("This is it? It's all downhill from here?"), it is extremely unlikely to be even remotely true—and thankfully so! Whether unconscious or deliberate, whether intended to comfort or simply dismiss, the fact remains that childhood is a complex, and often painful and confusing time of life. And while going to school can present a range of stresses, it's also true that all children encounter varying types and degrees of stress, in their families and neighborhoods, long before they come to school.

Since the mid-1980s, when the term was overused to the point of becoming cliché, it has become difficult to use the words, *dysfunctional family,* without evoking a certain degree of cynicism. Yet, many families are ill-equipped to accommodate a child's basic, emotional and developmental needs. Psychotherapist Robert Subby has identified four types of troubled family systems, including those with an alcoholic or chemically dependent parent, those with an emotionally or psychologically disturbed parent, those with a physically or sexually abusive parent, and those with a rigidly dogmatic parent (families with a one-dimensional and intolerant view of the world, with a strong emphasis on regimentation, order, discipline and sameness). He claims that these families operate with spoken and unspoken rules which "interfere with the normal process of emotional, psychological, behavioral and spiritual development, rules that close off and discourage healthy communication, roles that eventually destroy a person's ability to form a trusting relationship within themselves or [with] others."[18] Barbara Cottman Becnel concurs, identifying five models of parenting that leave a painful legacy for their children. She includes parents who are demanding and authoritarian, as well as those who are critical, overprotective, disengaging (not valuing their children) or ineffective (unable to provide what their children need).[19]

When we talk about stress in children's lives, what do we mean? In general terms, stress can be "anything that a child perceives as a threat . . . either to his survival or his self-image."[20] Despite a tradition that sanitizes—or at least minimizes—stress during childhood, the list of potential threats to a child's safety is a long and varied one. And any form of stress, threat or trauma can have a negative and long-lasting impact on how children grow, learn and behave.

Children's lives can be stressed by poverty, inadequate housing or poor nutrition. Stress can result from either excessive rules and punishment or excessive leniency, or from verbal, physical or emotional violence. It might stem from a relationship with a highly enmeshed or emotionally dependent parent, as well as any kind of abuse or trauma. It can come from extreme sibling rivalry or frequent moves, from parents' intense marital problems, or from a parent's prolonged illness, unemployment or death. It can involve a parent who is rejecting, uncaring or emotionally unavailable, or changes in or loss of support. It might stem from a parent's history of substance abuse, addiction or compulsive behavior, heavy recreational drinking or drug use, or a tendency to involve children in the parent's addiction (parents asking kids to get them a drink, light a cigarette for them or lie or cover for them when they've been using).

Children can experience stress when their feelings are consistently dismissed or ignored by people they value. Stress might result from infrequent or inconsistent expressions of love and acceptance. It might stem from patterns of conditional love based on the child's appearance, achievement or social competence, or how well the child takes care of the adult's needs. It might involve a disregard for personal boundaries, a lack of positive recognition or acknowledgment, or efforts to control with shame, guilt or even praise. It may appear as double standards, perfectionistic demands or expectations that are developmentally unrealistic or inappropriate. Or it may manifest in messages about the child's inadequacy or a denial of the child's reality.[21]

While much of the concern we read and hear about tends to focus on children with neglectful, unskilled or abusive parents, it is likewise true that overinvolved, demanding parents can create a great deal of stress in a child's life as well. "There is tremendous anxiety among many parents about educating their babies," write Robin Karr-Morse and Merideth Wiley. "With the growing understanding of baby brain development have come flash cards and music, math and reading programs that are being promoted as keys to a baby's success."[22] Many parents have taken the findings of brain research and assume that if sensory and emotional deprivation lead to damage, extra stimulation will make a child better than normal. This isn't necessarily so, claims author Michael Lemonick, who also expresses experts' concern that overloading young children, that is, "giving them more stimulation than they can handle, is more likely to cause them to shut down."[23] Educator Miriam Adderholdt-Elliot compares this trend to "hothousing" plants to force them to bloom early. This drive for a developmental boost, giving kids opportunities to develop skills in advance of other children their age, can lead to kids who are overscheduled and overstressed. What in moderation could be excellent activities often leads to competition, materialism, elitism, perfectionism and circuit overload.[24] Several teachers and counselors in schools serving high-end communities agree. "We're seeing more parents who are dedicated to getting their kids into every program, sports, musical, art and any other type of extracurricular program at all costs," said one counselor. But whether we're talking about parents playing Mozart or foreign-language tapes for infants *in utero* or parents who complete their children's homework projects for fear that their kids won't make it to the top of their class or get into the best schools,[25] it's a safe bet that such behavior "satisfies the parents' agenda, not necessarily the child's."[26]

Other stresses, in the form of specific life events, can also take their toll, with differing degrees of stress depending on the age of the child.[27] British researcher R. D. Coddington developed a Life Events Inventory, adjusting the rating scales for each of four different age groups from preschool to children sixteen and older.[28] This survey included a variety of events, and included gains and losses that require varying degrees of "readjustment" in order to cope with them. He surveyed teachers, pediatricians and social workers, asking them to rate each item. He assigned numbers to each event, with the highest numbers going to the most stressful experiences. In the end, however, it is the cumulative effect of stress that matters most, and if a child has experienced more than one stressful event, the numbers are added together to give a "cumulative stress figure."[29]

The most stressful events on the list include the death of a parent, getting married, an unwed pregnancy or acquiring a deformity. Beginning to date, changes in parents' marital or financial status, a parent's arrest or incarceration, being hospitalized, moving to a different school, becoming involved with drugs, or not being selected to be on a team or some other coveted extracurricular activity also figure significantly in the list for middle- and high-school kids.[30] Additionally, many of the teens I encountered, either at the middle school or day treatment center where I volunteered, had intensely stressful experiences that didn't show up on the lists I found. These included being targeted for bullying or ridicule; bullying others; having a parent introduce them to drugs; being raped or sexually abused; becoming sexually active at an early age; being verbally or emotionally abused; being physically abused; being thrown out of the house by a parent; being arrested; being committed to a juvenile detention center or residential treatment center; witnessing a parent's death from drugs, alcohol or murder; living with domestic violence or being affected in some way by community violence. Many of the kids I worked with also spoke of feeling overwhelmed, isolated, unsupported and often responsible for the family members who were still alive (whether in jail or not).

Even simple, everyday events can be stressful, and it can be easy to overlook the potential threat inherent in seemingly innocuous experiences. *Scholastic Parent & Child* magazine editor-in-chief Judsen Culbreth notes, "A young child might be worried about how to button a coat or zipper. A crowded school bus might be intimidating for elementary-school kids."[31] Family therapist June Buchanan recalled the terror of missing her bus stop on the way home from her first day of school at age five: "I went from total protectedness to being totally on my own. I was frightened and confused and continued to feel that way throughout my schooling if under any kind of pressure." Younger children may also be concerned with the size of the school or the number of other students, as well as issues of fairness, getting along with the teacher, the possibility of failure (regardless of how successful they may be), how they are treated by others, and how others will respond if they complain about these fears. Issues of popularity and social rejection also reckon prominently among children ten and older.[32]

The best time of their lives? Hardly. And for many children, childhood is downright devastating. The National Center on Child Abuse and

Neglect reported an increase in the number of children who suffered maltreatment at the hands of their parents or other caregivers from 1.4 million in 1986 to 2.6 million in 1990 to 2.9 million in 1994.[33] Bruce Perry, child psychiatrist, puts a conservative estimate at nearly twice that in the United States alone, including those exposed to trauma as witnesses or survivors.[34] Threats to a child's sense of security are not without their consequences, and early trauma is not just an inconvenience for children to buck up under or simply talk out in therapy at some point down the road. Abuse and neglect have a far more significant impact, affecting not only beliefs and behavior, but the actual structure and chemical balance in the child's developing brain.

When the Cradle Falls

It is absolutely unthinkable that a human being who, from the start, is given love, tenderness, closeness, orientation, respect, honesty and protection by adults should later become a murderer.

Alice Miller[35]

You need a particular environment imposed on a particular biology to turn a child into a killer.

Sharon Begley[36]

Millions of children are exposed to traumatic experiences each year. Over 30 percent of these traumatized children develop a clinical syndrome with significant emotional, behavioral, cognitive, social and physical symptoms called post-traumatic stress disorder.

Bruce Perry[37]

Stress necessitates an overemphasis on survival-oriented brain processing at the expense of rational, limbic and cortical functioning, especially within the frontal lobes. Consequently, stressed-out, survival-oriented humans have less opportunity to develop nerve nets into the frontal lobe and may exhibit learning difficulties as a result.

Carla Hannaford[38]

Take a class in child development and you'll probably hear about Harlow's classic work with baby monkeys, and how early care and interactions shape personal and social development. In his experiments, some of Harlow's monkeys were raised with their mothers, while others were raised by cloth-covered and wire mesh substitutes. All of the baby monkeys were well-nourished, physically, but in the absence of interaction and contact, in the case of the monkeys with the substitute mothers, the brain cells used in the development of self-regulation and social competence were not stimulated or nurtured. As a result, these baby monkeys grew to be agitated and withdrawn and had trouble dealing with other monkeys, patterns that stayed with them throughout their lives.[39]

Early attachment—and all the developmental goodies that go with it—appears to be centered in a part of the brain called the orbitofrontal cortex. This is the place where the limbic system and cortex are connected. It is stimulated by external sensory information and internal visceral input. This is the area that holds our earliest associations between our experience and our internal responses to these experiences. Its development is critical to our ability to regulate our emotions, inhibit inappropriate impulses and delay gratification in favor of long-term plans and goals.[40] Dr. Allan Schore of the UCLA School of Medicine claims that the development of this area is experience-dependent, and once again, the nature of the infant's relationship with primary caregivers is cited as the major influence. When the early relationship is abusive or neglectful, Schore claims that children grow up limited in their ability "to regulate the intensity, frequency and duration of primitive negative states such as rage, terror and shame."[41] Bruce Perry concurs: "Abuse and neglect early in life can have devastating consequences, tangling both chemistry and the architecture of children's brains and leaving them at risk for drug abuse, teen pregnancy and psychiatric problems later in life."[42] Further, children who have been abused not only come to believe that they are worthless and bad, but that they actually deserve the hurtful way they have been treated.

Inadequate stimulation to the orbitofrontal cortex combined with overstimulation of a child's alarm system is the perfect set-up for violence. If these experiences occur frequently and often enough, "a state of hyperarousal or of numbing may become a permanent trait in a child, setting the stage for a host of learning and behavioral problems."[43] Outcomes of long-term or ongoing abuse can include rage and cruelty or extremely passive victim behavior, a lack of tolerance for any frustration, or a tendency to act out disappointment with tantrums or self-destructive behaviors.[44] And one of the common threads in James Garbarino and Claire Bedard's research with children who commit murder is the experience of "poisonous environmental influences during their early years and beyond."[45]

In a *New York Times* article on PTSD, or post-traumatic stress disorder, Daniel Goleman states that "even a single instance of overwhelming terror" can alter brain chemistry.[46] The term PTSD, which entered the popular lexicon when it was used to describe a condition common to many Vietnam veterans, has since been extended to a more generic population, including children who have experienced repeated stress or extreme trauma. Of course, not all trauma results in PTSD and children can have many stress symptoms even if they do not meet the full criteria for a diagnosis of PTSD.[47] Potential damage increases, as does difficulty in treatment, when the trauma occurs over a prolonged period of time, when it is human in origin (particularly when involving someone close and trusted) and when the people closest to the traumatized person deny that the trauma occurred.[48] Even more damning is an accompanying sense of helplessness, and PTSD is more likely to occur when the victim is unable to do anything to stop the trauma.[49]

One of the most common characteristics of traumatized children is the development of a state of hyperalertness or hypervigilance in which they are constantly on the lookout for potential dangers. Hannaford has found that children who have been abused or traumatized tend to overdevelop their outer eye muscles, pulling their eyes toward an exaggerated peripheral focus, or "wall eye." These children have difficulty with visual tracking and focus needed for reading. In her work with special education students, she claims that "the eyes are always a factor."[50] Hypervigilance can also appear as distractibility and attention problems. Combined with other potential stress symptoms, such as impulsivity, restlessness or fidgeting, social avoidance, dissociation, sleep problems, anger or aggressive play, lying, psychic or emotional numbing, school failure, delayed development, regression to an early stage of development, and chronic anxiety, fear, confusion or unhappiness, childhood PTSD is often misdiagnosed with a variety of labels including ADHD (Attention Deficit Hyperactivity Disorder), depression, conduct disorder or separation anxiety.[51] Even without this array of symptoms, it's easy to see how difficult it would be for children to concentrate and perform in school when the bulk of their energy is being used to monitor the environment for danger or defending themselves against what is frightening or hurtful to them.

"Hypersensitivity can become wired in to basic brain chemistry and bodily functions," say Karr-Morse and Wiley. Especially when trauma occurs during infancy and toddlerhood, when the brain is most malleable, "the brain actually organizes itself around these conditions."[52] Sadly, a brain that becomes highly skilled at tuning into other people's emotional energy and physical cues may have trouble developing language and problem-solving skills. In comparing the brains of a group of neglected children to a control group, Bruce Perry found the cortex in the brains of the neglected children to be 20 percent smaller on average.[53] Hannaford explains, "With survival as their primary goal, the higher centers of thought and regulation may just not develop, though the full potential is there."[54] And Shannon Brownlee reports on a study in which Massachusetts psychiatrist Martin Teicher recorded electrical activity in the brains of abused and nonabused children. His findings show that the left hemisphere of abused children had fewer nerve-cell connections between different areas. Additionally, this research showed that "children with the most abnormal recordings were the most likely to be self-destructive or aggressive."[55]

"There seems to be a genetic component to the vulnerability that can turn into antisocial-personality disorder. It is only a tiny bend in the twig, but depending on how the child grows up, the bend will be exaggerated or straightened out," claims author Sharon Begley.[56] Once again, the role of the caregiver is critical. "A baby who is unreactive to hugs and smiles can be left to go her natural, antisocial way if frustrated parents become exasperated, withdrawn, neglectful or enraged. Or that child can be pushed back toward the land of the feeling by parents who never give up trying to engage and stimulate and form a loving bond with her."[57] Different responses actually create different brains, and different brains produce different behaviors.

So imagine a child's developing brain in the hands of an emotionally attuned caregiver, one who soothes and comforts, and is responsive to the infant's needs. Karr-Morse and Wiley claim that nurturing experiences and interactions create a positive emotional association for the infant. They also build an understanding that "strong emotional states can be entrusted to another and ultimately balanced or resolved in the context of the relationship. This reciprocal process of positive emotional exchanges is the foundation not only for attachment, but also for the development of empathy and constructive ability for emotional sensitivity in intimate relationships."[58] The neurological foundations for skills we value most, such as the ability to delay gratification, moderate one's own behavior and impulses, and behave with empathy and consideration for others, all develop within a relationship of trust and nurturing,[59] one in which children know that their needs will be met, one in which children feel safe.

7

"No, Really . . . I'm Fine": Coping and Compensating

The need for safety, belongingness, love relations and for respect can be satisfied only by other people, that is, only from outside the person. This means considerable dependence on the environment.

Abraham Maslow[1]

If the principal looks closely, he will recognize [the student's] laughter to be an anxious scream, a mask for the terror she feels. But what strength it takes for him to see through her bizarre laughter to the scared little girl beneath! Never has a child needed a hug more, and never has an adult been less inclined to offer it. . . .

L. Tobin[2]

Of course, as human beings, we all just want to feel that we fit in, we want to feel successful, we want to have energy, we want to be loved and appreciated and, boy, once kids spend a few years missing out on these things, you can't say you really blame them when they turn to anything that will satisfy those needs.

Joseph Lancaster
physician

The director introduced me, a new volunteer at a day treatment center for high-risk teens. I said I'd be working with them two days a week. Silence as they checked me out. Finally one girl walked up to me, her nose just inches from my face. "Well, if we're mean to you," she warned, "don't take it personal." What an interesting welcome! In one sentence, I encountered what I would often see and hear in my exchanges with the kids at this center, a touching mix of defensiveness and vulnerability. I was immediately smitten. How could I not be?

I deliberately hadn't asked for much background on the kids I'd be meeting, although I eventually learned that most of them had made a few stops through various stations in the juvenile justice system on their way to this place. Over the course of the next few months, I saw kids come and go for a variety of offenses. As bits and pieces of personal histories began to emerge, either in therapy groups or the occasional private conversation, I saw a pattern of early trauma, children who had grown up with chaos, abuse, abandonment and, often, horrific violence. These kids were survivors. Many reminded me of porcupines: They had built up a tough, prickly exterior to protect a soft, vulnerable inside, adaptations for a world that, to them, was not a safe place.

The suspicion and anticipation of betrayal was well entrenched at a very young age. Clearly the majority of the kids who ended up on this track had been denied the opportunity to master one of the first challenges of infancy: learning to trust. Lorraine B. Wallach cites Erikson's work regarding individual development, saying, "Trust provides the foundation for further development and forms the basis for self-confidence and self-esteem. The baby's ability to trust is dependent upon the family's ability to provide consistent care and to respond to the infant's need for love and stimulation."[3] When infant and parents fail to bond, or when the attachment between the infant and primary caregivers is disturbed, a resulting "attachment disorder" is common.[4] This was the thread common to most of the high-risk teens I met at the center. I saw kids continually reject or test the efforts of caring adults to get close to them. Many were seriously committed to proving that they weren't worth the time or faith the adults were willing to invest in them. Additionally, the combination of low hope and high despair had led kids to become dangerously reckless, angry and confrontative, suspicious and accusatory, or simply indifferent or severely depressed.

"When kids need us the most," contends educator Mary Ellen Simmons, "they act like they deserve it the least." Shannon Brownlee agrees, "Loving damaged children can be tough. One minute they are hostile, the next withdrawn."[5] But place these behaviors in the context of survival—once again, the primary job of the human brain—and for all of their acting out, what we're witness to is simply an adaptive way to get by in an often hostile world. Understanding this fact is crucial to our own ability to get past kids' off-putting survival behaviors and deal with "damaged" kids successfully. Besides, as one Brisbane principal cautions, "You can't help them by simply alienating them further."[6]

Fight, Flight or Freeze

Defensiveness can be as wise as daring.

Abraham Maslow[7]

It's no wonder these children have trouble trusting people. The ones who were supposed to model healthy relationships for them were fighting all the time, putting them in danger, forgetting their needs.

Susan Stiger[8]

If we lived in an unsafe environment, we probably also learned how to avoid danger.

Eric Jensen[9]

In the 1920s, Harvard physiologist Walter Cannon studying the link between emotional stimuli and autonomic nervous system responses, came up with the term "fight or flight" to describe the way living organisms respond to threat.[10] Both are survival responses that allow us to defend ourselves by attacking or intimidating, or protect ourselves by retreating, or running away. But what about infants and young children, for whom these options do not exist? If your parents fight and hit each other, if you're continually surrounded by yelling and threatening noise, if your needs for hunger or comfort are met by pain, and you can't fight back or run away, your brain resets for survival. You become very alert, existing in a state of hyperarousal, or you become very numb, living in a state of dissociation.[11] (The ability to dissociate, or emotionally remove oneself or mentally disconnect from a threatening reality, has led some experts to add "freeze" to the menu of possible stress responses.)

Educators Bernadette Donovan and Rose Marie Iovino suggest that we "regard the home environment as a learning environment—perhaps dangerous or barren or too fast-moving, but nevertheless the most powerful learning environment in [a] student's life."[12] In this environment, basic survival responses develop into behavior patterns early on. By their first birthdays, babies have developed a set of coping responses based on their previous experiences and interactions with their parents. Karr-Morse and Wiley cite research from the 1960s by Dr. Mary

Ainsworth, who examined attachment patterns in children between twelve and eighteen months of age. Observing the reactions of children whose mothers left them and then returned, she found that securely attached children cried when their mothers departed, but were cheerful and easily comforted upon the mothers' return. Children whose parents were more erratic or intrusive were agitated and anxious when Mom left, but resisted efforts to calm or comfort when she returned. The children of insensitive or emotionally unavailable parents had learned not to look to their mothers for reassurance and had very little response when their mothers came back into the room. And children of abusive parents had the most disorganized and distorted set of responses to the reunion, wanting closeness, but becoming sad, conflicted or fearful when the mothers returned, sometimes approaching their mothers backwards or simply freezing and staring off into space.[13]

By the time children reach school, most have developed a variety of self-protection strategies. Going to school will only add to their repertoire if the experience turns out to be unpleasant, unwelcoming or unsafe. "Psychologically, we react to a threatening situation in ways that have been successful to us in the past," claim Schultz and Heuchert,[14] or as early-childhood expert Elizabeth Crary says, "Kids do what works." But what "works" to ensure survival may not always "work" to ensure learning. Educators C. Lynn Fox and Shirley Forbing caution that many of the defense mechanisms children exhibit in these roles "result in behaviors which may cause a child to be labeled learning disabled, reluctant learner or behaviorally disordered."[15] Clearly, some survival behaviors can create even bigger problems for kids when exhibited in the classroom arena.

Taking Our Family Roles to School

I'm the only child of busy, successful parents. I'm busy, too. I really don't have time for the foolish things my seven-year-old classmates do. . . . You see, I need to grow up as fast as possible, so I won't be a bother at home.

Kristi[16]

There were fights on the playground from the first day of school. Where the staff was I do not know. I myself was not a fighter. So my way of dealing with the violence was to become a joker, and to be invisible.

Andy Quiñones
school-bus driver

I spent much of my childhood in a fog. I couldn't cope with anything that was going on in my life, and so I retreated into a fantasy land. My teachers thought I was stupid and inattentive. I wasn't. I was just trying to hide.

Candy

In the 1970s and 1980s, literature from the addiction and recovery field brought attention to ways in which children from troubled families cope with the abuse, neglect, disappointment or lack of predictability they experienced in their home environments. Originally focusing on children whose parent or parents were alcoholic, it quickly became clear that the same strategies were being employed by a much larger population. As psychologist Paul Clements notes, "In my experience, most of the problem kids come from homes that either are not safe or don't feel safe emotionally to the child."

But many children who don't *appear* to be "problem kids" are survivors nonetheless. From a family systems perspective, children typically adopt one of four roles as a way of surviving in a family in which their developmental needs are not being met. Each role, and the accompanying beliefs and behaviors, is a long-term, adaptive response to a perceived threat, serving both the child and the family in some way. According to author John Bradshaw, each role is "necessitated by the family's need for balance."[17] And while children may exhibit the behaviors of different roles at different times or in different situations, each has a predominant role or coping style, a fall-back position within the family that he or she will assume throughout childhood and, in the absence of intervention and support, throughout adulthood, as well.

The Family Hero

Sometimes labeled the Surrogate Parent or Superkid, this is the child, often the firstborn, who takes on the job of creating the impression that the family is functioning normally. Heroes provide a sense of worth and legitimacy to the family, and serve to make the family "look good." They are the overachievers, compliant and approval seeking. They stay safe by doing, and by doing well. They are often overlooked as being at risk, especially in the school setting, where their survival behaviors are supported and encouraged. However, they can be controlling and compulsive, workaholic and perfectionistic. They carry the burden of the family's dependence and the pressures that these responsibilities entail. Additionally, they are extremely vulnerable to even the slightest failure, and can be at high risk for eating disorders, amphetamine abuse, depression and suicide.[18]

The Invisible Child

If I were to ask a group of teachers to name the children in their homeroom classes, these are the kids they'd forget. Sometimes called the Lost Child, this group accounts for the loners, the daydreamers, the withdrawn kids who stay safe by making themselves as small a target as possible. These children provide the family the relief of being the one person in the family no one worries about. Quiet, shy and often isolated, they may miss valuable opportunities for care and nurturing by adults who are distracted by children who are louder, needier or more demanding (whether at day care, school or home). As with Family Heroes, the Invisible Child is rarely pegged as a high risk. However, these are the kids who fall through the cracks. When Invisible Children snap and end up in the headlines, it is much to the surprise of the adults in their lives.[19]

The Troublemaker

When these kids make headlines, almost nobody is surprised. This is simply the legacy of children who survive by acting out, seeking safety behind a wall of hostility, defiance and aggression. They serve as the family Scapegoat, taking the attention—and heat—off an addicted, alcoholic, compulsive, violent or otherwise troubled parent. These are the angry children, who frequently encounter rejection and failure. They are often the children whose brains are set on a hair-trigger alert. They may misinterpret benign events as threatening, and react intensely, explosively and violently. This group also accounts for children whose systems of stress hormones and emotional sensitivity have become impaired from chronic and long-term exposure to pain or violence. They may be the children who have lost their conscience, as well as their ability to feel. While many can, with help and support, eventually become courageous and realistic adults who are good under pressure, able to take risks and competent at helping others, without intervention, children in this group are at high risk for addiction, school failure, violence, unplanned pregnancy and problems with the law (involvement with crime).[20]

The Mascot

Super-cute, charming, funny and entertaining, the Mascot or Clown serves as comic relief for a troubled family. These kids cover pain, confusion and vulnerability with a joke, and may be quite popular with friends and adults alike. Often the youngest in the family, they may prolong their "baby" identity and be fairly immature at times. Their clowning may compensate for feelings of loneliness, inadequacy and fear. They are driven by a need for attention, whether positive or negative, and can be anxious, hyperactive and disruptive in a classroom setting. Many Mascots end up in special-education classes because of problems with attention, learning and self-control. However they, too, may be overlooked as being at risk, and may be experiencing far more pain and fear than anyone might imagine.[21]

The point of discussing these groups is simply to illustrate how different children, depending on a variety of factors including temperament and birth order, adopt different strategies for survival and self-protection. (Once again, the last thing I want to do is suggest the need for *more* labels for kids.) Many of these strategies will have begun to develop long before children enter kindergarten. And kids coming to kindergarten will have no reason to suspect that the school community is going to function any differently from the way their family system operates. So the defenses that helped them feel safe in their families get dragged into the classroom, just as surely as the crayons and lunch boxes do.

Survival Behaviors in the Classroom

So many troubled children keep jackets or caps on during the day. They need the physical protection for a fragile psyche; or perhaps they simply don't feel welcome and are keeping themselves ready to leave. The jacket will come off when the child feels a sense of purpose and belonging.

L. Tobin[22]

I'm sure the fact that my parents were alcoholic had a huge effect on how safe I felt. I was never sure how to act or what to do to get people to like me. All through junior high and high school, I was very much a super student, teacher's pet, people pleaser. I felt good when I looked good. I truly thought my self-esteem was wonderful! But I always had to do things to make people notice me. Good things, but I had to perform. I see now how emotionally unsafe I felt.

Beth K. Lefevre
behavior-management specialist

In a classroom setting, fight, flight and freeze responses can manifest in a bewildering array of behaviors. I remember my first day as a teacher, standing at the door of the classroom, greeting my students for the first time. One girl approached cautiously, oblivious to my enthusiastic anticipation of a wonderful year. She stopped in front of me, one hand grasping her notebook and pencil case, the other on her hip. She looked me squarely in the eye and announced, "I don't *do* reading," before ambling into the class. Only a few hours into my career, and here was a child telling me that I needn't bother teaching her reading, all before I'd had a chance to learn her name.

Oh, the pains these students took to create some semblance of safety in their school lives! Whether to guard against the inevitable demands of fifth grade, or the risk of failure and shame, what for me held the prospect of an exciting new year represented a serious threat to many of my students. This obviously wasn't personal—I was just starting off, and no one knew who I was—but all of my students had experienced various degrees of failure and frustration in the years before they crossed the threshold into my classroom that day, and all had devised a variety of strategies to insulate them from further stress and discomfort.

Some sat quietly in the back, withdrawn and isolated, hoping I wouldn't call on them. Others attempted to assert themselves, angry and aggressive, hoping to make themselves unapproachable and intimidating. Some refused to do any work, others tried to distract me with disruptive, attention-getting behaviors. I had world-class excuse-makers, overly compliant people-pleasers, often-entertaining class clowns. I had students who already knew everything, while others professed helplessness in the face of even the most uncomplicated tasks. I had students who lied, students who cheated on assignments and tests, students who stole anything that wasn't nailed down. Some slept through lessons; others professed illness every time they had to go to a class they didn't like. Some flaunted their indifference. Others had truly given up, defeated and despairing of any hope for success, and were convinced that there was no point in trying. In later years, I saw older kids who came to class high, who hid behind a fixation with makeup or clothes, who deliberately misbehaved to get thrown out of class (or school). And

I saw kids who ate compulsively, scarred their bodies, got pregnant or dropped out.[23]

I saw self-protective behaviors that ranged from ingenious and sophisticated to downright heartbreaking. But from the overachievers who strived for perfection (and crumbled at the slightest mistake) to the kids who deliberately underachieved in the hopes of keeping my expectations low, the goals were the same—achieving a sense of safety and control in this environment. These choices were neither particularly conscious nor calculated. They reflected instead a combination of temperament, patterns established in family roles, familiarity (what had worked in the past), and the options that seem to be available. Nonetheless, I spent so much time dealing with these adaptive survival behaviors that for weeks I wondered if I'd ever get to teach! I eventually came to realize that I would never make any serious headway until my students and I had made some kind of connection, and had connected in such a way as to convince them that their various styles of self-protection simply weren't necessary here, in our classroom.

The need for this connection, and the reassurances and trust that go with it, doesn't end with adolescence. I am always fascinated by the number of adult learners who demonstrate similar behaviors—like workshop participants who advise me up front that they "may have to leave early," or those who insist on sitting in the back rows, even when those rows have been roped off and marked with signs requesting that they please sit somewhere else! Even people who have paid to attend trainings and have a strong commitment to being there have no way of knowing, when they first walk in the room, just how invasive or intimidating—or boring—I'm going to be. We all need a safety net at times, and only when we know that we will indeed be treated with respect, when we know our needs (for personally relevant content, some interaction, a bathroom break, a mid-morning snack or some laughter, for example) will be met, when we know that we will not be embarrassed or set up to fail, only then are we willing to let our defenses down, and only then are we truly open to learning and growing.

8

Over the Edge: A World of Violence

Kids have more permission in their imaginations than ever before. On one hand, they can be more destructive, more dramatic and more violent. On the other hand, they can also be more inspired and more innovative.

Lynn Collins
educator

At the height of the Cuban Missile Crisis, the media was constantly giving us advice about what to do in case of a nuclear explosion. We couldn't really envision what the outcome could be, but it was enough to cause tension. I think the difference with kids today is that they can envision outcomes because they see images of other kids in horrific situations.

Michele Borba
educational consultant

As a rule . . . most children who kill have accomplices. It could be a detached mother trapped in poverty. An anonymous father. Dead-end role models. Drugs, abuse or neglect. A neighborhood awash in violence. Or a justice system too overburdened to recognize a child's cry for direction, or just plain love.

Maya Bell[1]

Mention the words "safety" and "schools" in the same sentence and the conversation invariably turns to guns and violence. Equating safety with violence prevention certainly makes sense in terms of where our cultural attention has been drawn in recent years, but this is indeed a small part of what a truly safe and caring school community is all about. Children can be remarkably resourceful when it comes to meeting their needs, but only a very small percentage will act out in the most extreme ways. The statistics say that youth crime has been relatively flat over decades, that the number of violent incidents is actually down. However the severity and lethality of those incidents have increased, and that's the part that gets our attention.[2] Still, many experts caution against sensationalizing the acts of a few, urging that we maintain our perspective in dealing with this very serious issue.

Schools have always had a fringe element, a handful of on-the-edge kids who act out their anger and frustration, or their need for power, attention or revenge, with verbal violence, vandalism or physical assaults—behaviors that range from impulsive and explosive to deliberate and premeditated. Nearly everyone I interviewed for this book had some memory that challenged the often-romanticized image of schools back in the "good old days." Director of Special Services Gary Myrah mentioned an article in the Sheboyan (Wisconsin) paper in the mid-1940s, discussing the need for all public officials to work together to reduce teenage violence. He also recalled films like *The Blackboard Jungle* and *To Sir with Love* for a sense of how challenging teaching could be decades ago. Even in the large, suburban high school I attended in New Jersey back in the mid-1960s, there was the occasional bomb scare, a fair number of fights in the halls and parking lot, and quite a few kids who routinely carried weapons, usually switchblades or other knives, although guns were not unheard of.

Nonetheless, with the exception of personal trauma experienced at the hands of bullies and cliques (which I'll address later in this book), according to the vast majority of respondents, violence in school was rarely perceived as a real threat, even by recent graduates. And while the number of teens who "always feel safe" in their school tends to decline following a well-publicized shooting,[3] most of the teens and young adults with whom I spoke were rather dispassionate, if not fatalistic, about their own vulnerability: If something was going to happen, it would happen.[4] Few bothered to give it much thought. If anything, their concerns were far more personal and immediate—insecurities about a boyfriend or girlfriend, fears of being ridiculed or "talked about" by their classmates, the dread of a "mean" or difficult teacher, or worries about their jobs, schoolwork, parents, futures, finances or friends, for example.

Things weren't much different for older respondents, most of whom never would have entertained the possibility of a school shooting when they were students. Safety concerns for them were far more likely to have been triggered by those ubiquitous duck-and-cover air-raid drills and the threat of nuclear attack, or specific events like the Cuban Missile Crisis or the Kennedy assassination. Montessori Director Pat Freeman, who was educated in England during the World War II, remembers days when "the largest portion of our lessons were done in the school bomb shelter. . . . During that time we were still expected to achieve and maintain good grades. I didn't see that as a bad thing, because it made you feel that you were going to have a future, otherwise why would your teachers or parents bother about such things?"

Throughout our history, school shootings and other forms of extreme violence have simply not been a part of our cultural reality. But at some point, a line was crossed. Overnight, it seems, the rules changed and the stakes became dangerously high. In only a few short years, the world has had far too many opportunities to confront the question of how in the world a child could get to a place where killing another human being could possibly register as an appropriate choice of action. We've faced unthinkable, stupefying headlines as players get younger, motives more obscure or absurd. And in the wake of each tragedy, there is a desperate search for answers, an intense pressure to do something, *anything,* to make sure this never happens again.

Violence in Kids' Lives

If you grow up with Dad shoving Mom around or Mom going after Dad with a knife, those scenes are laid down on your brain like so many nightly readings of Winnie the Pooh.

Susan Stiger[5]

Maybe what we're seeing is an indication that our saturation of violence is reaching a tipping point. And early adolescents are like the miner's canaries, the first to succumb to the poisoned air.

Dewey Cornell[6]

Teachers can do little to rectify the devastating home lives any children endure; but we can provide another reality when children are in school, creating an environment where they feel safe, accepted, nurtured and respected. In this environment, children can be taught alternatives to the violence that surrounds all of us, helping them perceive hopeful options for their futures.

Naomi Drew[7]

It never dawned on me, when I first started teaching, that I would need to add "no weapons" to the short list of ground rules for show-and-tell. This point was brought home by the fifth-grader who brought in a butcher knife, a souvenir from a fight he'd witnessed in his kitchen over the weekend. (Nobody was hurt with it, he assured me, only chased.)

For far too many of the kids I worked with during the past three decades, violence was very much a part of their lives. There was, for example, the student in the other fifth grade during my first year of teaching who was shot in the leg for riding his friend's bike. There was the twelve-year-old who saw her father stabbed as part of a gang initiation when she was six, and the fifteen-year-old who went to funerals for three different friends in two weeks. There were kids whose parents were injured by violence and kids whose parents were murdered. And not long ago, I observed an activity on expressing anger being run with a group of teenage boys which led to an eerily casual side discussion on whether the significant adults in their lives used "open or closed fists" on them. Domestic abuse and family violence are, for some, routine.

The correlations should hardly come as a surprise. Children are twice as likely to commit murder when they come from criminally violent families, have a history of being abused, belong to gangs and abuse alcohol or drugs. Throw in a few school problems, neurological disorders, prior arrests and weapons, and the odds are tripled.[8] Family violence, witnessed by more than three million children in the United States each year, will eventually "surface in the form of runaways, school dropouts, addicts, gangs, crime, suicides, homicides, homelessness, teen pregnancy and more," claims a report by Susan Stiger.[9] According to this same article, four out of five men in prison witnessed domestic violence as children, an experience that also quadruples a boy's likelihood of being physically abusive in dating relationships.[10]

Even in nonviolent homes, kids are exposed to much higher levels of violence and negativity than ever before. John Hoover and Ron Oliver, experts in bullying prevention, remind us that "American schools exist in a larger culture steeped in violence and seemingly fascinated with aggression."[11] Sharon Begley points to "the glorification of revenge in real life and entertainment."[12] And conflict-prevention specialist Linda Lantieri suggests that we shouldn't be surprised by the headlines, "given a society that glamorizes violence and that offers violence as the hero's choice."[13] And given what Dewey Cornell, the director of the

University of Virginia Youth Violence Project, calls "a saturation of violence" in our society, many psychologists and criminologists are surprised that things aren't much worse than they actually are.[14]

That's Entertainment

Do the ads reflect our cultural mind-set or do they help shape it?

Tom Shales[15]

The Internet credo is empowerment, and unfortunately that also applies to troubled teens sticking their toes into the foul water of hatemongering.

Steven Levy[16]

There's just not one clear answer (for the motive). . . . My mind wasn't capable of taking any more.

Jamie Rouse[17]

Jamie Rouse was one of the first teen gunmen involved in a school shooting. In November 1995 at the age of seventeen, he killed a teacher and a fourteen-year-old girl, and wounded another teacher with his .22-caliber rifle before he was wrestled to the ground. He is currently serving a life sentence without parole. In a recent interview, Rouse cited the influence of death-metal music on his behavior. While he doesn't specifically blame the music, he does claim that "it was a factor," one that helped him define who he was.[18]

It's a ritual that's becoming all too familiar: After the tragedies come the scapegoating and finger pointing. We seek comfort in finding something to blame, and if we could just nail it down to something tangible, this would help us make sense of it all. Yes, kids take in a remarkable amount of information—visually, conceptually, energetically—from television, music, movies, the Internet and video games. Some of this information is graphically cruel and violent, and the messages and images intensify as we seem to develop increasingly higher levels of tolerance. "Movies, photographs, video games and song lyrics that would have turned stomachs even five years ago, today don't raise an eyebrow," claims a 1999 article in the *Cincinnati Post.*[19] Often the bloodiest titles are the most popular among teens and younger kids. I've been astounded when way-too-young children tell me about movies they've seen that *I* couldn't sit through because they were too violent. And it's not just the odd choice of film or video game, either. Listening to group after group of troubled teens, I learned that for some kids, the products that offer high levels of gratuitous gore are the *only* ones that sustain their interest. This comes at a cost. "After a while, witnessing cruelty doesn't produce that empathic rush that generates concern for the victim," says noted author Michele Borba. Instead, she observes, children react "with indifference and emotional numbness."[20]

The media has come under close scrutiny, as well. "By telling a violent news story, are we risking imitation?" asks journalist Nancy Gibbs.[21] On a good day, the news can be depressing, even for world-weary adults. But for kids who watch footage of people their age being scared, hurt or killed by other people their age, what kind of impact do these images have? For kids without strong inner resources or solid external support, there is always a risk, especially if other factors come into play. It's tempting to condemn the media, as crimes that get the most attention are the ones most attractive to potential copycats—kids and adults alike.[22] Scott Johnson, the father of one of the Jonesboro, Arkansas, shooters, in a poignant essay writes, "I can't help but wonder if the nonstop pictures and commentary . . . somehow give desperate kids in need of attention a way to get it."[23] But the reporting is rarely enough on its own. "It starts with kids who are already somewhere close to the edge," says Harvard psychologist William Pollack.[24] Take, for example, the thirteen-year-old shooter in Oklahoma who claims to have been strongly influenced by the Columbine shootings, which had occurred a few months before. Many have wondered if this child would have been as likely to have acted out without the accompanying obsession with military tactics and the various prescription medications he had taken in the weeks before.[25]

Even a number of television programs and commercials, while perhaps not graphically violent, reflect a mean-spiritedness and callowness not previously seen. Commercials that once advertised candy bars "big enough to share" now pitch products with "two (pieces) for me, none for you," notes media commentator, Tom Shales.[26] In this same editorial, he denounces other television ads that seemed to endorse selfishness, greed and brutality as well as the products they were marketing. Along these lines, a popular advice column recently featured letters complaining about car commercials that glamorized dangerously aggressive, win-at-all-costs driving behavior.[27] Short, simple and obviously over-the-top perhaps, but what kind of messages do these ads promote?

A similar trend is evident in the gladiator mentality in talk shows that encourage public humiliation and judgment in the name of entertainment. (These shows were also a favorite among the teens in the center.)

According to Judith Martin, or Miss Manners, as she is also known, in recent years, many people have come to equate even a reasonable amount of privacy with shame. Add a desire "to be accepted for who they are," and people have a license to gossip, bad-mouth and embarrass their intimates.[28] What Martin calls "society's appetite for crass, crude behavior" also provides a blueprint for meanness and disrespect for anyone who watches. (I saw evidence of this over and over when kids—especially girls—would say the meanest things to one another, rationalizing with a dismissive, "I'm just being honest.") After a while, all this negativity can get pretty toxic. There is some genuine concern that these influences will, in time, erode not only courtesy, but the capacity for kindness and compassion, as well. Violence in particular can desensitize kids and, according to retired army lieutenant colonel and former West Point psychology professor, David Grossman, can even "help break down the natural inhibitions we have against killing."[29]

Still, not every child is affected. "It's like a virus spreading through a large population of people. Not everyone gets sick. Just the most vulnerable, and then with varying degrees of illness," claims Cornell.[30] And the most vulnerable kids are those who are lonely, angry, disempowered and disconnected. Take Jamie Rouse, for example. It would be easy to blame the music he liked—it's dismal and disturbing, with death-metal lyrics (about suicide, murder, rape and other violence) among the most extreme. But look at Rouse's profile and it becomes clear that this kid had a lot more than music going on in his life, including an obsession with death and suicide, a habit of smoking pot daily, his depression and a sense of never fitting in, a lack of anything positive to believe in, few friends, falling grades, car problems and a job he didn't like.[31] This isn't about making bad music go away. It's about inoculating kids against the potential comfort and guidance of toxic and dangerous influences they're likely to encounter at some point in their lives, and to minimize the likelihood that a hunger for these kinds of images and messages will ever develop.

Bang, Bang! You're Dead!

One-third of all eight-year-olds in this country have access to a gun.
Wendy M. Williams[32]

I've only been out of high school for two years, so I can remember a lot of the feelings I had. I don't remember ever feeling as if my life was threatened, although we knew some students carried weapons. In fact, I had a few friends who did, strictly for self-defense. They never bragged about them or showed them around. . . .

Joanna Carman

If you . . . choose to keep firearms at home, ensure that they are securely locked, that ammunition is locked and stored separately, and that children know weapons are never to be touched without your express permission and supervision.

from a bulletin on *"Stopping School Violence: 12 Things Parents Can Do"*[33]

We don't need gun control. We need bullet control.

Chris Rock
comedian

I was overseas, preparing for an afternoon inservice program, when I heard the news about the Jonesboro, Arkansas, shooting on a British Broadcasting news program. The report itself was bad enough. But for several devastating minutes, I got to see the United States through the eyes of an "outsider," a reporter who spoke as though this kind of thing was not only common but somehow accepted in America. This attitude is apparently more widespread than I'd ever imagined, as I noted when a principal from Slovenia recently asked, "Why do Americans let their children kill each other?" Despite my indignation, it's hard to condemn the perception. There are reportedly over 200 million firearms in this country. About half the homes in the United States have guns in them and more than 6,000 children are killed each year, either accidentally or intentionally, in incidents involving guns.[34] So it shouldn't be particularly surprising when guns make their way to school—in the hands of over 135,000 children nationwide every day.[35]

One of the things that make weapons especially dangerous in the hands of children is the fact that so few kids truly grasp the consequences of their use. "Children and most adolescents do not understand the finality of death," affirms Scott Poland of the National Association for School Psychologists.[36] This is partly developmental, partly a product of the version of death kids witness again and again in video games, movies and TV programming. Deborah Prothrow-Stith, assistant dean in the Public Health School at Harvard, acknowledges that "the reality of violence is appropriate in a movie which also attempts to show the pain and suffering it causes."[37] But a National Television Violence Study noted that 47 percent of all violent acts on television "fail to depict the harm to victims and 58 percent show no pain." Further, "73 percent of perpetrators go unpunished in these programs."[38] Compound this data with a disinclination to connect personal choices with the consequences of those decisions and the risks increase considerably. (One eleven-year-old at the center told me that it was his principal's fault that he was in the program: "If he hadn't searched me when I was holding, I wouldn't be here." And many of the kids couldn't understand why they weren't immediately let off the hook for their behavior if they simply said "Sorry" afterwards.)

Guns are frighteningly easy for kids to come by. Safety experts claim that many of the guns brought to school "are taken from homes where they are not stored securely."[39] Getting guns on the street does not seem to be much of a problem either. William Ayers has asked kids he's met at the juvenile detention center at which he volunteers how long it would take them to get him a gun if he were to give them two hundred dollars. "The response is uniform: 'Two hundred dollars? How many you want?' I could have three or four handguns by sundown," he says.[40] And according to Joan Gaustad, even in Washington, D.C., "which has one of the nation's toughest antihandgun laws, juveniles can easily buy guns on the black market. Or, for short-term use, a youth can even 'rent' a weapon."[41]

The easy availability of guns presents a reality that has polarized, and at times fragmented, every segment of American society, challenging common sense and cherished freedoms down to their constitutional foundations. But I fear for the energy that is exhausted even by the most worthy of arguments, and the degree to which potential efforts to connect with kids in positive and meaningful ways will be distracted. Because whether laws and sanctions become more restrictive or not, I'd like to see us move away from short-term, reactive thinking, focusing instead on what we can do to create the kinds of environments and relationships that would keep the idea of grabbing a gun and hurting another living being from *ever* entering a child's mind.

When Violence Happens in Schools: The Reactions

If there's a secret to running a school in post-Columbine America, it is to make sure the place keeps no secrets from you.

Nancy Gibbs[42]

We do not need more restrictive laws. Eric and Dylan would not have been stopped by metal detectors.

Darrell Scott
father of Columbine shooting victim, Rachel Scott

The worst time to prepare for a crisis is after it has already occurred.

Chester Quarles[43]

We don't need metal detectors, we need mental *detectors.*

Braulio Montalvo[44]
family therapist

In many schools across the United States, the days after the Columbine shooting were marked with a strange mix of hysteria and cynicism. School staff, anxious to avert the possibility of copycat incidents, implemented immediate and rigorous policies—no bookbags, no trenchcoats, no off-hand remark that might possibly be construed as threatening. Even in schools that had never had any hint of violence, a certain post-traumatic hypervigilance set in. And while some students were admittedly nervous, many saw the crackdowns simply as an annoying inconvenience. According to one principal in a suburban northeastern high school, students wryly responded to the restrictions on backpacks and purses by bringing their books to school in baby carriages and little red wagons.

Understandably, people get scared. However, when we react out of fear, the results are often a series of Band-Aids—simple, reactive, quick-fix approaches that rarely consider, much less seriously address, the underlying problems behind the desperate and misguided behaviors that make us so nervous in the first place. According to researcher Russell Skiba, "Schools continue to use 1950s remedies to address . . . complex risk factors. Suspension, expulsion and other punitive temporary removals from education are failed responses to signs of aggression." These reactions do nothing to teach new behaviors or deal with the emotional and social issues lurking behind the aggression.[45] Joan Gaustad agrees, noting that evidence "suggests that schools must work to improve discipline and physical security. These measures are not enough, however, to halt school violence; educators must go further and attack the roots of violence."[46] Of course, it will always be easier to make more rules and bigger punishments than it will be to modify the quality of the relationships within the school community, for example. And the idea of displaying posters with morality slogans around the school is certainly going to be a simpler option than, say, providing resources to support kids who are having trouble succeeding academically, socially or psychologically.

But so many of the knee-jerk reactions to violence that we see do little beyond assuaging an intense need to take some kind of action. Look at metal detectors, for example. About a quarter of the largest school districts use metal detectors, but according to the National School Safety Center, these devices have had little effect in reducing the number of violent incidents in school.[47] They may offer some comfort to policy makers and the public, but for many students, their presence can have an entirely different effect. Joanna Carman, a recent graduate whose high school had installed metal detectors a few years before Columbine, recalled, "Walking towards the building you could tell when they were using them because there were massive lines outside the doors." Carman spoke for many kids when she noted that most of her classmates thought the security devices were a joke, one that a truly determined student could easily circumvent.[48] Longtime advocate for safe and "invitational" schools, William Purkey cautions that "traditional law enforcement methods applied to schools carry major negative side effects," including "a significant financial burden, a reduction of time for classroom instruction and a decline in teacher and student morale."[49] Many people object to the way metal detectors change the overall atmosphere of the school. Some resent working or learning in an environment that "feels more like a correctional facility than a school." In fact, there is some evidence that such a presence can actually be more unnerving than comforting to students and staff who see these devices as evidence that there is more to fear than they had imagined. As a senior from Massachusetts told a national summit on school violence, "Too much security makes you wonder whether it is safe."[50]

Besides, as Lantieri and Patti note, "No metal detector on earth can stop people from bringing fear, prejudice and conflict to school, and no metal detector can prevent students from bringing that fear, prejudice and conflict back to the streets at 3 P.M."[51] Additionally, gang expert Richard Arthur warns of potential backlash to the lock-down approach to school safety: "It is true that using the police, enforcing school rules, excluding certain deviant students and having prudent dress codes may be helpful in creating a 'surface' kind of order in an otherwise chaotic school. However, at worst, they cause more crime and disruption than they stop."[52] Perhaps the greatest danger lies in the way the presence of metal detectors, and even armed guards, can create a false sense of security. An Infobrief Synopsis on preventing school violence issued by the Association for Supervision and Curriculum Development cautions that limiting "policy attention to the most visible manifestations of violence risks ignoring the broader origins of severe situations, including alienation, destructive values, lack of conflict resolution skills and disengagement in learning."[53] Author Kathryn Girard concurs: "The need for immediate fixes to problems may lead to unrealistic and inappropriate goals and expectations."[54] Besides, as Mary Ellen Simmons observes, "Metal detectors will never take the place of knowing your students. The human element is what makes schools safe places for kids."

There are times when it seems that the grownups are, indeed, grasping at straws. In the summer of 1999, the Louisiana state legislature passed a "Manners Bill," requiring students to address all adult school employees as "sir" or "ma'am."[55] The law was Senator Donald Cravins's well-meaning attempt to "stem the decline in his state's public schools: the soaring dropout rates, the violence, the rudeness."[56] Aside from the fodder for late-night television monologues, there was genuine concern from many experts who bemoaned the old assumption that enough rules and punishments can fix just about anything. There were also those who noted that the law seemed to present respect as a one-way street: Nowhere was there a mention of the kinds of behaviors adults would be expected to model. "What's the point of legislating politeness in schools when the adults have license to be rude and disrespectful—or worse—to children?" asked one educator.

And there are other problems, most notably, the scrutiny to which students' behaviors were suddenly subjected. The good news is that many adults have become much more aware—and much less tolerant—of student behaviors that hurt or marginalized other students, patterns which commonly have been ignored or excused. The bad news is that the reactivity sometimes went a bit over the top—or missed the point altogether. For example, some schools work to eliminate the presence of social misfits by encouraging students to be more tolerant and accepting; others approach the same problem as a dress-code issue.[57] (As one amused student commented, "They think there won't be any outcasts if we all look the same.") Psychiatrist Frank Ochberg expresses concern that there is a risk in this scrutiny, one "that could stigmatize and isolate boys and girls who superficially resemble certain stereotypes" or profiles.[58]

A year after Columbine, the Justice Policy Institute, a youth advocacy think tank, released a report on youth violence. This report notes that "youth violence is falling, but more children are paying the price of public fears driven by high-profile school shootings."[59] In what journalists Jerry Adler and Karen Springen call "a tremendous victory for bureaucracy over common sense," they note that "schools have made discipline issues out of violent imagery in creative-writing assignments."[60] Among the examples of hyperreactivity mentioned in various news reports is the seventh-grader who did jail time for completing an assignment to "write a horror story" with a story that was more horrifying than his teacher had bargained for,[61] the two five-year-olds who were suspended for pointing fingers at one another as though they were guns,[62] and the kindergarten student who was suspended for a day for wearing a fireman's costume that included a plastic ax.[63]

"In this atmosphere," says family therapist Braulio Montalvo, "what keeps getting lost is the child." Clearly, reacting is not enough, nor is superficial attention to surface details. "You need a gestalt cure for this," advises counselor Beverly Davies. Yet too often, the "cure" reflects an inclination to simply make the problem go away. Montalvo shared a story about a social worker who went to the principal with a list of kids who, she thought, were most at risk for violent behavior and needed special outreach. The principal responded by asking for the list: "I'll get them out of school immediately," she said.

And then what? How many of our policies help the school rather than the students? At some point we're going to have to learn how to run down the middle, because somewhere between ignoring and reacting is an effective combination of attention and prevention that *will* make a difference. And for this to happen, schools will have to take on a much larger role than most people concerned with education ever imagined.

9

Brave New World: The Changing Role of the School

The world is inherently orderly. And fluctuation and change are part of the very process by which order is created.

Margaret Wheatley[1]

It seems that rapid change is our only constant.

Carl Rogers and Jerome Frieberg[2]

Shift happens.

Rico Racosky
pilot, author, motivational speaker

There's this joke about a five-year-old boy who confides in his classmate, "I found a condom on the patio." His friend responds, "What's a patio?"[3]

There's no question that the world is changing, and that it's changing at a speed that seems to be constantly accelerating. Children know more, and at increasingly younger ages, than ever before. Where young people once received most of what they learned from within their families and communities, they are now, for better or worse, only a mouse-click away from an entire universe of information. For grownups, keeping up with new information, new technology and new demands of the workplace has, in itself, become a full-time job. For years, the byword of corporate leadership has been "learning to love change" in what Tom Peters calls "an era of unprecedented uncertainty."[4] Have our schools kept pace?

"Until now," writes futurist Alvin Toffler, "the human race has undergone two great waves of change, each one largely obliterating earlier cultures or civilizations and replacing them with ways of life inconceivable to those who came before."[5] For nearly a million years, humankind was primarily concerned with gaining some control over the environment. Early efforts to take care of basic survival needs eventually gave way, around 8000 B.C., to an agricultural revolution, or what Toffler calls a First Wave civilization. This way of life took thousands of years to play itself out, giving way to the Second Wave, an industrial society, sometime around 1700 A.D.[6]

It was during this Industrial Era that schooling became accessible to larger numbers of children from increasingly diverse segments of society, a time when formal systems of education were broadly established.[7] Not surprisingly, the structure and curriculum reflected the needs of this era, which included, among other things, the availability of a literate workforce for an industrial economy.[8] Toffler notes that in addition to the actual content taught in schools, there existed a "covert curriculum" that taught punctuality, obedience and rote, repetitive work. This made a great deal of sense at the time, as factory labor demanded workers who would show up on time, "take orders from a management hierarchy without questioning . . . [and] slave away at machines or in offices, performing brutally repetitious operations."[9]

But more change was afoot, and less than three hundred years after the industrial era started, there emerged a Third Wave, or the beginnings of an information economy. John Naisbitt pegs 1956 as the turning point, when, for the first time, American white-collar workers outnumbered laborers. This shift was cemented a year later when the Russians launched Sputnik, initiating global satellite communications.[10] Suddenly the world was a lot smaller, and for the first time in human history, workers were more involved in creating, processing and distributing information than they were in producing goods.[11] Advances in information technology and globalization throughout the last half of the twentieth century occurred at a mind-boggling rate, with all signs suggesting that we ain't seen nothin' yet!

There is one small problem, however: While our schools may have made strides to accommodate technological developments in the curriculum and the equipment available to students, our thinking, attitudes, relationships, communications, language and power dynamics are pretty much mired in First and Second Wave patterns. Behavioral expectations and instructional techniques that were built into the system more than 150 years ago to compel the standardization and uniformity necessary for a factory society have become anachronisms.[12] These patterns persist, although Toffler cautions that "old ways of thinking, old formulas, dogmas and ideologies, no matter how cherished or how useful in the past, no longer fit the facts." He also admits that the overlap is understandable, as is the chaos, disorientation and anguish that can be traced directly to the conflict "between the dying Second Wave civilization and the emerging Third Wave civilization that is thundering in to take its place."[13] We live in a world in transition. So it's only natural that we're going to run into difficulties when we attempt to educate Information Age children with methods and models suited for an industrial economy.

If one of the primary roles of schools is to prepare children to successfully enter the workforce, schools are going to have to deliver kids with the skills the workplace demands. As recently as the 1960s, about half of the people entering the workforce in America came with only six to eight years of schooling behind them. Where this background may have been adequate for a manufacturing-based economy, today, even a solid high-school education won't go far in the twenty-first century marketplace.[14] The Information Age has its own set of requirements in terms of content knowledge, technological competence and behavioral values. A 1997 survey of the Business Advisory Council in the Dayton area asked businesses to identify which core employment-related competencies were most in demand. The survey was intended to help area school districts prepare students for real-world work expectations. Interestingly, the skills on the low end of the list included basic math and writing skills, an understanding of business economics and basic computer skills. These competencies fell below attributes such as the ability to follow directions, literacy, ambition and flexibility. Skills most in demand included oral communications, people skills, telephone skills and character attributes such as honesty, cooperation, positive attitude and punctuality.[15]

"Factory model procedures in schools rarely work," write William Purkey and David Strahan. "Not only is production a poor metaphor for schooling, there is a growing recognition among leaders in business and industry that traditional 'assembly-line thinking' does not work in the private sector either."[16] Information Age businesses want people who can think—not just perform tasks well. David Thielen, a former senior software developer for Microsoft, describes the interviewing process at that company as one designed to identify people with competence in this area. "People who just perform tasks well often become a hindrance when their tasks change," he claims.[17] These companies are looking for knowledgeable people with high levels of creativity, curiosity and organizational skills, as well as a drive to grow and improve their abilities. They want employees who are willing to take risks, and who are willing to fail. And they want people whose intuition and judgment they can trust.[18] Where businesses once looked primarily for education degrees when considering prospective employees, they're now looking for vision and attitude.[19] But can a young person with "vision and attitude" survive in today's schools? Sure, sometimes, or in some classes, maybe. But schools, like all long-established institutions, can be notoriously obstinate in resisting change, and those that cling to factory-era values like uniformity and obedience probably won't feel welcoming, encouraging or safe to any child who doesn't fit that mold.

Rethinking Our Priorities

> *The only person who is educated is the person who has learned how to learn, the person who has learned how to adapt and change, the person who has realized that no knowledge is secure, that only the process of seeking knowledge gives basis in security.*
>
> Carl Rogers and Jerome Frieberg[20]

> *We are not interested in changing minds. Minds have always followed the passions of the heart. We are interested in opening hearts.*
>
> Ken Carey[21]

> *The task of the modern educator is not to cut down jungles, but to irrigate deserts.*
>
> C. S. Lewis[22]

When I first started working with kids, I was astounded by the extent of their needs. It wasn't just that they were far behind in academics or that their knowledge base and literacy skills were weak. That was, after all, why I assumed I was there. But no matter how enthusiastic I was, no matter how exciting and inspiring my lessons, no matter how beautifully I colored or laminated my materials, I never seemed to get anywhere academically. Even if I could get past their resistance and minimize the need for their various defenses, I kept tripping over a colossal lack of such basic attributes as initiative, decision-making skills or the motivation to achieve. Throw in their difficulties with planning and goal setting, self-control, critical thinking, self-expression and simple social competencies and efforts to focus exclusively on content became fairly pointless.

The challenge is almost beyond comprehension. Many educators complain that they're overloaded just dealing with cognitive issues and management, and they resent the demands of dealing with students' emotional, social, psychological, behavioral and personal-development issues, as well. "Schools are being forced to be homes," wrote Paul Clements. "School personnel can be a child's teacher, psychologist and principal, but they can't be Mommy and Daddy, too!" Author John Goodlad admits, "Our expectations for schools are both idealistic and grandiose, representing a synthesis of what many diverse segments of our population want. This is one of the problems of schools; there are so many expectations of them."[23]

In a 1996 report, UNESCO's International Commission on Education for the 21st Century proposed "four fundamental types of learning," including "learning to know" (acquiring knowledge and learning to learn), "learning to do" (dealing creatively with a variety of situations), "learning to live together" (understanding interdependence and participating cooperatively with others) and "learning to be" (developing autonomy, judgment, responsibility and potential).[24] To some extent, this is old news. Benjamin Bloom's 1956 taxonomy of cognitive skills was followed, a few years later, by a handbook for the affective domain, with objectives ranging from "simple attention to selected phenomena to complex but internally consistent qualities of character and conscience."[25] In the decades that followed, proponents of affective education, cooperative learning, humanistic education, holistic education and similar programs argued for a more comprehensive approach to teaching that would enhance the class climate, treat students as multidimensional beings and build prosocial skills.[26] Still, for many, if not most educational institutions, accomplishing the UNESCO Commission's worthwhile goals would require a significant degree of change—not only in content and teaching strategies, but in power dynamics and the way all individuals in the school community relate and interact with one another. A tall order, indeed, but in all likelihood the only alternative we have.

Naomi Drew cites a new set of "basics," among them respect for self and others, the ability to work cooperatively, a sense of empathy toward others, anger-management skills, a sense of hope, a sense of personal responsibility, nonviolent conflict-resolution competence and the understanding that our actions do have an impact on our world and our life.[27] She calls upon teachers' power to shape lives to guide the future of society in more peaceful, cooperative and respectful directions. And she is not alone. Linda Lantieri suggests the need for "a whole new vision of how we educate children" at all levels, one that would help young people to become competent not only academically, but socially and emotionally, as well.[28]

The need is certainly there. As Nathaniel Branden observes, "about 95 percent of people who work for a living do so in an organization—

they work with other people. If they lack the security and skills to relate competently, they are usually badly limited in what they will be able to accomplish."[29] This holds true in school and throughout life. And when we consider how many kids come to school with their anger, depression, alienation and prejudices, and without a positive support system, healthy outlets for their feelings, and the skill (or will) to control their impulses, then expanding the vision of education beyond the traditional Three R's makes quite a bit of sense. As a school social worker intern, Debra Sugar observed high correlations between students with both behavioral and academic problems and a lack of fundamental social skills. She cites research that confirms that "children with weak social skills are at higher risk for school dropout, juvenile delinquency, peer rejection, employment problems and mental health problems."[30] She noted that the lack of these skills, which are necessary for appropriate participation and cooperative interaction in class, were a major contributor to teacher stress. Finally, her work led her to determine that "basic social competence is prerequisite to learning readiness."[31]

Perhaps the best reason for addressing issues of interpersonal (social) and intrapersonal (individual) competence is the potential for positive impact. These are skills that can, indeed, be taught. Lantieri and Patti's *Resolving Conflict Creatively* program has shown that learning prosocial skills can lead to improvements in student relationships, behavior, attitudes, cooperation and achievement, and help to eliminate negative and antisocial behaviors, as well.[32] Author and educator Michele Borba has experienced similar results with her *Esteem Builders* program. Data on more than one thousand elementary students involved in this program indicated a 39 percent reduction in verbal aggression and a 41 percent reduction in physical aggression in an eight-month period. Additionally, 85 percent of all staff members at the three different sites reported improvements in prosocial skills, claiming students to be, as a result of their skill training, more tolerant, more respectful, more cooperative and better able to solve problems.[33]

In my last two years as a classroom teacher, I regularly sent my third-, fourth- and fifth-graders to help out in the kindergarten. Originally devised as a way to support the kindergarten teacher and the twenty-seven children in her full-day program, I soon realized that the older students were benefiting even more than the ones they were helping. Being able to experience a different kind of success, leadership and a sense of purpose—and be greatly appreciated and acknowledged for their contribution in the process—led to significant improvements in their work habits, quantity and quality of work submitted, behavior, attitude at school and at home, confidence, self-control, attendance and achievement.[34]

These are some compelling arguments for addressing noncognitive issues in school. And yet there is resistance. Author B. J. Wise notes that teachers complain about the added responsibility and don't understand why kids don't "just behave because they should." They also worry that by attending to issues they feel apply mostly to high-risk kids, that they are depriving those children who seem well-adjusted and are ready to learn (although Wise counters that it is even more unfair to deny children the skills they need to succeed).[35] There's a certain amount of scarcity thinking around this issue. Despite evidence that personal, social and learning competence actually increases and improves learning, the fear persists that spending time on noncognitive skills takes away from content learning.[36]

Support for the mental health and social development of students has faced a great deal of negative press in recent years. Educators William Purkey and David Aspy cite media criticism that blames school failure on time spent on "'frills' such as counseling services, affective programs and social development courses" even though "the linking of affective education and ineffective schools is both unwarranted and inaccurate."[37] And there may always be a certain polarity between the traditional basic-skills advocates and those leaning more toward a broader range of objectives. Sugar notes that "critics argue that until we have the basics down, and test scores up, we need to stay focused on academics," and suggests, conversely, that "education must address a broader spectrum of student needs before students will succeed, not only on tests, but in life."[38] Daniel Goleman notes that children lacking what he calls "emotional literacy" will benefit from this type of training: "In a time when too many children are lacking the capacity to handle their upsets, to listen or focus, to rein in impulse, to feel responsible for their work or care about learning, anything that will buttress these skills will help in their education. In this sense, emotional literacy enhances schools' ability to teach."[39] Rita Mercier concurs, noting that fluency in personal and interaction skills supports learning because it reduces the stress and negative emotions that interfere with higher-level thinking. Besides, she says, "ignoring the harmful effects of negative student behaviors and interactions is much more costly in terms of wasted learning time and losses in academic achievement."[40]

Perhaps it's time to rethink our goals and priorities in the face of societal demands and, more immediately, what the students sitting in our classrooms really need. What will we honor? In a time when school boards and legislators vote with their pocketbooks, we have educational communities in which boys' sports programs grab the lion's share of school resources. Sciences and technology programs continue to grow while the funding for the arts is cut back or, in some cases, eliminated altogether.[41] And some of the most effective programs for creating safety and achievement are dismissed as nonacademic "fluff." Do these priorities provide an emotionally safe school environment for all students? Is a more balanced approach not possible?

In the context of the school culture, B. J. Wise cites the adage, "Hurt people hurt people; healed people heal people." Wise also suggests that schools take on the responsibility of being healers.[42] While this role might never have occurred to our Industrial Age counterparts, it certainly bears consideration in our brave, new, twenty-first-century world.

Testing, Testing . . .

High scores—not high standards—have become the holy grail.

Barbara Kantrowitz and Daniel McGinn[43]

Excessive emphasis on testing can lead to low teacher morale, a narrowed curricular focus, a diminished sense of professionalism among teachers and unethical placement practices.

Larry Lashway[44]

Sometimes students who are not ready to show improvement and growth in the traditional assessment measures can be "caught" showing growth in other areas—areas that are many times taken for granted and go unnoticed and unmeasured.

Kristen Nelson[45]

We are not holding our profession accountable for learning, only for achievement on high-stakes tests.

Martin G. Brooks and Jacqueline Grennon Brooks[46]

Be a hero, take a zero.

students protesting high-stakes testing[47]

Imagine going to the doctor's for a physical. A few measurements are taken and afterwards, you receive a report with your height and weight, and the percentiles for each, telling you how you compare with others your age. How much does this information tell you about your overall health? Does it indicate how your body is strong or where it needs support? How it responds to vitamins, exercise or stress? Are the measurements reliable? Would a "good score" reflect the clinic's competence? Would a bad one mean you were sick?

If you are truly concerned about this issue, you probably would not be satisfied with such limited information, and would want to know what's going on with your cholesterol, blood pressure, hormones, internal organs, reflexes, eyesight, teeth and anything else that might have an impact on your physical well-being. But wait—there's more! To take this analogy one step further, now imagine that your doctors would no longer be able to practice if too many of their patients had "scores" below the range deemed acceptable! How would this pressure affect their priorities, not to mention their practices?

Assessment has always been a part of education, and standardized tests have been around for decades. When used as a tool for determining gaps in our students' understanding or to help us plan subsequent instructional strategies, their value is irrefutable. When justified as a motivational tool, the waters get a little murky, shifting the emphasis from the process of learning to the consequences of performing. And when those consequences begin to threaten students' promotion or graduation, educators' salaries and job security, district funding, schools' autonomy and even real-estate values,[48] testing—specifically, high-stakes standardized testing—can become downright dangerous.

A preoccupation with test results can have tremendous costs, instructionally and emotionally. Some students complain of a "test-taking frenzy" going on in their school, as well as a feeling that "real learning is being shoved aside as teachers focus on boosting test scores."[49] A California principal noted a shift from "the kind of hands-on, learning-by-doing teaching we did in the past" to a concentration on teaching to the test.[50] The pressure has led many an educator to present content and instruction to children who lacked the prerequisite skills needed to successfully incorporate the new knowledge. One teacher, doing a lesson on complex operations with fractions, had large numbers of learners who could not add or subtract whole numbers. When asked by her supervisor why she was teaching over her students' heads, she threw up her hands and said, "It's on the test!" Of course, by test time, her students could neither do the problems on fractions nor much of anything else. Teaching to the test, in this case, served no one.

This practice tends to breed a new version of the Three R's, or what Joseph Renzulli, of the National Center on the Gifted and Talented, calls the "ram, remember, regurgitate" curriculum.[51] This kind of "learning for the test" results in a shallow, disconnected and easily forgotten understanding of content, claims Linda McNeil, professor of education, undermining a solid academic curriculum.[52] Larry Lashway concurs, noting that the current accountability movement has a tendency "to drive non-tested content out of the curriculum."[53] And with most schools only beginning to get their curricular programs in sync with their state's exams,[54] one might wonder at the potential gap between what is being assessed and what is actually being taught—and learned—in any given classroom. Even districts that boast rising test scores may have little actual learning to back up the numbers. Such increases may simply reflect the alignment of the district's curriculum with the tests or local spending on improving test-taking skills. Research in one state suggests that test-score gains simply indicate that students are getting better at test-taking, rather than offering evidence of increased learning.[55]

It's hard to think of anything being "standardized" across the 55 million kids in U.S. public schools, whether we're talking about reading skills or shoe size. Many teachers question whether it's reasonable to expect every individual in, say, third grade, to know a particular set of skills simply because a number of others their age have mastered them (or because some bureaucrat or test publisher decided that those skills constituted appropriate knowledge for every child in that grade). Such a large population would certainly present vast differences in early support, readiness, personal experiences, cultural values, talents, abilities (and disabilities), skills for demonstrating knowledge and test-taking competence (and confidence). And with the typical emphasis on linguistic and logical-mathematical abilities, some experts note that while test results can be valuable in measuring a student's understanding in these areas, they "capture only a portion of student talents and achievements," ignoring students' strength, weaknesses and progress in other types of intelligence (such as spatial, bodily-kinesthetic, musical, naturalist, intrapersonal and interpersonal intelligences) as well as higher-order thinking skills in the areas they do test.[56] Plus, there is value in the unmeasurable. Principal Aaron Trummer cites an Irish proverb that warns, "You can't tell the quality of a sheep by weighing it." He mentions that even the best interpretation of a student's scores doesn't do justice to his or her talents. "Creativity, problem solving and intellect don't show up on tests." School success, claims Elliot W. Eisner, is far less evident in test scores than it is in "the kinds of ideas children are willing to explore on their own, the kinds of critical skills they are able to employ on tasks outside the classrooms, and the strength of their curiosity in pursuing the issues they will inevitably encounter in the course of their lives."[57] As teacher Mary O'Brien Merrigan remarks, "standardized tests measure only the bottom line, not the learning process."[58]

The impact of testing policies on emotional safety and morale—to students and staff—can be enormous. "We can kill children's enthusiasm for learning with pressure to perform well on these tests," says New Jersey educator Bonnie-Ann McLain.[59] And if students are feeling "panicked" or "under constant jeopardy"[60] because of standardized tests, what is this stress doing to performance, not to mention learning? In many parts of the country, testing has shifted from its original diagnostic purpose and is becoming increasingly threatening and punitive. One administrator told me that she had to reschedule an inservice training because the morale of her entire staff was decimated when a large area newspaper published a list of schools in their district, ranked according to the students' performance on the standardized exams. While reading the paper at home over the weekend, they (and the rest of the region's subscribers) discovered that their school's standing was near the bottom. Instead of devoting the day to professional development, she was scrambling to put together a program that focused, instead, on damage control.

To avoid the possibility of facing such public scrutiny and humiliation, much less the kinds of sanctions that would affect the school's autonomy or finances, some educators have resorted to strategies that run the gamut from strained ethics to outright criminal tampering. In recent years, teachers and administrators have been accused of—and in some instances prosecuted for—encouraging students to cheat on exams to drive scores up, excluding low-scoring students from the tests to raise overall results, giving students copies of earlier versions of exams to study, allowing children extra time to finish the tests, or pointing out incorrect answers and urging students to change them.[61] In some corners, even the idea of teaching to the test is considered a form of cheating, although there are those who defend this practice as a positive educational strategy.[62] Some say that the horror stories are inevitable, but what kind of priorities are we modeling for kids? Even young students are on to these tactics. What are they to make of incongruity between the "win-at-all-costs" messages underlying a school's lust for high scores and the character posters and ethics slogans that adorn their school's hallways?

Longtime education reformer Theodore Sizer claims that tests are an easy way out, a popular way to judge a school's effectiveness because "people are lazy. They're not asking questions." Tests, he claims, "have this façade of toughness and objectivity." And regardless of the impact these exams might have on kids and educators, they "put no burden on the people who most often demand them—the politicians."[63] Longtime teacher and antitest activist Susan Ohanian has been tracking what she calls "goofy test items," which are often sent to her by teachers who place themselves at great risk by speaking out against the tests. Arguing, among other things, that the content of the test often uses "wildly inappropriate reading levels" and content, that the design is "unprofessional, simplistic and error ridden" and that their purpose serves "corporate-led education reform" agendas and the needs of politicians looking for a quick fix, Ohanian pushes for greater media and public awareness of how dangerous and destructive standardized tests can be. She also makes a great case for spending the millions siphoned off by tests and testing on resources and facilities that would be of far greater benefit to kids who need them, and for focusing on the needs of individual students instead of seeing kids as an "undifferentiated mass into which information can be poured."[64] But even in the face of relentless testing, many schools (and individual teachers) are turning to more sophisticated assessment alternatives, such as rubrics, portfolios, conferencing, oral defense, narrative reports, anecdotal records, and student presentations or exhibits, to provide a broader picture of student performance, talent and mastery than a simple letter grade or a score from a standardized test can provide.[65]

If standardized tests must remain a part of the educational reality, then let's make sure they're done right, advises Nicholas Lemann. He suggests "using good tests, making sure they're administered under fair, secure conditions."[66] Focusing on their diagnostic value and refusing to use them punitively or competitively would be a real nice touch, too. (Withholding funding from the lowest-achieving schools makes about as much sense as withholding food from the hungriest children, especially when policymakers attach the caveat that the kids won't be fed until their hunger "improves.") Unfortunately, much of the best of what schools can accomplish—such as encouraging, inspiring, supporting, connecting with or believing in learners, for example—is rather hard to quantify. Likewise for many of the ways in which kids learn and grow. Is there space in this drive for accountability for an emotionally safe or "caring" curriculum, one that can have immense value even if, numerically, it's rather hard to pin down? Pulliam and Van Patten go back to the idea of preparing children for accelerating change, reiterating the inadequacy of attempting to meet future needs with curricula and practices developed to serve the past.[67] Being prepared for an unknown and uncertain world demands flexibility, creativity, openness to change and the ability to find out—skills that will also challenge our fascination with measurement and assessment.

Once again we need to ask ourselves what we in the educational community are doing here? What, indeed, do we value, respect and honor?

Author Marlow Ediger urges us to remember the value of "putting people first," valuing students above their cognitive accomplishments.[68] After all, numbers are nice, but let's not lose our perspective, or forget the fact that behind the numbers are a whole lot of individual learners—and a whole lot of ways to learn and appraise learning.

The Age of Connectedness

Our job is not to teach the kids we used to have, the kids we "should" have or the kids we wished we had. Our job is to teach the kids we do *have.*

Anonymous

The very intention to teach is an act of love.

Frank Siccone[69]

The classroom needs to be a safe haven where children feel secure and are able to establish a bond with a significant and empathetic adult.

Claire Thornton[70]

School is a place for laughing, learning and loving.

Esther Wright[71]

The Information Age came into being during my lifetime. In the true spirit of acceleration, I believe that the beginnings of the next major shift came right on its heels. This current "wave" has to do with the way human beings connect with everything around us, and the quality of our relationships with people, institutions and things. Perhaps an inevitable result of a deluge of information coupled with explosive breakthroughs in communications technology, this trend may also illustrate a need for balance, or what Naisbitt calls the "high touch" counterpart to "high tech."[72] This shift has begun to impact all of our relationships—from our personal affiliations to our "relationships" with our money and possessions, the businesses we frequent (and operate), the medical community (and our bodies), our political structures, our spiritual institutions, our problems (and our talents for solving them), nature and the environment, and the information, technology and resources available to us, as well!

This idea of "connectedness" represents a change in our awareness, too. It includes a growing realization that everything is interrelated, and that our actions—and, some say, even our thoughts—can have an impact beyond anything we may have previously imagined. It's about what Peter Senge calls "systems thinking," and the shift of mind "from seeing ourselves as separate from the world to connected to the world."[73] It's a mind-boggling leap from a thought structure that focuses on individual parts of a whole, to one that is moving toward holism, devoted to "understanding the system as a system, and giving primary value to the relationships that exist among seemingly discrete parts."[74] And while this notion certainly refers to more than just our connections with people, it also requires an acknowledgment that human growth and change happen most frequently in the context of human relationships—and that the nature of these relationships, and the energy dynamics within them, have an impact on the growth and change that occurs.

Education has always had an enormous "human factor," accounting for the influence of adults and peers in a school setting. Archbishop Desmond Tutu recounts his experiences in an impoverished South African ghetto school with "hardly any facilities to mention."[75] And yet, there was one math teacher, a Mr. Ndebele, who inspired extraordinary learning in his students. There were no discipline problems, and every one of his pupils passed the state public exams, many receiving distinctions for their achievements in this subject area. This success could hardly be attributed to the abundance of resources or technologies. The badly overcrowded church that was used as a school lacked even the most basic amenities such as desks and chairs. (The pews served both purposes, depending upon whether one sat on the seats or the floor.) Reverend Tutu attributes Mr. Ndebele's influence to the way he connected with his students: "He made us feel so special, and that was something, coming as we all did from an environment that conspired to make us feel utterly dejected, nonentities, whose parents counted for nothing in the land of their birth."[76]

I don't remember anyone ever telling me to look at my students with my heart instead of my grade book, but I know that I was able to connect better—and *teach* better, and get better results—whenever I was able to pull that off. The potential, indeed the necessity, exists for anyone who works with children. Being a knowledgeable, passionate teacher, skilled in instructional technique and entertaining delivery certainly counts for something, but I believe that the quality of the bond between a teacher and student will give passion and skill a place to take root. Any dimension of educational success, whether we're talking about academic achievement, discipline issues, or social and emotional development, for example, starts with a positive, healthy and meaningful connection between teacher and student. Successful teaching—which hopefully means more than simply transmitting information from teacher to learners—means successful relationships.

Unfortunately, much of the scant attention that has been paid to this aspect of education has focused on win-lose power dynamics, advanced in the name of discipline and control. In this regard, much of what has passed for conventional wisdom simply ends up creating *more* stress in the teacher-student relationship. For the most part, the idea of *any* relationship between teachers and students has frequently been very specifically discouraged. Comments like, "I don't care if they like me (as long as they respect me)," or "Don't smile before Christmas," insinuate that a close, enjoyable bond between an adult and child will preclude the possibility of adult authority, instructional success or mutual respect. In fact, these goals are typically *more* attainable in the context of a positive relationship—one in which both children and adults can feel respected, valued and safe. And for some children, as far as finding a place to connect with a positive, caring adult goes, school is the only game in town. So the quality of the relationships in this setting matters. A lot.

But there's something a little strange about relationships in this context of connectedness. It's not like our social concept, where we think of relationships in reference to people we like or choose to spend time with, or people we're thrown together with by virtue of our jobs or family relationships. Connectedness broadens the concept, and includes relationships with people (and things) we don't seem to actually have any real connection with. This is because the connection isn't necessarily a material, emotional, conversational or overtly interactive one. But make no mistake about it. At a certain level, there's definitely a connection, whether the individuals are interacting or not. It may be based on caring and respect; it may reflect hostility and mistrust. There's also energy in indifference, in being ignored, overlooked or marginalized. In a school setting, *any* connection has the potential for tremendous impact on children's learning and behavior, and on their feelings and beliefs, as well.

I like the idea of looking at education through this lens of connectedness. The concept encourages us to look beyond the content dimensions of instruction to the ways in which the energy dynamics inherent in our relationships and interaction patterns impact teaching and learning. It holds us accountable for the way we treat one another, the way we allow ourselves to be treated and the energy between us. In many cases, it will challenge us to examine and change some of the more destructive relationship dynamics that pervade the instructional environment and erode the emotional climate in these settings. But perhaps most importantly, it gives us a rationale for going through our priority list and, if it's not already there, elevating the concept of community to the top.

10

All Are Welcome Here: The Need for Community

In a school with a strong sense of community, students are more likely to feel valued and less likely to fall through the cracks.

Laura Kelly[1]

Teachers were always there for me in ways that my parents may not have been. I always felt that I could talk to at least one of my teachers about my concerns.

Sandy Murray
elementary-school principal

People make a difference. . . . Research supports it, common sense confirms it.

James Sweeney[2]

On December 31, 1999, I spent the day celebrating the arrival of the new year, time zone after time zone, with the entire world. From the comfort of my living room, I was able to partake in festivities around the globe, and witness and share the exuberance, joy and hope evident in the faces that appeared on my TV screen. It was a moving, humbling and powerful feeling to be a part of something so enormous, to be connected, via these electronic transmissions, with billions of others on this planet. The idea of a whole new millennium (by popular definition) was certainly profound in and of itself. But beyond any implications the calendar might have held, this experience thoroughly redefined my notion of community.

Communications technology—and, to be sure, the Internet—has dramatically opened up a whole new world of possibilities for this concept. Where community was once thought of in terms of extended family and local neighborhoods, this notion has expanded to include anyone with access to a telephone or modem.[3] But despite these changes, or perhaps because of them, the need for community is still critical to our social and emotional well-being. A sense of community provides evidence of our interconnectedness, and a place in which we can satisfy our need for belonging. Many personal and social ills have been linked to an absence of community, and the feeling of being disconnected from the whole.[4] High-school counselor Barbara Wills claims that this lack of connection "is a big factor in the lack of success" of many of the counselees she sees each day.

In survey responses from around the world, there was an extremely high correlation between feeling a sense of community and a sense of safety. Dozens of individuals identified good friends, caring teachers and a strong extended family as factors that contributed to their feeling safe as children. Many people cited living in small towns where "you knew almost everyone" or being in classes where "we all stuck together" as the basis for their security. Still others noted the presence of adults you could talk to and depend on. "Safety was the feeling that the adults in charge had a plan. Whether it was a fire drill or the air raid preparations, as a kid I knew that I was in the care of responsible adults," wrote educator Roberta Braverman. People remember feeling safe in settings where adults were present, visible and attentive. Retired teacher Elaine Lesse recalled how "the teacher stood on duty at recess and escorted us in and out." Author MaryAnn Kohl noted, "If your mother wasn't going to be home, a next door neighbor, sitter or good friend would be there to take care of you," and that kids couldn't get away with anything "because everyone watched out for kids, even if they were strangers." And school counselor Lynn Lowrance remembered feeling safe because "the environment was structured and predictable, routines and procedures were established, and calm, knowledgeable adults were there to help."

Nostalgia aside, there is good news in recent research which assures us that a majority of teens from all segments of society say they're close to their parents, and that they want the connections that come from listening, setting guidelines and spending time together. Additionally, many believe their schools are staffed with teachers and administrators who care about them.[5] Still, there seems to be a general consensus that many of the "external structures" that were common in the past, such as family, community and shared values, no longer exist.[6] On average, some reports claim that parents now spend 40 percent less time with their kids than they did thirty years ago.[7] Psychologist Paul Clements attributes some of the insecurity and problems he sees in kids to a lack of extended families. He also notes, "I don't see love in the homes as much as I would like." Stanford University professor Elliot Eisner remarks that the need for "someone in touch with the emotional and social aspects of the students' lives" is predicated by the absence of "strong nuclear families and strong social bonds" in the communities in which students live. "The school has always had a caring role to play," he asserts, "but this role is considerably more critical today."[8]

A Worthy Investment

I would probably do anything for a teacher I liked.

student, gang member[9]

I haven't met a child incapable of thinking and participating to some degree, if we let him know we value what he can contribute.

William Glasser[10]

Creating a respectful, caring and intentionally inviting learning environment is the surest way to encourage student achievement.

William Purkey and David Aspy[11]

When a truly caring and supportive community is available to a child, whether in the form of a family, neighborhood, peer acceptance or even one caring adult, the positive outcomes can be substantial. A 1997 survey of twelve thousand students from seventh to twelfth grade set out to identify factors that might affect young people's resistance to eight different risk areas (including violence, use of alcohol or drugs, sexual activity and suicide). The study found two significant protective factors: "connectedness to family (feeling close to and cared about by parents and other family members)" and "connectedness to school (feeling close to people at school, feeling fairly treated by teachers and feeling a part of the school)."[12]

The power of community can be seen in a number of areas. For example, special education supervisor Mary Finley reports that "a caring and supportive relationship with at least one person" is a "key protective factor" that helps inoculate kids against adversity and build resiliency.[13] Studies show that a sense of community also boosts academic motivation, enjoyment of school and trust and respect for teachers. Additionally, it also promotes socially acceptable attitudes and behaviors and can even increase the amount of time kids spend reading![14] The value of community can also be seen in character education and the development of positive values.[15] In fact, a sense of community can actually replace many of the structured prevention programs, claims author Eric Schaps, inspiring students to fit in and succeed: "Peer-group dynamics tend to work in support of, rather than contrary to, the school's goals and values."[16] This sense of community is also related to increased engagement in school activities, lower rates of student burnout, class cutting and thoughts of dropping out, and a higher likelihood of feeling bad when unprepared for class.[17] Further, research indicates that a "positive school climate where nurturance, inclusiveness and community feeling are evident" is common among schools with low levels of violent behavior.[18]

A sense of connection is important for learning and academic growth. Parent educator Ginny Luther found that, as a preschool teacher, her first job with any class was building safety and a sense of "team" in her classrooms. Luther found that students could be more successful academically once the relationships, trust and cohesion were in place to support learning: "No matter what the deadlines are for academic progress, none will be made if the kids don't have a sense of belonging, acceptance or safety in their classroom." Others would agree. Jane Nelsen associates each of Dreikurs's "mistaken goals" of children's behaviors—including attention, power, revenge and assumed inadequacy—to kids' perception of their ability to connect with others.[19] There is widespread acceptance of the positive relationship between school culture and student achievement.[20] Carl Rogers and Jerome Frieberg describe transforming a group of individuals into a "community of learners," leading to an excitement "almost beyond belief," and triggering curiosity, inquiry and personally meaningful exploration.[21] And William Glasser remarks that the preparation to live successfully demands involvement, not only with a curriculum that inspires thinking and problem solving, but also with the teachers who present this curriculum: Students cannot make better and more responsible choices, he claims, "unless they are strongly and emotionally involved with those who can."[22]

Claire Thornton asks teachers to be responsive and to offer the emotional security children need to concentrate on learning. She notes that "teachers cannot take away the pain, struggles and trauma of their students," but that by creating a secure environment, they can "ease negative life experiences."[23] Indeed, schools in which close bonds between teachers and students develop can be a "second chance" for many children, according to Nathaniel Branden. Schools, he says, can offer kids "an opportunity to acquire a better sense of self and a better vision of life than was offered in their home. A teacher who projects confidence in a child's competence and goodness can be a powerful antidote to a family in which such confidence is lacking and in which, perhaps, the opposite perspective is conveyed."[24]

Certainly a great deal of evidence supports these ideas. Over and over, I've heard stories of how one teacher—sometimes even one comment at just the right moment—made a life-changing difference for a child, often in the absence of just about any other support or protective factor in the child's life. Beth Lefevre still considers her third-grade teacher to have been her "salvation." At a time when Beth's parents "were drinking a lot," she writes, "I couldn't wait to get to school and I was the last to leave." Her connection with this teacher created the one place where she felt safe: "I never felt so incredibly loved, exactly the way I was." New Zealand educator Faye Hauwai moved frequently and felt that her "peer-bonding issues" contributed to a sense of inadequacy and self-doubt at that time. However, she claims, "I was an achiever at school and therefore I felt secure in the system and the way it rewarded me. Teachers made me feel confident about what I had to offer. . . ." And dozens of adults who grew up with parents who were drug dependent, physically or sexually abusive, mentally ill or emotionally unavailable, shared their recollections of that one special teacher who offered emotional sanctuary and encouragement.[25]

Connecting in School

Although students spend their academic careers in groups, schools often ignore the potential benefits of this group life.

Eric Schaps and Daniel Solomon[26]

The teacher-student relationship is easily lost in a confusing web of rules, limits and required objectives.

Carl Rogers and Jerome Frieberg[27]

At-risk youth cannot learn from anyone who doesn't like them.

Vicki Phillips[28]

When it comes to schools, there are communities and then there are communities. Just because we've got a number of people in the same physical environment doesn't ensure that the connections are going to be constructive or productive ones. John Goodlad observes that principals and teachers are isolated, and that people in schools need to get closer to kids.[29] And Kent Peterson and Terrence Deal write about the "blight of toxic cultures" in schools in which "staffs are extremely fragmented, where the purpose of serving students has been lost to the goal of serving the adults, where negative values and hopelessness reign."[30] Certainly external pressures have their impact. One report bemoaned the fact that "mandates and regulations govern many school systems in ways that make schools impersonal, indifferent and generally insensitive to the individuals within them."[31] Middle-school principal Barry Hopping commented on the erosive impact of "teacher bashing" and the "revenge mentality" of policy makers. He also described feeling betrayed by "mandates that allow no time for making connections with kids."

And then there is the experience of the school itself. Having visited classrooms on four continents, I would have to agree with J. Merrell Hansen and John Childs in their observations about schools: "They look alike and, some suggest, they even smell alike."[32] In a way, I find these similarities to be rather comforting: There's always been something magical for me about being in a school, and no matter where I am, it only takes one whiff of chalk dust to let me know that I'm "home." But there are differences, energetic variations that determine how schools *feel* when you walk in the door. Some are warm, lively and inviting, while others feel cold, indifferent, even hostile. Many factors contribute to a school's "personality." There are surface features, of course—the design, layout and landscaping, for example—but the attitudes, interactions and behaviors of the people (which are certainly influenced by the setting's physical attributes) pack an even bigger punch. This tone starts at the front office, and oftentimes, you can gain a pretty good sense of the quality, values and priorities of the school community from what you find there. Rita Mercier suggests examining a number of issues related to the school office, including whether adults and kids are greeted promptly and in a courteous and helpful way, whether the office serves mainly as a place to welcome people and exhibit student work and information about the school, and whether the office and administrative staff are available and responsive when parents or other professionals call, drop by or need assistance.[33]

A recent visit to an area high school gave me a clear example of how various elements can impact the school climate, and of how sharply this climate can be felt. One mid-December afternoon, I went to drop off a Christmas card for one of the kids I'd worked with at the day treatment center. A security guard waved me in, but after fifteen minutes of driving around with no success in finding a place to park, I wasn't feeling particularly welcome there. If there was visitor parking anywhere, I never found it. I chose a space with a no-parking sign (behind another car illegally parked there) over the "permit parking only" lots (which were full anyhow). I had no problem getting into the building—no one was there to greet me (or screen me). Once inside, I couldn't find the office, nor any signs to direct me there. There was little evidence of the upcoming holidays, and the building had this weird feeling of being deserted, although school was definitely in session and hundreds of kids and adults were there. Even when the halls were full, a lethargy was evident, a kind of numbness that was palpable, and more than a bit unnerving. When I got to the office (finally, with the help of a student), I found the staff to be helpful but harried. None of the adults I asked had heard of the student I was there to visit, until I finally hooked up with one of his special ed teachers—a close bond there, in that community-within-a-community. Otherwise, the overall sense was one of disconnectedness and apathy. Perhaps it was the time of year, or the time of day, but I couldn't help wondering about what this environment must feel like to the individuals who spend their days there.

Logistical Issues: A Sizeable Question

Students feel anonymous when they have no adult to turn to who knows them well and cares about their welfare.

James McPartland, Will Jordan, Nettie Legters and Robert Belfanz[34]

Our school district was small. Everyone knew everyone. Our schools were also, by their design, segregated. I don't believe this prepared me for working with diverse populations.

Wendy Paser
prekindergarten teacher

The point is not just to be small. Rather it is to change the relationships within schools.

Susan Klonsky and Michael Klonsky[35]

Some would argue that what I experienced on my visit to this high school is evidence of what happens in schools that are simply too big. There is, in many circles, a clamoring for smaller schools these days. I see this trend as both a reasonable reaction to the lack of community in many schools (regardless of size) and also, to some degree, as a reaction to recent episodes of school violence. There is quite a bit of research to support a move in this direction at all grade levels.[36] Studies have shown that, in general, the quality of school climate declines as school size increases.[37] According to the research, kids in smaller schools get better grades, are less likely to be involved in gangs or violence, have better attendance and lower dropout rates and are more likely to participate in extracurricular activities.[38] Most of the support for smaller schools speaks to greater possibilities for developing a sense of community, whether in a small setting or in a larger school divided into "smaller, semi-autonomous sub-units."[39]

In purely mathematical terms, the findings are hard to dispute. However, anecdotal reports do not uniformly support the research, and certain problems can occur in a smaller setting which the research does not address. The critical variable seems to be the *quality* of connections, which may or may not be a function of size. Given the right people, the right attitudes and the right opportunities, I believe that significant bonding and support can occur in any setting. I'm not convinced that meaningful and positive connections are guaranteed—or even more likely—for children or staff, just because they're in a small-school environment.

My concerns come, in part, from firsthand experience in both types of settings, having been a student for two years at a high school where my class alone had around one thousand students, and then at another school about one-third the size. Having lived in both cultures, I feel compelled to challenge the "smaller-is-better" conclusions because, as a student, I actually had the opposite experience. While both schools boasted high levels of instruction and student achievement, the larger school, by virtue of its size, was able to offer a much better variety of classes, resources and extracurricular opportunities—places for me to learn, belong and succeed that simply did not exist in the smaller school. And despite the relative enormity of the faculty at the larger school, I always felt as though I had adults I could talk to, people who valued and looked out for me. (A few of the relationships I established with teachers during the two years I was there continue to this day.) My experience in the smaller school was quite different, and it showed—in my commitment and, ultimately, in my grades. And while I'm well aware that neither school was "good" nor "bad" because of its size, I believe my experience to have been consequential enough to justify some caution in applying the conclusions of the research too literally.

Proponents of small schools claim that these environments "allow all kids to feel like they fit in."[40] Yet a strong community has little value to a student who isn't included in it. I saw plenty of "outcasting" in both of the schools I attended, and I've known plenty of individuals in both large and small settings who had problems with peer bonding. There is a certain advantage, however, for students in larger schools, as they have a wider variety of options for successful social connections if their attempts at affiliating with one group don't work out. Beyond size, there are issues of acceptance and tolerance also involved here. Is it fair to assume that a smaller school population will automatically be more welcoming than a larger group, particularly to a child who is perceived as an outsider, or even as simply being "different," for whatever reason?[41] Perhaps more important than size, particularly in these instances, is a school's willingness to embrace practices and policies that value diversity, respect differences and refuse to tolerate any form of discrimination or exclusion.

Being a student in a fairly homogeneous community can put some children at a distinct and sometimes relentless disadvantage. When Sherri Davidman worked as a middle-school counselor in a small suburban school district, she noticed that if a child picked up a label in kindergarten, it often lasted through graduation, even if that student had outgrown the label years before. (Many of Davidman's students didn't realize that there were others with whom they had anything in common until they got to college.) High-school counselor Eric Katz also sees some benefits in a bigger school, especially one with a large, heterogeneous population. Katz maintains that "the diversity and scale of our high school allows greater opportunities for students to find their social niche." He sees diversity as the primary variable involved in more students being able to find a place to fit in, with the physical size being vital to allowing "physical and psychological space for all the various ensembles to coexist in relative harmony."

Certainly any school community can be safe and welcoming with certain ingredients in place. Writer Linda Sorenson went to a big school and "loved it." She claims that teachers who knew her and took an active interest in things she cared about, as well as a principal who repeatedly expressed his caring and pride to the students, contributed to the sense of community she experienced there. Further, she felt that the school's excellence enhanced this community, and having "lots of engaging activities" and opportunities to explore personal interests added a sense of intimacy in this setting. At the opposite extreme, sizewise, student Erica Frenkel went to a private school at which the student body was so small that the largest class consisted of twenty-four students. "However," she says, "in my five years there, the school's size never once seemed limiting." What made this tiny elementary school "work" were the multiage classes (which "relieved the monotony of being with the same seventeen kids every year"), the social acceptability of friendships across grade levels, and a faculty and administration committed to creating a sense of family. Business manager Jerry Tereszkiewicz attended two different high schools. He attributes his relative comfort in the smaller setting not to its size, but to commitment of the staff: "Teachers cared. They did not tolerate nor participate in bullying or exclusion. Jocks were respected and valued but not revered. No students were forgotten or ignored." Although he didn't fit in everywhere, he and his friends never felt like outcasts either. And one principal who had worked, at various times and in different parts of the country, in a small rural school, a large urban school and a medium-sized suburban school confirmed that differences in the atmospheres in these various settings depended far more on the values and priorities of the adults in the school, and the way they interacted with one another, than on the number of people in the building.

Surprisingly, even class size—typically a more significant variable than school size—can, in the right hands, take a back seat to a teacher's skill and caring. Several people who had been in very large classes reported that they were able to establish powerful connections and feel quite close to their teachers. Victor Allan C. Ilagan, a lecturer in the Philippines, noted that his teachers were more like surrogate parents. "I felt loved and cared for, although we were usually forty-five to fifty students in a class," he claims. While such a crowd is hardly the ideal for either instruction or bonding, it obviously is not impervious to meaningful connections. (This is certainly true for counselors and teachers in departmentalized setting who see large numbers of students in the course of a day. Surely some of the most dramatic stories of a teacher's personal attention, dedication or faith in a student came from individuals who were, at the time, one of 150 students or more on that teacher's roster.) So once again, it seems that numbers don't tell the whole story. For most people, this issue boils down to the attitude of the administration and the teachers, a widespread commitment to the value of community, and a shot at a sense of place—or at very least, the freedom from exclusion. In all effective settings, the common thread is people, and the concern, acceptance and attention they offered.[42] As Tereszkiewicz notes, "Caring is what aids the education process, not size."

The Power of Advocacy

I am the decisive element in the classroom. It is my personal approach that creates the climate. It is my daily mood that makes the weather.

Haim Ginott

[The principal] knew every kid in the school by his first name, and not by accident. He was really concerned and everybody felt it. He knew what you were planning to do in life and how to help you get there.

Al Worden[43]

Relationships are the foundation of a personalized school. Opening students' minds to lifelong learning requires cultivating their trust and respect. Without a positive student-teacher relationship, many students aren't even willing to try.

Dennis Littky and Farrell Allen[44]

Verónica de Andrés, an educator in Argentina, claims that one teacher changed her whole life story simply by demonstrating that she believed in her. She feels that the most important factors in her sense of emotional safety included "feeling 'seen' and respected by the teachers and peers." This sense of "visibility" and value is critical. In a report on high school reform, anonymity is one of the primary sources of problems in a typical large high school. The antidote, the authors claim, is a "personalized atmosphere," one in which students and teachers get to know one another.[45] Another report, this one on issues involved in middle school philosophy, includes a recommendation for "adult advocates" to make sure that "no middle-level student feels isolated or alone." This report also sees advocacy as an important element of a nurturing climate, and as a way to create community "through varied organizational structures, such as advisor-advisee programs, homebase groups and team mentoring."[46] For as high-school principal Donald Wesley notes, "Anonymity is no match for teachers who choose to believe in their students, even on the slightest of evidence."[47] Although important in all settings, the need for this kind of connection is particularly valuable in a large school or new setting. Educator Cheryl Ficocello described her daughter Megan's experience in a high school with about three thousand students. The school has programs in place to explore students' preferences and ambitions—in Megan's case, an interest in becoming a nurse—and create schedules in such a way as to allow students with similar interests to connect with one another in at least a few of their classes. "This made the high school more palatable for her," says Ficocello.

If the need for a significant connection with an adult has benefits for all students, it is particularly critical for those kids at highest risk. Research suggests that along with achievement, "the attitudes of low socio-economic status and minority students are especially sensitive" to the benefits of a strong school community.[48] One report relates how some gang members who managed to turn their lives around credit the personal interest and attention they received from their schools' police officers and other caring adults.[49] Another found that few, if any of the dropouts in one particular study, "could recall any teacher whom they could consider a friend throughout their school years."[50] Author Karen Irmsher identifies two conditions characterizing schools that successfully serve at-risk kids. The first is that these schools function as "caring, cohesive communities." Second, "they operate under standards similar to high-reliability organizations," agencies like air-traffic-control towers that have the level of support necessary to achieve their goal of "100 percent failure-free operation."[51] Providing a thread of stability in a child's life seems to support this goal. For example, for some students, having five to seven teachers, typically for less than an hour each, may not offer adequate opportunities for establishing the kind of bond that would feel truly supportive.[52] Counselor Beverly Davies suspects that moving through a series of departmentalized settings can actually exacerbate "whatever attachment problems the kid may already be demonstrating." She believes in "self-containing the most dysfunctional kids so that they can attach to one teacher during the school year," and recommends that schools keep the teacher-child ratio low for these children and maintain the placement over a period of several years. Continuity is also a key to the success of Friends of the Children, a program that hires full-time mentors to oversee a small group of at-risk children throughout the children's school careers.[53]

This idea can be advantageous to all students—not just those at greatest risk. Speech therapist Sharon Tandy spoke of her high-school Russian class in which a small number of students studied the language and culture with the same teacher, most of them throughout the four years they attended the school. Tandy recalled a certain intimacy as the class became "more like a close-knit family," one that offered her a sense of acceptance, belonging, respect and fun. In another example, Cheryl Ficocello tells how, in her daughter's school, each student is assigned to a specific dean, ideally to stay with this same person for the entire four years. "Megan has always felt comfortable any time she needs to talk to somebody. She knows she can go to this woman and tell her what she needs and she'll at least give her an ear." Ficocello further notes that the deans really get to know their charges: "She doesn't need a file in front of her" when Megan goes in to visit. Author Nel Noddings considers herself a "firm believer" in this kind of continuity. Having taught one group of high school students for three consecutive years, she notes, "If teachers and students stay together by mutual consent for three years, you can do ever so much more than you can in one year."[54] She includes among the many benefits of spending this much time together a greater depth of connection and a sense of renewal for teachers.[55]

Some schools are trying to attract more men to the classroom, especially at the elementary level. Although nationally, only about 10 percent of teachers in kindergarten through sixth-grade classrooms are men, something can be said for the potential influence of gender in the classroom, "particularly in urban school districts where male role models are needed."[56] A male presence, especially for young children, helps boys personalize the value of learning, studying and doing their homework.[57] However Davies cautions that "filling the 'missing man' hole" will require more than just gender. We need "men who are clean and sober and available, and who are willing to allow attachment to occur," she says.

The need for advocacy and personal attention is also behind the numerous mentoring programs popping up in schools and around the country. The main goal of these programs is to provide children and teens with adults who will spend time with them and let them know they care for them.[58] Mentor programs have been shown to help kids improve in school and in their relationships with family and friends, as well. While often targeted specifically for at-risk kids, many believe that adult mentors can benefit all children, offering them "discipline, guidance and personal attention."[59]

But the benefits of a strong, caring school community don't happen in a vacuum. When it comes to connecting with students, teachers with certain positive and "facilitative" characteristics will always have an edge.[60] For example, effective advocacy requires a high degree of empathy, responsiveness and authenticity, as well as the ability to be warm and human in an authority relationship. Add in the willingness to treat students with acceptance and respect, a genuine appreciation for students' opinions, the ability to tailor discussions to the students' frame of reference and a general belief in the students' competence and potential, and these teachers have a great shot at creating an atmosphere of trust and belonging.[61]

Putting It All Together

Like throwing pebbles in a pond, the ripples go out from one small action and you never know how far they will reach.

Grace Mitchell[62]

It really boils down to this: that all life is interrelated. We are all caught up in an inescapable network of mutuality, tied into a single garment of destiny. Whatever affects one directly, affects all indirectly.

Martin Luther King Jr.[63]

I see communication as a huge umbrella that covers and affects all that goes on between human beings.

Virginia Satir[64]

Clearly community is a function of people and the quality of the connections among them. This feeling starts with relationships and interactions between individuals, and with classroom communities that are part of a larger school community. As with any set of personal values and priorities, we can't mandate the creation of communities, nor can we mandate the healthy and supportive relationships by which they are characterized. Nonetheless, schools and districts striving to build community typically work with some combination of vision, values, policies and practices to entice commitment from (and give direction to) everyone involved in achieving this goal. As a result, we can look to those schools that have established a sense of community to identify specific ingredients contributing to their success.

In the literature, the term *community* or *caring community* appears in a variety of contexts. (Even trends in architecture and city planning are looking to accommodate this hunger for connection, designing multifamily compounds and residential neighborhoods set up as self-contained villages in place of fragmented, isolating and impersonal sprawl.[65]) One educational program includes among its goals creating consensus on values related to school, building collegiality among staff members, extending teachers' roles beyond classroom instruction and building an "ethos of caring."[66] Another approach notes that relationships in schools that have achieved a sense of community include characteristics such as "shared vision, participation, shared sense of purpose, caring, shared values, trust, incorporation of diversity, teamwork, communication, respect and recognition."[67] Yet another promotes a set of "key beliefs and values," with requisites for success including the need for teachers to work together, respect all individuals in the school, feel valued, believe they make a difference, have some sense of control over the events that take place in the school, and exhibit traits of confidentiality, honesty, expertise and fairness.[68] Other community-building programs are more narrowly focused, emphasizing, for example, the comprehensive support for preschool-aged children and their families,[69] the importance of knowing students well so that they can be taught appropriately (based on their individual strengths, needs and experiences)[70] or the benefits of establishing a caring community in urban settings to accommodate the needs of low-income students of color.[71] But regardless of focus, creating community in schools seems to demand what Rogers and Renard call a "relationship-centered framework for teaching," the standards for which include students feeling cared about, successful, involved in meaningful learning, and physically and emotionally safe.[72]

One of the most effective tools for creating the climate and connections in which a healthy sense of community can emerge is simply listening to the people in the community and valuing what they have to say.[73] Author Jack Miller remarks, "Listening carefully to students and showing respect through small acts of attention build a sense of classroom community."[74] Katz suggests that "social standing or identity can be nurtured in any environment where there is a conscious desire to allow students a voice." And Barry Hopping claims one of the best programs in his middle school is the one in which advisors and students meet weekly to give the kids a chance to talk and be heard. In addition to promoting student involvement and building community, the process allows the staff to "stay on top of things" and attempt to resolve problems before they reach a crisis level. The importance of giving students a voice, and creating ways for them to share their concerns safely, is especially critical in light of findings that suggest that "peers often are the most likely group to know in advance about potential school violence."[75]

Sometimes the connections can come from the simplest things—positive acknowledgment and recognition, including apparently "throwaway" comments that may have much more significance than we might realize.[76] One of my favorite stories about teachers making a difference came from an individual who was deeply affected by a third-grade music teacher—simply because "she noticed me." It doesn't take much to touch the heart of a child in a deep and meaningful way. Clearly, even a smile and simple acknowledgment can go a long, long way.[77]

All the King's Horses . . .

The popular solution may not be the best solution.

Lauretta Buchanan[78]

Asking them to identify smaller, more specific problems was pushing them in exactly the wrong direction, because the real problems were big—bigger than anything I imagined.

Margaret Wheatley[79]

We are continually faced with great opportunities brilliantly disguised as insoluble problems.

Unknown[80]

The problem is not the problem. Coping is the problem.

Virginia Satir[81]

As the fairy tale goes, when Humpty Dumpty fell off the wall, his descent left him fractured beyond the best resources of king and country. There are those who would see Humpty's fate as a metaphor for our schools—too broken to fix, at least with the "pieces" we've currently got. More than a few people I interviewed, including a number of educators and high-ranking administrators, suggested that the best way to make schools safe and productive is to "tear 'em down and start over."[82] Ostensibly, many efforts at restructuring and reorganization have attempted to do just that. But even the best intentions rarely go beyond simply analyzing and rearranging the fragments that are scattered at the base of the wall.

The fallacy lies in our preoccupation with these fragments, and our failure to see our systems of education *as* systems, systems in which all of the individual elements—that is, the people, structures, procedures, roles, policies, beliefs, values, power dynamics, organizational design, resources and all the other elements that make up the system—are all interrelated, constantly impacting one another. In this age of connectedness, everything affects everything else. Nothing happens in isolation, and whatever happens at a distance also happens right here. Perhaps this is why the notion of community has such great appeal: Not only does it hold the promise of meeting such basic human needs as safety and belonging, but it also gives us a context for the interconnectedness that exists in such a rich and dynamic tapestry. Once again, this means that what we bring to this tapestry matters, because even seemingly insignificant actions have an impact on the whole. It also means that the truly profound changes are most likely to happen locally and incrementally, in this case, between individuals who are a part of the system. As systems theory expert Margaret Wheatley notes, "The challenge for us is to see beyond the innumerable fragments to the whole, stepping back far enough to appreciate how things move and change as a coherent entity."[83]

As we know, learning and achievement happen within an emotional environment—one created, at least in part, by the school community, regardless of the shape it's in. Throughout the years, we've been all over the map with our efforts to connect (or, in fact, disconnect) from students. Each choice we've made has impacted the climate of the classroom and the school. Kids and adults can connect with one another in innumerable ways, instructionally and emotionally. And while it's hard to argue with author Parker Palmer's idea that we lost our sense of community when we lost the middle ground "between invading one another and ignoring one another,"[84] it is also possible to create, in schools, a place of sanity and balance between those two extremes. If we're going to reach kids in schools that are challenging and stimulating and, at the same time, safe and welcoming, we will need to reclaim that space, and the healthy, functional behaviors that go with it. I don't believe that this will necessitate demolishing what we have in front of us, but I am certain that we're going to have to start looking at the tapestry in a far less fragmented way.

11

Snags in the Tapestry

You do not get out of a problem by using the same consciousness that got you into it.

Albert Einstein

Our biggest problem as human beings is not knowing that we don't know.

Virginia Satir[1]

Things in the environment that disturb the system's equilibrium play a crucial role in creating new forms of order.

Margaret Wheatley[2]

A few years back, a friend gave me a book of "magic eye" posters. On the front cover is an abstract design in turquoise, red, black and white, circles and lines that, on the surface, convey nothing in particular. But focus a bit beyond the picture as you hold it up and—if you don't go blind or crazy first—a three-dimensional image of three dolphins clearly appears. It's an old fad, but it still fascinates me. This may be in part because I'm pretty good at visually coaxing the hidden graphic off the page, and because I also enjoy the subtle victory inherent in unraveling a mystery. But even more intriguing is the idea of an unseen reality existing below what I initially perceive.

Extending this example as a metaphor for organizations (and life itself, really) isn't much of a stretch. Any educational setting will offer a first impression of how that institution is "working." But regardless of the information we take in at first glance, there is certainly more going on than meets the eye. Look a little deeper, and certain patterns begin to emerge. Certainly some are healthy and productive. But unfortunately, our most familiar and enduring relationship models have left us with some destructive patterns, as well. In many cases, these tendencies are so common and familiar that, having defined for decades what is normal and acceptable, they generally pass unnoticed and unquestioned. But these negative structures, behaviors and beliefs not only interfere with the objectives and intentions we profess to be priorities, they also, in fact, make things worse.

Author Juanita Ross Epp categorizes "any institutional practice or procedure that adversely impacts on individuals or groups by burdening them psychologically, mentally, culturally, spiritually, economically or physically" under the ominous heading of "systemic violence." Applied to the context of education, she uses this term to refer to patterns that harm students by preventing them from learning. Epp acknowledges, however, that systemic violence is not "intentional harm visited on the unlucky by vicious individuals. Rather it is the unintentional consequences of procedures implemented by well-meaning authorities in a belief that the practices are in the best interests of students."[3] But how to change these practices? We're talking about some subtle and well-entrenched patterns here. Add to that a rather pervasive and very human resistance to change. As John Goodlad notes, educators can be "extraordinarily adept at nullifying or defusing practices perceived to be in conflict with prevailing ways of doing things."[4]

The idea of school reform and restructuring has been around forever. But now, more than ever, this issue demands more than simply putting old "pieces" together in new ways. The challenge now is about thinking, instead, in terms of how the decisions we make affect this tapestry we call education. More recently, the notion of "reculturing" has emerged. This term goes beyond the idea of a new structure (although changes to the structure may certainly be involved) and refers, instead, to the challenge of "transforming mind-sets, visions, paradigms, images, metaphors, beliefs and shared meaning that sustain existing realities. . . . It is about inventing what amounts to a new way of life."[5] This means looking beneath the surface, and effecting change at a "deeper level of basic assumptions and beliefs that are shared by members of an organization, that operate unconsciously and that define in a basic, 'taken-for-granted' fashion an organization's view of itself and its environment," or what Edgar H. Schein calls the organization's "culture."[6] For regardless of the structural changes, building improvements, equipment upgrades, security devices, high expectations, motivational slogans, and our best efforts at testing and training, if the system is not built on a foundation of healthy beliefs and functional interactive patterns, there's a good chance that even apparently positive changes will be fairly superficial. Looking good isn't good enough. Below the appearances, beyond the numbers, an entirely different reality will exist, in this case, one that perpetuates the very problems we say we're trying to solve. But unlike the "magic eye" posters, where a three-dimensional treasure is hiding beneath the surface, in educational institutions, behind the most innocuous surface reality often lurks real danger.

The School as a Dysfunctional Family

Those who will not apply new remedies must expect new evils, for time is the greatest innovator.

Francis Bacon

We all have the power to change the scripts we have been given, to alter them so that they reflect accurately our values and the principles we decided to consciously embrace.

Vimala McClure[7]

Disorder can be a source of order. . . . Growth is found in disequilibrium, not in balance.

Margaret Wheatley[8]

Every organization within a school system has its own culture—from the various groups in a school to the district as a whole. For better or worse, each culture or group offers its own "situationally unique"[9] sense of family. When the beliefs, values and behaviors in these "families" support the developmental and emotional needs of the individuals involved (including safety and belonging needs), we say that group is healthy or functional. When these same patterns hurt members of the "family" or undermine their various needs, then the group's health and functionality are compromised. Although the joke's a bit stale, the comparisons between a dysfunctional family and most educational institutions still hold. As such, our commitment to creating emotionally safe schools, and the healthy relationships that support this climate, obliges us to take a closer look behind the surface, to identify the patterns which serve and those which do not. On closer inspection, we'll probably find that in the context of these goals, we've got a bit of baggage to unload. These are the dynamics at the heart of so many of the problems we see in schools—the patterns and obstacles that make schools operate like troubled families, and which sabotage our best intentions to encourage academic, social and personal success in kids.

I've identified a number of these patterns and, for manageability's sake, have grouped them into sets of related behaviors. My organization is fairly arbitrary, and most of my examples will involve a certain amount of overlap. (There are, in fact, a number of characteristics and tendencies, things like negativity, double standards or incongruence between goals and practices, which tend to occur in most of these categories. Few of the patterns I've identified will ever occur in isolation from many or most of the others.) Each category and the corresponding characteristics, as well as a list of healthier alternatives, is included in a chart at the end of the chapter. The point of this list is to help us start to notice the beliefs and interaction patterns that hurt in some way—either by inflicting pain on individuals in the system or by sabotaging worthwhile goals and intentions. Like all behaviors, these patterns reflect a desire for survival and safety, a way to protect the system and, to some degree, the individuals in it. But like any compensation strategy, there is, for each, a cost.

Impression Management

You're lucky you've got a job.

veteran teacher to frustrated first-year teaching intern

Don't confuse being "soft" with seeing the other guy's point of view.

George Bush[10]

The only way to solve problems is to confront them and tell the truth about them.

Shakti Gawain[11]

In some school settings, it doesn't take long for new teachers to figure out that sharing their frustrations and defeats in the teachers' lounge is not a particularly smart move. Rather than receiving validation or support that could lead to clarity and solutions, they often encounter impatience, pity or contempt. More than a few educators have reported that their anxieties were likely to be met with shaming or dismissive comments like, "Well, *I* never had a problem with them last year." I remember those comments, and similar feedback, which only added to my sense of despair and inadequacy. And I remember feeling this horrible pressure to say I was "fine" or "doing great" any time anyone bothered to ask. I avoided the lounges and cried in the relative safety of my classroom after the kids left every day. This went on for weeks. What saved me that year was being part of a group of twelve first-year teaching interns at this site. Whatever I was experiencing, I was not alone. Our after-school classes and meetings afforded me opportunities to realize that there were others in the same boat. As new teachers go, I was one of the lucky ones. I had a place where I could be myself, be imperfect, and still feel accepted and supported; a place where I could hear ideas that had worked for my colleagues, where I could gain a better notion of what was and wasn't working for me.

Without a strong sense of safety and acceptance, individuals in school communities—from the highest levels of administration to the students being served—can become quite adept at making a good impression. This is part of a survival repertoire, one that is necessary in a setting in which a call for help is seen as a sign of weakness—or worse, incompetence. A few teachers reported that asking for feedback and support left them vulnerable to criticism, or having unwanted scrutiny or agendas imposed on them instead. For some, even admitting to having a bad day puts them at risk. "In a system that demands perfection, mistakes are unacceptable," states author Anne Wilson Schaef. "We cannot learn from our mistakes, because we must pretend we never make any."[12]

When we're under pressure to look good, if it's not okay to not know, and if our sense of adequacy—or our job security—demands that we keep up certain appearances (whether internally or externally perceived), certain survival behaviors become particularly appealing. The need to be "right" can be an enormous obstacle in creating the trust and connectedness in relationships at the heart of a healthy and safe community.[13] Family therapist and former high-school counselor Lynn Collins notes, for example, how reluctant some teachers are to show compassion or understanding for a student who is upset with them because doing so would somehow convey the teacher's guilt or failure: "I'm not going to say 'I'm sorry you're upset' because I didn't do anything wrong." Likewise, the notion of an apology, even when the teacher clearly has made a mistake or violated a boundary, can be horrifying to people who believe that their honor, credibility or authority depend on always being right. These patterns are also evident at the systems level, as we've seen in the adult collusion behind cheating on standardized tests or on the football field to maintain the school's standings and prestige, instances in which this need to "look good" in the public eye overshadowed personal integrity.

In light of the severity of the negative press schools have received in recent decades, it is, in a way, understandable that we would be reluctant to do something that would make ourselves, our schools and our system of education any more of a target than they already are. However, many of the people I interviewed expressed concern at the frequency with which serious issues were swept under the carpet, ignored in the hope that they would disappear or that they would fail to manifest in a way that would draw fire. Denial is a common response to the desire to protect ourselves from the responsibility of dealing with difficult, painful or overwhelming challenges. One individual mentioned his experience in higher education with faculty members who had well-known drinking problems but "were protected by the dean of the college." He was not alone. This classic kind of enabling was evident in all types of educational settings, covering up problems that ranged from grade-tampering and backstabbing to verbal abuse and embezzlement. (Fortunately, many school systems now have Employee Assistance Programs and policies of confidentiality, which give staff places to go for help and support. Nonetheless, many educators have told me that even with these programs in place, their districts—or towns—are just too small for them to feel safe or comfortable seeking assistance in-house.)

Even when it comes to students' physical safety, it can be easier to just look the other way. One survey respondent recalled the number of times she walked the two miles from her school to her home when she was in second grade because the school bus driver was "often tipsy." Is it possible that a school system could be unaware of a problem that even a seven-year-old student knew to avoid? Apparently yes, and the problem goes even deeper. "I can't tell you how many pedophile teachers I've seen in twenty-nine years of teaching at the high-school level," says one school counselor. As of early 2000, nine states did not require background checks for teachers, and twenty-five states did not mandate screening for employees like bus drivers or janitors. Those that do checks often do not go beyond the borders of their own state.[14] But even with extensive investigations and clearance procedures, many individuals fall through the cracks. "These people may not have a legal record, but it's well known in the personnel office, and they keep transferring them hoping that they'll do better in the next spot," claims one counselor I interviewed. Studies concur. Some offenders simply cross state lines and resume teaching elsewhere. "To avoid costly legal action and bad press," states one report, "school administrators often allow teachers accused of crimes the chance to quietly move on." These incidents are common enough to have inspired a name for this practice. It's known as "passing the trash."[15]

Denial as a method of impression management is certainly a factor in issues of violence and bullying in schools. Collins was one of several individuals who noted that many "administrators are afraid, but they're not willing to admit they're afraid." There are good reasons, it seems, for insisting that everything is fine. "The public expects educators to maintain violence-free schools," says a report by educator Irene McDonald, "but any initiative taken by the school to reduce violence is often perceived as a failure of administrators to have maintained order and discipline." The pressure to maintain a positive image "constrains administrators' motivation to request resources for violence reduction."[16] Likewise, teachers are often reluctant to report assaults by students, either to their principals or to the police, out of concern that the incident could negatively impact their careers.[17]

A 1995 survey of junior-high students, teachers and administrators regarding their perceptions of the seriousness of specified violent behaviors was met with mixed responses. Many administrators hesitated to take part, fearing that students would exaggerate or misrepresent, for example, how knowledgeable and aware the staff actually were. Some insisted that "school violence isn't a problem here" but agreed to participate anyway. And one principal responded, "I find the whole matter of even suggesting that we have violence in our school to be rather offensive."[18] Not surprisingly, there were rather large discrepancies between the adults' perceptions and those reported by the students. Administrators, in particular, reported school violence to be less of a problem, adult awareness to be greater, and student satisfaction with the treatment of violent incidents to be higher than students reported. The disparity between adult and student perceptions would make one wonder about the effectiveness and relevance of programs and policies "developed on the basis of administrator or teacher perceptions of students' needs and concerns."[19]

Unless the symptoms are blatantly obvious, it's easy to overlook potential problems or the need for programs that address emotional development, life skills or social interactions.[20] For years, it was believed that the "good schools" with high academic achievement were immune from the extreme types of problems that plagued the inner city. However the shootings in "nice," suburban schools have helped our culture break through this denial. John Cloud reports that the vigilance that had led inner-city schools to "identify students early who may be prone to violence" and work on preventing and lowering the numbers of incidents "is finally creeping into the suburbs."[21] The past few years have made it abundantly clear that "affluence does not guarantee a safe learning environment for all students," as Rita Mercier notes. "The specific safety issues may differ from school to school, but financial resources or good intentions alone are of little benefit without the knowledge of how to help all students and staff interact successfully with one another."[22]

Denial can also come from parents and is a frequent complaint from educators and counselors trying to secure the support they need to help students. I've seen parents refute the possibility that their child could have done well-documented behaviors, or even that their child needed help, if they believed that such an admission would reflect poorly on them. (Granted, this defensiveness is often exacerbated by teachers and administrators who approach parents as if the child's failure or misbehavior in school is the parents' fault or responsibility to "fix." There are far more constructive ways for us to inspire parents' support and participation while maintaining our own accountability.) Others are reluctant to take the child's behavior or problem seriously. And when it comes to social skills or the child's emotional development, some parents will insist that their children already know—or don't need—the skills the school is trying to develop.[23] "Some of the most troubled kids have parents who don't want to cooperate," says school psychologist Jeanne Collin-Smith.[24]

Combine denial with blame—another classic defense mechanism—and more energy is diverted from potential prevention and solutions. This technique says that not only do I have to be right, but I also have to make somebody else wrong. As a snag in the fabric of a school community, this practice is far too common, destructive though it may be. Think back to the accusations that followed Columbine. Depending on which report we read or watched, inevitable questions included: Where were the parents (or the teachers or the cops or the Ten Commandments on the wall)? Which politician supported a policy that allowed this to happen? Where can we place criminal liability? It wasn't enough that this tragedy happened. It had to be somebody's fault.[25]

"As society seems to increasingly blame schools for low test scores, high dropout rates and unruly students, [school personnel] hold up their arms in exasperation and point the finger at parents," notes school social worker Debra Sugar.[26] The dynamics of blame were evident in a recent news report of three students who started a fire in their high school. The parents of one of the girls cited the heavy security in the school and said that the school was responsible because the teachers should have known where the girls were and what they were doing. In their view, the fire was the school's fault because the girls got away with setting it.[27] Is it any wonder that newsletters for administrators now feature articles advising principals to think carefully "whenever planning anything for school, even if it's positive," to consider "what possible chance there is for a lawsuit," and to "document like there's no tomorrow"?[28] Despite the logic and common sense in maintaining details of one's accountability and actions, if the fabric of the school community (particularly in the context of the local community) is fraught with suspicion and hostility, we can expect even more time, money and effort to be drained by "cover-your-back" policies and procedures.

Perhaps the most dangerous side effect of our investment in managing the impression others have of us is when our efforts to protect ourselves, or protect the system, end up sacrificing the individuals in the system. Sadly, I'm not sure to what degree our society will ever support the kind of authenticity required for a truly cohesive and safe school culture—or what it might cost us to truly be who we are, know what we know, and take whatever heat comes with these truths. So long as our schools exist in a cultural environment based in fear and judgment, it will be hard to shed the ways in which we compensate for our imperfections. For as long as we believe we have to please everyone (or at least not offend anyone), and until we can reconcile our need for approval (and our fear of reproach) with our own conscience, we will continue to make choices that, in the end, hurt us all.

Oversimplification

We don't understand the principle of duality that exists in the world, that you have to embrace the opposites. You have to always embrace the paradox. That's where peace comes from.

Shakti Gawain[29]

There are two ways to slide easily through life: to believe everything or to doubt everything. Both ways save us from thinking.

Alfred Korzybski

There is no contradiction between firmness and kindness, or between inviting educators and successful ones.

William Purkey and David Aspy[30]

One survey respondent told me about an incident that occurred in his high school thirty-five years before. In a threatening and terrifying gesture, a student was suspended from a third-story window by several of his classmates. As a result, all of the windows on the third floor of the building were eventually boarded up. That ended the threat of a student being thrown to the concrete below, although nothing was done to rectify the students' antagonism or stem the persistent violence that existed throughout the school. In the absence of the third-floor option, the students simply reverted to more traditional ways of intimidating and hurting one another.

As the pace of our lives—and the avalanche of new information that seems to go with it—continues to accelerate, we are losing our tolerance for complexity, conflict and paradox. Whether it's a matter of intellectual survival or simply a lack of time, we have developed a tendency to reduce things to their most basic, simplistic dimensions. We've become numb to all but the most extreme phenomena vying for our attention. In a world of sound bites and spin control, our patience has eroded and dimensionality can exhaust us. We either focus on one tiny aspect of a problem to the exclusion of its context, or we miss the point altogether.

This phenomenon of oversimplification is pervasive and corrosive, appearing in many guises. It is responsible for much misinformation and misunderstanding and, like other defensive or survival-oriented responses, can compound existing problems, and obstruct clarity and solutions. For example, when I first started talking about doing a book on emotional safety in schools, I was astounded when a handful of individuals bristled at the concept, accusing me of promoting everything from underchallenging learners to overprotecting them. The idea that we could create emotionally healthy school environments *and* hold children accountable for their behavior or challenge them academically did not seem possible. This kind of thinking goes to the very roots of our relationships in schools. "At some point in the history of education," write Purkey and Aspy, "a myth developed that education has to be either humane or effective, but that it is impossible to be both. The sad part about this myth is that it has been accepted as reality even though there is a wealth of data to refute it."[31] William Ayers acknowledges this myth in his reassurance that "personalizing our approach to juveniles does not mean that actions or behavior should have no serious consequences."[32]

These examples illustrate one of the most common forms of oversimplification: all-or-nothing thinking (sometimes called dualism, either-or thinking or black-and-white thinking). All of these terms refer to a very limited way of looking at a problem, restricting our options, typically, to two opposite extremes. In describing "debilitating environmental structures," Frederick Flach notes that it is the presence of these extremes that interfere with children's growth.[33] Whether we're talking about stubborn resistance to change or excessive fluidity, rejection of new ideas or the rejection of tradition, or a tendency toward punishment and vindictiveness or excessive forbearance,[34] we're talking about extreme, either-or options that exclude the potential for alternate, middle-ground possibilities. This kind of thinking is alive and well in school settings throughout the world. It dwells in the heart of the perfectionist who believes that anything less than an A+ is a dismal failure. It constrains the competitor to the role of either winner or loser, dismissing the value of the lesson or the game. It prompts the fear that "either I'm in control or my students are," and the thinking that makes the concept of win-win authority relationships so difficult to grasp. It is the dysfunctional pattern that screams out for balance, the one that, when examined and acknowledged, allows us to run down the middle and enjoy the trip. As educator and author Parker J. Palmer notes, "We must embrace the fact that teaching and learning—to say nothing of living—take the form of paradox: They require us to think 'both-and' instead of 'either-or.'"[35]

We cannot create community (at least not in a way that supports emotional safety) with only black-and-white options. Author Amitai Etzioni comments that "communitarians really seek to establish a New Golden Rule, one that seeks a balance between the still-valued needs of individuals and the larger society."[36] Fortunately, there are alternatives to either-or thinking, and thankfully, it truly is possible to have warm, friendly, mutually respectful relationships with students without compromising either our authority or what Etzioni calls the "common good." But in settings where we still hear incongruous comments like "I don't care if they like me as long as they learn," ideas like friendship and mutual respect remain hard sells. For many people, getting past the fear that connecting with students in positive ways would compromise their authority, their boundaries or their ability to hold kids accountable presents an enormous hurdle, even though research shows modeling respectful and nonviolent communications actually decreases disruptions and acting out.[37]

Our discomfort with the gray areas and our difficulty in approaching a problem from a variety of angles have contributed to what I call a "bumper-sticker-slogan" approach to complex issues. I see this especially in my work with teachers and parents on topics of discipline and power dynamics. Even teachers well prepared in areas related to resources and instruction often have little training in the relationship, authority and interaction patterns that contribute to the kinds of behaviors children exhibit. What information we do receive is usually a bumper-sticker-sized cliché like "Be consistent" or "Don't smile before Christmas." Our search for simple formulae like writing the name of a misbehaving child on the board (which, in actuality, only reinforces attention-getting behavior and makes what we're trying to discourage more likely to continue) or posting rules (with the expectation that their presence on the wall will generate a commitment from the students) does a disservice to everyone involved. The outcomes are disappointing and teachers feel betrayed. We move from one formula to the next, grasping at surface solutions, rarely giving even promising programs a chance to work.

For example, in the late 1970s, I worked with the district in which I was teaching on a five-year curriculum initiative. This was a comprehensive project designed to look at the needs of the community and the role of the school in that context. We surveyed teachers, parents, business leaders and other community members to identify the skills and abilities the schools needed to address to prepare students for success. The result was a complex matrix of academic skills, social skills, leadership and networking capabilities, inquiry skills, communication skills, conflict-resolution and people skills, and the development of personal qualities such as initiative and the desire and ability to continue learning. Extensive training began in 1979, and full implementation of the program was to be underway by 1981; shortly after I moved out of the district and across the country. Years later, when I called the former director to follow up, she told me that as soon as the program's funding ran out, the district moved on to other things, barely giving this project a glancing nod. I was also told that this project, which had consumed considerable resources, time and talent, had little if any impact on instruction, organization or leadership anywhere in the district. Political changes at the administrative level led to a more narrow (and simplistic) approach to curriculum, and "the project died on the vine." This practice is so common that no one who's been in this field for long is even remotely surprised when I recount this story. "Educational philosophy seems to cycle from progressive to 'back to basics,'" writes teacher Diane Varano, "but critics are unwilling to stick with an approach long enough to see whether it is effective. Strategies change from year to year, which leads to no discernible progress."[38]

Research by the W. T. Grant Consortium on the School-Based Promotion of Social Competence tells us that "programs designed to have an impact on students' behavior must recognize that change occurs over time."[39] But, we say, we don't have the luxury of time. So when something horrible occurs in our schools, "our natural response to these incidents is to look for quick-fix programs or treatments to keep such events from happening again," says a report on safe learning communities.[40] Rita Mercier notes that while some of these approaches, such as locks on gates, higher fences, classroom phones, intercom systems, video cameras (in classrooms, halls, bathrooms, cafeterias and on buses), metal detectors, alarm systems, visitor badges, school uniforms, crisis training or increased security "could help protect the school from vandalism, burglaries and the violent tendencies of some individuals," she cautions that "mutual respect and nurturing behaviors are not outcomes" we can expect from quick-fix responses.[41] Oh, but how much more appealing are these avenues compared to the challenge of reculturing a school!

Such is the nature of the quick-fix approach. Its legacy is often a series of "solutions" that misses the point of the problem, or at least misses an opportunity to address the real issues that allowed the problem to manifest in the first place. For example, one article championed smaller high schools on the basis of the assumption that fewer children would be excluded. "At the big schools, hundreds of students compete for the relatively few spots on the elite teams and squads, which can make everyone else feel like nobodies," the article cautions.[42] While I respect the good intentions here, I couldn't help wondering if perhaps it would be more constructive to work on deglamorizing these positions and making them less elitist, or providing opportunities for larger numbers of kids to fit in and excel in places that were valued at least as much as these "few spots." (The school would have to be awfully small for everyone in it to be on one of these teams or squads.) If you really want to stretch this point, getting rid of these elite positions entirely to avoid making someone feel like a "nobody" could also work! But this isn't about the teams, any more than it is about the numbers. Either we value every student—and the various and unique contributions each can make—or we don't.

This same mentality seemed to be at work at the high school that suspended a majorette for being four pounds over the weight limit determined by the band director. Despite assurances from the girl's doctor that her weight was well within a healthy range, the school upheld its requirement, ostensibly to protect the student from the jeers of the fans.[43] Once again, I'm curious: Do the classmates who refer to this girl as "Thunder Thighs" when she's on the football field treat her more respectfully in the school's hallways and classrooms? Does the name-calling stop when the four pounds come off? The bigger questions, once again, come back to the role of the school, and the potential we have to impact how kids see and treat one another, as well as the role we can play in helping them feel strong and comfortable in their own skins. These stories remind me of the protest organizers who were disappointed when the troops were recalled from Vietnam: Now that the U.S. involvement had ended, they would have to cancel the demonstration.

Teacher and author Tara Singh asks, "When are we going to come to right values?"[44] What is our real agenda here? What are our priorities? And what subtle messages and values do we convey in the choices we make?

I see this reliance on surface solutions in the attraction of school uniforms. While local ACLU offices are flooded with calls protesting this trend, many schools and parents are delighted with the prospect. Some justify the switch to uniforms or stringent dress codes with evidence of improvements in behavior and increases in honor rolls, or with the belief that dress codes will prevent kids from sneaking weapons in under loose or baggy clothes.[45] Others believe that uniforms will eliminate competition and discrimination among students, although dozens of kids and adults have told me that, in their experience, this rarely, if ever, happened. (Students simply found other targets—things like purses, lunch boxes, jewelry, hairstyles, accents, body size, disabilities or weaknesses—things that the school could not regulate, as a basis for their hierarchies.) The same goes for gang prevention. Although there is evidence that kids who dress "better" are treated with greater respect and courtesy by the adults in a school, simply putting them all in the same outfits has little impact on their fundamental values or behavior.[46] Kids in places that restrict all gang clothing, gestures and insignia still manage subtle and changing ways of communicating their affiliation. And, gang expert Richard Arthur reminds us that "some prisons, where all the inmates wear a uniform, are terrorized by rival gangs, and so are some schools, even though they have strict dress codes." He recommends, instead, that we focus on strategies like reducing alienation, ensuring success, improving values, and building mutual trust and respect[47]—processes that take time and often demand a great deal of patience and faith.

And it is exactly these demands that wear us down and wear us out. On a good day, most of us are overextended and pretty exhausted. It's easy to overload, easier still, sometimes, to just numb out. Even the headlines that shock and rouse us out of complacency don't seem to hold our attention for long. One month after Columbine, journalist Nancy Gibbs wrote, "We've had a chance to look at the precious microculture of our own household and study its condition. But how many of us actually did anything differently?"[48] When a local college invited nationally known experts on school violence to speak at a weeklong seminar in response to national and local concerns, they were dismayed when, less than three weeks before the program began, only thirty-eight individuals had signed up, far less than the minimum they had anticipated. Neither the relevance of the topics nor the chance to earn graduate-level credit, inservice credit or continuing education units were incentive enough to generate widespread participation, leading the program coordinator to conclude that "there is no sense of urgency because levels of violence haven't hit critical mass yet locally."[49] But local urgency may not be as big a factor as one might think. In Conyers, Georgia, on the night of the shooting there, large numbers of parents attended an award ceremony for their children, "but only forty or so remained for a school board meeting. And just one rose to suggest a parent volunteer project to combat violence. No one said much in response."[50] Transformative change demands commitment and effort at many levels. It will always be simpler to just board up the windows.

Reactivity

A spontaneous reaction is never of the same quality as a planned response.

Chester Quarles[51]

A really great teacher is someone who doesn't scream when you make a mistake.

Sammy[52]

For every dollar we invest in child care we save five dollars in crime costs down the line.

Hillary Rodham Clinton[53]

Motivational speaker Gail Dusa tells a story about a bridge that children had to cross on their way to school. Over the years, the bridge began to deteriorate and after a while the small holes in the bridge became big enough for children to fall through. In response, the children sold candy to raise money for stretchers. Experts were brought in to teach life-saving and CPR skills. And the town rallied and passed a bond initiative to buy a new ambulance. Everyone was much better prepared to deal with the injured children as the accidents occurred. But typical of dysfunctional systems dynamics, nobody had thought to just fix the bridge to keep the kids from getting hurt in the first place.[54]

Whether we're talking about disruptive behavior, academic failure, substance abuse, dropping out, pregnancy, depression or mental-health issues, or any of the numerous problems we encounter when dealing with kids, we generally pour more time, energy and financial resources into *reacting* to these problems than to preventing them. "We operate in this society on a crisis-and-punishment paradigm rather than prevention-and-promotion paradigm," says Linda Lantieri. "We spend money on young people when they get in trouble but not enough on prevention and health promotion."[55] Marie Kovacs, of the Western Psychiatric Institute and Clinic in Pittsburgh, notes that a preventative, or proactive approach to children's mental health is critical: "If you want to make a real difference in depression, you have to do something before the kids get sick in the first place. The real solution is in psychological inoculation."[56] But this is rarely the way it's done. "We have spent billions of dollars on the cognitive components of education, but we have spent next to nothing on creating positive emotional health," note Purkey and Aspy.[57] Even with a great deal of evidence to support the use of preventative, "inoculating" policies and practices, reactivity and tunnel vision can mire us forever in far less constructive patterns.

There is, behind any reactive approach, a short-term focus backed up by the rationalization that the ends justify the means. Reactivity may be most evident in our power structures, and in our admittedly macho approaches to problem solving—like the "wars" on everything from drugs and illiteracy to, incongruously, violence itself. It's more about fixing than preventing, and involves different processes—and different energy—than proactivity. Where reactivity relies on commands, rules and punishments, proactivity leans more toward generating buy-in, commitment and cooperation, and can accomplish these goals in more positive ways. The difference between reactive and proactive is also the difference between win-lose and win-win, the difference between getting tough and getting connected. Reactivity is outcome- or product-oriented; proactivity is willing to invest in process. Proactive approaches, therefore, typically take longer, and show results more slowly. They require us to think things out and think things through. They entice us to look for alternate routes and creative solutions. They demand that we do our homework and make sure that the practices and policies to which we commit are sound and reasonable in terms of what we know about how kids learn and what supports healthy growth. And proactive approaches also compel us to look beyond surface realities and make changes at a much more fundamental level.

Reactivity is often a panic or survival response. In schools, it's likely to show up as a rush to "make more rules" or "assign more work." We see evidence of the former tendency any time there is a shooting or similar crisis in a school, and we see evidence of the latter when we note a dip in test scores or achievement (or come up short in comparison to kids in some other part of the country or world). There is, of course, the desire to make things right, but the choices we make can't help but be influenced, at least to some degree, by the feeling that we also have to appease those who would judge us—or sue us. Sometimes, the outcomes are constructive and worthwhile, dealing directly with actual factors at the heart of a problem (like the authority on male violence hired a few months after the Columbine shooting to train the coaches and activity directors "about tolerance and the excesses of the jock culture"[58]). But often, the immediacy of many of these problems pushes us to settle for cosmetic changes, reaching, simply, for bigger, louder or more intense versions of what we've done in the past. Under pressure, we can easily succumb to the allure of the quick fix and the need to look like we're responding in some tangible way, whether the approach reflects sound, appropriate practice, or even makes sense.

Recently, after presenting a training program for parents, I was approached by four women, each with a child in the same first grade. The moms were quite upset about a new policy implemented at their children's school which, in a desperate bid to increase test scores, assigned to each first-grader two hours of homework a night. According to the parents, the assignments consisted mainly of worksheets and writing drills. Developmental inappropriateness aside,[59] the emotional toll was enormous. "My son cries the second he walks through the door," one woman said. The parents were doing their best to support the school policies and encourage their children, but they were all aware of the change in their children's attitudes. For although all four children had been very excited about embarking on their school careers, one mother seemed to speak for them all when she said, "It's only the third week of classes and my child already hates school." (Research has found that the amount of homework students have does not correlate with performance on achievement tests. Some districts are now pushing for more meaningful assignments and setting limits on the amount of homework kids have to reduce kids' stress and increase family time.)[60]

This is a terrific example of how we, in education, tend to shoot ourselves in the foot. As Purkey and Aspy note, "If schools ignore these stress-related pressures or try to force-feed the content of courses, the only thing the schools will accomplish is that students will develop an unquenchable distaste for what is being forced upon them" or for the learning process itself.[61] Common sense tells us this is true, and yet we persist with choices that make life and learning stressful, difficult and unpalatable. How often are our practices at odds with our goals? We want to promote achievement but set kids up to fail and hate learning. We preach community but encourage competition. We seek to eliminate bullying and violence in schools where paddling is accepted practice. We talk about teaching kids to take responsibility for their own problems while we refuse to drop our dependence on the office to punish them when they misbehave in our classrooms. To be sure, the messages inherent in such double standards are not lost on our students.

So I'm putting in my vote for reexamining our patterns and policies and asking some hard questions. Perhaps first and foremost: Are they, indeed, working? Are they working with the roots of the problem, or simply with the symptoms? What impact are they having on the emotional climate and school community? Because while we can certainly protect ourselves by putting up warning signs at the entrance to the bridge, in the long run, the repairs to the structure will be far less costly in every way imaginable than pulling bodies out of the river below.

Scarcity Thinking and Negativity

The myth is that in order for me to help you to do better, I have to make you feel worse.

Patti Present
middle-school counselor

Suspicion is the order of the post-Littleton day and distrust has been re-validated as the responsible act.

Ellen Goodman[62]

Surely there is enough for everyone within this country. . . . All our children ought to be allowed a stake in the enormous richness of America.

Jonathan Kozol[63]

In one of my undergraduate methods courses, we were given lists of local businesses that donated scraps and materials we could use in the classroom. We were taught to scour flea markets, write for free samples and make games out of recycled household trash. (I don't think any of my friends who went into medicine or business, for example, had one minute of their education devoted to 101 things you can create from old egg cartons.) I resented the fact that I had to spend a good portion of my annual salary every year on supplies and instructional materials, that I had to hoard and scrounge in order to do my job. Materials for hands-on activities or cooking activities, even books and reference materials, typically came out of my pocket. Even basic supplies were not a given. I remember at one point toward the end of my first year, having to run off activity guidelines on paper towels because my thirty-nine kids and I had used up our allotment of paper. And I remember marveling at the discrepancy between the expectations and demands being put on teachers (from everywhere, it seemed) and the amount of support we actually received.[64] By some standards, I had it made. I've since worked with people who have taught in converted bathrooms and storage closets, and many who spend their days dragging their materials around from one class to another in a school that doesn't have the space to assign a room to them. The disparity between schools just a few miles apart can be staggering, and it is a true testament to the resilience of the human spirit that anyone can learn or teach in "tiny, windowless and claustrophobic" rooms with inadequate resources, broken equipment, no cafeterias or playgrounds, and way too many kids.[65]

Even in well-funded, comfortable settings, the tunnel vision that keeps us focused on academics, along with the tendency to target nonacademic programs for blame any time there is a problem, has resulted in cutbacks that have affected many worthwhile programs. Inservice budgets have been scaled down, and superintendents are often under pressure to direct the funds they do have *away* from programs that would support teacher and student interactions and mental health.[66] One high-school teacher told me that she and her colleagues were hungry for ideas to reduce conflict and discipline problems but that every staff development program her district offered was devoted to some aspect of the state's testing regimen. In some districts, art and music have all but disappeared from the curricular landscape. And while James Garbarino warns that "the number of kids who need help has shot up significantly,"[67] the availability of services for kids has declined. School counselors—whose duties often include scheduling, bus duty, hallway and cafeteria monitoring and running parent conferences—can each be assigned to enormous numbers of children, thus reducing their potential effectiveness.[68] When Beverly Davies was the chemical dependency director at a local hospital, she notes that "we used to get kids for an average of one month to three months. Now the average is two and a half days." The agency that runs the day treatment program where I volunteered recently had to shut down several of its most effective programs. "Nobody's paying for them," my contact there told me. More kids needing help and fewer services available is, in the long run, a dangerous combination.

Scarcity thinking is grounded in fear, in the idea that there is somehow not enough to go around. This kind of thinking goes beyond the amount of resources or the kinds of salaries we have come to expect (something which, thankfully, has improved dramatically in many settings in the past three decades that I've been a part of this profession). It also speaks to the possibility of success for all children, to our sense of power and hope, to our optimism and perception of possibilities, to our tolerance for diversity and expression, to our willingness to take risks, to our ability to work together. The scarcity model strongly supports black-and-white thinking. It is a zero-sum belief system, reflected in ideas like "I can't win unless you lose" or "Either I have power or you do." It is the fear that celebrating someone's accomplishment will somehow deplete the recognition and achievement possible for us. It is perhaps nowhere more obvious than in the negativity many adults and kids experience in schools. Often a subtle undercurrent in addictive or dysfunctional organizations, negativism is related to both scarcity and perfectionism. "We are educated to be critical and judgmental. To be supportive and positive is viewed as being weak," says author Anne Wilson Schaef. "Rather than seeing the possibilities within and around us, we see only our limitations and the things we cannot do."[69] Imagine the impact this kind of thinking has on a school climate!

But schools are—without a more constructive intention and conscious effort—little more than a microcosm of the larger social context in which they exist. "The average parent in America spends only twelve and a half minutes per day speaking to his or her child," write educators Patti Present, Janet Cartozian and Susy Quinn. "Of that time, eight and a half minutes are spent in discouraging communication."[70] A study of three- and four-year-olds found that 85 percent of what these children heard was either about "what they [should] not do or how bad they were because of what they were doing."[71] These trends appear in school settings, as well. At the elementary level, children are likely to receive three negative comments for every positive comment they hear. By middle school, the ratio jumps to nine negative comments for every positive communication. And by high-school, kids might hear between eleven and seventeen criticisms before they hear one bit of encouragement.[72] Efforts to turn these numbers around come up against well-entrenched values and traditions. When one high-school counselor suggested that the adults in the school acknowledge and connect with the students—deliberately, positively and daily—his proposal was met with ridicule. Even the teachers considered to be the best in the school resisted. "To them it was silly," he said. Counselors Vic Fantozzi and J. D. Lucas acknowledged that high school environments can be particularly negative. In our interview, I proposed a scenario in which students enter the school and, throughout the course of the day, receive a hundred communications—verbal, nonverbal or written messages about who they are, how they look, how they perform, what they have to contribute academically and socially. Of those one hundred bits of feedback, I ask, how many would be positive and affirming? They both admit that, sadly, for many students, the answer would be zero. I've had this conversation with dozens of people since, and even the most generous were reluctant to suggest that more than a dozen or so comments would be positive, or even neutral. "I think the setup is that we're supposed to build your esteem by being critical," claims Fantozzi. He recommends turning our "entire mentality" on its head, noting that, "You don't teach by tearing down."

"It appears to me that society in general finds it a lot easier to make derogatory remarks than to make positive remarks," notes Lucas. "You have to be very secure to deal with that." But continual criticism and negativity can have a relentlessly corrosive effect, and even the most secure and devoted people will eventually succumb to its toxicity. William Purkey notes that the last two decades of the twentieth century "will surely go down as one of the most joyless and mean-spirited periods in American public education. Seldom, if ever, have schools and the people who live and work there received such ruthless condemnation."[73] The toll on teacher morale is enormous; the ultimate casualties, however, are the kids.

If this scarcity thinking is hard to shake, we certainly come by it honestly. It's only very recent generations who have had the privilege of living and growing up at a level beyond survival, and this experience is certainly not a global phenomenon. With all due respect to the large numbers of people still struggling with poverty and basic survival needs, we have, for the first time in human history, many individuals in the unique position of living, growing and relating to one another at levels that reach far beyond survival. The good news lies in the potential for more highly evolved, more productive, more gentle and more positive patterns in our lives. The bad news is in the paucity of models, or more than a hint of a map for those ready and willing to forge ahead into these largely uncharted waters. Perhaps just knowing that there is another reality beyond the surface, survival-oriented images most of us know best will be enough to allow us to take that next step.

In a reality based in abundance and positivity, you will never hear someone say, "If I let one person do it, I have to let them all do it," either because there is an abundance of opportunities for "them" to do other things, or someone's reckoned with the possibility that maybe letting them all do "it" isn't such a horrible idea. There is no bell curve in an abundant reality because all children can grow and learn and succeed, and the progress they achieve is respected in its own right (rather than in comparison to anyone else). With abundance (or prosperity) thinking, it's possible for feedback to be positive and encouraging without accepting the unacceptable. It's appropriate to teach in present time, building on where students actually are, rather than pushing them to achieve something "they'll need next year," regardless of their academic, intellectual or developmental readiness. With abundance thinking, it's unnecessary to compete for limited resources because somehow shifting into a belief system that says there's plenty for everyone seems to open the door to possibilities we may not have noticed before. It compels us to cooperate and connect, rather than run over one another in an effort to "exceed" and "surpass."[74] It eliminates the need for—and acceptability of—double standards, and creates space for a greater tolerance for diversity.

The notion of abundance requires a belief in possibilities, and faith in our ability to access them. The idea that I can grow beyond where I am, grow beyond the limits of my environment or grow beyond the expectations of others can most easily manifest in a setting supported by an abundance mentality. At a certain level we in education have accepted scarcity thinking as the norm. At some point, it is almost irrelevant to wonder whether the thinking created the reality or the reality created the thinking. Both the thinking and the reality will have to change in order for kids to benefit from the abundance of possibilities we can offer them.

Product vs. Process

Teaching the process of inquiry, we must show that questions are just as important as answers.

William Glasser[75]

Teach children to associate learning with life and experience, not only with school.

H. Stephen Glenn and Michael L. Brock[76]

Too often we give children answers to remember rather than problems to solve.

Roger Lewis[77]

I am not a humanist simply because I want to go around being nice to people. I am a humanist because I know that when I apply humanistic thinking to problems in teaching, students learn better.

A. Combs[78]

When we combine a scarcity mentality and competitive thinking with the need to look good and the tendency to reduce complex issues to their most simplistic terms, it's inevitable that we'll end up emphasizing product over process in our schools. The call for greater attention to various processes involved in learning, thinking, performance and assessment has long been a part of the educational landscape. We know that concentrating exclusively on product, or the final outcomes of these processes, can lead us to compromise the process, dismiss its importance or overlook problems behind the surface reality of the "product." This issue is at work any time we concentrate on a particular outcome or appearance with little regard for how we accomplished the results. It's at the heart of a belief system that allows us to rationalize ineffective or harmful practices as long as we have something significant to show for it. It's what allows us to settle for cosmetic changes when transformation is required.

I've seen the danger in this imbalance in many guises and many settings. It was a factor when I spent my summers doing electronic assembly, where meeting quotas often meant increased numbers of circuit boards with missing components and cold solder joints. It was a factor in a friend's compulsion to fit into small clothing sizes, seeing her reliance on diet pills and vomiting simply as a means to an end. It was a factor in a teacher's decision to take a job at a school after being enticed by the district's high test scores and prestige, only to find a culture, philosophy and set of practices that, in his estimation, were highly toxic and destructive.

The focus on product was also quite evident to the American teacher who spent three weeks visiting schools in Japan. In one setting, he got to hear a teenage girl offer a wonderful recitation of the preamble to the U.S. Constitution in near-perfect English. But despite her successful performance, she was unable to carry on even the most basic conversation in English, much to the surprise of the visitor. The performance was impressive, but clearly the students' high scores in this subject area reflected knowledge at only the most elementary recall (product) level.[79] I've seen this in schools throughout the world—where children could memorize and recite material of which they had no inherent understanding. Where children could retrieve a well-rehearsed answer only if the question was worded in a particular way. Where learning took place at such a superficial level that even when facts were stored long enough for students to retrieve them for a test or recital, this information did not seem to connect to anything in their brains and was not likely to linger long afterwards. And yet, this emphasis is so pervasive that, in a 1999 survey, the majority of those interviewed chose "giving knowledge to students" over "teaching children how to think critically" when asked to identify what they thought the main function of schools should be.[80] Product orientation stresses performance over learning, knowledge at a basic factual or procedural level. Alternately, process orientation is more complex, allowing more for understanding and application, learning to think and learning to learn. It accepts the importance of remembering factual knowledge—the simplest and most basic type of cognitive functioning—but only to the degree that we're able to use and apply what we remember.[81]

Product orientation can block thinking and problem solving. It's the impatience and apparent efficiency reflected in our directions to "just ignore her" or "just sit somewhere else" when a student has a problem with a classmate. Yet nowhere in this kind of an exchange is anything that would help the student become more confident and resilient around her peers, develop independent problem-solving skills, or feel supported in her affective response to her problem. If we truly wish for our students to "think better," we are likely instead to ask questions instead of giving answers.[82] We will look to more complex processes, encouraging kids to debate and discuss, develop stories and examples, or map ideas in nonlinear ways. We will honor feelings, allow for introspection and reflection, give kids time to think and plan,[83] encourage movement[84] or simply allow time for "messing about," giving them time to explore and create a mental model of the material and information with which they are working.[85] We will also provide feedback throughout the process, rather than simply returning a "product" with a number or letter on the top (and, sometimes, a few comments in the margins). All of these experiences involve both process and product, although the products will typically be far more complex than the outcomes of more product-oriented instruction.

In education, we have traditionally undervalued the journey and focused nearly exclusively on the destination. In doing so, we have missed much. Both product and process are important in learning, although as a teacher, I'm typically far more fascinated with *how* you got this answer, *why* you designed this product this way, or *what* led you to approach this problem this way than the actual products you turn in. By asking these questions and observing the thinking and logic behind your answer, I can discover far more about how you learn and think—and what you may need instructionally—than I can by looking at, say, the number 87 on your math paper, the shape of the boat you built for your science project or a book report you wrote from the perspective of a secondary character. This information doesn't fit neatly in those little boxes in my grade book, but it certainly can help me identify materials, resources, activities, information and approaches that will build on your current level of understanding. How different this is from a product-oriented focus, which endows us with a willingness to represent learning with measures that typically tell us very little about how a child learns or what he or she needs to be successful in a particular area. Work at the process level can have a tremendous impact on the quality of the final product, but the final product will probably challenge us to assess it on its own terms.

Product orientation is short-sighted and narrowly focused. It can fragment the curriculum into unrelated, isolated blocks of information we pour into students' heads when we see fit, even if there is no place for the message to land and take root. It revolves around *our* timetables and honors *our* agendas, often ignoring or dismissing our students' more immediate needs and curiosity. It can inspire severe tunnel vision that blinds us to opportunities to teach anything except what we've marked on our lesson plans. It's the pressure we feel to "get through the curriculum" rather than teach the students, the exasperation we feel when a student lacks the skills necessary for a lesson we feel compelled to teach anyway. It's what prevents us from reading to a math class, or acknowledging the strange and sudden change in the weather (and what that might mean) because we don't have science class until this afternoon. It is an issue when we attempt to do business as usual without addressing the concerns of students affected by some incident or event competing for their attention and emotional energy. And it was certainly a factor when a principal admonished me for answering the questions of a suddenly menstruating third-grader (who was completely uninformed, unprepared and, understandably, scared to death) because that content would be covered in her sixth-grade sex-education class.[86]

Product orientation lacks the cohesion and the multidimensional potential of a process-oriented approach to teaching and learning. It occurs when the message in our lessons doesn't jibe with what students see and "live" in their relationships with us. It's when the product of what we are teaching doesn't match the process by which we teach. For example, years ago, I had a chance to observe a teacher in a primary classroom. The morning's instruction included a brief lesson supposedly designed to build young learners' self-esteems.[87] The teacher sat amid a circle of students with a sock puppet on her hand, pleasantly chirping about how wonderful the children were and how they could be anything they wanted. A few minutes after the sock puppet was back in the drawer, this same teacher was screaming at these students, "I just explained that!" Whatever message the previous lesson was supposed to impart certainly wasn't supported by the teacher's outburst. More recently, a principal shared her plans for decorating an in-school suspension room, wanting something on the walls that would inspire better student behavior, or at least help the kids being punished "think about why they were there." But would the slogans on the posters she planned to install convey a stronger lesson than the verbal and emotional messages these kids were getting from their teachers and the interactive dynamics in which they all were engaged? Would they indeed get kids to think and make positive choices in the future? What was available was a simplistic penalty for misbehavior—which was "paid off" once the students had served their time. Very little learning at the process level was likely to occur here, regardless of what ended up on the walls.[88]

Educator James Comer notes the potential for these kinds of discrepancies when social or emotional programs are taught in isolation to the social context and the rest of the curriculum. "It's easy to get caught up in a specific curriculum that teaches various social skills but doesn't address the quality of life in the school," he says. "The key question is: Are the adults interacting in a way that creates a climate where children feel comfortable, safe and protected, where they can identify with and attach to adults?"[89] Clearly there's no point in trying to teach social and character skills without adult role models to back these efforts up. With or without programs specifically dedicated to these objectives, kids will learn a great deal from the attitudes and values expressed in our behaviors, body language, attitudes and power dynamics. "It is difficult to internalize a sense of well-being, high self-esteem and a passion for achievement in an environment that is chaotic, abusive or characterized by low expectations for students."[90]

The difference between teachers (and schools) that emphasize process (and recognize the innate complexity of putting dozens or hundreds of different individuals together in one setting for the purpose of learning) and those concerned more with products, is enormous—not just in how kids learn and think, but in how the adults and students interact and how those settings feel. It's the difference between "fixing" and guiding, between believing we know what's best and surrendering to the possibility that we might not have the answer. Process orientation understands that learning is rarely linear, consistent or smooth. It can acknowledge that good people sometimes write really bad papers and that no choice is a bad choice, but simply an opportunity for learning. And it's about trusting that our students are right on schedule, and that we are here simply to help them along their path.

There's this old saying that goes: If the only tool we have is a hammer, we tend to see every problem as a nail. We find a technique that works, say, with a simple, cognitive problem, so we reach for it to solve *all* of our problems, including those that are neither simple nor cognitive in nature. How willing are we willing to get—to step back and look at the big picture, to seek creative solutions rather than reacting out of habit, to wrestle with the multiple dimensions of complex human problems? At what point will we learn to live with the possibility that acknowledging, confronting and exploring a paradox may be far more satisfying and productive than simply looking for some two-dimensional "answer"? Are we willing to invest in the long haul or continue to be distracted and seduced by the empty promises of quick-fix, short-term formulae? How attached are we to traditions we know to be ineffective? Because if history is any indication, the negative patterns we don't consciously drop—and replace with more positive alternatives—will ultimately come back to haunt us.

I want to invite us all to take a good look at our schools, to stare a few inches beyond the surface, to see the realities that exist in schools, the realities that don't show up in a sound bite or a casual glance. To listen with our hearts, to feel it in our guts. To trust the intelligence in the messages we receive, and build the patience to allow process to happen. To witness with love and encouragement instead of competitiveness and fear. To take the long view, looking beyond the simplicity of numbers and appearances, embracing the complexity of the soul of the place. For it is only from this perspective that we will ever really know a school and the needs of the people in it, and it is only from this vantage point that things will begin to change.

Constructive Alternatives to Dysfunctional Patterns

OLD PATTERNS (Destructive, Counterproductive)	**NEW PATTERNS** (Constructive, Productive)
Impression Management	**Authenticity**
People pleasing, looking good, being fine; need for approval, fear of being judged, fear of lawsuits	Honesty, being oneself (safety to be); tolerance of disapproval from others; accountability
Denial, damage control	Conscientiousness, awareness
Ignoring, enabling, dismissing, excusing	Admitting, confronting, courage, awareness, clarity
Blame, need to fix (or be fixed)	Responsibility, support of others (within boundaries)
Dependence, codependence	Interdependence
Loyalty/disloyalty, dishonesty	Integrity, trust, honesty
Disregard for others, inconsideration	Concern, respect for others
Protecting the system	Advocating for the individual
Lack of communications; poor or miscommunications, triangulation	Healthy communications
Oversimplification	**Complexity**
Black-and-white thinking; dualism (win-lose); need for simplicity	Willingness to live with conflict and paradox
Misunderstanding, misrepresenting; reducing a concept to most simplistic (if incorrect) dimension	Ability to view and grasp multiple dimensions of a concept
Focusing on the irrelevant (missing the point)	Focusing on the relevant (getting the point)
Impatience, despair, quick fix	Persistence, patience, faith
Surface changes	Long-term, deep changes
Tunnel vision	Context
Attention to extremes (troublemakers, gifted kids, popular kids)	Attention to everyone
One set of values (assumptions)	Diversity of values (appreciation, acceptance)

Constructive Alternatives to Dysfunctional Patterns

Reactivity	Proactivity
Crisis orientation	Prevention orientation
"Get tough."	"Get connected."
Fear, pressure ("War on . . .")	Love, encouragement
Hierarchies, power-down, control	Networks, relationships, shared power
Commanding, ordering	"Selling," securing buy-in
Punitive orientation	Encouragement, reward orientation
Inspires avoidance of punishment, penalty or other negative outcome	Inspires seeking satisfaction, other positive outcome
Controlling	Asking, asserting what you want
Reliance on rules, punishment	Reliance on commitment
Complaining, blaming, "fixing"	Creating opportunities, making things better
Threats	Promises
Incongruence, mismatched goals and behaviors	Congruence, behaviors and policies support goals
Scarcity Thinking	**Abundance Thinking**
Negativity, pessimism, despair	Positivity, optimism, faith
Competitiveness	Cooperation, synergy
Resistance to change	Openness to possibilities
Attachment to tradition for tradition's sake (whether it makes sense or is good or not)	Willingness to drop or change destructive traditions; willingness to invite or invent new traditions
Judgments, discrimination	Acceptance, tolerance
Uniformity	Tolerance of diversity, variety
Suppressing	Expressing, tolerance for intensity
Victim thinking	Empowerment
Lack of resources, withholding resources	Creative uses of resources, availability of resources
Conditionality	Unconditionality
Double standards	Absence of double standards
Bell-shaped curve, success for a few, stinginess with grades (positive feedback)	Success for all, unwillingness to accept a percentage of student failures as a given (in every or any learning situation)

Constructive Alternatives to Dysfunctional Patterns

Product Orientation	**Process Orientation**
Learning to know, facts, procedures	Learning to learn, thinking
Fragmentation (linear)	Cohesiveness (multidimensional, holographic)
Telling (arrogance, *I know what's best)*	Asking (trusting, may not know what's best)
Expectations	Goals
Linear	Complex, multidimensional
Hypocrisy (incongruence between goals and behaviors)	Congruence (modeling, consistency)
Teaching according to curriculum	Teaching according to need
Past/future orientation	Present orientation (in context of goals, eye to future)
Fixing, knowing what's best	Guiding, trusting
Blocked awareness (to control)	Communications (to build commitment)
Eliminating problems	Correcting, solving problems

12

More Welcome than Others: Discrimination and Belonging

There were a few teachers that I bonded with, that had faith in me regardless of the bad things I did. They saw the good in every student, even the bad ones, and believed there was hope for everyone.

Joanna Carman

Belonging is the sine qua non of human effectiveness. A person without the protection of the group has only the stripped-down defenses of the loner.

Elizabeth Leonie Simpson[1]

Discrimination in any form is a barrier to teaching and learning. . . . Students can't learn when discrimination causes distractions. Students can't learn when they are victims of harassment.

Bob Chase[2]

Don't ignore or pretend not to see our rich differences. Acknowledging obvious differences is not the problem, but placing negative value judgments on those differences is!

Patti DeRosa[3]

No matter who you are, you're going to have to work with people who are different from you. You're going to have to sell to people who are different from you, and buy from people who are different from you, and manage people who are different from you.

Ted Childs[4]

In one of my all-time favorite *Twilight Zone* episodes, a young woman waits in a hospital room, her face swathed in bandages, waiting to see the results of a plastic surgeon's final attempt to reconstruct her face so that she can live among "normal" people.[5] In a feat of remarkable camera work, you don't actually see anyone's face throughout the entire show until the bandages are removed, revealing a perfectly lovely young woman—much to her horror and the horror of everyone around her. Only when the camera reveals the grotesquely distorted faces of the doctors and nurses do you realize that, in this society, the standards for beauty are quite different from those of the show's intended audience. I was nine years old the first time this show aired, and my notions of reality and "normalcy" were never quite the same afterwards. I've thought of this episode—and the relative criteria for belonging and acceptance—many times over the years. It comes to mind often when I hear conversations turn to judgments and criticisms, and particularly when I see young people who don't measure up to their culture's definition of beauty, value or worth.

In theory, we talk about celebrating diversity. And we acknowledge, fairly universally, the value of unconditional acceptance and belonging. But in truth, most schools offer these goodies within very narrow parameters. Remember, there are strong historical precedents here. For decades, children were expected to exhibit the same behaviors in schools that would later be required (and perhaps rewarded) in the factory-era workplace: compliance, conformity, hard work and obedience. Traits such as individuality, independence, initiative, freedom and flexibility were discouraged and, in fact, seen as threatening to the social order.[6] So in addition to providing for academic necessities, schools also took on the job of creating a social culture and power structure that would diligently encourage or inhibit these behaviors as need be. The cost of "fitting in" in such an environment was enormous—ranging from individual talents and capabilities that were restricted by gender, race or class, to the loss of cultural values, language and identity.[7] But if the idea of a melting pot defined this stage of our cultural and educational history, its days were numbered. Demographic changes toward the end of the twentieth century saw increasing enrollment of minority, non-English-speaking and handicapped students. Various segments of society brought forth their agendas and staked their claim to the American dream, triggering awareness, reform and changes in social consciousness.[8] With our increasing dependence on the global marketplace, the old structures are on even shakier ground. For even if it were possible (and morally justifiable) to somehow fit millions of children into the same mold, it no longer makes economic sense to do so.[9]

It is rather encouraging to see schools proclaim themselves places *Where Uniqueness Is Treasured*[10] or declare that *All Dreams Are Welcome Here.*[11] These slogans represent enormous shifts in our priorities and thinking. To be sure, things are better than they've ever been, with more opportunities for more children than ever before, at least in certain parts of the world.[12] But even in the best settings many of our teaching behaviors and traditions lag behind our best intentions. As is often the case, actual change follows consciousness, and for the most part, schools still function with factory-era power structures, social hierarchies, relationship dynamics, instructional strategies and even curricular expectations that conspire to exclude large numbers of students for a variety of reasons.

To complicate matters, many schools are saddled with at least one adult whose talents might be better suited to a less emotionally interactive calling. "Shouldn't teachers be required to at least *like* kids?" one parent asked, as her twelve-year-old daughter nodded her head in vigorous agreement. This ingredient seemed so basic that I probably wouldn't have mentioned it had so many people not brought it to my attention. (Not that I hadn't noticed. I suppose there's some small grace in the fact that this kind of thing isn't particularly easy to hide.) But there's another reason to bring it up beside the concerns expressed in interviews, conversations and survey responses. "All long-term learning takes place in the context of relationships," remarks psychology professor Maurice Elias. "Outside of a relationship, you get very little long-term, applied learning."[13] So the quality of the relationship between teachers and students is an important factor in the kind of learning we might expect to come out of that relationship. How teachers feel about their students, and how those feelings affect the way they treat the young people in their classes, matters more than we might surmise. In fact, according to Robert Reasoner, retired superintendent and president of the International Council for Self-Esteem, the single most important factor in a child's potential success in school—regardless of age, gender, socioeconomic status, quality of home life, ability and all other factors—is the child's perception that "my teacher likes me."[14] There is, after all, a degree of logic and common sense here. Feeling liked and accepted is a key component of emotional safety, and emotional safety is a key factor in school success. Even children who have no support elsewhere (or are actually being mistreated by other significant adults in their lives) can ultimately thrive with one caring adult in their lives. For many children that "one adult" is someone they encounter in a school setting.[15]

But if students experience their teachers as angry, impatient or indifferent, or if they feel invisible or devalued by their teachers, how safe are they likely to feel? How can we expect these relationships to impact their learning? "Students who believe their teachers support and care about them are more emotionally engaged with their work, value the work more and have higher academic goals and performance," says researcher Karin Frey. She also cites studies that connect declines in students' academic interest and aspirations at the secondary level to the students' perceptions that "teachers are less friendly and caring" there.[16] Educators Frank Siccone and Lilia López note that "research indicates that students pick up on teachers' attitudes even when the teacher is unaware of having negative feelings."[17] And keep in mind that the issue here is the child's perception. As Carl Rogers says, "I do not react to some absolute reality, but to my perception of this reality."[18] Whether the student feels valued and cared about, or disliked or overlooked, those feelings—and the consequences of those feelings—are real and valid, regardless of the teacher's actual sentiments or intentions. But these sentiments and intentions—whatever they are—are an important force behind teacher behavior. Eric Katz explains, "Our ability to recognize and appreciate the intrinsic value inherent in every student directly corresponds to whether we are actively engaged in creating an environment where all students can learn and achieve, or whether we are involved in creating excuses for not doing so."

In their list of characteristics of safe and responsive schools, researchers Dwyer, Osher and Warger include those schools that "treat students with equal respect." They note that "effective schools communicate to students and the greater community that all children are valued and respected. There is a deliberate and systematic effort . . . to establish a climate that demonstrates care and a sense of community."[19] I particularly like the "deliberate and systematic effort" part, and would like to add that "communicating appreciation" is not about going around saying, "Gee, I appreciate you," although verbal expression can certainly be a part of it. For the most part, our appreciation and caring will be communicated by our actions, whether we express affection or not. (For example, several Catholic-school alumni mentioned nuns who clearly cared about them although, as one respondent commented, "They weren't into all this touchy-feely stuff they have today.") True sensitivity, another ingredient of caring and responsive relationships, "doesn't merely involve crawling inside another person's head," write corporate trainers Craig Hickman and Michael Silva, "it includes acting to fulfill the needs and expectations you find there."[20] While I'm personally a big fan of verbal expression, kids will believe far more reliably what we do than what we say, and our words carry little weight without the behaviors and beliefs to back them up.

Decades ago, Rogers suggested applying the principles of acceptance, respect, understanding and trust that were at the heart of his therapeutic model to the field of education.[21] These themes also form the foundation of people-oriented leadership in successful businesses.[22] More and more, we're beginning to see an awareness that effectiveness in any field—whether education, health care, mental health, sales, business or other services—starts with the quality of relationships between the client and the person delivering the services. "Long before sociology was invented, Aristotle defined humanity as the sharing of life within a society," says Elizabeth Leonie Simpson. "All human development is social-situational—that is, it is the result of continued interaction between personal maturation and socialization into group life."[23] This interaction requires inclusion and acceptance.

As described by Maslow's hierarchy, the need for belonging or community is more basic than the needs for high achievement, accomplishment and status, much less personal development and self-actualization. In fact these higher-level goals can only be reached once lower-level needs, including the need for safety and belonging, are satisfied.[24] Research has shown a clear relationship between a "belief in personal efficacy and control" and feelings of belonging and acceptance by others; its absence is a significant factor in such outcomes as aggressiveness, juvenile delinquency, "weak self-image, little ability to defer gratification and much resentment toward authority."[25] Siccone and López confirm the correlation between the development of a student's "healthy sense of self" and the need for acceptance and belonging. "This can only really occur in a bias-free environment that sincerely values all people."[26]

One of the questions on the survey I sent out when I started researching this book asked people if they ever experienced or witnessed any type of discrimination in school. I was a bit overwhelmed, not only by the range of examples respondents offered, but by the vehemence of their responses as well. "Yes, yes, yes! Every day!" wrote Sione Quaass, a high-school student from Australia, before proceeding to catalog a list of offenses she'd witnessed. Despite trends that show improvement in the area of inclusion over the last few decades, when it comes down to individual experiences, we still have a long way to go. "Both the visible and invisible curriculum communicate to students that the school is a place of stratified opportunities," writes educator Hayes Mizell.[27] I'm concerned about this "invisible curriculum," the lessons kids get about who they are and what they're worth. And I'm concerned about how many ways there seem to be for kids to not be welcome in environments in which they spend a large portion of their lives.

One Fine Stew

Subtlety is not the only reason for the persistence of inequity. A false sense of accomplishment has also taken root. We have made wonderful advances, especially in the area of access to schools, courses and careers. Although bias is less problematic today, it still permeates and influences our classrooms.

David Sadker[28]

No child should ever feel—or physically be—excluded from official or informal school activities because of his or her heritage.

Francis Wardle[29]

Later, I remember, we came to the textbook section on Negro history. It was exactly one paragraph long.

Malcolm X[30]

Accomplishments have no color.

Leontyne Price[31]

For many children, school represents a somewhat alien culture, with values, rules, expectations and even language that can be quite different from those of the culture they bring from home. When their experiences are welcome and appreciated, and when school acts simply as a medium for gaining an understanding of a bigger, more diverse universe, children can thrive. But when the "alien culture" becomes the only acceptable culture, demanding behaviors that disregard or conflict with children's experiences and traditions, the impact can be quite different.

I remember seeing an African-American child, who had been brought up to understand that it was disrespectful to look a grownup in the eye, become embarrassed, angry and confused when a teacher demanded, "Look at me when I'm talking to you." One of my student teachers, working in a school whose population was predominantly Navajo, complained about various cultural taboos that were routinely violated, from showing pictures of certain animals on the bulletin boards at certain times of the year, to asking young children to pair up and hold hands with classmates whose clan relationship forbid such contact. Other Native American teachers told me how they, or an older relative, had gone to a government boarding school where they had their hair cut short and were punished severely for even the briefest lapse into their native language. "Emotional safety does not apply to kids who are made to feel that the society they live in favors other kids over themselves," commented insurance agent Richard Forer. Forer was one of several Jewish survey respondents who, as students, felt uncomfortable or compromised having to say prayers or celebrate holidays that honored Christian traditions, typically to the exclusion of any other. A number of individuals also complained about tests and important programs being scheduled during Jewish holidays when they would be out of school.

Emotional safety goes right out the window when kids are made to feel ashamed of where they are from. School-bus driver Andy Quiñones wrote, "For me, school was a mixture of danger and forced conformity, with just a smattering of being touched by a few good teachers." He recalls picking up a book about a red fire engine when he was in kindergarten, pretending he could read it. "I figured that way no one would know I spoke no English." Even as a five-year-old, Quiñones was well aware that "it was not considered proper or in good taste to speak Spanish." Even regional accents can become a source of stress. Therapist Kathy Jenkins recalled how people made assumptions about her values and her intelligence, correcting her speech to eliminate any vestige of the patterns she had learned in her native Texas. Similarly, artist and retired teacher Bobbie Yoakum spent five years in "developmental" classes when she moved from Mississippi to California. Bobbie was consigned to the lowest of three tracks (the equivalent of today's special education classes) by virtue of her Southern accent. She was sent to a speech therapist for her "impediment," and her parents were told "not to expect much from their mentally retarded daughter." Bobbie was finally reassigned to a "regular" class, but not until seventh grade, when her English teacher noticed Bobbie's true abilities.

When viewed through the lens of bias and stereotype, students can be burdened with expectations that bear little resemblance to who they really are. Chinese-American college freshman, Dorothy Lin, notes that "a lot of times teachers automatically assume that I am some genius because I am Asian, and I prove them wrong, which shocks them!"[32] In other settings, an American-born Muslim teenager fends off her classmates' taunts about her being a terrorist, and an African-American educator reports how surprised people are when they find out "I absolutely cannot dance!" Being targeted because of your background can create distress even when the intention seems positive. "Every year throughout elementary school, I was asked to tell the entire class about every Jewish holiday that came up," said one respondent. "I was severely shy and I always felt very self-conscious, but I was also the only Jewish kid in my class for six years." Even our multicultural perspectives can be pretty myopic. One graduate student, filling out various placement forms at a college that prided itself on its inclusive orientation, was offered three choices under the question that asked about his cultural background: Caucasian, Hispanic and Native American. This form sent a very strong, if unintentional, message to this African-American student. Similarly, multiracial and multiethnic students tend to fall into a bit of a vacuum when it comes to school. Although the number of biracial babies is increasing faster than the number of monoracial babies, multicultural programs tend to "ignore them or expect them to identify with the parent of color."[33]

What messages do children receive, asks author Adrienne Rich, when someone with a teacher's authority presents a picture of America "and you're not in it?"[34] With a historical tendency "to consider the practices of the dominant culture as 'standard' and those of other groups as 'variations,'"[35] it should come as no surprise when a lot of people end up feeling marginalized and excluded, and that these experiences can have serious negative consequences. "Many children, especially minority children, go through an entire educational experience without ever having been responded to accurately!" say Aspy and Roebuck. "It is no wonder that they are unable to learn from people who are unable to connect with them."[36] A 1991 report by the U.S. Department of Education's Indian Nations At Risk Task Force stated that "Native students frequently get categorized and treated as remedial students, thus lowering teacher expectations and increasing the risk of failure."[37] In other studies, dropout rates for black students were nearly double that of white students; more than three times as high for Hispanic, American Indians and Native Alaskan youth.[38] Foster-care worker Loretta Maase acknowledges, "When teachers and schools know that a child is a public placement (coming from a group home or foster care, for example), that child gets less attention or is met with lower expectations." Gender bias in school, which can start as early as first grade, may be a significant factor in a range of problems affecting girls, including a greater likelihood of stress and eating disorders than their male counterparts.[39] Other research on gender equity shows that "girls who repeat a grade are more likely to drop out of school than male grade repeaters" and that "they are less likely to return and complete school than boys."[40] Gender bias can also account for the fact that boys in school are far more likely than girls to be punished, suspended, retained or put on medication.[41] Gay and lesbian youth, 80 percent of whom report feeling "severe social isolation," are frequently targeted for harassment and violence at or on their way to school. This group is at high risk for drop-out, homelessness, substance abuse and severe depression, and accounts for 30 percent of all completed teen suicides.[42]

It is exactly statistics like these, along with rapidly changing demographics in American schools, that have brought the importance of concepts like sensitivity training, multicultural education and culturally responsive curriculum into the mainstream of teacher preparation.[43] Programs and materials developed to advance the notion of cultural pluralism have succeeded, to varying degrees, in increasing awareness of and respect for diversity, and encouraging understanding, acceptance, cooperation and interdependence.[44] But there have been problems, as well. Critics have noted that some programs approach pluralism as an isolated topic—yet one more subject to add to an already fragmented and overburdened curriculum. Others have identified problems such as invisibility and selectivity, with a focus on one or two cultural groups to the exclusion of others, or a one-size-fits-all approach that fails to acknowledge "that considerable cultural diversity exists" within cultural subgroups. Further complaints center on "sidebar" treatment, by which the "presentation of ethnic experience is limited to a few isolated events, frequently . . . set apart from the rest of the text," or a "superhero" approach, which acknowledges "only exceptional individuals, the superheroes of history from among that race or cultural group." And all too often, multicultural programs offer little more than a couple of "one-time activities, 'add-on' units or 'sprinkling' the traditional curriculum with a few minority individuals."[45] There are those concerned that some programs "suffer from political naïvete or turn out to bear a sophisticated hidden potential for the assimilation and political neutralization of minority groups," and others who argue for greater segregation as a way to preserve cultural identity.[46] There is, at times, a fair amount of all-or-nothing thinking around these issues. For example, one national forum advocating socially equitable middle schools noted that their efforts to promote opportunities for all students to meet high expectations were occasionally misinterpreted as advocating for a classless society.[47] Equity is not about pretending all students are exactly the same but is instead about a population of diverse individuals being equally entitled to basic rights such as respect, inclusion and success.

Despite the problems and controversies, there are reasonable arguments for implementing any program that will allow participants to examine their assumptions about people from different backgrounds and improve their ability to interact cooperatively and constructively. To stack the odds in favor of this goal, the concept of a multicultural approach to educating children has grown over the years, from its original racial orientation, to ultimately build inclusion and respect for every child in the school, regardless of racial, ethnic or religious background, gender, disability, sexual orientation or socioeconomic status.[48] Because while examples of racial, ethnic and religious prejudices have been documented for decades, discrimination casts a much larger shadow—and in doing so, affects an enormous number of students.

Pretty and Popular

She was a Cardinal, one of the children of the well-to-do who studied from nice books with bright pictures, and I was a Jaybird, one of the poor or just plain dumb children who got what was left after the good books were passed out.

Rick Bragg[49]

Upon graduating high school, I had many friends state that they would never, ever set foot in another classroom as long as they lived. And they haven't. They were finally free. Finally safe.

Mike Selby

For a few horrific hours in Littleton, Colorado, last week, the school outcasts finally had all the power—and they wielded it without mercy or reason.

Matt Bai[50]

We just tease somebody till they develop an eating disorder.

"Elaine"[51]

Be nice to nerds. Chances are, you'll end up working for one.

Bill Gates

When 1986 Teacher of the Year Award winner, Guy Doud, was a kid, he learned that "because my family wasn't one of the prominent families in the community and because my dad and mom struggled with alcoholism and because I was obese, I wasn't as important as other kids." Although he eventually came to realize that this message was "an out-and-out lie," the process of recovering his dignity and sense of worth was a long and painful one.[52] Many children get similar messages during their school experience; many of them spend years struggling to reclaim their sense of self.

We don't have to reach back too far in our history for well-documented examples of serious, widespread prejudice and discrimination in schools. After all, racial integration was mandated in schools during my lifetime; only recently have court rulings in favor of students targeted for harassment or violence put schools on alert, in some instances holding districts accountable with large financial settlements.[53] But while inclusion and protection may be compulsory from a legal standpoint, attitudes can be far more intractable. Even as individuals and systems struggle to assure that values such as acceptance and respect become an intrinsic part of our consciousness, personal experience suggests that the path of acceptability can, for some kids, be exceedingly narrow. "In today's schools, many of the outcasts are still the same," wrote one respondent, claiming that things haven't changed much in the past thirty-five years. "The fat students, the nerdy students, minority students or the poor students, they are still outcast. We have taught tolerance, but we have not taught respect."

A charming and articulate ten-year-old girl sitting next to me on a flight out of Dallas told me about her new school, to which she was returning after visiting her grandmother. She said it was a good school, but that teachers and classmates favored the kids who had money and dressed well. "You have to have nice clothes, expensive clothes, clothes that are in style," she said. Studies on student family income and social class support her claim. Rogers and Frieberg cite research that indicates that "schools perpetuate the separation of students based on social class and reinforce the perception that some students are unworthy. . . . The level of favoritism, unequal discipline, humiliation, labeling by teachers and students, and the feelings of powerlessness felt by the low-income students are a design for failure." They refer to one study that found that "student family income manifested itself in day-to-day interactions with teachers," noting that affluent students enjoyed certain entitlements, including being "talked to" or receiving standard punishments for infractions, while penalties for their lower-income classmates included the "expression of anger by school personnel, public humiliation and ostracism."[54]

One recent college graduate described this discrepancy from her own admittedly privileged perspective. She recounted that as a responsible and highly talented advanced-placement student, she was able to enjoy certain freedoms and flexibility not available to her classmates. She could, for example, leave school in the middle of a class to go out and get a latte, and noted that the principal and vice principal would wave to her as she drove away from a campus that was closed to everyone else. "I knew that other students couldn't have gotten out of the parking lot," she says. She also got away with double the maximum allowable absenteeism, in part because she managed to keep her grades up. She was well aware of the disparity in the rules and privileges—the "rich kids" were in sports, gifted classes ("Even stupid rich kids were in A.P.") and student government—and how this double standard just widened the gap between the "haves" and the "have-nots." As she observed, "It made the poor kids hate the rich kids even more."

Even more widespread was the elitism of the "jock culture," which routinely allowed special privileges for anyone associated with the school's sports teams. One person remembered a cheerleader who was given a warning for being late to her high-school geometry class after two other students in the same class had been given detention for the same offense several minutes before. I met people who, in college, had typed papers for members of the football team and later were shocked and angry when these individuals received higher grades than other students for papers that were "poorly written, copied or just plain junk." Student athletes at both the high-school and college levels are frequently protected from the consequences of their behavior. This practice was frequently identified as a possible contributing factor in the Columbine (and other) shootings. Non-athletes at the school complained that the athletes "received favorable treatment from school officials and often harassed those on whom they look down."[55] In studying peer intimidation and abuse, one group of researchers found that "teachers, particularly male teachers, often sided with student athletes accused of harassment, especially sexual," defending the athletes and focusing their advice on cautions to not get caught.[56] And would police officers have flushed a bag of marijuana down the toilet, thereby eliminating evidence for some of the more serious charges, if the student they arrested had not been a well-known member of the local college basketball team?[57]

As I explored the question of bias and discrimination in school, the issues of clothing, appearance and social cliques kept coming up. Even schools that were fairly homogeneous, ethnically and economically, broke down into groups whose names varied only by decade and geography. Tonia Wechsler notes that in her school, "there were the 'hoods,' the 'preps,' the 'nerds,' the 'scums.' Everyone was labeled." In another school, social cliques included "hoods" and "jocks," as well as "mods" in long hair and paisley, and the "conserves," short for the preppy, conservative kids who would brook only a few select clothing labels, styles and colors. In another setting, one woman, now a successful professional, spent much of her time in high school hanging out at the "freak wall," with other kids who were typically rebellious, indifferent to school, sexually active and involved with drugs and alcohol. Steering clear of the athletes, cheerleaders and homecoming court who hung out on the "jock wall," she remarks, "it was like we're all united here, bonded in not being able to make it in the functional world." When reflecting on various local gangs and groups of outcasts, she noted, "I understand wanting to be a part of something, even if that thing is bad, unhealthy or harmful." And while many of the respondents reflected on experiences that went back a decade or more, a series of interviews in 1999 indicated that far more recently, some teens still bear the burden of stereotypes and discrimination based on their clothing.[58] In some settings, the pressure to conform is intense, and intimidation and animosity between groups can have serious consequences. In some schools, the *real* dress code is the short list of designer labels the more powerful cliques require. As one female ninth-grader reported, "You coordinate your wardrobe or do your hair differently, just so you don't become a victim by being the way you are."[59] Here, too, the Columbine tragedy focused a great deal of attention on problems between social groups, in this case the shooters' affiliation with the "Trenchcoat Mafia" (and its "ties to the 'Goth' culture of black clothing, nihilism and funereal rock music") and the antagonism by some of the "jocks."[60] And the murder of Amarillo student Brian Deneke was reported to be rooted in hostilities between two of the school's social factions, the "jocks" and the "punks."[61]

However, not all discrimination comes at the hands of peers. Young people who don't fit in their particular culture's standards of acceptability, especially kids with their own sense of style and independence, often have the hardest time finding adults who truly appreciate them. Several people noted how obvious a teacher's ridicule or contempt could be, recalling sneers and jokes about students' outfits or hairstyles. One individual remembered overhearing teachers put down students, particularly the more artistic or rebellious kids. "If they didn't like you, they didn't hide it," she observed. Dress codes notwithstanding, a number of others noted differences in adults' attitudes and behavior toward young people based on how the students were dressed. College student Rob Kreuger recalled that in his high school, the only discrimination he witnessed was against the "Gothic" kids. By Kreuger's definition, heavy metal (music) fan, Lily Maase, fit in this category. However, as an accomplished writer, musician and honor student, Maase resented how some adults saw her as a "menace to society" just because her dress included black clothing, steel-toed boots and a chain around her neck. "Nobody entirely fits the stereotype," she said. "I am who I am."[62] And Richard Arthur discovered that teachers and staff at his school treated gang members quite differently when the kids, as part of a little experiment, came to school wearing suits and ties. "The clerical staff treated them with respect and commented on what good-looking young men they were. The gang members had not changed, but the clerical staff now treated them with the courtesy they deserved."[63]

But hierarchies go beyond fashion sense (or nonsense), and kids get hurt and left out for a variety of reasons. For example, despite the 1972 Title IX amendments prohibiting gender discrimination in schools,[64] researcher David Sadker suggests that as far as gender bias goes, "segregation still thrives in U.S. schools." He notes that "teachers unconsciously make males the center of instruction and give them more frequent and focused attention." Artist Linda McGinnis remembered this imbalance well. Excited about having a male teacher for the first time when she entered fifth grade, McGinnis was soon disappointed when "he interacted with the boys and ignored the girls in our class." But bias cuts both ways, and Sadker notes that "gender bias also affects males."[65] Columnist John Leo argues that "girls are better suited to schooling" and as a result boys are much more likely than girls "to have problems with schoolwork, repeat a grade, get suspended and develop learning difficulties." He noted a gender-equity backlash that has spawned pervasive anti-male attitudes in school.[66] High-school student Jason Krueger would agree. He observed that "the only discrimination I have seen has been female teachers giving female students an advantage and being hard on the males." One other male respondent was continually harassed by the girls in his home economics class with a teacher who didn't seem to notice what was going on. "The teacher was completely clueless," he added. Some teachers (and students) note that boys are still acknowledged for strength, speed and performance in math, science and technology, with girls more likely to receive reinforcement for their appearance, handwriting, artistic or writing skills. Clearly, both boys and girls are at risk here, particularly when stereotypes and policies limit potential or fail to accommodate differences in needs, or when the issue of equity becomes a highly politicized tug-of-war, one in which kids of both genders end up in the middle.

Sex-role expectations and gender bias are at the heart of many students' experiences in school. Beth Lefevre claims "I was very much a tomboy and believed I could do anything that they could do." Her accomplishments include being the school arm-wrestling champ in fifth grade and coming in first in shooting on the rifle range (although, she notes, "they wouldn't give me the trophy because I was the only girl"). By seventh grade she had "gotten the message" and started "acting like a girl," switching her attentions to "the acceptable sports—cheerleading and gymnastics." Kathy Jenkins discovered early on that being blond and pretty could be a liability. "I was never validated for my intellect," she comments. "I was immediately labeled and limited in terms of what people thought of me. It was as though I could either be attractive or intelligent, but not both." Their experiences are not uncommon; the messages girls get about what is acceptable and appropriate can be as limiting as they are pervasive. So it's not particularly surprising to discover that as girls approach adolescence, there is a tendency for them to decline in confidence and academic achievement, ratchet their dreams down a notch or two and become more passive.[67]

Systemic and cultural norms aside, girls' rules and standards for one another can be hurdles unto themselves. As a result, girls' social interactions can be heartbreakingly mean—in some cases truly vicious—especially in early adolescence. "Girls punish other girls for failing to achieve the same impossible goals that they are failing to achieve," says clinical psychologist Mary Pipher. "Girls who are smart, assertive, confident, too pretty or not pretty enough are likely to be scapegoated."[68] Once a group establishes some set of standards, it's not uncommon for the group's members to use various forms of direct and indirect bullying—such as social ostracism, backstabbing, manipulation, cattiness, verbal and physical aggression, malicious gossip, rumor-spreading or other attempts to dishonor or embarrass an adversary—to maintain social control.[69] "What's important is the message that not pleasing others is social suicide," says Pipher. Vivian Paley, an author and retired kindergarten teacher, sees fear of rejection as one fuel for the power of cliques. "Kids are afraid to buck their peers or they'll get picked on," she observes.[70] Even kids who feel bad about what they're doing and who are aware that they are hurting someone often lack the skills or the confidence to go against the crowd.[71] Nearly half the students in one study "agreed that befriending a scapegoat would result in reducing [their] social standing."[72] To be sure, acceptance can mean protection. Freelance writer Kathryn Tyler recalls hanging around with the "smart kids" in junior high. She notes, "I felt safe in school physically—there were never any incidents of violence—and within my clique emotionally. Outside of that group, I felt less comfortable." One hotel clerk told me that she finally found acceptance with "the wrong crowd" when she started smoking in eleventh grade. And Richard Arthur describes the appeal of gang life to one girl who saw her initiation as a vehicle for fun, excitement, camaraderie, autonomy from adults and a way to overcome the social rejection she'd experienced elsewhere.[73]

Male students who don't conform to their school culture's stereotypic norms are likewise at risk, particularly if they don't excel in sports or if they don't talk about having sex with girls (even in middle school).[74] Many male survey respondents also experienced school as anti-intellectual, noting that they would be targeted for "using multisyllabic words" or for having "oddball interests, like books with chapters." Educator Ronald Kimmel shared a prominent memory of what he termed emotional scarring: "I was not good at those sports which involved a ball. . . . Of course, I was always the last person chosen, which was humiliating and degrading. I also suffered while playing the game, treated like an annoyance and a liability. It was agonizing to be forced to spend forty-five minutes every day in this way." Attorney Charles Fisher noted that in his experience, "The ideal student model . . . is not an academic," although he noted that boys could get away with being academically gifted if they could "combine it with gifts on the sports field." Such rigid demands leaves a lot of kids vulnerable. As one educator noted, "Anyone who is not athletically competent is at risk, especially if he is 'artsy' or sensitive. These guys were almost uniformly identified as gay—which is probably the most dangerous label you can pick up in a school environment."

Research and personal commentary overwhelmingly concur. Often extreme and uncontested, homophobia compromises physical and emotional safety for thousands of students, gay and straight.[75] A 1997 study indicated that high school students hear an average of twenty-six anti-gay comments every day: 97 percent of them hearing derogatory remarks from peers, while 53 percent hear homophobic comments made by school staff (this last statistic supported by research that found 80 percent of prospective teachers reporting negative attitudes toward gays and lesbians).[76] Such prejudice affects not only homosexual students, but students with a homosexual parent, sibling or friend. High-school student Sione Quaass told of a classmate "who had to change schools because he'd get beaten up every day because people thought he was gay." Actual sexual orientation isn't necessarily the issue. But certainly the high degree of verbal and physical violence directed at students perceived to be gay is a factor in one study's finding that the "fear of being labeled a homosexual was much more common than fear of actually being one."[77] Despite changes in awareness, inservice training and actual school policies in a growing number of districts,[78] this is still land-mine territory for a lot of kids. As high-school counselor D. Moritz notes, "Perhaps one of the best indicators or barometers for evaluating if a safe climate exists for gay, lesbian, bisexual or transgender (GLBT) youth is to ask staff members how many GLBT youth have identified themselves as such. I work in a school with sixteen hundred students, in a guidance department of seven counselors. In the past fifteen years, fewer than ten students have self-identified. This tells me that we have not created a climate of support, and that GLBT youth are not feeling safe."

Sexual harassment to any child, for any reason, can have far-reaching consequences, negatively impacting victims physically and emotionally, and affecting their school experience and performance.[79] According to the Equal Employment Opportunity Commission's definition, this term refers to "any unwelcome sexual advances, requests for sexual favors and other verbal or physical conduct of a sexual nature. . . ."[80] There seems to be a perverse sense of normalcy about these types of attacks, with many students seemingly unaware of either the absolute inappropriateness or the hurtful consequences of this kind of behavior. As Barbara Wills notes, "male students, when counseled, often feel they have done nothing wrong." Although many who spoke up on behalf of this issue focused on the more prevalent (or better documented) "inappropriate sexual comments to young females," harassment affects boys as well, with abuse inflicted by both male and female classmates. Sexual harassment and violence in teen relationships is also an issue, particularly for young people who confuse anger, jealousy or possessiveness with love.[81]

When it comes to targeting kids for bullying or harassment, just about anything relating to a child's body or physical appearance can draw fire. One study conducted during the 1992 to 1995 academic years noted that physically mature girls were at high risk for sexual comments and demands from male classmates or for being labeled as promiscuous, and that "the double standard for girls remained strong." Girls considered unattractive or unstylish were frequently targets, as well.[82] Quaass noted how common it was for girls to be "getting a heap because their bust isn't big enough or their hips are too big." Not surprisingly, the issues of weight and body size were mentioned frequently in interviews and survey results. My ten-year-old travel companion complained that her classmates "are mean to fat kids." Sharon Tandy noted that when a girl was on the outs with friends, the girls would often gang up on the excluded child with taunts of "tubbo" or "fatty." Shakeshaft's study noted how routinely kids would embarrass girls who were targeted for being overweight, regardless of actual body size. They quote one student as saying, "The girl isn't fat, but they call her 'cow' and they moo at her."[83]

This report also noted that while comments about girls' weight were common, the practice was seldom directed at boys. Nonetheless, several male respondents reported being targeted—not only by peers but occasionally by a teacher as well. Therapist and trainer Bob Sugar recalled being anxious to get to lunch when his geometry teacher commented, "You look like you've got plenty to tide you over." Charles Fisher recounted his arrival at boarding school as one of three "fat boys," with Fisher outweighing the others by a few pounds. Since he did not "conform to the ideal model of the sporting English public-school boy," his classmates took it upon themselves to refuse to allow him to eat, which led to him volunteering to clear tables after as many meals as he possibly could, because it was the only way he could get any food at all. "I'd have to wait until the end of the meal and then I had to stuff my pockets with bread and boiled eggs." Fisher consumed his scraps "in the toilet because otherwise somebody [might] come and take this food away from me."

But this focus on the body goes another step further, and deplorably, any kind of physical irregularity also seems to be fair game for some kids. Manicurist Maria Stewart understands when kids with cleft palates are afraid to go to school. In addition to several surgeries throughout her childhood, Stewart also endured her classmates' teasing for the same thing. Quaass mentioned a disabled student "who gets pushed down the stairs and picked on" because he has cerebral palsy. And one Web site devoted to issues of teen violence in relationships includes in its list of abusive actions any behavior that "intentionally harasses, teases or takes advantage of a person with a disability," including "keeping something out of reach of a person who uses a wheelchair, making it hard for someone with hearing aids to hear you or deliberately trying to confuse someone with a learning disability."[84] As many people with disabilities can attest, "attitudinal barriers are just as restrictive as access barriers, but more difficult to break down because they are abstract and difficult to prove."[85]

Interestingly, research on bullying suggests that "external deviations play a much smaller role in the origin of bully-victim problems than generally assumed," although from student assessments of why certain children are bullied, certain of these features, such as "obesity, red hair, an unusual dialect or wearing glasses" do make certain kids more of a target. Nonetheless, not all children with these characteristics will be bullied. The cause of the bullying, according to expert Dan Olweus, is probably not the characteristic being ridiculed.[86] More likely, some personality trait such as shyness, sensitivity, passivity, anxiety or insecurity accounts for a student's vulnerability. Many reports and personal accounts cite weak verbal and social skills as contributing factors. One contributor reflected, "I would react by shutting down and becoming quiet. I feel I didn't have the skills to defend myself or vent [my feelings]. In this respect I felt unsafe and threatened daily by the words that 'might be said.'" Lack of confidence, lack of self-control and defensiveness can be veritable bull's-eyes, and kids with hot tempers or those who cry easily were observed to frequently end up as the butt of teasing by classmates who get power out of provoking a reaction. Others are targeted because they taunt or provoke bullies and several actually collude with bullies, allowing themselves to be scapegoated in order to remain in a group (not unlike kids "ranking in" to gangs, allowing their peers' abuses in order to be accepted).[87] Eric Katz believes that kids who lack the protection of social allies are most vulnerable. He has observed that students who are most isolated often appear the easiest and "safest" to victimize.

Such accounts make a strong argument for programs that build kids' emotional intelligence and social skills. They also speak to the need to redouble our efforts to encourage and teach not only tolerance and acceptance, but the even more positive attitudes toward differences, such as support, admiration, appreciation and nurturance.[88] "We probably don't need a Vegetarian Day or a Tactile Learners Parade at our school," said one somewhat cynical educator. "But we do need to accept and acknowledge the existence of these subcultures, and make it possible for the kids who identify with these groups to work and live in this community without fear of harassment, ridicule or failure."

Stand by Me

I know that I came to blame myself, for if no one would speak up and come to my defense, didn't that mean that I deserved what I was getting? Didn't it prove that the boys were right about me, and I really was the ugliest, stupidest and most hideous freak on the face of the planet? To me it proved all this and more.

Jan Rogers
student

He was very honourable . . . and held it as a solemn duty in the boys to stand by one another. He suffered for this on several occasions. . . . But he had his reward. Steerforth said there is nothing of the sneak in Traddles, and we all felt that to be the highest praise.

Charles Dickens[89]

Many educators are dismayed that while other countries are struggling for democracy, we, as a nation, seem to demand less of democracy when it provides the guiding principles for our own education system.

Victoria R. Fu[90]

Discrimination hurts. Whether experienced as a subtle message, lack of recognition, deliberate exclusion, verbal harassment or physical abuse, students whose school lives are marred by any form of prejudice are not safe. But if being the object of aggression by one's peers is devastating, having the important adults in one's life either ignore or participate in the experience is an even greater betrayal. "Adults . . . would not be subjected to racial taunting in the workplace or be expected to endure insults directed at body size, clothing or accent," says author Irene McDonald. "It would be rare in the adult world, for an individual to be shoved up against a wall, knocked to the ground, spat upon, groped, attacked by a group of colleagues for coffee money or denied access to the bathroom until they forfeited their ball caps."[91] Bullying expert Allan Beane agrees. "The law protects adults against crimes like extortion, slander and assault and battery," he reminds. "An adult who throws rocks and shouts obscenities at another adult will probably be arrested. This protection should extend equally to children who are generally considered more vulnerable and less able to defend themselves. Unfortunately, this isn't the case."[92]

In each of the numerous stories I received which detailed abuses that ranged from teasing to serious physical abuse were statements like "where the adults were, I don't know," "the school was not equipped to handle it" or "teachers would laugh and look the other way." One contributor, who requested anonymity, recalled school as "a torture." For educator Laurie Schmidt, "It was a terrifying experience." A number of male respondents compared their lives at school to the savagery in *Lord of the Flies,* and the term "survival of the fittest" came up often. Gary Myrah noted that occasionally the police would come and remove the ring-leaders, and for a time, "there was a sense of tranquility. . . . Unfortunately this would only be a temporary removal, and the anxiety would increase upon their return."

One survey respondent recalled a time during her freshman year when a girl sitting behind her hit her in the back. By the time the teacher dismissed the class, the attack had intensified, by now involving several of the girl's friends. "How could the teacher not have noticed?" she asked. "It was awful." Schmidt recalled being pushed and beaten on the school bus, one time blacking out from a blow to the head. "The bus driver just laughed and the other students yelled out, 'Cool! Do it again!'" She wasn't the only one targeted. "I saw kids shut in lockers, put up on the flag pole, beaten up and verbally and physically harassed—all in the presence of the teachers," she reports. Homemaker Sandra LaRose remembers teachers and administrators who didn't seem to know or care what was going on in the halls or bathrooms between classes, and when there was a problem "there wouldn't be anyone around to help you." In her experience, support that was available wasn't available to everyone: "Even the school counselors wouldn't help unless you were one of the popular kids." And Jan Rogers sent me a long, heartrending e-mail that traced her most recent suicide attempt back to years of torture at the hands of classmates. In addition to routinely being kicked, tripped, knocked down and spit on, Rogers was also beaten with a baseball bat (in front of one of the nuns) and repeatedly assaulted sexually. "By the end of my first year in that school, every nun, every lay teacher, and both priests knew at least some of what was going on. Not at any time did one of them do anything to stop it," she says. "I've tried to imagine how any adult, under any circumstances, can stand by and watch a group of children gang up on another child."

Good question. The literature uniformly insists that the awareness, attention and intervention of adults is imperative in ending peer discrimination, harassment and abuse. "Challenge discriminatory attitudes and behavior!" recommends Patti DeRosa. "Ignoring the issues will not make them go away, and silence can send the message that you are in agreement with such attitudes and behaviors." She also challenges adults to become aware of their own attitudes, as well as their hesitancies to intervene.[93] However, the literature also supports the contentions of individuals who had been harassed or attacked as children who claimed that the adults were either unaware of what was going on, made excuses for the abuser, ignored or accepted what was going on, or denied that there was a problem. All of these nonresponses are enabling behaviors, which not only allow the abuse to continue but appear to give kids permission to hurt one another. In one survey, junior-high students charged that teachers only responded to the most severe forms of violence, and that teachers and administrators generally were not aware of the violent behaviors that occurred at school. "Some things are so common, they are ignored," said one student. "Teachers don't care enough about name-calling, ethnic fights, teasing and stealing. They only care if blood is spilled so they can't be [sued]. . . ."[94] Olweus cites a 1983 survey, which concluded that teachers "did relatively little to put a stop to bullying at school, according to both the bullied and bullying students."[95] Researchers Merle Froschl and Nancy Gropper found that in their study, which focused on young children, "teachers or other adults, although present at all times, were uninvolved in or ignored 71 percent of the observed incidents."[96] Incidents of sexual harassment also generally "go unnoticed in the classroom. Students are not informed about ways to avoid harassment and defend their rights," comment authors Susan Strauss and Pamela Espeland. Likewise, adults have not been adequately trained to deal with these issues, despite findings that "harassment is most likely to occur in organizations where management fails to implement a strong philosophy and policy indicating that such behaviors won't be tolerated." The upshot of this neglect is that "schools have become environments that support sexual harassment," they claim.[97]

There is probably no one reason that adults hesitate to become involved; however, impression management may be a factor. Author Eric Jones recommends that school personnel acknowledge that "it is a well-known fact among adults that some children in every generation are nasty to others," instead of trying to hide these conflicts to try to make the school look good. Only then are teachers free to inform parents about the school's attitudes and policies regarding these issues. One other factor is the often-mentioned tendency to make or accept excuses for abusive behavior. Jones advises teachers to watch out for comments like, "We were only playing," "It was only a joke" or "It was an accident."[98] Strauss and Espeland also identify remarks like, "She asked for it," "She can't take a joke," "Boys will be boys" and "Everyone else does it" as common excuses for harassing behavior.[99] Certainly the values and personal biases of adults come into play, which may, in part, account for rather pervasive attitudes which suggest that victims "bring it on themselves" or that bullying builds character or "teaches about behavior acceptable to the group," beliefs that simply perpetuate the problems, encouraging students to believe that they are to blame for their own victimization.[100] And in one report, a school board member was reluctant to implement a sexual harassment curriculum in his district for fear that if the students knew their rights, the district would be vulnerable to lawsuits.[101]

Nonetheless, there are many schools and districts—not to mention large numbers of individual teachers, counselors and administrators—who routinely take a stand on behalf of any underdog, whose personal philosophies and actual policies and behaviors show a high level of commitment to creating safety at all levels, for all students. Barbara

Wills describes a number of features at her school that contribute to a widespread sense of security. There are, for example, offices placed throughout the building. "If students are being harassed by other students, they are a minute from an office that they can walk into. They are instructed to do this or go into any teacher's classroom, but never to the rest room as they may have no protection there."

Policies that invite students to seek refuge, and follow up with advocacy and support, can be the difference between life and death. In Port Huron, Michigan, a plot by four middle-school boys intending to outdo the Columbine killers was thwarted when a classmate reported their intentions to the school's assistant principal. This, however, is the exception rather than the rule. Several reports note that in most instances of school violence or suicide, there were students who knew in advance but did not tell anyone.[102] The fact that so many tragedies could have been prevented has raised serious questions about what appears to be a code of silence among kids in school. (In fact, one reason adults may have a distorted view of the social climate in schools might be because they seldom hear about problems.) But in light of the reception kids often encounter from adults—not to mention their peers—this is understandable. Not all schools are as inviting or supportive as the one Wills describes. In some settings, as bad as things can get for some students, telling makes it that much worse. "Typical adult responses to allegations of harassment in schools almost always discouraged students from further reports, seldom curbed harassment, and left kids feeling as though they had no place to turn for help," report Shakeshaft and her colleagues. "In many cases, staff and other students penalized them for going public by reporting a crime. In these cases, students were violated twice—first by the harassment and then by the treatment of adults and other students."[103] In one survey, students were more willing to report if the target was a friend, a younger student or someone unpopular. They were also more willing to report property damage and vandalism than "bullying, verbal threats, ethnic conflict or fights." The greatest determinants, however, were the age, physical size and popularity of the perpetrator. Still, a full 35 percent of students surveyed said they would never tell.[104] School psychologist Richard Lieberman claims that the fear of retribution is reasonable. "Schools need to assure students that they are doing the right thing by informing and that their identities will be protected."[105] A group of teens I interviewed told me that their teachers were responsive, and after any well-publicized school crisis, talked about how to prevent similar situations from occurring. The students were given numbers to call and instructions for reporting, but despite assurances of anonymity, they told me "many kids won't call because of caller ID, especially if the number they are trying to call won't accept blocked numbers."

In a long list of ways in which school policies, attitudes and environments can contribute to the incidence of peer conflict, authors Peter Stephenson and David Smith include the existence of many areas for students that are difficult to supervise, the use of untrained and underpaid staff to supervise at times like lunch and recess and a tendency to punish students who seek sanctuary inside the school during times they feel most vulnerable.[106] But failure to take action is probably the most common problem. Nearly all of the reports I read or received noted that little or nothing happened to the abuser, even when the abuse was witnessed by an authority. In McDonald's studies, "over half of the students were dissatisfied with the way victims of school violence were treated. . . . They were even less satisfied with the way the perpetrators were handled."[107] MaryAnn Kohl recalls that "there was a fair amount of 'silent' sexual harassment. . . . We were made to feel that we must accept it, ignore it, deal with it. It was very frightening to be harassed and have no one to go to, no one who would think it was important." When kids do not receive active support, when the reality of their experience is not respected, or when their confidentiality is not protected, it won't take long for them to get the feeling that there's no place to go, that no one is there for them and that there's no point in trying to get help. This message was certainly clear to many of the people who wrote in or interviewed with me. Perhaps it was a factor for Andrew Rudy, as well. When this fourteen-year-old high-school freshman committed suicide in the fall of 1999, many believed that the bullying he lived through daily was so vicious and severe that he felt there was no other way out.[108]

There are a number of compelling reasons for teachers to act—decisively and immediately—whenever they see any hint of discrimination or harassment. But unfortunately, in some schools, the trend has shifted from ignoring or accepting to simply expelling. One parent told me that her son had been suspended for a week for using an ethnic slur. With all due credit for the school's refusal to tolerate prejudice, one would have to wonder what this student actually learned from his punishment. Here was a wonderful opportunity to help a young man grow and develop more positive attitudes about others different from himself. But instead of counseling or diversity training, he got a week off, paid the penalty and went back to school, perhaps a bit more careful about how loosely he expressed his prejudices in the future. Actions do not need to be punitive, but they do need to be clear and firm. Daniel Goleman reported on research by Fletcher Blanchard, which showed that strongly expressed antiracist opinions led the people who heard these opinions to develop similar reactions. "When a few very vocal people express dismay at these acts, others are encouraged to do likewise." He continues, "His conclusion is that setting a tone that condemns acts of bias and hatred will, in fact, discourage them."[109] Besides, studies show that "prejudice that comes from ignorance and stereotyping is the easiest to change."[110] Recommendations for putting an end to peer conflict uniformly begin with adult awareness. But there are other important strategies as well, and experts also recommend starting young, breaking the code of silence, acting immediately, documenting all reported and witnessed incidents, photographing injuries, giving priority to the victims' distress before dealing with the perpetrator, training all adults who deal with students, modeling behaviors that respect and appreciate diversity, building students' social and emotional competence, and practical considerations such as reducing the adult-child ratios, particularly for supervising during breaks.[111]

The fear, anger and self-hatred borne of exclusion and harassment can linger long after graduation. Laurie Schmidt was one of dozens of people who told me they never went back. Years later she notes, "I have no desire to ever see those people again. The one friend I did have in middle school has since committed suicide." Among the numerous requirements for establishing emotional safety in schools is a conscious intention and effort to eliminate the attitudes, policies and behaviors that allow even one child to face another day at school with fear and dread. Because, for many, the consequences of not belonging can make a frightening and provocative episode of *The Twilight Zone* seem like a very tame version of their own lives.

Where Never Was Heard a Discouraging Word

After looking at my efforts with the paper and paints [the teacher] suggested that I should choose music. . . . I probably should have continued with the instruction in art. Later turns of creativity have even led some people to call me an artist, but I will never have the confidence to wear that label because that one offhand remark was branded so deeply into my adolescent soul.

Carol Nevius Jones
educator and children's book author

> *One time I worked really hard and earned an A in a class. The teacher announced to the entire class, "You know you are actually a C student. This grade is just a fluke."*
>
> Laurie Schmidt

> *The teacher—and I will always, always remember this—told me I would be much more comfortable with my own kind. I was six, but even at six you understand what it means to be told you are not good enough to sit with the well-scrubbed.*
>
> Rick Bragg[112]

According to Bob Reasoner, the longer one stays in school, the lower one's self-esteem.[113] How is it possible that twelve years in an educational system can have such a deleterious effect on such large numbers of students? As author Sonia Nieto reminds, "Students do not simply develop poor self-concepts out of the blue. Rather they are the result of policies and practices of schools and society that respect and affirm some groups while devaluing and rejecting others."[114] Too many people report spending much of their adulthood getting over the experience, struggling with negative and discouraging messages, occasionally achieving social, emotional, academic and other forms of success *in spite of* their education, rather than because of it.

Jean Potter is one example. A successful children's author and a former assistant secretary of education for the U.S. Department of Education, Potter once began a speech to the Pennsylvania State Guidance Counselors Association by stating, "I'm not supposed to be here." She went on to detail how, in high school, her efforts to apply to college were nearly derailed by a guidance counselor who determined that Jean was not "college material," and was destined, instead, for secretarial school. "You'll never make it through college," he told her. "You are interested in too many activities, and not always in your studies. Don't waste your father's money." His vote was overturned by Potter's determination and the insistence of her father, but the counselor's lack of confidence in Jean's ability dogged her for years. "Every time things got difficult, I would wonder if maybe this counselor had been right all along," she said. Her subsequent successes have validated a message she has for anyone who has a chance to touch a child's life: Never discourage a dream. "Don't ever discourage kids from doing what they think they can do. If a child's ambition exceeds his ability, he'll find out soon enough," she says. Encouragement and faith in his potential will go a lot farther. Rico Racosky agrees. His work with young people continually urges them to push the limits of what they can imagine for themselves: "None of us knows what great things we can achieve until we take positive action and find out for ourselves."[115]

Joseph Lancaster is another survivor, one who managed tremendous learning and success despite difficulties in a school setting. When Lancaster was in sixth grade, his teacher urged his father to pull him out of school, saying that Joseph was incapable of learning. He didn't fare much better in high school where he almost failed every class. But he did "a lot of talking and a lot of convincing to get into University," where he "stood first." The fact that Lancaster has accumulated a number of advanced degrees in medicine and education, as well as certification in twenty-two medical specialties, is surely a testament to the potential resiliency of the human spirit.

But why should school have to be an obstacle course for so many kids? History abounds with such stories—of hugely influential and successful individuals who never quite got the hang of school, or for whom school was a huge source of discouragement and failure. People like Pablo Picasso, whose father pulled him out of school at age ten and hired a tutor who soon gave up and quit. Beethoven, who never learned to multiply or divide, and whose music teacher told him he was "absolutely useless as a composer." Louisa May Alcott, whose teacher complained that she drew when she should have been doing addition. Bill Gates, who dropped out of Harvard. Charles Mingus, who was beaten and verbally abused by teachers who pronounced him unable "to keep up with the white pupils." Albert Einstein, who didn't speak until age four, couldn't read until age seven, flunked all of his math classes, failed his college entrance exams and generally disturbed his teachers with "unanswerable questions" and a tendency to smile "for no apparent reason." Sir Winston Churchill, who languished at the bottom of his class at one school and failed the entrance exams to another twice. Thomas Edison, who ran away from school after being beaten with a cane for fidgeting and not paying attention. Malcolm X, whose favorite teacher told him that Malcolm's dream of becoming a lawyer was "no realistic goal for a [black person]."[116]

And what of the others, people whose stories don't make it into books like these? Or the potential Picassos, Gates, Minguses and Einsteins who simply gave up and bought into the restricted vision some adult—whether well-meaning or mean-spirited—had for them? How dare we, any of us, presume to impose our picture of "realistic" on anybody, especially a child? Smothering a child's dreams, limiting her potential in any way, for any reason, surely must be the most grievous of sins. None of us can know the treasures in a child's soul that only the future—and perhaps a kind word of encouragement—can unlock. Who in their right mind would stand in this child's way? For even if one dream doesn't work out, its pursuit can lead to even better possibilities.

In a far more positive example, student and aspiring writer Rachel Harnish remembers the teacher who told her, "I know you're not sure of yourself, and that's okay. But when you win that Pulitzer, remember to mention my name." Would anyone doubt that this teacher's faith and encouragement will not reside in a corner of whatever confidence and success Rachel experiences down the road? As educators with extraordinary power to impact a child's life, which role will we play? Will we be the obstacle in a child's path or the light that helps her navigate its challenges?

13

How Does Your Garden Grow? More Diversity, More Discrimination

The Animal School: A Fable

Once upon a time the animals decided they must do something heroic to meet the problems of a "new world" so they organized a school. They had adopted an activity curriculum consisting of running, climbing, swimming and flying. To make it easier to administer the curriculum, all the animals took all the subjects.

The duck was excellent in swimming. In fact, better than his instructor. But he made only passing grades in flying and was very poor in running. Since he was slow in running, he had to stay after school and also drop swimming in order to practice running. This was kept up until his webbed feet were badly worn and he was only average in swimming. But average was acceptable in school so nobody worried about that, except the duck.

The rabbit started at the top of the class in running but had a nervous breakdown because of so much makeup work in swimming. The squirrel was excellent in climbing until he developed frustration in the flying class where his teacher made him start from the ground up instead of the treetop down. He also developed a "charlie horse" from overexertion and then got a C in climbing and D in running. The eagle was a problem child and was disciplined severely. In the climbing class, he beat all the others to the top of the tree but insisted on using his own way to get there. At the end of the year, an abnormal eel that could swim exceedingly well and also run, climb and fly a little had the highest average and was valedictorian.

The prairie dogs stayed out of school and fought the tax levy because the administration would not add digging and burrowing to the curriculum. They apprenticed their children to a badger and later joined the groundhogs and gophers to start a successful private school.

Does this fable have a moral?

George H. Reavis[1]

Perhaps the most fascinating thing about the story above is that Reavis wrote it while he was the assistant superintendent of Cincinnati schools back in the 1940s. I've shared this story with people from all over the world and find that its relevance is as widespread as it is current. Standards and high expectations are almost always fashionable—they make great fodder for political slogans and, quite frankly, seem to only offer alternatives like low expectations, "dumbing-down" the curriculum or a willingness to accept poor performance. But if standards can offer us a benchmark for performance goals, they can also be a source of another form of discrimination that many people experience in schools. Juanita Ross Epp defines standards as "a code name for an amalgam of current prejudice and the choices of this particular culture."[2] To be honest, standards are a fairly arbitrary collection of "shoulds" that generally speak to norms and averages across large numbers of students. In many cases, they have little to do with the actual needs or experiences, or the readiness of individual learners. And while this idea of "teaching to the middle" may have had its charm in the bell-curve mentality of a factory economy, our current economy, which demands a wide range of skills and talents, dictates that we can no longer afford the price of ignoring the kids on either end of a curve that has long since outlived its usefulness.

"People need an atmosphere in which they can specialize, hone their skills, and discover their distinctiveness," says Alan Loy McGinnis.[3] But how likely am I to grow into my own unique capabilities if the environment in which I am trying to grow is obsessed with sameness? Standards tend to reinforce the factory-era appeal of uniformity. As one high-school principal observed, "The very idea of having standards for student achievement assumes that all students are the same." When we

READER/CUSTOMER CARE SURVEY

HEFG

We care about your opinions! Please take a moment to fill out our online Reader Survey at **http://survey.hcibooks.com**. As a **"THANK YOU"** you will receive a **VALUABLE INSTANT COUPON** towards future book purchases as well as a **SPECIAL GIFT** available only online! Or, you may mail this card back to us.

(PLEASE PRINT IN ALL CAPS)

First Name ______ MI. ______ Last Name ______

Address ______ City ______

State ______ Zip ______ Email ______

1. Gender
- ❒ Female ❒ Male

2. Age
- ❒ 8 or younger
- ❒ 9-12 ❒ 13-16
- ❒ 17-20 ❒ 21-30
- ❒ 31+

3. Did you receive this book as a gift?
- ❒ Yes ❒ No

4. Annual Household Income
- ❒ under $25,000
- ❒ $25,000 - $34,999
- ❒ $35,000 - $49,999
- ❒ $50,000 - $74,999
- ❒ over $75,000

5. What are the ages of the children living in your house?
- ❒ 0 - 14 ❒ 15+

6. Marital Status
- ❒ Single
- ❒ Married
- ❒ Divorced
- ❒ Widowed

7. How did you find out about the book?
(please choose one)
- ❒ Recommendation
- ❒ Store Display
- ❒ Online
- ❒ Catalog/Mailing
- ❒ Interview/Review

8. Where do you usually buy books?
(please choose one)
- ❒ Bookstore
- ❒ Online
- ❒ Book Club/Mail Order
- ❒ Price Club (Sam's Club, Costco's, etc.)
- ❒ Retail Store (Target, Wal-Mart, etc.)

9. What subject do you enjoy reading about the most?
(please choose one)
- ❒ Parenting/Family
- ❒ Relationships
- ❒ Recovery/Addictions
- ❒ Health/Nutrition
- ❒ Christianity
- ❒ Spirituality/Inspiration
- ❒ Business Self-help
- ❒ Women's Issues
- ❒ Sports

10. What attracts you most to a book?
(please choose one)
- ❒ Title
- ❒ Cover Design
- ❒ Author
- ❒ Content

TAPE IN MIDDLE; DO NOT STAPLE

NO POSTAGE NECESSARY IF MAILED IN THE UNITED STATES

BUSINESS REPLY MAIL

FIRST-CLASS MAIL PERMIT NO 45 DEERFIELD BEACH, FL

POSTAGE WILL BE PAID BY ADDRESSEE

Health Communications, Inc.
3201 SW 15th Street
Deerfield Beach FL 33442-9875

FOLD HERE

Comments

overfocus on standards, we invariably leave out those students who have already achieved mastery and are bored, and leave behind those students who lack the prerequisite skills necessary to do the work that the standards demand. Standards tend to focus on product over process. They typically emphasize fairly linear kinds of tasks and thinking, and fail to appreciate, accommodate or acknowledge kids with more abstract, nonlinear means of processing or explaining. They also tend to elevate linguistic and mathematical intelligences (and related tasks) and disregard other ways of being "smart." And they also discriminate against kids who pay attention and take in information by just about any means other than sitting still, listening and looking at the teacher.

There's another problem with standards, and it's about what we do with them. Even if we had uniform consensus on a particular goal or expectation, what do we do with the duck who can't run or the rabbit who can't swim? There will always be children who aren't living up to our curricular expectations—either because they lack the skills and experiences necessary to acquire what we're trying to teach, or they aren't being taught in ways they can understand, or the content does not have any meaning or value to them, or their strengths lie in other areas or simply, perhaps, because their timetable is different from ours. Are the standards we have imposed on them, then, going to be used instructionally or punitively? To enhance, encourage and expand their experiences, or to label, limit and hurt?

Mel Levine is among many who have worked with talented kids with "normal or superior overall cognitive ability" who are struggling in school because "subtle but important variations" in their neurological "wiring" makes it hard for them to learn in traditional settings, and also because the adults in their lives often do not understand or know how to respond to their innate strengths and difficulties.[4] Thomas Armstrong saw similar trends in his work as a special-education teacher. He found that all of his students were capable of learning, and many were highly talented in one area or another. "What they all had in common," he observes, "was difficulty with the traditional classroom model of workbooks, lectures and standardized tests—a difference that sometimes showed itself in learning problems and sometimes in behavior or attentional problems."[5] The truth is, there are very few "eels" in our schools, kids who are naturally competent in all subjects, and who can withstand the gauntlet of the various academic, social and behavioral "filters" through which they are judged. As a result, "some students experience school as a place of possibility and growth, while for others, it is controlling and boring," says Hayes Mizell. "Some students get what they need to stride ahead, while the school permits others to fall behind or consigns them to persistently ineffective 'interventions.'"[6] Further, many students "have talents that traditional classrooms seldom tap," note researchers Noel White, Tina Blythe and Howard Gardner. "Educational standards do not have to be lowered for them, but should be expanded to offer a wider variety of opportunities for success."[7]

Even the most reasonable standards can hurt kids who can't accomplish them. Back in the 1960s, reports out of Washington expressed concern for the state of fitness in American children. In a scenario not too different from *The Animal School,* a list of skills for which *all* students would be held accountable made its way into the schools. Not long after, in gym classes throughout the country, teachers announced a series of tests students would all take the following week—or, in some instances, the following day! For all but a handful of strong or athletic kids, this was pretty scary stuff. I was surprised at how many people mentioned these physical-fitness tests when answering interview or survey questions for this book, and the degree of animosity the recall typically evoked. Those who remember the tests also remember neither being prepared for them nor having their performance used for any instructional purposes. No one I spoke to remembered those tests fondly. Even the woman at the library groaned when I told her I was looking for some documentation on the topic. "Oh yes," she said. "I remember *those!*"

Linda Sorenson remembers being among the "pretty pathetic characters" trying to hang by one arm from a "cold metal bar in those tacky one-piece blue gym suits as the seconds ticked off *way* too slowly." One workshop participant recalled what she still refers to as the "two-hundred meter, walk-run-throw up." Another regards taking the tests as "the most traumatic event of my adolescence." Now no one would argue against advancing the cause of youth fitness as a noble goal. But this approach actually had the opposite effect for a large number of students. Rather than inspiring greater physical activity, it created, for some of us, associations that, to this day, cast a certain pall of drudgery over any kind of endeavor more athletically demanding than, say, shopping.

Several years ago, in a very different kind of experience, I joined a gym that has, among its facilities, an indoor track. It's a small enough track that you have to go around twenty-seven times to run a mile. In the true spirit of an at-risk learner (for which I would certainly qualify in this setting), I was positive that I'd be able to run a mile on this track—since the laps were so short! Of course, by the time I was finishing my second lap, it had dawned on me that a mile was still a mile, even if the laps *are* little, and that, having run all of about 125 yards, I'd probably already outdistanced my best efforts to that point in my life—at which point I collapsed. Now when this kind of thing would happen in gym class, the result would usually involve criticism, impatience, ridicule or disgust. (None of these reactions, incidentally, whether from teachers or peers, taught me a thing about being a better runner, nor did they motivate me to improve.) However, this time I got something I'd never experienced before in the equivalent of a gym class: acceptance and encouragement. "Great start!" said the young lady taking me around to introduce me to the various facilities and machines. "Why don't you shoot for three laps next time?" And much to my surprise, I did! Where I had spent much of my adolescence dreaming up increasingly exotic excuses to get *out* of gym, I actually went back to this track, again and again. And to this day, I count my first mile—which took me five months to accomplish—among the greatest of my life's achievements. I will probably always be a bit of a duck when it comes to running, and I doubt I'll ever love physical exercise as much as I love certain other activities, but something has shifted in my confidence, and in my picture of my own capabilities—just because it was okay for me to be "the slowest kid in the class," and for me to simply start where I was and keep challenging myself to improve from there.

Stanley Greenspan cites critics who, in a classic example of black-and-white thinking and misrepresentation, "insist that our educational system is . . . catering to each child's idiosyncrasies in an overindulgent effort to build self-esteem by rewarding children for whatever they happen to do." The alternative they suggest is "returning to traditional methods of demanding higher standards" in order to "guide children toward academic mastery."[8] But what does this mean? Of course it's ridiculous to reward or praise substandard performance (which, incidentally, has nothing to do with what self-esteem is *really* about). And dumbing-down the curriculum is an insult to all children and teachers alike. But these are hardly our only alternatives. It's one thing to set developmentally appropriate curricular goals and build on the child's current knowledge and background to help children achieve these goals. It's another to demand that all children will perform a certain skill at a certain level regardless of their experience or the appropriateness of instruction offered—simply because we demand it. Over and over, we create one version of *The Animal School* after another and then shake our heads over the miserable outcomes. And the typical response to this scenario? More demands and even higher expectations, and the cycle continues. It's neither necessary nor wise to abolish standards if we use them as guidelines or goals, and if we focus our energies on finding ways for more and more kids to be appropriately challenged, growing toward—and beyond—our standards. And it hardly makes sense to punish students when they are not on our schedule. As physician and anthropologist Melvin Konner notes, "Consistently losing does not promote self-esteem, no matter how impervious to reality you may be."[9]

When the Elevator Only Goes Down

"Same" is the only definition of "fair" that most people understand.

Barb Nielsen
director of curriculum and instruction

If we are to treat our "patients" professionally, we need to stop punishing nonlearners and instead provide opportunities for their success.

William A. Owings and Susan Magliaro[10]

Good managers and good teachers . . . do not waste much time doing postmortems on the failures of their people. Instead, they look for strengths that others have overlooked and ways to encourage the gifts in their group.

Alan Loy McGinnis[11]

What did I learn? I learned that my natural instincts, interests and needs were not important. I learned to conform. I learned to get by. I can sit still and look at the board with the best of them. Worst of all, I learned to distrust my inner self.

Mike Selby
author

Even the best needles are not sharp at both ends.

Chinese proverb[12]

Counselor Hamidah Bahashwan grew up in Singapore, attending a school where students and staff shared the same culture, religion and language. Yet despite these similarities, Hamidah claims there was a great deal of discrimination—in this case, based on ability. "Too many teachers favored the 'good students.' Rather than encouraging and helping, they criticized and labeled the weaker students as lazy and inattentive, or compared them to students who had better grades." From her first year in school, Bahashwan and her classmates were ranked. She showed me report cards that indicated her academic standing in her class, and in the school as well, laughing about the scoldings she received when she dropped down to 15 out of 317! (I can only imagine what the student in 317th place must have been feeling that day.)[13] In some parts of the world, a child's entire future—including opportunities to pursue certain higher levels of education or various careers—are predicated on the basis of that student's performance, often on one set of tests, sometimes taken as early as age nine.[14]

Various forms of academic discrimination exist in schools throughout the world. For example, one U.S. principal saw his school's tradition of tracking students as damaging and restrictive for large numbers of kids. "Only Level 1 students—that's 6 percent of the school's population—are on a track whose curriculum is built around the aptitude test. Lower kids can't pass." In fact, in most settings, lower-tracked kids get caught in a vicious circle, as their placement precludes their being taught what they need to succeed on the test that determines the track to which they'll be assigned. There is research to suggest that low- and even middle-ability classrooms offer "fewer opportunities for higher-order thinking and place more emphasis on rote memorization and worksheet and workbook learning."[15] Some studies indicate that "tracking exacerbates differences by depressing the achievement of students in low tracks and boosting achievement of students in high tracks," although research on the benefits of tracking—or detracking—are somewhat ambiguous.[16] (My sense is that the relative benefits of either tracking or detracking are based on the assumption that, generally speaking, all students will be taught the same content at the same time and in the same way. I suspect that studies run in classes that attempt to accommodate a variety of academic skill levels, learning styles and intelligences will point to greater possibilities for success for larger numbers of students in untracked or detracked schools.)

Even in schools that do not use tracking, the tendency to classify and label kids according to ability still prevails. This is particularly true for children who have learning problems. "Efforts to help people with learning difficulties have often relied on the pigeonhole strategy: labeling a problem and thinking that greater understanding will follow from greater generalization," observes Carla Hannaford. "But more often than not, labeling leads to oversimplification and insensitivity to the very real, very unique people behind the label."[17] It's hard to resist the temptation to analyze and categorize kids according to various personality or temperament traits, or their personal learning preferences or intelligences. And few would argue with this type of assessment when the information is used to provide appropriate instruction, activities and resources. But more often than not, labeling can be a rather superficial process, claims Howard Gardner. "People label the kid as being linguistic or bodily kinesthetic, but then they teach the way they did before."[18] Many schools invest a great deal of time and effort in assessing their students and never using the information constructively—creating "data for data's sake," as author Theodore Sizer has observed.[19] But there isn't much point in determining individuals' learning needs unless we intend to accommodate them.

Indeed, labels *are* limiting—to the person being labeled as well as the people who live and work with that person. Cherry, Godwin and Staples note that once a student receives a label, "from that point on . . . future behavior is viewed according to that label. Once we categorize an individual, we stop observing. We create a set of expectations that clouds our view of that person."[20] Further, as Donovan and Iovino point out, labels tend to be negative, emphasizing disabilities, disorder and dysfunction, identifying students "on the basis of what they *can't* do, rather than what they *can* do." Seeing a child in terms of a label makes it harder to appreciate the child's abilities, positive traits and individual "genius." Additionally, they note, "children who are already struggling with self-doubts have these problems compounded when their difficulties are institutionalized through formal labels."[21] While we may not have formal testing procedures that ascribe kids to one future over another, as kids in some countries face, our attitudes can be just as confining. Mizell asks that we "cast aside assumptions about which students are and are not 'college material,'" for example, "and devote the attention and resources necessary to prepare all students to pursue postsecondary education."[22]

Labels also limit effort and self-perceptions. "Be careful what you say to children," cautions Nathaniel Branden. "They may agree with you."[23] Author and motivational speaker Les Brown agrees. "Most people do not realized how detrimental negative labels can be," he remarks, reflecting on his experience of having been identified as educable mentally retarded when he was in fourth grade. "I began to believe that I couldn't do certain things and if I encountered any classroom difficulty, I would stop."[24] As Claude Beamish maintains, it may take years before the brain is ready to myelinate in a certain area, which explains why many of us develop skills in our twenties, thirties or forties that we were unable to achieve as children in school. This is why labels are so pointless and unnecessary.[25] Many adults who insist "I can't spell" or "I can't draw," for example, make these claims more on the basis of having been labeled a poor speller or artistically inept as children than on the basis of actual efforts and experience, either as children or more recently, as adults. In fact, such labels can discourage those who can't see any point in trying to get better and, in fact, may take great pains to avoid being put in a position of having to demonstrate their lack of skill—simply because somewhere down the line, somebody said, "Oh, you're no good at this."

While Hannaford sees the value in investigating children's strengths and weaknesses, and in the assessments which yield profiles that tell us how individuals are likely to respond in certain situations, the problem, she claims, is when we use this information to make judgments or create a two-dimensional picture of who this individual is. "Everyone has the capacity to learn, but we tend to learn in our own unique ways," says Hannaford. "The last thing we need in education is more misleading and limiting labels."[26] Lyndall Schick recommends using more descriptive—and neutral—feedback rather than judgments or labels. "Getting to a neutral description from a negative one will help you start to think and feel differently about the child. It can also help prevent harmful, self-fulfilling prophecies." (Even positive labels can be harmful, especially when they are applied simply to artificially inflate a child's sense of self.) So, for example, rather than saying "He's such a good little worker" or "She's such a wild child," Schick suggests using specific, substantive feedback, which is far more honest and useful than labeling: "He can really stick with a job a long time" or "She has great energy and really loves to move."[27]

In addition to labels, we can also limit kids with failure and retention. "It's a lot easier to give a kid an F," said one workshop participant, "than to teach what he needs to get an A." Once a kid steps into "failure" territory, it can be a pretty slippery slide. Early in my career, when I was placed as a long-term substitute teaching math in grades four through eight, I was warned that the majority of eighth-graders had experienced few successes in this subject area. Their grades from previous years were low; their attitudes were resistant and hostile, almost daring me to try to teach them anything. Our books were new and curricular expectations were high—moving into complex concepts like square roots and reciprocals, pretty much right out of the gate. And yet, when I did a little preassessment to see what kind of skills I was working with, it turned out that nearly half of the kids in the class could not add if they had to regroup. No wonder they'd been failing all along! No wonder they hated math!

Of course, I had all sorts of support for simply diving in to square roots and reciprocals regardless of what these students knew or didn't know—it was, after all, in the book, it would be on the district's standardized tests, plus I had the district's criteria behind me. But I suspect that this was the rationale that had been used with these kids to teach over their heads, year after year, making math increasingly inaccessible and putting them further and further behind. The standards say they should already have mastered addition but the pretest confirmed an entirely different reality. I could *expect* them to know addition till the cows came home. I could wave the standards in their faces and yell at them for being so many years behind in math. And I could punish them with another year's string of failing grades. Would they know how to add *then?* My choices came down to this: Do I teach these students how to add (and move, eventually, through the other basic concepts and operations they had neglected to learn over the years) or do I teach them that they can't do square roots and reciprocals either? These are questions teachers everywhere face daily: Do I teach what the kids actually need based on where they are academically or do I simply "cover content"? How can I challenge these individuals appropriately, giving them success while continuing to raise the bar for their performance? Is there a way to use standards and curricular goals as a guidepost to help direct us in this sometimes delicate balancing act? Is there some way to turn failing students into successes without lowering our precious expectations?

I have a couple of gripes about this whole idea of expectations. I know it's been popular (even when I was in college in the early 1970s) to encourage parents and teachers to keep them high. But there's an illusion here—that expectations alone elicit behavior. I had my first inkling of this fallacy on my first day of teaching, when I ran through my rather onerous list of high expectations to a roomful of jaded fifth-graders who simply shrugged them off. It seemed that I was the only person in the room remotely committed to my high expectations. I was going to have to work a little bit harder to generate a commitment from them than just telling them what the expectations were. Further, expectations don't *teach*. Expecting kids to be able to put materials away neatly, head their papers properly or play well with others does not teach them how to do these things. The same holds true for academic skills, even if the skills are far more basic than those we had planned to teach.

Now if you want to talk about *beliefs,* or the kind of expectations that translate to *teacher* behaviors that increase the likelihood of building kids' commitment and success, I'm all for it! Because there's a difference between the behaviors and attitudes inspired by an expectation (*I* expect *these kids to make progress and catch up*) and the behaviors and attitudes inspired by a belief (*I* believe *that these students are capable of making great progress in math and catching up, given the right instruction and building on their current strengths and knowledge).*[28] Combine curricular goals with our faith in our students' abilities to grow, throw in some instructional strategies that can accommodate a variety of learning preferences and intelligences in an emotionally safe environment, and watch what happens to achievement. Sure, it'll be easier to sit back and brag about our "high expectations," but for the most part, they are, on their own, wishful thinking at best.

Preventing failure can have significant long-term consequences, for eventually, day-to-day failure can trigger a downward spiral that leads to retention for many students. A 1990 report noted that by ninth grade, "approximately 50 percent of all U.S. school students have been retained." Rates for retaining African-American and Hispanic students are twice the rates for white students. Although educators have typically viewed retention "as a means of reducing skill variance in the classroom in an attempt to better meet student needs" and as a way to allow "more time for students to develop adequate academic skills," research over the last seventy years suggests that retention accomplishes neither of these goals. (Note that these goals speak more to a tradition of maintaining uniformity, that is, keeping everyone on the same page for the convenience of the teacher, than to actually meeting individual academic needs.) One report showed that kids who had been retained did no better than those who were promoted with their classmates.[29] Other studies show a high correlation between retention and "significantly" lower test scores, negative student attitudes and behavior, lower achievement and dropping out.[30]

For some students, being held back is less about ability and achievement than it is about their behavior. There are many learners who grasp a concept but have a hard time "putting it in writing," explaining in traditional or linear terms, or demonstrating their understanding on tests, and many of these kids invariably fall between the cracks. Failure and retention are also, too often, used to punish or disempower noncompliant students. I spoke with many highly capable students and adults who believe that their poor grades were more a result of a power struggle or disagreement with a teacher, or their difficulty sitting still through boring lessons, than their actual knowledge or ability. Les Brown tells how he and a few other "troublesome students" were caught clowning around in fifth grade one day when the teacher had left the room unattended. Enraged, the principal pointed to a half-dozen students, Brown among them, saying, "These students are stupid, dumb, retarded. . . . They need to be put back." Brown reflects, "I remember the look on her face, the anger and the disgust her expression held. She was set on teaching us a lesson, on punishing us and making us pay." As a result, he was moved from fifth grade to a fourth-grade special-education class. "I was kept in that category all through high school. It has taken me a long time to escape that label," he admits.[31]

It will probably come as no surprise that "once students encounter difficulty," as one study confirmed, "there is little recovery. Academic failure in one course in the first semester often translates into worse performance in the second semester." Over time the gap widens, and students "who do not progress in a regular fashion" are at greatest risk of dropping out. Even kids with "good attendance and those who entered high school with good academic skills" are at risk.[32] Researchers Owings and Magliaro found that a large majority of retentions take place early in a child's school career—with two-thirds of retentions taking place between kindergarten and third grade. They also cite studies that show "an increased, cumulative negative effect of retention on achievement for at-risk students."[33] No wonder that "when children list things they fear, retention comes third—after losing a parent and going blind," reports Susan Ohanian.[34]

A number of developmental specialists, including authors Jim Grant and Louise Bates Ames, argue in favor of evaluating children's behavior as well as emotional and social readiness—rather than focusing exclusively on academic achievement—before placing a child in kindergarten or first grade. Both note that approximately one-third of all children "may definitely be overplaced and struggling with the work of a grade which is really beyond [their] ability." As Ames notes, "If we must choose an arbitrary calendar age, many people are beginning to believe that the age of seven might be better than six for starting first grade. We prefer, however, that it be the child's behavior and not his age in years which should decide his readiness for starting school."[35] There is much to support a readiness approach, particularly with regard to a child's ability to handle the details and two-dimensional aspects involved in reading and writing—skills to which the brain is better suited at age eight than at age five or six.[36] To be sure, when we "force children to read and work with verbal materials before they are developmentally ready, we are like a builder who, eager to see results, fails to put in the foundation before beginning work on the house."[37] Unfortunately, the problem is nearly always one of placement. In the traditional paradigm in which every student in a particular grade or class is expected to learn the same things, effective, success-oriented accommodations for low-readiness learners are often not available.[38]

Still, as this country moves to abolish social promotion, the overwhelming amount of research confirming the negative effects of retention has led the National Association of Elementary School Principals to urge individual schools, districts and states to carefully examine "any policies that deprive the child of age-appropriate relationships" and "seek alternatives to retention."[39] Once again, the question is not about whether or not to promote, nearly as much as it is about whether we are willing to meet children where they are academically, and to improve the variety of the tasks we assign, the appropriateness of the goals we set, the types of instruction we offer, the range of intelligences we encourage and the quality of the relationships kids (and adults) encounter in school.

Diversity 101: Lots of Ways to Learn

You cannot put the same shoe on every foot.

Syrus Publilius[40]

Not all learning problems reside within the child.

David Elkind[41]

Each of us has a particular pattern—a natural intelligence—our own way of taking information in, storing it, generating and expressing it.

Dawna Markova[42]

Students do not simply vary from one to another; they vary along several different dimensions.

Noel White, Tina Blythe and Howard Gardner[43]

If they don't learn the way you teach, teach the way they learn.

Peggy Corcovelos
program specialist

One of the first classes I took in graduate school introduced me to differences in individual learning styles, preferences and behaviors. At the time, I was teaching in a departmentalized elementary school with about 150 kids, most of them in grades four and five. As a part of my course requirements, I subjected a few of my classes to a number of assessments and surveys to determine how they differed, how they learned best and where some of their strengths resided. It was an eye-opening experience for me. For one thing, it not only helped me appreciate my kids on an entirely new level, but it also helped me realize the degree to which schools can discriminate against certain types of learners—and the degree to which my own preferences and my rather narrow definition of attentive or on-task student behavior contributed to this discrimination.

I had no recourse but to change how I taught, and to expand the number and types of choices I made available to my students. But as frightening as some of these changes were for me to implement, and as leery as I was about the prospects for success, the outcomes surprised me. For example, once I discovered that the majority of students in one class—94 percent—strongly preferred working with music or noise in the background (one child worked well with or without noise), we started playing tapes during certain seatwork activities or quiet time. Productivity nearly doubled. (As a "low-auditory" learner who is easily distracted by noise, it had never occurred to me that background music could actually improve concentration for some learners.) I moved a group of low-achieving kids from an early-morning reading group to the afternoon when I found that their "best times" were later in the day, and they practically flew through the material. I let kids choose a space to do their work and several who couldn't stay on task for five minutes sitting at a desk or table would sprawl out on the floor, for example, and remain absorbed in their work for an hour. I let kids work with partners or in small groups and saw higher levels of cooperation, interactions and even peer tutoring taking place. I had come into this profession with a certain picture of what learning was supposed to look like. This picture was, for the majority of my students, restrictive and stifling.

In any group of people, we will find enormous variations in their profiles as learners, with differences not only in their knowledge and experience, but in their personalities, preferences, interests, temperaments, sensory-motor development, social skills, physical and affective sensitivities, emotional development, learning strengths and how they mentally represent, remember and recall information. All of these factors play a part in how each individual will learn and in which arenas each will best perform. In the past several decades, we've learned much about differences in how people learn and achieve. But the study of our differences goes back much farther than that, starting with the ancient astrologers whose primary categories included fire, earth, air and water, and the various characteristics and influences of each. About two and a half millennia ago, Hippocrates identified four different types of human personalities. Since then, there have been many attempts to assess, explain and classify just about anything related to how people learn and behave. As a result, over two hundred quadrant models, charts and matrices have been developed to illustrate the various factors that make individual learners unique.

Counselor-education professor Shirley A. Griggs challenges us "to assess the learning-style characteristics of each student and to provide teaching and counseling interventions that are compatible with those characteristics."[44] And I certainly agree that the more sensitive we are to possible variations in these characteristics, the more options we'll be able to offer in a classroom (or clinical) setting. Ideally, the more information we have, the better able we'll be to accommodate each individual on her own terms. But there is a reality here in terms of the sheer volume of potential information and, to some degree, there is simply too much to know about any one child, much less 160 of them, for us to individually process, interpret and translate into teaching behaviors that would accommodate every profile presented to us.

Do you really need to know, for example, that my Myers-Briggs test shows me to be an ENFP, or that I'm highly visual and tactile, or that I'm more alert in the late morning than I am earlier in the day, or that my dominance profile suggests that I need to talk or write to process new information, or that I enjoy initiating and designing my own projects, or that under stress my auditory channels shut down, or that I'm an Aries with Cancer rising in order to successfully teach me a particular skill? Certainly your willingness to consider any or all of these factors will increase the likelihood of your designing instructional strategies and resources that will, indeed, get and sustain my attention. But since this is much more than most of us get to know about any of our students (and probably much more than most people would ever want to really know about me), perhaps it's enough to just realize that different kids have different profiles, and the more we can appreciate and accommodate this diversity, the more variety we can bring into our classrooms, the more ways we can allow kids to explore a particular skill or subject, and the more ways we can allow them to document or demonstrate their understanding, the more learners we are, indeed, going to reach. Perhaps the specifics for each child are less important than the simple realization that variations exist, and that each deserves attention and respect. And if I don't need a file an inch thick on each student (or adult, for that matter) whom I encounter in my life, I do need a bit of flexibility and skill in dealing with different preferences.

Let's look at a few of these factors that contribute to differences in personality types and learning needs, styles and preferences. In each area lies the potential for discrimination, as schools tend to cater to—and thereby feel safe for—a certain type of learner. For regardless of the wealth of information available, the image of the ideal learner as someone sitting and listening or writing quietly persists, even though this profile applies to relatively few actual learners. I'm sharing the following information, not for one second to suggest that we devote our lives to profiling (or labeling) our students, but simply to help us broaden the range of approaches we're willing to use, so that more students can feel safe, welcome and successful in school.

Is This Channel Open?

Highlight my strengths and my weaknesses will disappear.

Maori saying

It is, in fact, nothing short of a miracle that the modern methods of instruction have not entirely strangled the holy curiosity out of inquiry.

Albert Einstein[45]

Orderliness in the school was a fetish. Quiet was golden. A "good" class had children leaning over their desks, appearing to work diligently. The fact that most were quietly bored or seething with resentment or simply turned off made no difference.

Theodore Sizer[46]

Too many of us have been exiled from our native truth because we have not been taught to listen or speak in its tongue.

Dawna Markova[47]

I'm doing a training in a small town in the Midwest for about fifty local teachers. In between the various activities, I recount stories and examples to illustrate a point I'm trying to make. As I speak, I notice a variety of attending behaviors around the class. Many of the workshop participants are sitting and listening, nodding or smiling at various times. A few are taking notes as they listen, some writing or doodling the entire time I'm talking. One woman with back problems is standing up in the back of the room, occasionally walking or stretching as I speak. Another has moved from her seat to the floor. A woman in front of me is working on a cross-stitch project. One attendee is playing with a plastic straw, looking at me as I move about the room. Another folds and shreds a piece of paper. A man off to the side is whittling what will, by the end of the day, transform from a block of wood into a statue of a bear. Many are chewing gum, munching on bagels or muffins, or drinking their coffee, water or soft drink. All, I am convinced—by the comments, questions and interactions with one another that I encounter or witness throughout the day—are taking in a great deal of what I am sharing. Yet many are displaying behaviors that in most schools would get a lot of kids in a lot of trouble.[48]

The variety of attending behaviors indicate, among other things, differences in the learning styles and perceptual preferences of the individuals in the group. According to authors James W. Keefe and Barbara G. Ferrell, "learning styles are intimately interwoven with the affective, temperamental and motivational structures of the total human personality."[49] Learning styles has its roots in the psychoanalytic community, beginning with Carl Jung, who noted major differences in the way people took in information, how they made decisions and how active or reflective they were while interacting with others.[50] Depending on who you talk to, learning styles can refer to a number of factors that differentiate one learner from another. "Some learning styles are neurologically rooted and reflect individual preferences for sensory avenues," notes child development specialist David Elkind. "Other learning styles mirror individual differences in personality and temperament" while others "are more socially or culturally determined."[51] Many researchers focus their work, or a part of their work, on perceptual and sensory preferences, and ways that people with different preferences take in and process information. Some have explored modalities and learning in relation to brain-wave frequencies and states of consciousness.[52] Others, like Rita and Kenneth Dunn, examine how factors such as light, temperature, structure, motivation, persistence, social preferences, time of day, and the need for mobility or intake impact learning.[53] Still others have developed models that integrate personality theory and different types of intelligences.

The value of these various assessments is in their ability to "provide the basis for a more personalized approach to student advisement and placement, instructional strategy and evaluation of learning."[54] However, one of the greatest benefits of this work has been an increase in awareness and legitimacy for different styles of learning. Author and learning-style expert Dawna Markova remarks, "One of the biggest miseducations we suffer from is the assumption that all human beings use the same process for thinking."[55] These assumptions not only get in the way of learning, they get in the way of communicating and relating. (As a high-visual, auditory-limited person married to a high-auditory, communications-limited person, I can attest to this one personally! My husband and I tend to experience the same things quite differently, are each bothered by things that often escape the other's attention and, for years, were convinced that the neurological wiring that accounted for these differences existed purely to annoy one another.) The persistence of some of these assumptions may have something to do with the fact that the majority—75 percent—of teachers share a similar profile: logic (left-brain) dominant, right-handed, right-eye dominant and auditory-limited. This is significant in that fully three-fourths of teachers "tend to talk about details, not listen and expect students to look at them," particularly when the teachers are under stress.[56] Unfortunately, not all students can rise to these demands, and if their teachers lack the flexibility to provide information in other ways (and also respect that there are other ways to pay attention), these students are likely to have problems in school. As brain-based learning advocate Gordon Dryden observes, "Nearly all the 'dropouts' of society have learning styles different from their school's main teaching style."

Author Robert Sternberg relates that he did poorly in college courses in psychology and foreign languages, two fields in which he later excelled. His difficulty in his classes was not because of a lack of ability, as his teachers concluded, but because of "a mismatch between the way a course was taught and the way I think and learn," he said. Sternberg notes that certain teaching styles benefit some students but put others with a different style of learning at a disadvantage, and he recommends efforts to avoid mistaking a mismatch in style with a lack of a student's ability.[57] Some researchers note that our learning styles are not fixed, but can, to some extent, be shaped by our social environment and develop as we learn and grow.[58] Further, when different parts of our brains are communicating with one another, we have better access to a wider range of sensory input.[59] Nonetheless, we all have certain default systems, "lead functions," which develop *in utero* as a part of our survival mechanism. This development results in one hand, one eye, one ear, one leg and one side of our brain being stronger, or more dominant, than the other. While most of us can "grow beyond the constraints of [our] basal dominance profile," this profile will influence our behavior throughout our lives, particularly when we are learning something new or when we are under stress.[60] "Even when we are in balance, when both sides are 'on' and available for use, one side will always be dominant," claims educator and Brain Gym consultant Aili Pogust.

Hannaford notes thirty-two different possible combinations or dominance profiles. Some are better suited to a traditional educational environment than others. As schools are currently configured, the "ideal" student is left-brain dominant and has full sensory access (which is facilitated "when the dominant eye, ear, hand and foot are on the opposite side of the body from the dominant brain hemisphere"). These are the kids that schools tend to favor, "students who process linearly, take in information auditorily, look at the teacher when they are talking and can repeat the pieces of information back in a logical, linear fashion." In Hannaford's test population, only 15 percent of the students fell into this category, with the largest numbers of these students in gifted and talented classes. When the dominant eye, ear, hand or foot are on the same side as the dominant brain hemisphere, the corresponding channel and related abilities (visual, auditory, communications or movement) will be restricted under stress.[61] For example, the fact that my dominant brain hemisphere and ear are on the same side—both left—means that when I am nervous, rushed, anxious or distracted, I tend to shut down auditorily. You can give me very clear directions, and I will have no idea what you've said. You can call on me, and I might not hear you, even though I may be looking right at you. I can still communicate, move and take in information visually; however, I have significant difficulty processing information that comes through my auditory channels.

Hannaford notes that the most disadvantaged group of learners in traditional settings "are those who are 'full sensory limited,'" especially when they are gestalt, or right-brain dominant. (That is, right-brain dominant plus right-eye, right-ear, right-hand and right-leg dominant. Interestingly, this was Einstein's profile and perhaps a good part of the reason he had so many difficulties in school.) Five percent of gifted and talented kids tested "full sensory limited," although this profile accounted for 44 percent of the kids in special-education classes. These are the kids who tend to need quiet time alone, time to process through internal images and feelings, something few classrooms encourage or allow. They may have difficulty explaining themselves with words and get frustrated and act out when called on to respond verbally. They are typically highly kinesthetic learners who need to move in order to learn. And in a setting that demands immediate answers and high verbal skills from kids who can sit still, these are the children most likely to be labeled as having a learning disability, particularly Attention Deficit Hyperactivity Disorder (ADHD). Hannaford's work with "alienated" intermediate students revealed that their profiles "were simply not being accommodated by the current educational curriculum," and that, in general, a "discouraging incongruity" exists between how we teach and how a majority of our students learn.[62]

Modality preferences—usually identified as auditory, visual and tactile-kinesthetic senses—refer to the primary pathways by which information gets from our bodies and the environment to our brains. We usually receive information on all channels, although most people have one channel on which the information comes in more clearly. When we talk about modality preferences, we're usually referring to the channel a person relies on as his or her primary means of learning and expression.[63] People with different modality preferences or representational systems will experience similar things in different ways, and tend to use different language to describe these experiences. A person whose preferred modality is visual will, for example, come out of a movie talking about the colors or scenery or lighting, while the auditory person will be more likely to recall dialogue and the kinesthetic learner will be more focused on the action scenes. Neurolinguistic psychologists Byron Lewis and Frank Pucelik note that each representational system has its own language, and being able to communicate in someone's own language is important for building rapport and trust—and thereby safety—in the relationship.[64] This might include statements like, "I see what you mean," when talking to a visual, "I hear you" to an auditory, and "I can't get a handle on that" to a kinesthetic or tactile person.

Looking at the various sensory channels, we can see that our preferences and profiles affect how we learn and behave in an educational setting. Approximately half of all learners are visually limited, that is, their dominant eye is on the same side of the body as the dominant brain hemisphere. These kids can overload easily in a visually "busy" environment and when attempting to learn something new or challenging, they may either look away from the teacher or shut their eyes to concentrate and take in information through their other senses. Maps or charts with a lot of extraneous information can be confusing. (More than 70 percent of the special-education students in one study were identified as visually limited, compared to about a quarter of kids in the gifted and talented group.) High-visuals on the other hand, receive information by watching, looking, reading or being shown. They process information internally with insight and visualizations. They express by writing, drawing, designing, doodling or creating graphics. They need eye contact and they need to see the person who's speaking. They can do well with maps, charts, lists and diagrams. Specific eye dominance is a factor in learning, as well, specifically when it comes to reading and writing.[65]

Auditory learners receive information by listening, hearing and being told. They prefer having new information presented to them verbally. Internally, they process with self-talk, inner music or an inner voice. They express by speaking, singing, storytelling, selling, discussing, philosophizing or creating music. Over half of all learners are auditory-limited, which puts them at a significant disadvantage when new information is presented verbally, as it so often is. Low-auditory learners may tune out the speaker after a while, or may close their eyes and turn their head to the dominant ear to screen out distracting visual input, aid concentration or translate auditory information into an internal visual or spatial image. (High-auditory learners may also need to look away or shut their eyes if visual input is distracting, and may have difficulty talking or thinking when looking directly at someone.) Once again, to a high-visual, auditory-limited teacher, this behavior may look like inattention. Interestingly, in Hannaford's study, large numbers of both gifted and special ed students profiled as auditory limited. She explains this phenomenon by noting that because the vast majority of kids identified as gifted and talented are logic dominant, they are also verbal. Even though they may not take in what is being said, "they talk—and so are believed to be more intelligent. The opposite is true for the special education students, mainly gestalt dominant (right-brain), who are not verbal."[66]

Verbal ability relates to hand dominance. Learners with dominant left brains and right hands typically have strong verbal skills. Verbally able students can communicate with words even under stress, and like to talk about what they're learning. Under stress they may be kinesthetically limited. Stanley Greenspan notes that "some very verbal children may be overreactive to noise and certain types of touch and visual input. This makes paying attention to a task in a busy schoolroom very difficult." The opposite profile—right-brain-dominant left-handers—are usually stronger kinesthetically, but under stress, verbally limited. Right-brain-dominant right-handers are communications-limited as well, and left-brain-dominant left-handers can have a hard time expressing themselves both verbally and kinesthetically. In classrooms that rely mostly on books, lectures and worksheets, "students who are less proficient with verbal processes are required to learn in a manner that is unnecessarily difficult for them and are thus unable to function to their full potential," reflects Linda Verlee Williams. Despite our tradition of valuing verbal ability and equating it with intelligence, brain scientist Michael Gazzaniga assures that "extensive information process in the brain is going on independent of verbal processes."[67]

Kinesthetic learners would rather touch than look. They receive input through touch (or being touched), smell, taste or feelings and process internally by way of sensations. They may express with output such as handcrafting, building, driving, gardening, touching, clowning, dancing, moving, nursing (or other forms of healing) or participating in sports. Some researchers estimate that as many as 85 percent of all learners have strong kinesthetic preferences. Yet, "the typical school curriculum offers very few if any kinesthetic learning techniques," observes Hannaford. "All gestalt-dominant learners welcome movement to anchor learning," she adds, noting that movement (and talking) are normally restricted in classroom settings. In her studies, Hannaford found that 78 percent of all left-brain students (logic-dominant, high linear and verbal skills) were assigned to gifted and talented classes while an equal percentage of right-brain kids (gestalt-dominant, low linear and verbal skills) were placed in special ed.[68]

The goal, most experts agree, is "whole-brain" thinking and processing—being able to grasp both global overviews of the gestalt hemisphere and the details of the logic side, incorporating the right brain's gifts of creativity, movement, intuition, subjective reasoning and abstract thinking, with the left brain's talents for organization, language, linear functioning and objective reasoning. It's about integrating and stimulating the brain in such a way that we can see not only patterns, color and three-dimensional images, but also lines, details, symmetry and two-dimensional symbols. It's about providing experiences that encourage us to hear rhythm, tone, emotions and patterns in addition to words, context, sequence and syntax.[69] Gazzaniga cites early split-brain experiments that confirmed the existence of two separate mental systems, "each with its own capacity to learn, remember, feel emotion and behave." He argued that each hemisphere is not only a "separate and distinct" mental entity, but that each possesses "different specialized skills" as well as "distinct cognitive styles."[70] For optimal learning, we need both hemispheres working together.

The importance of a safe emotional classroom climate becomes clear, first when we recognize that, under stress, our nondominant senses are significantly compromised (as are the skills related to our nondominant hand and leg). We take in less information and have greater difficulty expressing ourselves. Further, our capacity to expand beyond our basal, survival profiles, and our ability to become "more whole-brained and multisensory in our behavior" depend upon the availability of "relaxed, familiar, non-stressful learning situations" in which we can develop new ways of taking in and processing information. Whole-brain learning, with access to all sensory information and effective movement and communication, requires strategies that go beyond the traditional talk-and-chalk approach: a greater tolerance for movement and student interaction (and demonstration of mastery or understanding), a greater variety of ways to absorb and process new information, and an emotional environment in which kids can learn in their own unique ways.

Personality and Temperament

If I'm not who I thought I was, and I can't be who I was told to be, then who am I?

Carolyn Kalil[71]

Students will change only if we honor who they are now and help them discover how they might become more of who they are now by making some changes.

Vicki Phillips[72]

The biggest problem we have with reality is that it differs from person to person and can change for each of us as we move to use different areas of our brain to react to . . . situations in our environment.

Claude Beamish[73]

A woman in one of my workshops approached me during the break. She proceeded to describe how many of her students did not value learning, were unwilling to do the work and didn't seem interested in taking advantage of any of the opportunities the school offered for them to grow. She was clearly saddened and more than a little frustrated by this incomprehensible absence in others of the values that drove her personal work ethic. I've also heard teachers talk about kids who "aren't motivated by anything" when what they're really talking about are kids who "aren't motivated by anything we're doing in our classroom." I know, I've done it myself. As with modality preferences and the skills that come with various hemispheric dominance profiles, it's easy to get locked into thinking that everyone is wired the same way we are, imagining that because we think something is important or fun, everyone else will. Unfortunately, when we project our own unique combination of priorities and values, modality preferences, learning styles, temperament and intelligences onto the rest of the world, we tend to view differences in priorities and in how others listen, learn or respond as flaws in their intelligence or character. Beamish notes that "it is perfectly normal for us to have differing needs, beliefs, behaviors, personalities and realities" from others in our lives. From a perspective of variations in myelination patterns in the brain, he suggests that at best, only 21 percent of the general population will share similar patterns—at the lowest end, less than 1 percent.[74] Overlay these percentages with other variables like experience and personal sensitivities and our uniqueness becomes even more evident. Expecting others to behave or believe just as we do is not only unrealistic, it can also cause stress and discord in our relationships. In the classroom, these expectations and assumptions will surely have their effect on the emotional climate, how safe and accepted kids feel and how well they will learn.

And as with certain modality and sensory profiles, kids with certain temperament and personality traits tend to do better in school than others. Jerome Kagan theorized that a child's temperament "reflects a specific innate emotional circuitry in the brain, a blueprint for his present and future expression, as well as his behavior."[75] Karr-Morse and Wiley identify temperament as "a subset of personality," referring to "children's basic orientation to emotions and arousal." They note that "these orientations are woven into the genetic endowment, underlie personality and shape how we respond to learning experiences."[76] Researchers Stella Chess and Alexander Thomas looked at various dimensions of temperament, identifying nine separate traits to indicate the different ways children deal with the world. They show each trait as a continuum that covers a range of ways a particular trait can present itself, with extremes at each end. While no traits are good or bad, the extremes can present certain challenges, particularly when kids place especially high or low in a number of temperament traits—more so when the adult and child have temperaments that are very similar or very different. Using this perspective can help adults learn ways to deal with a variety of temperament profiles, and the behaviors that go with various clusters of temperament traits, presumably to establish a "good fit."[77]

With regard to these temperament traits, most teachers would prefer working with students who place high on the scales for adaptability, persistence and regularity, and low on the scales for distractibility, intensity and sensory awareness (sensitivity to sound, light, smell or touch, for example). Schools tend to favor children whose activity levels are low to moderate (although some classes, like physical education can more easily accommodate children with higher energy levels). Of course there are many children who do not fit into these categories. Greenspan has found that the most frequent complaints from parents regard behaviors that cluster into roughly five categories: highly sensitive, self-absorbed, defiant, inattentive, and active or aggressive.[78] Not surprisingly, these are temperaments that tend to be difficult for educators to deal with, as well. But as with other factors that influence a child's learning and behavior, our awareness, sensitivity, empathy and flexibility can help us provide experiences that will enhance the children's strengths and offset their liabilities. For as Greenspan also notes, temperament is not fixed, and research suggests that certain sensitivities and tolerances can be moderated or strengthened through interaction, training and experience.[79] The object is making it possible for kids with different traits to succeed in the classroom. Problems are far more likely when teachers are inflexible and unaccepting or when we try to force kids to fit profiles that are completely unnatural for them.

For another perspective on human temperament and personality, we can look to the well-known Myers-Briggs Type Indicator (MBTI). In the

1920s, Katherine Briggs and Isabel Briggs-Myers, inspired by Jung's work on personality, developed this instrument with sixteen different categories based on four different scales. Over the years, David Keirsey refined the work of Myers and Briggs, distilling their sixteen personality types into four major temperament patterns.[80] For a number of years, this information has been offered in teacher-education classes and inservice programs to build understanding of different types (and why conflicts and misunderstandings can occur between people coming from these different realities), as well as different ways to work with each group successfully. A brief overview of the four groups will indicate, once again, how some kids can find safety, acceptance and success in schools and for others, it's a continual struggle. For each, I'll use Keirsey's temperament names and the letter code that came from the Myers-Briggs inventory. Keep in mind that each group describes a general temperament. Because of the other MBTI categories, there are variations that allow for four subgroups within each of the following temperaments.

The Guardian (SJ)

People in this group are planners and organizers. They value correctness, promptness, loyalty, stability, work before pleasure and the ability to follow rules and procedures. They are responsible and productive, concrete in their thinking and comfortable following the chain of command. They account for 38 percent of the general population, about equal numbers of males and females. In high schools, 43 percent of teachers and 45 percent of students are in this category; these numbers are even higher among administrators. People in this category differ in small ways—whether more extroverted or introverted, and whether they make decisions emotionally or analytically. They are upset when others question authority or don't follow rules, act disrespectfully, come late or unprepared, or don't take things seriously. Disorganization, inefficiency and unreliability are problematic for them.

The Artisan (SP)

People in this group are freedom-oriented. They need spontaneity, "active doing," flexibility and unstructured settings. They are playful and need work to be fun. Like their SJ counterparts above, they differ along the Introvert-Extrovert and Thinking-Feeling scales. They account for 38 percent of the population, also equal in males and females; however, only 7 percent of them end up teaching high school (usually in hands-on elective courses). This group also accounts for 40 percent of high-school students who, like SPs everywhere, resent limitations on their freedom or their random, concrete approach to learning. They can do high-quality work and are capable of tremendous concentration when it comes to things they like. They are troubled or stressed by boredom, predictability, rigidity, inflexibility, having to follow a plan, people without a sense of humor and rules in general. Understandably, the structure of a school—not to mention all those SJ teachers and administrators!—puts large numbers of SP students at high risk for power struggles and dropping out.

The Idealist (NF)

This group includes people who are empathetic, generally feelers and caregivers, who can see potential and encourage growth in others. They differ along the Introvert-Extrovert scale, and also as to whether they are process-oriented (more flexible, curious, nonconforming) or finish-oriented (more structured, organized, formal). They value acceptance, harmony, positive feelings, recognition, authenticity and integrity, and are abstract in their thinking. They are good at creative problem solving when it comes to relationships and associations, and are characterized by aesthetic experiences and reflective awareness. They are stressed by insensitivity and narrow-minded, judgmental behavior, and get upset when yelled at or treated impersonally. You can drive them crazy with details, procedures, regulations and red tape. This is a smaller group, about 12 percent of the general population, the majority of them women. NFs account for 35 percent of high-school teachers, but only about 9 percent of students.

The Rational (NT)

This group, sometimes referred to as the Thinker, is the most analytical and has the greatest need to know and understand how and why things are the way they are. People in this category value knowledge and competence, fairness and understanding, strategies and progress. They relate on an intellectual level, preferring logic and thinking to feeling. They enjoy a good debate and can usually explain things well. They differ in the same ways as the NFs above. They are most bothered by incompetence (especially by people in authority), meetings that have no purpose, arbitrary rules, emotional outbursts or anything that seems illogical. They are stressed if you question their knowledge, make fun of their ability or argue illogically. This, too, is a small group, accounting for 12 percent of the general population, the majority of them men. In high schools, they represent 15 percent of teachers and 6 percent of students.[81]

The important thing to remember here is that people in each group share certain similarities in their reality and their approach to the world, and that the people in one group operate from a different reality than people in the other groups. Schools that cater to one reality are ignoring enormous numbers of students (and teachers, too). Our ability to not only recognize that these differences exist, but also to appreciate them and, more importantly perhaps, to provide outlets for their expression, can greatly improve an individual's potential for emotional safety, belonging and success in school.

How Are You Smart?

For the first two years at University, I did all my exams orally because I found out I couldn't write. But, boy, I could sit down and give somebody a three-hour in-depth explanation. I knew my stuff really well and I passed with flying colors.

Joseph Lancaster
educator, physician

Each person exhibits a unique intellectual profile with preferred methods of approaching and solving problems. Thus, a standardized approach to education faces the serious problem of inevitably neglecting many students.

Noel White, Tina Blythe and Howard Gardner[82]

Morally, we must be cautious so that we do not mislead any child about the nature of his or her mind, nor misguide any teacher or parent responsible for setting favorable conditions for that youngster.

Anthony Gregorc[83]

When a theory about how people learn turns into a standardized program, it is a contradiction in both philosophy and purpose.

Pat Burke Guild and Sandy Chock-Eng[84]

When you hear the word "intelligent" in an educational setting, it's a pretty safe bet that we're talking about the kind of "smart" measured by standard IQ tests. Developed about a century ago, these tests look at aptitude through the rather limited lens of linguistic, logical-mathematical and, occasionally, spatial assessments. The focus is on linear, cognitive skills and the ability to manipulate certain symbolic fields, such as numbers, words and shapes. But this kind of testing—and certainly, this kind of thinking—ignores many other ways of being "smart," as well as virtues such as creativity, compassion or ethicality.[85] Further, intelligence tests tell us very little about a person's potential for further growth and achievement.[86] "Just as we look different from one another and have different kinds of personalities, we also have different kinds of minds," notes author Kathy Checkley. But here again, we see a strong bias in schools, which cater to "one profile of intelligence, the language-logic profile." For kids with this profile, life can be swell, at least academically. But this bias puts enormous numbers of learners at risk for difficulty and failure.[87]

A number of researchers have suggested various ways to look at intelligence and learning that go beyond the logical-verbal skills. Silver, Strong and Perini attempt to integrate the idea of multiple intelligences and learning styles, describing four styles of learning similar to Keirsey's categories.[88] Bernice McCarthy suggests that there are four types of learners—innovative, analytic, common-sense and dynamic—each with his or her preferences for perceiving and processing information.[89] David Kolb also identified four types of learners, as well. The quadrants in his model are created by one continuum for perception (with concrete experience on one end and abstract conceptualization on the other) and one for processing (with abstract experimentation on one end and reflective observation on the other).[90] Anthony Gregorc modified Kolb's work to create the Mind Styles Model, with four cognitive styles based on "the characteristic focus and flow of their thoughts: a concrete or abstract focus and a sequential or random flow."[91] Yale professor Robert Sternberg proposes that schools need to encourage analytical intelligence, creative intelligence and practical intelligence.[92] In a separate article, Sternberg uses various government-related terms to describe different dimensions of learning and thinking, or an individual's styles of "mental self-government."[93] David Perkins proposes three forms of intelligence: neural, experimental and reflective.[94] Educator Reynold Bean notes that verbal, creative, analytical, expressive, physical, artistic, perceptive and problem-solving skills are all forms of intelligence.[95] Meanwhile, Arnold Skromme, an engineer and inventor concerned with student discouragement and drop out, establishes individual intelligence profiles based on combinations of what he identifies as memory, creative, dexterity, empathy, judgment, motivation and personality IQs.[96] There is also a system designed to help teachers work with students whose intelligences and personalities align with the nine Enneagrams.[97] And DeBeaufort and Diaz list ten different types of specialized abilities under three umbrella headings of mental, emotional and behavioral intelligences.[98] Each of these models take the notion of intelligence far beyond the linguistic and logical dimensions emphasized in schools' instruction and evaluation. All advocate respect for different kinds of learners and recommend using a variety of approaches to accommodate and capitalize on the strength of each type.

In looking specifically at different types of intelligences (regardless of temperament, personality, learning styles or other factors), probably the most widely recognized categories are the ones proposed by Harvard education professor Howard Gardner; when people talk about theories of multiple intelligences, it is typically these classifications to which they refer. Gardner distinguishes between learning styles and multiple intelligences, insisting that the two are not interchangeable. Unlike learning styles, which emerged from psychoanalytical origins, multiple intelligence theory has its roots in cognitive science; it resulted from efforts "to understand how cultures and disciplines shape human potential." Where learning styles focuses on differences in the process of learning and different ways people think and solve problems, MI centers more on content and products. And while both learning styles and multiple intelligences share insights from the fields of biology, anthropology, psychology and medical case studies,[99] they operate from a different perspective and use a different language. Where learning styles, for example, might present a child as a visual learner, this same child would probably be described in MI terms as someone who "very easily represents things spatially, and can draw upon that strength if need be."[100] Gardner lists eight different types of intelligences. Briefly described, these include the following:

Linguistic. Skill with words; using language, expressing with words, either written or spoken, and understanding what is said or written. Related skills might include storytelling, memorizing, writing, discussing, debating, journaling, oration and reading.

Logical-Mathematical. Skill with numbers, puzzles, experiments; the intelligence of reasoning. Related skills include understanding principles and systems, problem solving, logic games and brainteasers, logical patterns, manipulating numbers and quantities.

Spatial. The ability to create or think in images, representing the spatial world internally (mentally); manipulating objects, understanding spatial relationships. Related skills include thinking visually, remembering visual details, enjoying movies or video games, building, drawing, sculpting, doing crafts activities, designing architecture or playing chess.

Bodily-Kinesthetic. The intelligence of physical skill; awareness of the body in space, capacity to use the whole body or parts of the body to solve a problem, make something or perform. Related skills include dance, athletics, role playing, getting "gut feelings" about things, acting, sports and physical games, building, movement, tactile or hands-on learning.

Musical. The intelligence of melody, tone and rhythm; hearing, recognizing, remembering or manipulating patterns of sound; a feel for rhythm. Related skills include singing, composing, playing an instrument. Can benefit from activities involving music, such as listening, singing along or playing.

Interpersonal. The ability to understand other people, sensitivity to others' needs. May manifest in strong social skills, the ability to cooperate and work with others, empathy for and enjoyment of others, and the presence of many friends. Related skills can involve leadership, volunteering, mentorship, teaching, counseling, listening, sales, mediation or politics.

Intrapersonal. The ability to understand the self; self-awareness, a good sense of personal strengths and weaknesses. May manifest in a desire to be alone, make choices, work independently and self-pace. Related skills include the ability to anticipate personal needs and possible reactions, pursue goals independently, reflect on and learn from experience.

Naturalistic. The ability to discriminate among things, identify patterns in the natural world, skill at classifying and organizing. Includes the tendency to be comfortable out of doors, touching and exploring, be attracted to things related to nature, as well as the ability to recognize and categorize things like plants, rocks, animals and other elements of nature; also includes the ability to recognize cultural artifacts (like cars or clothing).[101]

Just as we need different personality types, temperament strengths and modality preferences to make the world go 'round, we need different kinds of intelligences to function in life. Gardner notes that human beings are strong in each of the eight intelligences to varying degrees and that "no two people have the same blend of intelligences."[102] Even without taking all other factors into account, from purely a multiple intelligences perspective, it doesn't make much sense for schools to approach learning as though all children learn the same way.

The good news is that "intelligences are educable. Although determined to some extent by genetic predisposition, the development of intelligences is also a matter of culture and education."[103] Further, strength in one particular intelligence can manifest in a number of ways. For example, singers, composers, conductors and violinists can all be described as being strong in musical intelligence, although in each case their particular musical intelligence will be expressed differently (in part, because of individual strengths in other types of intelligence) and may not even overlap. So while insisting that everyone become accomplished at playing the violin may not be a realistic goal for each student, attempting to develop every child's musical intelligence is far more possible—if a variety of other options is available. As White, Blythe and Gardner observe, "each intelligence can be mobilized for a variety of tasks and goals" and "intelligences almost never operate in isolation." Even if students are not gifted in a particular domain, they can improve, "but they may need to begin by drawing on their stronger intelligences."[104]

From a practical standpoint, the idea of multiple intelligences does not suggest coming up with elaborate profiles for each individual student—certainly not simply for the sake of profiling. Nor does it dismiss the value of language-logic intelligences or suggest that every subject be taught seven or eight ways. As Checkley asserts, "The point is to realize that any topic of importance, from any discipline, can be taught in more than one way,"[105] and that by doing so, we will reach larger numbers of students. It may not be particularly realistic to expect that everyone involved in the life of a child develop high levels of understanding about developmental readiness, learning styles, perceptual preferences, temperament and multiple intelligences, and how these and other factors work together to create unique profiles for each learner. However, it is certainly possible to increase our awareness of and respect for the variety of differences that are possible, and improve our efforts to accommodate as many different types of learners as possible. Because schools do not have to be places of academic safety and success for some kids but not others. In fact, some simple changes in our picture of what constitutes learning, attention and achievement can make school a place where failure need not happen at all.

Part II

The Toolbox

Simple, quick-fix solutions are not benign; they make real solutions harder to implement later.

Kevin P. Dwyer[1]

Any system which cannot or will not adjust to and meet the needs of every individual becomes a destructive system.

David Aspy and Flora Roebuck[2]

After a week of teacher training overseas, I had two presentations scheduled in the Northeast before I'd get to come home. I had scheduled

a day in between my flight back to the States and the day of the presentation to give my body a chance to get on the local time and recharge a bit. I had a tight connection after clearing customs and although *I* arrived at my destination just fine, it would be another twenty-four hours before my luggage caught up with me. Normally, this wouldn't be a problem, as I can always pick up a few necessities at the hotel gift shop or in town nearby. I never imagined that this particular hotel would be in a remote industrial park with no gift shop or nearby facilities.

After a long day of travel, all I wanted was a long, hot shower, clean hair and about twelve hours of sleep. The "clean hair" part got to be a bit of a challenge. I had none of my normal supplies with me, but since, in my mind, there was no question as to whether or not I was going to wash up before I ventured out in public again, I worked with the tools I had. The hotel did supply a rather harsh shampoo but no cream rinse or conditioner, the absence of which would make combing out my wet hair a real challenge. Things got even more interesting when I realized that I didn't have my travel brush with me either. The closest I could get—I swear I'm not making this up—was a fork. In the end, I did achieve my goal. My hair was clean and reasonably presentable, and I felt human again. But it cost me. In addition to taking nearly twenty minutes to detangle my hair, the process was tedious and painful, and no matter how patient and careful I was, I lost a whole lot of hair.

My point is this: As educators, we sometimes use tools that are not the most appropriate ones for the job we wish to accomplish and, in fact, we can actually do harm—even though the apparent end results look the same. So, in this section, we'll take a look at the tools we commonly use to shape children's growth from five different perspectives, and the tools each requires. By means of introduction, I'd like to use an analogy that comes up often in the field of education—that of a starfish. I like this image for two reasons, besides the fact that I conveniently have five dimensions to explore. First, it recalls for me a story I heard years ago, when a staff development coordinator presented me with a starfish lapel pin at the end of my presentation. She retold a story I've heard dozens of times since, in various forms, of a man walking along a shoreline upon which thousands of starfish had washed up and lay dying on the beach. The man bent down and picked up a starfish and threw it back into the surf. He did this over and over, and after a while, another man came over to him. "You're wasting your time," he said. "Thousands of starfish are dying on this beach. What you're doing isn't going to make a difference." The other man looked at the starfish in his hand. He smiled as he threw it gently into the water. "I'll bet it'll make a difference to *this* one," he said. I find this story to be a great metaphor for the importance of doing what we can, when we can, for whomever we can. As educators, we encounter these opportunities daily, and these five chapters are intended to expand the picture of how we can rise to these occasions.

Second, William Purkey uses a starfish analogy to illustrate how consistently attending to various dimensions of a problem can lead to changes and solutions, much as pressure from the starfish's five tentacles on the shell of an oyster eventually yield to the starfish's dinner.[3] Use just one tentacle and the starfish goes hungry, just as focusing exclusively on one dimension of children's needs and development leaves us with imbalanced, superficial and short-sighted answers to complex, multidimensional problems. The following five chapters address what a comprehensive approach to educating children must, in fact, encompass. Because when we consider the idea of shaping how children grow—not just academically, but also socially, emotionally, physically and behaviorally—it will certainly serve us to examine the tools and strategies we tend to use to achieve these ends. Because no one would deliberately reach for a fork to comb wet hair when more appropriate—and less destructive—equipment and approaches are well within our reach.

14

Academic Safety: Learning and Success

So I'm failing English. I'm never gonna go to England.

Homer Simpson[1]

The great difficulty in education is to get experience out of ideas.

George Santayana

Knowledge which is acquired under compulsion obtains no hold on the mind.

Plato

No genius ever attributed his or her success to a worksheet.

Bernadette Donovan and Rose Marie Iovino[2]

"What do you learn in school, Hans Thomas?" Dad asked. "To sit still," I replied. "It's so difficult that we spend many years learning to do it."

Jostine Gaardner[3]

I'm observing an advanced-placement biology class in a high school in Iowa. The class is divided into two groups, each of which is charged with designing and maintaining a biosphere, kind of a sophisticated aquarium, keeping the various flora and fauna alive for as long as possible. The groups are planning what will and will not go into their spheres and the discussions are lively—much of it, frankly, over my head. They shoot questions at one another about whether certain life forms can get along with others, which plants and conditions they need to survive, how they can find answers to questions they have, and how the various tasks will be divided between them. The teacher hangs back, answering questions, reminding the kids to keep certain guidelines in mind, prompting new areas for consideration. I am mindful of the intensity of their engagement, of the various corners into which the students are mentally reaching for information they will need to get this project off the ground. There is no doubt that they are thinking at high levels—not just recalling, but analyzing, synthesizing and applying information they've learned beforehand.

In another setting, this one an inner-city primary classroom, groups of children are doing various Valentine's Day activities. But instead of the traditional card-making activities we normally associate with this holiday, one group is learning to use a stethoscope, graphing their heart rates before and after physical exercise. Another group is practicing fine motor skills, sewing and decorating tagboard Valentine card holders. A third group is using a balance scale to graph and weigh candy hearts. A fourth group is playing a board game that asks simple questions about the circulatory system as students proceed toward the finish line. Once again, the entire class is engaged and excited, learning and practicing a variety of skills, all centering around this holiday theme.[4]

Where most of us come from—ideologically, if not in actual practice—things like personal experience, inquiry, emotional engagement, an enriched environment, relevance, context and novelty are significant factors in how kids learn and behave in a classroom. We know that we need to design our classrooms and learning experiences to support the higher-level thinking that these factors can invoke, as knowledge at the recall level alone isn't going to cut it when kids venture out into a twenty-first century workplace. We know that new information needs a place to grow, breathe and make sense, that the authentic "Aha!" experience requires some risk on the part of the learner, and that a climate of trust and safety is essential for all of these things to happen.[5]

Academic safety is about our willingness to stimulate and encourage students, starting where they are, and providing the ingredients necessary for each to learn and grow. It requires an openness to a variety of viewpoints and a greater respect and tolerance for a diversity of student perspectives and opinions. In their definitions of emotional safety, many survey respondents included a reference to "the freedom to be who you are, expressing yourself as an individual . . . without fear of hurt, rejection, ridicule or belittlement," as Technology Outreach coordinator Wendy Marshall noted in her correspondence. But as basic as this "freedom" may seem, it is certainly not a given for many, if not most, students. "We were not supposed to think by ourselves and speak out our opinions, but only answer questions in the way the teacher explained," recalls Slovene educator Olga Sraj Kristan, speaking for many individuals I interviewed. "Otherwise we took the risk of being laughed at in front of the class."

Even when out-and-out ridicule is not the issue, not being able to have one's own thoughts and opinions can have a very real and negative impact on the climate in the classroom, and on the kinds of desirable learning behaviors students will exhibit. Educators Martin Brooks and Jacqueline Grennon Brooks tell of a seventh-grade teacher reviewing a poem who, although she responded in a respectful and encouraging manner, unintentionally shut down her students' willingness to volunteer their ideas. Two students suggested interpretations for the poem, but when the teacher "politely and calmly rejected their ideas when they failed to conform to her views," no other hands went up.[6] Many individuals remembered classes in which participation boiled down to a game of guessing how to get the teacher's conditional approval by offering up the "one right answer." Many also recalled a teacher's wrath at being questioned or challenged, even when students were simply trying to settle some incongruence between their experiences and the new information. Glasser stresses the importance of teaching children to "question without fear and to inquire into topics they don't understand."[7] But after a while, in an environment in which questioning and inquiry are met with negative or hostile teacher responses, it becomes sensibly self-protective to quit trying. Perhaps this is what communications professor Neil Postman had in mind when he observed, "Children enter school as question marks and leave school as periods."[8]

Jean Piaget recommends that a teacher be "a collaborator and not a master from a double point of view, moral and rational." He warns against trying to "transform the child's mind from outside," stating that kids are born with sufficient drive for exploration and cooperation "to ensure a normal intellectual development."[9] And Greenspan reminds us that higher-level thinking skills require the give-and-take necessary to appreciate a variety of experiential reference points.[10] This leaves little room for the "one-right-answer" approach when it comes to building skills that go beyond the factual recall level. Brooks and Brooks observe that "students bring their prior experiences with them to each school activity" and that it is crucial to connect our lessons to these experiences. "Initial relevance and interest are largely a function of the learner's experiences, not the teacher's planning," they say.[11] This is why, for example, it's easier for some children to learn a word like "dinosaur," which connects with internal images and emotions, than seemingly simpler, smaller words that are more abstract, like "the," "yes" or "can."[12]

Once students can attach some meaning or purpose to content, they are much more likely to "own" (and want) what we have to offer. I once spent a summer working with recent college graduates—most of whom had no experience or training as teachers—preparing them to teach in some of the nation's most challenging school districts. In our first meeting, I was to introduce issues related to discipline and classroom climate to help them get ready for the students and school cultures they were to encounter the following day. I was impressed by these bright, dedicated individuals who saw great value in education and in working with kids identified as disadvantaged. So I was rather taken aback when they sauntered into the classroom with such little interest in anything I had to say. These were kids who'd graduated at the top of their classes. They had a great deal to offer and were convinced that their enthusiasm, their commitment, their youth and their prior successes as students would be more than enough to guarantee their success as teachers. They had no questions, no doubts, no reason to listen to anything I might have to offer.

However, the next day, as the buses returned from some of the toughest schools in southern California, I noted a rather dramatic difference in their demeanor. They were quiet, dazed, some a bit in shock. I was actually sorry to see their confidence so rattled; they'd need that in the coming weeks. But there was a change in readiness, as well, even for those who had had a relatively good day, as they now saw a point to learning about things like how to connect with kids whose school (and life) experiences were worlds apart from their own. Their behavior and attitudes the previous day had been, at least in part, a reflection of my efforts to connect with something for which they had no frame of reference. I had been trying to present information that had no place to "land."

"Learning that is integrated through reflection and personal relevance is the learning that will last," says Jensen.[13] Racosky has had success in working with kids by starting with what the child wants, loves and dreams. As social theorist John Gardner observes, "Everyone has noted the astonishing sources of energy that seem to be available to those who enjoy what they are doing or find meaning in what they are doing."[14] Lack of relevance and meaning is often the source of boredom, low motivation and poor achievement in schools, and the passivity and other nonconstructive student behaviors that go with it.[15] "Meaningful content" is another of Kovalik's brain-compatible components,[16] and a part of what turns students from "tourists" who are just passing through into actively engaged citizens.[17]

For new information to lodge in memory, it has to connect to something that's already there. Starting with prior experience, learners take in new information and then create or recreate knowledge for themselves. As David Perkins remarks, "Messages from others are never logically sufficient to convey meaning. To some extent, the individual always has to construct or reconstruct what things mean."[18] From a brain perspective, in order to construct meaning, we need relevance to activate existing neural networks, emotion to release the neurochemicals that mark the learning experience as memorable, and some recognizable pattern to work into some familiar context.[19] Applying this information to actual teaching strategies puts educators in a very different role than simply delivering knowledge, and it creates a very different type of classroom than one in which students are passively taking in information in order to hopefully spit it back out at a later time.

Our most effective classrooms, then, are likely to be places of rich, multisensory input and stimulation that engage the students intellectually, emotionally and physically. In the early 1960s, researcher Mark Rosenzweig determined that rats in an enriched environment—one that offered a changing variety of toys, mobility and places to climb, play and explore—had heavier brains, with more dendritic branching, neural connections and support cells. He also noted that these rats demonstrated behavior that suggested improved intelligence compared to rats in more restrictive and less stimulating environments.[20] Similarly, studies by the University of Alabama's Craig Ramey found that young children who were immersed in an enriched learning environment with toys, playmates and good nutrition had higher IQs and lower rates of mental retardation and developmental difficulties than children in the control group.[21] Clearly, our brains thrive on rich, complex sensory input. Imagine the kinds of thinking and learning necessary, for example, for the "problem-based learning" that occurs in classes like the ones described by educational consultant Karoline Krynock and assistant principal Louise Robb. In these classrooms, "students receive a real or potentially real problem and devise a practical solution from the research that they do." The problems—like designing a mass transit system that would connect two cities separated by fifty-seven miles of Lake Michigan or designing a car to meet the growing needs of China—not only meet curricular objectives but also demand a variety of skills, including high-level thinking.[22] How different these classes are—in what kids learn and remember, and in how they *feel*—than classes that rely on memorization, linear-thinking processes and "drill and kill" worksheets.

"Teaching is a strategic act of engagement," writes educator James Bellanca, who notes the necessity of "the active engagement of students' minds" as a prerequisite to learning.[23] But how engaged are students likely to be when, in the average classroom, teachers do between 70 and

80 percent of the talking?[24] And although we know that textbooks rarely "activate curiosity, creativity, imagination or wonder," they account for 75 to 90 percent of all learning that goes on in schools, claim Donovan and Iovino. "Worksheets are even worse," they add. "Some children may go through an entire year of school filling out more than a thousand of these forms and bringing them home to parents who believe that worksheets represent meaningful learning experiences."[25] Similarly, the majority of questions in educational materials and activities leave much to be desired. Questions trigger the brain's thinking processes, but it doesn't take much thinking to answer the factual, recall kind of questions, which account for 80 to 90 percent of the questions kids encounter in their textbooks, classrooms and families.[26] To be sure, students can find a certain degree of safety and predictability in the structure of simplicity and routine. But once the brain's need for safety is satisfied, the cortex and midbrain start looking for pleasure, challenge and novelty to keep it engaged.

I remember a college professor talking about the need to keep things in the classroom environment fresh and, as an example, described how kids stop noticing things that have been up on the wall or on our bulletin boards for more than two or three days. Researcher Gordon Bower notes that we eventually adjust to the familiar, and that something new needs to be fairly different and distinctive to generate an emotional response, thereby gaining our attention.[27] Sometimes, for example, in a full-day workshop, I've seen presenters ask participants to move to a seat in another part of the room when energy or attention starts to lag. The changes in the participants' visual field and the novelty of the "view" from a different seat, as well as the movement itself, alters their level of alertness. I've also witnessed presenters who throw out packs of gum, shift to a brainstorming activity or a pair-and-share task, move to a part of the room they haven't spoken from yet, tell a joke, draw attention to a new overhead or handout page, or get people moving with a sensory integration exercise. The goal is to sustain attention, increase energy and alertness, introduce contradictions in experience or stimulate the brain into making new connections or seeing new perspectives. This is why novelty, surprise and variations in emotional and sensory intensity are so important to learning. Balancing these elements with routine and structure is a critical teaching skill—too much novelty leads to chaos and stress, while too much routine gives way to boredom and apathy.[28]

Pleasure and fun are also ingredients in a classroom that offers academic safety. I often ask workshop participants to imagine that they had a choice between attending two similar presentations. Assuming the rooms and seats to be equally comfortable and accessible, and the content and materials the same, which would they choose if they knew that one program was going to be more fun than the other? A bit of a no-brainer when it comes to our own learning needs, we sometimes forget that similar needs exist for kids. "As we learn more about the joy of learning, we might have less need to find out about its agonies," note Donovan and Iovino.[29] For there is much joy to be had in learning and most kids are born curious and hungry to learn. "Healthy children enjoy growing and moving forward, gaining new skills, capacities and powers," observes Abraham Maslow.[30] Even before that, Maria Montessori realized "if you create the right environment for learning, even very young children will explode into self-directed learning."[31]

New teachers tell me that they are *still* being admonished to "not smile before Christmas," even though we know that positive, playful exchanges contribute to learning and remembering. "He who laughs most, learns best," says comedian and former Monty Python member John Cleese. Author and teacher Ron Burgess agrees, urging teachers to practice "random acts of craziness," humor and general silliness to hold kids' attention, improve learning, reduce stress, increase recall and shorten the school day.[32] Positive elements in the learning environment also improve concentration and understanding, note Cherry, Godwin and Staples, who recommend that we keep learning "exciting, challenging, interesting, motivational and enjoyable."[33] And in terms of building a climate of connectedness and safety, it makes sense to incorporate humor and play—even into discussing serious topics—as a tool for engagement. As speaker Michael Pritchard says, "The shortest distance between two people is a good laugh."[34]

Power, Success and the Freedom to "Fail"

I think and think for months and years. Ninety-nine times, the conclusion is false. The hundredth time I am right.

Albert Einstein[35]

Confidence comes not from always being right but from not fearing to be wrong.

Peter T. McIntyre

You can get all As in school and still fail life.

Walter Percy[36]

I have found that failure is a far better teacher than success.
Bernard Baruch[37]

Learning should be an invitation, not an assignment.
Jerome Harste[38]

One day during my first year I saw an amazing shift take place when, instead of simply demanding that my students do an assignment, I gave them two different activities at the same time, telling them they could choose which one they wanted to do first. I remember them eyeing me suspiciously as a few tentatively made their selections. It struck me that the second they started doing one of the activities, they had not only made a choice, but they had made a commitment, as well—much more so than when they grudgingly got to work simply to avoid my nagging. I also remember how paralyzed some of my kids were at the prospect of making a choice, staring at the two assignments, unable or unwilling to make a choice. Even at this level, there was some question in their minds about how safe they would be, that there might be repercussions from making the *wrong* choice.

One of the most powerful ways to engage students is to give them input and choices about what they're learning. Glasser notes that planning and decision making are far more complex processes than following orders or answering factual questions—skills that are far more commonly emphasized in school. In fact, I've noticed that the longer kids stay in school, unless they're getting lots of choices at home or are in classrooms that encourage choice making, the more their confidence in making decisions is ultimately eroded. This is especially true for children well-versed in failure. "Failing children stall at making decisions to avoid the failure they believe will result no matter what course they take," Glasser observes. He also reminds that decision making is a critical ingredient in high-level thinking and socially responsible behavior.[39] Offering choices—as well as the time needed to reflect and decide—is a brain-compatible strategy that builds independence, confidence, commitment and decision-making muscle.[40] It's also one of the easiest ways to avert unnecessary power struggles by accommodating children's needs for control and autonomy without surrendering our authority as teachers.[41] "Giving the learners more control and allowing them to choose complex, interesting, life-like projects will focus their attention on their learning, instead of on their daydreams," claims Jensen.[42] But how are children to learn decision-making skills like evaluating options or anticipating outcomes when they get so little practice? One study showed that at best, 98 percent or more of assignments are teacher-selected, with no student input involved at all.[43]

"Choice is a huge motivating factor," claims Ron Newell, a consultant with a charter school in rural Minnesota. In this school, which serves 125 kids from grades seven through twelve, lead teacher Dee Thomas says, "We ask every student, 'What's your passion? If you could spend five weeks studying something in depth, and get credit for it, what would it be?'" Rather than having classes and bells, kids spend the year working on different projects of their own design. The kids document their time, apply what they learn to "real life" as well as the school's academic standards, use different types of resources and present their work to faculty, parents and interested community members.[44] Among the themes common to schools where students excel in academic achievement and enjoy learning is the idea of innovation. According to a PBS documentary about schools that kids love, one of the defining features of these schools was a respect for the teachers' creativity and judgment, which gave them the freedom to design activities based on the needs of their students. There is no cookie-cutter curriculum. Instead, the curriculum grows "from the lives of those who will live it."[45]

Unfortunately, it is far more common for the majority of lessons to be presented to the class as a whole-group lesson, with every child doing the same thing at the same time.[46] Whole-group activities may be entirely appropriate depending on the content, student readiness and potential for engagement and success for every child in the group. But too often, these lessons are presented with little regard for what children know, where their interests or strengths lie, or what they need to succeed with the material being presented. Australian educator Peter Westwood suggests that diagnostic teaching requires our understanding of what children can already do, what they can do with a little help, what the gaps are in their experiences and what levels of work would obviously be too advanced to introduce at this stage. Westwood's work focuses on children with learning disabilities, suggesting that *dyspedagogia,* or ineffective teaching, can be a contributing factor to many children's difficulties with learning.[47] (Diagnostic processes such as pretesting, observing, surveying or even gaining insight from preliminary discussions can be valuable with any group of learners in any grade or subject area.) Stanley Greenspan agrees with the importance of matching instruction to student readiness. "No human being . . . can master material presented in a form that its nervous system cannot handle," he writes. "Children given tasks beyond their capacities lose confidence, enthusiasm and very shortly, interest in succeeding in school."[48]

So, too, are children defeated when the value of the efforts and progress they *do* make are dismissed or ignored. As an example, Aspy and Roebuck describe the devastating experience of working with a "slow" child who eventually made one and a half years' progress in one year. Nonetheless, when an administrator invoked the school policy demanding retention for any child who scored below grade level two years in a row, the child was held back, despite her enormous gains and the teacher's protests. Not surprisingly, the following year, the girl became increasingly silent and withdrawn. She quit smiling and quit trying. "The system had won its point—but at the expense of the individual."[49] This story touched me, reminding me of a group of my students who suddenly "caught fire" and went through about a year's worth of material in a few months once their reading group was moved from the morning to the afternoon, a time when these particular learners were more alert and functional. Although they were still below grade level, they were doing excellent work—and large quantities of it! With my criteria based on quality and amount of work (for the grades I had to assign), I had no problem marking their report cards with As and Bs. Unfortunately, the principal had a different set of criteria and refused to release their report cards until she had changed all of their reading grades (to Cs and Ds) because the students were not reading at grade level. I didn't get much from those kids for the rest of the year—not only in reading, but the quality of their work and attitude declined in other subjects as well.

"Children are defeated by failure," says Glasser, particularly when their successes are reduced to failures because we have applied some arbitrary, external and relative measure against their individual growth.[50] As Charles Garfield notes, "suffocating organizations" can undo the inborn urge to grow, achieve and excel.[51] When children who try their best are still held back and torn down, many simply refuse to continue to try. Worse still, with no apparent point to even being in school, students often seek outlets in negative or destructive behavior. "Kids without any means to grow academically are frequently on the verge of aggression," says author and educator Erika Karres.[52] While Deborah Sunbeck advises us that defeated students can indeed be reclaimed, she recommends strategies like minimizing assessment, focusing on potentials and current strengths, doing nothing to embarrass them and being patient—*not* more failure![53]

Unfortunately, most school systems and curricula, as they are currently set up, are designed to ensure that at least some kids will fail, in some cases, continually throughout their school careers. Few curricular programs are based on actual student needs, and many are jammed so full of curricular expectations that trying to accommodate differences in achievement—much less learning styles or intelligences—comes at a cost. After speaking to a group of high-school math teachers on the necessity of starting where kids are and building on what they can do, I had the sense that most, if not all, agreed philosophically. But how does one start with where kids are when grade level or course standards say to students, "This is what we teach in this class, regardless of what you need or what you know. And by the way, this is the only class available at your grade level." One concerned teacher said that she was perfectly willing to teach kids what they needed to know to eventually get to the higher-level skills she was supposed to teach in the class (which a number of her kids couldn't do because they not only lacked the more basic skills they needed, but also came with an attitude that bespoke their conviction that they simply were no good at math). "Then what?" she asked. Those students could either repeat the class they had just taken—which meant having to fail despite the progress they had made—or moving into the only other "next class," which was even farther beyond what they could do than the one they'd have to repeat. If each teacher in that school was willing to "start where the kids are," this wouldn't be an issue. But so many teachers feel so much pressure to "get through the curriculum" that they simply forge ahead and hope for the best, or compensate as well as they can. For example, in one class I was visiting, the teacher spent the half hour between the time the kids left and the time our inservice started tutoring a couple of kids who needed a little more explanation on a particular type of problem. For other kids there's summer school or tutoring when they can afford it. And some schools offer "bridge" or intermediate classes for kids who aren't ready for the "regular" course requirements. But the mentality here is still based in an all-kids-on-the-same-page kind of thinking. Rigid and limited course designs that ignore student readiness offer no easy answers within the context of how most schools are currently set up. (Part of the problem results from our assessment and reporting techniques, which typically reflect a student's performance on a set of course standards or criteria rather than reporting specific skills, strengths or individual accomplishments.)

Is it any surprise that a National School Boards Association publication on school safety states their findings that "schools that offer opportunities for all students to experience academic success tend to have fewer discipline problems"?[54] Where are our students' investments in behaving cooperatively and nondisruptively—or even actively participating—when they believe that they are going to fail anyway? Please note that this is not about dumbing-down the curriculum or protecting kids from ever making a mistake. It is, however, about not punishing mistakes, slow progress or the need for additional instruction, or equating these experiences with failure. Nathaniel Branden notes that "effective teachers know that one can learn only by building on strengths, not by focusing on weaknesses."[55] And Rogers and Frieberg report that "students want teachers who help them succeed, not fail," describing successes at a "last-stop-before-prison" kind of school where, instead of yelling, punishing and suspending, teachers talked to kids, listened, gave students a chance to correct mistakes and get things right, and refused to let kids give up.[56] Encouragement, recognition and acceptance—critical ingredients in an academically safe classroom—can come from anywhere, often with dramatic results. Verónica de Andrés describes a first-grade boy whom she observed "daydreaming, avoiding work, remaining on the fringe of the group, hesitating in new situations and unwilling to express opinions." However, when one of his classmates commented on his talent as an artist, his entire attitude turned around.[57]

Fear of failure can cripple learning potential. "I felt safe when I was allowed to make mistakes," recalls Singapore business owner Faizah Alkaff. She echoed sentiments that ran as a common thread through many of the surveys and interviews I conducted, as many people recalled varying degrees of humiliation they felt when they made a mistake or didn't understand something. School secretary Judy Stilwell reflected on the day her classmates laughed at her when she read the word "nowhere" as though it were "now here," and how "just thinking back fills me with the same feeling." Debra Sugar remembers her frustration and embarrassment when the word "was" looked funny after she'd written it and was told to move her desk out to the hall for creating a disturbance after asking a friend for a reality check. Principal Sandy Murray defines emotional safety as "being able to say what I need to say without worrying about criticism" and "not being humiliated in front of others." And when I survey kids about the one thing they'd either keep or change in their schools, their answers almost always come down to their desire to be treated respectfully by their teachers and other adults in their lives.

In many settings, however, respect and acceptance are conditional, coming only when students are doing well and making what the adults consider to be the right choices. But anytime we attempt something new, we're bound to make mistakes and fail along the way. How safe we feel in any learning environment is largely a function of how others respond to our imperfect efforts. Ginny Luther found that her students "made the most progress when they were encouraged to push beyond their fears, focus on what they did right . . . and take responsibilities for their mistakes." She operates on the belief that "mistakes are only opportunities for learning." Mike Selby writes that schools in general neglect to teach people one of the great truths in life—that it's okay to fail. "Failure always precedes success. . . . If you are not failing, you are not trying," he says. Ken Fraser agrees, proposing a "no-lose" model of decision making, one in which we realize that any choice is simply an opportunity "to experience life in a new way," and that there are learning opportunities along any path we select.[58] Jensen reminds us that "wrong answers provide far more clues to learning than right answers," and that "there has to be room to 'fail' without stigma or embarrassment."[59] But even when teachers offer encouragement and are very tolerant of mistakes and errors, it may take kids a while to catch on—especially if they've had a history of being shamed or humiliated for past mistakes. "Tragically, for many children, the very adults who should provide security are instead a source of fear and mistrust," says Jillian N. Lederhouse. She recounts a story of a high-school senior who "had never had a hot lunch during four years of high school because he was absent the day freshmen learned how to gain access to the cafeteria line and he was too embarrassed to ask for help later."[60]

It's one thing to agree philosophically and encourage the kind of risk taking involved in new learning, and another to actually allow a child to miscalculate, fall flat or really mess up without attaching moral judgments, impatience, disappointment, criticism or punishment to the transgression. (This is the difference between failing at an attempt to master a skill and being a failure or, as one person remarked, the difference between *making* a mistake and *being* one.) Erica Frenkel relates how her music teacher had a sign on his wall which said, "Each student gets thirty-one mistakes, and after those are used up, they get thirty-one more." She recalls how that message gave her the confidence to take risks and try things in music—a subject in which she'd felt weak. This teacher's philosophy was simply a reflection of her school's attitude, which saw the mistakes children made as necessary to learning something as best they can.[61] This approach suggests the possibility that we could indeed have schools in which there would be no such thing as failure. "There is nothing radical about not labeling people as failures," writes William Glasser. In other areas of life, we concern ourselves with levels of success, "Almost everyone succeeds to some degree in any job. Only in schools are we so definitely labeled failure."[62] Failure-free schools are possible, but only if we're talking about success and encouragement for *every* child, regardless of where he or she comes into the loop, and the freedom to make mistakes—and, yes, "fail" along the way.

Author and educator Carol Ann Tomlinson has observed that teachers who differentiate instruction "strive to do whatever it takes to ensure that struggling and advanced learners, students with varied cultural heritages, and children with different background experiences all grow as much as they possibly can each day, each week and throughout the year."[63] The fact is, if I start with the objective that every child will know more, understand better or become more confident at a particular skill as a result of the time we spend together, I'm going to come from a very different place—instructionally, emotionally and in terms of the energy I bring to our interactions—than I would if my goal were simply to get through the lesson and assess kids according to how they compare in reaching whatever goal I've set for them all. It also means that I'm going to be much more oriented to a student's present-time academic and developmental readiness rather than teaching something simply because "it'll be on the test" or "they'll need this next year."

"Truly personalized learning requires reorganizing schools to start with the student, not the subject matter," claim authors Dennis Littky and Farrell Allen.[64] I often share examples of how teachers have successfully accommodated a wide range of student backgrounds and abilities in their classes, whether providing a variety of assignments around a particular skill or topic, allowing kids choices about topics or types of tasks, offering a variety of ways to demonstrate understanding or mastery, adjusting the amount of work assigned to different kids or assigning different children to tasks at different places in a sequence of skills. Nearly always, someone will say something like, "But it's not fair for some kids to have to do twenty math problems while others only have to do ten." (We seem to have some strange ideas about what is fair and equitable in schools, often confusing "fair" with "same." I rarely hear people complain that it's not fair that some children fail repeatedly because of our reluctance to offer them appropriate content and instruction.) In a truly fair classroom, we will, as Tomlinson suggests, "begin where students are, not the front of a curriculum guide," ensuring that all students "think and work harder than they meant to, achieve more than they thought they could, and come to believe that learning involves effort, risk and personal triumph." In this kind of environment, students can also learn that "success is likely to follow hard work."[65] Certainly, creating courses and curricular expectations that are responsive to students' actual needs—as opposed to some bureaucratic, political or corporate notion of where kids *should* be—would be a wonderful place to start. Brooks and Brooks advise, "Shifting our priorities from ensuring that all students learn the same concepts to ensuring that we carefully analyze students' understandings in order to customize our teaching approaches is an essential step in educational reform that will result in increased learning."[66] What could be more fair than that?

How 'm I Doing? Feedback and Assessment

Not everything that counts can be counted, and not everything that can be counted counts.

George Pickering[67]

Only the most gifted prodigies can develop their talents to any extent in the absence of external encouragement.

Noel White, Tina Blythe and Howard Gardner[68]

It was almost too much for me when I realized how I could totally destroy a player's self-confidence by uttering a single word, or even by giving the wrong facial expression at times. I remember praying and asking for help so that I would always keep the players and what was really important in their lives first and then worry about wins and losses second.

Michael T. Powers
high-school coach, author

Our job is not to document failure. Our job is to prevent *failure.*

Anonymous

Let's not look at things through the filter of short-answer tests. Let's look directly at the performance that we value, whether it's a linguistic, logical, aesthetic or social performance. . . .

Kathy Checkley[69]

We must show that questions are just as important as answers. Factual answers, the counterfeit currency of the educational system, are worthless unless they are integrated into ideas and thinking.

William Glasser[70]

In 1967, I enrolled in a high-school ceramics class with a first-year teacher who was enthusiastic, flamboyant and extremely unstructured, even by art-class standards. I was as excited about working with this very cool, creative, young woman as I was about learning to work with a new art medium. But in this teacher's efforts to not stifle her students' creativity, she failed to give anything that would have vaguely resembled directions, and most of us sat in class with no idea of what we were supposed to do, eventually picking up some clay and starting in on our ashtrays, bowls or sculptures, just to be doing *something*. Imagine our surprise when we presented our pieces for firing and the teacher tore them—and us—to shreds. I switched out of her class after three weeks.

There are few things more likely to compromise a student's sense of safety than a lack of clarity about what is required. Clear directions help. Sometimes simply waiting until we have our students' attention, and then not only giving directions verbally but also making sure we write them down for our more visual (and low-auditory) learners, will reduce the likelihood of failure and disruptive student behavior by a large measure. Besides, having a copy of the instructions, guidelines or requirements, for example, on the board, on a task card, on a criteria-based rubric or outline, can help us avoid the inevitable requests to repeat directions over and over. This is especially important if the directions are for a complex process or elaborate project. The more avenues we can provide for gaining or clarifying the information students need in order to be successful the more problems will be minimized for all concerned.[71] And yet, how many of us neglect this important step?

A similar threat to students' safety is the poor evaluation, low grade or negative feedback that seems to come out of the blue. For many kids—not to mention their parents—the first inkling that all is not well is a failing report card grade. (I've encountered parents who were shocked to find out, at the end of the year, that their child was being held back. "I've talked to the teacher many times and she never mentioned this as a possibility," one said. Another noted that the child's grades weren't great, but neither were they anything that would have suggested this outcome.) Many of the factors that most influence a child's final grades, promotion or graduation, things like an end-of-semester test or final project, provide feedback that is too infrequent and comes too late. Just as kids cannot succeed if they don't know what's going on, their progress and safety are likewise compromised when they're working in a vacuum with no idea whether they're on track or not.

Another safety-compromising tradition in education is the one that insists upon feedback being negative or critical. This tradition allows us to justify harsh judgments and even character attacks as being necessary to inspire learning, improvement or peak performance. But few people I spoke to suggested that being torn down contributed much to anything besides their eventual indifference or sense of inadequacy. Therapist and program director Emily Stafford recalled her explosive and intimidating high school band director who yelled and swore at her for making a wrong turn on the football field in practice one day. "I quit band after that year," she said. "I just decided that it really wasn't worth it to me." Others described teachers who were similarly critical, mean-spirited or downright abusive. One survey respondent spoke with her son and some of his friends about the emotional climate in their school. They admitted that some of the teachers yell and scream at the students, but that they've learned to tune it out. This mom implied that these particular boys may have been conditioned by their experience in athletic programs, in which, as many of the interviews suggest, humiliating outbursts from coaches often come with the territory. The boys assured her that "the student would not internalize it or even take it personally," but simply cope with the teacher's behavior and let it roll off his or her back. That is, however, not always the case, and even if a student can indeed endure a more Draconian approach with little negative impact to his or her dignity and confidence (and many, if not most, absolutely cannot), there are always better ways to get outstanding results. For example, Tony DiCicco, coach of the champion U.S. Women's Soccer team, learned that the women on the team "responded superbly to challenges, but terribly to chastisement." Although he had been used to coaching men who, he said, could better absorb tough criticism, in working with the women, he "tried to coach positive."[72] Likewise, Morgan Wootten, who was recently inducted into the Naismith Basketball Hall of Fame, is described as a coach who "doesn't scream at his players or humiliate them," but instead stresses dignity and discipline. (He, too, appreciates the potential lessons available in any failure. "You learn more from losing than from winning," he says.)[73] Education professor Richard Biffle remembered a teacher and football coach who "could coach exceptional talent out of his players . . . and was able to transmit his expectations without yelling, without screaming, without casting guilt. . . . He was a magical person."[74] Clearly, feedback—whether from coaches, teachers or parents—need not hurt to get results.

Jensen recommends that teachers give feedback to kids every thirty minutes or less. He also advises teachers to preestablish clear criteria for projects so that students can self-assess and give feedback to one another.[75] Krynock and Robb talk about the value of coaching students through the problem-solving process, and how teachers and other students can become "a community of analysts assessing one another's problem-solving skills."[76] As a special-education teacher, Thomas Armstrong videotaped his students to give them feedback about their behavior in class, much as some athletic coaches and their players review tapes to spot areas for improvement on the playing field. He found that doing so offered his students a way to become more aware of their behavior and take responsibility for making the necessary adjustments.[77] Rhoda Cummings and Gary Fisher encourage kids with learning difficulties to get involved in their own assessments, whether that means asking what the teacher is trying to find out, trying to have a say about when they would be tested, requesting a break if they get tired or stressed, finding out how long they'll have or inquiring afterwards about how they did.[78]

Students with different temperaments and personality styles can handle different types of feedback. Many are more responsive to feedback that focuses on goals (*How can we improve your performance?* or *This will be more efficient*), rather than on criticism (*That's a mistake).*[79] Feedback can range from reminders about guidelines and goals to questions about processes and intentions. It can help children understand the impact of their behavior on others and help them connect their choices to the outcomes of those choices. It can also include an acknowledgment of progress or effort, or comments that help kids maintain a sense of the bigger picture or context in which they are working. Regular feedback can also build trust and cooperation, particularly when its focus is positive. When I would send home brief, weekly progress reports (what my kids used to call "good notes") in some of my more challenging classes, simply reporting how my students had done that week had an enormously positive effect on student progress and behavior as well as home–school relationships. Even high-achieving kids need more frequent feedback than an occasional test score or report card every nine weeks.

Feedback can also provide a vehicle for sending kids back to the drawing board to enhance their understanding of a particular concept or fill in the gaps in their knowledge. Not long after I finished the initial draft of this book, I was invited to observe a number of high-school students giving oral reports in a world-religion class. One student was clearly struggling with his underprepared research on Hinduism. The criteria for this particular topic included a passing familiarity with the Hindu caste system—something with which this student was completely unfamiliar (although he *was* rather adamant about their "castle system," insisting that this cultural implication stemmed from the fact that "their buildings are way different from ours"). Now, certainly our traditions of negativity and scarcity thinking would justify our lowering this student's grade. But if our intention is to increase this kid's knowledge (rather than punish his lack of knowledge), we will simply send him back to the library or on-line resources so he can get the information he needs for a better understanding of the subject. Of course, time is a consideration and, quite frankly, some students—including a few I've encountered in graduate-level courses—are perfectly happy to accept a lower grade, rather than do the additional work, particularly if the topic doesn't hold a great deal of interest or relevance for them. But how often are students even offered the option of improving the quality of their work or of "getting it right"?

To have any real value, feedback needs to be honest. Few things are more insulting or transparently manipulative than praising poor products or performance, regardless of the intention. I've seen five-year-olds who quickly catch on when teachers use praise, as one young man described, "just to get you to do what she wants." If you want to acknowledge my efforts, my improvements or my persistence, fine! But don't try to tell me I'm good at something when I'm not or suggest that factually incorrect information is accurate just to build me up. Tell me what's working or what's right, ask me what I'm trying to accomplish and offer me pointers, information or resources to help me move forward.

Part of the problem lies in the limited ways in which we traditionally collect information about student progress and performance. "Most of what we can measure now behaviorally is neurologically immaterial to the optimal development of the brain," observes Goleman.[80] Linda Verlee Williams has concluded that "most tests are a major waste of teaching time" and have little impact on learning. Educators Claudia Geocaris and Maria Ross agree. "Although our instruction emphasized learning, our tests seemed to focus students' attention simply on a grade. The test had ceased to be a learning tool," they write. They set about to design a test that "would allow choice, address a diversity of learning styles and intelligences and demand that students think critically."[81] Research by Ruth Butler and Mordecai Nisan suggests that "the information routinely given in schools—that is, grades—may encourage an emphasis on quantitative aspects of learning, depress creativity, foster fear of failure and undermine interest. Generally, students were satisfied when they received "constructive, specific information" in written comments, and while those who received grades indicated that they would have preferred comments, they also indicated that they preferred normative feedback to no information at all.[82]

Some teachers question the necessity of paper-and-pencil tests in all instances or for all students. "If I can watch a child doing one math problem using the correct processes to get the correct answer, there is no reason for her to take a test with twenty of the same kind of problems on it," said one teacher. "I'd much rather use that time for instruction and building new skills." Other teachers defended their willingness to read test questions to the student or simply ask the students to explain a concept verbally. "My objective is to see if this child understands the historical significance of a particular event—not that he can *write* about his understanding," one high-school supervisor commented. "If the kids can write, or if the objective involves expressing a thought in writing, that's different. But writing may not be intrinsically necessary to demonstrating knowledge."

More and more, teachers are moving toward varied and open-ended assessments to determine student learning and progress. For example, rather than simply recording a bunch of letters or numbers in a grade book, many teachers now collect samples of students' work in portfolios. This strategy, which actually predates the tradition of using grades, can accommodate students at different levels, allowing them to demonstrate understanding in a variety of ways, and examine both product and process. Depending upon the purpose of the portfolio, the samples may be selected as evidence of students' best work, their process of learning or their progress over time. With a diverse set of materials, which may include writing samples, work samples, tests, drawings or videotapes, a portfolio certainly gives a better understanding of a learner's accomplishment than a simple letter grade or numerical score.[83]

Rubrics, another of these alternatives, describe varying levels of quality, usually for fairly complex or long-term projects. (While rubrics often translate to a final letter grade, they offer a meaningful description of what that grade signifies and how it was determined. If we must insist on continuing to represent learning with symbols, let's at least assign some meaning to the symbol that is relative to specific criteria related to the task and the student's performance.) Rubrics are designed "to give students informative feedback about their works in progress and to give detailed evaluations on their final products."[84] Other teachers defend oral defenses, journals or learning logs, physical projects, role-playing, debates or presentations for their ability to show what students are (or are not) learning, as well as their capacity to accommodate various abilities, assess individual growth, prevent cheating and make students think. One-on-one conversations with students can also offer teachers an avenue for immediate feedback and instruction, as well as a great way to connect with a child.[85] I see this move toward more descriptive assessments as a step toward the establishment of a system of education that truly respects individual students' knowledge, strengths and needs. But we're still far too attached to the tradition of filling the boxes in our grade books with nearly meaningless letters and number scores. And we still have a long way to go before we can truly break away from our insistence on grading kids against some arbitrary norm, rather than evaluating them relative to their own growth and development, which is, in the end, the only assessment that truly matters.

Winners All Around: Cooperation and Service

The competitiveness of school guarantees that some students will succeed and others will fail.

Eric Schaps and Daniel Solomon[86]

Most important, I believe, is getting rid of the bell-shaped curve! . . . If you wish to build motivation, have each student compete only with himself. Grade your students based upon their efforts and improvement, not based upon a comparison with other students.

Vicki Phillips[87]

If you treat people as if they are what they ought to be, you help them become what they are capable of being.

Goethe[88]

Everybody can be great because everybody can serve.

Martin Luther King Jr.[89]

After presenting a parent training in one of the nation's more upscale school districts, I was approached by an attendee who proudly told me, "My son is number fourteen." I had no idea what she was talking about. (I initially assumed it was his football jersey.) After a few seconds, however, she explained that he was ranked fourteenth in his class and had been accepted at one of the country's top colleges. In the following weeks, after working with other teachers from other similarly well-to-do and generally high-achieving districts, I learned that this practice of ranking students is alive and well. Clearly, teachers I spoke to were concerned about the kids on the low end of the list, but they were equally worried about kids whose parents push them to perform and achieve, and the degree to which some families seek prestige by their child's rank in class or admission to certain top colleges. (When I was talking to number fourteen's mother, I had the sense that his accomplishments were more about her needs than his.) The teachers spoke of students for whom competition for rank had become more about winning than learning. These are the students, I was told, whose parents fax their homework in when the kids leave it at home, whose parents pay the kids' fines, who bail them out of trouble and never let them experience the discomfort of what might otherwise be a great learning experience. The teachers also noted the number of parents who insisted that their children be placed in honors classes, more for the status than the necessity of advanced placement, parents who believe that their children's future hinged on their child's ability to beat out the other students in the school, to be the best at all costs. I will admit that the students I met appeared to be among some of the brightest, nicest, most grounded, confident and authoritative young people I've ever encountered. But I also heard widespread reports of irresponsibility, arrogance and entitlement, of drug and alcohol problems, and of three attempted suicides in one fifth-grade class alone.[90]

We can't talk about success and growth for all students—and the types of instruction and assessment that will make this possible—and continue to support the practice of defining a child relative to the behavior, achievement, accomplishments, appearance or status of others. Many educators are embracing the idea of ultimately eliminating the tradition of competition that allows only certain students to succeed. The use of ranking, relative grades and grade curves "places every student in an adversarial relationship to every other student," claims Nathaniel Branden. "If I cannot write a two-page essay without half a dozen grammatical errors, the fact that everyone else in the class made over a dozen errors does not make me an A student in English Composition."[91] Jensen agrees: "Please tell me what one student's evaluation and assessment has to do with another student's. Either you have a certain level of understanding and mastery in a subject or you don't."[92] As professor of education and administration Steve Tipps warns, "An emphasis on competition creates an emphasis on winning and losing." He notes that the idea of one winner and twenty losers in a classroom situation is not an effective message to give students—or their families—about learning. The bottom line is that we can't afford to have losers in education. "We want all children to be winners in learning," he adds. "Success is a great motivator, but real success comes from learning what you need to learn, not from beating other students."

William Purkey reminds us that "education is about inviting every single person who enters a school to realize his or her relatively boundless potential in all areas of worthwhile human endeavor."[93] The notion of competition, even as it is reflected in the popular call for schools to "exceed, excel and surpass," is incompatible with the notions of community, cooperation, success orientation, win-win power dynamics and brain-compatible learning.[94] I have known individuals who thrive on competition, but they tend to be people who win much of the time. Arguments in favor of competition tend to be based in win-lose, scarcity thinking, or the belief that competition has value in its ability to inspire kids to push the limits of their abilities or help them learn to handle the pressures of real-life challenges.[95] But there are plenty of brain-friendly, emotionally safe ways to build such skills without the potential cost of defeating students or labeling them as losers. We know we can motivate high achievement and build the necessary personal skills for dealing with stress and challenges without setting kids one against another. And as far as the other argument goes, the one about preparing kids for a cutthroat, competitive world? Even if we choose to accept this perception as reality, what better way to prepare kids than to continually challenge them to move forward in their own growth, experiencing themselves as strong, smart and successful along the way? No, this doesn't mean lowering the bar. It means setting the bar at just the right height to challenge children to reach farther than they have ever gone before, and that's going to look different from one child to another. If we really want to give kids a "competitive edge," then let's arm them, individually, with the academic, social and emotional skills they'll need to succeed.

"Schools that are serious about fulfilling every student's promise must develop structures and relationships that nurture the strengths and energies of each student," advise Littky and Allen.[96] A cooperative goal structure has a different feel, a completely different "energy" than a competitive environment and can allow for a different type of learning community and social environment to evolve from it. It provides a different level of emotional safety, particularly for kids who are reluctant to ask for help or help one another.[97] It's exactly the kind of philosophical foundation necessary to support our efforts to build social and personal skills like respect, compassion, empathy and consideration for others, as well as positive ways to resolve conflicts. (Schools that invest heavily in programs to build these kind of skills and then implement them against policies that contradict the goals of these programs end up giving kids mixed messages and undermining their objectives.) An emphasis on cooperation leaves the door open for students to work together in a number of positive ways.

Glasser suggests that we remember 10 percent of what we read, 20 percent of what we hear and 30 percent of what we see. At the other end of the scale are the things we experience personally, of which we remember 80 percent, and that which we teach someone else, of which we remember 95 percent.[98] Surely this is part of the reason we're seeing more and more support for peer and cross-age tutoring programs[99] and peer-mediation, peer-counseling or peer-facilitation programs, particularly with regard to drug abuse and violence prevention.[100] These programs can themselves enhance or create a climate of cooperation. There are other benefits, as well. In addition to the potential for building personal and interpersonal skills, programs that encourage kids to help other kids also have the capacity to improve learning and behavior. For example, the upper-elementary students from my classes who went to "work" in the kindergarten probably learned more from their experiences as helpers and tutors than from anything they found in a book. And when thirty-three members of a high-school baseball team volunteered to work with classes in a local elementary school, they had a great chance to strengthen their leadership skills and build connections within the district.[101]

"Peer and cross-age tutoring often improve the overall school atmosphere," claims Joan Gaustad. Teachers and parents report less competition, more supportive and accepting behavior and fewer derogatory remarks about classmates. And with some training, guidelines and adult feedback and interaction, these various peer-mentoring programs can be one of the best bets around for offering otherwise low-achieving kids a shot at success. Gaustad notes that "tutors who have struggled academically may be more patient and understanding than those who haven't."[102] My experience concurs. In the two years that kindergarten teacher Phyllis O'Brien graciously allowed my students to work in her class, some of the best helpers we saw were kids with a long history of academic and social difficulties (both of which, in many cases, improved dramatically as a result of the students' successes and their sense of being valued in this setting). For even the most challenging students, there is almost certainly someone on campus, either another child or an adult, whom they can help or support in some way, some place in which whatever strengths they have can be useful to others. Additionally, rethinking our organizational configurations frees us to create alternatives like multiage classrooms, which may be one of the most promising ways to allow for deeper connections and success-oriented approaches like differentiated instruction, flexible grouping, multiyear experiences and cooperative peer interactions.[103] (Block scheduling at the secondary level may also achieve many of these same goals.[104])

And as long as we're on the subject of cooperative goal structures, let's talk about another benefit of this orientation—service learning! Capitalizing on our basic need for purpose and success, these multidisciplinary, project-based learning experiences offer kids a chance to nurture their confidence, self-worth and sense of personal power, build leadership skills, enhance the connection between learning and doing, make meaningful connections in the community, expand their understanding of the world and others, enhance social consciousness, develop greater empathy and compassion for others, boost language and other skills, explore career possibilities and build up their resume to boot![105]

Service projects and volunteer opportunities also help kids counteract negative stereotypes as well. Unfortunately, some kids encounter mistrust and contempt simply because they are kids. Magazine editor Lee Kravitz acknowledges, "Across our nation, millions of young people are banding together to build stronger, more compassionate communities and a better world. Unfortunately, the majority of adults see young people [negatively]."[106] Nonetheless, millions of kids from all walks of life are engaged in service work, and opportunities for volunteers between the ages of ten and fourteen are on the rise.[107] The programs seem to have the greatest value for kids considered to be at risk. "Service learning is a transforming experience. Practitioners in the field witness these dramatic changes in students every day," remarks Sandra Krystal. "Young boys and girls who have been lost to the street are lured back to academics because of service learning," she adds.[108] Perhaps these kinds of programs will come to typify the work of the schools of the twenty-first century. For what better way to offer academic safety (and, yes, meet curricular objectives) than with projects that offer kids a sense of purpose, learning opportunities that connect to real and meaningful things in children's lives, and activities that build on their strengths and leave them with a sense of competence, success and the knowledge that they can make a difference—not just in their own lives, but in the world, as well.

15

Emotional Safety: Personal and Character Development

When you can't talk about the things that bother you, then you are likely to act them out. And the typical consequence of acting them out is that things get worse.

Robert Subby[1]

Lucky for me and others she has "rescued," [my teacher] Mary Sohns has an incredible talent for scoping out the kids that no one notices. She takes special care to reach out to the kid with the braces that make her talk funny, the one who walks with a limp, the one who is overweight or shy, or the one who is lost in the crowd. . . .

Rachel Harnish
student

The main point for me about emotional safety has to do with people being heard and valued. . . . In schools you cannot leave listening to chance.

Jenny Mosley[2]

Once again, I'm observing a teacher, this time in a busy kindergarten. What catches my eye is a large drawing of a little old lady, which is tacked to the bulletin board. Under the bulletin board is a step-stool on which a young man is standing, whispering to the picture. Puzzled, I asked the teacher, "Why do you have children talking to your bulletin boards?" She looked over at the little boy and laughed, "Oh, that's Mrs.

Murphy!" She went on to explain that if the students were having a problem and needed to talk, and she was busy with other students, they could go tell Mrs. Murphy instead. She said she kept an eye on students and typically followed up on anyone who seemed to be spending a lot of time with Mrs. Murphy, but frequently found that for most of her students, simply having "someone" in whom they could confide was enough. (Afterwards, when she questioned the children to see if they were okay, they would often inform her, "Oh, Mrs. Murphy took care of it.")

I have since met many other teachers who provide similar outlets for students who needed to talk. Some had stuffed animals (often a bunny with great big ears) or a quiet corner to which kids could retreat with their journals. One middle-school teacher, who had a simply drawn picture of an ear on the bottom half of a door in the back of the classroom, assured me that there were times when her seventh-graders actually lined up to "talk to the ear." This need for connection is particularly strong for kids in crisis. Many teachers had live animals—in one high-school classroom, this included a large lizard and a snake the students could hold during class—and found that these "friends" offered several benefits, much as studies with prisoners who had contact with animals not only found the animals calming, cheering and therapeutic, but also a vehicle for learning caring and compassion.[3] And of course, many teachers make a point of being available for students themselves whenever possible—or referring them to a safe person or place—when the students are troubled.

As I've noted in previous chapters, our schools' attention to children's affective needs has, in general, been rather limited. Perhaps this tradition explains the frequency with which survey respondents mentioned that having someone to listen or notice when they were having a hard time would have made it better. For many, just being able to have and express feelings would have been enough. Counselor Marla West defined emotional safety as "being able to share my feelings, both positive and negative, in an atmosphere of trust, with no repercussions." For many, the need for a personal connection and recognition was important. Roberta Braverman, an elementary-school teacher of gifted students, recounts the emphasis on the cognitive aspects of her development when she was a student: "I don't think many, if any, of my teachers knew who I was or responded to my essays or dreams with personal encouragement. They were more concerned with the structure of the language I used, the grammatical form."

Many reflected on having gone through tough times and feeling very much alone. Eric Katz recalled feeling isolated and unsafe in school. "The amount of emotional pain I was in could not have gone unnoticed by my teachers," he said. "But there was no response, no interaction." Katz believes that part of the problem was that he was not a disruption in school; even though his behaviors were indeed self-destructive, they weren't an obvious problem for anyone else. Others had similar priorities. Principal Sandy Murray included in her definition of emotional safety the need for "having someone notice when things just 'aren't right' with the way I am acting." One woman who moved in the middle of high school remembered starting in the new school, angry, afraid and severely depressed. "If anyone noticed, they never said a word," she recalled. "Not once did anyone ask how I was, or how I was handling the transition." She also said that there might have been someone who would have listened, but it never occurred to her to seek an outlet in school. "Counselors were there to make schedules and recommend a college. Nobody ever went to them for actual counseling." Although this happened in the mid-1960s, a number of younger respondents expressed similar sentiments. A respondent who attended high school in the early 1990s felt unsafe because she did not perceive the adults in her school as having her personal needs in mind: "They never seemed to take involvement in my life when I needed guidance." And when asked, "What would have made school feel better or more safe?" teen Sione Quaass wrote, "People listening."

Braverman speaks for dozens of people who complained about trying to squeeze time for "relating" and "connecting" into an already overburdened schedule. "Many educators feel so pressured and are often so busy with delivering content or curriculum, they almost have to have a planned time or class period assigned to show caring to individuals," she said. This is of particular concern to the numerous teachers who indicated that increasing numbers of kids across all socioeconomic lines seem to have no one to talk to much of the time. (Sure, peers count, and in many cases they're the only game in town. But this isn't much help for the "misfits" and "loners," kids who have difficulty connecting with others their age.) A study by Howard Haas and Alex Aitcheson confirmed these teachers' observations. These school administrators spent the summer of 1999 traveling more than ten thousand miles, talking to teens, ages thirteen to nineteen. Among their findings, Haas noted, "It was real clear to us that no one was talking to the kids." Despite adults' finger-pointing and pontificating, kids feel abandoned, either physically or emotionally, and complain that "adults aren't listening and paying enough attention to them."[4] An eleven-year-old student at a Youth Summit on Violence Prevention seemed a bit surprised in the teachers' interest in the opinions and solutions the students might have to offer. "Usually, adults don't want to hear what we have to say," she said.[5] But our interest *is* important, as William

Ayers advises: "Listen carefully to the voices of youth in crisis. Without that testimony, our work will be inaccurate."[6]

No one would argue the need for kids to be heard and valued, nor dismiss the importance of attending to their emotional development. The issue has been, to what degree do the schools shoulder this responsibility? For regardless of what families and communities *should* be providing for kids, if children aren't being supported in this aspect of their growth, for whatever reason, the availability of some caring person at school becomes that much more important. And many times, regardless of the emphasis on academics or the tradition of relegating feelings to nonschool arenas, this is exactly where some kids find the support and encouragement they need. A profile of a large Midwestern high school suggests that although the place sometimes seemed "like a police state," particularly after the spate of violent incidents in schools around the country, the atmosphere is not oppressive. "What keeps the place from feeling like North Korea," writes Nancy Gibbs, "is the genuinely benevolent interest the school's adults take in the lives of their students—on and off campus."[7] President Bill Clinton observed, "People who grew up in difficult circumstances and yet are successful have one thing in common. At a critical junction in their early adolescence, they had a positive relationship with a caring adult. Most often, that was a teacher."[8] And although many people leave school feeling unnoticed, dismissed, unsupported or worse, there are hundreds of stories of teachers who, perhaps instinctively, *were* there with an open heart, a willing ear and a strong shoulder. The significance and potential impact of simply being "seen" is inestimable, and many, many adults attribute their survival in school (or, in some cases, through certain periods of their life) to the fact that some caring and supportive teacher, counselor or coach was paying attention.[9] Making this kind of availability and support a more generic aspect of our role as educators is another important step in creating the kinds of caring communities we want schools to be.

I Been Down So Long . . .

Children who are depressed or angry can literally not learn.

Sandi Redenbach[10]

A pessimist sees the difficulty in every opportunity; an optimist sees the opportunity in every difficulty.

Winston Churchill

Almost every adult I ever asked for help or comfort used my pain to promote their own agendas. Either that or they didn't take me seriously or couldn't be bothered. If we're going to encourage kids to come to us when they're upset, we need to learn how to be there for them.

Juanita

You got to reach out to me even if that's the last thing I seem to want or need. You know a lifetime of worthlessness builds strong walls. But I'm told that love is stronger than strong walls.

Guy Doud[11]

Potential without the notion of optimism has very little meaning.

Martin E. P. Seligman[12]

Laura Gutman is a good example of why pessimism and depression in kids has significance for educators. A talented software and design instructor, as well as an accomplished artist and violinist, Laura has battled depression since adolescence. What saved her early on was having music—something in which she excelled—as an outlet for her talents. For many kids, school is *the* safe place in their lives, and, like Gutman, having one particular class or teacher can be a lifeline in an otherwise difficult or chaotic existence.

There are compelling reasons not only for providing opportunities for kids to connect with their passion—and with achievement and success, as well—but also for simply noticing how kids are doing and listening when they want to talk. The "astonishing growth of depression in the U.S. over the past thirty years" has inspired University of Pennsylvania professor of psychology Martin Seligman to refer to depression as "the common cold of mental illness," one to which children are especially vulnerable.[13] Depression in children looks different from adult depression, although the rates and intensity of depression are the same between school-age children and adults. It usually involves loss, such as a friend or a pet, separation or divorce, changes in school or the death of someone close to them. This term refers to a condition that goes beyond what we'd consider normal sadness, with symptoms that can include sleep problems, changes in energy levels, eating problems or loss of appetite, hyperactivity or increased distractability, changes in attending behavior, tearfulness, excessive worry, poor communications, change in grades, social isolation, increased aggression or irritability, despair or pessimistic outlook, weight loss (or gain) or the loss of pleasure in activities that were once enjoyed.[14] Clearly, depression can have an enormous impact on a child's success at school. But diagnosing depression in teens can be tricky, in part because their symptoms can manifest as irritability, acting out or other behavior problems—patterns many adults assume to be par for the course at that age. Further, kids may not realize that what they are experiencing is, indeed, depression and therefore are less likely to seek help.[15] Because many of the symptoms overlap, depression is often misdiagnosed as other conditions, particularly ADHD, conduct disorders or anxiety disorders (although depressed kids can indeed suffer multiple diagnoses).[16]

Depression can begin early in life, and while temperament and heredity can be factors, depression and general outlook are strongly influenced by external factors, suggesting that both depression and pessimism are primarily learned, not inherited.[17] (While depression and pessimism are not the same thing, pessimists are more vulnerable to depression and other health problems than people with more optimistic outlooks. Further, optimistic kids who get depressed tend to get better, while pessimists who get depressed are more likely to stay depressed.[18]) One of the most significant influences in a child's development in this area comes from having a depressed or pessimistic mother (or primary caregiver). Studies show a tendency for these children to copy their mothers' moods, focus on negative emotions and thoughts, have lower levels of motor activity and vocalization, make less eye contact, show little ability to engage in play, develop rigid emotional and cognitive survival patterns, and protest more frequently than children who grow up with a competent, nondepressed caregiver.[19] Both pessimism and depression can manifest as a result of repeated school failure, particularly when the child feels powerless to remedy the situation. Children's life crises also play an important part, particularly if the child feels unsupported, even more so if the crises don't let up.[20] Further, criticism that is likewise "permanent and pervasive" can trigger these feelings. For example, statements like *You never check your work* or *You're not very good in arithmetic* have a far more negative and long-lasting impact than more specific and temporary explanations like, *You didn't try hard enough* or *You weren't paying attention.*[21]

According to author Howard Chua-Eoan, when episodes of depression are not detected or treated in young teens, "depressive episodes can lead to severe anxiety or manic outbursts," both in adolescence and adulthood.[22] In one study of more than a quarter million young people, 69 percent indicated that they had hope, or a positive view of their personal future, among the internal assets contributing to their success.[23] In this statistic, however, is also the unfortunate implication that for nearly one-third of our youth, the view ahead is pretty bleak. I certainly saw this with the high-risk teens I've met. Different from the teen drama that suggests, "My life is ruined!" because of a curfew restriction or a zit, hopelessness is a far more pervasive sense of despair or indifference, the idea that opportunities for success or happiness are simply not forthcoming, no matter what. Several of these kids had also accepted the conviction with a chilling nonchalance that they wouldn't live to see their eighteenth birthday. Depression and pessimism are also related to substance abuse, eating disorders and suicide. (Various reports indicate rates of completed suicides by young people have doubled and tripled in recent years, depending on the ages of the children involved.[24]) This is particularly tragic, because childhood depression and the development of negative, pessimistic attitudes are preventable.

The potential for prevention matters for many reasons. For one thing, optimistic kids learn and behave differently than pessimistic children, typically outperforming their more negative counterparts in school, at work and at sports, for example. In studies with highly talented kids—some optimistic, some pessimistic—Seligman repeatedly found pessimists' performance to be below their potential while the optimists' performance exceeded it.[25] In general, young children are extremely optimistic, many of them seemingly immune to hopelessness. When they can retain their optimism, they tend to be more resilient, more resistant to upsets and less likely to give up in frustration than pessimistic kids. They see their successes as being global, long-term, meaningful and attributed to hard work. (Pessimists explain their successes as local, short-term and accidental.) By the same token, optimistic kids see their failures as short-term and related to specific causes or lack of personal effort. (Pessimists see failure as more global, long-term and significant. They are also more likely to blame their failures on others or some other permanent, unchangeable flaw, like being stupid, ugly or untalented.) Optimists may experience "some depressing effect" of bad events but are not defeated by failures or subject to "lifelong patterns of defeat." They are less likely to worry or imagine the worst when something bad happens and see setbacks as temporary and surmountable. In one study looking at success, it was found that teens' level of hope was a better indicator of college freshman grades than their SAT scores.[26] Perhaps most importantly, optimistic kids believe in their own capacity to change, or at least weather difficult situations.[27]

Fortunately, according to Seligman, "pessimists can learn the skills of optimism and permanently improve the quality of their lives." (The same skills can also be of value to optimists when they're having a hard time.)[28] The goal is not simply positive thinking or a denial of problems. It is about learning to interpret and explain events in such a way that even in the face of negative experiences, we can hold onto our sense of power to change things and make them better.[29] "Learned optimism works not through an unjustifiable positivity about the world but through the power of 'non-negative thinking,'" Seligman claims. He also cautions against relying on affirmations, as "merely repeating positive statements to yourself does not raise mood or achievement much, if at all." Instead, kids are more likely to change their customary reactions to negative events when we identify specific cause-and-effect relationships, dispute negative beliefs to show that they are factually incorrect, build resiliency and emotional adaptability and help kids to understand that what they think when something goes wrong actually changes the way they feel.[30] Additionally, I believe we're likely to see increases in optimistic behaviors in students as we become more conscious of the quality of the feedback we give kids, as we strive to model optimistic outlooks and work toward creating emotional environments in which kids can feel safe to see their mistakes and "failures" as steps along the path of learning, rather than flaws in their character or capability.

Bouncing Back: The Art of Resiliency

Resiliency is what happens when one regains functioning after adversity.

Norman Garmezy[31]

Resilience is not an exclusively interior quality. Its existence, growth and survival depend significantly on what and who fills the space around us and the nature of the balance that exists between ourselves and the outer world.

Frederic Flach[32]

Learning lessons in the school of life is the antidote to feeling victimized.

Al Siebert[33]

Fall seven times, stand up eight.

Japanese proverb[34]

Seligman's work has shown that people can learn to be more optimistic by setting and achieving goals for increasingly challenging tasks. The benefits of this approach include increased confidence, a stronger sense of personal control and competence, lowered anxiety, improved relationships and increased productivity. Being—or becoming—more optimistic is also considered a protective factor when it comes to kids' ability to cope and bounce back from adversity,[35] and many of the characteristics of resilient children are identical to those of optimistic kids. (Author Linda Winfield cites Garmezy's work, which also includes among the characteristics of resilient kids, positive interactions with peers and adults, low degrees of defensiveness and aggressiveness, and high levels of cooperation, participation and emotional stability.[36])

Resilience is about our response to stress. When you come right down to it, in predicting a person's capacity for resiliency, the math is pretty simple. It works out to a highly individualized balance between the risk factors in a child's life and the supports available, both externally and internally. Counselor and resiliency expert Tim Burns suggests that children are at risk when they face inner obstacles of unmet developmental needs and outer obstacles of increasing environmental stress.[37] Add to this equation the fact that during adolescence, the architecture of the brain changes, encouraging, among other things, greater risk-taking and exploration of the unknown as part of the evolutionary process toward independence and adulthood.[38] Unfortunately, surveys of young people for a number of risk factors (such as tobacco use, alcohol and substance abuse, antisocial behavior, sexual activity, vehicle safety, and depression and suicide) found that "students who exhibit at-risk behavior in one area often have a greater probability of being at risk in other areas, as well."[39]

However, not all kids succumb to high-risk behaviors, even when they are experiencing a great deal of stress or trauma in their lives, and resilience could well be a factor in their resistance. But resiliency does not evolve in a vacuum, and resilient children have the benefit of some combination of "assets" or protective factors behind them. As with so many other aspects of a child's life, for many kids, the influence of one important adult is crucial to their resiliency. An extensive study by Werner and Smith found that children who were at risk for school failure actually thrived when valued and supported by an important, caring adult.[40] Sociologist Troy Duster remarks on the American phenomenon by which we tend to view success and achievement with an image of a strong, rugged individual standing alone against all odds. "But if you look closer, what appears to be highly individualized achievement is often really about social support, a complex matrix, whether a family member, teacher or community, that assumes a kid is going to make it and taps them on the shoulder to say, 'Kid, you've got it.'"[41]

Other assets may include external factors such as support from family and others, extracurricular and community activities, positive peer influence and parental standards, monitoring, school involvement and support, and internal factors such as achievement motivation, empathy, sexual restraint, a concern with helping others, and skills in assertiveness, decision making, friendship making, planning and hope.[42] Flach further identifies external factors such as respectfulness, recognition, acceptance, tolerance of change, realistic limits, open communications, respect for privacy and a sense of community among the elements necessary to facilitate resilience.[43] Prevention specialist and resiliency researcher Bonnie Benard notes that resilient individuals are characterized by traits such as social competency, well-developed problem-solving skills, autonomy, and a sense of purpose and future.[44] And Siebert recognizes the importance of internal attributes such as curiosity, playfulness, adaptability and strong self-esteem, as well as the ability to learn from unpleasant experiences, value paradoxes within the self, trust and use intuitive hunches, form good friendships and loving relationships, practice empathy for difficult people and expect good outcomes.[45] The more of these "assets" or protective factors in children's lives, the better their shot at making choices that allow them to avoid, minimize or overcome the impact or allure of high-risk behaviors. Even better news is the positive correlation between the number of protective factors in a child's life and that child's ability to resist danger, maintain good health, help others, value diversity, succeed in school and delay gratification.[46]

Benson, Galbraith and Espeland's study included positive school climate and the availability of adult resources other than parents as two important assets, or protective factors, in a child's life.[47] "School administrators and teachers have the ability to change the structures, language and policies that affect individual belief systems," observes Winfield. She suggests that the process of fostering resilience requires that we take a long-term, developmental approach and change schools and communities so that they nurture protective processes necessary for kids to succeed. She also recommends focusing on children's strengths and assets rather than their deficits or the risk factors in their lives.[48] Benson, et al. agree. They prefer an asset-building approach over a problem-centered approach because the former sees kids as resources (not problems), benefits all kids (not just those in trouble), relies on individuals for solutions (not public funding), stresses cooperation and collaboration, sees the process as a long-term, lifetime commitment and sends a message of hope.[49] Finally, Winfield notes that we can foster resilience by altering risks children may be experiencing (or minimizing their exposure to those risks), reducing the negative chain reaction that typically follows exposure to risk, helping kids establish and maintain self-esteem and self-efficacy, and opening up opportunities for students to acquire skills and invest in prosocial activities.[50]

One more note on resiliency. In the spirit of oversimplified, all-or-nothing thinking, I've heard adults interpret resiliency studies as a justification for everything from withholding interventions and support to dismissing the need to change destructive policies. "Kids will bounce back anyway," they tell me. And to be sure, some will—by the grace of temperament, circumstance or dumb luck. But Burns cites research that provides "a sobering assessment about the limits of resilience when it comes to multiple risk children." The more risk factors present in a child's life, the worse the outcome is likely to be. "They cannot bounce back unless there are programs and people to supply the care and support that they are missing."[51]

The Myth of the Self-Esteem "Myth"

Self-esteem is not just about feeling good. Far more accurately, it is about having the belief that it is possible to deal successfully with any problem or crisis encountered and also the experience of feeling totally worthy of happiness, success and respect.

Murray White[52]

In any society, people with self-esteem are more productive and more able to contribute effectively to the development of the society. They know what they are good at and capable of performing and what are their weaknesses. They are sensitive to not only other people but also to the conditions around them. They are secure and confident about their position in the world. As such, they are more receptive to change and can adapt to new situations and conditions.

Siraj Zaibun[53]

Although one's self-evaluation is constantly in a state of flux to some degree throughout the life cycle, it is during childhood that initial self-assessments are most fluid and subject to the influence of others.

Gerry Dunne[54]

Positive and desirable qualities like optimism, resiliency and persistence typically go hand-in-hand with a solid sense of self-esteem. Unfortunately, there has been a tremendous amount of widespread misinformation and misunderstanding about this concept. Media coverage in the past several years has frequently represented self-esteem cynically, simplistically and inaccurately. For example, several years ago, the artwork on the cover of a national magazine used a sketch of a short, chubby guy seeing his reflection in a mirror as a tall hunk of a movie star, and labeled this delusion as self-esteem. When the producers of a major television show called prior to taping a segment on the topic, the efforts of several concerned educators to steer them to well-grounded programs that focused on personal accountability and social responsibility were ignored; instead, the program chose the low road, highlighting "feel-good" examples that would show self-esteem in the least flattering light.

Over the years, the term has been trivialized to the point of becoming cliché, popping up in commercials for everything from greeting cards to shampoo, equating personal mail and good hair with self-esteem. (A video game I've seen actually announces, *Your self-esteem must be fantastic!* after an occasional win.) It has appeared in a spate of programs offering frivolous, superficial and egocentric activities (which do a great disservice to programs and activities that address the significant and complex issues related to the development of genuine self-esteem). It has frightened some adults from correcting or confronting irresponsible or obnoxious children, and has justified others who feel compelled to shower praise on just about anything a child does, regardless of the quality, correctness or appropriateness of the work or behavior. It has been associated, when flattened into an almost meaningless notion of "feeling good about yourself," with young perpetrators of horrible violence who showed no remorse about the damage and pain they had caused. (In fact, attempts to prove the negative outcomes of having self-esteem have typically worked from this type of definition.) Perhaps understandably, these inaccuracies have inspired a certain degree of caution and cynicism among some parents and professionals who, unfortunately, won't touch this important concept with a ten-foot pole.

Part of the problem is the complexity and extensiveness of what authentic, strong self-esteem involves. Nathaniel Branden assures us that self-esteem is "much more than that innate sense of self-worth that presumably is our human birthright." Instead, he sees fully realized self-esteem reflected in our being "appropriate to life and to the requirements of life," including having the confidence to think, to cope with the basic challenges of life, to be successful and happy, to feel worthy and deserving, assert our needs and wants, achieve our values and enjoy the fruits of our efforts.[55] Terminology can further complicate matters. For example, Dunne distinguishes between self-image (the way we see ourselves) and self-concept (the way we think about ourselves), both components of the self-assessments that result in our overall sense of self-esteem.[56]

To better understand this concept, perhaps it might be easier to look at what self-esteem is *not*. For starters, authentic self-esteem is not narcissism, egotism, self-absorption, self-centeredness, self-indulgence, false confidence, arrogance, bragging, bravado, being delusional, being indifferent to the needs or rights of others, or feeling superior to others—concepts that have mistakenly been used to represent self-esteem. It's not about defining ourselves by our external trappings. (Wealth, success and beauty are hardly a guarantee for an even reasonable amount of self-esteem.) It is not about being protected from difficulties, challenges, mistakes or failure (although neither is it about deliberately knocking kids down to supposedly toughen them up). And, as Branden notes, self-esteem is reality-based, not "feelings generated out of wishes or affirmation or gold stars granted as a reward for showing up."[57]

Probably the best sales pitch for considering self-esteem as an important dimension of a child's emotional development lies not so much in its definition, but in its benefits. Psychologist Stanley Coopersmith, a pioneer in the field of self-esteem research, found that children with higher self-esteem were more outgoing, creative and inquisitive, more willing to make mistakes, more willing to develop their own opinions and express their views, and had better self-control than their peers with lower self-esteem.[58] The chart at the end of this section attempts to synthesize a number of definitions of self-esteem, translating them into the kinds of characteristics—beliefs and behaviors—that seem to manifest in people whose self-esteem is healthy or strong, contrasting them with characteristics of those whose self-esteem is low. (As you read through the list, consider which characteristics you would want in your classroom, in your living room and in your neighborhood.) When our definition includes ingredients like resiliency, social competence, sensitivity to others, respect, character strength, personal responsibility and the ability to take positive action to change one's behavior, attitudes, belief system or life in general, we can certainly see many good reasons for nurturing a child's self-esteem.

But once again, is this a job for the schools? Ken Fraser, who works with adults who have difficulty getting or keeping a job, noticed that his clients often had very negative experiences at school. He suspected that these experiences may have had something to do with his clients having difficulty acknowledging their personal competencies, despite the fact that they were typically quite talented. (This was particularly true for those who, as children, had been marginalized, or had suffered discrimination, abuse or poverty.)[59] But low self-esteem also affects high-achieving students as well, particularly those with strong perfectionistic tendencies. In fact, a 1984 study of university women found that "the higher the perfectionism score, the lower the self-concept score." It also suggested that these individuals tied much of their identity to their performance; even a little mistake could have an enormous and negative effect on their sense of worthiness.[60] Like it or not, schools play a part in this aspect of a child's development. Low self-esteem—which some studies have correlated with dropout, delinquency, crime, vandalism, violence, alcohol and drug abuse, teen pregnancy, depression, difficulty managing stress, vulnerability to peer pressure, cheating, occupational and social difficulties, and low academic achievement—often comes in the aftermath of repeated failure, humiliation, discrimination (ethnic, cultural and gender) and disempowerment in school.[61] Besides, as author and self-esteem expert Michele Borba notes, "Self-esteem is learned, therefore you can teach it."[62]

The potential impact of school experiences on a child's self-esteem (and all the behaviors and beliefs that go with it) obliges us to look at how our influence can be the most positive and effective. This doesn't mean creating a "self-esteem class" or trying to build these skills in isolation. Once again, creating emotionally safe schools will play an important role in building the kinds of beliefs and behaviors that reflect healthy self-esteem. For while no one can *give* us our self-esteem—it is, after all, a perception formed internally—our self-assessments can certainly be influenced by the feedback, judgments and reactions we get from others, particular throughout our school years.[63] Trust and respect are therefore paramount, notes Borba. She describes esteeming environments as ones in which kids are respected as individuals, perceive a sense of love and warmth, are provided with the security necessary to have ideas and opinions and try new things without fear of failure, have clear and consistent limits, a chance to succeed at their own levels and are accepted "with no strings attached."[64]

"If a teacher treats students with respect, avoids ridicule and other belittling remarks, deals with everyone fairly and justly, and projects a strong, benevolent conviction about every student's potential, then that teacher is supporting both self-esteem and the process of learning and mastering challenges," observes Branden. "Rationally, one does not focus on self-esteem per se; one focuses on the practices that support and nurture self-esteem, such as the practice of living consciously, of self-acceptance, of self-responsibility, of self-assertiveness, of purposefulness and of integrity."[65] Similarly, educator Lilian Katz notes, "Self-esteem is most likely to be fostered when children are esteemed and treated respectfully and receive the right kind of positive, meaningful feedback . . . rather than empty praise and flattery." She cites research that suggests "teachers are likely to engender positive feelings when they provide such a combination of acceptance, limits and expectations concerning behavior and effort." She also recommends avoiding "frivolous and cute," self-congratulatory activities, suggesting instead that we engage kids in projects that put them in the role of explorer or problem solver, and are worthy of their attention and understanding.[66]

Obviously, gold stars and flattery aren't going to have the impact that encouragement, acceptance, the potential for success and knowing someone has faith in your abilities will have. In fact, these kinds of superficial approaches invariably do more harm than good. For defeated or unmotivated kids, empty praise falls flat—and is likely to make us appear either manipulative, misinformed or downright stupid, even to young children. Frederic Flach advises against directly contradicting someone's insistence on having low self-esteem. "Such a strategy often intensifies his determination to prove . . . how worthless he really is."[67] Rather than arguing (*You are* too *worthwhile!*), we'll make much better gains by simply treating children with warmth and respect, providing for their security and safety needs, challenging them at a level at which they can achieve, allowing them to experience a sense of purpose and assuming that they are right on schedule. "Change takes place slowly," Borba reminds. "Don't expect dramatic results overnight. Remember, students have had many years to form their self-perceptions. Be patient."[68]

With healthy self-esteem, we get to be a "winner" whether we win or lose, and we have the strength, commitment and inner resources that allow us to keep on trying when nothing seems to be going right. Not unlike resiliency, self-esteem allows us to withstand the slings and arrows of life's little dramas and be able to heal and rebound. The goal of promoting self-esteem is not to have kids who walk around muttering, *I am special* or *I can do anything*. (In fact, that would make me more than a little nervous.) It's about creating an environment in which their value and uniqueness are never at issue, one in which they can formulate a realistic picture of their assets and limitations, so they can "dream dreams and aspire to ambitions that legitimately suit [their] talents and potentials."[69] For the true test of self-esteem comes not when I look in the mirror and imagine myself as a Hollywood goddess. It's when I look in the mirror and know, deep down in my soul, that I don't need to look, act, be or achieve like anybody besides the person staring back at me in order to have value, efficacy and purpose.

The Myth of the Self-Esteem Myth[70]

HIGH or Healthy Self-Esteem[71]	LOW or Weak Self-Esteem
Belief in my basic worth as a person regardless of others' opinions, or my achievements, for example.	Conditional belief in my basic worth, vulnerable to (or depending on) others' opinions or reactions, or my ability to achieve and succeed (or avoid failure). *Or* belief in my basic unworthiness, regardless of external factors, achievements, etc.
Belief in my own competence, capabilities, with an understanding and acceptance of the fact that I am better at certain things (and better at certain things at certain times) than I am at others.	Inflated sense of my abilities or my inabilities; all-or-nothing perception of my capabilities; shutting down or giving up in the presence of my inabilities, flaws or difficulties (being a victim).
Resistance to comparisons (and to defining myself in comparison to others); ability to maintain an internal and self-contained sense of my own value and capability.	Tendency to define self (and worth of self) in comparison to others, either better or more than, or less or worse than; difficulty appreciating or evaluating myself against internal standards.
Ability to enjoy and appreciate external appearance, status, possessions, acquisitions, without dependence on them in order to feel valuable, complete, worthwhile or attractive.	Reliance on external appearance, status, possessions and acquisitions to feel valuable, attractive, worthwhile or complete; a sense that I would be okay if only I had these external variables in my life.

The Myth of the Self-Esteem Myth

HIGH or Healthy Self-Esteem	LOW or Weak Self-Esteem
The ability to see myself realistically; the ability to acknowledge my current flaws, limitations and imperfections without being paralyzed or defeated by them; the ability to see myself realistically and still perceive myself as worthwhile.	The tendency to deny or ignore my current flaws, limitations and imperfections or to overcompensate for them by bragging, showing off, throwing my weight around or hurting others in some way.
The ability to enjoy and appreciate my relationships with others (a partner, my family, my friends and professional associates), without depending on them in order to feel valuable, complete, worthwhile or attractive.	Reliance on the existence and presence of these relationships in order to feel valuable, complete, worthwhile or attractive.
The willingness to take risks, make mistakes, and be wrong, without compromising my sense of self-worth.	Perfectionism, defensiveness, self-protection; resistance to promotions or additional responsibility; need for approval; need to be right.
The ability to say "no" and stick up for myself; the willingness to disagree and to maintain my integrity, even at the risk of disapproval, exclusion or abandonment; the willingness to be alone.	Difficulty saying "no," willingness to compromise my standards, limits and goals to receive approval and acceptance from others; the fear of being alone, *or* isolating to avoid rejection or disapproval.
The ability to recognize and value personal needs in relation to the needs of others (win-win); a willingness to give (service, compromise) without placing myself at risk (for harm, abuse, exhaustion, mental depletion, etc.).	Difficulty recognizing and valuing personal needs; self-sacrificing (lose-win); *or* indifference to the needs of others (win-lose).

The Myth of the Self-Esteem Myth

HIGH or Healthy Self-Esteem	LOW or Weak Self-Esteem
The ability to accept myself as I am, while continually attempting to grow and get better; belief that growth is possible.	Inability to accept myself as I am; pessimistic (Why bother?); perceiving myself as being unable to change.
The belief in my own power to change things I'm not comfortable with in my life or self; the ability to take positive action and make positive choices to improve things that I'm not happy with; high degree of persistence, even in the face of frustration, failure or discouragement.	Self-perception as a victim, helpless, disempowered; pessimistic (Why bother?); easily discouraged; high sensitivity to frustration, failure; tendency to give up or quickly adopt the idea that success is improbable.
The belief in my own deservingness; comfort with my achievements, accomplishments and acquisitions, as well as with compliments and gifts; the ability to receive; the ability to ask for what I want.	Difficulty receiving, especially compliments or gifts; tendency to be apologetic or feel guilty; lack of deservingness; *or* a sense of entitlement; difficulty asking for what I want (assumption I will be denied).
Willingness to associate and work with individuals of all races, creeds and lifestyles.	Inability to fully accept those perceived as different; threatened by those with different opinions; desire to be associated with those who will give me status.
Ability to set goals and make long-range plans, believing they can be achieved with effort and persistence.	Reluctance to set goals or take on challenges of difficult tasks.

Toward a Strong, Moral Character

The question of whether a school should engage in character education is an idle one. Schools cannot avoid influencing character. . . . A disorderly school affects character just as much as an orderly one; the only difference is the direction of the effect.

Amitai Etzioni[72]

If every child came to school with well-developed senses of responsibility, honesty, integrity and fairness, teaching would be easy. But since, both practically and developmentally, this is impossible, schools are left with no choice but to instill values right along with the other basics. They always have. They always will.

Terri Akin, Gerry Dunne, Susanna Palomares and Dianne Schilling[73]

When your world collapses around you, you can still choose your thoughts.

Viktor Frankl[74]

If we want our children to possess the traits of character we most admire, we need to teach them what those traits are.

William Bennett[75]

First Amendment neutrality doesn't mean being neutral on values.

Charles C. Haynes[76]

Values are caught, not taught.

John Connell[77]

The Joseph & Edna Josephson Institute of Ethics has been conducting nationwide teen character studies since 1992. The results point to what founder and director Michael Josephson calls "a hole in the moral ozone."[78] By many accounts, kids have become increasingly cavalier about lying and cheating, drinking and using drugs, coming to class drunk, damaging or stealing property, becoming sexually active, and hurting or disrespecting others—often at increasingly younger ages.[79] Obviously, these values, and the behaviors that accompany them, have their impact in a learning environment. "We may hope our children are good athletes, achieve in school, are artistically talented or good looking," says author and character-education expert Thomas Lickona, "but nothing is as important as their moral behavior. If our children are not honest, self-disciplined, kind, hard-working people, then they will not be happy or successful."[80]

Many would agree. Where the legitimacy of some self-esteem programs has been called into question, many of the same objectives have resurfaced in recent years in the guise of programs that promote character, resiliency, emotional intelligence and moral development. There is a great deal of overlap in the content, objectives and activities in the programs that have emerged under these particular headings, but all address issues related to various aspects of a child's personal and emotional development. "Today one speaks . . . of character training, perhaps spurred on by a more politically conservative perspective than the previous psychological models," notes John Steinberg. Where religious and politically conservative groups have balked at the idea of schools teaching values and morals, "there is renewed belief that the schools can also play an important role in ethic and character development."[81] But the question of whether schools should or should not assume a role in addressing these issues is largely academic. As Rita Mercier points out, "The truth is that values are taught, both directly and indirectly, on a daily basis." Whether through "the choices in the curriculum, in the ways that teachers interact with students, the types of discipline employed, books selected for reading, class discussions, the way the staff and students dress, the types of behaviors that are expected of students"[82] or any number of other factors, schools give kids messages about what is good, right, acceptable and appropriate all the time. "Like it or not . . . we are all role models. Our daily choices and actions will echo through generations," claims author and educator Anabel Jensen. "While we teach content, we teach our beliefs and values. Children see our attitudes, reactions, interactions with others, our approaches to problems. We teach children what we hate. . . . We teach children what we love. We are what we teach."[83] And, I believe, we teach what we are. How can our values and priorities not come across in everything we do? Authors Pam Schiller and Tamera Bryant agree. "Whether we realize it or not, we are always teaching values," they observe, "but we must put more conscious effort into that teaching."[84]

"When people talk about moral development, they are referring to their conduct and attitude toward other people in society," claims Ron Huxley.[85] Jean Piaget's studies with young children and Lawrence Kohlberg's work, which carried Piaget's findings into adolescence and adulthood, suggests that this development normally proceeds through a series of stages of increasingly flexible and sophisticated moral reasoning. Ultimately, we would hope that kids can distinguish right from wrong and learn to reason and make decisions based on "universal moral principles" or generic notions of "ethical fairness." However many children seem to have a hard time getting past the early, egocentric, safety-oriented concerns with not getting caught and punished or conforming for the approval of their peers. (I saw this often as a classroom teacher, in my work with high-risk teens and as a counselor with young patients being treated for sexually transmitted diseases.) Moral development can be influenced by a variety of factors, including the child's cognitive development, relevant social experiences, heredity and early experiences, modeling by important adults and older kids, the physical and social environment, the entertainment industry, and the communications media. Schools have been all over the map on this issue—from heavy-handed indoctrination to ignoring values instruction altogether. Interestingly, early research indicated that in-class discussions and activities had little impact on students' later patterns of moral conduct; far more significant were the effects of several factors related to school climate and culture, such as the quality of the relationships among the adults in the school, service learning opportunities and having the freedom and autonomy for students to interact and cooperate with one another (in order to get beyond an adult-imposed sense of duty to an internally developed sense of fairness and justice).[86]

Moral maturity requires a set of skills, values or characteristics necessary for navigating the ethical challenges and pressures we encounter in our lives. These "virtues" or moral habits contribute to the kind of character we develop and the kind of person we grow up to be.[87] "Character education is the deliberate effort to help people understand, care about and act upon core ethical values," writes Lickona. It assumes that destructive youth behaviors correlate to an absence of good character, that "good character" involves moral knowing, moral feeling and moral action; that good character does not develop automatically but is learned through intentional and focused efforts instead. Lickona insists on the need for values with universal validity and objective worth rather than "mere subjective preferences like taste in music or clothes."[88] And education professor Edward DeRoche recommends aligning the content of the program with the needs and values of the community. "The most successful character education programs are those that form strong partnerships with parents and the community," he advises.[89]

In general, various programs focus on the kinds of attributes that contribute to the making of a decent human being, and many schools deliberately attempt to build concepts like respect, responsibility, caring or helpfulness into their curriculum and school culture.[90] Authors Rushworth Kidder and Patricia Born note, "If you ask a diverse group of people to identify core shared values that matter to them most as they contemplate the future—the values they live by and would like to hand on to the next generation—they discuss scores of ideas." Nonetheless, they suggest that if pressed to choose the most important ideas, "they typically reduce the list to five key terms: compassion, honesty, fairness, responsibility and respect."[91] Clearly, there is a great deal of overlap among these programs, but regardless of the specific content objectives there is a tremendous potential to impact not only the behavior of individual students but the school climate, as well. Programs that were implemented intentionally, proactively and comprehensively and that had schoolwide and community support showed significant improvements in courtesy, respect for others, compassion, understanding others' point of view, self-discipline, accountability, responsibility, cooperation, caring and concern for others, goal setting, problem solving, confidence, staff cohesiveness and morale. The reports also include fewer office referrals and detentions, fewer incidences of violence and physical aggression, fewer incidents of name calling and verbal put-downs and decreases in bossiness, tattling, submissiveness with peers and inappropriate attention-seeking behaviors. Or, as one, second-grader put it, "[the character program] makes it easier not to get in trouble."[92]

Perhaps most important, however, is the environment in which these goals are taught, and the quality of relationships between the individuals involved. According to the Character Education Partnership, among the principles of effective character education programs are moral leadership from staff and students, opportunities for moral action and a school that serves as a caring community. "You can't just teach an attribute," says principal Brenda Hunter. "You have to show how to live it."[93] At some point, then, we need to examine our school policies and values to see if the messages they convey are indeed consistent with our character- and moral-education goals. For example, Etzioni looks at the difference between schools that use sports to teach the value of teamwork, personal commitment and playing well, and schools in which winning is the only thing that matters. He also mentions policies that use feedback and grades to flatter and inflate student egos versus those that recognize actual effort, progress and achievement. If a school truly values virtues like cooperation and hard work, the policies and attitudes it has about everyday issues and functions within the school will reflect these values—and do far more to communicate "character messages" than the cheery posters and catchy slogans kids encounter throughout the building.

The same holds true for the behaviors of individuals in the school. One elementary-school teacher shared how her school's office broadcasts a "character message" in the morning every day. However, she also saw serious inconsistencies between the messages and several teachers' behavior. "We heard this message about talking to people respectfully," she said, "but when I saw the way teachers were talking to the kids later that day, it was anything *but* respectful." Students worldwide express resentment at incongruities and double standards—teachers who drink coffee or soft drinks at their desk but refuse to allow kids to bring sodas or water bottles to class, who punish kids for being late but regularly come to class late themselves, who preach antismoking rhetoric in between trips to the teachers' lounge for a cigarette. (As an interesting little tangent, schools that permit smoking on campus graduate 25 percent more smokers than schools that don't.[94]) It doesn't take a rocket scientist to see that simply wanting—or *telling*—kids to demonstrate honesty, responsibility, empathy, fairness, kindness, tolerance and self-control isn't going to be especially effective if we adults can't pull off these attributes consistently and pervasively in our school communities ourselves. Any lesson on personal growth and character is certainly going to be enhanced when our behaviors and attitudes match those we request from our students.

Bearing Witness: Support for Children in Crisis

Teachers historically have been evaluated and rewarded for their academic performance. As a result, many teachers underestimate their own helping skills.

William Fibkins[95]

Tears are the language of the limbic brain. They ought not to be restricted.

Elaine DeBeaufort and Aura Sofia Diaz[96]

I write entirely to find out what I'm thinking, what I'm looking at, what I see, what it means. What I want and what I fear.

Joan Didion[97]

It was never a good idea to get too upset in school. If you cried, the kids would make fun of you, and the teachers would get disgusted or angry. Sharing (or even showing) my feelings always made it worse.

William

Listening is not the same as waiting to speak.

Anonymous[98]

Noted psychotherapist Alice Miller examined the early lives of a diverse group of well-known individuals who had suffered significant childhood abuse or trauma. In her studies, she found many who had overcome their abusive experiences and went on to achieve success as adults in positive and creative ways. Others, like Hitler and Stalin, went on to develop "monstrously destructive personalities." The difference boiled down to one common element—the presence or absence of a "sympathetic witness." The abused children who grew up to be successful, functional adults had, at some point in their history, an adult who listened to them and believed their stories, someone who was available to bear witness to the abuse they had endured at the hands of some adult in their lives.[99] I use this rather extreme example cautiously, as I believe that all children need to know they've got someone in their corner—not just those suffering from trauma or abuse. Sometimes a picture of "Mrs. Murphy" or a big stuffed animal is enough. But there are times when more personal and interactive support is called for.

Unfortunately, even teachers who are willing to provide this support are often so overscheduled and have so many students, they end up doing their listening and connecting on their own time or referring students in need when help is, indeed, available. More often than not, however, we are rushed, distracted and stressed when we are needed most. As a result, our responses—while occasionally expedient—aren't terribly supportive. Instead of making ourselves available to give a student attention, acceptance and validation, we give advice and admonishment. We lecture. We dismiss or mollify. We tell them to *just get busy.* We get angry and impatient. We criticize and blame. We compare them to someone who is worse off or tell them they're lucky their problems aren't bigger than they are. We minimize the seriousness of what is very real to them. We make excuses for the person who has hurt them. In short, we do all kinds of things that don't feel safe or supportive to someone who's upset.[100] The most effective responses come when we can be patient, objective and empathetic, which can be tough when we're getting ready to give a test or start a lesson. Acknowledging an upset student (*This is important. I want to hear what you have to say*) and setting aside a more convenient time to listen (*I'll be free when the bell rings,* or *Let's talk after I get this group started*) is a reasonable alternative, one that will generally appease even a fairly distraught student.

Another option involves providing a safe space for students in distress—something not readily available in most schools. Some facilities have a counselor, or perhaps a counselor's office, but as one teacher noted, "Faculty lavatories, which are small and private, are off-limits to the kids. The nurse's office is usually locked. With the exception of the occasional empty classroom, there aren't many places to go if you just need to have a good cry." In general, schools are not well suited—philosophically or architecturally—to private emotional expression and processing, or even solid one-on-one exchanges. In general, the message in most school settings is this: *You are emotionally safe as long as you suppress your emotions.* In our haste to get through the academic material, and our abiding focus on all things cognitive, we end up with an emotional environment in which children's feelings are inconveniences for us and liabilities for them. This is also the case in classrooms in which adults insist on perpetual cheerfulness, and those in which adults and children have not learned to respect certain feelings and sensitivities. Safety can also be compromised when peers ridicule or attack a child's emotional expression, especially when the adult does not advocate or support the distressed child.

But suppressed feelings take their toll, and the costs of repression can include the buildup of stress hormones, feelings of isolation and rejection, numbness and withdrawal, the desire to "blot out the pain" with nicotine, alcohol, drugs, food or other self-destructive actions, increased stress and physical illness, depression, passive-aggressive behavior, accusations against others, and the increased likelihood of an eventual blow-up or acting-out.[101] Further, Frederic Flach has observed that people who pride themselves on "never falling apart" have more difficulty learning from their experience, lack insight, create problems for those around them and are more vulnerable to the impact of change.[102] All emotions carry some kind of information or "message," say DeBeaufort and Diaz. Rather than suppressing or ignoring feelings, they recommend staying with the feelings until we grasp what they are trying to tell us.[103] But this option is rarely encouraged culturally, and perhaps even less so in a learning environment.

The majority of emotional "crises" most teachers encounter generally require little more than validation and, sometimes, a little time and space to regain some balance. I've seen extremely agitated children settle down quickly without having to repress or stuff their feelings (but instead, let go of their emotional upset and shift into more rational, cognitive functioning) when their complaints were met with understanding and acknowledgment. I remember one of the first times I was able to pull this off. It was shortly after learning about techniques like validation and active listening at a conference, when one of my students came in from the playground nearly hysterical because someone had called her a camel. This happened a few minutes before my class was returning and I was, conveniently, free to listen. After a minute or so, she took a deep breath and looked at me. I had to fight the impulses of some old, bad habits, and instead of responding with my usual, *What did you do to her?* or *Just ignore her,* I agreed that it hurt when people called us names. "Yeah," she said, exhaling, relieved. And that was it. I've always had the feeling that she didn't want answers, and she didn't want advice. (And I'm reasonably certain that she didn't want to be yelled at, either.) She just wanted permission to be upset. Once granted, she was, in a word, done.

A prerequisite to understanding and validating someone's emotional experience is the ability to listen well. In these busy times, listening has become something of a lost art, but listening well conveys our respect for another person's experience and reality. "When you listen carefully to another person, you give that person 'psychological air,'" says Karen Irmsher. "Once that vital need is met, you can then focus on influencing or problem-solving."[104] Listening provides a forum for learning to solve problems and express feelings responsibly. Good listening skills can also reduce a child's stress, build connections and lay the groundwork for greater cooperation. When we can make time to listen to what kids have to say—truly one of the greatest gifts we can give a child—there are a few things to keep in mind. Let's remember, for example, to focus on them, hear what they're really saying, offer eye contact and acknowledge the message we're hearing. Let's reflect and clarify as needed, encourage them to *Say more,* and respect the enormity of their trust by maintaining confidentiality and taking them seriously. (Some of the most painful betrayals I heard about came from people who had bared their souls to a teacher, counselor, coach or administrator and either had their confidence violated—typically, by having their concerns reported to their parents—or were punished, laughed at or told to apologize to someone who had been abusive to them.) Let's also watch the tendency to interrupt, show impatience or rush the speaker, ask trivial questions, make assumptions or jump to conclusions. And let's resist the urge to minimize or fix the problem, deny their concerns, cheer them up or use their problems as an excuse to promote our own agendas, say what we think they should have done, top their story or project what *we* would have done or how we would have felt.[105] A tall order, indeed—one for which few adults have had strong models or much preparation.

Finally, let's watch the temptation to rush to a solution. Good listening allows us to deal with the affect first. "When you accept as a simple fact that I do feel what I feel, no matter how irrational, then I can quit trying to convince you and can get about this business of understanding what's behind this irrational feeling," says a piece called *Could You Just Listen?* "When that's clear, the answers are obvious and I don't need advice."[106] When it's time for solutions—and this, by the way, comes *after* students have had a chance to process and disengage from the grip of the affect—we can help by *asking,* rather than telling. "We really don't need sympathy or advice from others," writes associate professor David Hagstrom, referring to the process of seeking clarity about crisis and concerns. "But what we do need are good, honest and direct questions that cause us to reflect on the situation differently. Clarity is what we need."[107] Lawrence Shapiro observes that we often fail to credit kids with the capacity for solving their own problems. "Too frequently, we jump in to help before help is really needed, or we assume . . . children should have decisions made for them," he says. He notes that kids are capable of solving even very complex problems when given the opportunity and encouragement to do so.[108] Working with the assumption that the students have the answers and the ability to figure out solutions allows us to interact in the role of a guide. The questions we ask help them explore their options, anticipate possible outcomes and take responsibility for working things out.

"I don't think that emotional safety has anything to do with being in an environment where you feel free to fall apart or spill your guts at the drop of a hat," claims school administrator Pat Freeman. Instead, she recommends creating an environment in which "a child understands that it is normal to have good days and bad days, successes and failures," one that emphasizes learning coping skills. Elaine DeBeaufort agrees: "The old choices were express and make outer trouble or repress and make inner trouble. . . . There is, however, a way out of this trap." Our brains are wired, she notes, to allow us to recall emotions that are registered in the long-term memory of the limbic brain, and deal with them in appropriate ways at appropriate times. It's also worth remembering that respecting people's feelings and creating a space for them to have feelings is quite different from pressuring them to express their feelings. Additionally, *feeling* an emotion and *describing* (or analyzing) it are different processes, using different parts of the brain. While there is value in each process, as DeBeaufort notes, "I believe our emphasis on expressing feelings has inhibited our freedom to feel."[109] Very often, simply allowing the feelings to be there, without "adding the burden of conscious expression," or asking the child to defend or explain the feelings is all we need to do.

For those times when feelings are too "big" to contain, or when they're likely to interfere with the learning or teaching process, it is possible to accommodate students in ways that don't disrupt instruction.

Simply sticking them behind a desk and demanding their attention is not likely to accomplish much. Upset students—in survival mode or in the throes of an emotional hijacking—don't have access to the parts of the brain needed to cognitively process, store or retrieve whatever it is we're trying to teach. A few minutes alone (perhaps out in the hall with a couple of tissues), a trip to the water fountain for a drink of water or a cool-down lap around the gym can work wonders, and get a child to a place, physically and emotionally, where that child can deal with the feelings from a less reactive or survival-oriented part of the brain. One high-school teacher told how, at the beginning of each semester, he would give each of his students a paper pass that said, *I'm having a bad day. Leave me alone.* He created the system to allow some flexibility for kids who were too upset to really get much out of the class academically but had nowhere else to go. He said that kids rarely used the pass unless something fairly extreme (and, typically, pretty recent) had happened. "It's more of a safety net," he said, one that allowed upset students to stay in class, safe to have their feelings.

Writing is another outlet for some students. Exasperated by a constant stream of complainers and tattletales, as well as her own difficulty in curbing her habitual nonsupportive responses when interrupted, one third-grade teacher developed a "tattling form" that her students could fill out when they were having a problem. The five parts of the form—your name, the name of the person bothering you, something nice about that person, and spaces to describe the problem and propose a solution—allowed upset students to get their feelings out on paper and focus on solving the problem, while buying the teacher a little time so she could approach the kids less reactively and at a more convenient time. Other teachers allow time for kids to go off to a more private corner of the room (or school) with a journal. "Journals are great listeners when you're sad, angry or grieving" writes teen author Jessica Wilber. "You can tell your problems and secrets to your journal."[110] Other teachers provide outlets in the form of activities such as group discussions and sharing circles, places in which kids can openly express feelings and look for solutions to problems. "More often than not, these are the troubles that children keep to themselves, obsessing about them alone at night, having no one to mull them over with," says Goleman. This type of activity, when structured to respect participants' needs for dignity and confidentiality, allows feelings and disagreements to be resolved before they escalate into something more overtly destructive.[111]

Certainly, school and community crises will require our attention to students' affective needs. Marla West recalls when, during the Vietnam War, one of the corporate weapons manufacturers held their annual stockholders' meeting in the auditorium of her junior high. While school was in session, busloads of protestors and police encircled the school. And although West recalls her teachers being calm and organized, none of them talked about it at all. Their silence did little more than "fuel the students' fears that a riot would break out and we would be captives." Fortunately, this tradition of silence seems to be changing somewhat. For example, students returning to Columbine after the April 1999 shootings had the benefit of mental-health counselors and nurses who were on hand if needed. There was also a "designated 'safe room' for those overcome by emotion."[112] Linda Lantieri noted that "most children want and need to talk about what happened." She also assured parents and educators who worried that talking about disturbing issues and events would be frightening to children, telling them that our silence could make the situation even more scary.[113] Students of all ages with whom I spoke after the tragedy agreed, confirming how reassuring it was to have had teachers who spoke with them about what had happened, and ask about how they were coping.

In the past, schools that responded to school and community crises often did so with help from outside mental-health resources. More and more, however, district personnel are being trained as crisis-response team members. Training may include building awareness of potential problems and reactions students may experience, learning to identify at-risk students, improving listening skills, implementing problem-solving techniques for students to use, dealing with parents or the media, long-term and ongoing intervention and specific skills for handling different types of crises.[114] These skills are valuable, not only for debriefing kids after a critical incident and making appropriate referrals, but also dealing with affective issues on a more immediate and day-to-day basis. Teachers are often the first line of defense in crisis prevention, even in schools in which counselors, psychologists or social workers are available. In some schools, a child's potential contact with support staff may be limited by high adult-student ratios and logistics. (And many of these individuals shared the frustration they felt when their energies were fragmented by paperwork, management or supervision duties and increasing demands for an ever-broadening range of expertise—including scheduling, career advice, crisis intervention, family support and clinical work, to name a few.) Consultant William Fibkins acknowledges that "not all counselors will be willing to share their helping role with teachers" and that "some teachers will say that helping students resolve personal problems is not their job." But he also calls this kind of territoriality and fragmentation a waste of valuable helping resources at a time when these resources are desperately needed.[115]

The Spirit of the School

As we observe our thoughts, emotions and other contents of consciousness, we become aware of our choices.

Annick Safken
professor of transpersonal psychology

Affairs are now soul-sized.

Christopher Fry

Education is a sorry enterprise if we teach little of what we ourselves acknowledge to be the central and defining experiences in our lives.

Charles Suhor[116]

No child in school will learn much on an empty spirit.

William Purkey and David Aspy[117]

People get nervous when notions of spirituality pop up in an educational context. Summoning the dictum of separation of church and state to their defense, there are those strongly opposed to anything remotely spirit-related in schools, even as others blame a host of problems on its absence. But I could hardly include a chapter on supporting students' personal and emotional development and ignore this important dimension. This isn't about the church or the state and, in this context, when I talk about spirituality in schools, I am not referring to religious traditions or practices. I am, however, talking about the ways in which we help students as they wrestle with the deeper questions in their lives in their quest for meaning and connectedness. I'm talking about the spirit of the students, the teachers and even the school, the energetic core of a person or place, the spark that yearns for success and wholeness and purpose and passion, buried and subdued though that spark, in some instances, may be. And I'm talking about connections—with information, with other people, with nature, with our past and future, with our inner wisdom and guidance. For I don't believe for a second that we can talk about feelings, values, empathy, self-esteem, resiliency, achievement or motivation and not, in some way, be talking about a person's spirit, as well.

Once again, the challenge is about finding our way to a middle ground. "As I explore ways to evoke the spirit in public education, I want neither to violate the separation of church and state nor to encourage people who would impose their religious beliefs on others," writes educator Parker Palmer. "But I am equally passionate about not violating the deepest needs of the human soul." And while Palmer rejects the imposition "of any form of religion in education, including so-called 'school prayer,'" he firmly advocates "any way we can find to explore the spiritual dimension of teaching, learning and living."[118] High-school principal Donald Wesley talks about spirituality as the "ascendancy of spirit," characterized as a journey "to becoming somebody unique and special—well before talents soar, awards are handed out and high-paying salaries are offered."[119] Others see it as fundamental to learning itself. "Spirit is at the heart of a meaningful education," claims educational program director Folásadé Oládélé.[120]

But regardless of how neutral or reasonably defined, these terms can take us into risky political and constitutional territory, and Charles Haynes cautions us to be very careful about the terms we use and the goals we set when we start talking about anything that could remotely be construed as spiritual. Consultant Charles Suhor agrees. "Our pluralism gives us access to many traditions, and there is no reason [to overreact] whenever exotic cultures are studied, Handel's *Messiah* is performed or silence is invoked as a relaxation exercise." Still, he reminds that "in the current climate, good reasoning is often absent,"[121] and good teachers with good intentions are likely to end up in the middle of extreme reactions from people on either side of the political fence. Nonetheless, like values and character education, "the spiritual is always present in public education whether we acknowledge it or not," as Palmer notes.[122] And regardless of what we call it, attention to this aspect of the human experience deserves more than a casual nod.

For one thing, addressing spiritual dimensions can satisfy a child's appetite for "something more, something non-linear, something full of imagination and fantastic resources," claims author Elia Wise.[123] Rachel Kessler defends the need to address student's spiritual needs from a more serious perspective, claiming, "drugs, sex, gang violence and even suicide may be both a search for connection and meaning and an escape from the pain of not having a genuine source of spiritual fulfillment."[124] Jack Miller agrees: "If we are to build a less violent and more compassionate world, we need to nurture this deeper sense of self."[125] Without a sense of spiritual connectedness, many of the higher-level values we hope to achieve in a classroom or school setting will be difficult to achieve; establishing a true sense of emotional safety and community may be all but impossible. Welcoming the soul into the classroom allows for the masks and defenses to drop. "Students dare to share the joy and talents they feared would provoke jealousy. They risk exposing the pain or the shame that might be judged as weakness," says Kessler. "Seeing deeply into the perspective of others, accepting what they thought unworthy in themselves, students discover compassion and forgiveness."[126]

In a setting so often consumed with the concrete and the measurable, it may be difficult to imagine the shift that would legitimize the nurturing of what DeBeaufort and Diaz call "intuitive intelligence" in a school setting. But many believe in the value of validating the "inner voice" that exists in the minds of most children. For as many scientists, artists, athletes, doctors, inventors, counselors, business people, law-enforcement officers and—yes—teachers will affirm, this inner wisdom and guidance can be a valuable resource in the contributions we can make during our lifetime.[127] Personally, I don't care what we call it. We don't need to insist on using words like *spirituality* or *transcendence* if it freaks people out or makes it difficult for us to do our jobs. But let's not kid ourselves about the fact that part of why we're here is to go deeper than surface contact (or what Palmer calls "technical triviality" and "cultural banality"[128]) both in the content we teach and the way we connect with one another—and to give meaning and purpose to the time and energy we spend in our schools.

16

Social Safety: Belonging and Interpersonal Competence

Although schools alone will not be able to create a peaceable society, there is little possibility that we will succeed in reducing violence without educating young people in the ways of peace.

Linda Lantieri and Janet Patti[1]

Impulse is the medium of emotion; the seed of all impulse is a feeling bursting to express itself in action.

Daniel Goleman[2]

I've got students who have absolutely no idea how to ask for what they want, set boundaries, walk away from a fight or stick up for themselves without hurting another kid or disrupting class. This takes up a whole lot of instructional time.

middle-school teacher

What it lies in our power to do, it lies in our power not to do.

Aristotle[3]

In a well-known impulse-control study conducted by psychologist Walter Mischel in the 1960s, four-year-olds were offered the choice between eating a marshmallow right now, or getting *two* marshmallows if they could wait for a few minutes while the researcher ran an errand. Left in the room with the one marshmallow, many of the youngsters gobbled up the treat as soon as the researcher left the room. However, others struggled against temptation, often covering their eyes or fidgeting to distract themselves until the researcher returned and gave them their reward—two marshmallows. Follow-up studies with these same children showed that the ones who, at four, had displayed better impulse control ended up being more socially and academically competent as teens. They were better students and scored higher on their SATs. (In fact, at this age, their ability to delay gratification was a much better predictor of success on the SATs than their IQ.) They were more assertive, more eager to learn, and better able to handle frustration than those who could not wait.[4]

Impulse control is a basic component of *emotional intelligence.* This term was coined by psychologists Peter Salovey and John Mayer, whose work was based on Gardner's personal intelligences (which include intrapersonal and interpersonal intelligences). Essentially, emotional intelligence, or EQ as it is commonly called, refers to the relationship between the thinking part of the brain and the emotional part of the brain.[5] It involves the ability to recognize, understand and choose how we think, feel and act, say Josh Freedman and his colleagues. "It shapes our interactions with others and our understanding of ourselves." And although EQ is difficult to measure or quantify, when it comes to leading a successful and happy life, EQ has been shown to make a far larger contribution than IQ.[6] A number of individuals also use the terms emotional literacy or emotional competence when talking about EQ, particularly when referring to specific skills and attributes.

Among the "EQ fundamentals," Freedman includes self-awareness and awareness of feelings, self-control and delayed gratification, self-motivation, empathy and optimism, the ability to socialize effectively and the willingness to commit to noble goals.[7] These fundamentals encompass a number of specific virtues and abilities, and various EQ programs address such topics as curiosity, accountability, courage, perseverance, adaptability, independence (also interdependence), forgiveness, humor, integrity, tolerance, initiative, conflict resolution, problem-solving skills, stress management, emotional control, decision making and communications as part of their training.[8] Clearly, many of these characteristics are the same as those listed in character-, values- and moral-education curricula, as well as various life-skills programs. In fact, my original intent was to include this section in the previous chapter on personal and emotional development. However, since EQ is most often presented in a social or interpersonal context (and since that chapter was getting kind of long, anyhow), I decided to include it here, in part, to serve as a bridge to discussing some of the serious problems we see when EQ in our students is low (or absent).

"Almost all students who do poorly in school lack one or more elements of emotional intelligence," says author Diane Schilling. "Study after study has shown that competence in emotional skills results not only in higher academic achievement on the part of the student but in significantly more instructional time on the part of the teacher."[9] Among the teachers Debra Sugar interviewed, the two behavior problems most commonly cited were impulsivity and aggression. "As one teacher put it," she writes, "the ability to control their anger and assess peer situations before impulsively acting are ultimately more relevant to her students' survival than their ability to read."[10] The issue of anger management or, more precisely, averting or quickly recovering from an emotional hijacking, is probably one of the most important and valuable goals of EQ training. As author Carolyn Shelton maintains, "It's possible for a child to keep an angry mood going (and growing) just by thinking (and talking) about it. . . . The more a child dwells on what made her angry, the more reasons and self-justifications she can find for being angry." She urges adults to help kids learn, instead, how to reframe the situation to gain some control over the emotions.[11] "'I am angry' is only one truth, one reality," asserts Elaine DeBeaufort. Becoming emotionally intelligent requires the ability to shift out of this feeling, she says, and learning to appreciate other people's perspectives and realities can help.[12]

Robert Sylwester advises, "We don't learn emotions in the same way that we learn a telephone number, and we can't easily change them. What we can learn is how and when to use rational processes to override our emotions or to hold them in check, and when to allow them free rein as an exuberant manifestation of life."[13] Freedman agrees. Even while flooded with stress hormones, we still have options. I remember hearing a "workshop story" years ago about a woman whose car broke down, who got stuck in the rain waiting for a bus and who, while she was standing in the aisle of the bus trying not to lose her grip on her wet packages, was bumped from behind, hard enough to nearly lose her balance. She turned around, ready to explode and encountered a very apologetic blind man who seemed to be having as much trouble that day as she was. The "explosion" never came. "You do not need to stay hijacked," says Freedman. "You can still choose actions." He recommends practicing patterns that lead to de-escalation before sensation turns into harmful actions. He insists that the neurochemicals need not persist but, with a deliberate shift, "they will dissipate in three to six seconds."[14]

In the shadow of all-or-nothing thinking, however, some EQ goals can be misinterpreted. Most adults would agree on the value of emotional self-control, for example. But as Freedman observes, "Sadly, many people think 'self-control' means 'do not feel.'" This is not the case. The goal of self-control is not to obliterate our feelings but to act, instead, with clarity and intention.[15] We *need* our feelings. (Damasio's research has shown that rational behavior and learning are absent when cognition is dissociated from the emotions.[16]) "The problem is not with emotionality, but with the appropriateness of emotion and its expression," says Goleman.[17] As Maslow notes, "Anger does not disappear with psychological health. Rather it takes the form of decisiveness, self-affirmation, self-protection, justified indignation, fighting against evil, and the like." But aggression in an unhealthy person—and this includes children who have grown up without nurturing or have been abused in some way—tends to take another path, one that is more cruel, malicious, destructive and sadistic.[18] These children, without intervention, support and more constructive outlets for their energies, are of great concern to anyone living and working with young people. Fortunately, for their sake—and for the sake of all children whose EQ may be lagging—the skills and attributes necessary for emotional and social well-being can be taught and strengthened. "Neuroscientists have confirmed that we have a wide window of opportunity to influence and strengthen our emotional social selves early on in life," report Lantieri and Patti. They share the encouraging research that points to the centers in the brain that control emotional impulses as being among the last to reach full maturity—in mid- to late adolescence. "From experience, we know we can intentionally reshape the emotional lessons learned in childhood, lessons which form the bases of our habits of the heart for the rest of our lives."[19]

When Kids Don't Play Nice

How can you absorb new information when you have to be in fear of your life every day? When you can't trust the other kids in the hallway? In the cafeteria?

Erika Karres[20]

You always had to be careful of who you bumped into in the halls, or who you looked at.

Joanna Carman

"Misfits" have a huge need for recognition and belonging and will eventually either act out or withdraw if their needs are not met.

B. J. Wise[21]

When I worked at the day treatment center, I wasn't particularly surprised to learn that many of the high-risk teens I met there had routinely carried guns or other weapons to school. What did surprise me, however, was the number of responsible, respectable adults—people of all ages, some of them teachers and counselors currently working in school settings—who reported that they had attended school similarly armed. These were not gang members or the typical troublemakers we often think of when we picture kids bringing weapons to school; they were simply kids who felt threatened enough by their classmates to believe that such a level of preparedness and self-protection was essential for them to get through the school day. If they were that frightened, they are in good company. "An estimated 160,000 children each day miss school for fear of being picked on by their peers," reports Michele Borba.[22] The seriousness of this problem has come under greater scrutiny in the past few years as more and more incidents of school violence and teen suicides are tied to high levels of peer harassment and abuse as possible causal factors.

When I've read the headlines, when I've worked with violent and troubled kids, I've seen two main themes at work. First, there's the need to help kids to just be *nicer*—more respectful, considerate, compassionate and accepting in their interactions with others. Second, I see a strong need to build the kind of confidence and groundedness, as well as the vocabulary and skills necessary to interpret social cues accurately, to deflect insults and "dirty looks" from peers, to not take things so personally, and to develop a repertoire of alternatives to the reactivity, defensiveness and explosiveness that are so much more familiar and automatic to so many kids. There are dozens of related skills—things like boundary-setting, courtesy, and knowing how and when to apologize—as well. No small tasks, to be sure, but once again, this issue of social competence is only one piece of a much bigger picture. As we work on the other pieces to reduce the degree of anger, resentment, failure and disempowerment many kids experience on a day-to-day basis, the desire to take these feelings out on a weaker, smaller (or less-well-armed) peer might just lose some of its appeal.

Clearly, the seeds for violent and bullying behavior are planted long before kids come to school, and early indications of problems are evident in some children well before kindergarten. The behaviors of these toddlers may range from a lack of compassion for a distraught classmate to overtly sadistic attacks, and are nearly always associated with the child's lack of self-regulation skills and a home life characterized by chaos, unpredictability, disruptions, drugs and alcohol, lack of parental love or warmth, harsh discipline, and parental behavior patterns of abuse and neglect (depending on the parents' moods).[23] An absence of healthy adult role models, few positive peer influences, viewing TV violence and misconduct or fighting in the home and community figure in, as well.[24] Other factors that predict aggression in children include having an emotionally cold or hostile caretaker who is also tolerant (or supportive) of the child's aggressive behavior, one who uses physical punishment and emotional outbursts to control the child. Also a factor, if slightly less important in this context, is the temperament of the child. On the other hand, research does not show a family's income or standard of housing, or a parent's level of education to be related to children's aggression, and bullying expert Dan Olweus claims that there is no evidence to suggest that these tough behavior patterns are a consequence of poor grades or school failure, or that they are actually a cover for anxiety and insecurity.[25]

As we have seen, when kids spend their early years without the love, warmth and support they need, they typically develop a cluster of behaviors based on what they witness from their primary caretakers and what they need to create a sense of safety in their lives. These emotionally protective behaviors include the tendency to overreact to what they perceive as a negative cue, and a pattern of tuning out anything that isn't immediately threatening, something that deprives them of the ability to notice ordinary expressions of kindness, friendliness or sympathy, claims family therapist Polly Drew. Additionally, she notes that children from violent and abusive homes "are expert physical fighters and have few inhibitions about using these skills they've learned at Mommy's or Daddy's knee." They are likewise proficient at rationalizing and justifying the aggression that is "encoded into their value system," and which they've learned to use to get what they want.[26]

But survival skills can become liabilities in school and, later, in life. In one thirty-five-year study, many of the individuals who were aggressive throughout their lives had been identified as school bullies by their schoolmates at age eight. Aggressive students tend to react with fewer facts, have difficulty perceiving alternative solutions and often fail to anticipate the consequences of their actions. Many of these children underperform in school and throughout their careers, and are likely to drop out. Other research confirms that when school bullies don't outgrow their behavior—and many don't—they become more aggressive as they get older and run a "clearly increased risk" of eventual criminality, alcohol abuse, mental health problems, antisocial personality disorders and difficulty in forming or maintaining healthy relationships with their spouses, children and subordinates at work.[27] Without some form of intervention and prosocial support, the future for these youngsters does not bode well.

Violent and aggressive students are driven by a need for power and a desire to dominate, control or subdue others. Many have no remorse for hurting other children and refuse to take responsibility for their behavior, justifying their actions by claiming to have been provoked, or by insisting that their target was "asking for it." (In fact, the belief that they are entitled to use violence in these situations can be so strong that they are surprised or puzzled by adults who call them on their behavior.) These students may also derive certain "benefits" from their behavior, which make it harder for them to give up the patterns that have "worked" for them. Besides a sense of power, aggressive students who have themselves been violated (by parents or peers) can also experience satisfaction from causing others to suffer. Their aggression can serve as an indirect way of getting back at their abuser, as well as a release of hostility or resentment when they inflict their pain on others. For some, there's the potential to acquire money, cigarettes, clothing or other things of value and, in some situations, prestige and acceptance among peers.[28] One study with 452 boys in upper-elementary grades show that tough, antisocial students are actually "rewarded with popularity," particularly when the boys are also friendly or athletic. (In general, bullies are perceived to have greater status and popularity than the individuals they antagonize.)[29] Although their popularity tends to drop off in the middle and upper grades, bullies often have a small group of followers and friends who seem to admire their power and their ability to do what they want and get their way with their peers. If these kids are still in school by late adolescence, they are generally disliked and rejected by the majority of the students. As their popularity wanes, their peer group generally consists of other bullies or, more seriously, a gang affiliation.[30]

When kids cannot get their needs met for things like safety, acceptance, belonging, identity, power, structure, respect, success, fun, love, status or recognition within conventional support structures, gangs start looking pretty good. In terms of these needs, "most young people who join gangs are often no different from those who do not," claims Richard Arthur. "The critical difference for gang members is that legitimate opportunities to achieve these ends are often—correctly or incorrectly—perceived as blocked."[31] According to a 1997 report by the Department of Justice, there are 25,000 different street gangs with 652,000 members in the United States.[32] Nonetheless, "relatively few young people join gangs," argues a report by Burnett and Walz. "Even in highly impacted areas, the degree of participation has rarely exceeded 10 percent." They also report that less than 2 percent of all juvenile crime is gang-related. However, a strong gang presence in a community can impact a school climate. Where once considered neutral territory, schools are increasingly seen by gang members as a place to hang out and exercise their influence. A gang presence in schools correlates with increases in weapons (among both gang members and nonmembers) and a greater fear among students of being victims of violence than students experience at schools without gangs.[33] The challenge then, as gang expert Louis Gonzales advises, is for schools and families to decrease the allure of the streets by being "the better gang."[34]

In previous chapters, we saw examples of various types of bullying, harassment, cruelty and abuse, and whether we're talking about direct physical or verbal violence or intimidation, or the more subtle and indirect forms of hurtful behavior seen in peer rejection, exclusion or neglect, we are talking about behaviors that hurt kids and jeopardize their ability to feel safe. We're talking about a problem with serious negative consequences for the emotional climate of a school and one that affects learning for thousands of students worldwide. Much of the literature—and there's quite a bit on this subject—focuses its attention on alerting educators and parents not only to the variety and seriousness of behaviors that can be hurtful or frightening (including those that aggressive students try to pass off as "just playing"), but also to the traditions in which significant adults have tolerated, excused or even modeled these kinds of behaviors. For we know that cruelty, intimidation and deliberate exclusion can cause a lifetime of pain. At the same time, however, there is much evidence for the possibility of a significant, positive impact when consistent and deliberate efforts are applied to prevent these behaviors from ever occurring, and to respond to them when they do occur.

The Other End of the Stick

Being left out of the circle is like being in a room without oxygen.

Russel Torres
kindergarten student[35]

A punching bag will only swing in silence for so long. Eventually, if you it hit hard and often enough, it will swing back at you, hard and uncontrollable.

Adam Kupersmith
student

You might even say that bullies are Self-Esteem Vampires.
Trevor Romain[36]

The continuum of peer aggression ranges from teasing to murder. When talking about bullying, standard definitions describe acts of harassment or intimidation that continue with regularity for a certain period of time (usually six months or more). However, since even single occurrences of violence—whether physical, verbal or emotional—can have a tremendous and long-lasting negative impact, in this context I'm referring to *any* act of aggression by peers that compromises the safety of the person being targeted for that aggression in any way. By this definition, it's probably not a big surprise that in various studies, 80 to 90 percent of kids claimed to have been harassed or abused by peers.[37] Likewise, belaboring the issue of what constitutes bullying or harassment is, for my purposes, pointless. "Bullying is an attitude rather than an act," says Besag. "It can be defined as bullying by measuring the effects the acts have on a vulnerable child."[38] This means "fun" is only fun if everybody involved agrees that it's fun. Even without malicious intent, if it hurts, if it's mean, if it excludes, if it frightens, it will impact a student's sense of safety. And students who experience or interpret their peers' actions in this way are at particular risk.[39]

Antagonism and harassment are dehumanizing, and "even after a short period of time, the loss of confidence and self-esteem is rapid," Besag asserts. She includes feelings of shame (for being disliked) and guilt (believing they deserve it), the loss of identity, increased vulnerability, lack of hope, depression, helplessness and misplaced emotions among the emotional effects of peer torment.[40] Harassment, rejection and abuse also cause difficulties in all areas of life, including a child's ability to learn. "Children who have trouble being accepted by their classmates are two to eight times more likely to drop out," says Sandi Redenbach, an educator and author, and a former dropout herself.[41] They are also two to three times more likely to suffer headaches and other illnesses than nonbullied peers. Follow-up research shows that even as young adults, individuals who were antagonized by peers were more likely to struggle with depression and poor self-esteem than those who were accepted or left alone.[42] Isolation often increases when scapegoated students are avoided by classmates, who fear being targeted themselves or risk losing status by their association.[43] While harassed adults have certain social, legal and logistical options available to them, "children cannot escape the school yard, the locker room or the cafeteria." For some, the prospect of another day of "torture and humiliation" makes suicide a viable and attractive option. For the rest, the scars can last a lifetime.[44]

And then, too, there is the risk of retaliation. Studies on friendships and conflicts have noted that children for whom revenge is "a very strong goal in their reaction to even everyday conflicts" tend to have fewer and poorer friendships than peers who respond less reactively and with less hostility.[45] Although the most common response of someone being bullied is "flight" or "freeze," targeted kids will occasionally fight when pushed far enough. In fact, quite a number of survey respondents, all of them male, said that the daily torment and fear they experienced as students did not cease until their self-control broke and they fought back. The men who wrote were lucky—they either were enraged enough or strong enough to make their point without doing much damage (or in one case, didn't need to fight at all when the attacker broke his own hand on the first punch).[46] But retaliation is ill-advised as bullies rarely back down. For most kids, any attempt in this direction typically only makes things worse.[47] After a while, some kids reach the point where they feel they have nothing left to lose; many of the kids in recent headlines had been on the receiving end of peer abuse long enough to spawn elaborate and deadly schemes to even up the score. As we've seen, these acts are often carried out in the same school settings in which the harassment allegedly occurred.

Bully-Proofing the Schools

The benefit of bringing bully problems out in the open is that the bully is no longer in control.

Trevor Romain[48]

If children are to make choices, they must believe that they have choices.

Martine Agassi[49]

It is preferable to teach social skills than to spend time dealing with behavior problems.

Debra Sugar[50]

The welfare and safety of both children are of concern in every dispute. All efforts to end hurtful behavior are directed in the best interests of the child who is the victim, as well as the child who is doing the hurting.

Chris Mattise[51]

When it comes to dealing with peer aggression, we need to address a number of dimensions. First, there are the aggressive kids, the kids who hurt others in some way. Then there are the kids whom these students torment. There are also students on the sidelines who, by their action or inaction, are a part of the dynamic, as well. And finally, there are the grownups, the teachers and parents who model (or don't) the kinds of skills kids need to get along with others and resolve conflicts that come up. Attempting to deal with just one of these components, or deal with this issue reactively or superficially won't cut it. Nonetheless, there is a certain amount of pressure to focus exclusively on the aggressors and react, decisively and emphatically. However, this pressure can distract us from more effective, long-term preventative approaches. "As a result of public demands to respond punitively to threats of violence at school through 'zero-tolerance' programs, schools often focus disciplinary actions on perpetrators of violence," says a position paper by the National Association of School Psychologists. "Policies that focus only on catching and punishing violent behaviors fall far short of the goal of creating safe school environments."[52] Garrity and her colleagues concur: "Unfortunately, the use of punishment is the most common intervention used with bullies. Many educators want the bullies to experience the pain they impose on others." But, they claim, "trying to meet the power of the bully head-on is very seldom productive."[53] In the next chapter, we'll look at power dynamics and structures that can help avert power struggles (and offer alternatives to adults who would otherwise seek to disempower these antisocial children). However, in the meantime, a more productive and multifaceted approach, one with positive interventions and behavior-management strategies—such as channeling students' power needs in prosocial directions and strengthening leadership skills—is more likely to get the results we want.

In dealing with aggressive children, there is also great advantage in getting an early start, preferably before kindergarten, or as soon as the first signs of aggression are noted. In the hands of loving and caring adults, children are capable of altruism and empathy at a very early age. Shapiro observes that by age six, most children have reached "the stage of cognitive empathy," that is, the ability to see things from another person's perspective. When this trait is nurtured, children learn to take other people's needs and feelings into account as they choose their behaviors. "Kindness and consideration are part of [a] child's genetic coding," he says, "But if these traits are not nourished, they will disappear."[54] Lantieri and Patti present the importance of helping little ones override the "predisposition to aggression," by teaching them things like how to cooperate, take turns, ask before taking things, share and get attention in constructive ways. They cite research which indicates that "when young people are taught social skills at an early age, they are less likely to commit violent crimes as adults." Another study showed reductions in juvenile court referrals, just by teaching young people how not to insult others, how to recognize others positively and how to accept feedback from others.[55]

Kids can be remarkably inventive when it comes to finding excuses for tormenting one another, but by far the most common characteristics of kids targeted for aggression by their peers is a lack of popularity, or not fitting in—understandably one of the greatest fears among adolescents and teens. Contributing to this status may be physical characteristics such as facial appearance, physical weakness, wardrobe or being overweight, but these do not seem to have nearly the importance of emotional characteristics like being insecure or unassertive, crying easily, being hot-tempered or having few friendship skills.[56] The fact that the least popular students are the most vulnerable makes a substantial argument in favor of the schools taking a part in reducing students' isolation and strengthening their personal and social competencies. Simply reacting to an aggressor will not end the problem or improve the social climate in the school. "Fighting back or ignoring the bully isn't the solution," insists author Trevor Romain.[57] Debra Sugar notes that the ability to adjust to social and behavioral demands of both teachers and peers are significant indicators of school success. "It is evident that focusing on reducing negative behaviors is not sufficient," she says. "It is necessary to replace these behaviors with positive, prosocial skills."[58]

Social-skills training generally concentrates on building confidence, assertiveness and independence—each an excellent antidote to being targeted. Training can also help kids develop an understanding of verbal messages and nonverbal cues, a good sense of timing and the ability to see the connection between their behavior and the impact that behavior has on others. Other skills addressed might include children's ability to interact with kids and adults flexibly, skillfully and responsibly, without sacrificing their own needs or integrity, as well as helping them learn to speak up for themselves, express feelings, make themselves heard and get help when they need it (rather than "holding it in" until they explode, emotionally and behaviorally).[59] Activities that help children identify strategies for dealing with specific and potentially dangerous situations—like finding a gun or drug paraphernalia—can also be helpful. Likewise valuable are "power skills" that help kids learn to do things like disengage from the energy and influence of the crowd, cool down (so they can think more clearly), observe and identify peers who play nicely, join games or find someone to play with during break times, allow others to have their opinions (without becoming defensive), disarm aggressors with humor or by agreeing with them, or call up calming and self-protective mental images to ward off the negative effects of teasing or criticism.[60]

Finally, effective skills training goes beyond slogans and mandates. It requires thinking and problem solving, using concrete, emotion-based problems in a familiar context. As Shapiro advises, "We must teach the emotional brain as well as the thinking brain."[61] But whose brains are we talking about here? Much has been written about identifying at-risk kids for placement in special programs to develop these skills. And while I see a value in improving our awareness that there are indeed young people in our school systems who need a fair amount of attention in this area, my preference would be that the kind of skills training that builds good friendships, positive interactions and constructive solutions to conflicts be made available to *all* students—not just the ones at the extremes or the ones who end up in the office. I say this, primarily, because I've met very few children who couldn't benefit in some way from polishing their social skills and personal competencies. I also believe these skills to be essential for functioning in just about all interactive situations throughout our lives, and that, quite frankly, the emotional climate of our schools depends upon our mediating weaknesses and difficulties any student may have in these areas. Besides, if we start picking and choosing kids in need of interventions, I'm concerned about the accuracy of our own observations and the impact of our biases and expectations. Outward appearances can be misleading. Many children, as part of their survival repertoire, become experts at appearing "fine," or have learned that *saying* they're "fine" is the best way for them to avoid retaliation from peers or minimize conflict, scrutiny or interference from adults. Likewise, while many of the more aggressive kids are easily identifiable, it's possible to overlook kids whose aggressive tendencies are somewhat less obvious. As one social worker told me, "I've worked with gangs for years, but when it comes to sheer viciousness, I don't think my toughest gangbangers could hold a candle to some of the 'nice girls' from 'nice families' that went to my high school." And finally, I call on Lantieri and Patti's recommendation to make social and emotional skills training a fairly generic part of the regular curriculum, and not something to trot out "when emotional outbursts, physical fights or racial slurs occur."[62]

One of the resources most often overlooked in dealing with peer aggression is the large group of students who are not directly involved in incidents of peer aggression. There is value in the idea of "mobilizing the masses" or utilizing this "caring majority of students" to take action—sometimes by simply setting a tone that says, "We treat others kindly here." These are the students who can refuse to watch or encourage bullying incidents, as the "arena mentality" can escalate and reinforce the aggressor's behavior. They are the ones who can intervene to support the children being targeted, the ones who can distract the bully, the ones who can discharge the tension in a threatening situation, the ones who can bear witness and report incidents—strategies that can make a significant difference in the school climate.[63] The children in this group may need special attention for other reasons. Mike Selby notes that highly sensitive children can be overwhelmed by aggression, even when it isn't directed to them. "When bullies pick on or physically hurt other people, the highly sensitive person will feel helpless and sick," he says. And these feelings do not necessarily come from a fear of being "next," but instead emanate from a sense of empathy or responsibility for the person being abused.

Drawing on the resources of the entire student population has proven successful in programs in which kids help other kids resolve their problems. Peer-mediation programs have cropped up around the country as a positive alternative to more traditional disciplinary reactions. In these programs, children are trained to step in and guide classmates to peaceful solutions to their conflicts, preparing for this role by learning skills such as listening without interfering or blaming, asking the right kinds of questions, concentrating on what is being said, staying calm and impartial in stressful situations, and helping kids involved in disputes communicate without making things worse. Generally used for noncriminal kinds of problems (name-calling, teasing, threats or rumor-spreading, for example), the process relies on honesty, respect, listening, communication, clarification, empathy, responsibility, an agreement by all parties to a certain set of ground rules and a desire to find win-win solutions rather than fixing blame or determining who is right or wrong. While not denying or obstructing the need for adult intervention, the use of peer mediation can be remarkably effective in creating safety for kids (by showing that their problems are taken seriously, by providing a forum where they can be angry or hurt instead of belligerent, and by allowing time and space for their problems to be addressed and, hopefully, resolved) and in building important life skills for all concerned.[64]

As adults, it's easy to make judgments and get impatient with kids on either side of the bully-target fence, but any healing that happens will start from a place of safety as well as one of acceptance—not of the hurtful or provocative behaviors, but acceptance of the individuals involved. I can think of few instances in which the advocacy of a caring adult—having someone who believes in you, someone who will support and encourage you—can have a more profound impact.

Respecting Differences, Changing Beliefs

Children aren't born with prejudice. But they will pick it up, unless we adults do a good job as role models and educators in our free society.

From a bulletin on "Respecting Differences"[65]

Cooperation widens your sense of who's in your group. It changes your thinking from "us and them" to "we."

Samuel Gaetner[66]

One day we've got to sit down together at the table of brotherhood.

Martin Luther King Jr.[67]

When author and consultant Rita Mercier started her leadership program for fourth-, fifth- and sixth-graders, student interactions in her school were "seldom kind or considerate," she admits. "Fear and intimidation were pervasive." As a part of the program, she paired some of the school's toughest kids with special needs children, putting them to work as peer helpers and tutors in special-education classes. This move was part of a larger effort that spurred a dramatic shift in the school climate. As Mercier observes, "That was the best diversity training we could have had."

The brain's capacity for classification and inference making helps us sort and interpret enormous amounts of information. "Modern humans make inferences reflexively and about almost everything," says Michael Gazzaniga. "They make inferences by correlating two events that take place contiguously," and then go on to make theories and assumptions based on these correlations.[68] These inferences are critical to the formation of our beliefs. However, if our assumptions are not, at some point, questioned, tested or further investigated, we can go through our lives operating from a set of beliefs that may or may not be particularly accurate. One of the most curious examples I've seen of this phenomena occurred when one of my third-graders came to school with her arm in a cast. By lunchtime rumors speculated when this nine-year-old would have her baby. A little confused, I asked one of the girls to explain. The answer was completely logical to these kids: "Fontaine's mother had a cast just like that and then she had a baby," they explained. Sometimes our assumptions can be very limiting, particularly when we start classifying and categorizing groups of people. Psychological experiments suggest that stereotypes and prejudices are unfortunate byproducts "of the way the mind categorizes all experience," asserts Daniel Goleman. "Essentially, the mind seeks to simplify the chaos of the world by fitting all perceptions into categories." The problem begins when people focus on the category and not the individual.[69]

Louise Derman-Sparks noted that children detect differences in people at a very early age, observing that "a two-year-old child already distinguishes differences in gender and skin color, and a child as young as three has already become aware of society's norms about gender, racial differences and physical disabilities." She claims that children as young as four have been heard "making biased comments based on racial, gender and physical differences."[70] Author Mary Beth Quinsey advises parents and teachers that it is perfectly normal for children to ask what we typically consider to be embarrassing (and usually loud) questions when they notice differences. She advises giving frank, simple and direct answers that are respectful both of the child's curiosity and the dignity of the person the child is asking about, and using these questions as a wonderful opportunity to help children explore and appreciate how wonderfully diverse people's appearances can be.[71]

Gordon Allport, a pioneer in the field of racial prejudice, found that children learn bigotry "by adopting the prejudices of their parents and by absorbing the lessons of the larger cultural environment when that environment fosters suspicion, fear and hatred of specific groups of people." His research tells us that "it takes the entire period of childhood and adolescence to master prejudice."[72] This is actually good news. As with any other learned behavior, prejudice can be unlearned, and although adults can certainly change their thinking, the potential to intervene before these beliefs are indeed "mastered" by the young people in our schools can be enormous.

Beliefs can change when a biased person is immersed in an environment in which the majority of people hold different, unbiased beliefs. "Students will appreciate diversity and work harder to resolve diversity-related conflict when they are in an environment that actively values diversity," claim Lantieri and Patti.[73] Goleman cites studies that show how people in authority "can play a crucial role in heading off expressions of ethnic and racial hatred simply by making it clear that they will not be tolerated." He gives an example of people who move from a part of the country where it is accepted to openly express a particular prejudice to another place where it is not. "People conform," says psychologist Stuart Cook. Adjusting behaviors to fit within local standards has an impact on the person's belief system. According to Cook, over time, "people change their beliefs to fit their behavior in order to relieve the tension that comes from feeling one way and acting another."[74] Such is the value of cognitive dissonance, and the difficulty of living in a state where there is a wide gap between a belief and an actual behavior or experience. "Something has to give," says Gazzaniga, "and it is usually the value or the belief."[75]

Part of our challenge in dealing with young people who have narrow experiences and values is to introduce a state of dissonance, as well as a shot at developing different, more accepting beliefs. I recall sitting in on a therapy group at the center with three teenage boys, two from rival ethnic gangs and the third, a white supremacist. (The mix was not deliberate, just who showed up that day.) The level of sheer insensitivity—what these boys thought was okay to say out loud—was, in itself, eye-opening. Fortunately, this group was led by a particularly gifted counselor, someone who was willing to calmly challenge an insulting remark by pointing out its potential impact or asking the boys to consider how a certain comment might sound to the others. It's hard to gauge the impact of being in an environment in which the staff were fairly unified in responding to slurs and derogatory remarks, as the majority of clients weren't there very long, but this brief contact with a different set of values at least introduced the possibility of another reality and value structure. Even a little step is a step.

Another way of introducing dissonance is through experiences that conflict with beliefs. Psychologist David Hamilton found that people can hold onto stereotypes even in the face of facts and experiences that challenge those beliefs. However, a number of experiences with people who do not fit a particular stereotype can give way to new beliefs.[76] One of the best ways to broaden experience (and expand beliefs) is to give kids a chance to interact with others who are different from them, preferably toward a shared goal. (Simply putting a bunch of different people together does not have anywhere near the effect of allowing them to work cooperatively. The "shared goal" seems to be the key.) Numerous studies have shown sharp reductions in prejudice and stereotyping, and a greater empathy and tolerance for diversity when children worked in band, for example, or participated in sports or learning teams toward a common purpose with others who were different from themselves.

Similar results have been found among children who worked together in cooperative learning activities, social clubs, service organizations or multiage settings, as well as kids who assumed the role of peer mentors or tutors with children who were different from them.[77] The bottom line is this: We do not change children's beliefs by forbidding or punishing them. What we do instead is create opportunities for success and cooperation beyond anything they could possibly imagine, and we believe in the power of possibilities these opportunities can generate.

The Teacher as Model

The most obvious—but crucial—point is that tackling bullying first of all requires teachers themselves to stop bullying.

Wendy Stainton Rogers[78]

It is not possible to teach [self] management skills when you are agitated yourself.

Joshua Freedman, Anabel Jensen, Marsha Rideout and Patricia Freedman[79]

Where there is a teacher in a school who intimidates, humiliates or degrades students, it affects the entire staff.

Robert Reasoner[80]

Humiliation is a psychological slap in the face.

Polly Drew[81]

Author, speaker and business owner Michael Powers, tells of a girl who had a crush on him in junior high and how she then became the brunt of his jokes. In an effort to be funny and accepted, he recalls going out of his way to make her life miserable. "I didn't fully realize what I was doing to the self-images of those around me," he wrote, especially to this girl. About halfway through the year, his physical education teacher—a man he looked up to like a father—approached him, saying he'd heard rumors, but that he didn't believe Mike could be capable of picking on this girl. That was pretty much all he said, but it was enough. The tormenting stopped immediately. It took a while longer, however, "before I fully realized the incredible way in which Mr. Greer had handled the problem. He not only made me realize the seriousness of my actions, but he did it in a way that helped me save some of my pride." In his tribute to this teacher (which was also an overdue apology to the girl he had hurt), Powers gives a striking example of how much learning and growth can take place in a moment of respectful and caring connection between a teacher and student.

Two of the most powerful factors in determining the actual extent of conflict and peer harassment that go on in a school are the attitudes and behaviors of the adults in the building. In earlier chapters, we saw how a teacher's avoidance or denial of bullying behavior contributed to its existence and, in some cases, its increasing severity. And while it is probably true that in most instances, more violence and intimidation go on than even the most attentive adults realize, certain beliefs make it easier to turn a blind eye. For example, attempting to cling to the notion that peer violence is simply one of the "rites of passage" of childhood, a normal or acceptable part of being a kid, or that the experience has "character-building" value, can have horrible repercussions on the emotional and social lives of the students, and on the emotional and social climate of the school, as well. And the entire school community (parents included) will take our efforts far more seriously if they know that our concerns are a regular part of school policies and objectives, not just the latest inservice flavor-of-the-week.[82]

Additionally, kids need models for "creative conflict resolution" and win-win problem solving if they are to learn to solve their own conflicts positively and nonviolently.[83] To this end, some social skills and bully-prevention programs include (or start with) training to strengthen adults' social skills. "Teachers and staff need to learn effective anger management, good communication skills and flexible problem solving to model prosocial behaviors," write Karen Summers and Angelique von Halle.[84] And Lickona asserts, "We teach respect for all persons by the examples we set. Nothing else is a more profound teacher in our children's minds."[85] This being the case, then we are likewise compelled to take a long, hard look at our discipline policies and procedures, as well as our own patterns of responding to kids when they are misbehaving, as it is in these situations that we are most likely to model the very behaviors we wish children to avoid.

Caring communities do not come about in an environment in which adults are "free to adopt patterns of behavior for themselves that they would not accept from pupils." Likewise it is impossible to contain bullying and aggression when adults "employ bullying tactics in controlling children."[86] And many of the traditional techniques teachers utilize are indeed behaviors we have come to identify as bullying, aggression or verbal violence when we see these behaviors in our students. "Whenever a teacher deliberately humiliates a pupil, then the teacher is, quite simply, engaging in bullying," advises Wendy Stainton Rogers. Rogers cites 1994 research that confirms that "most secondary pupils, at least, will tell you that in their school there are one or two teachers who regularly use intimidation, sarcasm, belittling or harassment towards pupils and that most teachers, on occasion, will resort to these kinds of behaviors."[87] And then out of the other side of our mouths we demand that kids treat each other respectfully? I don't think so. Don't "bully the bullies," says author Allan Beane.[88] If we're not walking the talk, they won't either.

Kids need to know that an adult will be there for them, and that we are capable of intervening and supporting them without making things worse. This means learning to listen, pay attention and take kids seriously in ways that perhaps we never have before. For many of us, it may also mean learning new skills for dealing firmly, immediately and consistently with incidents of meanness and harassment among students as well. We know, for example, that cornering a child who has been subjected to harassment and demanding the details of what happened, or the names of those involved, will only accentuate this child's distress, and yet, for many of us, this is a natural and logical response.[89] We know, too, that aggressive kids are only fueled by power struggles, but look at how reactive and disempowering many of our "get-tough" policies tend to be. We need another way, one that deals specifically, as Garrity suggests, with "the thinking processes and social problem-solving disabilities that the bullies have," one that rechannels their power needs in positive directions rather than engages them in a battle of wills.[90] This will challenge the traditional power dynamic present in most schools, and suggest a whole new way to think about what dealing with discipline and behavior issues really means.

17

Behavioral Safety: Discipline and Cooperation

Connecting at the heart does not mean letting people walk all over you.

teacher of at-risk students

They expect adults to be critical of them—to judge them and find them somehow lacking; this is how it's always been for them and why should you be any different?

Vicki Phillips[1]

There is no effort without error and shortcomings.

Theodore Roosevelt

When a student embarrasses, ridicules or scorns another student, it is harassment, bullying or teasing. When a teacher does it, it is sound pedagogical practice.

Juanita Ross Epp[2]

In the early 1980s, I coordinated a training-and-support program for first-year teaching interns. In our twice-weekly after-school seminars, I would plan activities covering a variety of topics. But week after week, all they ever wanted to talk about was discipline. Accordingly, this topic occupied much of the time we spent working together. Eventually, my observations of what was and wasn't working for these and other teachers culminated in a book and several classes and workshops on this issue.[3] Although I offered to speak on a variety of topics, everywhere I went, it seemed that behavioral concerns were at the top of everyone's list. What I found, as I worked with teachers (and parents, too, when I started doing similar trainings for them) was a startling similarity in the problems adults throughout the world were encountering with kids, as well as a similarity in their approaches to the children's challenging behaviors. Although most of the questions I encountered were about how to react to a particular type of misbehavior (*What do I do when . . . ?*), my work focused instead on the more complex (and for most people, less satisfying) answers that concentrated on *preventing* those kinds of problems in the first place. As this training evolved over the next two decades, I found, more and more, that talking about preventing discipline problems meant talking about building emotional safety in families, classrooms and schools. I began to notice that so much of the impudence, indifference and recalcitrance adults described were the result of misguided attempts by children to protect their safety and their closely related needs for identity, dignity, autonomy, success and peer acceptance. I also found that many of most common discipline policies and practices were actually exacerbating the problem, if not actually *creating* conflict that might not have occurred if the adults had approached the relationship in a different way. Finally, I found that adults who were able to create the kinds of authority relationships in which kids' needs were indeed considered typically encountered relatively few conflicts, outbursts and acts of defiance from the young people in their lives.

Although we can probably all think of a teacher who mistreated students, either verbally, emotionally or physically, I honestly believe that the majority of adults working with young people in schools are there because they care and want to make a difference in positive ways. If my purpose here is to look at which parts of the system allow these intentions to get lost, I certainly want to acknowledge the caring and intense dedication I see everywhere, and the fact that many, if not most, teachers treat students kindly and well—for some young people, the best they get anywhere in their lives. Nonetheless, if we're going to talk about discipline and emotional safety in the same breath, then we need to examine some of the habits and traditions that seem to entitle us to say or do things that hurt kids, compromise safety and create additional stress for us and them, behaviors we rationalize by insisting that, in the end, they serve the child's best interests.

Most people approach discipline issues wanting to know "what do I do when . . . ?" They—like much of the literature—equate the word *discipline* with *punishment,* often using the words interchangeably. Although discipline actually means to teach or train, it is far more common, particularly when we use "discipline" as a verb, for the context and connotation to be more punitive and reactive (and certainly less instructive) than this definition would imply. In our current paradigm, discipline is nearly always about responding in some way to a student's negative attitude, misbehavior or mistakes in judgment; most commonly, the responses are negative, and in some cases demeaning, cruel and vindictive. Efforts to improve this aspect of education have rarely gone beyond changes in terminology; the confines of a reactive and power-based model persist. Of all the dimensions of a safe emotional school climate, behavioral issues—and the policies related to them—are often the weakest link. Schools with resources in place to skillfully handle academic and cultural diversity, assure students' physical safety, accommodate a variety of intelligences and learning preferences, support emotional needs and build social competence, can still have difficulty in this area. Even if they get everything else right, if there's a place where the quality of the school climate is threatened or undermined, it's probably going to have something to do with discipline and power dynamics.

Simply put, teachers cannot teach kids who refuse to cooperate with them and little constructive learning will take place in a classroom overrun with disruptive, obnoxious students. However, part of the problem—or perhaps *the* problem—is our reluctance to shift out of a reactive, *what-do-I-do-when* paradigm, a model that keeps us in the precarious position of having to mobilize our efforts to control and disempower every time one of our students does something outside the bounds of what we consider to be acceptable behavior. Our models of win-lose authority relationships are so pervasive and so well entrenched that, perhaps, too, we resist letting go because at times the only available alternative seems to be somewhere in the neighborhood of permissiveness and neglect. But there is a middle ground. As author and speaker Vicki Phillips observes, "I believe we have reached a stalemate in our attempts to deal with at-risk youth in mainstream schools. We fear that too many students are out of control, yet our attempts to regain control simply escalate the crisis." Phillips suggests that it's time to shift to a new paradigm. In twenty-two years as a principal of an alternative high school, she found that the strategies most effective in dealing with difficult students were more therapeutic than punitive, and far more geared to changing behavior than controlling it.[4] In an alternative mind-set, we start thinking of "discipline" in terms of strategies like relationship building, success orientation and developing power dynamics that are more positive and cooperative than authoritarian and disempowering. As with many aspects of education, this approach may appeal to our philosophical and intellectual understanding. But up against the proverbial wall, when we reach for a solution, the win-lose, control model seems to be the one that most often ends up in our grasp.

Traditions of Disempowerment

People changed against their will are of the same opinion still.

proverb[5]

The real difficulty in changing the course of any enterprise lies not in developing new ideas but in escaping old ones.

John Maynard Keynes[6]

I will never forget my fifth-grade social studies teacher throwing a student into the garbage can, or the time my third-grade teacher said that anyone forgetting a math assignment would be made to walk home to get it.

Barbara Muller-Ackerman
elementary-school counselor

The power of the teacher as gatekeeper to success is often wasted and abused in attempts to maintain control.

Juanita Ross Epp[7]

In developmentally healthy humans, the first inklings of a need for autonomy and control emerges at about age two. This need for power—that is, the desire to influence and control our immediate environment—is normal, and it's necessary for eventually becoming independent and functional adults. Few of us would dismiss the importance of a sense of control in our own lives, and most of us understand that kids share this need as well. Now here's where that black-and-white thinking comes in again. If we're in a relationship with people who want power, and we believe that our only options are "winning" at their expense or "losing" in order to accommodate their needs, we've got a problem. With this kind of thinking to guide us, we will either end up putting a lot of our energy into making sure that we've got all the power in the relationship (by disempowering or controlling others) or we will simply give up and let them do whatever they want. But kids also need structure and limits for their sense of security, so either of these choices will leave certain needs unfulfilled.[8]

Of course, there is a middle ground, and the territory between winning and losing is called cooperation, or "win-win." This concept dates back to the 1920s, when educator Mary Parker Follett presented this alternative as a way for business managers to deal with conflicts in a way that attempts to accommodate the underlying needs of everyone involved.[9] One of the hardest ideas to sell to grownups is that win-win power dynamics are absolutely appropriate to authority relationships, and we need not relinquish our authority or power in order to accommodate kids' needs for autonomy. But few of us have had solid models for developing the kind of power structure in which the person in charge uses his or her power authoritatively and assertively—*not* to disempower, but to determine what is and is not negotiable, and within those limits, to encourage others to exercise their autonomy, make choices and experience a sense of control. To some degree, many teachers have moved in this direction academically or during nonconflict times, perhaps by giving kids choices about a topic they wish to investigate, which activity they would like to do (or do first) or where they would like to work. However, for the most part, all a student has to do is get out of line—and in some cases that might mean something as simple as talking, fidgeting or forgetting to bring a pencil—and the shadows of our win-lose legacy begin to emerge.

The notion that we have to make kids lose—that is, to hurt, denigrate or discomfort them in some way in order to change their behavior—has centuries of grim history behind it. If we go back to colonial New England, we know that the school "was not a pleasant place, either physically or psychologically. Great emphasis was placed on the shortness of life, the torments of hell and the fear that one's behavior might not be acceptable for salvation," write historians Pulliam and Van Patten. To keep kids in line, "a whipping post was commonly erected by the school door. Severe floggings were administered for misbehavior or breaking the rules, since Puritan philosophy called for literally beating the Devil out of the child."[10] Despite everything we have since discovered about learning and safety, in many settings, this mind-set has not changed much. "Unfortunately, too many school personnel see punishment as the only recourse in dealing with a student's misbehavior," says an article from a newsletter addressing issues of mental health in schools. "They use the most potent negative consequences available to them in a desperate attempt to control an individual and make it clear to others that acting in such a fashion is not tolerated." This punishment attempts to do something to the student "that he or she does not want done," includes a demand for future compliance and threatens even "harsher punishment if compliance is not forthcoming."[11]

The result is that many students find education to be "a constant struggle between 'them' and 'me' to see who will give in first."[12] Thomas Gordon explains: "When one person tries to control another, you can always expect some kind of reaction from the controllee." He notes that many of the take-charge, show-'em-who's-boss discipline approaches "advocate the use of power-based discipline with no mention of how children react to it. . . . This omission is important, for it implies that all children passively submit to adult demands, perfectly content and secure in an obedient role." Gordon also says that he's never found a shred of evidence to support this presumption.[13] Gazzaniga likewise suggests that problems can arise from our efforts to undermine people's need for power and control in their lives. "All modern experimental work points to how important for good health is the perception that an individual is in charge of his own destiny," he asserts. If we lack this sense of power—or even if we just *believe* that we lack this sense of power—we become susceptible to increased levels of stress.[14]

This stress plays itself out in the classroom, manifesting as an array of behaviors that can include increased negative attitudes toward school and school personnel, increased resistance (defiance, rebelliousness, insubordination or belligerence), retaliating (counterattacking, vandalism or violence) or taking it out on others (bossiness or bullying). Win-lose dynamics can also lead to additional power struggles and contention, temper tantrums, increased rule-breaking, aggression and antisocial behavior. Or students might react by withdrawing, shutting down, fantasizing, daydreaming, giving up, cutting classes or leaving school. For other students, the stress shows up as lying, tattling or blaming, cheating, competing (needing to win, making others lose), depression or illness, or in the apparent comforts of alcohol, food, nicotine, drugs or excessive dieting. And still other children respond to our efforts to control them with behaviors such as dependence, helplessness, submissiveness, fearfulness, people-pleasing, demands for approval or conforming and complying (including later vulnerability to peer pressure).[15] These are hardly the kinds of behaviors we want to encourage in schools. So why do we continue to use powering techniques when the outcomes consistently create the very behaviors we most dislike in children? There are several answers to this obviously rhetorical question. We keep doing what we do because it's what we know best. It's what we grew up with. It's what we continue to see around us, nearly everywhere we look. And because, once again with that black-and-white perspective, we are terrified that if we don't control *them,* they'll end up controlling *us*.

When teachers use reactive, punitive and win-lose methods to control and disempower, even the "good" students, those who aren't singled out (or caught), are affected. One of the teachers I worked with told me about her daughter, who remembered very little from her previous year in second grade other than the names of the "bad kids," which the teacher wrote on the board day after day. While her daughter was never targeted, she would get very upset by the teacher's yelling at the other kids and was often too distracted to concentrate. This kind of atmosphere is not particularly conducive to learning for anyone—unless our objective is to teach apprehension. And when these approaches do seem to work, they do so at great cost. "To me, the worst thing seems to be for a school principally to work with methods of fear, force and artificial authority," observed Albert Einstein. "Such treatment destroys the sound sentiments, the sincerity and self-confidence of the pupil."[16] The truth is, our traditions of disempowerment actually create more problems than they solve. Resentments simmer and sometimes explode, conflicts escalate, power struggles intensify—and so the cycle continues, leaving teachers searching for increasingly forceful ways to gain control.

Zero-Tolerance and Push-Out Strategies

The schools assume built-in motivation, but when it does not occur, they attempt to motivate children with methods analogous to using a gun. Although guns have never worked, the schools, struggling to solve their problems, resort to using bigger and bigger guns—more restrictions and rules, more threats and punishments.

William Glasser[17]

Students who break the rules are not welcome in school.

Juanita Ross Epp[18]

I was always the ringleader of my groups of friends. Instead of reeling me back in, teachers waged a war with me, and I, being stubborn and strong-willed, did not give in. In the end, we all ended up losing.

Cori Jennings
parent educator

Never underestimate the power of a child's need to save face.

middle-school teacher

As we've seen, the window of what is considered to be acceptable can be remarkably narrow in a school setting, and students who have trouble living up to academic, social or behavioral expectations can quickly find themselves on a pretty slippery slide. Many children who are identified as having behavior problems, some as early as kindergarten, experience similar patterns in school. Typically, the relationships with their teachers—undoubtedly the most important ingredient in preventing conflicts and disruptions—is not good. Most describe the impatience, accusations, sarcasm, criticism, insults, threats, contempt and humiliation they withstand from teachers as being remarkably common. Once labeled, these students are often the first ones suspected when anything goes wrong. (One of the teens I interviewed who had served time in a juvenile detention center for his increasingly violent outbursts in school admitted, "I was so tired of them accusing me of stuff I didn't do, I figured I might as well make it worth their while.")

Any students who do not fit the "ideal-student" profile—which generally includes qualities like being reasonably curious, industrious, cooperative, quiet and able to keep up with the rest of the class—are likely to encounter adult reactions intended to squeeze them into that role. Our most common strategies rely on our students' desire to avoid our anger or gain our conditional approval. In terms of achieving our short-term objectives, these strategies may work often enough, especially with some of our younger students, to persuade us to use them over and over again. But as Gordon suggests, the short-term outcomes may belie the costs. At some point, the need to impress peers or protect their dignity is going to come up against their need for teacher approval. And in terms of dealing with our anger and its repercussions, for some kids, the worst we can do to them is far less than what they get at home; confronted with our best threats, many of the children I've worked with just shrug. (And while some may see this observation as a means of justifying increasingly painful, objectionable or distasteful punishments, be assured that escalating our power struggles will, in the end, only make things worse.)

When we find ourselves more and more on the losing end of a win-lose (or, perhaps more appropriately, *no-win*) engagement with a student, at some point, it's going to get awfully tempting to make that student somebody else's problem.[19] Although we will talk mightily about wanting kids to take responsibility for solving their own problems, many of us can hardly resist the urge to send misbehaving students to the office, or rely on parents to correct the behaviors that are bugging or disrupting us. Here, too, there are certainly enough times that the office colludes or the parents take action that once again, we believe we are on the right track. But in the long run, these practices will come back to haunt us. Many teachers, on hearing that these long-sanctioned customs actually undermine their authority, credibility and professionalism, feel a combination of outrage and betrayal. I know I did. Fortunately, there are more effective alternatives. (However, if our thinking continues along the lines of worrying about what to do to the students for punishment *in place of* calling parents or sending them to the principal's office, we're still thinking inside the original win-lose, rules-and-punishment box.)

For many challenging children, the next step in our current system is a special-education placement—often in "behavior-disordered" or similarly named programs. Although certainly not the only reason for a referral, it's often the squeakiest wheels—or the most disruptive students—who are most quickly identified for placement, predominantly on the basis of how they act in class. (Improvements in student behavior that may occur in these classes may be a function of factors such as lower student-teacher ratio, greater structure or continuity, or a better match with the child's academic and learning-style needs.) Children who do not conform to behavioral demands can attract a variety of labels, with ADD and ADHD being perhaps the most common. However, there are those who suggest that many of these kids may not have attention deficits at all. Instead, as Thomas Armstrong argues, the "deficits" are actually in the area of what researcher Russell Barkley calls "rule-governed behavior,"[20] meaning that the children have a lower response (or greater indifference) to the possibility of negative consequences than some adults would like.

As with any procedure in a reactive, rules-and-punishment model, there are increasingly severe levels of displacement, and as students' behavior gets more disruptive, so, too, does the relative exile from the classroom. Students with more serious discipline problems can be suspended for a specific amount of time or barred from school altogether (expulsion). A report from Connecticut's State Department of Education indicated that "nearly 14 percent of public-school students in the state were expelled or suspended from school at least once during the 1998–99 school year." The report also noted that most of the violations "were minor infractions like cutting classes, talking back to teachers or using foul language," but that the numbers also represented "more violent offenses like fighting, making threats or bringing weapons to school." In the previous year, national statistics included more than 3 million suspensions and ninety thousand expulsions, although overall, the percentage of students involved is thought to be 7 percent or less.[21]

By any standards, the numbers are high. And they beg some important questions. For example, what happens to these kids? Do the actions imposed by the school bring them more in line with the behavioral standards we desire? What kind of support was offered to help the young people change the way they acted, or did the schools simply rely on the threat of more time away from school to effect a change? Suspension puts kids who are often already lagging academically even further behind in their classwork. One report claimed that these kids were at greater risk for missing classes and eventually dropping out. More disturbing was the implication that, at least in certain settings, "school officials encourage their departure," meeting with kids, once they start getting in trouble, to suggest that the kids either enroll in the local vocational institute or get a job instead of returning to school.[22] Punitive actions that restrict students' access to school affects large numbers of kids, with ethnic minorities as well as nontraditional learners most at risk.[23] To varying degrees, this practice has been going on for decades and is common enough to be known as a "push-out" policy.[24]

Nonetheless, these punitive practices received a big boost when policymakers started jumping on the zero-tolerance bandwagon. This movement began in 1994 when a number of states adopted federal guidelines that required mandatory expulsion for certain offenses. Originally focused on firearms possession on school property, in many states, this mandate grew "to include possession of drugs and alcohol, as well as a number of other objectionable behaviors." Supporters acclaimed the need "for tough laws to bring a sense of order to our schools."[25] This approach had additional appeal, however, suggesting that the use of by-the-book penalties would, by eliminating discretion, reduce the likelihood of protests and litigation from parents. But, this has not been the case. For, as columnist John Leo observes, "one-size-fits-all punishment merely removes one form of arbitrariness *(Shall we punish him or let him off with a warning?)* with another *(Shall we consider zinc cough drops a drug offense?).*"[26] And even in the absence of discretion, the uniformity supposedly built into these policies is rarely observed. A teacher from an upscale high school told me that one of her students had been suspended when it was discovered that he had been using pictures of his teachers for target practice in his garage. The student was reinstated after his parents showed up with "a bank of lawyers." (Evidently, suspended students whose parents can't afford lawyers tend to *stay* suspended until their penalty is served.) And according to a 1997 report by the Department of Education, despite a call for immediate dismissal, "only 31 percent of all students caught with guns on school property were expelled" during the previous school year. Additionally, "less than half were suspended for more than five days, and less than 20 percent were referred to alternative school programs."[27] Evidently, the value of zero is not absolute.

But that is hardly the issue. Kids whose behaviors range from annoying to dangerous get caught in this dragnet; along with the drugs and weapons violations, students are suspended for quarreling over a magazine, bringing a nail clipper to school, carrying a bottle of Advil or using mouthwash on school grounds.[28] (Is it any wonder that so many kids have so little respect for authority?) Once again, a policy lands in place that allows us to remove students rather than seeing their behavior as a call for interventions that would improve skills, sensitivity, self-control or common sense. From author Frank Blair's assertion that these "results have been moderately successful at best," I'm assuming that the "success" to which he is referring has to do with a slight decrease of these "objectional behaviors" (or perhaps a reduction in the number of student perpetrators) on campus, and not to changes either in the students' behavior or in the dynamics or climate that may have been a factor in students' perceiving these behaviors to be necessary in the first place. Besides, as more than one teen admitted, zero-tolerance policies did little more than challenge them to be more careful about getting caught.

The desire to get the disruptive kids out of the classroom may be entirely understandable, but it removes them from the very environment in which they could be doing some serious learning. Whether in "time out" or in the street, kids gain none of the potential benefits of classroom instruction and positive adult-student interaction. Educator Walter Doyle observes, "There is little evidence that suspension is, by itself, educative. Indeed, suspension denies educative opportunities for precisely those students who need them most." Additionally, Doyle says, "suspension can be inherently rewarding, a vacation from a setting the student is likely to find aversive."[29] (Barring kids from school as a punishment for lateness or truancy defies comprehension.) He goes on to cite one study which showed that schools with low suspension levels "had high levels of community involvement, emphasized instruction rather than control and had a student-centered environment."[30] McPartland and his colleagues acknowledge the fact that "some students are so hostile to authority that they need an alternative setting for their education. But at some point," they advise, our schools "must stop rejecting difficult cases and start finding ways to adapt school to the diverse needs of its students."[31] As schools broaden their picture of what constitutes "ideal students," I wholeheartedly believe we'll see significantly fewer incidents that would inspire the adults to remove kids from school. However, even under the best conditions, we need to think about adding or expanding some of the alternative programs that have been successful in reaching young people who have difficulty functioning in traditional settings. Some schools have had success with alternative programs, including those that offer services such as counseling, rehabilitation, community volunteers, business-mentorship programs, peer support, EQ and social-skills development, and appropriate academic placement and instruction, generally in low teacher-student ratio classes.[32] The untenable alternative, as Frank Blair cautions, results in large numbers of students being "expelled to the streets."[33]

Spare the Rod!

Give into the power of the teacher the fewest possible coercive measures, so that the only source of the pupil's respect for the teacher is the human and intellectual qualities of the latter.

Albert Einstein[34]

Corporal punishment does for childhood what wife beating does for marriage.

Jordan Riak[35]

How are we going to teach our children it is not okay to hurt others when we keep hurting them?

Jane Nelsen, Lynn Lott and Stephen Glenn[36]

The higher the incidence of corporal punishment in a school, the higher the level of vandalism and delinquency.

The National PTA Fact Sheet on Corporal Punishment[37]

During my first year of teaching, the interns who cotaught in the first grade had a student who was frequently referred for hitting and swearing on the playground. The teachers contacted the child's mother to let her know what was going on, and that they were working to correct this problem. Within the hour, the mother walked into the class and before anyone could stop her, reached under her coat and pulled out a long plastic strip from a model-car race track and proceeded to beat her son, swearing at him all the while.

There are so many things wrong with using corporal punishment as a disciplinary technique that it's hard to know exactly where to start. In the United States, this tradition traces its roots back to England—which, interestingly, was the last European country to ban its use in schools, in 1986 (Poland was the first, in 1783). According to an October 1998 report, school corporal punishment is prohibited in every industrialized country in the world except the United States, Canada and one state in Australia. In the United States, twenty-seven states have banned corporal punishment in schools; in ten other states, more than half the students are in districts with no corporal punishment. Nonetheless, during the 1993–94 school year, nearly half a million young people in the United States were subjected to this practice.[38] There is little equity in how this form of punishment is doled out. In the United States, the incidence of school paddlings are highest in the Southern and Southeastern states, while in the Northeast, where many states have outlawed this form of discipline, the frequency is much lower. Further, corporal punishment is more common in elementary and middle school than high school, more widely used in rural schools than on urban campuses, and inflicted more frequently on boys than girls, as well as disadvantaged children, disabled children and ethnic minorities.[39]

Those are the numbers. But behind every statistic is the heart of a child—and the impact of every incident that child has withstood—or witnessed.[40] "Human society has moved away from hitting other human beings. . . . The only beatable person left is the child," says Jordan Riak, director of Parents and Teachers Against Violence in Education.[41] A large and diverse group of professional organizations have come out against corporal punishment, and many have worked actively to abolish its use in families and schools, as the wide-ranging and long-lasting negative outcomes of this outdated practice become more well-known.[42] For all its hurtful potential, perhaps the most logical argument against corporal punishment is the fact that, in terms of achieving any long-lasting, positive outcomes, it simply does not work. The Society for Adolescent Medicine affirms that "physically punishing children has never been shown to enhance moral character development, increase the student's respect for teachers or other authority figures in general, intensify the teacher's control in class or even protect the teacher."[43] Retired principal Sid Leonard agrees: "The same ones kept coming back for more. Hitting children did not seem to improve their behavior. It seemed to be reinforcing the very behaviors I was attempting to eliminate."[44] Child advocate Penelope Leach notes that if corporal punishment worked, "you'd expect that one or two beatings would have been enough to 'teach a lesson' to any child." But, she argues, history tells the opposite story. Looking at "the naughtiest pupils" who supposedly needed physical punishments the most, she affirms that the beatings "did not make them into better pupils who 'needed' it less."[45]

Not only does corporal punishment not change students' behavior for the better, it can actually make it worse. "Physical punishment harms the child physically and emotionally," reports columnist Michael Pastore. "Hitting children increases their hostility and teaches violence. And because hitting creates a frustrated and unhappy child, hitting increases, not decreases, the child's antisocial behavior."[46] One long-term study confirmed that the more hitting children suffered at the beginning of the study period, "the higher the level of antisocial behavior at the end, independent of other traits that can affect such behavior."[47] Then, too, there is the risk of retaliation. Riak compares hitting a child to "pouring gasoline on a fire you want to extinguish."[48] In a report on crime in school in Australia, author Dennis Challinger warns, "Many students no longer accept punishment gracefully, and there is always the risk of a student reacting to violence with violence."[49] Leach cites as "the clearest evidence that physical punishments don't help to produce well-behaved, socialized people," studies of violent criminals and other "notorious individuals" whose childhoods included excessive physical discipline.[50] Many other studies and observations concur, suggesting a high correlation between corporal punishment and increased bullying, disruptions and other violent student behaviors.[51]

Corporal punishment is part of a product-oriented system that obstructs opportunities for children to experience valuable learning processes, like those involved in finding more constructive ways to get their needs met. Leach warns that no matter how calmly, logically or carefully we explain our reasons for hitting, "reason always gets lost in the feelings the punishment produces." Depending on the child's age, feelings can range from amazement and horror to rage and humiliation (which is often taken out on someone or something else). These feelings "leave no room for remorse or determination to do better in the future."[52] Keith and Janie Osborn share concerns about children whose behavior indeed appears to be inhibited by a fear of physical (or other) punishments, but who only comply until the authority turns his or her back. Once the threat of reprisal is removed, there is no internal reason for restraint. Even when this threat inhibits unwanted behavior, in and of itself, it fails to teach or inspire children to make more appropriate choices on their own.[53]

Corporal punishment has been linked to low self-esteem, depression, alcohol abuse, suicide and adult violence.[54] In schools, it contradicts our goal of connecting and creating community, and it significantly undermines emotional safety and a child's enthusiasm for learning.[55] (In addition to compromising emotional safety, the fact that, during the 1986–87 school year, somewhere between ten thousand and twenty thousand students in the United States required medical treatment as a result of school corporal punishment makes this a concern for children's physical safety, as well.[56]) Studies also show that corporal punishment has a negative impact on a child's intelligence. Researcher Murray Straus observed that while children who were hit "didn't get dumber," they did fall behind the average rate of cognitive development. He attributes the impact on intelligence to the fact that parents who did not hit tended to use more verbal interaction and cognitive stimulation in dealing with their children.[57] Corporal punishment has also been shown to aversely affect school achievement. By the same token, children raised without corporal punishment are more likely to complete a higher education and reap greater job benefits as adults.[58]

People argue the need for corporal punishment as a way for teachers to protect themselves, but using physical force to protect oneself or others from harm, to gain control of a weapon or protect property is not considered corporal punishment, and few, if any, would dispute the value of physical intervention in some survival situations. When we're talking about corporal punishment, whether we refer to it as part of a system of violent childrearing or, more euphemistically, as a spanking or a "swat," we're talking about the intentional use of physical force designed to cause a child physical pain, but not injury, ostensibly to correct or control the child's behavior.[59] And while its value is also professed as a "last resort" in favor of preserving order, evidence indicates that corporal punishment is often a *first* response, even for minor infractions, and that at worst, in schools where this practice is abolished, behavior remains about the same. (In fact, when more positive alternatives are invoked, there is usually a significant decrease in disruptive student behavior.)[60] But there is cause for hope. When Sweden became the first country to outlaw corporal punishment of children—not only in schools, but at home as well—Pastore reports that adults found "gentler and wiser ways to work with their children." In fact, in countries in which corporal punishment has been banned, a shift in thinking seems to have occurred, as well. Instead of seeing this practice as a normal, accepted method of teaching or parenting, adults who resort to physical punishments are widely thought to lack competence and skill in dealing with children, and seen as people in need of help.[61]

The bottom line will always come down to our intention: If our goal is to teach responsibility and self-control, build community and raise kids to be respectful, considerate citizens, we will choose different behaviors than we would if our goals included exacting revenge, causing pain or disempowering children. If our goals are positive, corporal punishment will not be among the intervention strategies we select, no matter how well-supported by tradition they may be. "Good school discipline should be instilled through the mind, not the behind," says president of the National Coalition to Abolish Corporal Punishment, Robert E. Fathman.[62] The sheer hypocrisy of using violence to try to teach respect, self-control or nonviolence should, in itself, stop us in our tracks. For it makes absolutely no sense for us to raise our hand to a child—much less a strap or a paddle—and then bemoan the rise of violence and antisocial behavior in our schools and communities. Hitting kids sacrifices values and long-term outcomes for an occasional short-lived victory. It makes us look weak, ineffective, unskilled and unprofessional. Cut it out. There is a better way.

A Discipline Paradigm for the New Millennium

Compassion and respect do not imply lack of firmness.

Nathaniel Branden[63]

If the system held people accountable for their behavior and taught personal responsibility, safety would be a secondary issue.

Lynn Collins
educator

Children need to learn to take care of their own behavior for themselves, not to please, placate or be rewarded by others.

Jean Illsley Clarke[64]

With young people, the most effective [discipline] strategy is to connect with them. Establish a relationship with them.

Marvin Marshall[65]

Children learn what is and what is not worthwhile to them and behave accordingly.

Janice T. Gibson[66]

When we look at our current systems for dealing with student behavior, our main problem is not that we haven't come up with harsh-enough punishments. It's more that the punitive, win-lose paradigm itself is ultimately destructive and stress-producing. Win-lose approaches end up undermining our goals and intentions—especially when these include creating community, emotional safety and opportunities for students to learn and grow from the choices they make. In a win-lose, penalty-based system, when students get caught doing something we don't want them to do (or refuse to do something we ask them to do), a penalty is imposed. Time is served, and the kids are free to do it again—until the next time they get caught.[67] The ultimate challenge in this paradigm is coming up with negative consequences that are more unpleasant than whatever satisfaction, power or other positive outcomes our students gain by their defiance. The whole system is antagonistic, pitting "us" against "them" in a battle of wits and wills. Where do we find community or collaboration in a model like this?

Parent educator Cori Jennings reports, "If my teachers could have realized my strong leadership qualities rather than trying to stifle them, they could have used them to their advantage." Educational consultant Joseph Ciaccio agrees. He recommends a "total positive response," shifting out of the admittedly more familiar punitive and reactive system to dealing with student misbehavior in positive ways. Combine this mindset with a willingness to demonstrate caring and total acceptance, particularly to difficult students, and he has seen evidence that referrals for misbehaviors will definitely drop off. "The most disruptive student could become one of your best pupils," he asserts.[68] When we can conceptualize being on the same side of the fence as our students, a number of win-win possibilities open up. In the meantime, we seem to be asking the wrong questions. "Tougher penalties for violent crime is not a deterrent," says Vicky Tyler. As evidence, she notes that in 1980 there were half a million people jailed in the United States, but despite stronger penalties and a major crackdown on crime in the decade that followed, there were twice as many people in jail ten years later.[69] Clearly, the solution has nothing to do with how we fight or punish these behaviors, or how we better control kids. We need a whole new way to think about our relationships with students and the kinds of power dynamics that can effectively get us what we want, one that will leave no casualties in its wake.

Imagine, for example, that I'm a student whose teacher is committed to eliminating as many obstacles to my sense of safety as possible. He's gotten to know me, personally and academically, establishing a connection right off the bat. I know he cares, that he's interested in my success and who I am as a person. He challenges me continually, setting hurdles that are appropriate for my level of skill, pushing me to grow, but at a place where success is within my grasp. He makes accommodations for things I need to know but somehow missed along the way. He models the behaviors he wants from me—talking to me respectfully, being on time, keeping his work area neat, controlling himself, even when he's upset. He doesn't have a lot of rules, but he does make a lot of requests, and his directions and boundaries are pretty clear.

When he asks for something, it's always stated in a positive way—not as a command or a threat. He never insults, demeans, yells or shames his students, no matter what we do. We laugh and have fun, but we listen, too. When I make a mistake, he shows me how to do it right, or gives me a chance to figure it out. He uses a variety of teaching strategies so I almost never have a chance to get bored. He gives me choices about my learning, and makes it possible for me to explore things that interest me in a way I like to learn. He's given me access to a great deal of freedom, power, dignity and success, all within a structure that helps me feel secure without feeling smothered. Clearly, I am not afraid here, but I would never deliberately cross the line. Why in the world would I disrupt, rebel, talk back, skip school or drop out of a class like this? After all, look what's in it for me to show up and cooperate. *What keeps me in line is having so little to fight against.*

Yes, Virginia, there *are* teachers like this, and perhaps there always have been.[70] Do they ever have problems with a kid? Of course. But in walking that fine line between an authoritarian approach and a permissive one, this kind of "win-win" teacher gets to avoid a whole lot of conflicts other teachers repeatedly endure. At the core, always, is our connection with the students, that fragile thread between our hearts and theirs. As one teacher from an alternative program in inner-city Los Angeles describes, simple acts of caring and respect can have far more power in them than any punishment. She tells how she greets kids on the first day of school by shaking hands, smiling and telling them how glad she is that they're going to be in her room. "If there was only one thing I could depend on, it would be relationships," she admits. "All the kids I work with are bigger and tougher than I am, so I can't threaten them with anything. They're not scared of anybody. So I have to rely on getting them to fall in love with me."[71]

When I work with teachers who are having discipline problems, the short answer to their dilemma is this: Change the relationship. Change the paradigm. Positive alternatives exist, and once we're willing to climb out of the confines of our power-based, win-lose traditions, an array of proactive, win-win and peace-promoting options suddenly becomes available. In suggesting this route, I do not for a second wish to imply that making the kinds of changes that result in fewer acts of disrespect, disruption or other forms of verbal or physical violence is going to emerge from some simplistic formula, or that under the best of circumstances, they will happen overnight. There is no quick fix here. These are process changes and they require time, faith and energy, as any significant shift in thinking will. But safety at the level of student behavior is crucial to the emotional climate of a school, and creating the kind of environment and power dynamics that inspires cooperation and a sense of community at the expense of conflict and hostility is certainly a worthwhile investment.

The Win-Win Classroom

The following teacher behaviors all play an important role in redefining how we interact with students, and each makes an important contribution to an emotionally safe climate.[72]

Establish a Win-Win Power Structure. Kids have power within limits. Control comes from students' self-management—not teacher's power. Make choices available; invite student input, opinions. Requires trust and faith in students' ability to self-manage. This approach values responsibility, collaboration, finding solutions and respecting one another's point of view. Primary question: *How can we* all *get what we want—without creating a problem for anyone in the process?*[73]

Deglamorize Obedience. If obedience was critical to the success of an industrial economy, information-age demands for initiative and critical thinking render it a liability. Inspire cooperation instead. (Cooperation does not rely on fear of punishment or disapproval.) Motivating cooperation builds commitment, engagement and resistance to peer pressure without compromising safety or putting the teacher-student relationship at risk.[74]

Respect the Students' Need for Dignity. Humiliation breeds anger; potential for escalated conflict or retaliation, or being turned inward, with self-destructive consequences. Avoid aggressive, intimidating, invasive or threatening gestures or words. Address problems in private. Inspire a sense of conscience (healthy guilt) and responsibility without embarrassing or implying inadequacy, defectiveness or low worth (shame). Allow leadership opportunities for all.[75]

Make the Connection. "The idea that you don't smile until Christmas is founded in folklore, not research," advise Rogers and Frieberg. Express a genuine interest—notice, value, acknowledge—without an agenda. This also means being human, sharing who we are. Develop a supportive, mutually respectful relationship. Obliterate that divisive sense of "us" and "them," and allow for everyone to be on the same side, working toward shared goals.[76]

Make Success Possible for Everyone. Eliminate discipline problems that arise when kids see no point in making a positive effort or behaving in class because they're going to fail anyway. Identify what they know and what they need and teach accordingly.

Stimulate and engage, conquer boredom and despair. Appeal to different modalities, preferences and intelligences. Reduce the threat of failure. Also build social skills and problem-solving capabilities as needed.

Eliminate Double Standards. "Walk the talk" that puts us on the same footing as our students. Act the way we want our students to act, model the values we would like them to adopt, use the words and tone we find acceptable from them, apologize when we blow it and respect the fact that they are driven by similar needs (power, structure, acceptance, fun, success, positive outcomes, etc.) as those that motivate us. Use care in picking battles. Ask: *Would this be a problem if another adult did it?*[77]

Set and Maintain Clear Boundaries. Reframe rules as boundaries that are clear, proactive, stated positively and designed to accommodate both teacher and student needs (win-win). Focus on positive outcomes. Give clear directions; make policies specific. Avoid warnings, excuses or delayed follow-through. If necessary, build in flexibility beforehand (requiring, say, thirty-seven out of forty homework assignments, allotting one "Get out of Jail FREE" card per student each quarter).[78]

Keep Consequences Positive. Shift thinking: Consequences are the *good* things we get or get to do as a result of cooperation. Use promises instead of threats to minimize resistance and place responsibility on students without undermining the quality of the relationship. Observe or interview students to determine a variety of meaningful positive consequences. Make as many of these options available to students to give them a stake in participating and cooperating. Eliminate and discourage reactive policies and punitive thinking; eliminate and discourage corporal punishment.[79]

Follow Through! Allow positive consequences only as long as (or as soon as) kids cooperate or come through on their end. Withdraw privileges or positive consequences immediately, until behavior changes or until a later time—no discussion, no warnings, no excuses. Hold kids accountable without shaming or punishing. (You break it, you fix it.) When appropriate, ask for a plan (how they'll handle it differently next time). Leave door open for self-correction.[80]

Depersonalize Conflicts. See conflicts as "problems to be solved, not battles to be won." Defuse potential conflicts before they have a chance to escalate. Watch the need to win or be right. Try not to be shocked or impressed by attention-getting behavior. Don't jump to conclusions about students' intentions. Avoid taking misbehavior personally. Stay calm, disengage and physically separate, if necessary. Learn to manage your anger.[81]

Focus on the Positive. Kids like school better when their teachers are positive. Acknowledge cooperation, progress, effort and achievement, using recognition statements. Avoid praise. Instead of judging, *describe* what you see and *tell* students how their choices pay off for them. *(I see you put the game away. Now you can go to the library.)* Allow positive consequences, when earned, as reinforcers. Call parents with good reports; regularly send home "good notes."[82]

Keep Kids in School Where They Can Learn to Do Better. To reduce gang violence and "turn an unsafe campus around," one school stopped expelling kids and put their energy into understanding and connecting with the street culture and offering special classes and job-placement assistance. Many students need far more than academic instruction. Develop resources and programs to support nontraditional learners and other kids "on the edge."[83]

Quit Judging Teachers by How Quietly Their Students Can Sit. As long as teachers feel a tremendous pressure to minimize the interaction, movement and noise in their classrooms, we're going to have struggles in the classroom that will not only result in a loss of potential academic growth, but an increase in kids being labeled, medicated or restricted, and an increase in stress for everyone concerned.

18

Physical Safety: The Student Body

For years, we've treated the mind and the body as if they were two different entities. Relative to physical location, perhaps, they are, but in other ways, they're not separate entities at all.

Eric Jensen[1]

Teenagers who want to sleep all day are not lazy; they are simply following the dictates of their biological clocks.

Shannon Brownlee[2]

We are all "learning-blocked" to the extent that we have learned not to move.

Paul Dennison and Gail Dennison[3]

A little bit stressed is like a little bit pregnant.

Sharon Promislow[4]

No picture of an emotionally safe school would be complete without some attention to the various factors that affect students physically. Anything that has an impact on kids' bodies can ultimately translate to the emotional climate of the classroom, as many of these factors directly affect the students' behavior, attitude and ability to learn. Still, our best efforts at improvement and reform tend to focus more on the intellectual, emotional and social aspects of our students' existence; the needs and responses of their actual bodies are often overlooked or ignored.[5]

In a recent full-day training, before one of the breaks, I announced that we'd be doing a brief writing activity when we returned. In preparation, I asked everyone to take a good, long drink of water, especially if they'd been drinking coffee, tea, soda or juice, as these actually dehydrate the body. This seemed like a strange request to many of the participants; however, drinking water is a cheap, brain-friendly trick that can actually improve behavior and academic performance. Most of us don't make this connection—it's just water, something we drink when we're thirsty, right? Sure, but there's more to it than that. (Especially because, if we're dehydrated enough, we tend to not even realize how thirsty our bodies actually are!) Water is what makes it possible for the brain and body to communicate. It helps the cells throughout our bodies maintain the electrical balance they need for nerves and muscles to function at optimal levels.

Normally we require about ten ounces of water for every thirty pounds of body weight each day, even more after caffeine, sugar or alcohol intake, while working at a computer, after exercise or when we're under stress. With adequate water intake comes many benefits. Water gives our brains an instant boost. It strengthens our immune system, gets rid of toxins, and protects against the effects of electromagnetic fields in the environment. It aids digestion and may reduce some headaches associated with dehydration. And adequate hydration improves academic skills. It significantly increases oxygen absorption in the blood, which improves brain functioning, and it reduces the stress response and agitation that can come when we're running dry. As water balances cellular polarity, we have more energy, increased alertness, better mental and physical coordination, and a greater ability to focus, concentrate and screen out irrelevant stimuli. Many people recommend drinking water before and during a test (or other situations in which performance is important).

Physical, psychological and environmental stress dehydrates our bodies. This decreases the functioning of our nervous system, which in turn can negatively affect behavior and performance. All of these benefits make good arguments not only for making schools emotionally safe to reduce the stress that can interfere with learning, but also for encouraging water-drinking throughout the school day to counter the stresses kids do experience.[6] The problem is, for most kids, when it comes to drinking water, school can be a very restrictive environment. (One of my sharpest memories includes my third-grade teacher reading us a story about a deer taking a drink of water at a cold, clear forest stream, as we sat in class on a hot, muggy day toward the end of the year. I was always a big water drinker and was painfully thirsty on this particular day, as were many of my classmates. Yet our requests to get a drink were repeatedly denied; we had an hour to go until lunch. It was one of the longest hours of my life.)

Fortunately, this tradition seems to be gradually losing ground, at least in some settings. Over the past couple of years, I have met teachers who have fountains or a sink in their rooms, invite kids to bring water bottles to class or have an open hall pass to be used as needed. When I offered this latter option to my students—with the concomitant obligation not to create a problem for anyone while they were leaving or out of the room—the first week or two were, predictably, rather chaotic, with a steady stream of kids coming and going. This is a major worry for teachers and administrators alike. (The kidneys take about a week to adjust to increased water intake.) But this was a prized "freedom," one the students were loath to jeopardize; it didn't take them long to figure out how to manage this routine responsibly. Overall, it served us all well. I didn't have to deal with nonstop interruptions from kids begging permission to leave the room, and after the initial fascination wore off, for most kids, just knowing they could leave at practically any time while they were in my class gave them enough security and power to not need to do so any more than necessary. (This went for bathroom use, as well.)

Having their most basic physiological needs accommodated is not a given for all children. In a recent e-mail, one mom told me about her seven-year-old son, whose second-grade class has between ten and fifteen minutes to line up for lunch, be seated and served, and quickly eat before being marched out to make room for the next bunch of students. Many of the children didn't have time to finish their meal. Even more troubling was the fact that they were then denied bathroom privileges unless they are willing to "trade in" five of their ten minutes of recess. "I feel that the basic rights of the children are being neglected," she wrote. She is not alone. I've heard dozens of stories from parents whose children are currently enduring problems in this area, and from adults who still carry the scars of bathroom-related traumas in school, from having to publicly report whether they had to go "number one" or "number two," to "messing themselves" in front of classmates when they were denied access to the toilet. "We had to put our hands up and ask. It wasn't unusual to be told to wait, or to be told off because you hadn't gone at playtime," wrote family therapist June Buchanan. "Children sometimes wet themselves. I don't think I did, but would sit holding on uncomfortably, more in fear of humiliating myself than able to relax and listen to what the teacher was saying." How much learning could possibly be going on when a student is consumed with having to go or the fear of being denied?

"The external control of another person's bodily functions is viewed as a human rights violation in the case of adults, but as an acceptable management tool in the case of children," writes Laurie Couture.[7] Indeed, few adults would tolerate having to recite the names of the presidents before being allowed to use the toilet or being restricted to three "emergencies" a week. Here, too, we have a tradition based on the fear of inevitable chaos, or that belief that "if one goes, they all go." (This is so well-entrenched that I've even had adult students in my classes who suffered under the assumption that I would "get mad" if they got up to take care of personal needs in between the breaks.) But while restricted or rigid schedules may accommodate "the caretakers' convenience or their need to assert power and control," they also present the risk of physical and psychological consequences that could be avoided.[8] Stress at this level will certainly take its toll on the students' sense of safety and the kind of learning that goes on. It is possible to work with a large group of children and allow them to self-manage these needs without losing control or inviting continuous disruptions. Perhaps we need more trust and respect than we've been willing to extend to our students, along with some discussion of what could be considered disruptive or problematic in order to make this work. But remember, in a win-win classroom, we rarely see kids using bathroom or water-fountain issues as a way to gain power or attention. I've been in many, many classrooms in which students took advantage of their rights to "go" when they felt the need, without creating a problem in or out of the classroom. In fact, in most of these classes, the students—even young ones—were quite respectful of the teacher's presentation and typically waited until the lesson or instructions were finished before getting up to take the pass.

Docking kids' recess time in exchange for a trip to the water fountain or bathroom is only likely to make things worse. With all due respect to the incredible pressure we all feel to get through the content in our curricular mandates, the "heads" into which we try to cram so much information are, in fact, connected to bodies that need far more movement than we typically allow. One of the important considerations here is the brain's need for oxygen. Although the brain makes up only 2 percent of the body's weight, it uses one-fifth of all the oxygen our bodies take in. (The distribution of oxygen to the cells is aided by the water we drink.) The brain needs oxygen to break down the food we eat and generate the electrical currents necessary to send messages throughout our nervous systems. Exercise and deep breathing help oxygenate the blood. Even a good yawn can increase circulation and oxidation, help detoxify the system, moisten dry, stressed eyes and relax the body. Movement, particularly aerobic activity, increases oxygen intake critical to learning. But more than half of all schoolchildren don't get the exercise necessary to keep their hearts and lungs healthy. Sitting still at a desk or table for long periods of time doesn't help. This common pattern gives kids few opportunities to get high levels of oxygen into their blood, can negatively impact levels of brain activation and attentiveness, and for some students can result in increased fidgeting in an effort to keep themselves alert. Sadly, the kids who need movement the most are typically the kids for whom recess—or even movement within the classroom itself—is most restricted. Some simple changes, like allowing kids to change seats after a while and varying instruction and activity levels throughout the class period can make a great difference in motivation and performance. Throw in a few live plants, and you've not only got a way to clean the air and add oxygen to the environment, but a means of also increasing negative ionization, which improves air quality and can improve alertness. Besides, plants can add warmth and welcome to the classroom's ambience. (For teachers who don't have much luck keeping plants alive, there's probably a student with a green thumb in every class who would be more than willing to take on this responsibility.)[9]

Time is another factor that affects students' learning and behavior. Throughout their entire school career, our students' brains are growing and developing in spurts and stages. Until certain regions in the brain develop, certain skills may be difficult, if not impossible to master. For example, the gestalt (right) hemisphere goes through a growth spurt between ages four and seven, followed by elaboration in the logic (left) hemisphere between seven and nine. When kids start kindergarten, they are certainly ready to learn, and the best and most natural way for them to do so "is through image, emotion and spontaneous movement," which can capitalize on their large vocabularies and wonderful imaginations. But instead, Hannaford notes, "We do just the opposite. We teach children to sit still, learn letters and numbers in a linear fashion . . . and read books with simplistic vocabulary, no emotion and few images." Even the use of printing at this age is highly linear, something easier to grasp once the development of the logic hemisphere kicks into gear, and five-year-olds typically find it much more natural to use cursive script.[10] Likewise, it's easy to look at a teenager and expect certain levels of functionality and judgment. Yet inside those increasingly adultlike bodies are brains that are still in "in some ways, closer to a child's brain than an adult's." It may be a while before their brains develop the more adult capacities for handling ambiguous information and making decisions, accurately assessing risk in various situations, modulating emotional responses or even interpreting facial and nonverbal information reliably.[11] Do our behavioral expectations and instructional requirements account for their developmental capabilities?

Our energy runs in cycles, in various rhythmic patterns, which results in changes in our memory, mental functioning, intellectual performance and mood throughout the day. The implications for instruction, assessment and our constant demand for students' attention are significant. There are also major implications for administrators who often "judge the quality of learning by how much attention" a teacher can sustain, instead of focusing on learning, acquisition and meaning.[12] Kids will also show preferences for certain times of the day (like my reading group who, much like their teacher, was far more functional and alert later in the day than first thing in the morning).

Kids go through changes in their body clocks, particularly during the teen years. Between ages twelve and twenty-two, there is a "biological preference for later bedtime and waking hours."[13] Research shows that teens need more sleep than they did when they were younger, "and their biological clocks tell them to catch those extra winks in the morning." According to sleep physiologist Mary Carskadon, most teens need nine and a quarter hours of sleep a night, with their brains, generally speaking, not ready to wake up until eight or nine in the morning.[14] (Many kids have a hard time getting anywhere near this much sleep, in part, because of jobs or internships, homework, sports or youth group commitments, babysitting, social activities or stress in general.[15]) In response to these findings, a number of districts around the United States have changed their school schedules to accommodate teens' needs for a later start time. For example, at the beginning of the 1999–2000 school year, all of the high schools in Brownsville, Texas, modified their opening bell from 7:20 until 8:45. According to instructional facilitator Betsy Sheets, despite the initial resistance to change (and the need for several of the kids to adjust their after-school work schedules), when we spoke four months into the semester, things seemed to be going smoothly. As a final time consideration, moving to a year-round schedule offers among its benefits a lower impairment of memory and retention, which is weakened far more by a three-month break than by shorter intervals.[16]

Things That Go Bump in the Environment

We humans are not simply machines; we are mental, emotional, spiritual as well as biochemical and physical beings. A blow to any of these levels impacts the equilibrium of our whole.

Sharon Promislow[17]

Why didn't anyone understand? I was working hard! I was trying my best. But a classroom of thirty felt like one with three hundred. The lights bothered me. The gymnasium violently hurt my ears. Trying to learn something new in this environment drained the life out of me. I tried to concentrate but was usually too exhausted.

Mike Selby
author

Light: God's first creation.

Francis Bacon[18]

As of 1998, the average public-school building in the United States was forty-two years old, with the oldest schools in communities serving higher proportions of kids living in poverty. Only about a quarter of all public schools were built after 1969; slightly more than that before 1950. According to one study, much equipment needs to be replaced in schools twenty to thirty years old. Add on another ten years and the roof and electrical equipment need updating. "After forty years, a school building begins rapid deterioration, and after sixty years, most schools are abandoned." Nearly a third of the schools in the country are considered to be in the "oldest" condition; that is, they were built before 1970 and either never renovated or renovated prior to 1980.[19] However, older schools do not necessarily mean more dangerous environments. In fact, some of the more unhealthy buildings are those tightly sealed "energy efficient" structures built since the early 1970s. (One report cites the American Lung Association's estimation that "as many as 20 percent of the country's schools are troubled with poor indoor air quality and even more have inadequate ventilation systems."[20])

But many schools present environmental hazards, and sometimes, work done to rehabilitate older buildings can involve products, substances and procedures that create problems. In fact, in 1995, the National Education Association published a handbook on fighting the "Sick Building Syndrome" and eliminating environmental hazards around the school. Using the combined expertise of environmental scientists, physicians, engineers, psychologists, educators and advocates, the handbook addresses such issues as indoor air quality, cleaning substances, floor coverings, radon and asbestos, classroom lighting, electromagnetic fields, pest management, lead poisoning, mold and formaldehyde, all of which can have an impact on the health and behavior of the individuals in the building. In addition to affecting learning, many of these factors "are believed to be responsible for illness in many sensitive students and staff."[21]

Environmental risk factors are of particular concern to kids and adults with certain allergies, asthma or chemical sensitivities. Within the United States and Canada, these individuals represent about 30 percent of the general population.[22] Regardless of outdoor air pollution, for these individuals, the air *inside* the school can be a source of a variety of problems, including "headaches, nausea, respiratory problems, allergic reactions, irritability, mental confusion, distractibility and aggressive behavior."[23] While environment-friendly building products and techniques currently exist, availability and cost have sometimes obstructed their widespread use, although this, too, seems to be changing significantly.[24] In some cases, schools have averted problems by not allowing buses to idle near intake vents or by collecting dirt and pollen in floor mats in building entrances, using the least toxic substances for pest control, painting or roofing during school breaks, and drying wet carpets quickly or eliminating them altogether to avoid the chemicals in the glues or in the carpets themselves.[25] Air conditioning—which is commonly funded for prisons but not for schools—can help alleviate indoor air pollution, protect equipment and make the learning environment more comfortable for everyone.[26] Even replacing scented school supplies and traditional markers, which contain keotone and acetates, with less irritating products can be a boon for some kids and adults.[27]

Another environmental factor is the quality of light in a school. Light can indeed have an impact on kids' health and learning. In fact, some schools have gone as far as removing the conventional fluorescent lighting in their buildings altogether, replacing them with full-spectrum lighting instead. These bulbs come close to duplicating the light rays from the sun, while conventional fluorescent bulbs provide only a portion of the wavelengths and lack the benefits natural daylight has to offer. Follow-up studies on the students in these classrooms showed some impressive results. In various settings, students under full-spectrum fluorescent lamps showed significant improvements in attendance, higher test scores, and improvements in achievement, growth and development. Another school saw a reduction in eyestrain, depression and illness, and yet another noted that the lights had a calming effect on otherwise hyperactive children (whose learning skills improved under full-spectrum lighting). There were even fewer dental cavities among students in a full-spectrum lighting environment, possibly because the ultraviolet rays help our bodies absorb vitamin D, which is necessary for the absorption of calcium. The change in lighting, according to one principal, "changed the whole atmosphere throughout our school."[28] Other research showed that students in natural or nonfluorescent light had "fewer visual problems, less fatigue, fewer posture problems and increased academic achievement."[29] None of this surprises me, perhaps because I'm pretty light-sensitive myself. I've been in many schools in which several, if not most, of the rooms had very limited natural light. (Many of the trainings I do are in auditoriums or hotel conference rooms that get absolutely no natural light. If I don't get some sun on my face periodically throughout the day, I am exhausted and nearly incoherent by the end of the training.) If the architecture doesn't let the sunshine in, full-spectrum bulbs seem to hold great promise as an alternative.

School-bus safety was another issue. According to the National Highway Traffic Safety Board, in 1999, 23 million children rode buses to school. Almost all buses lack seat belts; however, there is some argument against the 1960s technology in lap belts and that in an accident, they could actually cause pelvic injuries. However, others argue that some of the children who have been killed or injured in school bus accidents might well have been saved or protected by a lap belt. Nonetheless, the NHTSB is looking into the overall design, which might call for more padding in the seats and a stronger structural design.[30] Several of the parents and students I interviewed also mentioned school buses as a problem; however, the majority of their complaints focused more on kids being mistreated by other kids on the bus or severe overcrowding (three or four high school students to a seat, according to several students from one school).

Noise can also be an issue for some auditory-sensitive kids. Armstrong cites a study in which "students at an elementary school situated near Los Angeles International Airport had more difficulty solving math problems and tended to give up sooner on learning tasks than control groups because of airplane noises." A number of educators suggest that music in the learning environment can improve learning and retention. One method of accelerated instruction, developed by Georgi Lozanov, uses music to relax learners into an optimum state for learning, and presents and reviews new information against a background of music.[31] Music can also increase attention and time on task. I saw work production nearly double in my own classroom when listening to music during certain activities was an option, and many teachers swear by its motivational potential, as well. Armstrong also noticed that many hyperactive kids who had trouble attending to words had no trouble attending to music. "In fact . . . for some of these kids, music serves as a real asset in helping to calm and focus them during study periods." Interestingly, although most educators assume that only quiet or classical music is appropriate in a classroom, this may not be the case. Although various classical pieces can be effective to reduce hyperactivity, control anger or promote relaxation, Armstrong cites research which indicates that kids labeled as ADHD showed a significant decrease in motor activity when they listened to rock music through individual headsets.[32]

As we get increasingly "wired" with electric and electronic equipment in our homes and schools, there is an increased risk from the electromagnetic fields these appliances produce.[33] Of these, television presents a number of issues worth examining. Most children spend more time watching TV during their elementary school years—about five thousand hours—than they actually spend in their classrooms. During this time, the average student will have seen eight thousand murders and one hundred thousand acts of violence, including content from children's programs; they have also watched more than twenty thousand commercials a year. And while some see the potential for television to be "a wonderful resource to expand children's worlds, bringing them people and places they will otherwise never see, enriching their vocabularies and introducing complex ideas,"[34] it can also have a negative impact on body, mind and values. Both TV and video games present rapidly changing stimuli and high-contrast images to maintain attention. "Our brains are very sensitive to quick movements, sudden noises and color changes that might signal danger," says Hannaford, "so we prepare for fight or flight to protect ourselves. . . . Because there is a natural physical reaction to danger and there is no outlet for the impulse when watching TV, the watcher may develop overactivity, frustration or irritability that can affect other areas of his life."[35]

Although it activates a survival response, television can, in the long run, actually reduce our natural vigilance and instinctive reaction to danger. Research suggests a connection to shortened attention spans, and educator Jane Healy reports a reduced ability "to remain actively focused on events taking place in the real world." She also connects television watching with increased aggression and violent behavior. Social critic Jerry Mander is among many concerned with the fact that TV takes kids away from "activities that are more active, multisensory, and intellectually, socially and emotionally nourishing."[36] Hannaford agrees. TV viewing is passive and lacks the "internal mental, emotional and physical involvement necessary for cognitive development," she claims. It does little to develop imagination or creative reasoning.[37] Donovan and Iovino cite three "subtle but nevertheless devastating threats to the genius of students" that can come from "the vast majority of TV, video and Internet fare that kids are exposed to, including stereotypical images, insipid language and mediocre content."[38] And recent studies report decreases in grade-school kids' verbal and physical aggression when the students participated in a program that reduced their viewing.[39]

Bedtime television viewing can be a stimulant for some kids, and children who watch a lot of television, "especially at bedtime or on a TV set in their bedroom, are more likely to resist going to bed, have trouble sleeping or wake up more" during the night. The American Academy of Pediatrics notes the connection between television watching and kids tending to be overweight from a lack of physical activity, as well as increases in violent and sexually active behavior. They recommend no television at all for children under two years of age and urge in favor of the feedback and socialization gained from one-on-one interactions, which children can't get from TV.[40] (Healy and others go one step further, recommending a ban on TV viewing for children under eight.[41]) A large number of authorities recommend strict limits on TV viewing for kids—generally two hours a day or less, especially during weekdays—and keeping televisions out of kids' bedrooms. They urge parents to become involved in their children's viewing by monitoring what they watch, looking for good programming, watching together and talking about the content, helping kids distinguish between what's real and make-believe and using TV to teach. They also encourage a variety of alternative, TV-free activities.[42] There are cautions against leaving the television on all the time, as well, as studies suggest that background television can interfere with kids' abilities to perform challenging cognitive tasks, and that kids who routinely combine homework, reading and other intellectually demanding activities with television are likely to be missing out on the benefits of the work they're doing while the TV is on.[43] (Although computers don't take nearly as much heat as television, there is some concern for the possibility of muscle strain and eyestrain, repetitive stress injuries, obesity and a distraction from social interactions.[44]) All in all, the issue here is a call to a greater degree of consciousness and mindfulness in our use of television, finding ways to reap the benefits it may have to offer without allowing it any more of a presence in our lives than is good for us all—grownups and kids alike.

Yummy, Yummy, Yummy, Is There Food in Your Tummy?

In spite of the substantial evidence to the contrary, several prominent public and private health organizations—and researchers themselves—have ignored, downplayed or dismissed any relationship between diet and children's behavior.

Michael F. Jacobson and David Schardt[45]

The diets of children with learning difficulties are often deficient in proteins.

Carla Hannaford[46]

Many who readily accept the link between diet and heart disease, or other chronic physical conditions find it hard to imagine that nutrition could have a direct and determining effect on human behavior and personality dysfunctions.

Joseph D. Beasley and Jerry J. Swift[47]

So what's wrong with a bit of petrol in your popsicle?

from an article on artificial coloring in foods[48]

Much of what I first learned about the impact of diet on learning and behavior came from firsthand observations, taught to me by fourth-graders who came to school eating the powder used to make sugary drinks, their fingers and mouths stained bright purple or orange or green or red. It was what I learned from kids who ate even less than that and couldn't keep their heads up by 10:00 in the morning. It was the frustration I experienced every time I tried to do anything remotely challenging in the afternoons on "cupcake day." Various studies—along with the observations of other educators and many parents—confirmed my experience. "Research shows that school-age breakfast skippers often feel tired, irritable or restless in the morning," writes columnist Teresa Farney, "but those who regularly eat a morning meal have a better attitude toward school and more energy by late morning." Hungry kids can exhibit symptoms of depression, anxiety, irritability or hyperactivity; they have trouble thinking clearly and are more prone to fatigue or complaints of tummy aches and dizziness.[49] And when kids do eat, the quality of their diet often makes learning and behaving in school even more of a challenge.

Physician Joseph Lancaster is amazed at how well some teachers do with kids who are "physiologically unprepared" to succeed, or even *be* in school. "Even kids who are fed well at home often sneak junk food, trade lunches and drink sodas at school," he observes. "This only makes things worse." Many experts point to high sugar intake as a culprit, implicated for its potential to negatively impact learning and health. Physician Carolyn Dean suggests that if we can't eliminate all refined, concentrated sugar from our diets, we should try to consume less than five teaspoons a day. Considering the fact that a single can of soda contains at least twice this amount, most experts agree that a large portion of the population—including many children and teens—are taking in way more of the sweet stuff than is good for them.[50] Both sugar and carbohydrates can throw off the brain's chemical balance, resulting in restlessness, irritability and inattention. Armstrong mentions a study in which hyperactive kids who had carbohydrates and sugar for breakfast had a lower attention span than kids who had eaten a healthier breakfast. Interestingly, these same children actually did better at attention tasks than nonhyperactive kids when they ate a high-protein, no-sugar breakfast.[51] Hannaford reckons that every nonintegrated, stressed-out, survival-oriented individual she ever worked with had a diet high in sugar and carbohydrates.[52] (Several studies indicate that on its own, sugar may not be a major player in negatively affecting children's behavior, although on purely nutritional grounds, it's probably a good idea for most kids to eat fewer sugary foods.[53] Many experts are even more concerned with the potential harm in kids' consumption of artificial sweeteners. Despite extensive testing to affirm the safety of these substances, some physicians warn of possible neurological and biological effects, particularly on children.[54] Further, a number of health practitioners and parents reported positive changes in some children's behavior and health after being off artificial sweeteners for several weeks.)

Sugar sensitivity is just one of a number of nutritional issues. Numerous dietary deficiencies can impair brain functioning and learning—among them, iron, potassium, sodium, calcium, trace elements and certain types of enzymes and fats.[55] (Children with learning or attention difficulties may be lacking in a number of specific nutrients. Some experts feel that supplements can be very helpful when tailored to the needs of the individual child.[56]) However, of growing concern for many parents and professionals is an upsurge in food allergies and sensitivities, as well as the increasing presence of chemical additives in our food in recent years. Of these, synthetic food dyes made from petroleum, artificial flavoring and antioxidant preservatives seem to have the most harmful effects on some individuals, and many believe children to be the most vulnerable. On their own, many of these chemicals might not be a problem for most people. But combined with environmental pollution and allergens, impurities in air and water, and overprocessed food from which many of the nutrients and much of the fiber has been removed (and which may contain pesticides, hormones or antibiotics), a human nervous system can take a serious hit, particularly if that nervous system is sensitive to any of these stressors in the first place.

Children who react to these substances can display physical symptoms, such as a stomachache, headache, earache, hives, poor muscle control, bedwetting, or difficulty writing, drawing or speaking. Or their symptoms might be behavioral, evident in children who are overactive, aggressive, impulsive, excessively talkative, compulsive or easily frustrated. Or these substances could affect specific learning skills like difficulty paying attention, reading a story, remembering a spelling word, writing or doing a math problem. Allergies or sensitivities to specific foods—in children, these commonly include wheat, milk, corn, peanuts, soy, chocolate, eggs, yeast, citrus and sugar—can produce many of the same outcomes. Because these reactions are so similar to many of the behavior patterns in hyperactive or attention deficit children, some children identified as ADHD may not actually have this disorder, but may, instead, be allergic or sensitive to certain foods or to some of the substances in what they eat and drink. For many of these children, adhering to diets that eliminate specific foods or additives to which they react can make a tremendous difference in their ability to function in school and at home.[57]

Am I crusading for nutritional perfection? Hardly. (Certainly my own behavior would not be much of a testament in this direction, either. This issue continues to challenge my best intentions on a fairly regular basis.) What the research and anecdotal reports suggest to me, however, is that for kids who seem to be having a hard time, behaviorally and academically, a little attention to their diet might not be a bad place to start. Whether scientifically "proven" or not, a great deal of evidence implies that at least some children can experience dramatic improvements in their behavior, attention, memory, motor skills, academic performance and emotional control simply by eliminating certain foods or food additives, with no further intervention necessary.

I'm Hyperactive, You're Hyperactive

Public schools have begun to issue ultimatums to parents of hard-to-handle kids, saying they will not allow students to attend conventional classes unless they are medicated. In the most extreme cases, parents unwilling to give their kids drugs are being reported by their schools to local offices of Child Protective Services, the implication being that by withholding drugs, the parents are guilty of neglect.

Lawrence H. Diller[58]

Desks were uncomfortable, but it was not wise to move around much, and fidgeting earned you a day in the corner. Shameful!

Elaine Lesse
retired teacher

There is no "ADD child," but many different kinds of children who are hyperactive and inattentive for many different reasons.

Thomas Armstrong[59]

When faced with an ADHD labeled child, adults have two divergent choices: transform themselves and then the education system, or suppress the child.

Carla Hannaford[60]

When I can't stop diddlin', I just takes me Ritalin. . . .

Bart Simpson

I think I have Attention Surplus Disorder.

Lauren[61]

In the time I've been researching the various topics for this book, perhaps no single subject has triggered the intense reactions and controversy as those related to Attention Deficit Hyperactive Disorder (ADHD)[62] and its treatment. During this time, I met a few educators who saw the growing numbers of students on medication as an answered prayer (a few of whom fretted about the increasing resistance from parents when approached with suggestions to go this route). But the majority of respondents and interview subjects were more than a little nervous about this trend. Looking at the statistics, these concerns are understandable.

One of the problems seems to be the gap between the portion of the student population who would supposedly qualify for a true ADHD diagnosis and the portion of the population actually being identified and treated. The exact number of kids with ADHD is not known, although typical estimates range between 3 and 5 percent of school-age children.[63] But take a look at how many kids have been labeled as ADHD—and are on medication for this condition—and the numbers are significantly higher. In 1970, 150,000 individuals were identified as ADHD. This number grew to a million in 1990, with 6 million reported ten years later. This number represents 12 to 13 percent of the schoolchildren in the United States. In schools in high poverty areas, the percentages may run as high as 20 to 30 percent of the entire student body.[64] And in certain programs for troubled kids, more than half of the students were reported to be on ADHD medication.

Further, the trend to medicate children is reaching into an increasingly younger population. According to a study of more than 200,000 preschool-aged children, "the number of two- to four-year-olds on psychiatric drugs, including Ritalin and anti-depressants like Prozac, soared 50 percent between 1993 and 1995."[65] In another study, this one of 223 children under three who exhibited developmental or behavioral problems, 57 percent were being treated with drugs, most commonly Ritalin, clonidine and dextroamphetamine; one third were medicated with more than one prescription. (Some of the children on Ritalin required an additional prescription to counteract Ritalin's side effects.[66]) Joseph Coyle of Harvard Medical School's psychiatry department calls the dramatic increases in prescriptions to preschool-aged children troubling, "given that there is no empirical evidence to support psychotropic drug treatment in very young children and that there are valid concerns that such treatment could have deleterious effects on the developing brain."[67]

Diagnosing ADHD is another source of controversy. "There are no objective brain-based tests that are routinely used to detect the presence or absence of these behavior disorders," report Karr-Morse and Wiley. Therefore, ADHD is typically diagnosed fairly subjectively, using a series of behavior checklists that are completed by the parents, teachers and, usually, a professional diagnostician.[68] The checklists typically include a set of inattentive behaviors, such as being easily distracted by irrelevant sights and sounds, failing to pay attention to details, making careless mistakes, not following directions, losing or forgetting things, or avoiding tasks that require sustained mental effort. They also include a list of behaviors that reflect hyperactivity and impulsivity, such as being restless, fidgeting or squirming, leaving a seat when sitting or quiet behavior is expected, running or climbing when expected to sit quietly, seeming to be "driven by a motor," blurting out answers or showing difficulty waiting in line or for a turn. In some cases, individuals will meet the criteria from one list or another; in others, they will be characterized by behaviors from both lists.[69]

As educational coordinator and ADHD specialist Linda Classen observes, without a "pure scientific way to diagnose ADHD, we will identify it the same way we identify a duck." In other words, if it looks like ADHD and sounds like ADHD, we're gonna call it ADHD.[70] The only problem is, many of the behaviors on this list can be explained by—or overlap with—a number of diagnoses besides ADHD. Depending on who you talk to, what we might be seeing are the "look-alike" symptoms of

Sensory Integration Dysfunction,[71] Post-Traumatic Stress Disorder,[72] Reactive Attachment Disorder,[73] Oppositional-Defiant Disorders and Conduct Disorders,[74] fetal alcohol syndrome,[75] chronic middle-ear infection, sinusitis, visual or hearing problems,[76] poor diet, emotional problems,[77] sensitivity to food additives, lack of clear guidelines, inadequate feedback, lack of natural light, too-warm temperatures,[78] inadequate instructional stimulation (lack of novelty, relevance, choices or opportunities to self-manage),[79] depression,[80] bipolar disorder,[81] child abuse and neglect (particularly during the first thirty-three months of life),[82] or thyroid problems.[83] Additionally, Greenspan suggests that certain children might be identified as ADHD because of temperament-related patterns, such as an oversensitivity to sounds or sights, difficulty sequencing movements or processing visual or auditory input, or a tendency to be distracted by details.[84]

Other mismatches of learning styles can lead to an ADHD diagnosis. Remember, high-visual, auditory-limited teachers look for eye contact and the ability to sit still as evidence of a student's attention or interest. As Jensen observes, "Neither of these two behaviors will come from a dominantly auditory or kinesthetic learner [who is] likely to be talkative and mobile."[85] Armstrong agrees. "Sitting quietly in a classroom is totally against the natural inclinations" of children whose strength lies in their bodily-kinesthetic intelligence.[86] Hyperactivity may also represent a child's attempt to manually stimulate his brain to compensate for weak electrical firings at certain neurochemical sites, says Deborah Sunbeck,[87] or an effort to mobilize his vestibular system in order to take in more information from the environment.[88] Drug counselor Beverly Davies also includes amphetamine abusers among those who are frequently diagnosed as ADD or conduct disordered. (Ironically, several drug counselors noted that this type of drug is among those most frequently prescribed for these kids.) Finally, the behavioral emphasis of an ADHD label may have more status for students than any type of a learning disability classification. As Fassler and Dumas assert, some children who are having a hard time learning will deliberately misbehave "because they'd rather be labeled 'bad' than 'dumb.'"[89]

Armstrong argues, "Essentially . . . ADD appears to exist largely because of a unique coming together of the interests of frustrated activist parents and a highly developed psychopharmacological technology." Certainly, the attempt to create a medical diagnosis makes it easier to justify using a pharmaceutical remedy. However, as Armstrong notes, "unlike other medical diseases, such as diabetes or pneumonia, this is a disorder that pops up in one setting, only to disappear in another."[90] Conventional wisdom points to some neurological disturbance in the brains of ADHD-affected children; however, research has not borne this out. In November 1998, the National Institutes of Health confirmed, in a consensus development conference dealing with the diagnosis and treatment of ADHD, that "there are no data to indicate that ADHD is due to a brain malfunction."[91] This has led large numbers of individuals to conclude that this condition is far more behavioral than organic, with the strongest opponents citing the interests of the pharmaceutical industry in the overpromotion of both ADHD and the drugs used to treat it.[92]

But economics and politics aside, there are some real dangers inherent in the use of any drugs, particularly with children. Psychiatrist Peter Breggin, a major opponent of the use of these drugs, recites a litany of concerns, beginning with their potential for addiction and abuse, which, not surprisingly, many proponents deny.[93] Although several special education specialists cited research which suggests that kids who are identified and treated early are less likely to self-medicate with street drugs, a number of individuals (including drug counselors and educators) with whom I spoke claimed that more than a few kids are indeed using "street drugs," as well as selling and trading their prescription meds in school. (There is also research to suggest a relationship between prescribed stimulant use in childhood and the use of nicotine and cocaine in adulthood.[94]) The abuse of stimulant drugs is an increasing and significant problem, and many teachers feel that their drug education programs—particularly their efforts to head off their students' impulses to "take something" to solve a problem, are being undermined by the trend that often seeks medication far too immediately, "substituting chemistry for coping."[95] Columnist Walter Kirn shares his concerns about the emergence of an "institutional drug culture," warning that "a profoundly mixed message is being sent to teens when certain substances are demonized for promoting the same subjective states touted on the labels of other compounds."[96]

But there are enough other threats to a child's physiology, according to Breggin, to qualify psychotropic drugs as a potential risk to their physical safety in and of themselves. Consider the capacity for methylphenidate (Ritalin and other brands) to produce long-lasting and sometimes permanent changes in the biochemistry of the brain, disrupt neurotransmitter systems and hormone production, or endanger the cardiovascular system. (Although ADHD advocates often point to abnormalities in the brain as a cause, Breggin counters that "any brain abnormalities in these children are almost certainly caused by prior exposure to psychiatric medication.") Other adverse effects can include depression, psychosis, irritability, insomnia, nervousness, dizziness and attacks of Tourette's or other tic syndromes. Likewise, there is a concern that the drug can actually worsen the very symptoms it is meant to improve, including hyperactivity and inattention, with a potential for eventual impairments in thinking ability, memory and the ability to learn.[97] And although there is no direct link between the use of prescription drugs and violence, there have been some grumblings about the number of violent kids, in particular, the high-profile school shooters, who were on these drugs.[98]

Proponents of the use of medication often point to an improvement in symptoms, which, in turn, they claim, can improve behavior, relationships and learning.[99] And while it's true that many of these drugs can indeed help kids focus, opponents often ask, "Focus on what?" Hannaford concedes that drugs like Ritalin may allow kids to attend to "repetitive school work, detail and rote memorization," but beyond these lowest levels of cognitive functioning, "there is no evidence that Ritalin improves learning or academic performance."[100] Nor does it help avert future problems, like school failure or delinquency, claims Breggin.[101] Further, this drug locks the brain into an organized, or focused, state of consciousness, preventing kids from shifting into an open or receptive state, which is necessary for learning.[102] Emotionally, Ritalin (and other brands of methylphenidate) have an impact as well, depressing spontaneity, curiosity, exploration, socializing and playing. Several parents complain that the drugs turn kids into "zombies" or "robots," or that it "robs them of their bubbly personality." Additionally, observes Breggin, "the drugs increase obsessive-compulsive behaviors, including very limited, overly focused activities."[103]

There are issues of responsibility to consider, as well. Stephen Morris, a former parochial-school chaplain, observes, "Challenges that teachers used to handle are being handed over to psychiatrists."[104] And Lawrence H. Diller, a behavioral-pediatrics physician who prescribes Ritalin for children, is nonetheless "alarmed by the widespread and knee-jerk reliance on pharmaceuticals by educators who do not always explore fully the other options available to deal with learning and behavioral problems in the classroom."[105] To some, medication is simply the latest weapon in our arsenal to force conformity among children. Breggin suggests that the entire purpose of the diagnostic checklist is "to redefine disruptive classroom behavior into a disease," claiming the behaviors considered for a diagnosis of ADHD simply represent "a list of the behaviors that most commonly cause conflict or disturbance in classrooms, especially those that require a high degree of conformity."[106]

Advocates for medicating kids with ADHD symptoms (and those more tolerant of an approach that includes medication) note that the meds are just a part of a comprehensive, multimodal treatment approach, which includes counseling for the individual and the family, parent training, esteem building, anger management and an appropriate educational program.[107] But many children get prescriptions without the benefit of these other services. Alternatives to using drugs to change children's behavior and learning abilities require more effort on the part of adults. Debra Sugar suggests that in many instances, medicating kids give the grownups an excuse not to change. "Parents and teachers stop asking questions once kids are on meds," she says. The same may hold true for some kids. Several teachers commented on kids "using" the label to their advantage. One noticed that as soon as one of her students was diagnosed, "he stopped bothering to control his mouth. 'I'm ADD,' he'd tell me." Perhaps this can also explain how some children can go for long periods of time between check-ups once that initial prescription is filled. Psychologist Shannon Croft suggests having prescriptions monitored on a monthly basis.[108] But more commonly, psychiatrists write prescriptions for six to twelve months at a time, and several educators told me that some of the kids in their classes hadn't had their prescriptions checked or changed in more than two years.

To be honest, I don't care whether we label this cluster of behaviors as ADD, ADHD or something else altogether. Likewise, I'm less concerned with whether these behaviors represent a "disease," per se, or simply an annoyance. These behaviors are a reality for many kids, and their teachers and parents, as well. What concerns me most, however, is how we, the adults, deal with them, and the degree to which we are willing to change our *own* behaviors and approaches, particularly with regard to instruction and discipline, as well as the physical and environmental factors we're willing to consider, examine and modify as needed. It will always be easier to medicate children, but regardless of the apparent improvements this approach may seem to offer, I think we owe it to our students to consider the cost, including the very real potential for serious, long-term harm. My point is that whether "scientifically proven" or not, there are a number of other less invasive and less potentially harmful alternatives to medication that I believe, can offer the solutions and relief we all are seeking, alternatives that don't require trying to fit every peg into the same square hole.

I would challenge us all to make a few small and subtle changes here and there and see what happens. Accommodate a wider variety of learning and temperament styles, modality preferences and intelligences, and increase factors like novelty and relevance in our instruction. Encourage good breathing, water consumption and frequent movement in and out of the classroom. Try minimizing television, cleaning up the physical environment and becoming more conscious of what we feed kids. Improve the quality of our discipline and motivation strategies and give students more input and choices within the limits we set for them. Be respectful of kids' needs, maintain good boundaries, build trust and mutual respect, and make a conscious effort to accept and value and reinforce them all. Do any or all of these things and then see if we can't get by on fewer prescriptions. Because any one of these changes might just reduce some of the ADHD-like behaviors we're seeing. But our cautions about drugging children go even deeper than these results. They speak to priorities, coping skills and problem-solving abilities—and, to some degree, our willingness to withstand the allure of a quick fix. For in the long run, perhaps we'll all be well served if we can resist the urge to "take the edge off" the way kids experience life—or the way we experience kids.

Taking the Path Less Traveled

The best teacher is not necessarily the one who possesses the most knowledge, but the one who most effectively enables his students to believe in their ability to learn.

Norman Cousins[109]

Educate—don't medicate.

Peter Breggin[110]

As a child, I got in trouble mostly because I was so hungry for attention. It was not important whether it was positive or negative attention. I just wanted someone to notice that I existed.

Sandi Redenbach[111]

It feels easier to read. What just happened?

fourth-grader after doing Brain Gym exercises[112]

The problems we face in education today are going to tax our creativity and courage like never before—creativity, so we can reach beyond the cognitive approaches so common and familiar in this field. (Many of these problems are not exclusively cognitive or intellectual in nature; nor do they generally suffer from a lack of talking, reasoning or information.) And courage because we can make ourselves a target for anything from raised eyebrows to having our competence called into question whenever we attempt to do something that isn't widely known, accepted or well-supported in conventional quarters. The good news here comes in the form of new discoveries in a number of areas, but particularly in the field of brain research. Many recent findings confirm and strengthen old arguments for expanding our concepts of teaching and learning well beyond the academic and cognitive dimensions. Others suggest a world of possibilities that didn't exist even a few years ago.[113]

As mentioned earlier in this book, early experiences create neural pathways in a child's brain. The fact that each of us develops different patterns as a result of a number of unique biological and environmental factors accounts for vast differences from one person to the next, in talent, ability, personality, temperament and so on. When kids come to school, they bring with them the benefits or disadvantages of the experiences they've had along the way. If they've missed certain developmentally important experiences, or if their early lives have been characterized by abuse, neglect, abandonment or other trauma, their neural development can present significant challenges for the teachers and counselors working with them. To some degree, an exciting, enriched school environment can fill in some of the gaps for some children, but for many kids, even the most stimulating academic experiences won't be enough. Emotional nurturing and encouraging can also play a big part, particularly in children with their survival mechanisms set on high. However, for many children, some of the most promising avenues for help may lie in strategies that address the child's needs from a mind-body perspective. Many of these approaches borrow from techniques used in the fields of physical or occupational therapy, neurolinguistic psychology, counseling and psychology, chiropractic, acupressure and kinesiology, for example, and may be at least somewhat unfamiliar in an educational setting. And while less radical or invasive than a pharmacological approach, many of these ideas may be seen as rather controversial when applied to learning.

The idea behind many of these strategies is that the brain is typically blessed with a certain neural plasticity that endows us with the ability to learn new things, and to relearn or adapt in response to stress or damage. And perhaps while not all damage can be undone, many educators and practitioners hold out great hope for improvement and change, particularly when our efforts are specifically directed to modifying the brain's circuitry with certain experiences. Shapiro claims that although kids are "born with specific emotional predispositions . . . [they] can learn new emotional and social styles that will create new neural pathways and more adaptive biochemical patterns." But because of the human stress-response system "and its impact on brain development . . . for children with developmental disabilities or damage, cognitively based therapy may be an exercise in futility," warn Karr-Morse and Wiley. They recommend interventions directed at the limbic system and midbrain for greater effectiveness.[114] (Play is a great way to achieve this objective—something we typically restrict, if not completely discourage in most school settings.) The goal of many interventions is to actually "develop alternative neural pathways" and changes in the ways kids receive, interpret, categorize, store and utilize the information their brains take in. Although many of the therapies designed to change neural circuitry are not likely to make their way into the classroom, they may present a viable alternative in a clinical setting, particularly for people who have been frustrated by a lack of progress or success in using more cognitive or analytical approaches, and those desiring an alternate route to using medication.[115]

What we probably *will* start seeing in more and more classrooms are the kind of exercises and tactile experiences geared to integrating, balancing and "waking up" the brain and body to get it ready for learning or testing. This will require having our students use their bodies for more than sitting, listening, reading and writing. Certainly, if a child has a sensory integration problem or some degeneration of the vestibular system, we aren't likely to *talk* him out of it, no matter how articulate or pushy we are. If we want to help kids who have a hard time neurologically organizing the information they get from their bodies and the world around them, we'll have much better luck when we offer them a "balanced sensory diet" that includes a combination of alerting, organizing and calming activities, nearly all of which will involve some form of movement or tactile experience.[116] (This is a good idea for *all* kids, not just those who have learning or integration problems.)

In the past few years, I've worked, talked and studied with Brain Gym consultants from Singapore to South Jersey. These individuals are achieving remarkable successes with the children in their classes and centers, including kids identified as hyperactive, autistic, learning disabled, speech impaired, ADHD and conduct disordered.[117] The exercises they use with their students are designed to increase the electrical activity between different parts of the brain, develop neural pathways and restore an integrated, balanced energy flow throughout the brain and the body. This integration is necessary for successful brain functioning and learning. The various movements put the students into a "state" that is better prepared for learning. They can improve learners' ability to take information in through all their senses (not just their preferred modality channels), can help anchor new learning and increase myelination, dendritic branching and new nerve growth throughout the brain. By getting the different parts of the brain "talking" to one another, we move neural focus away from the survival centers in the brain to allow for better intellectual, emotional, motor and creative processing. Further, integration can interrupt an emotional hijacking, calm the body and prepare the brain for more rational thinking. It can improve attention, self-regulation and formal reasoning and decrease hyperactivity as well. It can also repair damaged tissue in the vestibular system and help kids who may have missed important developmental stages to "catch up." And integrating activities have also been shown to improve concentration, memory, organization, listening, coordination, communication, and academic performance, achievement and test scores with kids of all ages (compared to control groups who did not use these activities).[118]

Some of the most touching stories I've heard in the past few years have come from individuals who were willing to stand up to the pressures from authorities or tradition, people who chose to detour down a road less traveled, perhaps just to see where it ended up. Diet was a frequent topic of discussion, with several parents noting dramatic improvements in their children's behavior when certain foods were eliminated. I've talked to parents whose kids responded to nutritional supplements, and others who saw positive changes when their kids used herbal or homeopathic remedies.[119] One of the most interesting stories came from a woman who discovered that her son was especially sensitive to fluorescent lighting and found certain colors to be particularly distracting. Rather than putting her child on medication as the school advised, she asked the school to allow him to wear a baseball cap in class and cover his desk with blue paper.[120] An unorthodox approach, to be sure, but the child showed great improvement and, as a result, was able to avoid more aggressive measures to control his behavior.

Sometimes the simplest and least obvious solutions can be incredibly effective. In a couple of different settings, I've seen enormous changes in kids' participation, posture, level of alertness, communication skills, ability to sit quietly and listen, and willingness to wait their turn to speak when they were allowed to play with bean bags or other "fidget" toys during the activity or in their groups. Two of these observations occurred in the center with high-risk teens. One was in a therapy group with three boys whose reticence to sit up and share seemed to vanish once the toys were introduced. Another was with an extremely hyperactive, highly medicated kid I got to spend some time with one-on-one. I had suspected some sensory integration problems and was not at all surprised to see that after he had selected five different fidgets—one in each hand and three in his lap—he was much more focused, grounded and articulate. Other teachers have told me about programs that engaged children with different crafts techniques that were highly tactile. Others note improvements in learning when kids are allowed to talk and interact with one another.[121] Still others have seen improvements using sound therapy to treat learning difficulties, lateral organization problems, perceptual disturbances, speech and voice problems, social and postural problems, anxiety problems, impaired hearing and deafness, concentration and memory problems, and a number of developmental delays.[122] And one karate program geared specifically to ADHD kids saw improvements in concentration, focus, social skills, motor skills, self-control and behavior that the kids were unable to achieve in a regular classroom setting.[123]

The majority of these alternative approaches would fall into the category of low-risk interventions. They cost nothing or next to nothing, are easy to manage and, in general, if they don't work, nobody gets hurt. Added to classroom routines one at a time, they don't typically result in anarchy or chaos either. And chances are, just about anything will work with somebody's child some of the time. As educator and Brain Gym consultant Aili Pogust advises when teachers question the value of a new technique, "Try it for three weeks and take a break for a week. Then observe the changes. If the technique had an impact, continue using it." It's kind of like finding the right diet or workout, one that fits an individual's unique combination of physiological needs, comfort and motivation levels, interests and lifestyle—and actually gets results. It may take some experimentation, or at least a certain degree of openness to a wider variety of tools than those we may have previously considered.

Schools can no longer pretend to be one-size-fits-all organizations. Until the unlikely day that we stumble across some magic formula that works for all kids, all the time, what we really need is a bigger menu, one that expands our options in dealing with all aspects of a child's existence—academic, of course, but also emotional, social, behavioral and physical, as well. Whether we are dealing with one child or a few hundred, the more options we're willing to try, the greater our chances of success with larger and larger numbers of kids. This will require changes in how we're taught to teach and the degree to which we are willing to come together to bring a range of expertise and ideas to a child's life. It will, in short, require a change in what schools are.

Part III

The Grownups

If you were born to be a teacher, then you must recognize that you are in the most noble and important profession on this earth. You are the primary difference in a student's success and failure and for many kids, their only chance for a decent future. When the world turns kids off, it is you who turns them back on.

Lauretta Buchanan[1]

Teachers, too, can suffer from the darkness of anonymity. It comes to us through isolation from colleagues and parents and through the effects of delayed gratification. Not only are we members of a team with whom we rarely meet, but also we rarely see the fruit of our labors.

Donald C. Wesley[2]

I talk with a lot of educators in my work. In the time that I've been collecting data for this book, I've noticed a strange phenomenon. It has to do with the reactions I faced when I mentioned to someone who is currently working in an educational setting that I was doing a book on creating emotional safety in schools. In a number of instances, when these individuals heard the words "emotional safety" and "schools" in the same breath, they didn't just respond—they *detonated!* Instead of the usual nod or acknowledgment I might have expected, what I received instead were intense and emotional discourses on how unsafe *they* felt. Not only did this happen in workshops and at conferences, but also in casual encounters—on planes, at the gym, in the store where I was doing my holiday shopping. "Let me tell you about emotional safety," one veteran teacher said to me, as she recounted a series of events involving her school's administration, nearly backing me across the room with the force of her frustration.

Clearly children are not the only ones at risk here. Although a handful of teachers commented that they feared for their physical safety, the majority of discontent centered more on management issues, particularly around things like job security, respect and accountability. I've heard a succession of offenses from every level of personnel from the classroom to the highest administrative offices, horror stories that ranged from people supposedly being fired via e-mail messages, to instances of administrators hedging their support for teachers, backing down in the face of an angry parent or potential litigation. I heard the term "sticking it out for another few years" more often than I would have liked, and met so many teachers and administrators taking early retirement that I sometimes wondered if there would be any adults left in our schools in the next few years. I met teachers too young and too new to the profession to be as jaded and disillusioned as they were. And despite the intense levels of commitment and dedication I sensed or observed, by the end of the fall semester of 2000, I was convinced that in the nearly three decades in which I've been a part of this profession, I had never seen morale so low.

"In the context of our national debate about public education, public criticism and dissatisfaction have led to a growing sense of demoralization among teachers and other personnel who already work long hours, with little support, for low wages," observes Debra Sugar.[3] Among the loudest complaints I heard were feelings of not being valued, appreciated, respected or supported. There were also a number of comments from individuals who believed that they were being held accountable for factors over which they had very little control—things like students' home lives, previous academic experiences or enormous gaps between what students were expected to learn and what they actually brought with them. For many, the issue of standardized test scores being used as the measure of their competence, much less the basis of their salaries (which already lag behind other professions[4]), cut straight to the heart, challenging the entire point of what drew people into teaching in the first place. There was a thread of resentment among others, for the initiative, expertise and professional judgment they saw as being denied to them. Many showed the strain of what they described as increasing demands and decreasing power—clearly a corrosive combination. "Teachers are being stretched to the limit," writes Linda Lumsden. "Expectations placed on them seem to be expanding exponentially."[5]

Now certainly, I met a lot of educators who love their job, who enjoy the kids they work with, who are very excited about the programs they have going on in their classrooms and schools, who look forward each day to going to work. I met large numbers of people who, despite what they described as clearly child-unfriendly decisions going on at the state or political level, refused to give up their faith in public education. And I believe that the majority of professionals in this field remain convinced of their capacity to make a difference in children's lives regardless of any constraints or lack of support they may concede exist. But the negative press, the weight of the bureaucracy and the trend that reduces the whole of what teaching is about down to a few sets of numbers have taken the wind out of a lot of people's sails. "With the growing discontent for public education and constant rejection and condemnation in the media, it is hard for educators to feel emotionally safe," asserts principal Sandy Murray. "Many times these feelings are reflected in the way educators treat children. In order to have emotional safety in a school, all persons need to feel safe."

Adults feeling isolated, frustrated, stifled, unsupported and unsafe is not only dangerous to kids, it's risky for the profession, as well. "We will never really improve American education until we elevate the teaching profession," said Education Secretary Richard Riley.[6] Now more than ever, the stakes are way too high for the field of education to be anything *but* rewarding and exciting, and for those on the front lines, in particular, to feel anything except the highest levels of respect and support.

19

Teacher Safety: Protecting the Protectors

[I was] dying a little every day. I had begun to feel like a shock absorber, taking in the pressures, the anxieties and frustrations of students, parents, administrators, teachers, the board of education and the community, trying to be, at the same time, an advocate for student growth and learning. It seemed to me that everyone was losing, especially me.

school counselor[1]

How does one compensate professionals for inadequate books and supplies, large classes, disruptive students, public criticism, limited assistance, increased duties and the lowest salaries paid to highly educated personnel in the nation?

David J. Parks[2]

Like the queen on a chessboard, the teacher with the most moves has the most options and the greatest degree of influence.

Bob Garmston and Bruce Wellman[3]

After completing my internship in the spring of 1974, I practically moved into the waiting room outside the office of the personnel director for the district in which I wanted to work. At that time, positions for classroom teachers were few and far between, opening only if someone already in a classroom moved, retired or, to be blunt, died. The director told me that, at most, they only expected three openings for the entire year. "That's okay," I assured him. "I only need one." Right before Thanksgiving, when opportunity finally knocked, it didn't stop to ask me if the grade level, subject area, neighborhood or pay scale would work for me. If you wanted to work, you grabbed whatever came along.

Fast-forward to the fall of 2000 and in a classic reversal of supply and demand, schools throughout the United States now struggle with vacancies they can't fill. Rising enrollments and a push for smaller classes are coming up against a teacher shortage that is already sending some districts into a panic. And with a million veterans ready to retire and others lured away by private industry, an estimated 2.2 million public school teachers will need to be hired by 2010.[4] School districts are getting creative—enticing teachers to their schools with higher pay and better professional development opportunities, or incentives like health-club memberships, signing bonuses, paid moving expenses, better pensions, graduate school tuition, college loan reimbursements or low-interest mortgages. Districts in places like Las Vegas, which in the fall of 2000 was still growing by about one thousand kids a month, pitch their climate, especially to teachers going through a nasty winter.[5]

Rather than depending exclusively on teacher education training programs at local colleges and universities—many of which aren't turning out enough graduates to meet current demands—districts have extended their resource pool as well. Some are drafting people from the ranks of substitutes (which are already seriously dwindling in some areas), from other positions in the school, from overseas, or people with university or military training experience. Many recruit mid-life career switchers and people with expertise in other areas (especially math and science) who can pursue alternate routes for certification, but whose main preparation for teaching will come on the job. And there's the rub. Oftentimes new teachers—whether straight out of college at twenty-two or changing careers at fifty—end up in schools with high turnover, or with classes nobody else wants. But even with a terrific placement, and even for individuals coming from a successful student teaching experience with full teaching certification, first-year teachers can be in for a bit of a shock when faced with the realities of running a classroom on their own.[6]

It's rarely a question of commitment or enthusiasm. A recent survey of more than twenty-two hundred teachers with less than five years' experience shows that 96 percent love their work and 68 percent get a lot of satisfaction out of teaching. (School administrators concur, with 98 percent categorizing most new teachers as "highly motivated and energetic.") But no amount of enthusiasm, dedication or even creativity can compensate when a teacher lacks the skills necessary for organizing, motivating and managing a group of kids, particularly when those kids are unmotivated or poorly prepared. Parent educator Cori Jennings observes, "Teachers are taught what they should teach but not taught how to get children to learn." Veteran teachers and administrators agree. Despite their appreciation for these spirited commitment they saw in the new recruits, the fact remains that the majority of newly certified teachers are still seen as better versed in theory than in facing the practical challenges of day-to-day classroom life, and are weakest when it comes to discipline concerns and issues related to getting and keeping their kids on task.[7] Most agree that the average requirement of seven to ten weeks of student teaching or other field training simply doesn't offer preservice teachers adequate training before being "thrown into a classroom alone."[8] When things don't work out, teacher dismissals rarely have much to do with a lack of knowledge about the subject area an individual is teaching. According to district personnel director Cory Butler, "Teachers are let go because they lack instructional skills, like not being able to manage a classroom, and for not getting along with people."[9] For teachers coming from other fields without the luxury of an extended student teaching or supervised clinical experience, the road can be even more bumpy.

So the challenge for school districts is how to capitalize on the altruism and passion most people bring to this field, without allowing these qualities to be eroded or squelched. Second, there is the need to secure the loyalty and commitment of people already in the classroom, make better use of the talent and leadership skills many veterans have to offer, and in some cases, restore the morale of the disheartened. And finally, there is the question of skill building, offering support to fill in the gaps in instructional and relationship skills so that every member of the staff can be effective and successful. While there are a number of factors involved here, perhaps most important is the nature of the emotional climate and the quality of the relationships in the school and district, and in the larger context of the community, as well.

Teachers as Learners

Teaching is the only job where people who are just beginning are expected to do the same thing as people who have been [in the classroom for] twenty-five years.

Bob Chase[10]

As a teacher I can tell you that I have not met this subject in the process of my education. We did not get information on how to ensure feelings of safety in class.

Olga Sraj Kristan
teacher

> *When faced with the contrary, day-to-day classroom pressures that do not take into account the environmental conditions for effective transfer, teachers can abandon the less familiar and risky new practice for the safety and security of their usual approach. Even the teacher most excited about the possibilities of a newly acquired practice needs the right school environment to sustain it.*
>
> James Bellanca[11]

There are, of course, the expectations. "What we need above all, many say, is educators who have a deep understanding of the subjects they're teaching so they can help students meet higher standards," write Barbara Kantrowitz and Pat Wingert. "A teacher should also be up on the latest research on how kids' minds work, understand how to use technology and be comfortable working with students from many different ethnic and economic backgrounds."[12] And if you talk to administrators, it's a safe bet that they're also going to want people who can keep misbehaving kids—and angry parents—out of their office, as well. But even if a district is lucky enough to get qualified applicants for the vacancies it needs, what is the likelihood that each person will be able to pull off all of the above? Some schools offer mentors and on-site support programs, but these are generally reserved for new teachers—where they exist at all. What about the rest of the staff?

Inservice training is certainly a possibility. It offers educators access to new skills and the latest research, generally without requiring the time, financial commitment or outside work that college courses and degree programs typically entail. Inservice programs can also help educators meet certification requirements and qualify for pay increases or career advancements. But this avenue, for some teachers, is limited at best. In a rubric prepared by the Bay Area School Reform Collaborative, one of the criteria is the development of a professional learning community, one in which "schools nurture an environment in which the structure, climate and working conditions support learning for and collegiality among adults." From the strongest to the weakest criteria, the existence of professional-development opportunities for all staff members is a given, with evidence for the highest levels of accomplishment including features such as programs being linked to school standards, the existence of multiple networks and a norm of critical inquiry and lifelong learning, which permeates the entire school.[13] I must admit that I read these criteria with some degree of amusement; even the most minimal standards listed in this rubric were miles ahead of anything I ever experienced. (I once had a principal who believed that attending a local conference—which we had to pay for ourselves and use a personal day to attend—was simply an excuse "to get out of work." Never mind that this unusual opportunity offered outstanding national speakers addressing issues that were very pertinent to our school.) Teachers still report that they get little or no financial support from their district, and for years, administrators and staff-development coordinators have complained about their professional-development budgets being the first items to be cut. However, this situation now seems to be changing for the better. With more than 12 percent of all newly hired teachers coming on board without any teacher training, many schools wishing to avoid a steady stream of new recruits—since poorly trained teachers are generally the first to hightail it out of the profession—the demand for support programs is stronger than ever. And as many states and districts mandate a certain number of professional development hours each year, budgets and schedules are giving way to better opportunities for all staff.[14]

Still, a number of issues bear consideration. One is the degree of input any school staff has on the training it receives. (Although I generally ask ahead of time, I can always tell the minute I walk in to do an inservice training whether the staff in attendance has requested the program or has simply been *sent* to hear what I have to share.) Just as kids tend to be more committed and open to doing things in which they have had some say, so it goes with adults. From talking to large numbers of educators, the main concerns they express have to do with whose decision it is for them to attend a training, the relevance of the material being presented, and the amount of work any new skills or changes will require. Sugar mentioned one staff-development specialist she interviewed who attributed her success in effecting change to the relationship-building efforts she made before attempting to share new information. Her initial approach, she claimed, was supportive and empathetic, one that avoided making demands on the teacher. And one social worker saw her effectiveness increase "when the teacher has already expressed some interest in the topic, feels supported rather than threatened or criticized, and when the school's administration is supportive of the intervention."[15] Many people also recommend that experience, expertise, participation in ongoing professional development or advanced degrees be acknowledged and rewarded in some meaningful and significant way.

The greatest obstacle, however, seems to be time, particularly when it comes to learning programs with complex processes or content that requires significant shifts in thinking, behavior and attitudes.[16] There is something wryly incongruous about having the highest standards in the world for the uncertified or inadequately trained people some districts are fortunate to get their hands on, particularly if no structures are in place to provide the time or resources to grow into the position. But even well-trained professionals who genuinely wish to keep up with the latest and greatest discoveries in the field can find themselves stressed and burned out trying to work one more thing into a schedule already teeming with logistical, clerical, energetic and time demands. (Many people I spoke with felt that they could do a good job in the classroom or they could stay abreast of the professional literature, but in their current circumstances, they could not do both.)[17] Some of the most effective programs happen in districts with plans in place to practice, follow up, troubleshoot and refine their application of new ideas or practices long after the initial training is over. Author Ismat Abdal-Haqq cites research that criticizes traditional inservice efforts as being "fragmented, unproductive, inefficient, unrelated to practice and lacking in intensity and follow up." He proposes professional development that is ongoing, accessible and inclusive, and includes opportunities for individual reflection, group inquiry, discussion, coaching or other followup procedures. He suggests that the approach be collaborative, offering teachers a chance to work with peers, and respectful of teachers as professionals and adult learners. And he recommends getting away from "inflexible and counterproductive school schedules" that restrict the potential value of professional development programs and impose upon teacher's personal time, either before or after school or during the summer.[18]

The quality of the school culture has a lot to do with how opportunities for new learning are received. Inviting people to step outside of their comfort zone and try new behaviors and approaches can require a great deal of convincing, and even the best presentation of the latest ideas and research are only going to go so far in the absence of an environment that feels safe, supportive and encouraging. (And it goes without saying that change initiated by criticism or threats are doomed to be superficial at best.) As Maslow's hierarchy suggests, schools in which the staff feel their needs for survival, belonging, esteem and power are effectively being met are going to be much more receptive to trying new ideas or approaches than a school in which the faculty is fighting an antagonistic administration, community or legislature, for example. Toxic schools, those dominated by negativity, opposition, frustration and hopelessness, are likewise going to need some work before new learning will have a place to land and take root. Authors Peterson and Deal describe one high school in which "disgruntled staff came to faculty meetings ready to attack new ideas, criticize those teachers concerned about student achievement and make fun of any staff who volunteered to go to conferences or workshops."[19]

Change can be difficult to inspire, and school settings can be notoriously attached to the status quo, even when nobody seems to be happy with what that represents. "A school's readiness for change is influenced by teachers' psychological state," maintains Louise Stoll. "Neglecting interpersonal and psychological processes leads teachers to behave defensively to protect themselves from innovations that might expose their inadequacies, whereas valuing individuals as people and their contributions enhances teachers' self-esteem and builds trust."[20] Donovan and Iovino reflect on the existence in schools of "cainotophobia," the fear of new things, and "psychosclerosis," or what they call "the hardening of the mind." Additionally, they cite "all too many cases of teachers who are spurned by their colleagues for showing too much creativity, outspokenness, innovation and vitality."[21] I heard similar stories from teachers, counselors and administrators worldwide; indeed, as part of my work with first-year teachers, I spent a good bit of time talking about ways to protect themselves from those who might discourage or sabotage their optimism and enthusiasm.[22] Clearly, for some teachers, the passion, curiosity and hunger for new knowledge they bring to the profession can make finding emotional safety in their work environment a rather elusive goal.

The State of the Teacher

Knowledge is power, but knowledge about self is the greatest power.

Carl Rogers and Jerome Frieberg[23]

I see a number of strong parallels between the emotional safety that a student feels in school and the emotional safety that a staff member feels. . . . [When staff do not feel safe,] productivity is affected—lower test scores, less teacher effort, shallow or strained relationships, low levels of trust, and an unwillingness to take risks.

Lindsay Shepheard

What kind of school plan you make is neither here nor there; what matters is what sort of person you are.

Rudolph Steiner[24]

A teacher is like the downstairs maid. My God, there isn't a single teacher on the New York City Board of Education. It's preposterous! Can you imagine a board of surgery that didn't include a surgeon?

Frank McCourt[25]

Teaching is one's life, but also one's death.

Victor Allan C. Ilagan[26]

In a 1997 report prepared by the National Center for Education Statistics, teachers identified "more administrative support and leadership, good student behavior, a positive school atmosphere and teacher autonomy" as the working conditions most closely associated with job satisfaction. There are several good reasons for protecting teacher morale and job satisfaction, notes Linda Lumsden, as these factors can have "far-reaching implications for student learning, the health of the organization and the health of the teacher." Lumsden also cites research which found that "where morale was high, schools showed an increase in student achievement." Conversely, she states that a drop in morale and job satisfaction can lead to "decreased teacher productivity and burnout," as well as "a loss of concern for and detachment from the people with whom one works, decreased quality of teaching, depression, greater use of sick leave, efforts to leave the profession and a cynical and dehumanized perception of students."[27]

Healthy school environments promote teacher morale, while at the same time, physically and psychologically healthy teachers help create a positive, healthy school environment. British educator Jenny Mosley suggests that adults in a school system need to feel "emotionally safe within themselves," to be grounded and healthy and capable of meeting their own needs, before they can implement the kinds of programs that would promote emotional safety throughout the system. Counselor Beverly Davies concurs: "People in the teaching field need to be pretty healthy mentally. They also need to have a lot of expertise in mental health issues." Since teachers inevitably act on their attitudes, beliefs and feelings, Schultz and Heuchert note that "wherever the teacher is with regard to self" will have an influence on the students, and on how they act in similar situations.[28] And New Zealand child advocate Robin Warnes, who suffered a number of physically and psychologically painful incidents as a student, recommends that a psychological profile be done "on all prospective candidates to find out if they are suitable to work with children" before they enter into the field.

Teacher educator Juanita Ross Epp asks her students to "describe critical incidents from their own school experiences" as a part of their preservice training. She notes that her students are often "amazed at the intensity of emotion that they feel in recalling these events," and are likewise surprised by the degree to which they had excused or accepted mistreatment from adults as normal, or never bothered to question the appropriateness or necessity of these behaviors. She also notes "the potential dangers of an uninspected past" for anyone going into this field.[29] Similarly, Parker Palmer encourages teachers to do what he calls "professionally relevant inner work."[30] However, few teachers I've spoken to included any such reflection as a part of their professional training. (Those who had indeed done personal work—whether or not it was related to their work with kids—pursued their healing on their own through private channels, or through the districts' Employee Assistance Program.) Certainly, unresolved issues with parents, childhood wounds, anger or addictions are going to creep into classroom relationships, particularly when we're under stress. Even something as basic as learning to recognize one's own "anger triggers"—those words, behaviors or attitudes that can set off an emotional hijacking—can help teachers learn to manage their feelings and avoid becoming abusive or getting out of control in their dealings with kids and others.[31] Perhaps at some point, attention to this dimension of personal development will become more commonplace in actual teacher-preparation programs.

Of all clichéd, unquestioned beliefs, one of the most disturbing I've heard is "I don't care if my students like me, as long as they respect me." I still hear this one from time to time, though not nearly as often as I did when I first started teaching. Aside from the sheer unlikelihood of being respected and disliked by the same person at the same time, it would serve our profession quite well to care deeply about how our students feel about us. (Likewise, for those individuals who argue that there is no place in their classrooms for relationships, take heed.) A tremendous amount of research data shows a high correlation between teachers' interpersonal skills and students' learning. Aspy and Roebuck cite studies from the 1970s by the National Consortium for Humanizing Education that indicate "positive and statistically significant relationships between teacher levels of interpersonal functioning and almost all aspects of student self-concept." When teachers were able to provide higher levels of understanding, genuineness and respect, their students learned more. High levels of interpersonal skills also correlate with lower levels of disruptive student behavior. Unfortunately, data from pilot studies of teachers in ten different states showed that "most teachers were providing levels of interpersonal skills which tended to retard rather than facilitate learning." However, these studies also see the potential benefit of teachers participating in programs designed to enhance their communications and interpersonal skills. The NCHE studies concluded that kids simply learn better from people they like better, and they tend to most like teachers who function at high levels of interpersonal competence.[32] Author Chester Quarles notes that interpersonal skills, the ability to form relationships and positive involvement in students' lives also decrease the likelihood of being targeted for violence by students. "Teachers who are well-liked are much less likely to become victims than teachers who are disliked."[33] And I've heard numerous reports from teachers who have worked to become more positive, accepting, encouraging and respectful of the students in their classes, with benefits ranging from having more fun and less stress, to increased cooperation, higher levels of academic engagement and performance, and fewer discipline problems.

If we want the system to get better, we need for the individuals *in* the system to get better. And individuals don't have a chance to "get better" when they are stuck in a mode of self-protection and survival. To some degree, a teacher's job satisfaction and morale is a matter of personal responsibility; there are many things we can do, personally and individually, to stay inspired and enthusiastic about our work. But just as important is the climate in which we work and the degree to which we feel "nurtured, supported and valued by the broader school community."[34] Systems fueled by negativity, gossip and backstabbing are destructive and exhausting, and ultimately the quality of education and learning suffers. Positive cultures—where the emotional climate is underscored by laughter, support and caring—presents an entirely different realm of possibilities. But positive cultures and great working conditions don't just happen. They are a product of work and shared vision. They are a product of strong leadership.

Are You at Risk?*[35]

Risk factors** include a tendency for teachers to:

- feel personally responsible for a student's successes and failures
- measure personal success by student behavior and achievement, or by approval from others
- have an overwhelming need to avoid conflict and generate approval from others (which can manifest as attention-seeking,

* At risk for lots more stress, frustration and conflict than you would like.

** We're probably all guilty, to some degree, of all of the above from time to time. This list is simply a sample of the ways at-risk factors can show up in the classroom. These patterns become problematic when they become typical of a teacher's feelings and behaviors.

maintaining status quo, passive-aggressiveness or rebelliousness)
- compromise student needs to avoid conflict or “rocking the boat,” either with administrators, parents or other students
- believe that the job would be easier to perform if only the students, their parents, the administration or “the system” would change
- have difficulty setting and maintaining boundaries between self and other people
- have difficulty setting and maintaining boundaries between self and job
- have difficulty forming or maintaining close or intimate relationships
- deny personal needs
- exhibit rigidity in behavior or attitudes
- lean toward perfectionism (unrealistic expectations of self and others)
- have difficulty adjusting to changes
- deal with discipline problems by shaming, blaming, complaining, manipulating, ignoring or dumping them on someone else (parents, principal, vice principal or other support staff)
- feel disempowered (“Nothing I do would make any difference.”)
- feel threatened by another teacher’s progress or success
- feel as though “things would completely fall apart if it weren’t for me”
- swing from chaos, helplessness and victimization to moral superiority and self-righteousness
- often rescue students by ignoring misbehavior, offering inappropriate second chances or failing to follow through on previously expressed boundaries
- protect a student from failure or negative consequences in an effort to feel successful, valuable or powerful
- overidentify with, and even adopt, another person’s feelings
- appear to be “fine” and “in control”
- probably deny that any of the above are personally relevant

These patterns can ultimately interfere with teachers’ ability to:

- interact with students without violating their dignity or self-worth
- interact with school staff effectively
- meet students’ academic and learning-style needs
- behave consistently within the framework of their own values
- feel worthy and successful
- detach from the job
- take care of themselves

Other contributing factors:

- a tradition of dysfunctionality (which now feels "normal")
- the tendency for the organization to promote and reward workaholism, codependence, loyalty and self-sacrifice (over self-care or care of one's family)
- a scarcity of healthy, functional role models
- the absence of a healthy, functional system to support people trying to operate in healthy, functional ways
- the very human tendency to resist change

Some assumptions on reducing risk factors:

- It is possible to adopt healthy patterns of behavior, even in unhealthy and unsupportive environments.
- "The system" is not likely to rescue, protect or take care of (or support) a teacher's needs regardless of that teacher's enthusiasm, instructional skills, dedication or good intentions.
- Change happens best in supportive environments; teachers tend to function effectively, grow professionally and personally, and avoid stress and burnout when they can create a support network for themselves, either in or out of school—and preferably in both environments.
- Change is most effective when individuals take responsibility for their own growth, rather than attempting to change or blame others.
- Change is most effective when encouraged rather than coerced.
- "The system" is not likely to change all by itself.
- As individuals change, "the system" will change.

Follow the Leader

The most productive team is the one in which every individual is important, and in which every individual is at the same time committed to the common mission of the team.

Charles Garfield[36]

I do not believe that there is any safety in a workplace where the staff is managed like buffaloes and vision is not valued. I find that the energy of some of my [colleagues] is constantly drained by fear and micromanagement. And I am having to accept the fact that supreme effort and a passion for doing the right thing for kids do

not mix with politics or someone's personal "I gotcha" agendas.
educational program coordinator

I never had a boss that tried to sit on me, and I think that's essential. If you expect people to develop, you have to give them responsibility, you have to tell them what their objectives are, and then you have to let them do it.
David M. Roderick[37]

Schools that have stars rather than facilitators as their leaders leave a hollow legacy.
Carl Rogers and Jerome Frieberg[38]

As part of his daily routine, John McClellan, principal of an inner-city high school, taught one class a day. His assistant principals taught regularly scheduled classes as well. Clearly their presence in an instructional capacity had an impact on the climate of the school. "You know, after the first week, the kids don't care who you are," he maintains. "They don't know you're a [Ph.D.] . . . that don't mean zip to them. They just want to know, 'You care about me.' And we did.'"[39] Although negative relationships with principals was a common theme, I was delighted to hear from a handful of educators who wrote in to tell me about wonderful things their principals did, and the positive impact this relationship had on the teachers' loyalties, attitudes and commitments, and on the climate of the school in general. One news report quoted a teacher who was moved and inspired when she came in at the end of the summer and found her principal painting the bathroom doors in preparation for the beginning of school. This involvement at a core level sent a strong message to the staff, and the community as well.[40]

Just as interpersonal skill is a positive factor in relationships between teachers and students, it is likewise an important quality in a strong school leader. Data from the National Consortium for Humanizing Education investigations found that the principal is pivotal in a school's program: "Teachers whose principals demonstrated high levels of interpersonal functioning reported more favorable perception of their school environment and their teaching tasks than did teachers whose principals were functioning at low levels." This study showed that the principal's behavior sets the pattern for the entire school, affecting the school climate and classroom communications—for better or worse. Aspects of the principal's behavior that were highly related to teacher-student behaviors and interactions included the principal's level of respect for the teacher or student, plus his or her level of empathy, use of praise and acceptance of ideas proposed by teachers or students.[41] In a lovely example of this trickle-down effect, one woman reflected on her experience as a teacher whose principal "trusted us to do the very best job possible, and in turn, we trusted the students who came to us to do the very best job possible."[42]

By the same token, teachers who perceived their principals to be negative, mistrusting or antagonistic had the opposite experience. One educator transferred schools because the tension got to be more than she could bear. "You never knew who you could talk to and who you couldn't," she said. "Everything would get back to the principal. She had her favorites. If you were on her 'good list,' you could do anything." After a year of witnessing unequal demands made on certain teachers, special privileges for the principal's "pets," and staff being pitted one against the other, she and several colleagues moved on, taking assignments at other schools in the district. Unfair or preferential treatment—whether it had to do with receiving supplies, getting support for programs and proposals, having schedule or grade-level preferences accommodated, being supported in conflicts with parents or getting permission to leave early—came up often. Unresponsive leadership was another concern. One high-school teacher submitted a list of physical-safety and crisis-management issues she felt needed to be addressed after her school went through three bomb scares right after the Littleton shootings. "The principal stuck them in a drawer," she said. When she went in with other teachers to reiterate the request, they were told that they were being paranoid and emotional. "What a charming environment to work in," she added.

One of the most common complaints came from teachers who don't feel they can trust their administrators to back them up when it comes to teaching certain content, or setting grading, homework or discipline policies. To the extent that these teachers were unwilling to share or discuss their policies with their principals before implementing them, however, the disagreements may be understandable. Recently at a training for a large high school, the principal took me aside at lunch to complain about a teacher who started off the year with a three-page, single-spaced discipline code that was extremely negative and punitive. "This office is not prepared to support his program because it goes against the school's mission and philosophy, and stands in violation of several board policies," she said. Meanwhile, the teacher had approached me earlier, feeling as though the administration had hung him out to dry any time he had a conflict with a kid. When asked if either had attempted any kind of collaboration to come up with a policy that both teacher and administration could live with, it became clear that neither party felt safe or comfortable enough to attempt to find a win-win solution to this problem. As a result, the teacher perceived the administration to be hostile and antagonistic, and the administration viewed this teacher as secretive, passive-aggressive and uncooperative.

Corporate and teacher educator Stephen Haslam includes in his definition of emotional safety "whether employees feel safe enough to disagree without fear of reprisals." And while ideally, all teachers would see the logic and ultimately self-protective value in clearing personal policies and procedures with the office early in the game—if only to help avoid surprises down the road—being able to do so assumes that teachers and administrators see themselves as being on the same side of the fence, committed to finding equitable solutions, and that teachers feel safe opening up to their principals. But in many settings, teachers believe that any attempt to secure support beforehand could come across as an admission of weakness, insecurity or incompetence, and leave them vulnerable to administrative sanctions, criticisms, restrictions or worse. It's not surprising, then, that many teachers keep themselves as isolated as possible. "It's easier to beg forgiveness than ask permission," came up as a personal philosophy more times than I could count. Rita Mercier stresses the need for dialogue, disagreements and even heated debates, even if it means bringing in a trained facilitator for these discussions.[43] Without a basis of trust necessary for these kinds of interactions to occur, the results can range from whiny compliance or passive-aggressive sabotage to outright defiance and insubordination. One teacher admitted that some days, she spent more time documenting, self-protecting, laying low and covering her tracks than she did teaching. None of us does our best work when we're in survival mode, and none of these survival responses does much for the emotional climate of a school.

But principals can get caught in the middle, and getting everybody on the same page can be an overwhelming challenge, especially for principals new to an especially toxic site. Several principals I spoke with talked about having to break up cliques among the staff. As one explained, "Without this [step], we won't have safety for anyone." One principal sent me a long, detailed correspondence in which she described taking over a school after the previous "harmful person" in her position had "forcibly retired," leaving "a concentration of angry, dissatisfied and uncaring people," the likes of which the new principal had never encountered in more than two decades in education. "It is amazing how one person can cause such a cancerous situation to occur," she wrote. The district administration was supportive, but the teachers were bitter, the parents angry and aggressive. New staff she brought on board often come to her in tears "because of the abuse they receive from the venomous veteran staff." In a follow-up e-mail toward the end of the first semester, the principal's efforts had started to pay off. Months of relentless positivity, focused on the core of positive people she hired, eventually gave way to subtle changes in the culture of the school. Some of the most negative and hostile people either retired or moved on, their remaining colleagues somewhat less negative—or at least less verbal—as their ranks dwindled. The principal closed with the following advice: "Anyone who manages a school must be cognizant of the effects that negativity, meanness, inconsistency, lack of caring and disrespect have on a community, which is what a school is." Clearly it takes a very special person to hold onto a vision and maintain a positive focus with an oppositional staff—many of whom returned the posters and gifts the principal had gotten for them, or spitefully threw them in the office trash can—but if a school like this can change, there is no reason for any school staff to abandon hope.

"A leader is someone with whom others will go where they wouldn't normally go themselves," claims Spence Rogers.[44] Corporate speaker and author Charles Garfield has identified three skills that high-performing team builders develop and use. The first of these is the ability to delegate. Effectively delegating responsibility not only multiplies the leader's strength but also gives power and control to the employees—in this case, the teachers and other staff members in the school. Empowering teachers doesn't just satisfy one of the most frequently identified criteria for higher morale, it also contributes to higher levels of performance. As Garfield notes, in first-rate organizations, "the source of excellence is peak performers who never assume that they are powerless. Even in organizations that others perceive as hopelessly complex and unresponsive, the peak performers retain a sense that they control their own actions." Delegating to empower means being able to refrain from "making decisions others better make themselves" and understanding the difference between working with people and interfering with them. (One study showed that there is less violence in schools where principals provide opportunities for teachers and students to participate in decision making.[45]) Second, effective leaders are skilled at building on strengths and stretching the abilities of others. Finally, they are willing to encourage educated risks and to identify and eliminate the obstacles that stand in the way of others' successes.[46] Lumsden notes that principals build morale by actively standing behind their teachers, involving staff in decisions about policies and practices, acknowledging their expertise and supporting their sense of self-determination and purpose.[47]

In author James Liebig's data on visionary leaders throughout the world, common threads include concerns for enhancing social equity, enabling human creativity and seeking to serve higher purposes.[48] Swedish educator John Steinberg describes school leaders who manage to accomplish seemingly impossible goals "despite massive opposition or an apparently hopeless economic situation." The leaders he described had among their skills: the ability to identify goals and priorities, create consensus among the staff, influence the right people, investigate conventional and unconventional funding sources, present information in ways that suit the decision makers and never give up. "They can say 'no' once, twice, or even three times," said administrator Jan-Anders Andersson. "But the fourth time they say 'yes.'" Teachers working with these administrators believed that their school leaders were on their side and on the side of the children; they had likewise bought into the principals' optimistic belief that "nothing is impossible."[49]

Rogers and Frieberg cite research by Wayne Hoy, John Tarter and Robert Kottkamp, which indicates the importance of trust in the relationship between the principal and staff, and suggests that the primary role of the principal is to "improve instruction indirectly through the development of an open, healthy and trustful climate" in the school. Their studies show that teachers tend to be mistrustful of principals when they are not given the freedom to make professional judgments and are watched closely. "The more supportive and open the principal is, the more trust the teachers had in their principal," the study concludes. Further, they note that principals have a direct role in developing trust between themselves and their teachers, as well as an indirect role in developing collegiality and trust among the staff members.[50] Peterson and Deal suggest that principals shape school culture by communicating core values and the mission of the school through their own actions, by honoring and recognizing those who have worked to serve the students and the purpose of the school and by observing rituals and traditions to support the school's heart and soul. "They recognize heroes and heroines and the work these exemplars accomplish . . . celebrate the accomplishments of the staff, the students and the community."[51]

Other studies show the importance of the principal's encouragement and support in sustaining successful, long-term change.[52] But this brings up another handy skill principals need to manage schools effectively, that is, the ability to handle conflict, anger and fear within the organization. "Creativity, innovation and growth all produce conflict," observes educational consultant David Cowan. "Remembering that conflict is a process, those organizations that are creative, innovative and growing are organizations that are taking charge of conflict and turning it into a productive process." It is not enough to come to the job armed only with instructional and managerial skills; school leadership demands skills for not only interacting successfully with others, but also for helping to build these skills where necessary among staff members. (I've known technically brilliant teachers who had a tremendous grasp of how to put a lesson together, develop materials and present information but whose lack of people skills and their inability to deal with conflict kept them from ever having a chance to be particularly effective in an actual instructional setting.) By the very nature of the job, principals can end up catching conflicts from—or among—students, staff, parents, upper administration and the community. Cowan speaks to the necessity of having skills like diffusing and containing confrontations, strategically managing conflicts at every level, harnessing the creative energy underlying most conflicts and training staff to prevent and productively resolve conflicts. Other skills are likewise essential, like listening, valuing and respecting other people's perspectives, helping others become more successful and managing anger, moods and criticism, as well as knowing when to dominate, collaborate, compromise, get help, postpone, integrate, use humor or just walk away.[53]

In the what-to-avoid category, one common theme was rigidity. Keeping in mind that the majority of administrators fall in the SJ (Guardian) category, it's not surprising that this issue came up. These are the people with a greater fondness for rules, procedures and the chain of command than the rest of the population. They are absolutely essential for providing the structure necessary for schools to operate and, in truth, we'd be lost without them. But, as DeBeaufort and Diaz caution, the rational processes that work so well in dealing with issues such as finances, scheduling or logistics, will fail us when dealing with interactions and relationships.[54] One principal cited increased flexibility and revamping policies that weren't "people friendly" as the keys to her success. Balancing these skills with an eye to the human side of running a school and, perhaps, a "people first" philosophy, is probably the best way to go.

Even more dangerous than rigidity is the impact of intimidation on a sense of school climate. Regardless of the intention, intimidation is a great way to destroy community and back people into survival. "Intimidation pushes people away from concerns for the team," down to a focus on self-protection and preserving one's own safety, claims Garfield. "It causes many individuals to lose their grip on the higher values of collaboration and affiliation. It leads to regression rather than growth." Additionally, in an environment in which people's needs for dignity and autonomy are not being met, those with "adequate ego strength and a secure sense of their worth" are likely to jump ship and seek employment in a setting in which they'll be valued and respected. "Replacing them takes time, money and training," and does not solve the problems that eat away at the quality of the school culture.

And finally, because empowerment also involves responsibility, effective principals will help teachers acquire the necessary skills for preventing and resolving their own problems—particularly discipline issues and conflicts around student behavior—rather than taking responsibility for them. There is a fine line between supporting teachers and enabling them, and if this is going to work, principals are going to have to create the kind of environment in which teachers can approach school leadership, either to work out policies, procedures and preventative strategies that fit within the school's ultimate mission, or to tap into their expertise for assistance without putting themselves at risk. At the same time, teachers are going to have to be able to trust the administrators in the building, using administrators as resources to observe, offer feedback and brainstorm solutions—rather than using them, as some still do, as a dumping ground for children or problems they don't wish to deal with. For when principals, teachers and all school staff stand together, as a strong, cohesive community, the possibilities for learning, improved achievement and morale, and success within the context of the larger community are endless.

Administrative Behaviors That Motivate, Empower, Value, Inspire and Build Commitment and Trust[55]

- Working to change any negative aspects of the school's culture that may be undermining staff esteem and productivity
- Making the school a professional learning community
- Giving staff members opportunities to suggest topics and resources for inservice and staff development programs
- Presenting options for scheduling, room assignment or grade level
- Trying to accommodate staff members' needs for input and choice when making administrative decisions that concern them
- Treating staff members as professional consultants, people with their own perspectives on the practices and needs of the school
- Creating an open interactive environment in which people can share ideas and views

- Allowing time for ideas to develop and mature, for people to implement new strategies and try out new skills
- Planning and budgeting for innovation; following through on innovative ideas suggested by staff
- Helping staff keep the big picture in mind (school's mission, district goals, community values)
- Providing the most direct channels possible for access to supplies, resource personnel and yourself
- Modeling the beliefs, behaviors, language patterns and attitudes you would like your teachers to adopt
- Discouraging dependence or victim behavior by helping teachers explore and evaluate options (rather than solving problems for them)
- Offering acceptance, feedback and support while encouraging teachers to solve their problems themselves
- Resisting the habit to get in the middle of—and take responsibility for—squabbles between kids and teachers, even if you have in the past
- Refusing to punish students for infractions you did not witness
- Helping teachers resolve conflicts with other staff members or parents without assuming responsibility for the solution of the problems
- Encouraging the development or creation of a reward-oriented school environment; helping teachers find ways to increase the number of positive options they can offer to students
- Providing resources or support necessary to help teachers develop success-oriented instruction and routines (in order to make success possible for students at a variety of ability levels)
- Being visible in nonconflict arenas; visiting every classroom, as often as possible, to offer feedback or just help out
- Respecting teachers' professional judgment, as well as their need for freedom and power in their work experience
- Being committed to finding and encouraging win-win solutions (as opposed to blaming or discouraging ideas)
- Inviting feedback from staff
- Finding something positive to say about every member of your staff
- Making time to regularly acknowledge the contributions your staff members make (including casual, informal verbal or written messages of recognition and appreciation) and encouraging (not requiring) your staff to do the same for one another
- Using motivators and rewards to show appreciation, recognize special achievements or just break up routines

- Identifying and changing negative, reactive school policies
- Maintaining regular and positive communication with the community
- Taking care of yourself; learning to let go, delegate, set and maintain boundaries

Work-Environment Questionnaire[56]

To complete the questionnaire, read and then rate each statement according to the following scale:

4 Strongly Agree
3 Agree
2 Disagree
1 Strongly Disagree

For the purpose of this survey, the word "employer" may refer to the principal, superintendent or the district's board of education. (Note that in some instances, a different response might apply for each.)

____ My employer provides an environment in which I feel safe and secure.
____ My employer provides an environment in which honesty and openness are valued.
____ The culture and emotional climate of the workplace is generally positive and supportive.
____ I feel accepted and am treated with courtesy, listened to and invited to express my thoughts and feelings by my principal.
____ I feel accepted and am treated with courtesy, listened to and invited to express my thoughts and feelings by the upper administration.
____ I feel accepted and am treated with courtesy, listened to and invited to express my thoughts and feelings by the community.
____ I feel accepted and valued by my colleagues.
____ I feel like I am a part of a team (shared mission, values, efforts and goals).
____ I feel challenged and am given assignments that inspire, test and stretch my abilities.
____ My professional judgment is respected by my employer; I have adequate freedom to exercise my judgment and expertise.
____ My efforts are recognized and acknowledged in tangible ways.

____ I receive constructive feedback in a way that emphasizes positives, rather than negatives.
____ Innovation is expected of me, and I am encouraged to take the initiative.
____ I have clear-cut and noncontradictory policies and procedures in my workplace.
____ I am encouraged to solve as many of my own work-related problems as possible.
____ I see my employer as a resource (rather than an obstacle).
____ The rewards for success are greater than the penalties for failure.
____ There is consistency between my employer's professed philosophy and the behavior of the leaders and managers.
____ I believe in and take pride in my work and my workplace.
____ At work, I am accepted for the person I am.
____ It is safe to go to my employer if I'm having difficulty with some aspect of my job (a particular student or class, an angry parent, improving learning in some particular area).
____ I have a clear understanding of the goals and objectives of my employer.
____ I trust my employer to be there for me and back me up.
____ I feel safe sharing my plans, programs and policies with my employer.
____ My employer is committed to finding win-win solutions to problems.
____ To the degree that it is possible, I believe that my employer considers my needs and preferences when making decisions that affect my work life.
____ I feel in control of my work and capable of competently carrying out my daily tasks.
____ I tend to see problems as challenges, rather than as obstacles.
____ I am encouraged to give honest feedback to my supervisor.
____ I am able to keep encounters with other staff work-centered, rather than ego-centered.

Other ways my employer affects my sense of safety (esteem, belonging, power, identity or other needs):

20

The Collaborators: Parents and Community

Trying to educate children without the involvement of their family is like trying to play a basketball game without all the players on the court.

Bill Bradley[1]

In dealing with parents, a teacher has two alternatives. Parents will be either allies or adversaries. There is little middle ground.

Fredric H. Jones[2]

Practitioners who want to assist children must assist parents simultaneously.

Robin Karr-Morse and Merideth Wiley[3]

When former college president John Dunworth read about a community fighting to save its "small, over-budget, low-performing" elementary school in rural Florida, he was so moved by the community's determination that he offered "to come out of retirement and be principal for a year—for the whopping salary of one dollar." Despite enormous obstacles, Dunworth had a lot going for him, including four hand-picked teachers, parents pitching in as school volunteers, college students tutoring the schools' pupils and contributions of computers and other equipment from nearby military bases and local businesses. Inspired by the principal's dedication and his commitment to "respect, belief, leadership and parents and teachers working as a team," the teachers' efforts along with the parental and community involvement paid off. In addition to dramatic academic gains, costs were cut and the enrollment, which had been decreasing as parents pulled their children out of the failing school, stabilized and is expected to increase.[4] In a similar success story, Rita Mercier's efforts to change her school from a "nightmare" to a "model for social skills" relied, in part, on "a multitude of partnerships" that were nurtured among community organizations who provided tutors, recreational activities, special events and collaborative social services—all of which had a positive impact on the total culture of the school.[5]

Teachers and principals who invest the time and skill to build bridges into the community have a tremendous edge over those who fail to cultivate the rich and diverse resources and support that may be available. These connections work to the advantage of everyone. "Families today don't have the luxury of spending as much time together as our own parents spent with us, teaching us the lessons of the heart," write Lantieri and Patti. "Our communities are no longer functional villages, responsive to children's needs. Kids are growing up further and further away from a deep sense of community."[6] Professor of child psychiatry James Comer agrees. "The reason we need to strengthen the ties between families and schools is that the nature of our society has changed. . . . Neighborhoods are not natural communities anymore." He sees the need to "create a tighter fabric of support for children's development," one that can counter the negative aspects of the technology and information with which kids are being bombarded, often without the benefit of adults who can filter what they encounter.[7] Indeed, a renewed hunger for community by families who believe that "raising children may now take a little help from the rest of the village," has even shown up in architectural and community design plans for "neotraditional neighborhoods," which are built like small towns with services, stores, entertainment and schools all within walking distance.[8] The desire for a tighter social fabric places the school right at the heart of the action. I believe there has never been a better time to capitalize on this trend and become an integral part of the "village." But once again, we can't hope to do so successfully from an adversarial or defensive position.

In a study of beginning teachers, 86 percent of those surveyed said they would decline a significantly higher salary in favor of "well-behaved students and supportive parents."[9] Positive home-school relationships is high on many teachers' priority lists, and with good reason. Partnership between parents and teachers adds to the instructional potential for the significant adults in a child's life and can reduce some of the stress, isolation and burnout to which teachers can be vulnerable.[10] Parent involvement can boost students' grades and achievement, improve their social skills and behavior, and keep their attitudes about school more positive. It can also improve the overall climate of a school.[11] Parents can add to the adult presence in school, and increase the adult-to-child ratio in providing supervision, support, individual attention and mentoring. Their involvement can improve safety on school grounds, keep students safer as they travel between home and school and increase awareness of the potential for violence before it occurs.[12] It can also bring a wealth of specialized talents and expertise into the classroom to enrich existing programs and help teachers understand cultural differences in their students' backgrounds.[13]

Unfortunately, relationships between parents and teachers are often strained and rarely achieve their maximum potential. In my work as a parent educator, the complaint I hear most often has to do with parents rarely being contacted by the school unless there is a problem or their child has misbehaved. A close second is not hearing from the school until an academic or behavior problem that has been building up for a while—and which probably could have been circumvented if confronted early enough—results in a suspension, failing grade, retention or other serious negative outcome. Plus, many parents simply don't feel comfortable in a school environment. "Look into the eyes of some parents when they're at school and you can actually see fear," advises a newsletter for promoting family involvement.[14] But if some parents feel dumped on, ignored, uncomfortable or intimidated, teachers often complain of having their efforts unsupported or undermined by uncooperative parents. "For some of us, the real school bullies are the parents," claimed one teacher. And more than one principal reported how it only took one or two hostile, antagonistic or controlling parents to ruin an otherwise pleasant school environment—and work experience—for an entire year. Although many educators talk about how tough it is connecting with poorly educated, low-income parents who are functioning at a survival level, older, better educated and more assertive parents can present their own kind of challenges, as well. But regardless of which end of the socioeconomic spectrum parents represent, it's a fair bet that their main concerns are the success, happiness and well-being of their children in our classrooms. Nonetheless, these concerns don't always translate to supportive collaboration when it comes down to the relationships and actual interactions between parents and teachers.

Historically, few teacher education programs have paid much attention to this aspect of the job. Certainly nothing in my training could have prepared me for the Open House for which only three parents showed up, one of them drunk and another—a woman I had never seen in my entire life—who came into my room screaming at me about what a terrible teacher I was until she realized that her son wasn't in my class.

"Few teachers choose their career because they enjoy making presentations to parents," remarks assistant superintendent William Ribas. "Although some do look forward to Curriculum Night as an opportunity to meet parents and share with them the year's plans, other teachers dread the meeting and consider the ultimate objective to be survival."[15] Remember, we don't do our best relationship building from the survival parts of our brain. Wearing down resistance and building collaboration is possible, but if things are going to change for the better, schools are going to have to shoulder a great deal of burden, at least for initiating the change.

I remember calling a parent early in my career to complain about her son's misbehavior. Although many of the parents indicated that they wanted to know when something went wrong, I underestimated how quickly I would wear out my welcome when such was the nature of nearly all of my contacts. The turning point for me came when this parent responded to my complaint by telling me, "Hey, he's *your* student," and politely ending the conversation.[16] But after a few days, my resentment and self-righteousness eventually gave way to the realization that this approach wasn't working. Not only was it not achieving positive results, it was creating obstacles in my relationships with the parents and, in many cases, with my students, as well. In trying to make the situation better, I was actually creating more stress for everyone involved. There had to be a better way. The "better way" wasn't all that complicated, but it did require certain changes in my own attitude and behavior. One of the first things I did was to start calling parents whenever something *positive* happened. Interestingly, the first couple times I called, the parents seemed to miss the part about "Jerome turned in a great report in science class" or "Nicole has made huge improvements in reading." All they heard was "this is your child's teacher" and immediately assumed something was wrong. (I actually had one parent respond to "He's doing fantastic in math" with, "Yeah? What do you want?") All this did was reinforce how badly strained the relationships between the school and the parents had gotten, and how badly needed these positive connections were.

Eventually I decided to add to my priorities a weekly report that emphasized students' strengths and progress. Generally consisting of a checklist of five or six desirable behaviors, all stated positively, I committed to checking off as many behaviors as possible for each student each week. (Early in the process, I deliberately added one or two "sure things" that just about every student was certain to achieve.) Whenever possible, I added a few words about positive changes in attitude or work habits, or specific accomplishments or things I genuinely appreciated about the child.[17] The nearly immediate change in parents' attitudes was only one of the benefits. Even more profound was the shift in my perceptions of the students. I started to notice what they were doing well and what they were doing right. I was able to relax and enjoy them more and, quite frankly, my time in the classroom got to be far less stressful and far more fun.

A third change, which evolved somewhat more slowly, emerged in the way I approached parents when a child was having a hard time or some incident occurred. Rather than trying to get the parent to take responsibility for fixing the situation, as I had in the past, I simply reported what was going on and how I was dealing with the situation. In fact, I deliberately attempted to keep the problem from becoming the parent's problem. (Paradoxically, I found that the more responsibility I was willing to assume, the more supportive the parents were. There is a big difference between asking parents to collaborate and asking them to rescue. And I certainly couldn't keep hounding my kids to take more responsibility for their problems as long as I kept looking to others to bail me out of mine.) What eventually came to pass was a true partnership, with parents often suggesting approaches that had worked in the past that might not have occurred to me, or providing insights to help my understanding of the situation. Don't forget, I'd already put a lot of effort into establishing relationships through the phone calls and weekly progress reports, so ideally, by the time a problem popped up, I had had quite a few positive contacts with each parent. I also worked to improve my followup and called back after a few days to let them know how the situation was progressing.[18]

There are a number of other tools and techniques to help build positive, mutually supportive relationships between home and school. One is a class or school newsletter. Many of my first-year interns had their classes prepare newsletters and found that the information they sent home every month was well received. This was a great way to keep parents informed about upcoming programs, special projects or units the class would be studying, reminders about class policies, parenting tips or things parents could do to help their kids with certain skills; it was also a nice place to feature students' work. Others suggest a school bulletin including school and community news, activity calendars, articles reprinted from other sources, book reviews (perhaps written by students), regular columns, fund-raising updates, brief reports on important educational issues—and, of course, work by and about students. Besides written communications, many teachers make an effort to attend or participate in community, sporting or cultural events in which their students are involved. Others sponsor a number of in-school meetings that range from informal get-acquainted parties to more structured conferences in which the progress and needs of individual children are examined in greater detail. Providing childcare for these events, whenever possible, can significantly boost attendance and participation. The personal phone calls or home visits, when possible, are a good investment of time and energy, too.[19] (I met one assistant principal of a large middle school who made a point to contact every parent once a semester. Using a master checklist of the entire student population, he'd deliberately seek something positive about eight or ten children a day and call home just to pass on the good news. He said the average length of each call was less than twenty seconds, and it kept him in touch with every parent in the school.)

Other recommendations include being sensitive to cultural differences and child-rearing beliefs and using translators to interact with parents in their native language for both written and oral communications.[20] Develop and promote an "open-door policy," including a schoolwide attitude that welcomes parents throughout the school and invites buy-in and ownership on their end. (Starting with a parent-friendly school office is particularly important.)[21] Surveys to parents can help provide valuable information about their children's interests and experiences, parents' goals and concerns, and specific skills or talents they may wish to share with the school.[22] Developing volunteer programs or finding "essential roles" for parents can help utilize their energy and skills in a focused way, and can be particularly valuable when they involve parents at an instructional or decision-making level—and not just for fundraising, for example. (Studies show that we increase the potential effectiveness of volunteers when the programs include specific goals, adequate resources, training and ongoing guidance and public recognition of volunteers for the contribution they've made.)[23] Schools that have had the greatest successes in implementing specific programs—for building students' social and emotional skills or preventing violence, for example—typically have included parents and the community as a part of the planning and implementation team.[24] Scheduling parent-related events at varying times of the day or week can accommodate a variety of schedules and attract greater numbers of parents to school programs and events.[25] And recruiting individuals from local businesses, community services, law enforcement agencies and students from higher grades or local college programs to connect with kids and support school programs and goals can expand the concept of the "village" on school grounds.[26]

Many districts work to broaden the concept of education to encompass the entire community. Offering free or low-cost workshops as part of an ongoing parent-education program can work to everyone's advantage; so can creating a parents' resource library with books, tapes, brochures and handouts with additional information that will make their job as parents easier. Likewise, providing inservice training as needed to help staff to work effectively with families can be a valuable way to explore faculty attitudes, assess needs and improve commitment to this aspect of the school's mission.[27] This sounds like a lot of work, but keep in mind that ultimately, parent involvement will ease the load—not add to it.[28] Besides, the most important aspect of any of these efforts shows up in the message that kids invariably get when they know that their parents and teachers are on the same team, working together, committed to similar goals. This partnership gives kids a lot less wiggle room when it comes to working within structures that all of the significant adults in their lives support.

As with just about any other aspect of education, the key to successful relationships with parents are the interpersonal and intrapersonal skills educators bring to the table. According to one study, "several teacher attributes have been found to positively influence teacher relationships with children and parents." These include "sensitivity, warmth, reliability, accessibility, openness and flexibility." This study cites research that also includes teachers' involvement in professional growth opportunities, positive attitudes, personal competence and actively involving parents in specific activities as attributes highly correlated with successful parent involvement. From the parents' perspective, "desirable teacher attributes consist of characteristics such as warmth, closeness, approachability, positive self-image, positive discipline, nurturance, child-centeredness, effective classroom management, trust, reliability and effective teaching strategies."[29] And like any healthy relationship, interactions with parents require healthy boundaries, even if only to clarify teachers' availability, or how and when they would like parents to contact them.[30] (I used to give out my home phone number to parents, and while that was never a problem in the entire time I was teaching, I've had teachers look at me as though I were crazy for doing so. Obviously a decision like this depends on personal preferences, the community in which one is working, previous experience and, perhaps, the kind of technology a teacher has access to for intercepting calls at untoward hours.)

When teachers treat parents with warmth and appreciation, when they respect the parent's values and competence, when they don't depend on parents to solve their problems for them, when they welcome parents' input and involvement and maintain regular, positive communications, it's only fair to hope that parents would return the courtesies.

"Please don't ask me to keep little Johnny in from recess because he wet the bed or broke your favorite lamp," one teacher begged. Another was distressed by the number of requests she was getting for a phone call or handwritten note reviewing a child's behavior or performance each day. But by far the most upsetting parent behaviors were those that called a teacher's expertise or professionalism into question or accused a teacher of lying or exaggerating when describing a student's misbehavior. The more we can focus on solutions—instead of blame—to determine avenues that best support a child's growth and development, the better served this whole process will be.

Dealing Successfully with Your Students' Parents[31]

- Get acquainted early in the year, either by note, phone, in-school conferences, welcome meetings or home visits. Keep first meetings positive.
- Keep parents informed about your policies and goals. If you have certain specific requirements about how you want work done, when assignments are due, or other boundaries they may have some questions about, let them know ahead of time.
- Keep them informed about your classroom projects and practices. For example: If you are doing a special program, or allowing new behavior options—like allowing students to leave the class to work in the library or sitting on the floor to read or do special assignments—let the parents know.
- Maintain regular positive contact. Best bet: a weekly progress report that focuses on responsible learning behaviors necessary for success in the classroom. Having the students (or one student) put the names on the forms will leave you free to quickly fill in the progress. I have found that these reports work best when we only mark the skills that had indeed been demonstrated (only positive marks, rather than "grading" each skill) and when we make sure that each student gets at least two stars or smiley faces every week. (I frequently checked all five, as often as possible!) Make a point, when you can, to write a few words on the back or bottom of the form—always something positive! "Doing great in math!" "Self-control is improving." "Great sense of humor!" "Very helpful and caring with other students." The little time you put in will pay off in a big way.

- Make positive "surprise" contact. Example: an unanticipated phone call or note home about something special that happened or something that you noticed. These calls don't need to take more than a minute. Pick one class that really needs a lot of encouragement. Attempt to get back to the parents of each child in the class—say once a month, or even once a semester.
- Create (or supervise the creation of) a monthly newsletter. Be sure to include samples of the students' work—including all students in some way during the course of the year. Tell about new projects, guests, field trips or special events. You might also include reviews of parenting resources, parenting tips and ideas, or excerpts from books, magazines or Web sites. (Be sure to reference them correctly.)
- *Proofread* all correspondences that go home or, better yet, have someone else check for spelling, punctuation, grammatical and even format errors. Make sure your correspondences reflect your care and professionalism.
- Invite parents to visit your classroom, to see your class in action, to help out or to share their own expertise in some area.
- Be respectful of constraints on parents' time. Begin and end meetings on time.
- If a student is experiencing difficulty, either with the work or social behavior, or if the student is demonstrating behaviors that are interfering with her potential success in school, get in touch with the parents right away. Don't allow yourself to be placed in the embarrassing position of having to explain why you didn't contact the parents until the behavior became enough of a problem to affect the student's grades, progress or placement.
- *If there is an incident,* call only to report what happened. Watch your tone and any tendency to judge. Stick to the behavior—what you saw—rather than trying to interpret or analyze the child's intent. Avoid blaming or criticizing, or making judgments about personalities, character or values that might leave parents feeling defensive, protective, shamed, anxious, angry or resentful.
- When reporting an incident, watch the tendency to suggest that this is the parent's problem or demand that they solve it for you. Best bet: Describe the problem and how *you* plan to deal with it. You might ask for input or suggestions, but avoid asking the parent to "talk to him" or punish him for you. Offer to follow up in a few days (and then make sure that you do).
- You have specialized knowledge that makes you qualified for your line of work. Do not use that knowledge against the parent by using jargon or talking down to him or her.

- Work with parents toward a mutual goal: the child's success and well-being in school. Do not presume to care more about the student than the parent does.
- Do not speak ill of coworkers, the administration or other students, teachers or parents. At all times, keep your actions and interactions professional.
- If confronted with an angry parent, *stay calm* and maintain your boundaries. Speak softly if they speak loudly. Acknowledge the parent's anger as well as how important it is for you to hear what he or she has to say. If you need to, suggest going to an appropriate place for this kind of discussion. Encourage the parent to talk about what's going on and *listen!* Take notes as they talk. Resist the urge to argue, get impatient, condescend or attack. Try to avoid getting defensive or making the parent wrong for being upset. If you feel the least bit threatened, make sure to include (or call for) another teacher, administrator or support staff. It is okay for parents to get angry and blow off steam. It is not okay for anyone to use their anger as an excuse to violate teachers or other staff members!
- Watch out for requests from parents for you to punish a child in the classroom for misbehaviors that happened at home. It is neither appropriate nor necessary for you to withhold privileges for events you did not witness, although you can suggest resources or classes for parents who are having problems and seem open to receiving such information.
- Parents may ask you to do something that is not feasible or comfortable. Rather than talking about what you *can't* do, focus your answers on what is possible or what you are able to do. Also, don't be afraid to request time to reflect, find out more or take an issue under advisement before getting back to a parent with a decision.
- DOCUMENT, DOCUMENT, DOCUMENT. Keep track of all contact with parents in which you have shared important information or discussed a student's progress or behavior. Note the date, the purpose of the call, the parent's response and the outcome. Alert administrators to problems you may be having. Also make a note to follow up as necessary and then do so.

Rethinking Our Priorities, Part II: Valuing the People Who Work with Our Kids

Many studies have shown that kids learn best in schools where teachers feel respected and connected to their colleagues and the community.

Barbara Kantrowitz and Pat Wingert[32]

Personal value is a component of emotional safety. We treat well that which we value highly, and keep it safe. And for me, that starts with the individual.

Anne Naylor
author, lecturer

Bad news travels faster than good. This can be evidenced by how long it takes for the TV cameras to get to your school if there is a problem. How much PR time does it take to get them there for a positive event?

Barbara Wills
professional counselor

If someone lasts four to five years, they see that they can teach, but they can't support themselves or their families.

Sandra Feldman[33]

People have said to me, "You have these computer skills. Why are you just a teacher?"

David Eisenstat[34]

There is a moment, I think, for most teachers, when the lure of working with kids surpasses all logic. We know, we just *know,* that we are meant to teach. But in the day-to-day crush of details and bus duty, politics and paperwork, or kids without their homework for the eighth day in a row, life can erode passion and distract us from our sense of purpose.[35] But if teaching were only tough on the *inside,* it would be bad enough; knocks from outside the profession can wring out those last drops of commitment and resiliency from even the most dedicated teacher. We pick up the newspaper and read about how our schools are failing. We meet young people who are considering a teaching career against the advice of family and friends who urge them to get "a real job" instead. We are confronted—usually by someone who wouldn't last ten minutes in most classrooms—and told that we "sure make a lot of money for people who only work five hours a day, seven months a year."

Most of us have simply learned to ignore the perception of a second-class status, at least at the cultural level. We turn off the TV, we avoid people who just don't get it. We roll our eyes at the people who believe that teaching attracts either suckers or saints, or people who still think "those who can't, teach."[36] But the message is clear and over time, without some kind of buffer or internal support, it will take a mighty toll on this profession. It's when that status hits us in our pocketbooks that hurts the worst. In what threatens to become a bitter, no-win contest as contracts in districts across the United States come up for renewal, teachers in the system are pushing for bigger salaries and fewer restrictions, while district officials, caught up in the nationwide fever of educational reform, are pushing back—with fewer freedoms, increased demands and longer days.[37] In one district, a speech therapist told me that management offered the staff a 5-percent pay raise, but also proposed extending the school day to eight hours and adding days on to the school year. "In the end, we are losing money," she said. And if the hours don't get you, the added responsibility will. "We're expected to do all this extra stuff to look good to the community," one teacher expressed. "We're putting on conferences and assemblies. We're assigned to committees. We've got meetings before school and after school. Why don't they just let us teach?"

Many teachers around the country work second jobs or seek summer employment to make ends meet. (This has been the case for as long as I've been a part of this profession. No amount of budgeting could have gotten me through the year without waitressing or writing curriculum on the side. This cuts into valuable time that could be used for professional development opportunities or advanced degrees—or even keeping up with the literature.) One district found that they were losing teachers who had been in the profession for a few years. Just as they were becoming established and proficient, the pay scale began to level off. Looking at offers from other states, it quickly became clear that the longer they stayed where they were, the more money they were losing.[38] One educator noted that his district was losing almost as many teachers as were coming in, lured away from their classrooms by industries, other agencies or other school systems that had better financial packages.[39] "In other professions, including medicine, law, accounting and engineering, a shortage usually leads to higher salaries, better working conditions and efforts to give the professional some control, and ultimately freedom over his or her destiny," observe Rogers and Frieberg.

"In teaching, when there is a shortage, the opposite occurs." They cite a trend toward more restrictions, prepackaged curricular programs (which are supposedly "teacher-proof") and evaluations meant to control, rather than enhance the profession.[40]

Even before we get into the classroom, the priorities are obvious. Richard Biffle, the associate dean for a college of education, notes that, traditionally, universities budget for recruiting, marketing and funding relative to financial support the various colleges and departments receive. In many institutions, schools of education come in at the bottom of the list. He spoke of universities that have all but eliminated their colleges of education—cutting back funding for graduate programs and dropping tenured full professors. There is a sad irony to the fact that schools of education often come under attack for failing to prepare beginning teachers to deal with the myriad of new educational mandates, performance standards, benchmarks and outcomes (dictated by people outside the field of education), even as their budgets and programs continue to shrink. Biffle says, "Teacher-training programs are working against all possible odds. What is normally endowed to other departments—whether it's facilities, computer labs or other resources—schools of education have to beg for, and rarely get." In what is likely to be absolutely no help to public schools being hit by the teacher shortage, Biffle observes that universities tend to favor the colleges and departments that attract large endowments and research funding—rarely the strong suit for a school of education. He predicts that as long as education departments are seen as a liability in a university's bid for higher rankings, "the economics of running a program that doesn't seem to show up on anybody's radar screen" will continue to put teacher training programs at risk.

Administrative decisions at the district level can also be disheartening, even when seemingly unintentional. How respected can teachers feel, for example, when they're not assigned to a school or grade level until a day or two before the kids show up? Very often, enrollment determines an eleventh-hour placement, and new or transferring teachers are generally the most vulnerable. This was true for many of my interns who often had less than twenty-four hours to get ready for their first group of students. And then, to add insult to injury, it was not uncommon for them to be moved to a different class or grade level a month or two into the school year when enrollment profiles changed. (Imagine the flexibility and resiliency needed to switch lesson plans, bulletin boards and curricular materials—sometimes with less than twenty-four hours' notice—to accommodate kids who are four years younger or older than the ones you spent the summer planning for, all within the first few weeks of your career!) And what kind of message did the members of a graduate education class receive when the university found comfortable, air-conditioned, adult facilities for its other classes but assigned their class to a hot, crowded elementary-school library with chairs and tables designed for eight-year-olds? Even kids are getting the message. A rather insightful fifteen-year-old, Sione Quaass, reflected on the fact that public education in her native Australia would be a whole lot better if the government "gave it a little funding once in a while." She mentioned that officials "found that literacy and numeracy were at low levels in public schools in Australia, so they gave us hours of tests to show us how bad we are. Surely that'll encourage people to go to school," she added.

It's not much better for principals either. One administrator told me that despite her 200-day contract, she put in 350 days during the previous year. (Among many of those I spoke with, this is the norm, not the exception, and few were at all surprised by those numbers.) She, too, depends on parents, community resources and creative budgeting to get by. But in the meantime, her greatest concerns, like many people in the profession, centered on job security and respect. She spoke of principals losing their jobs if test scores in their schools did not hit certain benchmarks, and how many had resorted to cheating just to survive. "Our time and skills are not respected or valued at the district level," she said. "Calls aren't returned. No one has or shares information that affects us." Additionally, she cited as major sources of stress in her work life a "horrendous" rumor mill and the necessity of being conniving and manipulative to get what her kids and teachers needed.

Once again, the question comes down to this: As a culture, as a society, what will we honor? A recent poll determined that the majority of the public still believes in the potential of the public school system, favoring improvements to the existing system over alternatives.[41] Yet, at the same time, "a record number of education questions" appeared on state ballots in the November 2000 election with issues such as whether to fund private school vouchers for parents, shut down certain programs, base teacher salaries on student performance or restrict content teachers could discuss—hardly a public-school-friendly agenda.[42] In all of the arguments, our priorities get fuzzy. As an excerpt from one teacher's journal denotes, "With the demands of society for budget cuts and higher test scores, we are failing to realize that we are dealing with students who are feeling, total human beings."[43] As are the adults with whom the students work. When the adults don't feel valued, respected or safe, this feedback is bound to have an effect on their teaching, and on the kids they teach—assuming they stay in the system.

So here's another challenge: Are we willing to shift our focus to what these adults are doing right, and what they're doing well? There's no telling what sorts of brilliance a more positive lens might reveal. Nothing I've seen suggests that merit pay proposals include unmeasurable phenomena to acknowledge the success of a teacher who helped a child regain her confidence or sense of belonging, or the teacher who opened up a world of possibilities for a child who'd seen himself as a failure, or the teacher whose passion and enthusiasm lit a fire under a group of kids for some skill or subject area. And yet this is where teachers are surely making the most significant strides. Can we, as individuals, as a profession and as a culture, look beyond numbers and competitive rankings? Are we willing to acknowledge the need to make schools emotionally safe for adults, places that not only engage their talents and creativity and commitment, but treasure them, as well?

As you read this book, did you think of the teachers who, at some point in your life, had a hand in the skills and perhaps the desire for knowledge that brought you to this page. Is it not time to start saying "thanks"? I would encourage anyone who appreciates a teacher's efforts and impact, past or present, to *please* take the time to express the sentiment. Teachers' lives can feel pretty isolated at times and most of us go through periods (at least) that feel like we're working in a complete vacuum. I've never yet met a teacher who suffered from too much appreciation. A simple "thank you" can lift a heart more than anyone will ever know.[44] (I have moved a half-dozen times since I started teaching, including one move that took me across the country. Very few of my possessions survived all this time and transition, but I still have the "appreciation" notes I received from parents and kids in the early 1970s.) We are all living and learning together, changing and being changed by the people whose lives we touch. We are products of a multitude of influences, and much of our knowledge, abilities and beliefs came to us from outside ourselves. For the gifts we and our children receive from these teachers, let's take the time to remember. Go find someone who is helping people grow. Say "Thanks." For by this small act of grace, and the ripple effect it may inspire, we can't begin to imagine how many hearts we will ultimately touch.

Epilogue: Are We Almost There Yet?

The greatest change happens on the edge of chaos.

from a commercial for the Showtime cable channel

No matter how far you have gone on the wrong road, turn back.

Turkish proverb

If we open a quarrel between the past and the present, we shall find that we have lost the future.

Winston Churchill

Disorganization, then reorganization.

Unknown

What gives hope its power is not the accumulation of demonstrable facts, but the release of human energies generated by the longing for something better.

Norman Cousins[1]

The reward for attention is always healing.

Julia Cameron[2]

If you're ridin' ahead of the herd, take a look back every now and then to make sure it's still there.

Will Rogers

I recently read a great sports story that spoke to the possibility of breaking impossible barriers. This story goes back to 1976, and the world of weight lifting. At the time, it was assumed that lifting 500 pounds was beyond all human capability. Russian weight lifter Vasily Alexeyev set out to reach this goal, but try as he might, he could not achieve this record. One day, his trainers gave him a bar and told him it weighed 499.9 pounds, revealing to Alexeyev only after he had successfully lifted it, that the bar actually weighed 501.5 pounds. Once he had broken through this 500-pound ceiling, he continued setting new records, eventually going on to lift 564 pounds.[3] Clearly the greatest obstacle here was a mental one; once the long-held assumptions were circumvented, his achievement surpassed anything ever imagined possible.

If changes in our thinking are the most difficult to make, they are also the most freeing. There are places in our current reality and cultural belief systems that are outdated, inaccurate and no longer serviceable in an era of information and connectedness. But I believe that we have choices about what we define as our reality in education, and in the end, the world of status and judgments and artificial criteria may only be as real—and as limiting—as we choose to believe it to be. We will ultimately prove whichever reality we choose to accept, so it pays to choose wisely. As bleak as the picture can appear at times, I'd like to throw in with Toffler's challenge to resist "the chic pessimism that is so prevalent today." Becoming aware of the darkness is simply a step toward bringing these elements into the light. They are only opportunities to learn and change; they are not cause for despair. We are in transition and with transition always come chaos, fear and, to a certain degree, grief. Most of the conflict we're seeing is the result of political battles waged by people jockeying for control while desperately trying to preserve "the dying industrial order." But as Yogi Berra once said, "There's no stopping the future." And Toffler notes that the Third Wave civilization "could, with some intelligent help from us, turn out to be the first truly humane civilization in recorded history."[4]

As new information emerges about how people learn and interact most successfully, it will be harder and harder to ignore the ways in which our current attitudes and behaviors lack congruence. The call for schools to operate as conscious entities has never been louder. We can't continue to get away with doing business as usual when such methods are so obviously undermining our goals. Rita Mercier urges us to continually question and self-assess, create an atmosphere that welcomes challenges, introspection and a search for contradiction within our system. "Even if school policy chooses to ignore research," she suggests, "do it consciously, and then check back from time to time to see if the policy is working and serving your needs." Reevaluate goals and where policy isn't serving, adjust as necessary. One contributor likened the process of change to a climb up the mountain, encouraging those needing the courage to stay in the moment: "Your rope is as long as it needs to be, and you can always tie a knot, hang on and yell for help. The worst case is not falling off the mountain. It is never daring the summit."

When people approach me to ask if I think a particular strategy will or will not work, I typically answer with a question: "What is your ultimate goal?" Our sense of the big picture, our mission and direction is often the first casualty in the crunch of daily life. I would urge that we stay mindful of what we're doing here and what we're truly trying to accomplish in any decision we make, and urge a deliberate resistance to the monumental appeal of the quick fix. I also believe that this whole issue of change will challenge us to examine our individual roles and personal responsibility in the process as never before. Jordan Riak remarks, "Reform only takes a loud, strong minority." For those awaiting the initiative of the majority, counting on the System to change, I will call upon the wisdom of personal growth expert Nathaniel Branden, who counsels: "No one is coming." Each of us in education faces the probability of being called upon, if only by our own conscience, to be a pioneer, a visionary, a salesperson and a healer. And hopefully, somewhere between denial, panic and despair, each of us can carve a path on which, together, we can accomplish our goals.

Are there problems and bad habits we need to address? You bet. And yes, we still have miles to go before we sleep. But along the way, what I would wish for everyone on this planet is this: To experience, just once, that magic moment when a light goes on in the eyes of a child, when resistance breaks, when hearts connect—for these are moments that make the challenges of teaching worth every second, and remind us of why we are here in the first place. They are the moments that will keep the good ones in the game, putting in more hours than most people will ever know, juggling the demands of a job that, when done right, can match any other, in its complexity, and in the enormity of its potential impact.

We will change as we are already changing. But the most significant changes, I believe, will come not from new mandates and performance criteria, as well meaning as these, perhaps, are intended to be. The potential for healing lies not in the system of rules and punishments, but in a system that celebrates curiosity and caring, discovery and joy. And yes, in the process, we will make it better and we will make it safe. One heart at a time.

Appendix A

Survey: Is Your School an Emotionally Safe Place?

This survey lists a number of practices that characterize a school with an emotionally safe climate. It has been included to help you evaluate your school's goals, policies and intentions, as well as the degree to which each exists in actual practice. The list is deliberately idealistic and comprehensive. Studies suggest that each item is an important component of an emotionally safe school environment, and that emotional safety is built on a combination of *all* of the characteristics listed in this survey. As schools strive to achieve the specific behaviors each item suggests, they will no doubt see improvements in the culture of the school, as well as in the performance, commitment, behavior and interactions that occur within its walls. Likewise, as schools increase the agreement with each of the items in this survey, they can expect a reduction of stress commonly associated with failure, rebelliousness, disruptiveness and passive student behavior.

You may wish to use this survey to evaluate the degree to which your school is committed to each item in terms of its philosophy or vision, as well as the degree to which the behaviors described in each item regularly occur in actual practice. You can rate each item for an individual classroom, or according to your perception of the school environment or district as a whole.

Use the following scale to rate each item:

1- Strongly agree
2- Somewhat agree
3- Somewhat disagree
4- Strongly disagree

Need for Meaningful Outcomes (Positive Consequences), Structure, Boundaries (Limits) and Follow-Through

___ We make a deliberate effort to anticipate what students and teachers (and parents) will need in various situations in order to prevent problems from occurring.

___ We have and communicate boundaries and policies that clearly describe desirable and acceptable student behaviors.
___ We have and communicate boundaries and policies that clearly describe desirable and acceptable staff behaviors.
___ The school environment is reward oriented (as opposed to being punishment oriented): Rules and boundaries emphasize the *positive* consequences of cooperation and compliance.
___ Our goal is to motivate through access to positive outcomes, rather than through avoidance or fear of negative outcomes.
___ We attempt to motivate students with the promise of a positive outcome, rather than using statements that offer conditional approval or safety (avoidance of disapproval, punishment) for cooperation (threats).
___ We attempt to follow through consistently, withholding (or withdrawing) positive outcomes until students follow through on what is required on their end.
___ We are committed to avoiding warnings, threats, and meaningless or delayed (negative) consequences.
___ We make students and their parents aware, as soon as possible, of changes in behavior or performance that could affect grades, promotion or graduation.
___ We communicate with parents on a regular basis about what their kids are doing well.

Need for Respect, Belonging and Dignity

___ We attempt to avoid equating students' worth with their behavior or achievement.
___ We attempt to avoid humiliation, shaming, sarcasm, ridicule or other forms of attack with regard to students' personality, achievement or behavior.
___ We attempt to avoid depending on negative adult reactions (anger, punishment, disappointment) in order to motivate students (or control their behavior).
___ We recognize that students have a need to experience meaningful positive outcomes, just as adults do.
___ We treat our students with the same respect we want them to show us and one another.
___ We recognize that our students have a need for dignity, purpose, success, impact (seeing outcomes of choices and behaviors), acceptance, belonging, attention, structure, power and fun, among other things.
___ We encourage students to have and voice their own thoughts and opinions.

___ We encourage students to speak up for their own instructional needs (for example, more help, additional information or resources, clarification, other learning needs).

___ We encourage inquiry and debate, and attempt to avoid negatively reacting to students who challenge or disagree with adults (although we do ask students to present their positions respectfully).

___ We attempt to adhere to the same standards of behavior (including language and tone of voice) that we expect or require from our students.

___ We regard—and use—a students' mistakes simply as opportunities for new learning.

___ We avoid responding with impatience, anger or disappointment to a student who is having difficulty understanding or mastering a new concept or performing a new skill.

___ We respect students' affective needs and are committed to listening and supporting their feelings in positive ways.

___ We work to eliminate prejudices toward students based on their racial or cultural background, physical appearance; academic, artistic or athletic competence; sexual orientation; family history; prior achievement or performance.

___ We avoid gossiping about students or their families.

___ We strive to stay aware of put-downs expressed by students or staff, especially those that involve the use of slurs or derogatory names or remarks.

___ We respond immediately to put-downs, slurs, and derogatory names or remarks (rather than ignoring or excusing them).

___ We respond to such incidents as opportunities to teach (build connections, empathy, social skills and respect for diversity), rather than punishing the students involved.

___ We have programs in place to encourage in students service work (mentoring, helping, etc.) within the school and/or community.

Need for Autonomy (Power and Control)

___ We accept the importance of students learning decision-making and self-management skills.

___ We encourage kids to set goals and evaluate options in order to take responsibility for solving their own problems, rather than "rescuing" them or telling them what they should do.

___ We allow students to self-manage with regard to materials and resources.

___ We encourage students to self-manage their personal needs within clearly stated boundaries (for example, drinking water or using the rest rooms as needed).

___ We allow and encourage students to have input in and make decisions about their learning (topics, presentation, media, sequence, assignments, need for additional practice, readiness for the next skill or topic, etc.).
___ We allow and encourage students to have input in and make decisions about how, where and with whom they work.
___ We hold students accountable for their behavioral choices without blaming, shaming, attacking or punishing (for example, withholding positive outcome, privileges, credit for work due).
___ Students are encouraged to initiate and take risks regarding their own learning.
___ We allow and encourage students to create, design, request or renegotiate projects and assignments to make them personally meaningful and relevant.

Need for Recognition, Attention and Emotional Safety

___ We attempt to recognize positive behavior with statements that emphasize a positive outcome or meaningful benefit *to the students,* rather than using statements that emphasize the students' worth ("goodness"), our happiness or pleasure, or the students' ability to please us.
___ We attempt to reinforce positive behavior by allowing positive outcomes to occur, continue or become available, contingent, for example, on work completion or nondisruptive behavior.
___ We attempt to meet students' needs for attention in positive, constructive and proactive ways in order to diminish the tendency for them to act out to get these needs met.
___ We strive to stay aware of changes in patterns in students' behavior and to maintain a sense of how students are doing (that is, not just focusing on their academic performance).
___ We attempt to create emotional safety by noticing and supporting students in crisis.
___ We provide appropriate outlets for students in crisis.
___ Our students know that if they need to talk, we are willing to listen (or set a time when we can listen, or refer them to someone who can listen).
___ We respect students' needs for confidentiality to the degree that doing so will not put that student or anyone else in danger.
___ We strive to maintain awareness of how students treat one another.
___ We immediately respond to incidents we witness that involve any form of bullying, harrassment or threat to a student's safety.

Need for Options as a Learner (Individuality)

___ We attempt to determine what interests and motivates our students and use this information in our planning and instruction.
___ We attempt to identify various aspects of our students' individual learning needs (such as learning styles, modality preferences, dominance profiles, temperament or personality profiles), and use this information in our planning and instruction.
___ We attempt to identify various types of intelligences (linguistic, musical, logical-mathematical, spatial, bodily-kinesthetic, naturalistic, interpersonal and intrapersonal) and use this information to capitalize and build on students' strengths.
___ We provide resources and activities to accommodate a variety of intelligences in each class.
___ We attempt to accommodate a variety of modality strengths (visual, auditory, tactile and kinesthetic preferences) in our directions and activities.
___ We attempt to accommodate a variety of learning styles and preferences in our instruction and assignments.
___ We recognize and attempt to accommodate the needs of tactile and kinesthetic learners (as well as high visual, verbal and auditory learners).
___ We acknowledge and appreciate the fact that some students may pay attention without sitting up straight and making continual eye contact.
___ We make sure kids have ample opportunities to move during the day.
___ We teach children ways to self-regulate (maintain appropriate alertness for the particular class or activity) without disrupting others.
___ We attempt to accommodate a variety of learning preferences by offering choices, particularly during independent work time (for example, seating or location in room, affiliation, music or sound, intake, etc.).
___ We offer a variety of assessment tools to allow students to demonstrate mastery in ways besides paper-and-pencil tests.

Need for Success (Academic, Social, Intrapersonal)

___ We assess student ability before beginning instruction or assigning tasks.
___ We attempt to accept students exactly the way they come to us, build on what they know and encourage growth from wherever they start.

___ We attempt to provide opportunities for success for each child in the school, even if he or she is far behind curricular expectations.

___ We attempt to match instruction and assignments to individual student needs according to their current skill or mastery levels or prior experience.

___ We have adopted the belief that the primary purpose of evaluating a student's work is to determine what type of instruction or resources that particular student needs next.

___ We invite and consider student input and self-assessment when assigning placement, follow-up work or grades.

___ If a student fails to master a concept or skill, we see our role as that of improving understanding, rather than simply evaluating their performance before moving on to the next concept.

___ We encourage students to use our feedback to improve their work and resubmit (for a higher grade, for example, or until they get it right).

___ We attempt to build interpersonal skills such as communication skills, respect, tolerance, compassion, resistance to teasing and peer pressure, and other positive social behaviors.

___ We attempt to build intrapersonal (character) skills such as persistence, responsibility, honesty, integrity, as well as confidence, the ability to stick up for oneself, problem-solving skills and resistance to failure, defeatism or victim thinking.

Areas of greatest strengths:

____

____

____

____

____

____

____

____

____

____

____

____

Areas most in need of improvements:

Appendix B

Building Emotional Safety Worksheet

Goal:

____

____

____

____

____

Evidence of need for improvements:

____

____

____

____

____

Existing strengths we can capitalize on to achieve this goal:

____

____

____

____

Existing support for achievement of this goal:

____

____

____

____

____

Existing constraints and obstacles:

____

____

____

____

____

Potential constraints and obstacles:

____

____

____

____

____

____

What we need to accomplish this goal:

____

____

____

____

____

____

____

Resources (persons, programs, literature, etc.) that can help us:

____

____

____

____

____

Steps and processes (timetable) for achieving this goal:

____

____

____

____

____

How we'll know we achieved this goal (observable indicators):

____

____

____

____

____

Chapter Notes

Introduction

[1] Carol Silverman Saunders, *Safe at School* (Minneapolis: Free Spirit Publishing, 1994), 7.

[2] H. Jerome Freiberg, "Measuring School Climate: Let Me Count the Ways," *Educational Leadership,* vol. 56, no. 1 (September 1998). Available: *Association for Supervision and Curriculum Development* Web site, [Internet, WWW], Address: *http://www.ascd.org/safeschools/e19809/freibergclimate.html.*

Part I
Dimensions of a Very Big Picture

[1] Joshua M. Freedman, Anabel L. Jensen, Marsha C. Rideout and Patricia E. Freedman, *Handle with Care: Emotional Intelligence Activity Book* (San Mateo, Calif.: Six Seconds, 1998), 54.

[2] Quoted in Naomi Drew, *The Peaceful Classroom in Action* (Torrance, Calif.: Jalmar Press, 1999), xiii.

[3] Quoted in Jeff Hartzer, "Chaos Journal," 11 November 2000. Available: *Aquilaarts* Web site, [Internet, WWW], Address: *http://aquilaarts.com/chaosjournal.html.*

Chapter 1
What Safety Is

[1] Wire report and articles appearing in the *Albuquerque Journal,* 22 November 1999: A1–A3.

[2] Greene, Leon, "Beyond Violence," *Principal* 79, no. 1 (September 1999): 4.

[3] Greene, 4; also "Annual Report on School Safety," October 1998. Available: The U.S. Department of Education Publications Web site, [Internet, WWW], Address: *http://www.ed.gov/pubs/AnnSchoolRept98,* "Executive Summary." Additionally, William Ayres reports that the vast majority of children have been by adults, not other kids. (William Ayres, "I Walk with Delinquents," *Educational Leadership,* vol. 55, no. 2 [October 1997]. Available: Association of Supervision and Curriculum Development Web site, [Internet, WWW], Address: *http://www.ascd.org/pubs/el/oct97/extayers.html,* also, *http://www.ascd.org/safeschools/el9710/oct97toc.htm.)*

[4] Ibid., "Introduction."

[5] Charles L. Whitfield, *Healing the Child Within* (Deerfield Beach, Fla.: Health Communications, Inc., 1987), 18.

[6] Carl Rogers and H. Jerome Frieberg, *Freedom to Learn* (New York: Macmillan College Publishing Co., Inc., 1994), 25. Note: I doubt that the same survey given in a similar district would yield significantly different results.

[7] Rita Mercier, *Your Right to Know: An Insider's Parent Guide to School Safety, Elementary Edition,* unpublished manuscript (Encinitas, Calif.: Educational Consultant Services, 1999).

[8] For more information, refer to Mattise's book, *The Hurt-Free School Program,* or her Web site at *http://www.hurt-free-character.com.*

Chapter 2
The Heart of the Matter: Feelings and School

[1] Linda Lantieri and Janet Patti, *Waging Peace in Our Schools* (Boston: Beacon Press, 1996), 3.
[2] Bernard J. Baars, "Can Anyone Overstate the Significance of Emotions?" (no date). Available: Virginia Tech Web site, [Internet, WWW], Address: *http://server.phil.vt.edu/assc/watt/baars1.html.*
[3] Quoted in Elaine DeBeaufort with Aura Sofia Diaz, *The Three Faces of Mind* (Wheaton, Ill.: Quest Books, 1996), 131.
[4] Carla Hannaford, *Smart Moves: Why Learning Is Not All in Your Head* (Arlington, Va.: Great Oceans Publishers, 1995), 51, citing research findings by Antonio Damasio and his colleagues.
[5] Quote found on the University of North Carolina, Wilmington, PDS School Systems and UNCW Combined Calendar, 2000–01.
[6] Robert Sylwester, "How Our Brain Determines What's Important," *A Celebration of Neurons (Chapter 4).* Available: ASCD Web site, [Internet, WWW], Address: *http://www.ascd.org/pdi/brain/read4_1.html.*
[7] John Steinberg, "A History of Affective Education," *EQ Today* (19 March 1999). Available: 6seconds Web site, [Internet, WWW], Address: *http://www.6seconds.org/jrn/jpca.html.*
[8] Ibid.
[9] I worked in a number of classrooms and schools during much of the 1970s and 1980s, either as a classroom teacher or at the university level, and despite this era's reputation for permissiveness, in actual practice, this rarely ended up being the case. It didn't take very long to realize that simply providing an exciting environment with a ton of resources and materials and telling a roomful of kids to spend the day "creating meaningful learning experiences" just wasn't going to wash, particularly when working with kids who had few independent learning skills and no history of working in an unstructured environment. Teachers who didn't figure this out fairly quickly rarely lasted long in the classroom.
[10] Stanley I. Greenspan with Beryl Lieff Benderly, *The Growth of the Mind* (Reading, Mass.: Addison-Wesley Publishing Co., Inc., 1997), 2.
[11] Anne Wilson Schaef, *When Society Becomes an Addict* (San Francisco: Harper & Row Publishers, 1987), 8.
[12] Sylwester, "How Our Brain Determines What's Important."
[13] Ibid.
[14] Eric Jensen, *Completing the Puzzle* (Del Mar, Calif.: The Brain Store, Inc., 1997), 13.
[15] Gordon H. Bower, "How Might Emotions Affect Learning?" *The Handbook of Emotion and Memory: Research and Theory.* Sven-Ake Christianson, ed. (Hillsdale, N.J.: Lawrence Erlbaum Associates, Publishers, 1992), 8.
[16] Diane Schilling, ed., *50 Activities for Teaching Emotional Intelligence, Level II: Middle School* (Torrance, Calif.: Innerchoice Publishing, 1996), 4.
[17] Greenspan, *The Growth of the Mind,* 1.

Chapter 3
Safety: It's a Brain Thing

[1] Greenspan, *The Growth of the Mind,* 212.
[2] Sandi Redenbach, *Autobiography of a Dropout: Dear Diary* (Davis, Calif.: Esteem Seminar Programs and Publications, 1996), 94.
[3] Daniel Goleman, *Emotional Intelligence* (New York: Bantam Books, 1995), 8.

[4] Eric Jensen, *Brain-Based Learning* (Del Mar, Calif.: Turning Point Publishing, 1996), 29, quoting the work of Antonio Damasio.
[5] Ibid.
[6] Robin Karr-Morse and Meredith S. Wiley, *Ghosts in the Nursery* (New York: The Atlantic Monthly Press, 1997), 32.
[7] This information was condensed from a number of resources, including Goleman, 11–17; Carla Hannaford, *The Physiological Basis of Learning and Kinesiology* (course manual, 1998); Jensen, *Brain-Based Learning,* 21–22; Jensen, *Completing the Puzzle,* 16–17; Karr-Morse and Wiley, 32; David A. Sousa, *How the Brain Learns* (Reston, Va.: The National Association of Secondary School Principals, 1995), 2–3; and Mary Sue Williams and Sherry Shellenberger, *How Does Your Engine Run?* (Albuquerque, N. Mex.: TherapyWorks, Inc., 1996), 1:6–7.
[8] Hannaford, *The Physiological Basis of Learning and Kinesiology;* Jensen, *Brain-Based Learning,* 21–22; Jensen, *Completing the Puzzle,* 16–17; Karr-Morse and Wiley, 32; and David A. Sousa, 2–3.
[9] Ibid.
[10] Lawrence E. Shapiro, *How to Raise a Child with a High EQ* (New York: HarperCollins Publishers, Inc., 1997), 13.
[11] Goleman, 11–17; LeDoux, Joseph, *The Emotional Brain* (New York: Simon & Schuster, 1996), 50; Michael D. Lemonick, "Smart Genes?" *Time* magazine, No. 39 (27 September 1999): 50; Schilling, 4–5; and Sylwester, "How Our Brain Determines What's Important."
[12] Schilling, 4.
[13] Goleman, 13–16; Schilling, 4–5; Shapiro, 13–14; and Robert Sylwester, "How Emotions Affect Learning," *Educational Leadership* 52, no. 2 (October 1994). Available ASCD Web site, [Internet, WWW], Address: *http://www.ascd.org/pdi/brain/read4_2.html.* Note: LeDoux forecasts the evolutionary possibility that future humans will be better able to control their emotions, as cortical connections to the amygdala "are far greater in primates than in other mammals, suggesting the possibility that as these connections continue to expand, the cortex might gain more and more control over the amygdala" (303).
[14] Karr-Morse and Wiley, 32; and LeDoux, 50.
[15] Karr-Morse and Wiley, 32.
[16] Schilling, 5.
[17] Karr-Morse and Wiley, 40.

Chapter 4
Learning and the Brain

[1] Michael Gazzaniga, *Mind Matters* (Boston: Houghton Mifflin Co., 1988), 14.
[2] Sousa, 9.
[3] Quoted in Hannaford, *Smart Moves,* 27.
[4] Karen Stone McCown, Joshua M. Freedman, Anabel L. Jensen and Marsha C. Rideout, *Self Science: The Emotional Intelligence Curriculum* (San Mateo, Calif.: Six Seconds Publishing, 1998), ix.
[5] Marcia D'Arcangelo, "How the Brain Learns: The Brains Behind the Brain," *Educational Leadership* 56, no. 3 (November 1998). Available: Association of Supervision and Curriculum Development Web site, [Internet, WWW], Address: *http://www.ascd.org/pubs/el/nov98/extd'arcangelo.html;* Gordon Dryden and Jeannette Vos, *The Learning Revolution* (Rolling Hills Estates, Calif.: Jalmar Press, 1994), 110; Hannaford, *Smart Moves,* 18; and Sousa, 4–5.
[6] Hannaford, *Smart Moves,* 24.
[7] Robert Valiant, "Growing Brain Connections: A Modest Proposal," *Schools in the Middle* 7, no. 4 (March/April 1998): 24.
[8] Claude R. Beamish, "Knowledge About the Brain for Parents, Students, and Teachers: The Keys to Removing the Invisible Roadblocks to Learning and High Self-Esteem for

All Students." Conference paper, *The Oregon Conference Monograph,* vol. 7 (1995), 23–25; Hannaford, *Smart Moves,* 18–20; Sousa, 4–5; and Valiant, 24.

[9] Hannaford, *Smart Moves,* 18–21.

[10] Beamish, "Knowledge About the Brain," 23.

[11] Ibid. Note: In a personal interview, Dr. Beamish noted that it may take years before the brain is ready to myelinate in a certain area, explaining why many of us develop skills and abilities in our adult years that we were unable to develop as children in school.

[12] Sousa, 10.

[13] LeDoux, 278; Sousa, 12; and Sylwester, "How Our Brain Determines What's Important."

[14] Ledoux, 270–271; and Sousa, 14–15. Note: The number of items an individual can process changes with age, generally from about two items at preschool to an average of seven through adolescence and adulthood. Likewise, we vary with age in the amount of time we can work with this information before we lose our focus, approximately ten to twenty minutes for adolescents and adults.

[15] Hannaford, *Smart Moves,* 50–55; Jensen, *Brain-Based Learning,* 186–187; and Sousa, 15–17.

[16] Quoted in LeDoux, 272.

[17] Bruce Joyce and Marsha Weil, *Models of Teaching,* 2d ed. (Englewood Cliffs, N.J.: Prentice-Hall, Inc., 1980), 75–78. Note: The authors cite David Ausubel's work with Advance Organizers to improve the effectiveness of lectures, presentations and other forms of receptive learning. Ausubel argued that "whether material is meaningful depends on the learner and the material, not the method of presentation."

[18] Sylwester, "How Our Brain Determines What's Important."

[19] Karin Frey, "Social-Emotional Learning: A Foundation for Academic Success," *Committee for Children Prevention Update* (spring 1999): 1.

[20] Quoted in Jane Bluestein, *Mentors, Masters and Mrs. MacGregor: Stories of Teachers Making a Difference* (Deerfield Beach, Fla.: Health Communications, Inc., 1995), 177.

[21] LeDoux, 206.

[22] Bower, 15.

[23] Stanley I. Greenspan with Jacqueline Salmon, *The Challenging Child: Understanding, Raising and Enjoying the Five "Difficult" Types of Children* (Reading, Mass.: Addison-Wesley Publishing Co., 1995), 21; also Greenspan, *The Growth of the Mind,* 5, 32.

[24] Greenspan, *The Growth of the Mind,* 21.

[25] LeDoux, 181, 209, 224.

[26] Ibid., 202–204.

[27] Sousa, 34.

[28] LeDoux, 211. Also Bower, 22.

[29] Ibid. Note: Many individuals in recovery have shared experiences in which they had to relearn skills they had mastered while they were still using. One reported that for months after she quit smoking, she had to actually hold an unlit cigarette in her hand to recall the details of a particular conversation or event that had occurred while she still smoked. Nonetheless, according to counselor Beverly Davies, this particular example of state-dependent learning may become increasingly rare if support for treatment opportunities continue to decline.

[30] Gordon Dryden and Jeannette Vos, "Teaching Breakthroughs," The Learning Web Web site. Available: [Internet, WWW], Address: *http://www.thelearningweb.net/teaching_breakthroughs.htm.*

[31] Charles Dickens, *David Copperfield,* George H. Ford, ed. Original publication date, 1849–1850 (New York: Houghton Mifflin Co., 1958), 79.

[32] Karr-Morse and Wiley, 33.

[33] Neil Blacklock, "Fear Cripples," from "Facts and Arguments," *Globe and Mail* (18 August 1997). Available: PTAVE Web site, [Internet, WWW], Address: *http://nospank.org/blklock.htm.*

[34] Chester L. Quarles, *Staying Safe at School* (Thousand Oaks, Calif.: Corwin Press, Inc., 1993), 24.

[35] Michael Okuda, Denise Okuda and Debbie Mirek, *The Star Trek Encyclopedia: A Reference Guide to the Future* (New York: Pocket Books, 1994), 224.
[36] Beamish, personal interview. Also Hannaford, *Smart Moves,* 54.
[37] Bobbie Faulkner and Patricia Faiveley, "Multi-Age from the Ground Up," in *Multi-Age Classrooms,* Karen Gutloff, ed. (Washington, D.C.: NEA Teacher-to-Teacher Books, National Education Association, 1995), 85.
[38] William W. Purkey and David N. Aspy, "The Mental Health of Students: Nobody Minds? Nobody Cares?" Reprint from *Person-Centered Review,* vol. 3, no. 1 (February 1988): 46.
[39] Schilling, 5.
[40] Gazzaniga, 206.
[41] O. Tanner, quoted in Edward W. Schultz and Charles M. Heuchert, *Child Stress and the School Experience* (New York: Human Sciences Press, Inc., 1983), 29.
[42] Sylwester, "How Our Brain Determines What's Important."
[43] S. B. Cotler and J. J. Guerra, from *Assertion Training* (Champaign, Ill: Research Press, 1978), quoted in Schultz and Heuchert, 30; also Robert Schacter and Carol Spearin McCauley, *When Your Child Is Afraid* (New York: Simon & Schuster, 1988), 24.
[44] Beamish, "Knowledge About the Brain," 24–25; Hannaford, *The Physiological Basis of Learning and Kinesiology;* Jensen, *Introduction to Brain-Compatible Learning,* 37; and Sousa, 13. Note: The term "downshifting" was coined by researcher Leslie Hart.
[45] Claude R. Beamish, "Reality, Changing Realities, and the Causes of Realities," The MindLift Foundation Web site. Available: [Internet, WWW], Address: *http://www.mindlift.com/reality.htm.*
[46] Jensen, *Brain-Based Learning,* 23.
[47] Beamish, "Reality, Changing Realities, and the Causes of Realities"; Hannaford, *Smart Moves,* 156; and Sylwester, "How Our Brains Determine What's Important."
[48] Gazzaniga, 200.
[49] Shannon Brownlee, "The Biology of Soul Murder," *U.S. News & World Report,* 11 November 1996. Available: PTAVE (Parents & Teachers Against Violence in Education) Web site, [Internet, WWW], Address: *http://nospank.org/11trau.htm.* Note: This article cited the work of Megan Gunnar, a University of Minnesota developmental psychobiologist who studied children in Romanian orphanages.
[50] Gazzaniga, 200; Hannaford, *The Physiological Basis of Learning and Kinesiology;* and Sylwester, "How Our Brains Determine What's Important."
[51] LeDoux, 19.
[52] Bower, 14.
[53] Clare Cherry, Douglas Godwin, and Jesse Staples, *Is the Left Brain Always Right?* (Torrance, Calif.: Fearon Teacher Aids, 1989), 132.
[54] From B. Philips, *School, Stress and Anxiety* (New York: Human Sciences Press, 1978), 146, as quoted in Schultz and Heuchert, 31.
[55] Schultz and Heuchert, 31.
[56] Many of the items on the list appeared in Schultz and Heuchert, 21, 53–54. Other sources include Jensen, *Completing the Puzzle,* 83; Jensen, *Introduction to Brain-Compatible Learning,* 43. Other sources include interviews, surveys, insights and experiences shared by workshop participants, plus personal observations and experience (as both teacher and student), plus input from conversations or communications with Carla Hannaford, Mike Selby, Andy Quiñones, Claude Beamish, Jan Rogers, Mary Sue Williams and Sherry Shellenberger. (Many items suggested in the literature overlapped or were repeatedly expressed in interviews and surveys.)

Chapter 5
Body and Mind

[1] From the introduction to a class on The Physiological Foundations of Educational Kinesiology.
[2] Linda Verlee Williams, *Teaching for the Two-Sided Mind: A Guide to Right Brain/Left Brain Education* (New York: Simon & Schuster, 1983), 144.
[3] Ibid., 146.
[4] Carol Stock Kranowitz, *The Out-of-Sync Child* (New York: The Berkley Publishing Group, 1998), 268.
[5] Quoted in Jane Bluestein, *Mentors, Masters and Mrs. MacGregor: Stories of Teachers Making a Difference* (Deerfield Beach, Fla.: Health Communications, Inc., 1995), 72.
[6] Kranowitz, 132–33.
[7] Ibid.; Deborah Sunbeck, *Infinity Walk* (Torrance, Calif.: Jalmar Press, 1996), 89–90; Linda Verlee Williams, 144–45.
[8] Hannaford, *Smart Moves,* 101.
[9] Ibid, 95, 99; also Hannaford from Physiological Foundations of Educational Kinesiology class; also Jensen, *Brain-Based Learning,* 33.
[10] Hannaford, *Smart Moves,* 99.
[11] Julia Cameron with Mark Bryan, *The Artist's Way* (New York: G.P. Putnam's Sons, 1992), 22.
[12] Hannaford, *Smart Moves,* 99.
[13] Ibid., 96.
[14] Sheila Ostrander and Lynn Schroeder, with Nancy Ostrander, *Superlearning* (New York: Delacorte Press, 1979), 9–15.
[15] Ibid., 7.
[16] Paul E. Dennison and Gail E. Dennison, *Brain Gym,* Teacher's Edition, revised (Ventura, Calif.: Edu-Kinesthetics, Inc., 1994), introduction; also Sunbeck, 55, 126, 177.
[17] William Revelle and Debra A. Loftus, "The Implications of Arousal Effects for the Study of Affect and Memory," *The Handbook of Emotion and Memory: Research and Theory,* Sven-Ake Christianson, ed. (Hillsdale, N.J.: Lawrence Erlbaum Associates Publishers, 1992), 115.
[18] Williams and Shellenberger, 1–5.
[19] Cherry et al., 134.
[20] DeBeaufort and Diaz, 144.
[21] Williams and Shellenberger, A-55.
[22] All of these examples were taken from the "Sensory-Motor Preference Checklist (for Adults)" in Williams and Shellenberger, A-55.
[23] Most teachers tell me they have fewer problems in this regard when they communicate their intentions with parents, administrators and other staff *before* implementing non-traditional options in their classes, and especially when the behavior of their students does not interfere with other classes.
[24] Sunbeck, 126.
[25] Jensen, *Completing the Puzzle,* 51.
[26] Jane Bluestein, *21st Century Discipline: Teaching Students Responsibility and Self-Control* (Torrance, Calif: Fearon Teaching Aids, Frank Schaffer Publications, 1999), 143.

Chapter 6
Monsters in the Closet: Where Children Are Coming From

[1] Karr-Morse and Wiley, 24.
[2] Survey response via e-mail.
[3] Nathaniel Branden, *The Six Pillars of Self-Esteem* (New York: Bantam Books, 1994), 195.

[4] Greenspan, *The Growth of the Mind,* 220; also Lorraine B. Wallach, "Violence and Young Children's Development," *ERIC Digest* (June 1994). Available: ERIC Web site, *U.S. Department of Education,* [Internet, WWW], Address: *http://www.ed.gov/databases/ERIC_Digests/ed369578.html.*
[5] Greenspan, *The Challenging Child,* 26–27.
[6] Renchler, Ron, "Poverty and Learning," *ERIC Digest,* no. 83 (May 1993). Available: ERIC Web site, U.S. Department of Education, [Internet, WWW], Address: *http://www.ed.gov/databases/ERIC_Digests/ed357433.html.*
[7] Karr-Morse and Wiley, 13.
[8] "Education Indicators," *America's Children 1998.* Available: Forum on Child and Family Statistics, ChildStats Web site, [Internet, WWW], Address: *http://www.childstats.gov/ac1998/edtxt.htm;* also "Health Indicators," *America's Children 1998.* Available: Forum on Child and Family Statistics, ChildStats Web site, [Internet, WWW], Address: *http://www.childstats.gov/ac1998/toc.htm.*
[9] Nathaniel Branden, 171–72.
[10] Abraham Maslow, *Toward a Psychology of Being* (New York: D. Van Nostrand Co., 1968), 51.
[11] Karr-Morse and Wiley, 24.
[12] Rogers and Frieberg, citing Ronald Koutulak's summary of brain research originally published in the *Chicago Tribune* in 1993.
[13] Hannaford, *Smart Moves,* 62.
[14] Katherine Corcoran, citing the work of Alison Gopnik, Andrew Meltzoff and Patricia Kuhl in *The Scientist in the Crib: Minds, Brains and How Children Learn,* in "Authors Say Babies Can Learn Without Gimmicks," *Albuquerque Journal* (26 December 1999).
[15] Greenspan, *The Growth of the Mind,* 10.
[16] Corcoran.
[17] Quoted in Catherine Sullivan-DeCarlo, Karol DeFalco and Verdell Roberts, "Helping Students Avoid Risky Behavior," *Educational Leadership,* vol. 56, no. 1 (September 1998). Available: *Association of Supervision and Curriculum Development* Web site, [Internet, WWW], Address: *http://www.ascd.org/pubs/el/sep98/sullivan.html.*
[18] Robert Subby, *Lost in the Shuffle* (Deerfield Beach, Fla.: Health Communications, Inc., 1987), 10–12, 15.
[19] Barbara Cottman Becnel, *The Co-Dependent Parent* (San Francisco: Harper San Francisco, 1991), viii.
[20] C. P. Anthony and G. A. Thibodeau, from *Textbook of Anatomy and Physiology* (St. Louis: C. V. Mosby Co., 1979), p. 672, quoted in Schultz and Heuchert, 23.
[21] The sources of stress listed in these two paragraphs were compiled from a number of sources, including: "Risk Check for Your Child," handout from Garfield Middle School, Albuquerque, New Mexico; Branden, 194–95; Jodi Freeman, *How to Drug-Proof Kids* (Albuquerque, N. Mex.: The Think Shop, Inc., 1989); Schultz and Heuchert, 74–75.
[22] Karr-Morse and Wiley, 295.
[23] Michael Lemonick, "Fast-Track Toddlers," *Time* magazine, vol. 154, no. 7 (16 August 1999): 76–77.
[24] Adderholt-Elliot, 9. Note: The author also notes that the pressure on first-born children is usually the most intense.
[25] Nancy Gibbs, "If We Have It, Do We Use It?" *Time* magazine, no. 39 (27 September 1999): 53; Lemonick, "Fast Track Toddlers"; Craig Wilson, "Bugged by Parents Who Make the Kid's Grade," *USA Today* (27 October 1999).
[26] Ibid.
[27] Other factors affecting the impact of stress may include the child's temperament, the type and amount of support available to the child in the family, school and community, and the number of stressful events the child experiences.
[28] J. H. Monaghan, J. O. Robinson and J. A. Dodge, "The Children's Life Events Inventory," *Journal of Psychosomatic Research.* vol. 23, no. 1 (1979): 63–68.
[29] David G. Fassler and Lynne S. Dumas, *"Help Me, I'm Sad"* (New York: Viking, 1997), 20–23.

[30] Fassler and Dumas, 23.
[31] Judsen Culbreth, appearing on *CBS This Morning,* as quoted in "Stressed-Out Kids," 28 August 1999. Available: The CBS Worldwide Inc. Web site, [Internet, WWW], Address: *http://www.cbs.com/flat/story-180058.html.*
[32] Reynold Bean, *How to Help Your Children Succeed in School* (Los Angeles: Price Stern Sloan, 1991), 51–53; 66; Schacter and McCauley, 133, 144, including a reference to *USA Today*'s 1985 report on the Search Institute's poll of 8,000 children, aged 10–14.
[33] Claire Thornton, "Needed: Responsive Teachers," *Momentum,* vol. 29, no. 2 (April/May 1998): 77; also "Statistics Desk," *National Clearinghouse on Child Abuse* (12 November 1998). Available: Committee for Children Web site, [Internet, WWW], Address: *http://www.calib.com/nccanch/services/stats.htm.*
[34] Perry, Bruce D., "Post-Traumatic Stress Disorders in Children and Adolescents," originally published in *Current Opinions in Pediatrics,* vol. 11, no. 4 (August 1999). Available: The Child Trauma Academy of Baylor College of Medicine Web site, [Internet, WWW], Address: *http://www.bcm.tmc.edu/civitas/PTSD_opin6.htm;* also Eitan D. Schwarz and Bruce D. Perry, "The Post-Traumatic Response in Children and Adolescents," originally published in *Psychiatric Clinics of North America,* vol. 17, no. 2 (1994): 311–26. Available: The Child Trauma Academy of Baylor College of Medicine Web site, [Internet, WWW], Address: *http://www.bcm.tmc.edu/civitas/ptsdChildAdoles.htm.*
[35] Alice Miller, *Banished Knowledge* (New York: Doubleday, 1988), 28.
[36] Begley, 32.
[37] Perry, Bruce D., "Post-Traumatic Stress Disorders in Children and Adolescents," originally published in *Current Opinions in Pediatrics,* vol. 11, no. 4 (August 1999). Available: The Child Trauma Academy of Baylor College of Medicine Web site, [Internet, WWW], Address: *http://www.bcm.tmc.edu/civitas/PTSD_opin6.htm.*
[38] Hannaford, *Smart Moves,* 133.
[39] Janice T. Gibson, *Living: Human Development Through the Lifespan* (Reading, Mass.: Addison-Wesley Publishing Co., 1983), 143–46. Note: Earlier studies noted that baby monkeys preferred contact with the soft, padded substitute, even though the harder, wire-mesh substitute offered the baby food, demonstrating that "contact comfort is more important to the development of a strong affectional response in baby monkeys than is satisfaction of the hunger drive."
[40] Rita Carter, *Mapping the Mind* (Berkeley, Calif.: The University of California Press, 1998), 182, 196–197; also Karr-Morse and Wiley, 36–37.
[41] Quoted in Karr-Morse and Wiley, 38.
[42] Quoted in Brownlee article.
[43] Bruce Perry quoted in Karr-Morse, 34.
[44] Fassler and Dumas, 27.
[45] Cited in Wendy M. Williams, "Preventing Violence in School: What Can Principals Do?" *NASSP Bulletin* (December 1998). Available: National Association of Secondary School Principals Web site, [Internet, WWW], Address: *http://nassp.org/publications/bulletin/dec98bul.htm.*
[46] Daniel Goleman, "A Key to Post-Traumatic Stress Lies in Brain Chemistry, Scientists Find," *The New York Times* (12 June 1990).
[47] Perry, 2.
[48] Whitfield, 56.
[49] Goleman, "A Key to Post-Traumatic Stress . . ." Note: In laboratory experiments, brain changes did not occur when the animals facing stress were able to escape or control the threat.
[50] Hannaford, *Smart Moves,* 107.
[51] Perry, 2; Schultz and Heuchert, 23; Whitfield, 55–58; also Kendall Johnson, *Trauma in the Lives of Children* (Alameda, Calif.: Hunter House Publishers, 1998), 54–56; Lorraine B. Wallach, "Violence and Young Children's Development," *ERIC Digest* (June 1994). Available: ERIC Web site, U.S. Department of Education, [Internet, WWW], Address: *http://www.ed.gov/databases/ERIC_Digests/ed369578.html.* Note: According

to Shannon Brownlee, "as many as half of children from some violent neighborhoods show symptoms of ADHD compared with about 6 percent of the general population."
[52] Karr-Morse and Wiley, 159.
[53] Brownlee.
[54] Hannaford, *Smart Moves,* 166.
[55] Ibid.
[56] Sharon Begley, "Why the Young Kill," *Newsweek* (3 May 1999): 34.
[57] Ibid.
[58] Ibid., 194; also Greenspan, *The Growth of the Mind,* 119.
[59] Greenspan, *The Growth of the Mind,* 145; Hannaford, *Smart Moves,* 60; Karr-Morse and Wiley, 45.

Chapter 7
"No, Really . . . I'm Fine": Coping and Compensating

[1] Maslow, 34.
[2] L. Tobin, *What Do You Do with a Child Like This?* (Duluth, Minn.: Pfeifer-Hamilton Publishers, 1991), 12.
[3] Lorraine B. Wallach, "Violence and Young Children's Development," *ERIC Digest* (June 1994). Available: ERIC Web site, U.S. Department of Education, [Internet, WWW], Address: *http://www.ed.gov/databases/ERIC_Digests/ed369578.html.*
[4] Fassler and Dumas, 43.
[5] Brownlee.
[6] Michael Ware, "Death-List Bid Defused by School," *Courier-Mail,* Brisbane, Queensland, Australia (24 May 1999). Sent via e-mail by Hazel Walker.
[7] Maslow, 54.
[8] Susan Stiger, "Fractured Lives: The Silent Victims of Family Violence," *Sage Magazine,* vol. XI, no. 4 (April 2000).
[9] Jensen, *Completing the Puzzle,* 36.
[10] Morton Hunt, *The Story of Psychology* (New York: Doubleday Dell Publishing Group, Inc., 1993), 163, 487–88; Karr-Morse, 162.
[11] Karr-Morse, 162. Note: Susan Stiger's article, "Fractured Lives," quotes Dr. Victor La Cerva, medical director of the Family Health Bureau of the New Mexico Department of Health, as stating, "If you're being tortured yourself, you're more likely to dissociate. If you're watching, you're more likely to be aroused."
[12] Bernadette Donovan and Rose Marie Iovino, "A Multiple Intelligences Approach to Expanding and Celebrating Teacher Portfolios and Student Portfolios" (Paper presented at the annual meeting of the Northeastern Educational Research Association, October 1997), 34.
[13] "Resolving Conflict with Linda Lantieri," 20 April 1999. Interview published by *EQ Today,* Available: 6seconds Web Site, [Internet, WWW], Address: *http://www.6seconds.org/jrn/jpclantieri.html.*
[14] Schultz and Heuchert, 21.
[15] C. Lynn Fox and Shirley E. Forbing, *Creating Drug-Free Schools and Communities: A Comprehensive Approach* (New York: HarperCollins Publishers, 1992), 16.
[16] Quoted in L. Tobin, 12.
[17] John Bradshaw, *Healing the Shame That Binds You* (Deerfield Beach, Fla.: Health Communications, Inc., 1988), 31.
[18] Miriam Adderholdt-Elliot, *Perfectionism: What's Bad About Being Too Good?* (Minneapolis: Free Spirit Publishing, 1987), 34, 37–40, 110–13; Bean, 66; Fox and Forbing, 17; Sharon Wegscheider-Cruse, *Choicemaking* (Deerfield Beach, Fla.: Health Communications, Inc., 1985), 23.
[19] Fox and Forbing, 17; Wegscheider-Cruse, 43.
[20] Begley, 32–33; Fox and Forbing, 17; Stiger, 12; Wegscheider-Cruse, 43. Note: While many kids in this group may respond to traditional therapy or a loving, nurturing bond

with a significant adult, severe trauma survivors typically need extensive, multimodal and longer-term interventions.

[21] Fox and Forbing, 17; Hannaford, *Smart Moves,* 166; Wegscheider-Cruse, 43. Note: Hannaford has found about 95 percent of the students she's encountered who have been labeled with various learning problems assume the Mascot survival role.

[22] Tobin, 12.

[23] Many of the adaptive behaviors I witnessed are included as responses to stress in interviews with students conducted by Schultz and Heuchert, 38, 51–52.

Chapter 8
Over the Edge: A World of Violence

[1] Maya Bell, "Alone, Confused and Armed," *Albuquerque Journal* (28 November 1999).

[2] Bill Jordan, head of "Not Even One," a Gun Violence Prevention Program, speaking on "School Violence: A Town Hall Meeting Live," *KOAT-TV Special Report,* which aired 29 June 1999. Also William Ayers, "I Walk with Delinquents," *Educational Leadership,* vol. 55, no. 2 (October 1997). Available: Association of Supervision and Curriculum Development Web site, [Internet, WWW], Address: *http://www.ascd.org/pubs/el/oct97/extayers.html* and *http://www.ascd.org/safeschools/el9710/oct97toc.htm.*

[3] "Report: Students Optimistic," 3 September 1999. Available: CBS News Web site, [Internet, WWW], Address: *http://www.cbs.com/flat/story_175277.html.* Note: Some high school principals mentioned a brief period of rumor-fueled hysteria following Columbine, although several others noted that in their schools, this event made barely a ripple. I heard from a number of counselors and administrators who were surprised that their students saw this incident as isolated and "far away," unrelated to their lives or the reality of their personal experience.

[4] Journalist John Cloud wrote about students in Conyers, Georgia, after a shooting by classmate, T. J. Solomon. "When asked why no one told a teacher or the principal that T. J. recently threatened to bomb a classroom, the students shrug and look away, dragging on their cigarettes," he writes. "The look on their face is not of shock or horror, but a numb roll of the eyes, as if they've already begun to see the shooting as some sort of campus ritual, akin to the nuclear-attack drills of the 1950s."

[5] Stiger, 11.

[6] Quoted in Lisa Popyk, "Blood in the School Yard," *The Post* (7 November 1998). Available: *The Cincinnati Post* Web site, [Internet, WWW], Address: *http://www.cincypost.com/news/1kill110798.html.*

[7] Drew, xii.

[8] Wendy M. Williams.

[9] Stiger, 11, 15.

[10] Ibid., 15.

[11] John R. Hoover and Ronald Oliver, *The Bullying Prevention Handbook: A Guide for Parents, Teachers and Counselors* (Bloomington, Ind.: National Education Service, 1996), 8.

[12] Begley, 35.

[13] "Resolving Conflict with Linda Lantieri," 20 April 1999. Interview published by *EQ Today,* Available: 6seconds Web site, [Internet, WWW], Address: *http://www.6seconds.org/jrn/jpclantieri.html.*

[14] Popyk, "Blood in the Schoolyard."

[15] Tom Shales, "Vicious Commercials Send Sad Message," *Albuquerque Journal,* 24 June 1999.

[16] Steven Levy, "Loitering on the Dark Side," *Newsweek* (3 May 1999): 39.

[17] Quoted in an article by Thomas J. Cole, "Music a Prelude to School Shooting," *Albuquerque Journal* (4 June 2000).

[18] Cole.

[19] Popyk.

[20] Michele Borba, *Building Moral Intelligence: The Seven Essential Virtues That Teach Kids to Do the Right Thing* (San Francisco: Jossey-Bass, 2001), 170.
[21] Gibbs, Nancy, "Introduction: Time Special Report on Troubled Kids," *Time* magazine, vol. 153, no. 21 (31 May 1999): 33.
[22] Adam Cohen, "Criminals as Copycats," *Time* magazine, vol. 153, no. 21 (31 May 1999): 38.
[23] Scott Johnson, "One Father's Unique Perspective," *Newsweek* (3 May 1999): 38.
[24] Quoted in Cohen's article.
[25] "Oklahoma Boy Influenced by Columbine," Associated Press wire service report appearing in *The Albuquerque Journal* (12 June 2000). Note: This article did not suggest these drugs were the cause of this child's violent outburst but did mention his recent prescriptions as one of a number of possible factors contributing to his behavior.
[26] Shales.
[27] Letters appearing in "Dear Abby," *Albuquerque Journal* (12 June 2000).
[28] "Civil Servant," interview with Judith Martin (Miss Manners), *People* magazine, vol. 52, no. 18 (8 November 1999): 109–10. Note: I suspect that Martin may be referring to an exaggerated interpretation of work done in the recovery field which focuses on breaking through the childhood shame associated with the silence and secrets typically present in families wrestling with abuse and addiction.
[29] Joshua Quittner, "Are Video Games Really So Bad?" *Time* magazine, vol. 153, no. 18 (10 May 1999): 50–59. Note: In the article, Grossman was talking specifically about certain violent video games.
[30] Popyk, "Blood in the Schoolyard."
[31] Ibid.
[32] Wendy M. Williams citing research by Cornell psychologist James Garbarino.
[33] "Stopping School Violence: 12 Things Parents Can Do" (no date). Available: National Crime Prevention Council Web site, [Internet, WWW], Address: *http://www.ncpc.org/2schviol.htm.*
[34] "Children and Guns," *NAESP Report to Parents.* Alexandria, Va: National Association of Elementary School Principals, September 1999.
[35] From a 1991 study by the Children's Defense Fund reported in Quarles's book. Also a 1987 study published by the National School Safety Center, reported in Joan Gaustad, "Schools Attack the Roots of Violence," *ERIC Digest,* no. 63 (October 1991). Available: ERIC Web site, U.S. Department of Education, [Internet, WWW], Address: *http://www.ed.gov/databases/ERIC_Digests/ed335806.html.*
[36] Popyk, "Blood in the Schoolyard."
[37] Vicky Tyler, "We Need to Make Violence 'Uncool'" (7 September 1994). Available: [Internet, WWW], Address: *http://freecenter.digiweb.com/education/abuse/nonviol.html.*
[38] Ibid.
[39] "Children and Guns."
[40] Ayres.
[41] Gaustad.
[42] Gibbs, "A Week in the Life of a High School," 69.
[43] Quarles, 17.
[44] Quoting a comment made by a psychiatrist which he overheard at a conference.
[45] Kevin P. Dwyer, "Children Killing Children," *Communiqué,* Newsletter of the National Association of School Psychologists, special edition (spring 1999): 3.
[46] Gaustad.
[47] Remboldt, *Solving Violence Problems in Your School,* 7.
[48] Numerous interviews and survey responses; also reflects feedback from students in an article by Fred Bayles, "Students Say They Feel Safe," *USA Today* (29 October 1999).
[49] William Watson Purkey, "Creating Safe Schools Through Invitational Education," *ERIC Clearinghouse on Counseling and Student Services* (1999).

[50] Bayles. Note: Rita Mercier supports this idea, claiming, "Overemphasis on security in and of itself can cause students and staff to feel afraid and stressed."
[51] Lantieri and Patti.
[52] Richard Arthur with Edsel Erickson, *Gangs and Schools* (Holmes Beach, Fla.: Learning Publications, Inc., 1992), 135.
[53] "Preventing School Violence: Policies for Safety, Caring and Achievement," *An ASCD Infobrief Synopsis* (August 1996). Available: Association for Supervision and Curriculum Development Web site, [Internet, WWW], Address: *http://www.ascd.org/issues/violence.html.* Note: The day after the Columbine shootings, NRA president Charlton Heston appeared on ABC's *Good Morning America.* The "Perspectives" column in the 3 May 1999 issue of *Newsweek* quoted him as having said, "If there had been even one armed guard in the school, he could have saved a lot of lives and perhaps ended the whole thing instantly." The column also noted that later reports indicated there was indeed an armed guard at the school.
[54] Kathryn L. Girard, "Preparing Teachers for Conflict Resolution in the Schools," *ERIC Digest* (1995). Available: ERIC Web site, U.S. Department of Education, [Internet, WWW], Address: *http://www.ed.gov/databases/ERIC_Digests/ed387456.html.*
[55] Walaika Haskins, "Legislating Respect," the *Newsweek.com* Web site. Available: [Internet, WWW], Address: *http://www.newsweek.com/nw-svr/issue/25_99a/tnw/today/ps/ps05we_1.htm.*
[56] "Mouth Watch," *People* magazine, vol. 52, no. 10 (13 September 1999): 76.
[57] "Fear Clouds School Openings," Sept. 3, 1999. Available: CBS News Web site, [Internet, WWW], Address: *http://www.cbs.com/flat/story_177930.html.*
[58] Miguel Llanos, "FBI Tool Weighs Student Threats" (6 September 2000). Available: *MSNBC News* Web site, [Internet, WWW], Address: *http://www.msnbc.com/msn/456069.asp?cp1=1.*
[59] Anjetta McQueen, "School Violence Stereotypes Spurring Student Crackdown," *The Albuquerque Journal* (12 April 2000).
[60] Jerry Adler and Karen Springen, "How to Fight Back," *Newsweek* (3 May 1999): 37.
[61] Josh Romonek, "Teen Ends Jail Stint Over Essay," *Albuquerque Journal* (4 November 1999).
[62] John Leo, "Schools Teach Boys How to Suppress Masculinity," *Albuquerque Journal* (16 July 2000).
[63] Adler and Springen, 38.

Chapter 9
Brave New World: The Changing Role of the School

[1] Margaret J. Wheatley, *Leadership and the New Science* (San Francisco: Berrett-Koehler Publishers, Inc., 1994), 18.
[2] Rogers and Frieberg, 152.
[3] I first heard this joke told by educator and motivational speaker, Gail Dusa.
[4] Tom Peters, *Thriving on Chaos* (New York: Alfred A. Knopf, 1987), 7.
[5] Alvin Toffler, *The Third Wave* (New York: William Morrow & Co., Inc., 1980), 26.
[6] Toffler, 26, 30; also Arthur W. Combs, "Humanistic Education: Too Tender for a Tough World?" *Phi Delta Kappan,* vol. 62, no. 6 (February 1981): 446.
[7] James D. Pulliam and James Van Patten, *History of Education in America,* 6th ed. (Englewood Cliffs, N.J.: Prentice-Hall, Inc., 1995).
[8] Debra Sugar, "Social Skills Instruction in Albuquerque Public Schools: An Intervention Proposal." Research paper submitted to New Mexico Highlands University School of Social Work, spring 1999.
[9] Toffler, 45.
[10] John Naisbitt, *Megatrends* (New York: Warner Books, 1982), 12.
[11] Ibid., 12–14.
[12] Greenspan, *The Growth of the Mind,* 218; also, Naisbitt, 13; Pulliam and Van Patten.
[13] Toffler, 18, 29.

[14] "BASRC 1997 Annual Report" (1997). Available: Bay Area School Reform Collaborative, [Internet, WWW], Address: *http://www.fwl.org/basrc/rubrics/annualreport.pdf*, 6.

[15] "Survey of Education Needs," *Final Report* of the South Metro Chamber of Commerce Business Advisory Council. Dayton, Ohio: Paragon Opinion Research, Inc., 19 June 1997. Similar skills were also listed in John O'Neill, "Building Schools as Communities: A Conservation with James Comer," *Educational Leadership,* vol. 54, no. 9 (May 1997): 7; also Joe Hoff, "Avoiding the Cold Within: Instructional Relationships Systematically Applied," *Schools in the Middle,* vol. 8, no. 2 (October 1998), 36.

[16] William Watson Purkey and David Strahan, "School Transformation Through Invitational Education," *Research in the Schools,* vol. 2, no. 2 (1995): 4.

[17] David Thielen, "Management Secrets from Former Microsoft Superstar," *Bottom Line/Personal* (1 July 1999): 7–8.

[18] "MIT's Lester Thurow Welcomes You to the Brainpower Era," *Bottom Line/Personal* (15 October 1999): 7–8; also Thielen, 7–8.

[19] Rico Racosky, "Shift Happens: Making Sense of Changing Times," presentation materials and handouts, 1998.

[20] Rogers and Frieberg, 152.

[21] Ken Carey, *The Third Millennium* (San Francisco: Harper San Francisco, 1991), 59.

[22] Quoted in Donald C. Wesley, "Believing in our Students," *Educational Leadership,* vol. 56, no. 4 (December 1998/January 1999): 45. The original source of this quote is Lewis's 1947 book, *The Abolition of Man: How Education Develops Man's Sense of Morality* (New York: Macmillan).

[23] Goodlad, 34.

[24] Louise Stoll, "Enhancing Schools' Capacity for Learning." Paper presented at Innovations for Effective Schooling Conference, Auckland, New Zealand (August 1999).

[25] David R. Krathwohl, Benjamin S. Bloom and Bertram B. Masia, *Taxonomy of Educational Objectives, Handbook II: The Affective Domain* (New York: David McKay Co., Inc., 1964), 7.

[26] Combs, 446; John (Jack) P. Miller, "Making Connections Through Holistic Learning," *Educational Leadership,* vol. 56, no. 4 (December 1998/January 1999): 46–48; and Lantieri and Patti, 18.

[27] Drew, xiii.

[28] "Resolving Conflict with Linda Lantieri."

[29] Branden, 220.

[30] Sugar, 4.

[31] Ibid., 3, 5.

[32] Lantieri and Patti, 15.

[33] Based on as yet unpublished research on Dr. Michele Borba's *Esteem Builders* program (Jalmar Press, Torrance, Calif.), compiled by Wright State University. Borba attributes the success of the program to the fact that it was school-based (that is, the fact that the staff of each school shared a common language, set of skills and purpose, and all reinforced the same skills together), and to the deliberateness with which the program and the skills were taught. "Developing prosocial behaviors is not automatic," she asserts. "It must be taught, deliberately and systematically."

[34] Jane Bluestein, *Developing Responsible Learning Behaviors Through Peer Interaction.* Unpublished doctoral dissertation, University of Pittsburgh, 1980; also documentation from pilot program which ran during the 1978–79 school year. Note: Initially sent to help with play-type activities, buttoning coats, opening milk cartons or cleaning up, the older students quickly started moving into tasks of an instructional or academic nature: reading stories, doing math activities, putting on plays or puppet shows.

[35] B. J. Wise, "'Vaccinating' Children Against Violence," *Principal,* vol. 79, no. 1 (September 1999): 14–20.

[36] Lantieri and Patti, 21; also Mercier.

[37] William W. Purkey and David N. Aspy, "The Mental Health of Students: Nobody Minds? Nobody Cares?" Reprint from *Person-Centered Review,* vol. 3, no. 1 (February 1988): 43.

[38] Sugar, 2.
[39] Goleman, 284.
[40] Mercier.
[41] Juanita Ross Epp, "Schools, Complicity, and Sources of Violence," *Systemic Violence: How Schools Hurt Children,* Juanita Ross Epp and Ailsa M. Watkinson, eds. (London: Falmer Press, 1996), 18.
[42] Wise.
[43] Barbara Kantrowitz and Daniel McGinn, "When Teachers Are Cheaters," the MSNBC Web site, 11 June 2000. Available: [Internet, WWW], Address: *http://www.newsweek.com/news/419167.asp?cp1=1.*
[44] Larry Lashway, "Accountability," *Research Roundup,* published by the National Association of Elementary School Principals, vol. 16, no. 1 (Fall 1999), 3. Note: This was the starting premise of research by Mack McCary, Joe Peel and Wendy McCloskey in "Using Accountability as a Lever for Changing the School Culture" (Greensboro, N.C.: SouthEastern Regional Vision for Education, 1997).
[45] Kristen Nelson, "Measuring the Intangibles," *Classroom Leadership,* an ASCD Newsletter for K-12 Classroom Teachers, vol. 3, no. 5 (February 2000): 1, 8.
[46] Martin G. Brooks and Jacqueline Grennon Brooks, "The Courage to Be Constructivist," *Educational Leadership,* vol. 57, no. 3 (November 1999): 21.
[47] According to one principal I interviewed, this was the slogan for a number of high-achieving Massachusetts students who deliberately failed the achievement tests in their district to protest the pressure to excel and the importance assigned to these tests.
[48] Kantrowitz and McGinn; Daniel McGinn, "The Big Score," *Newsweek* (6 September 1999): 47; Sue Rardin, "Getting Tough on the Tough Teach," *Trust,* vol. 2, no. 4 (fall 1999): 16; Evan Thomas and Pat Wingert, "Bitter Lessons," the MSNBC Web site, 11 June 2000. Available: [Internet, WWW], Address: *http://www.newsweek.com/news/419168.asp.*
[49] McGinn, 47. Note: This report cited a group of high-achieving eleventh-graders who deliberately failed portions of a standardized test in protest; however, it reflected feedback from a number of students I interviewed or surveyed.
[50] Ibid., 50.
[51] Kantrowitz and McGinn.
[52] Ibid.
[53] Lashway, 1.
[54] McGinn, 51.
[55] Brooks and Brooks, 20; also Walter Haney and George Madaus, "Searching for Alternatives to Standardized Tests: Whys, Whats and Whithers," *Phi Delta Kappan,* vol. 70, no. 9 (May 1989): 684.
[56] Tom Hoerr, "Reporting What We Respect," *Classroom Leadership,* an ASCD Newsletter for K-12 Classroom Teachers, vol. 3, no. 5 (February 2000): 2–3; also Kay Burke, *The Mindful School: How to Assess Authentic Learning: Revised Edition* (Arlington Heights: IRI/SkyLight Training and Publishing, Inc., 1994), 21.
[57] Elliot W. Eisner, "What Really Counts in Schools," *Educational Leadership,* vol. 48, no. 5 (February 1991): 11.
[58] Contribution in "Testing and Student Success: Helping Parents Understand Standardized Test Result," *Classroom Leadership,* an ASCD Newsletter for K-12 Classroom Teachers, vol. 3, no. 5 (February 2000): 7.
[59] Ibid.
[60] McGinn, 51.
[61] Kantrowitz and McGinn; Lemann; and Thomas and Wingert.
[62] McGinn, 50.
[63] "Tests Are an Easy Way Out," interview with Theodore R. Sizer and Nancy Faust Sizer, *Newsweek* (6 September 1999), 51.
[64] Susan Ohanian, "Silence Ain't Golden: Spread the Word" (26 September 2000). Available: *Interversity* Web site, [Internet, WWW], Address: *http://206.68.56.30/events/resisting_conf/texts/Ohanian1000.php;* Gary S. Stager, "An Interview with Susan

Ohanian," *Curriculum Administrator,* April 1999 issue (10 May 1999). Available: Gary Stager's Web site, [Internet, WWW], Address: *http://www.stager.org/articles/ohanian.html.*

[65] Heidi Goodrich Andrade, "Using Rubrics to Promote Thinking and Learning," *Educational Leadership,* vol. 57, no. 5 (February 2000), 13; Anne Davies, "Seeing the Results for Yourself: A Portfolio Primer," *Classroom Leadership,* an ASCD Newsletter for K-12 Classroom Teachers, vol. 3, no. 5 (February 2000): 4; Hoerr, 2; Kantrowitz and McGinn; Kathie Nunley, "In Defense of the Oral Defense," *Classroom Leadership,* an ASCD Newsletter for K-12 Classroom Teachers, vol. 3, no. 5 (February 2000), 6.

[66] Lemann.

[67] Pulliam and Van Patten, 1, 255–56.

[68] Marlow Ediger, "Caring and the Elementary Curriculum." Report, Truman State University, Kirksville, Missouri, 1998.

[69] Quoted in Esther Wright, *The Heart and Wisdom of Teaching* (San Francisco: Teaching from the Heart, 1997).

[70] Thornton, referencing an article by J. Exline in "Children in Crisis in the Classroom," *Momentum,* vol. 24, no. 2 (1993), 12–16. Note: In the original context, Thornton made this comment regarding children who live with violence and fear. While certainly appropriate for this population, I believe that the need for a "safe haven" and "a bond with a significant and empathetic adult" would benefit any child coming to school.

[71] Esther Wright, *Loving Discipline A to Z* (San Francisco: Teaching from the Heart, 1994), 84.

[72] Naisbitt, 39.

[73] Peter M. Senge, *The Fifth Discipline: The Art and Practice of The Learning Organization* (New York: Doubleday, 1990), 12.

[74] Wheatley, 9.

[75] Quoted in Bluestein, *Mentors, Masters and Mrs. MacGregor,* 306.

[76] Ibid., 306–7.

Chapter 10
All Are Welcome Here: The Need for Community

[1] Laura Kelly, "Schools as Communities: Communication, Collaboration and Caring," *ASCD Curriculum Update* (fall 1999), 8.

[2] James Sweeney, "School Climate: The Key to Excellence," *NASSP Bulletin 76* (547), November 1992: 69.

[3] Daniel Okrent, "Raising Kids Online: What Can Parents Do?" *Time* magazine, vol. 153, no. 18 (10 May 1999): 38–43. Note: Okrent calls the Web community a "shadow community," one in which interaction is actually contact with "the facsimile of a human being." I agree with his concerns, especially when an electronic community comes to substitute for actual human contact and social interaction—even more so when we're talking about young people. I will, however, argue for the potential for positive connections and support that can develop around common interests and experiences, and for the information that these communications can provide.

[4] A brief report entitled "Psychologist Warns Teens' Solo Lifestyles Lead to Less Sense of Social Responsibility" refers to a speech by William Damon at a conference on youth development, in which Damon claims adolescent isolation increases eventual detachment "from the larger civil society" and a lack of a sense of their role in the community. And Sharon Begley cites a lack of emotional connection, whether from outcasting or abandonment, as a factor in extreme youth violence.

[5] "Report: Students Optimistic." Also, Cal Thomas, "Parenting a Way to End Violence," *Albuquerque Journal* (16 October 1999).

[6] Frederic Flach, *Resilience: Discovering a New Strength at Times of Stress* (New York: Fawcett Columbine, 1988), 7; Eric Schaps and Daniel Solomon, "Schools and Classrooms as Caring Communities," *Educational Leadership,* vol. 48, no. 5 (February 1991): 40.

[7] John Cloud, "Just a Routine School Shooting," *Time* magazine, vol. 153, no. 21 (31 May 1999): 34–43.

[8] Elliot W. Eisner, "What Really Counts in Schools," *Educational Leadership,* vol. 48, no. 5 (February 1991): 16; also the research of Nel Noddings, cited in Bonnie Benard, "Fostering Resilience in Children," *ERIC Digest* (August 1995). Available: ERIC Web site, U.S. Department of Education, [Internet, WWW], Address: *http://www.ed.gov/databases/ERIC_Digests/ed386327.html.*

[9] Quoted in Arthur and Erickson, 48.

[10] Glasser, 97.

[11] Purkey and Aspy, 45.

[12] Eric Schaps, "The Child Development Project: In Search of Synergy," *Principal,* vol. 79, no. 1 (September 1999): 22; also Eric Nagourney, "Vital Signs: Behavior: Stopping School Trouble Before It Starts" (14 November 2000). Available: *The New York Times* Web site, [Internet, WWW], Address: *http://partners.nytimes.com/2000/11/14/science/14SCHO.html.* Note: Schaps reports that the protective factors applied to all eight risky behaviors except pregnancy.

[13] Mary Finley, "Cultivating Resilience: An Overview for Rural Educators and Parents," *ERIC Digest* (1994). Available: ERIC Web site, U.S. Department of Education, [Internet, WWW], Address: *http://www.ed.gov/databases/ERIC_Digests/ed372904.html;* also Margery Stein, "For Every Child, a Full-Time Friend," *Parade* magazine (28 May 2000): 16; also Bonnie Bernard, "Turning It Around for All Youth: From Risk to Resilience," *ERIC/CUE Digest,* no. 126 (1997). Available: ERIC Web site, U.S. Department of Education, [Internet, WWW], Address: *http://www.ed.gov/databases/ERIC_Digests/ed412309.html.*

[14] Ibid.; also Rogers and Frieberg, 254.

[15] Philip Cohen, "The Content of Their Character: Educators Find New Ways to Tackle Values and Morality," *Curriculum Update* (Spring 1995). Available: Association for Curriculum and Supervision Development Web site, [Internet, WWW], Address: *http://www.ascd.org/pubs/cu/spring95.html.*

[16] Schaps, 22–24.

[17] Mark A. Royal and Robert J. Rossi, "Schools as Communities," *ERIC Digest,* no. 111 (1997). Available: ERIC Web site, U.S. Department of Education, [Internet, WWW], Address: *http://www.ed.gov/databases/ERIC_Digests/ed405641.html;* also Spence Rogers and Lisa Renard, "Relationship-Driven Teaching," *Educational Leadership,* vol. 57, no. 1 (September 1999): 35; also Ron Roberge, "Project P.O.D.S.: Providing Opportunities for Developing Student Success," *ERIC Digest* (1995). Available: ERIC Web site, U.S. Department of Education, [Internet, WWW], Address: *http://www.ed.gov/databases/ERIC_Digests/ed401499.html,* which listed first among its main objectives in lowering the 30–35 percent national and provincial dropout averages (based on the number of students starting tenth grade who did not finish high school), "developing among at-risk students a sense of belonging, identification and membership within the school community."

[18] Dean Walker, "School Violence Prevention," *ERIC Digest,* no. 94 (March 1995). Available: ERIC Web site, U.S. Department of Education, [Internet, WWW], Address: *http://www.ed.gov/databases/ERIC_Digests/ed379786.html;* also K. Dwyer, D. Osher and C. Wagner, "Early Warning, Timely Response: A Guide to Safe Schools," Washington, D.C.: U.S. Department of Education, 1998.

[19] Jane Nelsen, *Positive Discipline* (New York: Ballantine Books, 1987), 46, 64.

[20] Cindy C. Kratzer, "Roscoe Elementary School: Cultivating a Caring Community in an Urban Elementary School," *Journal of Education for Students Placed At Risk (JESPAR).* Available: Center for Social Organizations of Schools, Johns Hopkins University Web site, [Internet, WWW], Address: *http://www.csos.joh.edu/jespar/tableofcontents/2.4kratzer.htm;* also James Sweeney, "School Climate: The Key to Excellence," *NASSP Bulletin* 76 (547), November 1992: 69–73.

[21] Rogers and Frieberg, 153.

[22] William Glasser, *Schools Without Failure* (New York: Perennial Library, 1975), 19.

[23] Thornton.
[24] Branden, 202.
[25] Bluestein, *Mentors, Masters and Mrs. MacGregor,* numerous stories, as well as a number of survey responses.
[26] Eric Schaps and Daniel Solomon, 38.
[27] Rogers and Frieberg, 33.
[28] Vicki Phillips, *Empowering Discipline* (Carmel Valley, Calif.: Personal Development Publishing, 1998).
[29] From *What Schools Are For,* cited in J. Merrell Hansen and John Childs, "Creating a School Where People Like to Be," *Educational Leadership,* vol. 56, no. 1 (September 1998). Available: Association for Supervision and Curriculum Development Web site, [Internet, WWW], Address: *http://www.ascd.org/safeschools/el9809/selhansen.html.*
[30] Kent D. Peterson, and Terrence E. Deal, "How Leaders Influence the Culture of Schools," *Educational Leadership,* vol. 56, no. 1 (September 1998). Available: Association for Supervision and Curriculum Development Web site, [Internet, WWW], Address: *http://www.ascd.org/safeschools/el9809/petersoninfluence.html.*
[31] Hansen and Childs.
[32] Ibid.
[33] Mercier.
[34] McPartland, et al.
[35] Susan Klonsky and Michael Klonsky, "Countering Anonymity Through Small Schools," *Educational Leadership,* vol. 57, no. 1 (September 1999), 41.
[36] Charles M. Achilles, Jeremy D. Finn and Helen Pate-Bain, "Class Size: It's Elementary," *Streamlined Seminar,* Alexandria, Va.: National Association of Elementary School Principals, vol. 18, no. 1 (September 1999); Sue Galletti, "Small Schools Create Communities with Results," *Schools in the Middle,* vol. 8, no. 1 (September 1999). Available: [Internet, WWW], Address: *http://nassp.org/publications/schools_in_the_middle/galletti.htm;* James McPartland, Will Jordan, Nettie Legters and Robert Balfanz, "Finding Safety in Small Numbers," *Educational Leadership,* vol. 55, no. 2 (October 1997). Available: Association for Supervision and Curriculum Development Web site, [Internet, WWW], Address: *http://www.ascd.org/safeschools/el9710/oct97toc.htm.*
[37] Sweeney, 70. Note: He also reports that "suburban schools tend to have more positive climates than rural schools. Urban schools generally have the least positive climates. Finally, elementary schools tend to have more positive climates than secondary schools, even when the analysis controls for size."
[38] Nicole Christian, with reporting by Maggie Sieger, "Is Smaller Perhaps Better?" *Time* magazine, vol. 153, no. 21 (31 May 1999): 43; also Galetti.
[39] Royal and Rossi.
[40] Ibid.
[41] Information from survey responses, interviews, comments from workshop participants and casual conversations indicate that individuals throughout the world experienced exclusion as students because of their race, ethnicity, religion, sexual orientation (real or imagined), clothing, hair style or length, weight or body size, academic or athletic weaknesses, learning differences, physical disabilities, musical preferences, accents, their parents' marital or financial status, the part of town they lived in, or if they came to this setting from someplace significantly more urban or more rural. Interestingly, many teachers I've spoken with have complained that they had difficulty finding acceptance in their professional environments, particularly when working in smaller communities, for many of the same reasons. As with children, exclusion was an even bigger issue for people who came from outside the district or school after an initial community had been established.
[42] Joe Nathan, "State Could Raise the Grade Following Chicago's Lead," *St. Paul Pioneer Press* (21 August 2000). Note: The success of smaller schools is tied to a number of factors, including low adult-student ratios, strong advisor programs, ties to the community, goal-setting and encouragement, relevant and appropriate curriculum, and a commitment to having every child in the school have some adult who knows him or her well.

[43] David N. Aspy and Flora N. Roebuck, *Kids Don't Learn from People They Don't Like* (Amherst, Mass.: Human Resource Development Press, Inc., 1977), 16. Quoting Astronaut Al Worden talking about his high school principal as "the one person in his life who had done the most to promote his real growth as an individual."
[44] Dennis Littky and Farrell Allen, "Whole Student Personalization, One Student at a Time," *Educational Leadership,* vol. 57, no. 1 (September 1999): 26.
[45] McPartland, et al.; also Klonsky and Klonsky, 38.
[46] Judy Pollack and Kimberly Hartman, "The ABCs of Middle Level Teacher Training," *Schools in the Middle,* vol. 8, no. 7 (May/June 1999). Available: [Internet, WWW], Address: *http://nassp.org/publications/schools_in_the_middle/pollack.htm.*
[47] Wesley, 42.
[48] Galletti. This report strongly advocates smaller schools to achieve this sense of community.
[49] Gaustad. Also, Karr-Morse and Wiley report on the promising outcomes of after-care programs for juveniles who have served time in detention or jail. As they attempt to reenter their communities, they are assigned to individual advocates "who provide mentoring, regular telephone contact and weekly meetings with youths and their families to keep them on track" (p. 258).
[50] E. Timothy Burns, *From Risk to Resilience* (Dallas: Marco Polo Publishers, 1996), 106.
[51] Karen Irmsher, "Education Reform and Students at Risk," *ERIC Digest,* no. 112 (April 1997). Available: ERIC Web site, U.S. Department of Education, [Internet, WWW], Address: *http://www.ed.gov/databases/ERIC_Digests/ed405642.html.*
[52] Eisner, 16.
[53] Margery Stein, 16.
[54] Quoted in Joan Montgomery Halford, "Longing for the Sacred in Schools: A Conversation with Nel Noddings," *Educational Leadership,* vol. 56, no. 4 (December 1998/January 1999): 32.
[55] Ibid.
[56] John Welbes, "Men Are Rare in Elementary Classrooms," *St. Paul Pioneer Press* (27 May 2000).
[57] Ibid.
[58] "Mentoring Improves Youth Attitudes and Behaviors," *Catalyst,* vol. 19, no. 1 (February 1999). Available: National Crime Prevention Council Web site, [Internet, WWW], Address: *http://www.ncpc.org/cat9902b.htm.*
[59] Ibid.
[60] Rogers and Frieberg, 255.
[61] Arthur and Erickson, 47; Aspy and Roe, quoted in Rogers and Frieberg, 255; Bluestein, *21st Century Discipline;* Rogers and Frieberg, 5, 6, 43, 154, 156, 157, 255; Byron Lewis and Frank Pucelik, *Magic of NLP Demystified* (Portland, Ore.: Metamorphous Press, 1993), 14–15; Thornton, 77–78.
[62] Quoted in Karen Miller, "Memorial to Grace Mitchell," *Child Care Information Exchange* (March 2000): 68.
[63] Siccone and López, 101.
[64] Virginia Satir, *The New Peoplemaking* (Mountain View, Calif.: Science and Behavior Books, Inc., 1988), 51.
[65] Tim Padgett, "Saving Suburbia," *Time* magazine, vol. 153, no. 7 (16 August 1999): 50–51; also Sue McAllister, "Neighbors Matter to New Buyers," *Albuquerque Journal* (23 July 2000).
[66] Mark A. Royal and Robert J. Rossi, "Schools as Communities," *ERIC Digest,* no. 111 (1997). Available: ERIC Web site, U.S. Department of Education, [Internet, WWW], Address: *http://www.ed.gov/databases/ERIC_Digests/ed405641.html.*
[67] Irmsher.
[68] Sweeney, 71.
[69] "Caring Communities," *NCREL Policy Briefs, Report 3,* analysis of the national School Readiness Task Force report (1993). Available: North Central Regional Educational

Laboratory, [Internet, WWW], Address: *http://www.ncrel.org/ncrel/sdrs/areas/issues/envrnmnt/go/93-3care.htm.*

[70] "Statements . . . About Students," extracted from the Bay Area School Reform Collaborative Home Page (no date). Available: Costaville, California Web site, [Internet, WWW], Address: *http://www.costaville.com/aboutstu.htm.*

[71] Kratzer.

[72] Rogers and Renard, 34–37.

[73] Stoll.

[74] John (Jack) P. Miller, 47.

[75] Dwyer, Osher and Warger, 4.

[76] Ken Fraser, *Positive Choices: A Modern Journey to Samarkand,* course manual, Kindston, ACT, Australia: Work Resources Centre, Inc., 1998.

[77] Bluestein, *Mentors,* 11.

[78] Lauretta Buchanan, "Helping Kids Bridge the Gap Between a 'Troubled Now' and a Better Tomorrow!" S.M.A.R.T.S. Learning System. Handouts from the Kentucky Behavior Institute, 1999.

[79] Wheatley, 101.

[80] Quote found on the University of North Carolina, Wilmington, PDS School Systems and UNCW Combined Calendar, 2000–01.

[81] Virginia Satir, John Banmen, Jane Gerber and Maria Gomori, *The Satir Model: Family Therapy and Beyond* (Palo Alto, Calif.: Science and Behavior Books, Inc., 1991), 17.

[82] One critic, Bard College president Leon Botstein, recommends creating a new system rather than trying to fix what we have, particularly with regard to high schools, which he feels have outgrown cultural and biological changes that have occurred since the system was initially set up. Botstein specifically recommends "a secondary school that turns students out into the world at 16," to pursue educational, vocational or service opportunities at that time. Quoted in Patrick Rogers, "Enough Already: Interview with Leon Botstein," *People* magazine, vol. 52, no. 1 (12 July 1999).

[83] Wheatley, 41.

[84] Parker J. Palmer, "Evoking the Spirit in Public Education," *Educational Leadership,* vol. 56, no. 4 (December 1998/January 1999): 11.

Chapter 11
Snags in the Tapestry

[1] Quoted on the The Women's History Web site. Available: [Internet, WWW], Address: *http://womenhistory.about.com/homework/womenhistory/library/qu/blqusati.htm.*

[2] Wheatley, 19.

[3] Epp, 1.

[4] John I. Goodlad, *A Place Called School* (New York: McGraw-Hill Book Company, 1984), 16.

[5] J. Prosser, "School Culture," *Research Matters,* The School Improvement Network's Bulletin, Institute of Education, University of London, no. 9 (autumn 1998), citing G. Morgan, *Images of Organization* (Thousand Oaks, Calif.: Sage, 1997), 143.

[6] Ibid., referencing Edgar H. Schein, *Organizational Culture and Leadership* (San Francisco: Jossey-Bass, 1985), 6.

[7] Vimala McClure, "Parenting in the New Millennium," *The Fabric of the Future: Women Visionaries Illuminate the Path to Tomorrow* (Berkeley, Calif.: Conari Press, 1998), 337.

[8] Wheatley, 20.

[9] Ibid. This term comes from H. Beare, B. J. Caldwell and R. H. Milliken, *Creating an Excellent School: Some New Management Techniques* (London: Routledge, 1989).

[10] Quoted in "Quotable Quotes," *Reader's Digest* (March 2000): 69.

[11] Shakti Gawain, "Moving Toward the New Millennium," *The Fabric of the Future: Women Visionaries Illuminate the Path to Tomorrow* (Berkeley, Calif.: Conari Press, 1998), 276.

[12] Schaef, 69.
[13] Jane Bluestein, "26 Stress-Producing Obstacles in Relationships," *The Parent's Little Book of Lists: DOs and DON'Ts of Effective Parenting* (Deerfield Beach, Fla.: Health Communications, Inc., 1997), 96–99.
[14] Hal Karp, "Who's Going to School with Your Kids?" *Reader's Digest* (March 2000): 78.
[15] Ibid., 79.
[16] Irene McDonald, "Expanding the Lens: Student Perceptions of School Violence," in *Systemic Violence: How Schools Hurt Children,* Juanita Ross Epp and Ailsa M. Watkinson, eds. (London: Falmer Press, 1996), 90.
[17] Quarles, 7.
[18] Ibid., 84.
[19] Ibid., 89–90.
[20] Lantieri and Patti, 129.
[21] Cloud, 38.
[22] Mercier.
[23] Ibid.
[24] Polly Summar, "Troubled Students Hard to Identify, Counselors Say," *Albuquerque Journal* (24 January 2000).
[25] Ellen Goodman, "Dream Parents Can Raise Nightmares," *York Daily Record* (4 May 1999); also Margaret Carlson, "An Outrage That Will Last," *Time* magazine, vol. 153, no. 18 (10 May 1999): 35; Patrick Rogers, et al., "The Youngest Victims," *People* magazine, vol. 53, no. 13 (3 April 2000); Cloud, 38; various television, print and Internet news reports following the shooting. Note: There are subtle energetic, process and outcome differences between examining situations to learn about the factors that may have contributed to them and looking for a scapegoat.
[26] Sugar, 1.
[27] KRQE-TV News segment (17 December 1999).
[28] June Million, "Creative PR Could Keep You Out of Court," *Communicator,* Newsletter of the National Association of Elementary School Principals, vol. 23, no. 3 (November 1999): 5.
[29] Gawain, 277.
[30] Purkey and Aspy, 47.
[31] Ibid.
[32] Ayers.
[33] Flach, 216–17. Note: Flach's list specifically refers to factors that do not support the development of resilience in children; however, many of the items on the list also appear in descriptors of dysfunctional families (Bradshaw, Subby, Wegscheider-Cruse and others) or addictive systems (Schaef).
[34] Ibid.
[35] Palmer, 10.
[36] Amitai Etzioni, "Balancing Individual Rights and the Common Good," *Tikkun* magazine (January-February 1997). Available: *Tikkun* Web site, [Internet, WWW], Address: *http://www.tikkun.org/9701/etzioni.html.*
[37] "Annual Report on School Safety," October 1998.
[38] Editorial by Diane Varano, *Educational Leadership,* vol. 56, no. 4 (December 1998/January 1999).
[39] Lantieri and Patti, 14–15.
[40] "Safe Learning Communities: Strategies and Resources" (1999). Available: NCREL (North Central Regional Educational Laboratory, Oak Brook, Illinois) Web site, [Internet, WWW], Address: *http://www.ncrel.org/sdrs/areas/issues/envrnmnt/drugfree/sa3resil.htm.*
[41] Mercier.
[42] Christian, 43.
[43] Joan Jacobs Brumberg, *The Body Project* (New York: Random House, 1997), 126–27.
[44] Tara Singh, *Nothing Real Can Be Threatened* (Los Angeles: Life Action Press, 1989), 106.

[45] Andrea Schoellkopf, "Many Students Starting Class in Uniform," *Albuquerque Journal* (14 August 1999); Susanna Laurenti, "Dress Code Works," *Boca Raton News* (14 November 1999).
[46] Arthur, 134.
[47] Ibid., 66–75; 133–34, 144–49.
[48] Nancy Gibbs, introduction.
[49] Melissa Tyrrell, "Create Safer Study Environments," *York Daily Record* (25 May 2000).
[50] Cloud.
[51] Quarles, 16.
[52] Quoted in Bluestein, *Mentors,* 213.
[53] Anjetta McQueen, "Study Links Day Care, Less Crime." Associated Press Report submitted via e-mail, 28 April 2000. Note: This research determined that "youths who spent their early years in quality day care were half as likely to be arrested" and that "troubled tots who didn't go to preschool and receive home visits from social workers were five times as likely to become chronic lawbreakers—arrested four or more times—by age twenty-seven."
[54] In case anyone was wondering, Gail assures me that this is not a true story about a real town—just an anecdote she uses to make a point.
[55] "Resolving Conflict with Linda Lantieri" interview.
[56] Quoted in Fassler and Dumas.
[57] Purkey and Aspy, 47.
[58] Richard Woodbury, "Taking Back the School," *Time* magazine, vol. 154, no. 7 (16 August 1999): 32–33.
[59] Hannaford, *Smart Moves,* 84; Nanci Hellmich, "Cut the Homework and the TV Time," *USA Today* (28 September 2000). Note: Regardless of the dubious value of many of the assignments these students were bringing home, the brain handles detail-oriented work better at age eight than at six. Hellmich's article cites recommendations by pediatrician T. Berry Brazelton and child psychiatrist Stanley Greenspan (in their book, *The Irreducible Needs of Children*) which recommend "for children six to nine, no more than one hour a day" for homework or TV, and an average of two hours or less for children in middle and high school. They recommend more time with family instead. And early childhood consultant Frances Ryan notes that the work is far more appropriate and motivating if the children choose to do it on their own. She also leans more toward activities like cooking or playing or talking with parents instead of drillwork to practice basic skills.
[60] Jeffrey Gold, "N.J. School District Limits Homework," *Albuquerque Journal* (23 October 2000); Tom Duffy, "Give Me a Break!" *People* magazine (27 November 2000): 209–10. Note: Heavy doses of homework became standard procedure in the U.S. after the Russians launched Sputnik—and a panic for making kids in American schools more competitive—in 1957. It is not unusual for high school kids to complain of having four to six hours of homework on an average night. Trying to work these demands around after-school jobs, sports and social commitment, time with family and the need for sleep creates a great deal of stress for many students and their families.
[61] Purkey and Aspy, 46.
[62] Goodman.
[63] Jonathan Kozol, *Savage Inequalities* (New York: HarperPerennial, 1991), 233.
[64] An evening news segment (*ABC News,* 31 August 2000) reported that "by one estimate, half a million teachers pay for materials schools don't cover out of their own salaries." They interviewed teachers who spent between $1,000 and $5,000 a year on materials and supplies, noting that the practice was so widespread that advertisers have started offering incentives (such as donating a percentage of money teachers spend back to the schools of their choice) to get teachers' business.
[65] Kozol, 85–87.
[66] Purkey and Aspy, 47.
[67] James Garbarino, *Lost Boys: Why Our Sons Turn Violent and How We Can Save Them,* quoted in Cloud, 38.

[68] Summar; also Cloud. Note: These articles identify school districts in Texas, New Mexico and California with ratios that range from 350 to 1,000 students for each counselor.
[69] Schaef, 78–79.
[70] Cartozian, Present and Quinn, introduction.
[71] Robert Fritz, *The Path of Least Resistance* (New York: Fawcett Columbine, 1989), 17.
[72] I have heard these ratios consistently reported in workshops I've attended and feedback I've gotten from other educators, writers and speakers. I have been unsuccessful in numerous attempts to locate the original studies from which these numbers were determined. My faith in their credibility comes from the variety of sources from which I've heard them, the consistency with which they've been reported, anecdotal feedback from adults and kids, and personal experience as well. Regardless of the numbers, my point here is that the amount of feedback kids receive is overwhelmingly negative, and that it gets worse the older they get and the longer they stay in school.
[73] William Watson Purkey, "The Coming Revolution in American Education: Creating Inviting Schools," Guest Editorial, *Values Realization Journal 2000.* Reprint.
[74] Purkey, "The Coming Revolution in American Education." Note: Purkey comments that "even the most progressive and socially aware educational groups and journals have bowed to these gods. Yet, after two decades of exceeding, excelling and surpassing, the schools remain largely the same and the criticism continues unabated."
[75] Glasser, 77.
[76] H. Stephen Glenn and Michael L. Brock, *Seven Strategies for Developing Capable Students* (Rocklin, Calif.: Prima Publishing, 1998), 36.
[77] UNCW Calendar.
[78] Quoted in Schultz and Heuchert, 138.
[79] "The Japanese Way," KOB-TV News 4 report (27 February 2000). Note: While this report was in no way meant to disparage Japanese schools, it did effectively point out the discrepancies between apparent achievement evident in a student's performance and degrees of understanding and mastery which, in this case, did not extend beyond the ability to perform.
[80] Marge Scherer, "Perspectives: The C Word (Constructivism)," *Educational Leadership,* vol. 57, no. 3 (November 1999): 5. Note: The survey was conducted by National Public Radio. Fifty-eight percent chose "giving knowledge" as the main function, 35 percent chose focusing on "teaching children how to think critically rather than worrying about how much detailed knowledge they have," and 7 percent endorsed both ideas. (Scherer wondered if these 7 percent might have been educators.)
[81] Benjamin S. Bloom, ed., *Taxonomy of Educational Objectives, Handbook I: The Cognitive Domain* (New York: Longman, 1956), 28–29, 33.
[82] Bluestein, *21st Century Discipline;* Bluestein, *The Parent's Little Book of Lists;* also Jane Bluestein, *Parents, Teens and Boundaries: How to Draw the Line* (Deerfield Beach, Fla.: Health Communications, Inc., 1993).
[83] Jensen, *Brain-Based Learning,* 165.
[84] Paul Dennison and Gail E. Dennison, *Brain Gym* (Ventura, Calif.: Edu-Kinesthetics, Inc., 1986), in introductory message to parents and teachers; Hannaford, *Smart Moves,* 13; Dawna Markova, *How Your Child Is Smart* (Berkeley, Calif.: Conari Press, 1992), 70, 177.
[85] John Holt, *How Children Learn* (New York: Dell Books, 1967), 165.
[86] The student was ten or eleven years old, and I swear I am not making this up.
[87] In an all-too-familiar example of oversimplification and misrepresentation, this teacher (and this program) had confused genuine self-esteem with superficial, feel-good flattery and empty encouragement. More on this later in this book.
[88] I share this example with great compassion and respect for this administrator, who is new to her job and very much concerned with the toxic and negative culture she had just inherited. I know she is indeed working hard to install a number of processes to build relationships and deal with student behavior in much more constructive ways,

and that she is quite devoted to ultimately changing a culture and belief system that were well established before she got there.

[89] O'Neil, 146.

[90] Ibid.

Chapter 12
More Welcome than Others: Discrimination and Belonging

[1] Elizabeth Leonie Simpson, "The Person in Community: The Need to Belong," *Feeling, Valuing, and the Art of Growing: Insights into the Affective,* Louise M. Berman and Jessie A. Roderick, eds. (Washington, D.C.: Association for Supervision and Curriculum Development, 1977), 190.

[2] Bob Chase, "Statement on GLSEN Report Card at the Back to School Press Conference" (NEA Policy Statement), 1998. Available: GLSEN (Gay, Lesbian, and Straight Education Network) Web site, [Internet, WWW], Address: *http://www.glsen.org/pages/sections/news/back-to-school/1998/bobchase.*

[3] Patti DeRosa, "Guidelines for Challenging Racism and Other Forms of Oppression" (24 July 1996). Available: Ben and Jerry's Online, Address: *http://euphoria.benjerry.com/esr/challenge.html.*

[4] Quoted in "Fast Company," *American Way* (15 October 2000): 104. Note: T. J. "Ted" Childs is IBM's vice president of global workforce diversity.

[5] Saul Jaffe and Lauren Weinstein, "Twilight Zone Episode Guide," the Sci Fi Network Web Site. Available: [Internet, WWW], Address: *http://www.scifi.com/twizone/season2.html.* Note: This episode, entitled "Eye of the Beholder," aired during the 1960–61 television season. I believe Donna Douglas played the unfortunate young woman.

[6] Bluestein, *21st Century Discipline,* 21–23.

[7] Arends, 203–4.

[8] Ibid.; also "Population and Family Characteristics," *America's Children 1998.* Available: Forum on Child and Family Statistics, ChildStats Web site, [Internet, WWW], Address: *http://www.childstats.gov/ac1998/poptxt.htm.* Note: According to anecdotal reports from educators who work there, students in the Glendale, California school district represent sixty different native languages, and fourteen different languages spoken by students in one San Jose area junior high alone.

[9] "Diversity Training and Consulting." Available on the National MultiCultural Institute Web Site, [Internet, WWW], Address: *http://www.nmci.org/training.htm#train.* Note: This group advises, "Organizations that value and take advantage of their diversity, both among their employees and clientele, will be better prepared to build a cohesive and effective workforce to serve existing and emerging markets." Also, Brigitte Greenberg, "Learning Disabled Seeking Education," *Albuquerque Journal* (10 February 2000).

[10] "The Regional Multicultural Magnet School." Available: [Internet, WWW], Address: *http://www.rmms.k12.ct.us/index.html.*

[11] University of Cincinnati billboard.

[12] I make this claim with caution and do not suggest it to have universal validity, at least not at this time. According to an Associated Press release by Brian Murphy ("Back to School Around the World: The Three R's vs. Poverty, Disease, Violence and More"), as the 2000-01 school year began, some children in Indonesia could not afford the monthly dollar for school fees. A high school teacher in Senegal divided his 108 students into two groups, each to be taught on alternate days. Committees in the Balkans and on the Korean peninsula faced the task of replacing textbooks that reinforce ethnic stereotypes. And in Afghanistan, educational opportunities for female students (and teachers) simply ceased to exist.

[13] "Emotionally Intelligent Parenting: An Interview with Elias, Maurice," *EQ Today* (21 April 1999). Available: *6seconds* Web site, [Internet, WWW], Address: *http://www.6seconds.org/jrn/elias.html.*

[14] Reasoner cites a study conducted in New Zealand by Woolens entitled "Project Resiliency." He believes the data to have been presented in a workshop in British Columbia by Debbie Kokay.
[15] Bluestein, *Mentors*.
[16] Frey, 2.
[17] Siccone and López, introduction.
[18] Carl R. Rogers, *Client-Centered Therapy* (Boston: Houghton Mifflin Company, 1951), 484.
[19] Dwyer, Osher and Warger, 3–4.
[20] Craig R. Hickman and Michael A. Silva, *Creating Excellence* (New York: New American Library, 1984), 128.
[21] Rogers, 384, 427.
[22] Thomas Gordon, *Leadership Effectiveness Training* (Toronto: Bantam Books, 1977), 58; also Thomas J. Peters and Robert H. Waterman, Jr., *In Search of Excellence: Lessons from America's Best-Run Companies* (New York: Warner Books, 1982), 236, 238.
[23] Simpson, 185, 189.
[24] Gordon, 22–24. Note: While the satisfaction of safety needs is listed as a prerequisite to belonging and acceptance, I personally believe that there is a bit of reciprocity and overlap here, and that safety, at least from an emotional and psychological standpoint, relies to a certain extent upon acceptance and belonging.
[25] Simpson, 187, 192, 193. Note: These findings reflect outcomes of several different studies.
[26] Siccone and López, introduction.
[27] Hayes Mizell, "Choosing a Path: Making School Equity at the Middle Level a Reality," *Schools in the Middle,* vol. 8, no. 6 (April 1999): 18.
[28] David Sadker, "Gender Equity," *Educational Leadership*, vol. 56, no. 7 (April 1999): 23. Note: While Sadker was referring to the persistence of gender bias in this quote, I believe it applies, to varying degrees, to all forms of discrimination.
[29] Francis Wardle, "Children of Mixed Race—No Longer Invisible," *Educational Leadership,* vol. 57, no. 4 (December 1999/January 2000): 71.
[30] Malcolm X (as told to Alex Haley), *The Autobiography of Malcolm X* (New York: Ballantine Books, 1964), 33–34.
[31] Quoted in Siccone and López, 150.
[32] Livia King, "Bridging Cultures," *Albuquerque Journal* (4 January 2000).
[33] Wardle, 68.
[34] Quoted in Siccone and López, introduction.
[35] Fu.
[36] Aspy and Roebuck, front pages.
[37] Robin A. Butterfield, "Blueprints for Indian Education: Improving Mainstream Schooling," *ERIC Digest* (June 1994). Available: ERIC Web site, U.S. Department of Education, [Internet, WWW], Address: *http://www.ed.gov/databases/ERIC_Digests/ed3278989.html.*
[38] Phillip Kaufman, Steve Klein and Mary Frase, "Dropout Rates in the United States: 1997," National Center for Education Statistics, U.S. Department of Education Office of Educational Research and Improvement. Available: National Dropout Prevention Center Web site, [Internet, WWW], Address: *http://www.dropoutprevention.org;* also Lyric Wallwork Winik, "There's a Generation with a Different Attitude," *Parade* magazine (18 July 1999): 6.
[39] Susan Strauss with Pamela Espeland, *Sexual Harassment and Teens* (Minneapolis: Free Spirit Publishing, 1992), 18. Note: Reporting on the findings of the Minnesota Women's Fund "Reflections of Risk: Growing Up Female in Minnesota," a report on the health and well-being of adolescent girls in Minnesota (Minneapolis: Minnesota Women's Fund, 1990).
[40] Sadker, 24.

[41] Leo, John, "Schools Teach Boys How to Suppress Masculinity," *Albuquerque Journal* (16 July 2000).

[42] Patricia Cloud Duttwiler, "Gay and Lesbian Youth at Risk," *The Journal of At-Risk Issues,* vol. 3, no. 2 (winter/spring 1997). Available: National Dropout Prevention Center Web site, [Internet, WWW], Address: *http://www.dropoutprevention.org/2levelpages/statistics/WhosAtRisk/5lvlstatswhogaylesb.htm;* "GLSEN: Teaching Respect for All in our Schools," handout packet published by the *Omaha Chapter of Gay, Lesbian and Straight Education Network;* "Research Begins to Bare the Facts," *Caucus Connection* (December 1997): 7–8; Wendy Schwartz, "Improving the School Experience for Gay, Lesbian and Bisexual Students," *ERIC Digest,* no. 101 (1994). Available: ERIC Web site, U.S. Department of Education, [Internet, WWW], Address: *http://www.ed.gov/databases/ERIC_Digests/ed377257.html.*

[43] Joan T. England, "Pluralism and Education: Its Meaning and Method," *ERIC Digest* (December 1992). Available: ERIC Web site, U.S. Department of Education, [Internet, WWW], Address: *http://www.ed.gov/databases/ERIC_Digests/ed347494.html;* also Arends, 204–206. Note: While the importance of these issues has been increasingly recognized in past decades, there are vast differences in the degree to which such topics are emphasized from one teacher training program to another, and in many instances, treatment is fairly superficial. For example, Sadker notes that "two-thirds of education professors spent less than two hours teaching about gender equity" and that "they rarely provided practical classroom strategies to neutralize bias."

[44] Ismat Abdal-Haqq, "Culturally Responsive Curriculum," *ERIC Digest* (June 1994). Available: ERIC Web site, U.S. Department of Education, [Internet, WWW], Address: *http://www.ed.gov/databases/ERIC_Digests/ed370936.html;* England; Fu; Arends, 202.

[45] Abdal-Haqq; also Kathy Escamilla, "Integrating Mexican-American History and Culture into the Social Studies Classroom," *ERIC Digest* (September 1992). Available: ERIC Web site, U.S. Department of Education, [Internet, WWW], Address: *http://www.ed.gov/databases/ERIC_Digests/ed348200.html.*

[46] Carmen Treppte, "Multicultural Approaches in Education: A German Experience," Available: ERIC/EECE Web site, [Internet, WWW], Address: *http://ericeece.org/pubs/books/multicul/trepptke.html.* Note: There is also a move, in some quarters, toward single-gender classes, although Sadker cautions that this "is not a substitute for ensuring equitable public education for all our students."

[47] Mizell, 18.

[48] Richard Arends, *Learning to Teach* (New York: Random House, 1988), 202; Cathy A. Pohan and Norma J. Bailey, "Including Gays in Multiculturism," *The Education Digest* (January 1998): 52.

[49] Rick Bragg, *All Over but the Shouting* (New York: Pantheon Books, 1997), 55.

[50] Matt Bai, "Anatomy of a Massacre," *Newsweek* (3 May 1999): 25.

[51] From a rebroadcast of a *Seinfeld* episode, September 1999 which dealt with high-school social rituals.

[52] Guy Doud, "From Hero to Zero." Available: The Life Story Foundation Web site, [Internet, WWW], Address: *http://www.lifestory.org/doud1.html; /doud2.html; /doud3.html.*

[53] Duttweiler; Siccone and López, introduction.

[54] Rogers and Frieberg, 235, 237.

[55] Eric Pooley, "Portrait of a Deadly Bond," *Time* magazine, vol. 153, no. 18 (10 May 1999): 30; also mentioned as a possible factor in the Conyers, Georgia, shooting in Cloud's article.

[56] Charol Shakeshaft, Laurie Mandel, Yolanda M. Johnson, Janice Sawyer, Mary Ann Hergenrother and Ellen Barber, "Boys Call Me Cow," *Educational Leadership,* vol. 55, no. 2 (October 1997). Available: Association for Supervision and Curriculum Development Web site, [Internet, WWW], Address: *http://www.ascd.org/safeschools/el9710/shakeshaftcow.html.*

[57] "Walker Charged with Misdemeanor," *Albuquerque Journal* (10 August 1999).

[58] Zach Ewing, "Not Everyone Who Is a Jock Is a 'Jock,'" *Albuquerque Journal*

(2 November 1999); Joshuah G. Flores, "Baggy Pants Give Off Phony Fashion Cues," *Albuquerque Journal* (2 November 1999); Livia King, "Metal Fans Experience Discrimination, Mistrust," *Albuquerque Journal* (2 November 1999).

[59] McDonald, 86.

[60] Bai, 26.

[61] "A Deadly Rift: Aftermath in Amarillo," segment broadcast on ABC's *20/20* (6 July 2000).

[62] King, "Metal Fans Experience Discrimination."

[63] Arthur, 134. Note: Arthur also found that some of the most dangerous kids in the school got away with a lot more and were bothered less by teachers and security guards than other, less menacing students simply because they had learned to dress "straight," 34.

[64] "Title IX, Education Amendments of 1972." Available U.S. Department of Labor Web site, [Internet, WWW], Address: *http://www.dol.gov/dol/oasam/public/regs/statutes/titleix.htm.*

[65] Sadker, 23–24.

[66] Leo, citing information in Christina Sommers's book, *The War Against Boys.*

[67] Patricia Freedman, "A Girl's Place is in the Universe" (21 December 1998). Available: 6seconds Web site, [Internet, WWW], Address: *http://www.6seconds.org/jrn/jpcgirls1.html.* (This is for the first part of this article. For parts 2 and 3, the URL is the same except for ending with *jpcgirls2.html* and *jpcgirls3.html.*)

[68] Mary Pipher, *Reviving Ophelia* (New York: Ballantine Books, 1994), 68; also Brotman.

[69] Valeria E. Besag, *We Don't Have Bullies Here,* handbook for Schools (Newcastle upon Tyne, U.K.: Valerie E. Besag, 1992), 38; Barbara Brotman, "Mean Streak," *St. Paul Pioneer Press, Express* (23 August 1999); Natalie Southworth, "Experts Report Girls as Aggressive as Boys, but in Verbal Ways," *The Globe and Mail,* Toronto (23 October 1999); Olweus, 10; Pipher, 68; Shakeshaft et al.; "Teacher Talk: Violence in the Schools" (June 1997). Available: *Indiana University Center for Adolescent Studies* Web site, [Internet, WWW], Address: *http://education.indiana.edu/cas/tt/v213/violence.html;* "Teacher Talk: Female Fighting and the 'Male Dance'" (June 1997). Available: *Indiana University Center for Adolescent Studies* Web site, [Internet, WWW], Address: *http://education.indiana.edu/cas/tt/v2i3/female.html.*

[70] Quoted in Brotman.

[71] Bowers, Cynthia. Segment on a teen suicide resulting from bullying. *CBS Evening News,* 2 September 1999.

[72] Hoover and Oliver, 15. Note: These statistics included both boys and girls.

[73] Arthur, 31.

[74] Shakeshaft, et al.

[75] Epp, 19; also Hoover and Oliver, 14; "Back to School Campaign: Report Card on Making School Safe for All Students," 1998, Available: GLSEN (Gay, Lesbian, and Straight Education Network) Web site, [Internet, WWW], Address: *http://www.glsen.org/pages/sections/news/back-to-school/1998/key,* and *http://www.glsen.org/pages/sections/news/back-to-school/1998/districtsbygrade;* Sister Mary Ellen Gevelinger, O.P. and Laurel Zimmerman, "How Catholic Schools Are Creating a Safe Climate for Gay and Lesbian Students," *Educational Leadership,* vol. 55, no. 2 (October 1997). Available: Association for Supervision and Curriculum Development Web site, [Internet, WWW], Address: *http://www.ascd.org/safeschools/el9710/geveling.htm;* also a number of personal interviews.

[76] "Just the Facts" (1998). Availability: *Blackboard On-Line,* the GLSEN (Gay, Lesbian and Straight Education Network) Web site, [Internet, WWW], Address: *http://www.glstn.org/pages/sections/library/reference/006.article.*

[77] Shakeshaft, et al.

[78] Nicole Ziegler Dizon, "Schools Struggle Over How to Protect Gay Students," *Albuquerque Journal* (8 October 2000).

[79] Strauss, 3, 14.

[80] Ibid., 55.

[81] "Love Doesn't Have to Hurt," from the Partners in Program Planning in Adolescent

Health. Available: American Psychological Association Web site, [Internet, WWW], Address: *http://www.apa.org/pi/pii/teen/teen1.html.* through *teen8.html.*

[82] Shakeshaft, et al.

[83] Ibid.

[84] "Love Doesn't Have to Hurt."

[85] Michael Quaass, "Reduce the Social Barriers Which Inhibit and Prevent People with a Disability from Entering Vocational Training and Education," course handout; also Garrity et al.

[86] Dan Olweus, *Bullying at School* (Oxford, U.K.: Blackwell Publishers, 1993), 30–32.

[87] Allan L. Beane, *The Bully-Free Classroom* (Minneapolis: Free Spirit Publishing, 1999), 6; Cynthia Bowers, Segment on a teen suicide resulting from bullying, *CBS Evening News* (2 September 1999); Laurie Dhue, Segment on bullying, "Newsfront: Coalition for Children, Inc.," *MSNBC* (25 April 2000); Martin E. P. Seligman, *Learned Optimism* (New York: Alfred A. Knopf, 1991), 138; Beate Schuster, "Mobbing, Bullying and Peer Rejection." Available: American Psychological Association Web site, [Internet, WWW], Address: *http://www.apa.org/psa/julaug96/sb.html;* also Arthur; Besag, 38; Garrity, et al.; Hoover and Oliver, 13; Olweus, 32–33.

[88] "Attitudes Toward Difference: The Riddle Scale," handout distributed by GLSEN Omaha with an adaptation of Dr. Dorothy Riddles' Scale of Homophobia, 1987. Note: This continuum considers tolerance and acceptance to be negative attitudes, just above repulsion and pity. Positive attitudes include support, admiration, appreciation and nurturance at the highest level. Although originally focused on attitudes toward homosexuals, I believe the scale applies to attitudes toward other types of "differences" as well.

[89] Dickens, 77.

[90] Victoria R. Fu, citing the work of H. A. Giroux (in *Postmodernism, Feminism and Cultural Politics: Redrawing Educational Boundaries,* Albany: State University of New York Press, 1991), "Culture, Schooling and Education in a Democracy." Available: ERIC/EECE Web site, [Internet, WWW], Address: *http://ericeece.org/pubs/books/multicul/fu.html.*

[91] McDonald, 83.

[92] Beane, 8.

[93] DeRosa; also Beane, 7; Olweus, 66; Shakeshaft, et al.; John H. Hoover and Glenn Olsen, *Teasing and Harassment: A Guide for Parents and Teachers* (Unpublished manuscript, National Education Services, 1999), 56; Merle Froschl and Nancy Gropper, "Fostering Friendships, Curbing Bullying," *Educational Leadership,* vol. 56, no. 8 (May 1999): 72; Eric Jones, "Practical Considerations in Dealing with *Bullying in Secondary School," Bullying: A Practical Guide to Coping for Schools,* 2d ed., Michele Elliott, ed. (London: Pitman Publishing, 1997), 13; Carole Remboldt, *Violence in Schools: The Enabling Factor* (Minneapolis: Johnson Institute-QVS, Inc., 1994), 23–29.

[94] McDonald, 87.

[95] Olweus, 20.

[96] Froschl and Gropper, 72.

[97] Strauss and Espeland, 7.

[98] Jones, 12–13.

[99] Strauss and Espeland, 74.

[100] Hoover and Oliver, 14–15; also Peter Stephenson and David Smith, "Why Some Schools Don't Have Bullies," *Bullying: A Practical Guide to Coping for Schools,* 2d ed., Michele Elliott, ed. (London: Pitman Publishing, 1997), 170–73; Hoover and Olsen, 50. Note: McDonald's research suggests that many students share these beliefs, and see bullying and peer conflict as a natural part of growing up and, as one eighth-grade girl noted, "learning to stick up for themselves." Several students would prefer that teachers "mind their own business" as they went about what they felt was a normal step in their initiation into adulthood.

[101] Strauss and Espeland, 8.

[102] Michael A. Rettig, "Seven Steps to Schoolwide Safety," *Principal,* vol. 79, no. 1 (September 1999): 10; also Adler and Springen; Cloud.

[103] Shakeshaft; also Larry Calloway, "Court Rules APS Has No Duty to Protect Against Attack," *Albuquerque Journal* (30 September 1999). Note: In this report, a student who was eventually stabbed in school attempted to get support from authorities in school, telling administrators of the numerous threats that had been made to her by this one girl. She was met with disbelief and "warned that she would be suspended if she got into a fight."
[104] McDonald, 87.
[105] Quoted in Adler and Springen, 37; also Dwyer, Osher and Wagner; Rettig.
[106] Stephenson and Smith, 170–73.
[107] McDonald, 87.
[108] "Warding Off Child Bullies," 3 September 1999. Available: CBS News Web site, [Internet, WWW], Address: *http://www.cbs.com/flat/story_182257.html;* also Bowers.
[109] Daniel Goleman, "New Ways to Battle Bias: Fight Acts, Not Feelings," *The New York Times* (16 July 1991).
[110] Lynn Duvall, *Respecting Our Differences* (Minneapolis: Free Spirit Publishing, 1994), 16.
[111] "CSPV Fact Sheet," 18 June 1999, prepared by the Center for the Study and Prevention of Violence, using information excerpted from "Evaluations of School-Based Violence Prevention, by F. Samples and L. Aber in *Violence in American Schools: A New Perspective,* by D. S. Elliott, B. Hamburg and K. R. Williams, eds., 217–52. New York: Cambridge University Press, 1998. Available: University of Colorado Web site, [Internet, WWW], Address: *http://www.colorado.edu/cspv/factsheet/factsheet10.html;* Rudi Keller, "Expert: Identify Violent Kids Early," *Albuquerque Journal* (12 February 2000); Beane, 83, 85; Stevenson and Smith, 170–73; Jones, 15; Olweus, 25; Strauss and Espeland; numerous others.
[112] Bragg, 55.
[113] Reasoner bases his conclusion on research by Coopersmith and an AAUW study, both of which noted negative changes in self-esteem measures as students progressed through the grades. In addition, he notes "in standardizing my Student Self-Esteem Inventory, which assesses self-esteem in the context of the school, and thus really 'academic self-concept,' I found that I had to develop separate norms for boys and girls for each grade level. I standardized [the inventory] over 14,000 students and found that I had to adjust the norms at each grade level because the scores declined through the grades, with the lowest scores at grades eleven and twelve."
[114] Siccone and López, introduction.
[115] Richard J. Racosky, *dreams + action = Reality* (Boulder, Colo.: ActionGraphics Publishing, 1996), ii.
[116] Malcolm X, 41; also Adderholt-Elliott, 16; Sunbeck, 47–50; Markova, 25–26; [Liner notes from] Charles Mingus, "The Clown" (CD); Mike Selby, *Self Worth Now!* (Sedona, Ariz.: Allisone Press, 2000), 53.

Chapter 13
How Does Your Garden Grow? More Diversity, More Discrimination

[1] George H. Reavis, *The Animal School* (Peterborough, N.H.: Crystal Springs Books, 2000). This story is in the public domain, however it is currently as a full-color, illustrated book from this publisher.
[2] Epp, 5.
[3] McGinnis, 35.
[4] Mel Levine, "Misunderstood Minds." Available: *All Kinds of Minds* Web site, [Internet, WWW], Address: *http://www.allkindsofminds.org/library/articles/MuMinds.htm;* Barbara Kantrowitz and Pat Wingert, "Doctor's Orders," *Newsweek* (2 October 2000), 44–47. Note: According to this second article, Levine helps teachers understand "neurodevelopmental constructs," or ideas about differences in "attention, language, memory, neuromotor function and social cognition."
[5] Thomas Armstrong, *The Myth of the ADD Child: 50 Ways to Improve Your Child's*

Behavior and Attention Span Without Drugs or Coercion (New York: Dutton, 1995), 92.
[6] Mizell, 18.
[7] Noel White, Tina Blythe and Howard Gardner, "Multiple Intelligence Theory: Creating the Thoughtful Classroom," in *Multiple Intelligence: A Collection,* Fogarty, Robin and James Bellanca, eds. (Arlington Heights, Ill.: IRI/SkyLight Training and Publishing, Inc., 1995), 180.
[8] Greenspan, *The Growth of the Mind,* 212.
[9] Quoted in Greenspan, *The Growth of the Mind,* 213.
[10] William A. Owings and Susan Magliaro, "Grade Retention: A History of Failure," *Educational Leadership.* vol. 56, no. 1 (September 1998). Available: ASCD Web site, [Internet, WWW], Address: *http://www.ascd.org/pubs/el/sep98/owings.html.*
[11] Alan Loy McGinnis, *Bringing Out the Best in People* (Minneapolis: Augsburg Publishing House, 1985), 28.
[12] Quoted in Siccone and López, 175.
[13] I was surprised to find that this practice of ranking students still occurs in the United States. I hadn't heard of this happening for years and wrongly assumed that schools had stopped ranking children with competitive placements.
[14] "The Japanese Way"; also conversations with parents and educators from various places overseas. Note: There was also mention of class discrimination in some settings, in which children were at risk for being limited by the kind of work the parents (typically the father) did. Children of laborers were, in these settings, sometimes discouraged from, or flatly denied, opportunities for careers that demanded higher education. But as Ohanian and others point out, American kids are increasingly at risk for have their future success in school and work limited by a single test score.
[15] Donovan and Iovino, 37.
[16] Tom Loveless, "Will Tracking Reform Promote Social Equity?" *Educational Leadership,* vol. 56, no. 7 (April 1999): 28–29.
[17] Hannaford, *Smart Moves,* 132.
[18] "Howard Gardner on: The Acceptance of Multiple Intelligence Theory," from *Reinventing Our Schools.* Available: Penn State Educational Systems Design Web site, [Internet, WWW], Address: *http://www.ed.psu.edu/insys/ESD/Gardner/AcceptMI.html.*
[19] Theodore Sizer, *Horace's Hope* (Boston: Houghton Mifflin Co., 1996), 9.
[20] Cherry, et al., 89.
[21] Donovan and Iovino, 36–37.
[22] Mizell, 21.
[23] Branden, 179.
[24] Les Brown, *Live Your Dreams* (New York: Avon Books, 1992), 63.
[25] Beamish, "Knowledge About the Brain"; "Realities, Changing Realities."
[26] Hannaford, *Dominance Factor,* 47.
[27] Lyndall Shick, *Understanding Temperament: Strategies for Creating Family Harmony* (Seattle: Parenting Press, 1998), 75–77.
[28] There's also a subtly different "energy" in each of these statements. Say each one and listen, watch and feel the effect on your nervous system. Each has a different energetic impact on the emotional climate in a classroom as well.
[29] Susan Ohanian, "An Antisocial Idea" (6 March 2000). Available: *The Nation* Web site, [Internet, WWW], Address: *http://past.thenation.com/issue/000306/0306ohanian.shtml.*
[30] Reported in Owings and Magliaro; also "To Promote or Retain: The Debate over Social Promotion Continues," *Communicator,* Newsletter of the National Association of Elementary School Principals, vol. 23, no. 1 (September 1999): 1–3.
[31] Brown, 62–63.
[32] "Thoughts on Risk and Recovery from Course Failure," *Forum* (International Alliance for Invitational Education), vol. 21, no. 1 (April 2000): 16–17.
[33] Owings and Magliaro.
[34] Ohanian, "An Antisocial Idea."
[35] Louise Bates Ames, *Is Your Child in the Wrong Grade?* (Rosemont, N.J.: Modern

Learning Press, 1978), 4; also Jim Grant, *I Hate School* (Rosemont, N.J.: Modern Learning Press, 1986); 5–10.

[36] Hannaford, *Smart Moves,* 84; also Sunbeck. Note: Hannaford cites the policies of the Danish school system, which does not teach reading until age eight. She believes this fact, and the fact that children do not start school until age six or seven, contributes to Denmark's 100 percent literacy rate.

[37] Linda Verlee Williams, 146.

[38] Some schools have "transitional kindergartens" or special "bridge" classes for kids who fall behind. However, the context is still one of uniformity, and kids (and staff) often perceive these classes as places for "dumb kids."

[39] "To Promote or Retain."

[40] Quoted in Wright, *The Heart and Wisdom of Teaching.*

[41] David Elkind, *Reinventing Childhood* (Rosemont, N.J.: Modern Learning Press, Inc., 1998), 143.

[42] Dawna Markova, *The Open Mind: Exploring the Six Patterns of Natural Intelligence* (Berkeley, Calif.: Conari Press, 1996), 17.

[43] White, Blythe and Gardner, 184.

[44] Shirley A. Griggs, "Learning Styles Counseling," *ERIC Digest* (December 1991). Available: ERIC Web site, U.S. Department of Education, [Internet, WWW], Address: *http://www.ed.gov/databases/ERIC_Digests/ed341890.html.*

[45] Quoted in Markova, *How Your Child Is Smart,* 19.

[46] Sizer, x.

[47] Markova, *The Open Mind,* 16.

[48] Luckily, I'm a good match for a group like this. My visual channel is my preferred modality, or my primary means of perceptual processing. Most of the time, I am not easily distracted by people moving around and doing different things. (My weakest modality is my auditory channel; I find certain sounds and noises far more disruptive to my concentration.) I also know that, with my secondary tactile/kinesthetic preferences, I listen better if I'm doing something with my hands, so I've come to respect people's needs to doodle or knit while I talk.

[49] James W. Keefe and Barbara Ferrell, "Developing a Defensible Learning Style Paradigm," *Educational Leadership* (October 1990): 57.

[50] Harvey Silver, Richard Strong and Matthew Perini, "Integrating Learning Styles and Multiple Intelligences," *Educational Leadership,* vol. 55, no. 1 (November 1997): 22.

[51] Elkind, 95.

[52] DeBeaufort and Diaz; Markova, *The Open Mind;* Sunbeck; Hannaford, *Physiological Foundations,* 6.

[53] Kenneth Dunn and Rita Dunn, *The Educator's Self-Teaching Guide to Individualizing Instructional Programs* (Englewood Cliffs, N.J.: Parker Publishing Co., 1975).

[54] Keefe and Ferrell, 57.

[55] Markova, *How Your Child Is Smart,* 34.

[56] Hannaford, *Smart Moves,* 191. Note: Just for the record, I am among these 75 percent. This is my profile exactly.

[57] Robert Sternberg, "Allowing for Thinking Styles," *Educational Leadership,* vol. 52, no. 3 (November 1994): 36.

[58] Silver, Strong and Perini, 23; Markova, *The Open Mind,* 170; Sternberg, 36; Carla Hannaford, *The Dominance Factor* (Arlington, Va.: Great Oceans Publishers, 1997), 48.

[59] Dennison and Dennison, *Brain Gym,* Teacher's Edition, "Message to Parents and Educators"; also Sharon Promislow, *Making the Brain Body Connection* (West Vancouver, Can.: Kinetic Publishing Corporation, 1999), 33.

[60] Hannaford, *Dominance Factor,* 15. Note: Some suggest that our dominance profiles can change depending upon the task.

[61] Ibid., 33, 146.

[62] Ibid., 151, 10–11.

[63] Linda Verlee Williams, 145.

[64] Lewis and Pucelik, 41–42.

[65] Markova, *The Open Mind,* 37; Hannaford, *Smart Moves,* 188; Hannaford, *Dominance Factor,* 25; Lewis and Pucelik, 60; Linda Verlee Williams, 85.
[66] Hannaford, *Smart Moves,* 187–88; also Hannaford, *Dominance,* 26–28; Markova, *Open Mind,* 37; Lewis and Pucelik, 61; "How a Teacher Can Work with a Child Diagnosed with ADD," *Pure Facts,* newsletter of the *Feingold Association of the United States* (September 1996): 3. Note: According to the Feingold report, children with a super-sensitivity to noise "will tune out the world around him when he is trying to focus."
[67] Gazzaniga, *The Social Brain,* 28; Greenspan, *The Challenging Child,* 169; Hannaford, *Dominance,* 28–30; Hannaford, *Smart Moves,* 181, 190; Linda Verlee Williams, 7.
[68] Lewis and Pucelik, 142; Linda Verlee Williams, 151; Hannaford, *Smart Moves,* 181, 183, 188; Hannaford, *Dominance,* 30, 152; Markova, *Open Mind,* 37.
[69] Hannaford, *Physiological Foundations,* 18, 20, 25; also Jensen, *Completing the Puzzle,* 21; "The 4MAT System," Available: *About Learning Inc.* Web site, [Internet, WWW], Address: *http://aboutlearning.com/aboutlearning/4MATsys.html.*
[70] Gazzaniga, *The Social Brain,* 44, 46.
[71] Carolyn Kalil, "Follow Your True Colors to the Work You Love," excerpt from book of same title. Available: *Follow Your True Colors* Web site, [Internet, WWW], Address: *http://www.truecolorscareer.com.*
[72] Phillips, 23.
[73] Beamish, "Reality, Changing Realities."
[74] Ibid.
[75] Quoted in Shapiro, 18.
[76] Karr-Morse and Wiley, 129.
[77] Ibid., 132; Schick, 23, 65; Helen Neville and Diane Clark Johnson, *Temperament Tools* (Seattle: Parenting Press, Inc., 1998), 11, 15–16. Note: Karr-Morse and Wiley observe that babies perceived as "having difficult temperaments are at higher risk of child abuse and the resulting behavioral problems arising from conflict between parents and children that can precede violent behaviors." I also believe that a poor match between teacher and student can predict a variety of learning and discipline problems.
[78] Greenspan, *The Challenging Child,* 2.
[79] Ibid., 7, 28; also Karr-Morse and Wiley, 129; Shapiro, 18–19; Schick, 12–13; "Learning Styles and the 4MAT System: A Cycle of Learning." Available *University of North Dakota "Volcanoes" Program* Web site, [Internet, WWW], Address: *http://volcano.und.nodak.edu/vwdocs/msh/11c/is/4mat.html.*
[80] "About True Colors." Available *True Colors* Web site, [Internet, WWW], Address: *http://truecolors.org/general/about_true_colors.htm;* also Phillips, 5. Note: In the late 1970s, Don Lowry began working with Keirsey's research and developed a system using color to identify these four groups, making the concept more accessible for practical application in a work, school, family or clinical environment.
[81] All of the information about these four categories comes from David Keirsey, *Please Understand Me II: Temperament, Character, Intelligence* (Del Mar, Calif.: Prometheus Nemesis Book Co., 1998). "About True Colors"; Phillips, 7–12; Beamish, "Reality, Changing Realities"; and Claude R. Beamish, "A Brief Look at the Children of the Four Major Groups," The MindLift Foundation Web site. Available: [Internet, WWW], Address: *http://www.mindlift.com/4cmajorgrps.htm;* Barbara Barron-Tieger and Paul Tieger, "What's Your Personality Type?" *New Woman* (August 1998), 68–73.
[82] White, Blythe and Gardner, 182.
[83] Anthony Gregorc, "Frequently Asked Questions on Style." Available: *Gregorc Associates, Inc.* Web site, [Internet, WWW], Address: *http://www.gregorc.com/faq.html.*
[84] Pat Burke Guild and Sandy Chock-Eng, "Multiple Intelligence, Learning Styles, Brain-Based Education: Where Do the Messages Overlap?" *Schools in the Middle,* vol. 7, no. 4 (March/April 1998), 40.
[85] Kathy Checkley, "The First Seven . . ." *Educational Leadership,* vol. 55, no. 1 (November 1997): 10; Greenspan, *The Growth of the Mind,* 128–29.

[86] Howard Gardner, *Frames of Mind: The Theory of Multiple Intelligences* (New York: Basic Books, 1983), 18.
[87] Checkley, 10.
[88] Silver, Strong and Perini. Note: These include Mastery Style Learner (concrete, sequential, valuing clarity and practicality), Understanding Style Learner (abstract focus, learning through questioning and reasoning, values logic and evidence), Self-Expressive Style Learner (uses images, feelings and emotions, values originality, aesthetics, surprise) and the Interpersonal Style Learner (concrete, social learner, values the potential to help others).
[89] "The 4MAT System"; also "Major Premises of 4MAT." Available: *About Learning Inc. Web site, [Internet, WWW], Address: http://aboutlearning.com/aboutlearning/4premis.html;* "Learning Styles and the 4MAT System."
[90] "Learning Styles" (February 1996). Available: *Algonquin College of Applied Arts and Technology* Web site, [Internet, WWW], Address: *http://algonquinc.on.ca/edtech/gened/styles.html.*
[91] Rick Aster, "SAS Programming for All Types." Available: Rick Aster's Web site, [Internet, WWW], Address: *http://www.rickaster.com/globalstatements/gregorc.html;* also Anthony Gregorc, "Frequently Asked Questions on Style." Available: *Gregorc Associates, Inc.* Web site, [Internet, WWW], Address: *http://www.gregorc.com/faq.html;* also "Learning Styles." Note: The four categories include Concrete Sequential, Concrete Random, Abstract Sequential, and Abstract Random.
[92] Wendy M. Williams.
[93] Sternberg, 38. Note: He includes Legislative, Executive and Judicial functions (creating, following directions or evaluating); Monarchic, Hierarchic, Oligarchic and Anarchic forms (method of handling and prioritizing multiple tasks); Global and Local levels (big-picture vs. details); Internal and External Scope (working alone or with others); and Liberal or Conservative learnings (defying or following conventions).
[94] Valiant, 25.
[95] Bean, 13.
[96] Arnold B. Skromme, *The Cause and Cure of Dropouts* (Moline, Ill.: The Self-Confidence Press, 1998).
[97] Janet Levine, "The Enneagram System: Understand Yourself to Understand Your Students." Available: *Enneagram-Edge* Web site, [Internet, WWW], Address: *http://www.enneagram-edge.com/journal.html.*
[98] DeBeaufort and Diaz, 345–54. Note: The mental intelligences they list include Rational, Associative, Spatial and Intuitive intelligences; emotional intelligences include Affectional, Mood and Motivational intelligences; and behavioral intelligences are identified as Basic, Pattern and Parameter intelligences.
[99] Silver, Strong and Perini, 22.
[100] Checkley, 13.
[101] Information about these categories came from several sources, including "Harvard's Howard Gardner Teaches Parents to Nurture Children's Natural Gifts for Learning," *Bottom Line Personal,* vol. 20, no. 17 (1 September 1999): 11–12; also Gardner, *Frames of Mind;* Armstrong, 92–95; Checkley, 12; Silver, Strong and Perini, 26; Ginger Kelley McKenzie, "Multiple Intelligences Put into Practice," *The National Montessori Reporter 99,* vol. XXIII, no. 3 (fall 1999): 3–5.
[102] "Harvard's Howard Gardner," 11.
[103] White, Blythe and Gardner, 183; also Checkley; Lantieri and Patti, 9.
[104] White, Blythe and Gardner, 183.
[105] Checkley, 10; White, Blythe and Gardner, 186; also Thomas Armstrong, "Multiple Intelligences: Seven Ways to Approach Curriculum," *Educational Leadership,* vol. 52, no. 3 (November 1994): 26.

Part II
The Toolbox

[1] Dwyer, 2.
[2] Aspy and Roebuck, 3.
[3] Purkey and Strahan, 2.

Chapter 14
Academic Safety: Learning and Success

[1] Quoted in Wright, *The Heart and Wisdom of Teaching.*
[2] Donovan and Iovino, 38.
[3] Jostine Gaardner, *The Solitaire Mystery* (New York: Farrar, Straus & Giroux, 1996), 48.
[4] Tamara Gerrard, *Com-Packs: Kids' Committees for Integrated Learning,* Albuquerque, N. Mex.: I.S.S. Publications, 1987. Note: As Tami's supervisor during her first year of teaching, and later as a friend, I often visited her classroom and was privileged to see these and many similar units being conducted in her class.
[5] Charles Suhor, "Spirituality—Letting It Grow in the Classroom," *Educational Leadership,* vol. 56, no. 4 (December 1998/January 1999): 15; also David H. Elkind and Freddy Sweet, "Classroom Dialogue Stimulates Respectful Relationships," *Schools in the Middle,* vol. 8, no. 2 (October 1998), 43.
[6] Brooks and Brooks, 22.
[7] Glasser, 77.
[8] Quoted in Donovan and Iovino, 34.
[9] Jean Piaget, *The Moral Judgment of the Child* (New York: Free Press Paperbacks [Simon & Schuster, Inc.], 1997), 404.
[10] Greenspan, *The Challenging Child,* 21.
[11] Brooks and Brooks, 22.
[12] Hannaford, *Smart Moves,* 85.
[13] Jensen, *Completing the Puzzle,* 121.
[14] Quoted in Charles Garfield, *Peak Performers* (New York: William Morrow & Co., Inc., 1986), 80.
[15] Glasser, 49; Rogers and Frieberg, 9; Linda Verlee Williams, 170.
[16] Faulkner and Faiveley, 85.
[17] Rogers and Frieberg, 9.
[18] David Perkins, "The Many Faces of Constructivism," *Educational Leadership,* vol. 57, no. 3 (November 1999): 8.
[19] Jensen, *Completing the Puzzle,* 36–38.
[20] Gerd Kempermann and Fred H. Gage, "New Nerve Cells for the Adult Brain," *Scientific American* (May 1999): 51.
[21] Karr-Morse and Wiley, 27.
[22] Karoline Krynock and Louise Robb, "Problem Solved: How to Coach Cognition," *Educational Leadership,* vol. 57, no. 3 (November 1999): 29.
[23] James Bellanca, "Teaching for Intelligence: In Search of Best Practices," *Phi Delta Kappan,* vol. 79, no. 9 (May 1998): 658.
[24] Rogers and Frieberg, 265.
[25] Donovan and Iovino, 38.
[26] Joshua Freedman et al., 46. Note: The authors recommend "interpretive" or "fusion" questions (similar to Bloom's "analysis," "synthesis" and "evaluation" questions) to truly engage the brain in higher-level thinking.
[27] Bower, 10.
[28] Bower, 16; Cherry, Godwin and Staples, 79; Donovan and Iovino, 59; Jensen, *Completing the Puzzle,* 26–27, 92; Sylwester, "How Our Brain Determines What's Important."
[29] Donovan and Iovino, vii.

[30] Maslow, 23–24.
[31] "Montessori: The Rebirth of a Legend." Available: *The Learning Web* Web site, [Internet, WWW], Address: *http://www.thelearningweb.net/montessori.htm.*
[32] Ron Burgess, *Laughing Lessons: 149½ Ways to Make Teaching and Learning Fun* (Minneapolis: Free Spirit Publishing, 2000), 1, back cover.
[33] Cherry, Godwin and Staples, 132.
[34] Elkind and Sweet, 43.
[35] Quoted in Joshua M. Freedman, Anabel L. Jensen, Marsha C. Rideout and Patricia E. Freedman, *Handle with Care: Emotional Intelligence Activity Book* (San Mateo, Calif.: Six Seconds, 1998), 82.
[36] Wright, *The Heart and Wisdom of Teaching.*
[37] Ibid.
[38] Catherine Kellison McLaughlin, *The Do's and Don'ts of Parent Involvement: How to Build a Positive School-Home Partnership* (Torrance, Calif.: Innerchoice Publishing, 1993), 107.
[39] Glasser, 76–78.
[40] Faulkner and Faiveley, referring to Susan Kovalik's eight brain-compatible components, 85.
[41] Bluestein, *21st Century Discipline,* 107–12.
[42] Jensen, *Completing the Puzzle,* 28.
[43] Rogers and Frieberg, 250–51, citing research collected by the National Center for Education in the Inner Cities during the 1991-92 school year. Observing 128 classrooms at different grade levels, this study determined that at the elementary level, only .14 percent of activities were student selected. In middle school, the average was 2.03 percent; in high school, .93 percent.
[44] Kristina Torres, "New Country School Breaks Mold," *St. Paul Pioneer Press* (7 September 2000).
[45] Rogers and Frieberg, 17–18, describing the documentary, "Why Do These Children Love School?" by Dorothy Fadiman.
[46] Rogers and Frieberg, 250–51, citing findings by the National Center for Education in the Inner Cities in 128 classes at the elementary, middle and high school levels. This study reported that 78 to 88 percent of lessons (depending on grade level) were presented in this way in the classrooms studied.
[47] Peter S. Westwood, from a paper on Learning Disabilities (Flinders University of South Australia, School of Education, 1982), 6, 18.
[48] Greenspan, *The Growth of the Mind,* 213.
[49] Aspy and Roebuck, 2.
[50] Glasser, 97.
[51] Garfield, 62.
[52] Erika V. Shearin Karres, *Violence Proof Your Kids Now: How to Recognize the Eight Warning Signs and What to Do About Them* (Berkeley, Calif.: Conari Press, 2000), 73.
[53] Sunbeck, 180.
[54] Cited in Quarles, 22.
[55] Branden, 221.
[56] Rogers and Frieberg, 7.
[57] Verónica Martínez de Andrés, "Developing Self-Esteem in the Primary School: A Pilot Study," Intervention study submitted as part of graduate study, Oxford Brookes University, Oxford, U.K., 1996.
[58] Fraser, 69.
[59] Jensen, *Completing the Puzzle,* 115.
[60] Jillian N. Lederhouse, "You Will Be Safe Here," *Educational Leadership,* vol. 56, no. 1 (September 1998). Available: Association for Supervision and Curriculum Development Web site, [Internet, WWW], Address: *http://www.ascd.org/safeschools/el9809/ sellederhouse.html.*
[61] Ibid.
[62] Glasser, 96.

[63] Carol Ann Tomlinson, *The Differentiated Classroom: Responding to the Needs of All Learners* (Alexandria, Va.: Association for Supervision and Curriculum Development, 1999), 2.
[64] Littky and Allen, 25.
[65] Tomlinson, 2.
[66] Brooks and Brooks, 21.
[67] Quoted in Garfield, 156. Note: This statement is purported to be one of Einstein's favorite quotes.
[68] White, Blythe and Gardner, 184.
[69] Checkley, 12.
[70] Glasser, 77.
[71] Bluestein, *21st Century Discipline,* 77–80.
[72] Mark Starr and Martha Brant, "It Went Down to the Wire . . . and Thrilled Us All," *Newsweek* (19 July 1999): 46–54.
[73] William Plummer, "Wootten's Way," *People* magazine, vol. 54, no. 21 (20 November 2000): 166, 169.
[74] Quoted in Bluestein, *Mentors,* 42.
[75] Jensen, *Completing the Puzzle,* 62–63.
[76] Krynock and Robb, 31.
[77] Armstrong, *The Myth of the ADD Child,* 196–97; also Starr, 51–52.
[78] Rhoda Cummings and Gary Fisher, *The School Survival Guide for Kids with LD* (Minneapolis: Free Spirit Publishing, 1991), 40–42.
[79] Janet Levine.
[80] Goleman, *Emotional Intelligence,* 5.
[81] Claudia Geocaris and Maria Ross, "A Test Worth Taking," *Educational Leadership,* vol. 57, no. 1 (September 1999): 29–30.
[82] Ruth Butler and Mordecai Nisan, "Effects of No Feedback, Task-Related Comments, and Grades on Intrinsic Motivation and Performance," *Journal of Educational Psychology,* vol 78, no. 3 (1986): 215.
[83] James Bellanca, Carolyn Chapman and Elizabeth Swartz, *Multiple Assessments for Multiple Intelligences,* 3d edition (Arlington Heights, Ill.: IRI/SkyLight Training and Publishing, Inc., 1997), 207–8; William L. Beckley, *Creating a Classroom Portfolio System* (Dubuque, Iowa: Kendall/Hunt Publishing Co., 1997), 6; Anne Davies, "Seeing the Results for Yourself: A Portfolio Primer," *Classroom Leadership,* an ASCD Newsletter for K-12 Classroom Teachers, vol. 3, no. 5 (February 2000): 4.
[84] Heidi Goodrich Andrade, "Using Rubrics to Promote Thinking and Learning," *Educational Leadership,* vol. 57, no. 5 (February 2000), 13.
[85] Kathie Nunley, "In Defense of the Oral Defense," *Classroom Leadership,* an ASCD Newsletter for K-12 Classroom Teachers, vol. 3, no. 5 (February 2000): 6; also Deborah Him and Carolyn Moore, "Sailing the Sea as We Build the Boat," in *Multi-Age Classrooms,* Karen Gutloff, ed. (NEA Teacher-to-Teacher Books, Washington, D.C.: National Education Association, 1995), 35; Krynock and Robb, 31.
[86] Quoted in Rogers and Frieberg, 233.
[87] Phillips, 46.
[88] Thomas Armstrong, *Awakening Genius in the Classroom* (Alexandria, Va.: Association for Supervision and Curriculum Development, 1998), 65.
[89] K. Lynne Mainzer, Patricia Baltzley and Kathleen Heslin, "Everybody Can Be Great Because Everybody Can Serve," *Educational Leadership,* vol. 48, no. 3 (November 1990): 94.
[90] Note: I'm not suggesting for one moment that all wealthy districts are founded on competition or that high-achieving kids in these areas all have status-crazy parents. My point is that even in the most successful schools, when the goal structure is competitive, when achievement and status are relative, and when large numbers of individuals operate with a value system that says "only the best is any good," there's going to be another population that gets lost in the shuffle, including those kids who aren't at the top of the academic or social heap, those who are but can't handle the pressure or

those whose natural intelligences may not be appreciated or recognized in this kind of setting.

[91] Branden, 221–22.

[92] Jensen, *Completing the Puzzle,* 84.

[93] Purkey, "The Coming Revolution in American Education."

[94] Epp, 3; Purkey, "The Coming Revolution"; Jensen, *Completing the Puzzle,* 83; Rogers and Frieberg, 233; Lantieri, 18.

[95] "The Joys of Competition," *Imagine,* vol. 7, no. 1 (September/October 1999): 4–5.

[96] Littky and Allen, 24.

[97] Robert E. Slavin, "Cooperative Learning and Student Achievement," *Educational Leadership,* vol. 46, No. 2 (October 1988): 31–33.

[98] Hannaford, *Physiological Basis of Learning and Kinesiology* handbook.

[99] Joan Gaustad, "Peer and Cross-Age Tutoring," *ERIC Digest,* no. 79 (March 1993). Available: ERIC Web site, U.S. Department of Education, [Internet, WWW], Address: *http://www.ed.gov/databases/ERIC_Digests/ed354608.html;* Audrey Gartner and Frank Riessman, "Peer-Tutoring: Toward a New Model," *ERIC Digest* (August 1993). Available: ERIC Web site, U.S. Department of Education, [Internet, WWW], Address: *http://www.ed.gov/databases/ERIC_Digests/ed362506.html.*

[100] Fox and Forbing, 184; "Peer to Peer Instruction," *Program Ideas: Youth Mobilization* (no date). Available: National Crime Prevention Council Web site, [Internet, WWW], Address: *http://www.ncpc.org/3you1dc.htm;* "Preventing School Violence: Policies for Safety, Caring and Achievement"; Caroline E. Mohai, "Peer Leaders in Drug Abuse Prevention," *ERIC Digest* (December 1991). Available: ERIC Web site, U.S. Department of Education, [Internet, WWW], Address: *http://www.ed.gov/databases/ERIC_Digests/ed341892.html.*

[101] June Million, "A Win-Win Situation—Teaming Up with Your High School," *Communicator,* Newsletter of the National Association of Elementary School Principals, vol. 23, no. 4 (December 1999): 5.

[102] Gaustad, "Peer and Cross-Age Tutoring."

[103] Kristie Colwell-Cornett, Monica R. Louderback-Gibson, and Chandra E. Napier, "When Students Resist," in *Multi-Age Classrooms,* Karen Gutloff, ed. (NEA Teacher-to-Teacher Books, Washington, D.C.: National Education Association, 1995), 35; Him and Moore, 45, 48; Faulkner and Faiveley, 75; "Working in a Multiage Classroom: Can Students of Different Ages Work Together?" *Communicator,* Newsletter of the National Association of Elementary School Principals, vol. 23, no. 2 (October 1999): 1–2.

[104] Thomas L. Shortt and Yvonne V. Thayer, "Block Scheduling Can Enhance School Climate," *Educational Leadership,* vol. 56, no. 4 (December 1998/January 1999): 76–81.

[105] Barbara A. Lewis, *The Kid's Guide to Social Action* (Minneapolis: Free Spirit Publishing, 1998), 3; Barbara A. Lewis, *The Kid's Guide to Service Projects* (Minneapolis: Free Spirit Publishing, 1995), 3–4; Mary K. Nebgen and Kate McPherson; "Enriching Learning Through Service: A Tale of Three Districts," *Educational Leadership,* vol. 48, no. 3 (November 1990): 92; "Teens Who Volunteer Do Well by Doing Good," *The Family News Network,* vol. 2, issue 6 (August/September 1999): 17; Sandra Krystal, "The Nurturing Potential of Service Learning," *Educational Leadership,* vol. 56, no. 4 (December 1998/January 1999): 58–60; Mainzer, 95; "Emotionally Intelligent Parenting."

[106] Michael Ryan, "Together, We Transform the World," *Parade* magazine (5 September 1999): 4–7. Note: A survey by *Public Agenda* found that 71 percent of adults surveyed view teens as undisciplined, disrespectful and unfriendly; 53 percent say kids are spoiled and out of control.

[107] Ryan, 6; "Teens Who Volunteer," 17; Jackie Waldman, *Teens with the Courage to Give* (Berkeley, Calif.: Conari Press, 2000), xi–xii; Joshua Freedman, et al., 79.

[108] Krystal, 60.

Chapter 15
Emotional Safety: Personal and Character Development

[1] Subby, 33.
[2] Jenny Mosley, *Quality Circle Time in the Primary School,* vol. 1, Camb LDA, 1996.
[3] Susan Schindette, "Of Felons and Felines," *People* magazine, vol. 52, no. 18 (8 November 1999): 115–16.
[4] Theresa Walker, "Educators Seek Roots of Violenced Among Teens," *Albuquerque Journal* (28 November 1999); also Howard Haas and Alex Aitcheson, "Meet Howard Haas and Alex D. Aitcheson." Available: The *Children's Crusade* Web site, [Internet, WWW], Address: *http://www.childrenscrusade.com/meet.htm.* Note: The purpose of their investigation was to identify the kids' perspective on why they are killing one another.
[5] Kelly Pearce, "300 Kids at Summit on Stopping Violence," *The Arizona Republic* (15 April 2000).
[6] Ayers.
[7] Gibbs, "A Week in the Life," 75.
[8] Quote provided by Robert Reasoner.
[9] Bluestein, *Mentors.*
[10] Redenbach, 95.
[11] Doud (part 2).
[12] Seligman, 154.
[13] Quoted in Robert Owens Scott, "It's Called Optimism," *Spirituality & Health* (Spring/Summer 1999): 23–24.
[14] Seligman, 235; Schracter and McCauley, 243; Fassler and Dumas, x, 50, 55, 59.
[15] Howard Chua-Eoan, "Escaping from the Darkness," *Time* magazine, vol. 153, no. 21 (31 May 1999): 44–49.
[16] Fassler and Dumas, 63, 65–66.
[17] Karr-Morse and Wiley, 212, 215; Seligman, 127.
[18] Scott, 23; Seligman, 4, 144.
[19] Karr-Morse and Wiley, 212, 215.
[20] Seligman, 135.
[21] Seligman, 127, 129–30; also Fassler and Dumas, 106. Note: School failure can refer not only to kids with repeated failures, but also to perfectionistic, high-achieving kids with occasional failures.
[22] Chua-Eoan.
[23] Peter L. Benson, Judy Galbraith and Pamela Espeland, *What Kids Need to Succeed* (Minneapolis: Free Spirit Publishing, 1995), 137.
[24] Brent Q. Hafen and Kathryn J. Frandsen, *Youth Suicide: Depression and Loneliness* (Evergreen, Colo.: Cordillera Press, Inc., 1986), 10, 27–28; "Kids Killing Kids & Kids Saving Kids," Video by Arnold Shapiro Productions, Inc., 1991; Fassler and Dumas, 71, 104; Schacter and McCauley, 160; Rogers and Frieberg, 32; Karr-Morse and Wiley, 7; Robert Weller, "Columbine Student Hangs Himself," *Albuquerque Journal* (6 May 2000). Note: Statistics vary regarding teen suicides in the United States, with estimates as high as seven thousand suicides annually, making it the second leading cause of death among teens (one report placed it third). Frequency of completed suicides ranges from one child every six hours to an even more staggering estimate of one death per ninety minutes. Despite these inconsistencies, the literature concurs, however, that depression is a leading factor in youth suicide.
[25] Seligman, 154.
[26] Joshua Freedman, et al., 54.
[27] Seligman, 4–5, 43–47, 52, 137, 144; Scott, 23–24; Shapiro, 4; Susan C. Vaughan, "Optimists Live Better Lives than Pessimists," *Bottom Line Personal,* vol. 21, no. 24 (15 December 2000): 13; "Teaching Optimism," *EQ Today* (20 April 1999). Available: 6seconds Web site, [Internet, WWW], Address: *http://www.6seconds.org/jrn/jpcoptimism.html.*

[28] Seligman, 207.
[29] Scott, 23.
[30] Seligman, 211, 218, 221, 236; Fassler and Dumas, xi; "Teaching Optimism."
[31] "Resiliency and the Individual" (no date). Available: The National Network for Family Resiliency, University of Maryland Web site, [Internet, WWW], Address: *http://hartwick234.umd.edu/nnfrdocs/general/pub_ind.html.*
[32] Flach, 209.
[33] Al Siebert, "How Resilient Are You?" (1999). Available: *Thrivenet* Web site, [Internet, WWW], Address: *http://www.thrivenet.com/articles/resilien.html.*
[34] Quoted in Joshua Freedman, et al., 94.
[35] "Resiliency and the Individual."
[36] Linda Winfield, "Developing Resilience in Urban Youth," *NCREL Monograph* (1994). Available: *NCREL* (North Central Regional Educational Laboratory, Oak Brook, Illinois) Web site, [Internet, WWW], Address: *http://www.ncrel.org/sdrs/areas/issues/educatrs/leadrshp/le0win.htm.*
[37] Burns, 13.
[38] Tom Siegfried, "Teen Behavior Linked to Brain," *Albuquerque Journal* (4 September 2000).
[39] Penelope P. Soule and Joyce Sharp, "Safe and Drug-Free Schools and Communities," Student Survey conducted by the Nevada Department of Education, February 1997; Burns (referring to a report entitled "Patterns of Co-Occurrence Among At-Risk Behaviors," published by the Search Institute in Minneapolis, 1990), 15.
[40] "Resiliency and the Individual."
[41] Patricia Leigh Brown, "The Pomp of Graduation After Overcoming Difficult Circumstances" (14 June 2000). Available: *New York Times* Web site, [Internet, WWW], Address: *http://partners.nytimes.com/library/national/061400oakland-edu.html;* also Greenspan, *Growth of the Mind,* 123; also Bluestein, *Mentors*; Benard.
[42] Benson, et al., "What Kids Need to Succeed," 3–4; also Soule and Short. Note: Although geared more to building "success" than resiliency per se, the study by Benson, Galbraith and Espeland shows a remarkable similarity in outcomes when these protective factors are present.
[43] Flach, 213.
[44] "Resiliency"; Finley; Burns, 100.
[45] Al Siebert, "How to Develop Survivor Resiliency" (1999). Available: *Thrivenet* Web site, [Internet, WWW], Address: *http://www.thrivenet.com/articles/excelnt.html;* Siebert, "How Resilient Are You?"
[46] Peter L. Benson, Judy Galbraith and Pamela Espeland, *What Teens Need to Succeed* (Minneapolis: Free Spirit Publishing, 1998), 13–17; Benson, Galbraith and Espeland, "What Kids Need to Succeed," 5; Winfield; "Resiliency."
[47] Benson, Galbraith and Espeland, 3–4.
[48] Winfield.
[49] Benson, et al., "What Teens Need," 2–3.
[50] Winfield.
[51] Burns, 111.
[52] Murray White, "Magic Circles: The Benefits of Circle Time." Unpublished paper, 1999.
[53] Siraj Zaibun, "Change, Challenge and Commitment: Programmes to Develop Self-Esteem and the Potential of Youths in Singapore." Unpublished paper presented at the International Conference for Self-Esteem, San Francisco (June 2000).
[54] Terri Akin, David Cowan, Gerry Dunne, Susanna Palomares, Dianne Schilling and Sandy Schuster, *The Best Self-Esteem Activities for the Elementary Grades* (Spring Valley, Calif.: Innerchoice Publishing, 1990), 4.
[55] Branden, 3; also Nathaniel Branden, "Answering Misconceptions about Self-Esteem," *Self-Esteem Today,* vol. 10, no. 2 (spring 1998). Available *National Association for*

Self-Esteem Web site, [Internet, WWW], Address: *http://www.self-esteem-nase.org/journal01.shtml.*

[56] Akin, et al., 2.

[57] Branden, 204.

[58] Janice T. Gibson, *Discipline Is Not a Dirty Word* (Brattleboro, Vt.: The Lewis Publishing Co., 1983), 82–83.

[59] Fraser, 10–12.

[60] Adderholt-Elliot, 15.

[61] "Summary of Self-Esteem Research Supporting the Significance of Self-Esteem," compiled by Robert Reasoner, cited in Sandi Redenbach, *Self-Esteem: The Necessary Ingredients for Success* (Davis, Calif.: Esteem Seminar Programs and Publications, 1991), 4–10; also Akin, et al., 2; Sylwester, "How Our Brain Determines What's Important"; Dianne Rothenberg, "Supporting Girls in Early Adolescence," *ERIC Digest* (September 1995). Available: ERIC Web site, U.S. Department of Education, [Internet, WWW], Address: *http://www.ed.gov/databases/ERIC_Digests/ed386331.html;* Stephanie Marston, *The Magic of Encouragement: Nurturing Your Child's Self-Esteem* (New York: Pocket Books, 1990), 25–26.

[62] Michele Borba, *Esteem Builders* (Torrance, Calif.: Jalmar Press, 1989), 2.

[63] Borba, *Esteem Builders,* citing Stanley Coopersmith's work, 7; Joseph Donnelly, Anthony T. Procaccino Jr. and Maryam Donnelly, "Impressionable Years: Forming Empowerment in Adolescents Through Fostering Self-Esteem," *Journal of the National Association for Self-Esteem,* vol. 1, no. 1 (winter 1999): 7; Akin, et al., 4; Rothenberg. Note: Rothenberg cites research that shows kids in the middle grades, especially girls, are the most vulnerable.

[64] Borba, *Esteem Builders,* 7.

[65] Branden, "Answering Misconceptions," 4.

[66] Lilian G. Katz, "Self-Esteem and Narcissism: Implications for Practice," *ERIC Digest* (1993). Excerpted from a paper entitled "Distinctions Between Self-Esteem and Narcissism: Implications for Practice." Available: ERIC Web site, U.S. Department of Education, [Internet, WWW], Address: *http://www.ed.gov/databases/ERIC_Digests/ed358973.html.*

[67] Flach, 137.

[68] Borba, *Esteem Builders,* 8.

[69] Flach, 135.

[70] This chart includes several ideas graciously contributed by Robert Reasoner, president, International Association for Self-Esteem.

[71] Please note that some authors make a distinction between healthy and high self-esteem. Certainly, by more superficial (feel-good) definitions, "it is possible to have such high, unhealthy self-esteem that we live a life of delusion," and likewise "possible to have low, healthy self-esteem and be living a life of humility," as authors H. Stephen Glenn and Michael Brock point out (*Seven Strategies for Developing Capable Students,* Rocklin, Calif.: Prima Publishing, 1998, 173). I understand their concern, however taking the full set of characteristics into account, high—or healthy—self-esteem precludes the possibility of delusion, and certainly leaves plenty of room for humility and any number of other desirable traits.

[72] Amitai Etzioni, *Pillars of Character Education* (1998). Available: *Christian Science Monitor* Web site, [Internet, WWW], Address: *http://www.csmonitor.com/durable/1998/05/26/p1951.htm.*

[73] Terri Akin, Gerry Dunne, Susanna Palomares and Dianne Schilling, *Character Education in America's Schools* (Spring Valley, Calif.: Innerchoice Publishing, 1995), 1–2.

[74] Quoted in Fraser, 76.

[75] Cited by Thomas Lickona, "Educating for Character: A 12-Point Comprehensive Approach" (no date). Available: *Center for the Fourth and Fifth Rs, State University of New York College at Cortland* Web site, [Internet, WWW], Address: *http://cortland.edu/www/c4n5rs/descr_iv.htm.*

[76] Charles C. Haynes, "Averting Culture Wars over Religion," *Educational Leadership,* vol. 56, no. 4 (December 1998/January 1999): 26.
[77] John Connell, "8 Cardinal Points of Effective Teaching," course handout.
[78] Gisele Durham, "Study: Many Teenagers Lie, Cheat," *Albuquerque Journal* (17 October 2000).
[79] Borba, *Moral Intelligence,* 1–2; Durham; "Teen Drinking on the Rise," *Parade* magazine (19 December 1999), 17; Karr-Morse and Wiley, 259; Arthur and Erickson, 18–19; Eva Marx, "Health and Learning: A Coordinated Approach," *Principal,* vol. 79, no. 1 (September 1999): 6; Lickona, "Educating for Character"; Karen S. Peterson, "Sex, Not Sex: For Many Teens, Oral Doesn't Count," *USA Today* (16 November 2000).
[80] Thomas Lickona, "Raising Moral Children," excerpt from *Raising Good Children* (New York: Bantam Books, 1983). Available: Salem-Keizer Public Schools Web site, [Internet, WWW], Address: *http://ssc.salkeiz.k12.or.us/counsel/parentlibrary/respect/moral.htm.*
[81] Steinberg.
[82] Mercier.
[83] Anabel Jensen, "Building a Role Model," *EQ Today* (21 April 1999). Available: *6seconds* Web site, [Internet, WWW], Address: *http://www.6seconds.org/jrn/jpcw98.html.*
[84] Pam Schiller and Tamera Bryant, *The Values Book: Teaching 16 Basic Values to Young Children* (Beltsville, Md.: Gryphon House, 1998), 6.
[85] Ron Huxley, "Moral Development of Children: Knowing Right from Wrong." Available: *Parenting Toolbox* Web site, [Internet, WWW], Address: *http://parentingtoolbox.com/hand/moraldev1.html.*
[86] Piaget, 319–20; Huxley; William Huitt, "Moral and Character Development." Available: [Internet, WWW], Address: *http://chiron.valdosta.edu/whuitt/col/morchr/morchr.html;* Mary Elizabeth Murray, "Moral Development and Moral Education: An Overview." Available: University of Illinois at Chicago Web site, [Internet, WWW], Address: *http://www.uic.edu/~lnucci/MoralEd/overview.html;* "Lawrence Kohlberg" (2000). Available: The Psi Cafe Web site, [Internet, WWW], Address: *http://www.psy.pdx.edu/PsiCafe/KeyTheorists/Kohlberg.htm;* "An Introduction to Life Span Development: Lawrence Kohlberg" (2000). Available: Prentice-Hall Distance Learning Web site, [Internet, WWW], Address: *http://cw.prenhall.com/bookbind/pubbooks/feldman4/chapter1/custom12/deluxe-content.html.*
[87] Borba, *Moral Intelligence,* 3.
[88] Thomas Lickona, *"What Is Character Education"* (no date). Available: Center for the Fourth and Fifth Rs, State University of New York College at Cortland Web site, [Internet, WWW], Address: *http://cortland.edu/www/c4n5rs/ce_iv.htm;* Thomas Lickona, "What Is a Comprehensive Approach to Character Education?" (no date). Available: Center for the Fourth and Fifth Rs, State University of New York College at Cortland Web site, [Internet, WWW], Address: *http://cortland.edu/www/c4n5rs/comp_iv.htm.*
[89] Edward F. DeRoche, "Creating a Framework for Character Education," *Principal,* vol. 79, no. 3 (January 2000): 33–34.
[90] "Johnny Be Good: Teaching Character in America's Public Schools," *Communicator,* Newsletter of the National Association of Elementary School Principals, vol. 23, no. 4 (January 2000): 3.
[91] Rushworth M. Kidder and Patricia L. Born, "Resolving Ethical Dilemmas in the Classroom," *Educational Leadership,* vol. 56, no. 4 (December 1998/January 1999): 39. Note: For Amitai Etzioni ("Pillars of Character Education"), it boils down to self-discipline and empathy. The Josephson Institute identifies six "pillars of character," including trustworthiness, respect, responsibility, fairness, caring and citizenship (reprinted in Akin, *Character Education,* 4), and Borba has identified seven essential virtues, including empathy, conscience, self-control, respect, kindness, tolerance and fairness (*Moral Intelligence,* 5).
[92] Kate Rauhauser-Smith, "Schools' Three Rs Now Include Respect," *York Daily Record* (22 November 1999); "Johnny Be Good"; Michele Borba, "Esteem Builder Pilot

Schools," *Preliminary Research Summary* (Torrance, Calif.: Jalmar Press); "Moral Classrooms: The Development of Character and Integrity in the Elementary School." A research report by The Teel Institute for the Development of Integrity and Ethical Behavior (Kansas City, Mo.: The Teel Institute, 1998); "Learning for Life: A Program for Education." Results of study with twenty-five hundred elementary school students conducted by Syndics Research Corporation and Kevin Ryan of Boston University. Irving, Texas: *Learning for Life*.

[93] "Johnny Be Good," 3.

[94] "Substance Abuse Alert," *NAESP Report to Parents,* Alexandria, Va.: National Association of Elementary School Principals, September 1999.

[95] William Fibkins, "Training Middle School Teachers to Be Effective Helpers," *Schools in the Middle,* vol. 8, no. 6 (April 1999): 7.

[96] DeBeaufort and Diaz, 123.

[97] Quoted in Jessica Wilber, *Totally Private and Personal: Journaling Ideas for Girls and Young Women* (Minneapolis: Free Spirit Publishing, 1996), 128.

[98] Quoted in Siccone and López, 195.

[99] Burns, 92–93, citing Miller's work in her book, *The Untouched Key: Tracing Childhood Trauma in Creativity and Destructiveness* (New York: Doubleday, 1990).

[100] Bluestein, *Parents, Teens and Boundaries,* 141–49; Bluestein, *21st Century Discipline,* 128–29.

[101] Whitfield, 100; Dwyer, Osher and Warger, 4; DeBeaufort and Diaz, 125; Hannaford, *Smart Moves,* 58–59, 171.

[102] Flach, xiv.

[103] DeBeaufort and Diaz, 148.

[104] Karen Irmsher, "Communication Skills," *ERIC Digest,* no. 102 (January 1996). Available: ERIC Web site, U.S. Department of Education, [Internet, WWW], Address: *http://www.ed.gov/databases/ERIC_Digests/ed390114.html.*

[105] Schultz and Heuchert, 87–88; Bluestein, *21st Century Discipline,* 136–38; "How You Can Support Columbine High School" (1 May 1999). Available: *University of Colorado* at Boulder Web site, [Internet, WWW], Address: *http://www.colorado.edu/ Chancellor/columbine/*; Larry Barker and Kittie Watson, "Power Listening Lessons," *Bottom Line Personal,* vol. 21, no. 24 (15 December 2000): 1; "Listen to Your Children," *NAESP Report to Parents,* Alexandria, Va.: National Association of Elementary School Principals, September 1999; Harriett Brittenham, "How Are You Communicating?" *Resources,* Newsletter of the Brittenham Consulting Group (August 1999). Note: If the confidentiality is conditional, let the student know ahead of time. For example, as a volunteer, I felt obligated to report any information which suggests that the kids I was working with intended to harm themselves or others and they knew this going in. Anything else went in the vault.

[106] Reprinted in Fox and Forbing, 106.

[107] Hagstrom, 54.

[108] Shapiro, 135.

[109] DeBeaufort and Diaz, 99.

[110] Wilber, 129. Note: I wholeheartedly agree. I've been keeping a journal for close to four decades and can attest to its value in my life—not just in helping me understand and release what I'm feeling, and increase my awareness and accountability, but to brainstorm solutions and, occasionally, keep from saying or doing things I'd be sorry for later.

[111] Goleman, *Emotional Intelligence,* 266–67; Akin, et al., *Character Education,* 9–18.

[112] Woodbury, 32.

[113] "For Immediate Release: Guide Provides Help to Parents and Educators After Littleton" (1999). Available: Educators for Social Responsibility Web site, [Internet, WWW], Address: *http://www.esrnational.org/pressrelease.html.*

[114] Fibkins, 6–9; Kendall Johnson, 1; Marina London, "Providing Critical Incident Services to Children and Adolescents," *EAP Digest,* vol. 19, issue 5 (July/August 1999): 19; David Hagstrom, "Seeking Clarity About Crisis," *Educational Leadership,* vol. 56, no.

4 (December 1998/January 1999): 53–57; Debbie Waddell and Alex Thomas, "Disaster: Helping Children Cope," *Communiqué,* Newsletter of the National Association of School Psychologists, special edition (spring 1999): 12–15.
[115] Fibkins, 6.
[116] Suhor, 14.
[117] Purkey and Aspy, 48.
[118] Palmer, 6.
[119] Wesley, 42.
[120] Folásadé Oládélé, "Passing Down the Spirit," *Educational Leadership,* vol. 56, no. 4 (December 1998/January 1999): 62.
[121] Suhor, 13.
[122] Palmer, 8.
[123] Elia Wise, "Back to School It Is . . . Why Not Forward? Educating Children for a World that Works" (September 2000). Available: *The Edge* Web site, [Internet, WWW], Address: *http://edgenews.com/columns.htm.*
[124] Kessler, 49.
[125] John Miller, 48.
[126] Kessler, 50.
[127] DeBeaufort and Diaz, 61–68.
[128] Palmer, 8.

Chapter 16
Social Safety: Belonging and Interpersonal Competence

[1] Lantieri and Patti, 12.
[2] Goleman, *Emotional Intelligence,* xii.
[3] Quoted in Freedman, et al., supplemental cards included at the end of the book.
[4] Frey, 2; Goleman, *Emotional Intelligence,* 80–82.
[5] Shapiro, 5, 8, 12; Lantieri and Patti, 9.
[6] Schilling, 6; Goleman, *Emotional Intelligence,* 44–45.
[7] Freedman, et al., 1.
[8] Ibid.; Shapiro, 5; Schilling, 1–2; Karr-Morse and Wiley, 10. Note: Many of these qualities and skills are evident in Kovalik's list of life skills as well (Faulkner and Faiveley, 82–83).
[9] Schilling, 6.
[10] Sugar, 8.
[11] Carolyn Sheldon, *EQ in School Counseling* (Torrance, Calif.: Innerchoice Publishing, 1996), 11. Note: Sylwester comments that emotional "eruptions can generally be avoided because the participants have enough time to insert reason into the equation while negative emotions are only simmering" (Sylwester, "How Our Brain Determines What's Important").
[12] DeBeaufort and Diaz, 62.
[13] Sylwester, "How Our Brain Determines What's Important."
[14] Joshua Freedman, "Hijacking of the Amygdala," *EQ Today* (21 April 1999). Available: 6seconds Web site, [Internet, WWW], Address: *http://www.6seconds.org/jrn/hijack.html;* also Alan McCluskey, "Emotional Intelligence in Schools," 28 February 1997. Available: *Connected* Web site [Internet, WWW], Address: *http://www.connected.org/learn/school.html.*
[15] Freedman, et al., 96.
[16] Hannaford, *Smart Moves,* 51.
[17] Goleman, *Emotional Intelligence,* xiv.
[18] Maslow, 162.
[19] Lantieri and Patti, 8.
[20] Karres, 8.
[21] Wise, 15.

[22] Borba, *Moral Intelligence,* 1; also Carole Remboldt, *Violence in Schools: The Enabling Factor* (Minneapolis: Johnson Institute-QVS, Inc., 1994), 4.

[23] Goleman, *Emotional Intelligence,* 196–97; Keller; Beane, 1; "CSPV Fact Sheet"; Hoover and Oliver, 8; Ron Banks, "Bullying in Schools," *ERIC Digest* (April 1997). Available: *ERIC* Web site, U.S. Department of Education, [Internet, WWW], Address: *http://www.ed.gov/databases/ERIC_Digests/ed407154.html.* Note: According to Goleman, the "capricious" discipline depended not as much on the child's behavior as on how the parent felt at the time. When these parents were in a good mood, they ignored their children's behavior (and misbehavior); if they were in a bad mood, the children would be severely punished. Also, according to other sources, many children on the receiving end of peer aggression have parents and home lives with similar characteristics. The presence of the factors described do not guarantee that a child will become violent and sadistic, but are fairly common among those who do.

[24] Dewey G. Cornell and Ann B. Loper, "New Studies of Attitudes and Behaviors and School Violence" (9 August 1996). Available: American Psychological Association Web site, [Internet, WWW], Address: *http://www.apa.org/releases/schlviol.html.*

[25] Olweus, 28, 34, 39, 42. Note: This research focused on *boys'* aggression. And while socioeconomic status did not seem to figure into the equation, Olweus admits that it might be more of a factor in "countries with greater socioeconomic inequalities" (like the United States).

[26] Polly Drew, "Adults Must Protect Kids from Themselves," *The Milwaukee Journal Sentinel* (31 May 1998). Available: *The Milwaukee Journal Sentinel* Web site, [Internet, WWW], Address: *http://www.packerplus.com/news/sunday/lifestyle/0531polly.stm.*

[27] Olweus, 36; Kate Ruahauser-Smith, "Bully for Good Relations," *York Daily Record* (23 October 1999); Lantieri and Patti, 13; "What to Do About Bullying," *NAESP Report to Parents,* Alexandria, Va.: National Association of Elementary School Principals, September 1999; Schuster; Banks; "More Information on Bullying" (no date). Available: Bully B'ware Web site, [Internet, WWW], Address: *http://www.bullybeware.com/moreinfo.htm.*

[28] Olweus, 35; "More Information on Bullying"; Beane, 16; "Bullying Common in Middle School," *OT Week* (16 September 1999), reprinted from *American Psychological Association* (20 August 1999).

[29] John Casey, "Some Antisocial Boys Reap Rewards as Adults" (26 November 2000). Available: *AOL* Web site: [Internet, WWW], Address: *http://aolsvc.health.cbshealthwatch.aol.com/aolmedscape/p/G_library/article.as;* Hoover and Oliver, 12; Olweus, 35.

[30] "More Information on Bullying"; also Olweus, 35; Beane, 5; Hoover and Oliver, 10. Note: Hoover and Oliver have identified the middle-school years as the worst for bullying.

[31] Thornton, 77.

[32] Gary Burnett and Gary Walz, "Gangs in the Schools," *ERIC Digest,* no. 99 (July 1994). Available: ERIC Web site, U.S. Department of Education, [Internet, WWW], Address: *http://www.ed.gov/databases/ERIC_Digests/ed372175.html;* also "Teacher Talk: Gangs and School Violence" (June 1997). Available: *Indiana University Center for Adolescent Studies* Web site, [Internet, WWW], Address: *http://education.indiana.edu/cas/tt/v2i3/gangs.html.*

[33] Arthur, 37. Note: C. Horswell, in a 1991 article in the *Houston Chronicle* identified the key reasons for joining a gang were "the lack of a vision for the future and the fact that 'no one cares.'" (Quoted in Rogers and Frieberg, 232.)

[34] Bluestein, *Book of Lists,* 95.

[35] "Green Circle" (human relations) program participant quoted in "With Respect to Diversity." Bi-annual newsletter published by the York (Pennsylvania) Jewish Community Center's Prejudice Reduction Task Force, spring 1999.

[36] Trevor Romain, *Bullies Are a Pain in the Brain* (Minneapolis: Free Spirit Publishing, 1997), 8.

[37] Schuster; "More Information on Bullying"; Hoover and Oliver, 9; "Bullying Common in Middle School."

[38] Besag, 26.
[39] Although the word "victim" is what is most commonly used to refer to kids who are on the receiving end of their peers' aggression, I am reluctant to use the word here. This term carries a certain energy that feels more negative, disempowered and permanent than alternate words (such as "target"). Most people would use the terms interchangeably, or might argue the need for an energetically "stronger" term like "victim" to justify giving this issue the attention it deserves. Chalk it up to personal bias, but I don't agree.
[40] Besag, 27–28.
[41] Redenbach, 104; also Frey, 2.
[42] Olweus, 33.
[43] Banks.
[44] "More Information on Bullying."
[45] "A Penchant for Revenge Can Make It Tough to Find a Friend," *University of Illinois at Urbana-Champaign Newsletter* (March 1995). Available: University of Illinois at Urbana-Champaign Web site, [Internet, WWW], Address: *http://www.admin.uiuc.edu/nb/9903/friendship.html.* Note: This tendency to interpret nonaggressive behavior and perceive others as being more hostile than they actually are is a common trait among angry children—whether they are aggressive kids or withdrawn social outcasts. (Goleman, *Emotional Intelligence,* 235.)
[46] All of the men, without exception, shared that they resisted for as long as they could and found their out-of-control outbursts deplorable (as well as the fact that that kind of behavior seemed to be the only thing anyone in that environment understood or took seriously). The men also noted that they only had one incident in which they turned violent in their lives and in general, the event was traumatic, frightening and, to varying degrees, life-changing.
[47] Frank J. Barone, "Bullying in School: It Doesn't Have to Happen," *Phi Delta Kappan* (September 1997): 94.
[48] Romain, 63.
[49] Martine Agassi, *Hands Are Not for Hitting* (Minneapolis: Free Spirit Publishing, 2000), 32.
[50] Sugar, 12.
[51] Chris Mattise, "The Helpful-Hurtful Policy: Addressing Social Harassment in the Elementary School Setting," Staff Handbook (1998), 5.
[52] "NASP Position Statement: School Violence," *National Mental Health and Education Center for Children and Families.* Available: National Association of School Psychologists Web site, [Internet, WWW], Address: *http://www.naspweb.org/center/safe%5Fschools/safeschools%5Fviolence.html.*
[53] Garrity, et al.
[54] Shapiro, 52–53; also Lantieri and Patti, 8; Hannaford, *Smart Moves,* 60; Karr-Morse and Wiley, quoting Nancy Eisenberg, 188. Note: Hannaford claims that children show signs of this type of caring at around three years of age; Eisenberg claims empathy has been observed in children as young as fourteen months.
[55] Lantieri and Patti, 14; also Karr-Morse and Wiley, 308.
[56] Hoover and Oliver, 12–13; Schuster; Banks; Garrity, et al.; "More Information on Bullying," Schacter and McCauley, 159–60.
[57] Romain, 93.
[58] Sugar, 6.
[59] Schilling, 7; also "What to Do About Bullying."
[60] Thornton, 79; Matt Gerber and Kim Jones, "Kids Keeping the Peace: Resolving Conflict on the Playground" (24 July 1996). Available: *Ben and Jerry's Online,* Address: *http://euphoria.benjerry.com/esr/playgrd.html;* Cummings and Fisher, 129; Beane, 109, 111; Armstrong, *The Myth of the ADD Child,* 106.
[61] Shapiro, 138, 285.
[62] Lantieri and Patti, 6.
[63] "Tips & Strategies: Action Plan for Bullying" (no date). Available: Bully B'ware Web

site, [Internet, WWW], Address: *http://www.bullybeware.com/tips.htm;* Lantieri and Patti, 146; Garrity, et al.; "More Information on Bullying."

[64] Duvall, 36–38; Sally Angaran and Kathy Beckwith, "Peer Mediation in Elementary Schools," *Principal,* vol. 78, no. 5 (May 1999): 27–29; also Christopher Newton, "School Kids to Learn Mediation," *York Daily Record* (12 January 2000); "Teacher Talk: Peer Mediation" (June 1997). Available: Indiana University Center for Adolescent Studies Web site, [Internet, WWW], Address: *http://education.indiana.edu/cas/tt/v2i3/peer.html.*

[65] "Respecting Differences," *NAESP Report to Parents,* Alexandria, Va.: National Association of Elementary School Principals, September 1999.

[66] Quoted in Daniel Goleman, "Psychologists Find Ways to Break Racism's Hold," *The New York Times* (5 September 1989).

[67] Quoted in Duvall, 35.

[68] Gazzaniga, *The Social Brain,* 163.

[69] Daniel Goleman, "Psychologists Find Ways"; also Lewis and Pucelik, 5–8. Note: From a neurolinguistic psychology perspective, Lewis and Pucelik quote Bandler and Grinder as having identified three mechanisms used to create a model that represents our perceptions and experiences. These include the processes of generalization, deletion and distortion.

[70] Quoted in Lantieri and Patti.

[71] Mary Beth Quinsey, *Why Does That Man Have Such a Big Nose?* (Seattle: Parenting Press, 1985).

[72] Quoted in Lantieri and Patti, 16.

[73] Lantieri and Patti, 17.

[74] Goleman, "New Ways to Battle Bias."

[75] Gazzaniga, *The Social Brain,* 80.

[76] Cited in Goleman, "Psychologists Find Ways."

[77] Beane, 62, 73; Lantier and Patti, 17; Goleman, *Emotional Intelligence,* 159; Goleman, "New Ways to Battle Bias"; Goleman, "Psychologists Find Ways"; Hoover and Oliver, 15; Bluestein, *Developing Responsible Learning Behaviors*; Colwell-Cornett, et al., 34; "Respecting Differences." Note: Changes in attitudes extended not only to racial and ethnic differences, but differences in gender, age and ability. Although I do not have specific data, I suspect that working cooperatively with any kind of differences would engender greater empathy, appreciation and understanding.

[78] Wendy Stainton Rogers, "Promoting, Permitting and Preventing Bullying," *Bullying: A Practical Guide to Coping for Schools,* 2d ed., Michele Elliott, ed. (London: Pitman Publishing, 1997), 66.

[79] Freedman, et al., *Handle with Care,* 3.

[80] Robert Reasoner, *Self-Esteem and Youth: What Research Has to Say About It* (Port Ludlow, Wash.: International Council for Self-Esteem, 2000), 31.

[81] Polly Drew.

[82] Olweus, 26; Barone, 94; Garrity, et al; Banks; "More Information on Bullying"; Stephenson and Smith, 170–73.

[83] "Creating Peaceable Families," 24 July 1996. Online guide developed by the Resolving Conflict Creatively Program (RCCP) National Center. Available: *Ben and Jerry's Online* Web site, Address: *http://euphoria.benjerry.com/esr/peaceable-young.html.*

[84] Karen Summers and Angelique von Halle, "From the Classroom to the Staff Room: Helping Staff Model Prosocial Behaviors," *Committee for Children Prevention Update* (spring 1999): 6.

[85] Lickona, "Raising Moral Children."

[86] Stephenson and Smith, 170–73.

[87] Wendy Stainton Rogers, 66.

[88] Beane, 122.

[89] Besag, 28.

[90] Garrity, et al.

Chapter 17
Behavioral Safety: Discipline and Cooperation

[1] Phillips, 19.
[2] Epp, 20.
[3] Bluestein, *21st Century Discipline.*
[4] Phillips, 1.
[5] Quoted in Marvin Marshall, *Discipline Without Stress, Punishments or Rewards: How Teachers and Parents Promote Responsibility and Learning* (Los Alamitos, Calif.: Piper Press, 2001).
[6] "Behavior Problems: What's a School to Do?" Feature article from the newsletter, *Addressing Barriers to Learning,* of the Clearinghouse of the Center for Mental Health in Schools of the University of California, Los Angeles, vol. 2, no. 2 (1997): 1.
[7] Epp, 10.
[8] Bluestein, *21st Century Discipline,* 37–44; Bluestein, *Parents, Teens and Boundaries,* 77–79; Jane Bluestein and Lynn Collins, *Parents in a Pressure Cooker* (Rosemont, N.J.: Modern Learning Press, 1989), 25–33.
[9] Lantieri and Patti, 19.
[10] Pulliam and Van Patten, 33. Note: Additionally, "Massachusetts law allowed for children to be confined in stocks for some offences and fathers had a legal right to execute their children if they could not be controlled, although this extreme was never practiced." Discipline could also include instances of torturing students with a whispering stick (a flat stick of wood placed between their teeth like a bit), making them kneel on hard pebbles or making them wear heavy wooden yokes.
[11] "Behavior Problems," 1–2.
[12] Aspy and Roebuck, iv.
[13] Thomas Gordon, "How Children *Really* React to Control," *Discipline That Works: Promoting Self-Discipline in Children,* New York: Plume/Penguin, 1989, 78–81. Available: PTAVE Web site, [Internet, WWW], Address: *http://nospank.org/gordon.htm.*
[14] Gazzaniga, *Mind Matters,* 205. Note: Studies indicate that individuals in top management positions feel less stress than middle managers who have less authority and power to change their environment or situation. And considering the risk for peer pressure, approval seeking and dependence, Thomas Armstrong wonders why there isn't a parent advisory group or professional organization designed to treat *overly* compliant children (*The Myth of the ADD Child,* 18).
[15] Gordon, "Discipline"; also Bluestein, *21st Century Discipline,* 29–31, 39–44; Epp, 10; "Behavior Problems," 3; Blacklock; Wegscheider-Cruse, 8; Lisa Popyk, "Violence Is Seductive to New Breed of Killers," *The Post* (9 November 1998). Available: *The Cincinnati Post* Web site, [Internet, WWW], Address: *http://www.cincypost.com/news/2kill110998.html;* "Anthropologist Finds Psychological Seed of War in Baby Spanking," *The Boston Globe* (5 January 1941). Available: PTAVE Web site, [Internet, WWW], Address: *http://nospank.org/montagu3.htm.* Note: One of the exercises I do in many of my trainings is to ask participants to identify behaviors kids employ to get their needs for power and safety met. Regardless of where I do this activity, or the nature of the population with whom the participants are in contact, their lists are nearly identical to the behaviors listed here.
[16] Albert Einstein, "Force and Fear Have No Place in Education," *Out of My Later Years,* New York: Philosophical Library, Inc., 1950, 33–35. Available: PTAVE Web site, [Internet, WWW], Address: *http://nospank.org/einstein.htm.*
[17] Glasser, 19.
[18] Epp, 20.
[19] In many settings, this step is reserved for the fourth or fifth violation of a particular rule, although this number is fairly arbitrary and depends on the particular formula being used. I've seen various systems set up with warnings or punishments of increasing severity depending on the number of times students get caught doing the

same thing over and over. There is no incentive for children to change their behavior until it gets uncomfortable enough for them to consider not repeating it, which, incidentally, doesn't always happen. Further, most of these warnings or "consequences," such as yelling, verbal reminders or writing the student's name on the board, do little more than give attention to the misbehavior. For kids whose misbehavior is indeed attention-seeking, these tactics only serve as reinforcers, actually strengthening the very behaviors they're supposed to extinguish. This is one of the reasons many of us find ourselves punishing the same kids all the time.

[20] Armstrong, *The Myth of the ADD Child,* 18.

[21] Paul Zielbauer, "Discipline Figures Prompt Call to Improve School Behavior" (7 July 2000). Available: *The New York Times* Web site, [Internet, WWW], Address: *http://www.nytimes.com/library/national/regional/070700ct-students-edu.html.* Note: The report noted that the national statistics "revealed only the number of these punishments, not the number of students who received them."

[22] Rudi Keller, "Some Dropoouts Claim Schools Pushed Them," *Albuquerque Journal* (29 April 2000). Note: At one high school, typically only 50 percent of the freshman class makes it to graduation.

[23] Zielbauer; Quarles, 24; McQueen, "School Violence Stereotypes."

[24] Quarles, 24; Keller, "Some Dropouts."

[25] Frank E. Blair, "Does Zero Tolerance Work?" *Principal,* vol. 79, no. 1 (September 1999): 36.

[26] John Leo, "'Zero Tolerance' Policies Distort Discipline of Schools," *Albuquerque Journal* (10 December 1999).

[27] Blair, 37.

[28] Leo, "Zero-Tolerance."

[29] Walter Doyle, "Classroom Management Techniques and Student Discipline." Paper prepared for the Student Discipline Strategies Project, sponsored by the Education and Social Division of the Office of Research, OERI, U.S. Department of Education, December, 1986; also Quarles, 24.

[30] Doyle.

[31] McPartland, et al.

[32] Quarles, 24; Doyle; Sugar.

[33] Blair, 37.

[34] Einstein.

[35] Quoted in Patricia Daigle, "Opposing Corporal Punishment in Two Lands," *Contra Costa Times* (13 December 1986).

[36] Jane Nelsen, Lynn Lott and Stephen Glenn, *Positive Discipline A-Z* (Rocklin, Calif.: 1999), 152.

[37] "Corporal Punishment: Myths and Realities," Fact sheet prepared by The National PTA (1991). Available: PTAVE Web site, [Internet, WWW], Address: *http://nospank.org/pta.htm.*

[38] "Facts About Corporal Punishment," presented by the *National Coalition to Abolish Punishment in Schools* (20 October 1998). Available: Center for Effective Discipline Web site, [Internet, WWW], Address: *http://www.stophitting.com/facts_about_corporal_punishment.htm;* also "Corporal Punishment in Schools," Position Paper of the Society for Adolescent Medicine, *Journal of Adolescent Health* (1992): 13:240–246. Available: PTAVE Web site, [Internet, WWW], Address: *http://nospank.org/sam.htm.*

[39] "Corporal Punishment in Schools" (Society for Adolescent Medicine); "Corporal Punishment: Myths and Realities"; "Corporal Punishment," Position Statement of the National Association of School Psychologists (18 April 1998). Available: PTAVE Web site, [Internet, WWW], Address: *http://nospank.org/nasp2.htm.* Note: Compare the 1984 statistic in which one in two thousand students were physically punished in Connecticut and Utah, with Arkansas' ratio of one in eight.

[40] Robin Warnes, "Childhood Abuse: Corporal Punishment, A Survivor's Testimony." Available: [Internet, WWW], Address: *http://www.angelfire.com/sk/abuse/index.html.* Note: Warnes was one of a number of people who felt that the act of observing a

classmate being humiliated, berated or paddled was a serious trauma for most children.

[41] Quoted in Augustin Gurza, "Spanking: An Idea Whose Time Has Gone," *Los Angeles Times* (21 March 2000). Available: PTAVE Web site, [Internet, WWW], Address: *http://nospank.org/gurza.htm.*

[42] Among these organizations are the American Medical Association, the Society for Adolescent Medicine, The National Center on Child Abuse Prevention, the American Academy of Pediatrics, the American Bar Association, the National Education Association, the National PTA, the National Association for the Education of Young Children, the American Association for Counseling and Development, the American Psychiatric Association, the American Psychological Association, the Association of Junior Leagues, the Council for Exceptional Children, the National Association of Elementary School Principals, the National Association for the Advancement of Colored People, the National Association of School Psychologists, the National Association of State Boards of Education, the National Committee to Prevent Child Abuse, the National Mental Health Association and the United Nations Committee on the Rights of Children.

[43] "Corporal Punishment in Schools" (Society for Adolescent Medicine).

[44] "Facts about Corporal Punishment."

[45] Penelope Leach, "Spanking: A Shortcut to Nowhere" (1999). Available: PTAVE Web site, [Internet, WWW], Address: *http://nospank.org/leach.htm.*

[46] Michael Pastore, "Too Many Parents Still Hitting on Wrong Idea," *Philadelphia Inquirer* (16 January 1999).

[47] Brenda C. Coleman, "Study: Do Not Spank," *San Francisco Examiner* (15 August 1997); also "Spanking Makes Children Violent, Antisocial," excerpt from *The American Medical Association News Update* (13 August 1997). Available: PTAVE Web site, [Internet, WWW], Address: *http://nospank.org/straus.htm.* Note: In this study, antisocial behavior was defined as "cheating or lying, bullying or being cruel or mean to others, not feeling sorry after misbehaving, breaking things deliberately, disobeying at school or not getting along with teachers. Also note: In this same study, researchers discovered that children who had been spanked even once during the week before the base interview showed an increase in antisocial behavior two years later. (Physical punishments other than spanking were not included.)

[48] Quoted in Carol E. Robinson, "Alamo Advocate Aims to Ban Punishment at Home, School," *San Ramon Valley Times* (3 July 1994).

[49] Quoted in Quarles, 23; also Derril Farrar, "Hands Off!" *Sunday Telegraph* (4 September 1983).

[50] Leach; Alice Miller, *For Your Own Good: Hidden Cruelty in Child-Rearing and the Roots of Violence* (New York: Farrar, Straus & Giroux, 1984), 142–45; Jordan Riak, *Plain Talk About Spanking* (Alamo, Calif.: PTAVE, 1996), 4–5.

[51] "Corporal Punishment in Schools (RE9207)," Position Statement of the American Academy of Pediatrics, Committee on School Health (1991). Available: PTAVE Web site, [Internet, WWW], Address: *http://nospank.org/aap2.htm;* "When Discipline Silences, Forever," *The Philadelphia Inquirer,* Metro Section (14 January 1999). Available: PTAVE Web site, [Internet, WWW], Address: *http://nospank.org/silenced.htm;* "Corporal Punishment in Schools," Policy Statement by the American Academy of Child and Adolescent Psychiatry (Approved, June 1988). Available: PTAVE Web site, [Internet, WWW], Address: *http://nospank.org/aacap.htm;* "Corporal Punishment: Myths and Realities"; Coleman; "Spanking Makes Children Violent, Antisocial"; Pastore; Beane, 125; "United Nations Committee on Rights of Child," Eighteenth Session, Geneva (18 May–5 June 1998). Available: PTAVE Web site, [Internet, WWW], Address: *http://nospank.org/uncrc.htm;* Adele Faber and Elaine Mazlish, "Experts Speak Out on Punishment," *How to Talk So Kids Will Listen & Listen So Kids Will Talk* (New York: Avon Books, 1980), 115–17.

[52] Leach.

[53] D. Keith Osborn and Janie Dyson Osborn, *Discipline and Classroom Management* (Athens, Ga.: Education Associates, 1977), 27; also Doyle; "Corporal Punishment: The

Position of the American School Counselor Association" (Adopted 1995). Available: PTAVE Web site, [Internet, WWW], Address: *http://nospank.org/asca.htm.*

[54] Laurie A. Couture, "Corporal Punishment: Society's Remaining Acceptable Violence." Available: Child Advocate Web site, [Internet, WWW], Address: *http://www.childadvocate.org/AcceptableViolence.htm;* Pastore; "Spanking Makes Children Violent, Antisocial"; "Corporal Punishment in Schools" (American Academy of Pediatrics).

[55] Jordan Riak, "Abuse in Schools Is Out!" Article reprint prepared by Parents and Teachers Against Violence in Education. Alamo, Calif.: PTAVE (Copyright waived, no date); Rogers and Frieberg. Note: In addition to condemning the use of corporal punishment, Couture also notes that being subjected to corporal punishment *as a witness* is traumatic itself.

[56] "Corporal Punishment in Schools" (Society for Adolescent Medicine). Note: This report suggests that these numbers represent fairly conservative estimates.

[57] "Want Smarter Kids? Don't Spank Them," Reuters (August 3, 1998). Available: PTAVE Web site, [Internet, WWW], Address: *http://nospank.org/straus4.htm.*

[58] Pastore; "Spanking Makes Children Violent, Antisocial"; "Corporal Punishment in Schools" (American Academy of Pediatrics).

[59] "Spanking Makes Children Violent, Antisocial"; Couture.

[60] "Corporal Punishment in Schools" (Society for Adolescent Medicine); Doyle; "Corporal Punishment: Myths and Realities." Among the infractions that resulted in physical consequences reported in the literature and survey responses were incomplete homework, not singing loud enough, talking, not understanding an assignment, laughing, not holding pencils correctly (Epp, 15), whispering, giggling, not finishing their milk ("Corporal Punishment: Myths and Realities"), not being able to spell a word, being late to class, forgetting gym shorts, touching sports equipment left on the playing field (Warnes), spilling milk or talking in class.

[61] Couture; "Bigotry by any other name . . ." *Report to Friends—August 1999.* Available: PTAVE Web site, [Internet, WWW], Address: *http://nospank.org/msg4.htm*; "A Lesson Learned: Spare the Rod," *Bangkok Post* (15 September 2000). Available: PTAVE Web site, [Internet, WWW], Address: *http://nospank.org/thai2.htm.*

[62] "Facts About Corporal Punishment," presented by the National Coalition to Abolish Punishment in Schools (20 October 1998). Available: Center for Effective Discipline Web site, [Internet, WWW], Address: *http://www.stophitting.com/facts_about_corporal_punishment.htm.*

[63] Branden, 217.

[64] Jean Illsley Clark, *Time-In: When Time-Out Doesn't Work* (Seattle: Parenting Press, Inc., 1999), 7.

[65] Marshall.

[66] Gibson, *Discipine,* 15.

[67] I saw this often with kids in the treatment center. Occasionally we'd get a client who seemed committed to turning his or her life around, to staying clean, keeping off the streets, getting through school. But the majority were simply putting in their time, their main objective being the desire to distance themselves from their probation officers and mandatory drug testing so they could give their old lives another shot until they got caught again. Even those who hadn't given up the possibility of their making it in conventional society, didn't have much of an incentive for giving up what they knew best.

[68] Joseph Ciaccio, "A Teacher's Chance for Immortality," *Schools in the Middle,* vol. 8, no. 2 (October 1998): 26, 28.

[69] Tyler.

[70] This profile was compiled from survey and interview responses about what makes a great teacher, the best thing a teacher ever said or did, and teacher behaviors that create a sense of safety. Unfortunately, many teachers also report being "written up" or given a great deal of grief from administrators when they do these things, even though this approach created enormous successes, improved student behavior and achievement, and far less of a need for intervention from the office. This kind of "ideal" is

much easier to achieve in a system committed to building safety, community and win-win.

[71] Jim Fay and David Funk, *Teaching with Love and Logic* (Golden, Colo.: The Love and Logic Press, Inc., 1995), 312–313.

[72] Please note that this list is an extremely condensed presentation of the kinds of behavioral processes can turn a classroom around.

[73] Bluestein, *21st Century Discipline,* 37–44; Bluestein, *The Parent's Little Book of Lists,* 49–65; Bluestein, *Parents, Teens and Boundaries,* 77–79; Bluestein and Collins, 25–40; Garfield, 29; "Discipline," *NAESP Report to Parents,* Alexandria, Va.: National Association of Elementary School Principals, September 1999; Rogers and Frieberg, 6, 7, 221, 229–30; Connell; Ciaccio, 27.

[74] Bluestein, *21st Century Discipline,* 25–31; *The Parent's Little Book of Lists,* 22–27; Bluestein and Collins, 9–17; Piaget, 404.

[75] "Teacher Talk: Respect" (June 1997). Available: Indiana University Center for Adolescent Studies Web site, [Internet, WWW], Address: *http://education.indiana.edu/cas/tt/v2i3/respect.html*; Whitfield, 44; Shapiro, 72–73; Bradshaw, 18; Bluestein, *The Parent's Little Book of Lists,* 32–33; Bluestein, *Parents, Teens and Boundaries,* 61–65; Bluestein, *21st Century Discipline;* Ciaccio, 26; Wright, *Loving Discipline,* 38–39; Tracy Dingmann, "Punishment Won't Curb School Violence," *Albuquerque Journal.*

[76] "Teacher Talk: Tips for Creating a Peaceful Classroom" (June 1997). Available: Indiana University Center for Adolescent Studies Web site, [Internet, WWW], Address: *http://education.indiana.edu/cas/tt/v2i3/peaceful.html*; Connell; Rogers and Frieberg, 233; Phillips, 19–22; Fay and Funk; Wright, *Loving Discipline,* 21.

[77] Bluestein, *21st Century Discipline,* 64–67; Bluestein and Collins, 71–73; Bluestein, *Parents, Teens and Boundaries,* 135–39; Bluestein, *The Parent's Little Book of Lists,* 232–33; Connell.

[78] Bluestein, *21st Century Discipline,* 47–50; Bluestein, *The Parent's Little Book of Lists,* 67–78; Bluestein, *Parents, Teens and Boundaries.*

[79] Gazzaniga (citing David Premack's research), *The Social Brain,* 161; Bluestein, *21st Century Discipline,* 92–102; Bluestein, *Parents, Teens and Boundaries,* 119–25; Bluestein, *The Parent's Little Book of Lists,* 79–83; Diane Heacox, *Up from Underachievement* (Minneapolis: Free Spirit Publishing, 1991), 36.

[80] Bluestein, *21st Century Discipline,* 140–161; Bluestein, *Parents, Teens and Boundaries,* 109–15; Bluestein, *The Parent's Little Book of Lists,* 73–78; Glasser, 23; "10 Guidelines for Raising a Well-Behaved Child," presented by End Physical Punishment of Children, (22 November 1998). Available: Center for Effective Discipine Web site, [Internet, WWW], Address: *http://www.stophitting.com/EPOCH.htm.*

[81] Bluestein, *The Parent's Little Book of Lists,* 239–47; Bluestein, *Parents, Teens and Boundaries,* 57–60, 103–8, 173–80; "Creating Peaceable Families"; Phillips, 67–88; Sam Horn, "How to Handle Someone Who Is Angry, Manipulative, Intimidating or Just Plain Rude," *Bottom Line/Personal* (1 July 2000): 1.

[82] Rogers and Frieberg, 233; Subby, 20, 22; Branden, 185; Bluestein, *21st Century Discipline,* 115–22; Bluestein, *Being a Successful Teacher,* 167–68; "Parental Contacts," *Teacher Talk,* Newsletter for first-year teachers serving students with exceptionalities, University of New Mexico (September 1999): 1; Pam Belluck, "New Advice for Parents: Saying 'That's Great!' May Not Be" (18 October 2000). Available: *New York Times* Web site, [Internet, WWW], Address: *http://partners.nytimes.com/2000/10/18/national/18PRAI.html.*

[83] Arthur, 139–49; "Independence Alternative High School," school profile and SRO program. Available: [Internet, WWW], Address: *http://home.if.rmci.net/paulrh/.*

Chapter 18
Physical Safety: The Student Body

[1] Jensen, *Completing the Puzzle,* 25.
[2] Shannon Brownlee, "Slugabeds: Why Teens Need More Snooze Time," *U.S. News and World Report,* vol. 127, no. 6 (9 August 1999): 54.
[3] Dennison and Dennison, *Brain Gym,* teacher's edition, 2.
[4] Promislow, 42.
[5] There are an enormous number of physical or body-related factors that have a bearing on children's learning and development. I have chosen to focus on basic physiological needs, factors in the immediate school (and home) environment, nutritional issues and food sensitivities, and traditional and nontraditional approaches to dealing with children identified as ADHD. The physical implications of abuse and neglect were presented briefly in earlier chapters. Other factors for consideration might include prenatal care and nutrition, low birth weight, deficits in specific neurotransmitters, physical disabilities, systemic yeast and fungal overgrowth, ear infections and antibiotics, specific allergies (like asthma) or diseases, and the recreational use of cigarettes, drugs and alcohol (both actual use by the child or prenatal use by the mother).
[6] All of the information regarding the importance of drinking water is from the following sources: Hannaford, *Smart Moves,* 138–45; Promislow, 36, 57; Jensen, 89; Dennison and Dennison, *Brain Gym,* teacher's edition, 24. Note: The amounts recommended for water intake apply to non-malnourished individuals with no medical restrictions on water intake. It is not recommended that we attempt to prescribe specific amounts for individual students, but encourage them to drink as needed.
[7] Laurie A. Couture, "Forced Retention of Bodily Waste: The Most Overlooked Form of Child Maltreatment." Available PTAVE Web site, [Internet, WWW], Address: *http://nospank.org/couture2.htm.*
[8] Couture, "Forced Retention of Bodily Waste"; "Health Risks to Children Associated with Forced Retention of Body Waste: A Statement by Medical Authorities" (October 1999). Available PTAVE Web site, [Internet, WWW], Address: *http://nospank.org/trbw.htm.* Note: According to a number of authorities, health risks can include kidney or urinary tract infections, incontinence, urinary reflux up to the kidneys, constipation, bowel obstructions and desensitization of the brain to cues that signal the need to use the toilet.
[9] Hannaford, *Smart Moves,* 146–47, 158–59; Dryden and Vos, 137; Jensen, *Completing the Puzzle,* 87–90; Dennison and Dennison, *Brain Gym Teacher's Edition,* 29; Promislow, 110. Note: In a related issue, making some informal seating available can also help.
[10] Hannaford, *Smart Moves,* 83–84. Note: It is much more natural for five-year-olds to write in cursive script. In fact, many European countries never teach printing, although kids have no trouble "going from writing in cursive to reading block printed text, usually at the age of eight."
[11] Shannon Brownlee, "Inside the Teen Brain," *U.S. News and World Report,* vol. 127, no. 6 (9 August 1999): 46–48; Robert Hotinski, "Missed Signals: You Were Angry?" *U.S. News and World Report,* vol. 127, no. 6 (9 August 1999): 50.
[12] Jensen, *Completing the Puzzle,* 50–51.
[13] Jensen, *Introduction to Brain Compatible Learning,* 68.
[14] Brownlee, "Slugabeds," 54.
[15] Connie López, "Dozing Off: Overbooked Teens Too Busy, Stressed to Get Enough Sleep," *Albuquerque Journal* (26 December 2000).
[16] Jensen, *Completing the Puzzle,* 134–35.
[17] Promislow, 42.
[18] Quoted in Dale Dauten, "Lighting Deserves a Look," *Albuquerque Journal* (25 January 2000).
[19] "America's Aging Schools," *Principal,* vol. 79, no. 2 (November 1999): 11.

[20] "Back to School, and Back to 'Sick Buildings'?" *Pure Facts,* newsletter of the Feingold Association of the United States (September 1997): 1.
[21] "NEA Offers Solutions for 'Sick Schools,'" *Pure Facts,* newsletter of the Feingold Association of the United States (September 1995): 1. Note: The NEA's Professional Library Guidebook is entitled *The Healthy School Handbook: Conquering the Sick Building Syndrome and Other Environmental Hazards.*
[22] "Dream Builders," *HGTV* broadcast on 19 August 1999 (Report on environmentally safe building products and procedures); Jane Hersey, *Why Can't My Child Behave?* (Alexandria, Va.: Pear Tree Press, Inc., 1999), 346.
[23] "Back to School, and Back to 'Sick Buildings'?"
[24] "Dream Builders." Note: One retailer interviewed claims that the healthy building products he sells are no more expensive or, in some cases, even less expensive than conventional products. Others claim that slightly higher up-front construction costs pay off in the long run.
[25] "Back to School, and Back to 'Sick Buildings'?"
[26] Saunders, 143–44. Note: The comfort factor has implications for increasing learning and cooperative behavior, and by reducing irritability likely to accompany being overheated, can reduce conflict and violence as well.
[27] "Getting Started on a Great School Year," *Pure Facts,* newsletter of the Feingold Association of the United States (September 2000): 1–3; "Dry Erase Markers Can Really Smell Up a Classroom," *Pure Facts,* newsletter of the Feingold Association of the United States (October 2000): 5.
[28] "The Many Effects of Daylight," *Pure Facts,* newsletter of the Feingold Association of the United States (March 2000): 1–5; also Dauten; Hannaford, *Smart Moves,* 148. Note: Hannaford also noticed a decrease in agitation in students when the conventional fluorescent lights were turned off.
[29] Jensen, *Completing the Puzzle,* 134; also Dauten. Note: Dauten also cites studies which show that natural lighting (in this case, from the addition of skylights) also reduced accidents in warehouses and increased sales in stores.
[30] "School Bus Safety," *CBS News* segment, 20 September 1999.
[31] Dryden and Vos, 179–80.
[32] Armstrong, *The Myth of the ADD Child,* 98; also Ostrander and Schroeder, 63. Note: In using music in my own classroom, I left the choice up to my students, as long as the volume didn't disturb any of the other classes and the lyrics didn't include anything "mean or obscene." Other teachers tell me that their classes have responded well to a variety of genres. In one instance the kids alternated between the preferences of the school's two main social factions, in this case country music and heavy metal, with one day a week set aside for "teacher's choice." Many teachers report observable improvements in attendance, cooperation, concentration and on-task time, and a reduction in lateness and unpreparedness.
[33] Hannaford, *Smart Moves,* 148–50. Note: Perhaps the most significant issue here is the tendency for humans to become more excitable or agitated when subjected to low frequency and extremely low frequency electromagnetic fields. Hannaford that the effects seem to relate to "a combination of field intensity and frequency" and quotes researchers who advise "a prudent avoidance of EMFs, especially with children."
[34] "TV Savvy for Kids," *NAESP Report to Parents,* Alexandria, Va.: National Association of Elementary School Principals, September 1999; also "How Parents Can Turn Off TV Violence," *NAESP Report to Parents,* Alexandria, Va.: National Association of Elementary School Principals, September 1999.
[35] Hannaford, *Smart Moves,* 172; also Sylwester, "How Our Brain Determines What's Important."
[36] Armstrong, *The Myth of the ADD Child,* 75–77. Note: Healy and Mander are quoted on these pages.
[37] Hannaford, *Smart Moves,* 67.
[38] Donovan and Iovino, 42.
[39] Lindsey Tanner, "Reducing TV Lowers Aggression in Kids," *Albuquerque Journal* (15

January 2001). Note: The study included the number of hours of television viewing, plus viewing videotapes and playing video games. The content of their viewing was not assessed.

[40] "Kids and TV Research," study that appeared in the Internet version of *Pediatrics,* a journal published by the American Academy of Pediatrics, sent via e-mail by a survey respondent; also Lemonick, "Fast Track Toddlers."

[41] Hannaford, *Smart Moves,* 66.

[42] Armstrong, *The Myth of the ADD Child,* 77; Shapiro, 36; "Raising Children to Resist Violence: What You Can Do" (1996). Available: American Psychological Association Web site, [Internet, WWW], Address: *http://www.apa.org/pi/pii/raisingchildren.html*; "How Parents Can Turn Off TV Violence."

[43] G. Blake Armstrong and Bradley S. Greenberg, "Background Television as an Inhibitor of Cognitive Processing," *Human Communication Research,* vol. 16, no. 3 (spring 1990): 355–386.

[44] Karen Jacobs, "Computers Can Be Hazardous to Your Health," *Principal,* vol. 79, no. 1 (September 1999): 32–34; Greene, 4; "Re-Evaluate School Computers," Associated Press article forwarded via e-mail (12 September 2000).

[45] Michael F. Jacobson and David Schardt, *Diet, ADHD and Behavior: A Quarter-Century Review* (Washington, D.C.: Center for Science in the Public Interest, 1999), 12.

[46] Hannaford, *Smart Moves,* 152.

[47] Authors of the *Kellogg Report: The Impact of Nutrition, Environment and Lifestyle on the Health of Americans,* quoted in "The Kellogg Report—A Landmark Study," *Pure Facts,* newsletter of the Feingold Association of the United States (December 1990/January 1991): 1.

[48] "Color Johnny Hyperactive/ADD," flyer published by The Feingold Association of the United States, Inc.

[49] Teresa J. Farney, "Mom Knew, Breakfast Most Important Meal," *Albuquerque Journal* (20 September 2000); also Marx, 6; Catherine Masters, "Empty Tummies Dictate Timing of School Days," *New Zealand Herald* (4 October 1999).

[50] Carolyn Dean, "Sweet Conspiracy," *Natural Health* (January/February 2001): 70–76. Carolyn Dean, "Ask the Experts: Teen with ADD," *Natural Health* (January/February 2001): 42. Note: Teenage boys in the U.S. consume and average of thirty-four teaspoons of sugar a day; the average for teenage girls is twenty-four teaspoons. For both boys and girls, approximately 40 percent of their daily sugar intake comes from soft drinks, many of which also contain caffeine and other chemicals.

[51] Armstrong, *The Myth of the ADD Child,* 68.

[52] Hannaford, *Smart Moves,* 155.

[53] Jacobson and Schardt, 17. Note: High-fat diets may also be a factor. According to an article by Andrew Skelly ("High-Fat Diet May Impair Learning and Memory" [21 Feburary 2001]. Available: WebMD Health Web site [Internet, WWW], Address: *http://my.webmd.com/content/article/3207.2689*), a study by Toronto researchers found that "fat—particularly saturated fat—impairs cognitive function."

[54] Hersey, 75.

[55] Dryden and Vos, 138; Jensen, *Completing the Puzzle,* 46; "Lack of Iron in Infancy Can Have Lasting Effects," the allHealth Web site. Available: [Internet, WWW], Address: *http://www.allhealth.comealth/followup/print/0.4197.5001_174415.00.html*; "How Foods and Additives Affect the Brain," *Pure Facts,* newsletter of the Feingold Association of the United States, special issue on brain chemistry: 1–4.

[56] Leo Galland, "Alternative Medicine Clinic." This page was faxed to me with no support information; Dean, "Ask the Experts."

[57] Jacobson and Schardt, 10, 19–24; "Color Johnny Hyperactive/ADD"; "How Foods and Additives Affect the Brain"; Hersey, 19–20, 48; "E.E.G. Confirms Food-Induced Abnormalities in ADHD Children," *Pure Facts,* newsletter of the Feingold Association of the United States, special issue ontreatments for ADD/ADHD: 1–4. Note: Copies of work samples sent to me by Jane Hersey of F.A.U.S. showed dramatic differences between children's drawing, writing, spelling, printing and handwriting samples which were done while adhering to the Feingold diet and those which were done after

children had eaten food containing substances to which they were sensitive. This diet focuses on the impact of synthetic dyes, artificial flavors, certain preservatives and foods that contain natural salicylates. Clinical and anecdotal studies have shown this diet to be effective. Although it has never been proven in double-blind, placebo-controlled studies, many efforts to *disprove* the effects of these dietary changes have been attempted without success.

[58] Lawrence H. Diller, "Just Say Yes to Ritalin!" Available: Mothers Who Think Web site, [Internet, WWW], Address: *http://salon.com/mwt/feature/2000/09/25/medicate/index.html.*

[59] Armstrong, *The Myth of the ADD Child,* 34.

[60] Hannaford, *Smart Moves,* 198.

[61] Character on the short-lived TV series, *It's Like, You Know,* 31 August 1999 broadcast.

[62] This includes attention problems, hyperactivity and impulsivity, which are commonly associated with ADHD.

[63] Jacobson and Schardt, 1; "Ritalin Overprescribed and Dangerous, Study Says," reprinted from *Health Watch* newsletter (February 2000); Sandra Reif, *Reaching and Teaching Children with ADD/ADHD,* resource handbook to accompany training (Bellevue, Wash.: Bureau of Education and Research, 1999), 12. Note: Reif cites the existence of studies which suggest that as many as 8 percent of students would qualify.

[64] Fred A. Baughman, "The Rise and Fall of ADD/ADHD" (19 Oct. 2000). Available: [Internet, WWW], Address: *http://sightings.com/general4/add.htm*; Peter Breggin, "On the Impact of Psychoactive Drugs on Children," transcript of testimony presented before the Subcommittee on Oversight and Investigations, Committee on Education and the Workforce. Available: Sightings Web site, [Internet, WWW], Address: *http://sightings.com/general4/addpsy.htm.*

[65] Lindsey Tanner, "Psychiatric Drug Use Up for Children," *Albuquerque Journal* (28 February 2000).

[66] "Pampers, Pacifiers and Prozac," *Pure Facts,* newsletter of the Feingold Association of the United States (September 1998): 1; Kelly Patricia O'Meara, "Doping Kids," vol. 15, no. 24, 28 June 1999. Available: *Insight on the News Online* [Internet, WWW], Address: *http://www.insightmag.com/investiga/apec11.html.*

[67] Tanner.

[68] Karr-Morse and Wiley, 110. Note: Diagnosis is similar for other "disruptive behavior disorders," including Oppositional-Defiant Disorders and Conduct Disorders.

[69] Jacobson and Schardt, 2 (adapted from *Attention Deficit Hyperactivity Disorder,* National Institute of Mental Health, 1994); "The Disability Named AD/HD: An Overview of Attention-Deficit/Hyperactivity Disorder" (2000). Available: *CHADD* (Children and Adults with Attention-Deficit/Hyperactivity Disorder) Web site, [Internet, WWW], Address: *http://www.chaddlorg/facts/add_facts01.htm*; Reif, 8–9. Note: In general, the *DSM*'s guidelines suggest that the behaviors appear before age seven and continue for at least six months. "Above all," note Jacobson and Schardt, "the behaviors must create a real handicap in at least two areas of a person's life, such as school, home, work or social settings."

[70] Classen asked me to clarify that "even in a clinic setting, where many kinds of tests and history taking would be done," the diagnosis is still generally based on observable symptoms. Part of Classen's work focuses on gathering data in the context of a public school setting, in order "to evaluate a child for possible protection from discrimination by Sec. 504 of the Rehabilitation Act." She and others insist that the process is detailed and deliberate to ensure that the diagnosis is *not* "casually thrown around."

[71] Kranowitz, 17. Note: The main difference between ADHD and Sensory Integration Dysfunction being "a child's unusual responses to touching and being touched, and/or moving and being moved."

[72] Perry, 2.

[73] "What Is Attachment Disorder?" Available: [Internet, WWW], Address: *http://members.tripod.com/~radclass/slide02.html.* Note: "Experts in R.A.D. (Reactive Attachment Disorder) estimate that this disorder has been misdiagnosed as Bi-Polar Disorder or Attention Deficit Disorder in 40 to 70 percent of the cases."

[74] Karr-Morse and Wiley, 110.
[75] Kathryn Shea and Stephen Winners, "Educating Children with FAS/FAE." Available: Northeast Consultation and Training Center Web site, [Internet, WWW], Address: *http://www.taconic.net/seminars/fas-c.html.*
[76] Janet Zand, "Hyperactivity," excerpted from *Smart Medicine for a Healthier Child* (1994). Available: Health World Web site, [Internet, WWW], Address: *http://healthy.net/asp/templates/article.asp?PageType=article&ID=1589.*
[77] "Ritalin Overprescribed and Dangerous."
[78] Jensen, *Completing the Puzzle,* 47.
[79] Armstrong, *The Myth of the ADD Child,* 13, 128.
[80] Fassler and Dumas, 65, 71.
[81] Demitri Papalos. Handout from a workshop entitled "Keepers of the Storm," submitted by a contributor who attended Papalos's presentation on Bi-Polar Disorder.
[82] Karr-Morse and Wiley, 123.
[83] "Thyroid Disease: Related Conditions" (2000). Available: *About.com* Web site, [Internet, WWW], Address: *http://thyroid.about.com/health/thyroid/cs/relatedconditions/index.htm.* Note: ADD/ADHD was included among a number of "conditions and diseases that are related to or worsened by thyroid disease." This condition was also included among the personal experiences of certain survey respondents and others involved in the development of this book.
[84] Greenspan, *The Growth of the Mind,* 150.
[85] Jensen, *Creating the Puzzle,* 47.
[86] Thomas Armstrong, "Learning Differences—Not Disabilities," in *Multiple Intelligence: A Collection,* Fogarty, Robin and James Bellanca, eds. (Arlington Heights, Ill.: IRI/SkyLight Training and Publishing, Inc., 1995), 226.
[87] Sunbeck, 81. Note: Sylwester suggests that "lower metabolic activity and specific neurotransmitter deficiencies in brain stem and limbic system structures" might also play a role.
[88] Williams and Shellenberger, 1–7; Hannaford, *Smart Moves,* 35, 118.
[89] Fassler and Dumas, 72.
[90] Armstrong, *The Myth of the ADD Child,* 13.
[91] "Inconsistencies, Confusion in the Treatment of ADHD," *Pure Facts,* newsletter of the Feingold Association of the United States, special issue on treatments for ADD/ADHD: 1; also Baughman; Breggin.
[92] Breggin; Baughman. Note: Pediatric neurologist Fred Baughman calls it "the single, biggest health care fraud in United States history." Indeed, a number of major lawsuits have been brought against Novartis, the manufacturer of Ritalin for conspiracy and fraud in advancing their aims at the expense of children.
[93] Breggin; "Connecting with Kids," *News 4 KOB-TV* (28 July 1999). Note: Ritalin is pharmacologically similar to cocaine and is classified as a Schedule II drug, the most addictive in medical usage (O'Meara). Psychologist Shannon Croft, quoted in the television interview, notes that Ritalin can be "quickly addictive" when snorted.
[94] Breggin; O'Meara.
[95] Armstrong, *The Myth of the ADD Child,* 45. Note: Most of the teachers and counselors, including some substance abuse specialists, are far more concerned about what they see as an overprescription for stimulant drugs than they are about other drugs like anti-depressants.
[96] Kirn, 48–49.
[97] Breggin; O'Meara; "Ritalin Overprescribed and Dangerous."
[98] O'Meara; "What Every Citizen Must Know About Psychiatric Drugs." Available: The Juice Guy Web site, [Internet, WWW], Address: *http://www.sni.net/healthinfo/violence.html.*
[99] "Medical Management of Children and Adults with Attention-Deficit/Hyperactivity Disorder" (2000). Available: CHADD (Children and Adults with Attention-Deficit/Hyperactivity Disorder) Web site, [Internet, WWW], Address: *http://www.chaddlorg/facts/add_facts03.htm.* Note: It may be worth noting that CHADD, which claims that

"for most children and adults with AD/HD, medication is an integral part of treatment," is financially supported by Novartis, the pharmaceutical company that makes Ritalin.

[100] Hannaford, *Smart Moves,* 199–200; also Breggin.

[101] Breggin; "Ritalin Overprescribed and Dangerous."

[102] "How Food and Additives Affect the Brain," 3; Hannaford, *Smart Moves,* 199.

[103] Breggin; Tanner; "Ritalin Overprescribed and Dangerous." Note: As someone who used a variety of diet pills and other stimulants—prescription and street drugs (including Ritalin)—for a number of years, I can personally attest to all-nighters that ended up being devoted to making sure all the pencils in the house were the same size instead of studying or finishing a term paper. And although I was sure that these drugs made me quite articulate, I'm equally certain that my professors would have preferred papers with sentences that didn't run on for two pages.

[104] Quoted in Walter Kirn, "The Danger of Suppressing Sadness," *Time* magazine, vol. 153, no. 21 (31 May 1999): 48–49.

[105] Diller.

[106] Breggin.

[107] Chua-Eoan, 48; Fassler and Dumas, 64; Hannaford, *Smart Moves,* 201; "The Disability Named AD/HD: An Overview of Attention-Deficit/Hyperactivity Disorder."

[108] "Connecting with Kids."

[109] Quoted in Wright, *The Heart and Wisdom of Teaching.*

[110] Quoted in "Ritalin Overprescribed and Dangerous."

[111] Redenbach, 90.

[112] Cecilia K. Freeman and Joyce B. Sherwood, "Brain Gym and Its Effect on Reading Ability: A Report on the Brain Gym Reading Pilot Project at the Saticoy Elementary School, Ventura, California, School Year 1998–99." Unpublished paper, February 2000, 28.

[113] Kempermann and Gage, 49, 52–53; Paul Recer, "Brain Regenerates Thinking Cells, Princeton Study Says," *Albuquerque Journal* (15 October 1999); Jim Wilson, "Caution: Brain Work Ahead," *Popular Mechanics,* vol. 177, no. 3 (March 2000): 72–75, 133; Janet McConnaughey, "Growth of Dead Brain Cells Excites Scientists," *Albuquerque Journal* (6 November 2000). Note: Recent findings show that our brains actually generate new cells throughout our lives, and that enriched environments and movement increase nerve growth and learning performance (even very old mice showed improvements in these areas). Brain scientists have known for a while that the brain can compensate for damage by creating new neural pathways among surviving neurons, but the potential for nerve regeneration was never previously confirmed. Although new cells do not "regrow whole brain parts or restore lost memories" when a brain has been damaged, these findings certainly speak to a potential for self-repair, with significant implications for the treatment of certain diseases and, perhaps, to the repair of damage to certain sites in the brain important for learning and growth. The new cells are generated in the hippocampus.

[114] Karr-Morse and Wiley, 33.

[115] Paula Pickle, "Neurodevelopmental Therapy/Attachment Therapy: An Integrated Approach." Available: The Attachment Center at Evergreen, Inc. Web site, [Internet, WWW], Address: *http://www.attachmentcenter.org/neurodevelopmental.htm*; Ricky Greenwald, *EMDR: A New Treatment for Traumatic Memories/Children Helped by EMDR* (13 October 1999). Available Child Trauma Web site, [Internet, WWW], Address: *http://www.childtrauma.com/chpemd.htm.* Note: There is a wide variety of therapies which work with neural circuitry and, in some cases, traumatic memories. These avenues are beyond the scope of this book. I'm not about to attempt to squeeze an evaluation, recommendation, or even a presentation of the various approaches or their effectiveness into a footnote. However, personal experience and observations, and the reports of a few respondents, suggest that some of these approaches might be worth exploring when an alternative to "talk therapy" or medication is called for.

[116] Kranowitz, 42, 185–88. Note: Degeneration of the vestibular system, critical for taking information in from the environment, can occur when children suffer ear infections,

allergies or being shaken as an infant, or from keeping the head still for long periods (watching TV). Damage to the vestibular system is present in almost all children identified with dyslexia and learning disabilities, and many identified as ADHD. Movement helps repair damaged tissue in the vestibular system and increases the development and myelination of new nerve networks (Hannaford, *Smart Moves,* 157–159).

[117] Hannaford, *Smart Moves,* 164; interviews and conversations with Aili Pogust, Sumiati Said and other Educational Kinesiologists certified in Brain Gym. Note: Hannaford talks about dramatic success with autistic and speech-impaired children using Brain Gym exercises, particularly those involving the calf muscles, to improve speech development.

[118] Dennison and Dennison, *Brain Gym Teacher's Edition;* Hannaford, *Smart Moves,* 164; Promislow, 16–18; Carla Hannaford, "The Brain Gym Option for Hyperactivity," *Australian Journal of Remedial Education,* vol. 26, no. 1; "About Brain Gym," Brain Gym Web site. Available: [Internet, WWW], Address: *http://www.braingym.org/about.html*; "About Educational Kinesiology," Edu-Kinesthetics Web site. Available: [Internet, WWW], Address: *http://www.braingym.org/info/info.html*; "Research Report" (including experimental research, field studies, anecdotal research and theoretical information on Educational Kinesiology), compiled by the Educational Kinesiology Foundation, Ventura, Calif.; Freeman and Sherwood, 28–30; also interviews and conversations with a number of Brain Gym specialists, Kinesiologists and others certified in different types of brain-body work. Note: The Brain Gym movements were developed from early work that promoted the relationship between movement and learning. The field in which this work is applied is called Educational Kinesiology, or Edu-K for short.

[119] Also Zand.

[120] The child's sensitivity was determined by a Certified Kinesionics Practitioner who used muscle testing to determine substances and factors to which his nervous system responded negatively, and which had a negative affect on his behavior and attention.

[121] Includes research cited in Elizabeth G. Cohen, "Making Cooperative Learning Equitable," *Educational Leadership,* vol. 56, no. 1 (September 1998). Available: Association for Supervision and Curriculum Development Web site, [Internet, WWW], Address: *http://www.ascd.org/safeschools/el9809/cohencoop.html.*

[122] Forrest Lien, "SAMONAS Sound Therapy." Available: The Attachment Center at Evergreen, Inc. Web site, [Internet, WWW], Address: *http://www.attachmentcenter.org/samonas.htm.* Note: This therapy is based on the work of Alfred Tomatis, a French physician. This approach uses filtered sounds to achieve results.

[123] Rhoda Fukushima, "Karate Kids," *Albuquerque Journal* (10 July 2000).

Part III
The Grownups

[1] Buchanan.

[2] Wesley, 42.

[3] Sugar, 3.

[4] Steven Greenhouse, "Autumn of Teachers' Discontent Is Dawning" (20 September 2000). Available: *New York Times* Web site, [Internet, WWW], Address: *http://partners.nytimes.com/2000/09/20/national/20TEAC.html.*

[5] Linda Lumsden, "Teacher Morale," *ERIC Digest,* no. 120 (1998). Available: ERIC Web site, U.S. Department of Education, [Internet, WWW], Address: *http://www.ed.gov/databases/ERIC_Digests/ed422601.html.*

[6] Anjetta McQueen, "The Fight to Find, Keep Teachers," *Albuquerque Journal* (4 July 2000).

Chapter 19
Teacher Safety: Protecting the Protectors

[1] Quoted in Rogers and Frieberg, 139.
[2] Quoted in Lumsden.
[3] Quoted in Stoll.
[4] Barbara Kantrowitz and Pat Wingert, "Teachers Wanted," *Newsweek* (2 October 2000): 37; McQueen, "The Fight to Find, Keep Teachers"; John Balz, "U.S. Schools Face Rising Enrollment," *Albuquerque Journal* (21 August 1999). Note: Despite relatively enormous gains in salaries over the past few decades, starting pay for teachers still lag far behind entry-level positions in other fields. In 1997–98, the average beginning teacher earned $25,735; new college grads in engineering earned $42,862, in computer science, $40,920 (McQueen).
[5] Kantrowitz and Wingert, 38; McQueen, "The Fight to Find, Keep Teachers"; Rudi Keller, "New Mexico Loses Experienced Teachers to Better Pay," *Albuquerque Journal* (9 July 2000); Abby Goodnough, "Sensing Higher Calling in the Classroom" (1 August 2000). Available: *New York Times* Web site, [Internet, WWW], Address: *http://partners.nytimes.com/library/national/regional/080100ny-teach-edu.html*; Lynette Clemetson, "Wooing Them with Elvis," *Newsweek* (2 October 2000): 39.
[6] Kantrowitz and Wingert, 38; Goodnough; McQueen, "The Fight to Find, Keep Teachers"; Daniel McGinn, "There's Just No Substitute," *Newsweek* (2 October 2000): 42; Rudi Keller, "Teacher Course Put on Hold," *Albuquerque Journal*. Note: When the participants accepted for the first-year intern training program that I coordinated in the early 1980s were among the best beginning teachers in the state. But even with supervision, support and validation from others in the program with whom they met twice weekly, the realities of that first year could be pretty harrowing. Yet, of all the first-year teachers in the district, only the twelve interns in this program had this level of support. Others started off far more on their own and often, it showed—in their performance, morale and how long they stayed in the job. Principals generally rated the performance and professionalism of intern teachers higher than other, unsupported first-year teachers as well.
[7] Tamara Henry, "New Teachers Are Passionate but Unprepared," *USA Today* (24 May 2000).
[8] Anjetta McQueen, "Teacher Training Advocated: Congress Lectures College Officials," *Albuquerque Journal* (17 September 1999).
[9] Juan A. Lozano, "Wanted: Recipe for a Better School Teacher," *Albuquerque Journal*, 27 June 1999.
[10] Quoted in Kantrowitz and Wingert, 40.
[11] Ibid.
[12] Kantrowitz and Wingert, 38.
[13] "School Membership Rubric." Available: *Bay Area School Reform Collaborative* Web site, [Internet, WWW], Address: *http://www.fwl.org/basrc/rubrics/SchoolRubric.pdf.*
[14] Kantrowitz and Wingert, 40.
[15] Sugar, 10.
[16] Ismat Abdal-Haqq, "Making Time for Teacher Professional Development," *ERIC Digest,* vol. 95, no. 4 (October 1996); Girard.
[17] Note: In case it isn't obvious, this is not an argument for lowering standards or expectations. Rather, I believe it speaks to the concept of educators as life-long learners and professionals who frequently have to sacrifice personal or preparation time in order to gain new knowledge, and the need for whatever kind of supports are necessary to make this kind of growth an inherent part of the profession.
[18] Abdal-Haqq, "Making Time for Teacher Professional Development." Note: The author suggests making use of colleagues, aides, interns and parents to cover classes to free up time for teachers, restructured time with regularly scheduled release days, better use of time in staff or district meetings, common planning periods for colleagues having similar assignments or establishing a substitute bank of thirty to forty days a year

"which teachers can tap when they participate in committee work or professional development activities."

[19] Peterson and Deal.

[20] Stoll, referring to ideas proposed by David Reynolds.

[21] Donovan and Iovino, 50.

[22] Note: What seemed to work best were strategies like finding like-minded colleagues, like the other interns in the programs and certain other members of their school staff or university program, becoming more discerning about where, when, how much and with whom they were willing to share, and, in several cases, simply avoiding the teachers' lounge.

[23] Rogers and Frieberg, 119.

[24] Quoted in Donovan and Iovino, 49.

[25] Quoted in Charles Hirshberg, "How Good Are Our Schools?" *Life* (September 1999): 42.

[26] Note: Ilagan elaborates, "By this I mean that teaching is the most fulfilling of all professions as one partakes not only in the dissemination but likewise the creation of knowledge. Teaching is the noblest of all professions as they say. One grows in it. Teaching therefore can be said [to be] Life. On the other hand, teaching can, for some, mean Death in the sense that teachers are overworked and underpaid. . . ." He mentions other stresses that can drain and exhaust a teacher's life force.

[27] Lumsden.

[28] Schultz and Heuchert, 30.

[29] Epp, 14.

[30] Palmer, 11.

[31] "Creating Peaceable Families."

[32] Aspy and Roebuck, front, ii, 5–6, 42, 46, 255. Note: The NCHE studies also found teachers' physical fitness and health to be a factor in "their ability to employ interpersonal skills in a sustained manner" throughout the school day. Although all participants studied started at the same level of effectiveness, the performance of teachers in the "low fitness group" deteriorated significantly about halfway through the five-hour day.

[33] Quarles, 57. Note: Reasoner cites a Wisconsin study that asked students to identify the "most outstanding teacher they ever had and the one they learned the most from." The results showed 85 percent of respondents "described that teacher as 'caring,' 'supportive in positive ways,' or 'made me feel special'" (Reasoner, 32).

[34] Lumsden.

[35] Bluestein, *21st Century Discipline,* 183–84; some additional material from Subby, 16–17; Wegscheider-Cruse, 29–31.

[36] Garfield, 91.

[37] Chairman, United States Steel, quoted in Garfield, 184.

[38] Rogers and Frieberg, 120.

[39] Quoted in Rogers and Frieberg, 111.

[40] "Celebration of Learning," Eyewitness News 4 segment (27 August 1999).

[41] Aspy and Roebuck, 39–41.

[42] Rogers and Frieberg, 5; also Peterson and Deal.

[43] Mercier.

[44] Spence Rogers, *Teaching Tips: 105 Ways to Increase Motivation and Learning* (Evergreen, Colo.: Peak Learning Systems, Inc., 1999), 41.

[45] *Helping Children Grow up in the '90s: A Resource Book for Parents and Teachers,* Bethesda, Md.: National Association of School Psychologists, 1992.

[46] Garfield, 88, 181–85.

[47] Lumsden.

[48] James E. Liebig, *The Merchants of Vision* (San Francisco: Berrett-Koehler Publishers, 1994), 2.

[49] John Steinberg, "The Fourth Time They Say 'Yes,'" *Strategier,* no. 352 (1998). Available: John Steinberg's Web site, [Internet, WWW], Address: *http://www.steinberg.se/english.html#anchor245039.*

[50] Rogers and Frieberg, 118.
[51] Peterson and Deal.
[52] Bellanca.
[53] David Cowan, *Taking Charge of Organizational Conflict* (Spring Valley, Calif.: Innerchoice Publishing, 1995), iii, 37, 113–17, 138–43, back cover.
[54] DeBeaufort and Diaz, 22–24.
[55] Adapted from Bluestein, *21st Century Discipline,* 191. Note: Some new material added from Fraser, *Values in the Workplace,* 12.
[56] This is an expanded version of the survey in Ken Fraser, *Values in the Workplace,* course manual, National Agency for Self-Esteem & Responsibility (Kingston, ACT, Australia: Work Resources Centre, Inc.), 5–6, which was adapted from Nathaniel Branden's *Self-Esteem at Work* (San Francisco: Jossey-Bass, 1998).

Chapter 20
The Collaborators: Parents and Community

[1] McLaughlin, 51.
[2] Fredric H. Jones, *Positive Classroom Discipline* (New York: McGraw-Hill Book Company, 1987), 72.
[3] Karr-Morse and Wiley, 109.
[4] Bill Kaczor, "Dollar-a-Year Principal Saves School" (23 September 2000). Available: Messenger-Inquirer Web site, [Internet, WWW], Address: *http://www.messenger-inquirer.com/features/education/2319491.htm.*
[5] Mercier.
[6] Lantieri and Patti.
[7] O'Neill, 147.
[8] Padgett.
[9] Henry.
[10] McLaughlin, 17.
[11] "Family Involvement Keeps Paying Off in Middle School," (2000). Available: Parent Institute Web site, [Internet, WWW], Address: *http://www.parent-institute.com/nl/deliver.asp?issueID=midaug00sample&itemID=12053*; Fran Pulver, "Increasing Family Involvement: Steps to a Successful Parent Night," *Committee for Children Prevention Update* (Fall 1999): 7; "Why a Coalition for Parent Involvement?" Available: The National Coalition for Parent Involvement in Education Web site, [Internet, WWW], Address: *http://www.ncpie.org*; "Getting Parents Involved: One School's Approach," *Communicator,* Newsletter of the National Association of Elementary School Principals, vol. 23, no. 2 (October 1999): 3.
[12] "Parent Participation Crucial in Preventing Drug Use" (2000). Available: Parent Institute Web site, [Internet, WWW], Address: *http://www.parent-institute.com/nl/deliver.asp?issueID=enaug00sample&itemID=11959*; "Neighborhood: Making Safer Schools" (no date). Available: National Crime Prevention Council Web site, [Internet, WWW], Address: *http://www.ncpc.org/2schools.htm*; "Adult Presence Critical in Keeping School Grounds Safe," (2000). Available: Parent Institute Web site, [Internet, WWW], Address: *http://www.parent-institute.com/nl/deliver.asp?issueID=enaug00sample&itemID=11966*; "Developing Family/School Partnerships: Guidelines for Schools and School Districts." Available: National Coalition for Parent Involvement in Education Web site, [Internet, WWW], Address: *http://www.ncpie.org/ncpieguidelines.html; Safer Schools: Strategies for Educators and Law Enforcement Seeking to Prevent Violence within Schools.* Washington, D.C.: National Crime Prevention Council, 1998. Note: Many schools also take advantage of city police officers, school resource officer programs and area residents to increase safety and reduce violence in schools.
[13] Pei-Pei Yow, "Speech to Cupertino City 5Cs about AAPA" (1 December 1999). Available: Asian American Parents Association Web site, [Internet, WWW], Address: *http://www.geocities.com/CapitolHill/Parliament/572/aapa/articles.html*; Lakshmi Sukumar, "Unity in Diversity" (Sept. 1, 1998). Available: Asian American Parents

Association Web site, [Internet, WWW], Address: *http://www.geocities.com/CapitolHill/Parliament/572/aapa/articles.html*; "Family Involvement Keeps Paying Off in Middle School"; Gail Burd, "Brain Awareness Week: A Classroom Primer" (March/April, 1996). Available: Society for Neurosciences Web site, [Internet, WWW], Address: *http://www.sfn.org/nl/1996/March-April/mar-apr_BrainAwarenssWeek.html.*

[14] "Use a Multi-Faceted Approach to Help Parents Feel Comfortable at Your School" (2000). Available: Parent Institute Web site, [Internet, WWW], Address: *http://www.parent-institute.com/nl/deliver.asp?issueID=enaug00sample&itemID=11960.*

[15] William B. Ribas, "Tips for Reaching Parents," *Educational Leadership,* vol. 56, no. 1 (September 1998). Available: Association of Supervision and Curriculum Development Web site, [Internet, WWW], Address: *http://www.ascd.org/pubs/el/sep98/ribas.html.*

[16] Jane Bluestein, "I'm Calling Your Mother! Boundary-Setting with Your Child's Teachers." Article reprint (Albuquerque, N. Mex.: I.S.S. Publications, 1999): 1.

[17] Bluestein, *Being a Successful Teacher,* 167–68.

[18] Bluestein, *21st Century Discipline,* 166–68.

[19] Bluestein, *Being a Successful Teacher,* 17–20; "Teachers as a Crucial Link in Partnership Between Parents and Schools: Self-Teaching Module for Teachers." Available: University of Wyoming Web site, [Internet, WWW], Address: *http://www.uwyo.edu/ag/ces/FAMILY/Dream/Parent/Kits/Tkit.htm*; Dan Jesse, "Increasing Parental Involvement," *Schools in the Middle,* vol. 7, no. 1 (September/October 1997), 22–23; McLaughlin, 132–35; "Use a Multi-Faceted Approach to Help Parents Feel Comfortable at Your School." Note: It's easy to overlook certain quiet (or "invisible") kids who need this positive attention as much as anyone. It might help to keep track of calls or individual notes to make sure everyone in the class gets on. Also, when I worked in departmentalized settings with 140 to 160 kids, I tended to focus on my more challenging classes for the more frequent contacts.

[20] "Use a Multi-Faceted Approach to Help Parents Feel Comfortable at Your School"; "Teachers as a Crucial Link in Partnership Between Parents and Schools."

[21] "Use a Multi-Faceted Approach to Help Parents Feel Comfortable at Your School"; Jesse, 22.

[22] June Million, "Getting the Word out on Safety," *Communicator,* Newsletter of the National Association of Elementary School Principals, vol. 23, no. 2 (October 1999): 5; "Developing Family/School Partnerships: Guidelines for Schools and School Districts." Available: National Coalition for Parent Involvement in Education Web site, [Internet, WWW], Address: *http://www.ncpie.org/ncpieguidelines.html*; "Seven Tips to Building a Successful Partnership" (1998). Available Partnership for Family Involvement in Education Web site, U.S. Department of Education, [Internet, WWW], Address: *http://pfie.ed.gov/seventbuilding_partnership.htm.*

[23] "Clear Goals, Training Can Help You Create a 'Powerful' Volunteer Program at School" (2000). Available: Parent Institute Web site, [Internet, WWW], Address: *http://www.parent-institute.com/nl/deliver.asp?issueID=enaug00sample&itemID=11962.*

[24] Fran Pulver, "Increasing Family Involvement: Steps to a Successful Parent Night," Committee for Children Prevention Update (Fall 1999): 7; Alan McCluskey, "Emotional Intelligence in Schools," 28 February 1997. Available: Connected Web site [Internet, WWW], Address: *http://www.connected.org/learn/school.html;* "A Blueprint for Safe Schools" (18 June 1999), produced by the Center for the Study and Prevention of Violence. Available: University of Colorado at Boulder Web site, [Internet, WWW], Address: *http://www.colorado.edu/cspv/factsheets/factsheet15.html;* Sullivan-DeCarlo, et al. Note: Increased communication and a win-win approach can help overcome parents concerns about the schools' involvement in their children's emotional development and personal lives.

[25] "Use a Multi-Faceted Approach to Help Parents Feel Comfortable at Your School."

[26] *Safer Schools,* 3; "Seven Tips to Building a Successful Partnership"; "A Blueprint for Safe Schools"; "Police Training Academy in a Middle School," *Catalyst,* vol. 19, no. 1 (February 1999). Available: National Crime Prevention Council Web site, [Internet, WWW], Address: *http://www.ncpc.org/cat9902a.htm;* Jesse, 22; "Helping Every

Student Attend a Safe School: The Center for the Prevention of School Violence." Available: *North Carolina State University* Web site, [Internet, WWW], Address: *http://www.ncsu.edu/cpsv/helpeveryst.htm*; Million, "A Win-Win Situation," 5; "School Resource Officer Program" (4 July 1999). Available: Northampton, Massachusetts Police Department Web site, [Internet, WWW], Address: *http://www.orthamptonpd.com/School_Resource_Officer_Program/General_General_r.html.* Note: The need for an expansive network is becoming increasingly clearer as children's physical, social, emotional, behavioral and academic health needs tax the expertise of even the most well-rounded individuals in a school setting. Children who have problems in any of these areas are likely to benefit more from a team approach than expecting one individual—particularly a teacher who most likely is dealing with a number of such children—to handle all dimensions of the problems kids present on his or her own.

[27] "Developing Family/School Partnerships"; "Teacher as a Crucial Link."

[28] "Teachers as a Crucial Link."

[29] "Teachers as a Crucial Link in Partnership Between Parents and Schools"; also "Warmth, Flexibility Are Among Teacher Qualities that Improve Family Involvement" (2000). Available: Parent Institute Web site, [Internet, WWW], Address: *http://www.parent-institute.com/nl/deliver.asp?issueID=enaug00sample&itemID=11968.*

[30] Ribas; Bluestein, *21st Century Discipline,* 167.

[31] Jane Bluestein, workshop handout; also Bluestein, *Being a Successful Teacher,* 17–27. Note: The point about focusing answers on what is possible when parents have unrealistic expectations is from William Ribas.

[32] Kantrowitz and Wingert, 38.

[33] Quoted in Kantrowitz and Wingert, 40.

[34] Welbes.

[35] Jane Bluestein, from the back-cover blurb for Esther Wright, *Why I Teach* (Rocklin, Calif.: Prima Publishing, 1999).

[36] Examples reported in interviews, surveys and conversations.

[37] Greenhouse.

[38] Keller, "New Mexico Loses Teachers"; also Susan Montoya, "Teachers Leave N.M. for Better Pay," *Albuquerque Journal* (17 August 1999). Available: *Albuquerque Journal* Web site, [Internet, WWW], Address: *http://www.abqjournal.com/news/5news08-17-99.htm.*

[39] McQueen, "The Fight to Find, Keep Teachers."

[40] Rogers and Frieberg, 296.

[41] "Poll Shows Public Still Likes Public Education," *Communicator,* Newsletter of the National Association of Elementary School Principals, vol. 23, no. 2 (October 1999): 1.

[42] Jacques Steinberg, "Education Initiatives: Frustrated Parents Hope Their Votes Will Change Schools' Ways" (10 October 2000). Available: *The New York Times* Web site, [Internet, WWW], Address: *http://partners.nytimes.com/2000/10/10/politics/10SCHO.html.*

[43] Rogers and Frieberg, 33.

[44] Jane Bluestein, "Thank a Teacher." Article reprint. Albuquerque, N. Mex.: I.S.S. Publications (1999): 1–2.

Epilogue: Are We Almost There Yet?

[1] Quoted in Drew, xii.

[2] Cameron, 53.

[3] Linda Verlee Williams, 160.

[4] Toffler, 19, 27, 453.

Recommended Resources

In preparing this section, I had a tough call to make. I could either include the complete bibliography (with somewhere around eight hundred resources actually used in this book) or I could cut out significant portions of various chapters. Being a bit greedy with the text portion of this book (all of which is annotated rather thoroughly in the chapter notes), I came upon a compromise: I would include a number of the more significant resources used in this book under the heading of Recommended Resources, and I would post the entire bibliography on my Web site.

Any reader who wants the complete listing can visit my site at *http://www.janebluestein.com* and click on the "handouts" button. The link to "handouts for educators" will take you to the first page of the bibliography (at *http://www.janebluestein.com/hnd_bib.html*).

"About True Colors." Available *True Colors* Web site, [Internet, WWW], Address: *http://truecolors.org/general/about_true_colors.htm.*

"Behavior Problems: What's a School to Do?" Feature article from the newsletter, *Addressing Barriers to Learning,* of the Clearinghouse of the Center for Mental Health in Schools of the University of California, Los Angeles, vol. 2, no. 2 (1997).

"Clear Goals, Training Can help You Create a 'Powerful' Volunteer Program at School" (2000). Available: Parent Institute Web site, [Internet, WWW], Address: *http://www.parent-institute.com/nl/deliver.asp?issueID=enaug00sample&itemID=11962.*

"Corporal Punishment," Position Statement of the National Association of School Psychologists (18 April 1998). Available: PTAVE Web site, [Internet, WWW], Address: *http://nospank.org/nasp2.htm.*

"Corporal Punishment: Myths and Realities," Fact sheet prepared by The National PTA (1991). Available: PTAVE Web site, [Internet, WWW], Address: *http://nospank.org/pta.htm.*

"Corporal Punishment in Schools," Position Paper of the Society for Adolescent Medicine, *Journal of Adolescent Health* (1992): 13: 240–46. Available: PTAVE Web site, [Internet, WWW], Address: *http://nospank.org/sam.htm.*

"Corporal Punishment in Schools," Policy Statement by the American Academy of Child and Adolescent Psychiatry (Approved, June 1988). Available: PTAVE Web site, [Internet, WWW], Address: *http://nospank.org/aacap.htm.*

"Corporal Punishment in Schools" (RE9207), Position Statement of the American Academy of Pediatrics, Committee on School Health (1991). Available: PTAVE Web site, [Internet, WWW], Address: *http://nospank.org/aap2.htm.*

"Developing Family/School Partnerships: Guidelines for Schools and School Districts."

Available: National Coalition for Parent Involvement in Education Web site, [Internet, WWW], Address: *http://www.ncpie.org/ncpieguidelines.html.*

"The Disability Named AD/HD: An Overview of Attention-Deficit/Hyperactivity Disorder," (2000). Available: CHADD (Children and Adults with Attention-Deficit/Hyperactivity Disorder) Web site, [Internet, WWW], Address: *http://www.chaddlorg/facts/add_facts01.htm.*

"Diversity Training and Consulting." Available on the National MultiCultural Institute Web Site, [Internet, WWW], Address: *http://www.nmci.org/training.htm#train.*

"Getting Parents Involved: One School's Approach," *Communicator,* Newsletter of the National Association of Elementary School Principals, vol. 23, no. 2 (October 1999): 3.

"An Introduction to Life Span Development: Lawrence Kohlberg" (2000). Available: Prentice-Hall Distance Learning Web site, [Internet, WWW], Address: *http://cw.prenhall.com/bookbind/pubbooks/feldman4/chapter1/custom12/deluxe-content.html.*

"Johnny Be Good: Teaching Character in America's Public Schools," *Communicator,* Newsletter of the National Association of Elementary School Principals, vol. 23, no. 4 (January 2000): 1–3.

"Lawrence Kohlberg" (2000). Available: The Psi Cafe Web site, [Internet, WWW], Address: *http://www.psy.pdx.edu/PsiCafe/KeyTheorists/Kohlberg.htm.*

"Learning Styles and the 4MAT System: A Cycle of Learning." Available University of North Dakota "Volcanoes" Program Web site, [Internet, WWW], Address: *http://volcano.und.nodak.edu/vwdocs/msh/11c/is/4mat.html.*

"Major Premises of 4MAT." Available: About Learning Inc. Web site, [Internet, WWW], Address: *http://aboutlearning.com/aboutlearning/4premis.html.*

"Moral Classrooms: The Development of Character and Integrity in the Elementary School." A research report by The Teel Institute for the Development of Integrity and Ethical Behavior. Kansas City, Mo.: The Teel Institute, 1998.

"NASP Position Statement: School Violence," *National Mental Health and Education Center for Children and Families.* Available: National Association of School Psychologists Web site, [Internet, WWW], Address: *http://www.naspweb.org/center/safe%5Fschools/safeschools%5Fviolence.html.*

"Peer to Peer Instruction," *Program Ideas: Youth Mobilization* (no date). Available: National Crime Prevention Council Web site, [Internet, WWW], Address: *http://www.ncpc.org/3you1dc.htm.*

"Population and Family Characteristics," *America's Children 1998.* Available: Forum on Child and Family Statistics, ChildStats Web site, [Internet, WWW], Address: *http://www.childstats.gov/ac1998/poptxt.htm.*

"Preventing School Violence: Policies for Safety, Caring and Achievement," *An ASCD Infobrief Synopsis* (August 1996). Available: Association for Supervision and Curriculum Development Web site, [Internet, WWW], Address: *http://www.ascd.org/issues/violence.html.*

"Raising Children to Resist Violence: What You Can Do" (1996). Available: American Psychological Association Web site, [Internet, WWW], Address: *http://www.apa.org/pi/pii/raisingchildren.html.*

"Research Report" (including experimental research, field studies, anecdotal research and theoretical information on Educational Kinesiology), compiled by the Educational Kinesiology Foundation, Ventura, California.

"Resiliency," 1999, from Pathways to School Improvement Resources. Available: North Central Regional Laboratory Web site, [Internet, WWW], Address: *http://www.ncrel.org/sdrs/areas/issues/envrnmt/drugfree/sa3resil.htm.*

"Seven Tips to Building a Successful Partnership" (1998). Available Partnership for Family Involvement in Education Web site, U.S. Department of Education, [Internet, WWW], Address: *http://pfie.ed.gov/seventbuilding_partnership.htm.*

"Spanking Makes Children Violent, Antisocial," excerpt from *The American Medical Association News Update* (13 August 1997). Available: PTAVE Web site, [Internet, WWW], Address: *http://nospank.org/straus.htm.*

"Teacher Talk: Gangs and School Violence" (June 1997). Available: Indiana University Center for Adolescent Studies Web site, [Internet, WWW], Address: *http://education.indiana.edu/cas/tt/v2i3/gangs.html.*

"Teacher Talk: Peer Mediation" (June 1997). Available: Indiana University Center for Adolescent Studies Web site, [Internet, WWW], Address: *http://education.indiana.edu/cas/tt/v2i3/peer.html.*

"Thoughts on Risk and Recovery from Course Failure," *Forum* (International Alliance for Invitational Education), vol. 21, no. 1 (April 2000): 16–17.

"Title IX, Education Amendments of 1972." Available U.S. Department of Labor Web site, [Internet, WWW], Address: *http://www.dol.gov/dol/oasam/public/regs/statutes/titleix.htm.*

"To Promote or Retain: The Debate over Social Promotion Continues," *Communicator,* Newsletter of the National Association of Elementary School Principals, vol. 23, no. 1 (September 1999): 1–3.

"TV Savvy for Kids," *NAESP Report to Parents.* Alexandria, Va.: National Association of Elementary School Principals, September 1999.

"United Nations Committee on Rights of Child," Eighteenth Session, Geneva (18 May–5 June 1998). Available: PTAVE Web site, [Internet, WWW], Address: *http://nospank.org/uncrc.htm.*

"Warmth, Flexibility Are Among Teacher Qualities that Improve Family Involvement" (2000). Available: Parent Institute Web site, [Internet, WWW], Address: *http://www.parent-institute.com/nl/deliver.asp?issueID=enaug00sample&itemID=11968.*

"What Is Attachment Disorder?" Available: [Internet, WWW], Address: *http://members.tripod.com/~radclass/slide02.html.*

"Working in a Multiage Classroom: Can Students of Different Ages Work Together?" *Communicator,* Newsletter of the National Association of Elementary School Principals, vol. 23, no. 2 (October 1999): 1–2.

Abdal-Haqq, Ismat. "Making Time for Teacher Professional Development," *ERIC Digest,* vol. 95, no. 4 (October 1996).

Achilles, Charles M., Jeremy D. Finn and Helen Pate-Bain. "Class Size: It's Elementary," *Streamlined Seminar.* Alexandria, VA: National Association of Elementary School Principals, vol. 18, no. 1 (September 1999).

Adderholdt-Elliot, Miriam. *Perfectionism: What's Bad About Being Too Good?* Minneapolis, Minn.: Free Spirit Publishing, 1987.

Akin, Terri, Gerry Dunne, Susanna Palomares and Dianne Schilling. *Character Education in America's Schools.* Spring Valley, Calif.: Innerchoice Publishing, 1995.

Ames, Louise Bates. *Is Your Child in the Wrong Grade?* Rosemont, N.J.: Modern Learning Press, 1978.

Andrade, Heidi Goodrich. "Using Rubrics to Promote Thinking and Learning," *Educational Leadership,* vol. 57, no. 5 (February 2000): 13–18.

Angaran, Sally and Kathy Beckwith. "Peer Mediation in Elementary Schools," *Principal,* vol. 78, no. 5 (May 1999): 27–29.

Arends, Richard I. *Learning to Teach.* New York: Random House, 1988.

Armstrong, Thomas. *Awakening Genius in the Classroom.* Alexandria, Va.: Association for Supervision and Curriculum Development, 1998.

———. *The Myth of the ADD Child: 50 Ways to Improve Your Child's Behavior and Attention Span without Drugs, Labels or Coercion.* New York: Dutton, 1995.

Arthur, Richard with Edsel Erickson. *Gangs and Schools.* Holmes Beach, Fla.: Learning Publications, Inc., 1992.

Aspy, David N. and Flora N. Roebuck. *Kids Don't Learn from People They Don't Like.* Amherst, Mass.: Human Resource Development Press, Inc., 1977. *http://www.ascd.org/safeschools/el9710/oct97toc.htm.*

Baars, Bernard J. "Can Anyone Overstate the Significance of Emotions?" (no date). Available: Virginia Tech Web site, [Internet, WWW], Address: *http://server.phil.vt.edu/assc/watt/baars1.html.*

Balz, John. "U.S. Schools Face Rising Enrollment," *Albuquerque Journal* (21 August 1999).
Banks, Ron. "Bullying in Schools," *ERIC Digest* (April 1997). Available: ERIC Web site, U.S. Department of Education, [Internet, WWW], Address: *http://www.ed.gov/databases/ERIC_Digests/ed407154.html.*
Barone, Frank J. "Bullying in School: It Doesn't Have to Happen," *Phi Delta Kappan* (September 1997): 93–96.
Baughman, Fred A. "The Rise and Fall of ADD/ADHD" (19 October 2000). Available: [Internet, WWW], Address: *http://sightings.com/general4/add.htm.*
Beamish, Claude R. "A Brief Look at the Children of the Four Major Groups," The MindLift Foundation Web site. Available: [Internet, WWW], Address: *http://www.mindlift.com/4cmajorgrps.htm.*
———. "Knowledge About the Brain for Parents, Students, and Teachers: The Keys to Removing the Invisible Roadblocks to Learning and High Self-Esteem for All Students." Conference paper, *The Oregon Conference Monograph.* vol. 7 (1995).
———. "Reality, Changing Realities, and the Causes of Realities," The MindLift Foundation Web site. Available: [Internet, WWW], Address: *http://www.mindlift.com/reality.htm.*
Bean, Reynold. *How to Help Your Children Succeed in School.* Los Angeles: Price Stern Sloan, 1991.
Beane, Allan L. *The Bully-Free Classroom.* Minneapolis: Free Spirit Publishing, 1999.
Begley, Sharon. "Why the Young Kill," *Newsweek* (3 May 1999): 32–35.
Bell, Maya, "Alone, Confused and Armed," *Albuquerque Journal* (28 November 1999).
Bellanca, James. "Teaching for Intelligence: In Search of Best Practices," *Phi Delta Kappan,* vol. 79, no. 9 (May 1998): 658–60.
Benard, Bonnie. "Fostering Resilience in Children," *ERIC Digest* (August 1995). Available: ERIC Web site, U.S. Department of Education, [Internet, WWW], Address: *http://www.ed.gov/databases/ERIC_Digests/ed386327.html.*
Benson, Peter L., Judy Galbraith and Pamela Espeland. *What Teens Need to Succeed.* Minneapolis: Free Spirit Publishing, 1998.
Besag, Valerie E. *We Don't Have Bullies Here,* handbook for schools. Newcastle upon Tyne, England: Valerie E. Besag, 1992.
Blacklock, Neil. "Fear Cripples," from "Facts and Arguments," *Globe and Mail* (18 August 1997). Available: PTAVE Web site, [Internet, WWW], Address: *http://nospank.org/blklock.htm.*
Blair, Frank E. "Does Zero Tolerance Work?" *Principal,* vol. 79, no. 1 (September 1999): 36–37.
Bloom, Benjamin S., ed. *Taxonomy of Educational Objectives, Handbook I: The Cognitive Domain.* New York: Longman, 1956.
Bluestein, Jane. *21st Century Discipline: Teaching Students Responsibility and Self-Control.* Torrance, Calif.: Fearon Teaching Aids, Frank Schaffer Publications, 1999.
———. *Being a Successful Teacher.* Torrance, Calif.: Fearon Teaching Aids (Frank Schaffer Publications), 1989.
———. *Developing Responsible Learning Behaviors Through Peer Interaction.* Unpublished doctoral dissertation, University of Pittsburgh, 1980.
———. *Mentors, Masters and Mrs. MacGregor: Stories of Teachers Making a Difference.* Deerfield Beach, Fla.: Health Communications, Inc., 1995.
———. *Parents, Teens and Boundaries: How to Draw the Line.* Deerfield Beach, Fla.: Health Communications, Inc., 1993.
Borba, Michele. *Building Moral Intelligence: The Seven Essential Virtues That Teach Kids to Do the Right Thing.* San Francisco: Jossey-Bass, 2001.
———. *Esteem Builders.* Torrance, Calif.: Jalmar Press, 1989.
Bower, Gordon H. "How Might Emotions Affect Learning?" *The Handbook of Emotion and Memory: Research and Theory.* Sven-Ake Christianson, ed. Hillsdale, N.J.: Lawrence Erlbaum Associates Publishers, 1992.

Bradshaw, John. *Healing the Shame that Binds You.* Deerfield Beach, Fla.: Health Communications, Inc., 1988.
Branden, Nathaniel. "Answering Misconceptions about Self-Esteem," *Self-Esteem Today,* vol. 10, no. 2 (Spring 1998). Available National Association for Self-Esteem Web site, [Internet, WWW], Address: *http://www.self-esteem-nase.org/journal01.shtml.*
———. *The Six Pillars of Self-Esteem.* New York: Bantam Books, 1994.
Breggin, Peter. "On the Impact of Psychoactive Drugs on Children," transcript of testimony presented before the Subcommittee on Oversight and Investigations, Committee on Education and the Workforce. Available: Sightings Web site, [Internet, WWW], Address: *http://sightings.com/general4/addpsy.htm.*
Brooks, Martin G. and Jacqueline Grennon Brooks. "The Courage to be Constructivist," *Educational Leadership,* vol. 57, no. 3 (November 1999): 18–24.
Brown, Les. *Live Your Dreams.* New York: Avon Books, 1992.
Brownlee, Shannon. "The Biology of Soul Murder," *U.S. News & World Report,* 11 November 1996. Available: PTAVE Web site, [Internet, WWW], Address: *http://nospank.org/11trau.htm.*
———. "Inside the Teen Brain," *U.S. News and World Report,* vol. 127, no. 6 (9 August 1999): 44–54.
Brumberg, Joan Jacobs. *The Body Project.* New York: Random House, 1997.
Burgess, Ron. *Laughing Lessons: 149 1/2 Ways to Make Teaching and Learning Fun.* Minneapolis: Free Spirit Publishing, 2000.
Burke, Kay. *The Mindful School: How to Assess Authentic Learning,* revised edition. Arlington Heights: IRI/SkyLight Training and Publishing, Inc., 1994.
Burnett, Gary and Gary Walz. "Gangs in the Schools," *ERIC Digest,* no. 99 (July 1994). Available: ERIC Web site, U.S. Department of Education, [Internet, WWW], Address: *http://www.ed.gov/databases/ERIC_Digests/ed372175.html.*
Burns, E. Timothy. *From Risk to Resilience.* Dallas: Marco Polo Publishers, 1996.
Butler, Ruth and Mordecai Nisan. "Effects of No Feedback, Task-Related Comments, and Grades on Intrinsic Motivation and Performance," *Journal of Educational Psychology,* vol. 78, no. 3 (1986): 210–216.
Butterfield, Robin A. "Blueprints for Indian Education: Improving Mainstream Schooling," *ERIC Digest* (June 1994). Available: ERIC Web site, U.S. Department of Education, [Internet, WWW], Address: *http://www.ed.gov/databases/ERIC_Digests/ed3278989.html.*
Carter, Rita. *Mapping the Mind.* Berkeley, Calif.: The University of California Press, 1998.
Cherry, Clare, Douglas Godwin, and Jesse Staples. *Is the Left Brain Always Right?* Torrance, Calif.: Fearon Teacher Aids, 1989.
Christian, Nichole, with reporting by Maggie Sieger. "Is Smaller Perhaps Better?" *Time* magazine, vol. 153, no. 21 (31 May 1999): 43.
Chua-Eoan, Howard. "Escaping from the Darkness," *Time* magazine, vol. 153, no. 21 (31 May 1999): 44–49
Ciaccio, Joseph. "A Teacher's Chance for Immortality," *Schools in the Middle,* vol. 8, no. 2 (October 1998): 24–28.
Clark, Jean Illsley. *Time-In: When Time-Out Doesn't Work.* Seattle: Parenting Press, Inc., 1999.
Cohen, Elizabeth G. "Making Cooperative Learning Equitable," *Educational Leadership,* vol. 56, no. 1 (September 1998). Available: Association for Supervision and Curriculum Development Web site, [Internet, WWW], Address: *http://www.ascd.org/safeschools/el9809/cohencoop.html.*
Cohen, Philip. "The Content of Their Character: Educators Find New Ways to Tackle Values and Morality," *Curriculum Update* (Spring 1995). Available: Association for Curriculum and Supervision Development Web site, [Internet, WWW], Address: *http://www.ascd.org/pubs/cu/spring95.html.*
Combs, Arthur W. "Humanistic Education: Too Tender for a Tough World?" *Phi Delta Kappan,* vol. 62, no. 6 (February 1981): 446–48.

Cornell, Dewey G. and Ann B. Loper. "New Studies of Attitudes and Behaviors and School Violence" (9 August 1996). Available: American Psychological Association Web site, [Internet, WWW], Address: *http://www.apa.org/releases/schlviol.html.*

Cowan, David. *Taking Charge of Organizational Conflict.* Spring Valley, Calif.: Innerchoice Publishing, 1995.

Cummings, Rhoda and Gary Fisher. *The School Survival Guide for Kids with LD.* Minneapolis: Free Spirit Publishing, 1991.

Dean, Carolyn. "Sweet Conspiracy," *Natural Health* (January/February 2001): 70–76.

de Andrés, Verónica Martínez. "Developing Self-Esteem in the Primary School: A Pilot Study," Intervention study submitted as part of graduate study, Oxford Brookes University, Oxford, U.K., 1996.

DeBeaufort, Elaine, with Aura Sofia Diaz. *The Three Faces of Mind.* Wheaton, Ill.: Quest Books, 1996.

Dennison, Paul E. and Gail E. Dennison. *Brain Gym,* teacher's edition, revised. Ventura, Calif.: Edu-Kinesthetics, Inc., 1994.

DeRoche, Edward F. "Creating a Framework for Character Education," *Principal,* vol. 79, no. 3 (January 2000): 32–34.

DeRosa, Patti. "Guidelines for Challenging Racism and Other Forms of Oppression" (24 July 1996). Available: Ben and Jerry's Online, Address: *http://euphoria.benjerry.com/esr/challenge.html.*

Dizon, Nicole Ziegler. "Schools Struggle Over How to Protect Gay Students," *Albuquerque Journal* (8 October 2000).

Donovan, Bernadette and Rose Marie Iovino. "A Multiple Intelligences Approach to Expanding and Celebrating Teacher Portfolios and Student Portfolios." Paper presented at the annual meeting of the Northeastern Educational Research Association, October 1997.

Doud, Guy. "From Hero to Zero." Available: The Life Story Foundation Web site, [Internet, WWW], Address: *http://www.lifestory.org/doud1.html; /doud2.html; /doud3.html.*

Doyle, Walter. "Classroom Management Techniques and Student Discipline." Paper prepared for the Student Discipline Strategies Project, sponsored by the Education and Social Division of the Office of Research, OERI, U.S. Department of Education, December 1986.

Drew, Naomi. *The Peaceful Classroom in Action.* Torrance, Calif.: Jalmar Press, 1999.

Dryden, Gordon, and Jeannette Vos. *The Learning Revolution.* Rolling Hills Estates, Calif.: Jalmar Press, 1994.

Dunn, Kenneth and Rita Dunn. *The Educator's Self-Teaching Guide to Individualizing Instructional Programs.* Englewood Cliffs, N.J.: Parker Publishing Co., 1975.

Duttwiler, Patricia Cloud. "Gay and Lesbian Youth at Risk," *The Journal of At-Risk Issues,* vol. 3, no. 2 (winter/spring 1997). Available: National Dropout Prevention Center Web site, [Internet, WWW], Address: *http://www.dropoutprevention.org/2levelpages/statistics/WhosAtRisk/5lvlstatswhogaylesb.htm.*

Duvall, Lynn. *Respecting Our Differences.* Minneapolis: Free Spirit Publishing, 1994.

Dwyer, K., D. Osher and C. Wagner. "Early Warning, Timely Response: A Guide to Safe Schools," Washington, D.C.: U.S. Department of Education, 1998.

Ediger, Marlow. "Caring and the Elementary Curriculum." Report, Truman State University, Kirksville, Mo., 1998.

Eisner, Elliot W. "What Really Counts in Schools," *Educational Leadership,* vol. 48, no. 5 (February 1991): 10–17.

Elkind, David. *Reinventing Childhood.* Rosemont, N.J.: Modern Learning Press, Inc., 1998.

England, Joan T. "Pluralism and Education: Its Meaning and Method," *ERIC Digest* (December 1992). Available: ERIC Web site, U.S. Department of Education, [Internet, WWW], Address: *http://www.ed.gov/databases/ERIC_Digests/ed347494.html.*

Escamilla, Kathy. "Integrating Mexican-American History and Culture into the Social Studies Classroom," *ERIC Digest* (September 1992). Available: ERIC Web site, U.S. Department of Education, [Internet, WWW], Address: *http://www.ed.gov/databases/ERIC_Digests/ed348200.html.*

Etzioni, Amitai. "Balancing Individual Rights and the Common Good," *Tikkun* magazine, (January-February 1997). Available: Tikkun Web site, [Internet, WWW], Address: *http://www.tikkun.org/9701/etzioni.html.*

———. *Pillars of Character Education* (1998). Available: *Christian Science Monitor* Web site, [Internet, WWW], Address: *http://www.csmonitor.com/durable/1998/05/26/p1951.htm.*

Ewing, Zach. "Not Everyone Who Is a Jock Is a 'Jock,'" *Albuquerque Journal* (2 November 1999).

Fassler, David G. and Lynne S. Dumas. *"Help Me, I'm Sad."* New York: Viking, 1997.

Faulkner, Bobbie, and Patricia Faiveley. "Multi-Age from the Ground Up," in *Multi-Age Classrooms,* Karen Gutloff, ed. Washington, D.C.: NEA Teacher-to-Teacher Books, National Education Association, 1995.

Finley, Mary. "Cultivating Resilience: An Overview for Rural Educators and Parents," *ERIC Digest* (1994). Available: ERIC Web site, U.S. Department of Education, [Internet, WWW], Address: *http://www.ed.gov/databases/ERIC_Digests/ed372904.html.*

Flach, Frederic. *Resilience: Discovering a New Strength at Times of Stress.* New York: Fawcett Columbine, 1988.

Fox, C. Lynn and Shirley E. Forbing. *Creating Drug-Free Schools and Communities: A Comprehensive Approach.* New York: HarperCollins Publishers, 1992.

Fraser, Ken. *Values in the Workplace,* course manual, National Agency for Self-Esteem & Responsibility. Kingston, ACT, Australia: Work Resources Centre, Inc.

Freedman, Joshua M., Anabel L. Jensen, Marsha C. Rideout and Patricia E. Freedman. *Handle with Care: Emotional Intelligence Activity Book.* San Mateo, Calif.: Six Seconds, 1998.

Freeman, Cecilia K. and Joyce B. Sherwood. "Brain Gym and Its Effect on Reading Ability: A Report on the Brain Gym Reading Pilot Project at the Saticoy Elementary School, Ventura, California, School Year 1998–99." Unpublished paper, February 2000.

Freiberg, H. Jerome. "Measuring School Climate: Let Me Count the Ways," *Educational Leadership,* vol. 56, no. 1 (September 1998). Available: Association for Supervision and Curriculum Development Web site, [Internet, WWW], Address: *http://www.ascd.org/safeschools/el9809/freibergclimate.html.*

Frey, Karin. "Social-Emotional Learning: A Foundation for Academic Success," *Committee for Children Prevention Update* (spring 1999): 1–3.

Froschl, Merle and Nancy Gropper. "Fostering Friendships, Curbing Bullying," *Educational Leadership,* vol. 56, no. 8 (May 1999): 72–75.

Fu, Victoria R. "Culture, Schooling and Education in a Democracy." Available: ERIC/EECE Web site, [Internet, WWW], Address: *http://ericeece.org/pubs/books/multicul/fu.html.*

Gardner, Howard. *Frames of Mind: The Theory of Multiple Intelligences.* New York: Basic Books, 1983.

Garfield, Charles. *Peak Performers.* New York: William Morrow & Co., Inc., 1986.

Garrity, Carla B., Kathryn Jens and William W. Porter. "Bully Proofing Your School: Creating a Positive Climate" (July 1999). Availability, First Search Web site, [Internet, WWW], Address: *http://firstsearch.oclc.org.* Note: This article was sent to me by a friend who found it on a firstsearch library system. I do not have a more complete address nor do I know the original source of the article, though I do have a full text copy.

Gartner, Audrey and Frank Riessman. "Peer-Tutoring: Toward a New Model," *ERIC Digest* (August 1993). Available: ERIC Web site, U.S. Department of Education, [Internet, WWW], Address: *http://www.ed.gov/databases/ERIC_Digests/ed362506.html.*

Gaustad, Joan. "Schools Attack the Roots of Violence," *ERIC Digest,* no. 63 (October 1991). Available: ERIC Web site, U.S. Department of Education, [Internet, WWW], Address: *http://www.ed.gov/databases/ERIC_Digests/ed335806.html.*

Gazzaniga, Michael S. *Mind Matters.* Boston: Houghton Mifflin Co., 1988.

———. *The Social Brain: Discovering the Networks of the Mind.* New York: Basic Books, 1985.

Geocaris, Claudia and Maria Ross. "A Test Worth Taking," *Educational Leadership,* vol. 57, no. 1 (September 1999): 29–33.

Gerber, Matt and Kim Jones. "Kids Keeping the Peace: Resolving Conflict on the Playground" (24 July 1996). Available: Ben and Jerry's Online, Address: *http://euphoria.benjerry.com/esr/playgrd.html.*

Gibbs, Nancy. "A Week in the Life of a High School," *Time* magazine, vol. 154, no. 17 (25 October 1999): 66–115.

———. "Introduction: Time Special Report on Troubled Kids," *Time* magazine, vol. 153, no. 21 (31 May 1999): 33.

Gibson, Janice T. *Living: Human Development Through the Lifespan.* Reading, Mass.: Addison-Wesley Publishing Co., 1983.

Girard, Kathryn L. "Preparing Teachers for Conflict Resolution in the Schools," *ERIC Digest* (1995). Available: ERIC Web site, U.S. Department of Education, [Internet, WWW], Address: *http://www.ed.gov/databases/ERIC_Digests/ed387456.html.*

Glasser, William. *Schools Without Failure.* New York: Perennial Library, 1975.

Glenn, H. Stephen and Michael L. Brock. *Seven Strategies for Developing Capable Students.* Rocklin, Calif.: Prima Publishing, 1998.

Goleman, Daniel. "A Key to Post-Traumatic Stress Lies in Brain Chemistry, Scientists Find," *The New York Times* (12 June 1990).

———. *Emotional Intelligence.* New York: Bantam Books, 1995.

———. "New Ways to Battle Bias: Fight Acts, Not Feelings," *The New York Times* (16 July 1991).

Goodlad, John I. *A Place Called School.* New York: McGraw-Hill Book Company, 1984.

Goodnough, Abby. "Sensing Higher Calling in the Classroom" (Aug. 1, 2000). Available: *New York Times* Web site, [Internet, WWW], Address: *http://partners.nytimes.com/library/national/regional/080100ny-teach-edu.html.*

Gordon, Thomas. "How Children *Really* React to Control," *Discipline That Works: Promoting Self-Discipline in Children.* New York: Plume/Penguin, 1989, 78–81. Available: PTAVE Web site, [Internet, WWW], Address: *http://nospank.org/gordon.htm.*

———. *Leadership Effectiveness Training.* Toronto: Bantam Books, 1977.

Grant, Jim. *I Hate School.* Rosemont, N.J.: Modern Learning Press, 1986.

Greene, Leon. "Beyond Violence," *Principal,* vol. 79, no. 1 (September 1999): 4.

Greenhouse, Steven. "Autumn of Teachers' Discontent Is Dawning" (20 September 2000). Available: *New York Times* Web site, [Internet, WWW], Address: *http://partners.nytimes.com/2000/09/20/national/20TEAC.html.*

Greenspan, Stanley I., with Jacqueline Salmon. *The Challenging Child: Understanding, Raising and Enjoying the Five "Difficult" Types of Children.* Reading, Mass.: Addison-Wesley Publishing Co., 1995.

Greenspan, Stanley I., with Beryl Lieff Benderly. *The Growth of the Mind.* Reading, Mass.: Addison-Wesley Publishing Co., Inc., 1997.

Gregorc, Anthony. "Frequently Asked Questions on Style." Available: Gregorc Associates, Inc. Web site, [Internet, WWW], Address: *http://www.gregorc.com/faq.html.*

Griggs, Shirley A. "Learning Styles Counseling," *ERIC Digest* (December 1991). Available: ERIC Web site, U.S. Department of Education, [Internet, WWW], Address: *http://www.ed.gov/databases/ERIC_Digests/ed341890.html.*

Guild, Pat Burke and Sandy Chock-Eng. "Multiple Intelligence, Learning Styles, Brain-Based Education: Where Do the Messages Overlap?" *Schools in the Middle,* vol. 7, no. 4 (March/April 1998): 38–40.

Hafen, Brent Q. and Kathryn J. Frandsen. *Youth Suicide: Depression and Loneliness.* Evergreen, Colo.: Cordillera Press, Inc., 1986.

Hagstrom, David. "Seeking Clarity About Crisis," *Educational Leadership,* vol. 56, no. 4 (December 1998/January 1999): 53–57.

Halford, Joan Montgomery. "Longing for the Sacred in Schools: A Conversation with Nel Noddings," *Educational Leadership,* vol. 56, no. 4 (December 1998/January 1999): 28–32.

Haney, Walter and George Madaus. "Searching for Alternatives to Standardized Tests: Whys, Whats and Whithers," *Phi Delta Kappan,* vol. 70, no. 9 (May 1989): 683–87.

Hannaford, Carla. *The Dominance Factor.* Arlington, Va.: Great Oceans Publishers, 1997.
———. *Smart Moves: Why Learning Is Not All in Your Head.* Arlington, Va.: Great Oceans Publishers, 1995.
Hansen, J. Merrell and John Childs. "Creating a School Where People Like to Be," *Educational Leadership,* vol. 56, no. 1 (September 1998). Available: Association for Supervision and Curriculum Development Web site, [Internet, WWW], Address: *http://www.ascd.org/safeschools/el9809/selhansen.html.*
Hawley, Jack. *Reawakening the Spirit at Work.* New York: Simon & Schuster, 1993.
Haynes, Charles C. "Averting Culture Wars over Religion," *Educational Leadership,* vol. 56, no. 4 (December 1998/January 1999): 24–27.
Heacox, Diane. *Up from Underachievement.* Minneapolis: Free Spirit Publishing, 1991.
Henry, Tamara. "New Teachers Are Passionate but Unprepared," *USA Today* (24 May 2000).
Hersey, Jane. *Why Can't My Child Behave?* Alexandria, Va.: Pear Tree Press, Inc., 1999.
Hickman, Craig R. and Michael A. Silva. *Creating Excellence.* New York: New American Library, 1984.
Hoerr, Tom. "Reporting What We Respect," *Classroom Leadership,* an ASCD Newsletter for K-12 Classroom Teachers, vol. 3, no. 5 (February 2000): 2–3.
Holt, John. *How Children Learn.* New York: Dell Books, 1967.
Hoover, John R. and Ronald Oliver. *The Bullying Prevention Handbook: A Guide for Parents, Teachers and Counselors.* Bloomington, In.: National Education Service, 1996.
Huitt, William. "Moral and Character Development." Available: [Internet, WWW], Address: *http://chiron.valdosta.edu/whuitt/col/morchr/morchr.html.*
Hunt, Morton. *The Story of Psychology.* New York: Doubleday Dell Publishing Group, Inc., 1993.
Irmsher, Karen. "Education Reform and Students at Risk," *ERIC Digest,* no. 112 (April 1997). Available: ERIC Web site, U.S. Department of Education, [Internet, WWW], Address: *http://www.ed.gov/databases/ERIC_Digests/ed405642.html.*
Jacobson, Michael F. and David Schardt. *Diet, ADHD and Behavior: A Quarter-Century Review.* Washington, D.C.: Center for Science in the Public Interest, 1999.
Jensen, Anabel. "Building a Role Model," *EQ Today* (21 April 1999). Available: 6seconds Web site, [Internet, WWW], Address: *http://www.6seconds.org/jrn/jpcw98.html.*
Jensen, Eric. *Brain-Based Learning.* Del Mar, Calif.: Turning Point Publishing, 1996.
———. *Completing the Puzzle.* Del Mar, Calif.: The Brain Store, Inc., 1997.
Jesse, Dan. "Increasing Parental Involvement," *Schools in the Middle,* vol. 7, no. 1 (September/October 1997).
Johnson, Kendall. *Trauma in the Lives of Children.* Alameda, Calif.: Hunter House Publishers, 1998.
Jones, Eric. "Practical Considerations in Dealing with Bullying in Secondary School," *Bullying: A Practical Guide to Coping for Schools,* 2d ed., Michele Elliott, ed. London: Pitman Publishing, 1997.
Joyce, Bruce, and Marsha Weil. *Models of Teaching,* 2d ed. Englewood Cliffs, N.J.: Prentice-Hall, Inc., 1980.
Kantrowitz, Barbara and Pat Wingert. "Teachers Wanted," *Newsweek* (2 October 2000): 37–42.
Kantrowitz, Barbara and Daniel McGinn. "When Teachers Are Cheaters," the MSNBC Web site, 11 June 2000. Available: [Internet, WWW], Address: *http://www.newsweek.com/news/419167.asp?cp1=1.*
Karp, Hal. "Who's Going to School with Your Kids?" *Reader's Digest* (March 2000): 76–83.
Karr-Morse, Robin, and Meredith S. Wiley. *Ghosts in the Nursery.* New York: The Atlantic Monthly Press, 1997.
Karres, Erika V. Shearin. *Violence Proof Your Kids Now: How to Recognize the Eight Signs and What to Do About Them.* Berkeley, Calif.: Conari Press, 2000.
Katz, Lilian G. "Self-Esteem and Narcissism: Implications for Practice," *ERIC Digest* (1993). Excerpted from a paper entitled "Distinctions between Self-Esteem and

Narcissism: Implications for Practice." Available: ERIC Web site, U.S. Department of Education, [Internet, WWW], Address: *http://www.ed.gov/databases/ERIC_Digests/ed358973.html.*

Kaufman, Phillip, Steve Klein and Mary Frase. "Dropout Rates in the United States: 1997," National Center for Education Statistics, U.S. Department of Education Office of Educational Research and Improvement. Available: National Dropout Prevention Center Web site, [Internet, WWW], Address: *http://www.dropoutprevention.org.*

Keefe, James W. and Barbara Ferrell. "Developing a Defensible Learning Style Paradigm," *Educational Leadership* (October 1990): 57–61.

Keirsey, David. *Please Understand Me II: Temperament, Character, Intelligence.* Del Mar, Calif.: Prometheus Nemesis Book Co., 1998.

Keller, Rudi. "Some Dropouts Claim Schools Pushed Them," *Albuquerque Journal* (29 April 2000).

Kelly, Laura. "Schools as Communities: Communication, Collaboration and Caring," *ASCD Curriculum Update* (Fall 1999).

Kempermann, Gerd, and Fred H. Gage. "New Nerve Cells for the Adult Brain," *Scientific American* (May 1999): 48–53.

Kessler, Rachel. "Nourishing Students in Secular Schools," *Educational Leadership,* vol. 56, no. 4 (December 1998/January 1999): 49–52.

Kidder, Rushworth M. and Patricia L. Born. "Resolving Ethical Dilemmas in the Classroom," *Educational Leadership,* vol. 56, no. 4 (December 1998/January 1999): 38–41.

King, Livia. "Metal Fans Experience Discrimination, Mistrust," *Albuquerque Journal* (2 November 1999).

Kirn, Walter. "The Danger of Suppressing Sadness," *Time* magazine, vol. 153, no. 21 (31 May 1999): 48–49.

Klonsky, Susan and Michael Klonsky. "Countering Anonymity Through Small Schools," *Educational Leadership,* vol. 57, no. 1 (September 1999): 38–41.

Kozol, Jonathan. *Savage Inequalities.* New York: HarperPerennial, 1991.

Kranowitz, Carol Stock. *The Out-of-Sync Child.* New York: The Berkley Publishing Group, 1998.

Krathwohl, David R., Benjamin S. Bloom and Bertram B. Masia. *Taxonomy of Educational Objectives, Handbook II: The Affective Domain.* New York: David McKay Co., Inc., 1964.

Krynock, Karoline and Louise Robb. "Problem Solved: How to Coach Cognition," *Educational Leadership,* vol. 57, no. 3 (November 1999): 29–32.

Krystal, Sandra. "The Nurturing Potential of Service Learning," *Educational Leadership,* vol. 56, no. 4 (December 1998/January 1999): 58–61.

Lantieri, Linda, and Janet Patti. *Waging Peace in Our Schools.* Boston: Beacon Press, 1996.

Lashway, Larry. "Accountability," *Research Roundup,* published by the National Association of Elementary School Principals, vol. 16, no. 1 (Fall 1999).

Lederhouse, Jillian N. "You Will Be Safe Here," *Educational Leadership,* vol. 56, no. 1 (September 1998). Available: Association for Supervision and Curriculum Development Web site, [Internet, WWW], Address: *http://www.ascd.org/safeschools/el9809/sellederhouse.html.*

LeDoux, Joseph. *The Emotional Brain.* New York: Simon & Schuster, 1996.

Lemonick, Michael. "Fast-Track Toddlers," *Time* magazine, vol. 154, no. 7 (16 August 1999): 76–77.

Leo, John. "'Zero Tolerance' Policies Distort Discipline of Schools," *Albuquerque Journal* (10 December 1999).

Levine, Janet. "The Enneagram System: Understand Yourself to Understand Your Students." Available: Enneagram-Edge Web site, [Internet, WWW], Address: *http://www.enneagram-edge.com/journal.html.*

Levine, Mel. "Misunderstood Minds." Available: All Kinds of Minds Web site, [Internet, WWW], Address: *http://www.allkindsofminds.org/library/articles/MuMinds.htm.*

Lewis, Barbara A. *The Kid's Guide to Service Projects.* Minneapolis: Free Spirit Publishing, 1995.

Lewis, Byron and Frank Pucelik. *Magic of NLP Demystified.* Portland, Ore.: Metamorphous Press, 1993.

Lickona, Thomas. "Educating for Character: A 12-Point Comprehensive Approach" (no date). Available: Center for the Fourth and Fifth Rs, State University of NY College at Cortland Web site, [Internet, WWW], Address: *http://cortland.edu/www/c4n5rs/descr_iv.htm.*

———. "Raising Moral Children," excerpt from *Raising Good Children* (New York: Bantam Books, 1983). Available: Salem-Keizer Public Schools Web site, [Internet, WWW], Address: *http://ssc.salkeiz.k12.or.us/counsel/parentlibrary/respect/moral.htm.*

Liebig, James E. *The Merchants of Vision.* San Francisco: Berrett-Koehler Publishers, 1994.

Littky, Dennis and Farrell Allen. "Whole Student Personalization, One Student at a Time," *Educational Leadership,* vol. 57, no. 1 (September 1999): 24–28.

López, Connie. "Dozing Off: Overbooked Teens Too Busy, Stressed to Get Enough Sleep," *Albuquerque Journal* (26 December 2000).

Loveless, Tom. "Will Tracking Reform Promote Social Equity?" *Educational Leadership,* vol. 56, no. 7 (April 1999): 28–32.

Lozano, Juan A. "Wanted: Recipe for a Better School Teacher," *Albuquerque Journal,* 27 June 1999.

Lumsden, Linda. "Teacher Morale," *ERIC Digest,* no. 120 (1998). Available: ERIC Web site, US Department of Education, [Internet, WWW], Address: *http://www.ed.gov/databases/ERIC_Digests/ed422601.html.*

Mainzer, K. Lynne, Patricia Baltzley and Kathleen Heslin. "Everybody Can Be Great Because Everybody Can Serve," *Educational Leadership,* vol. 48, no. 3 (November 1990): 94–96.

Markova, Dawna. *The Open Mind: Exploring the Six Patterns of Natural Intelligence.* Berkeley, Calif.: Conari Press, 1996.

Marston, Stephanie. *The Magic of Encouragement: Nurturing Your Child's Self-Esteem.* New York: Pocket Books, 1990.

Marx, Eva. "Health and Learning: A Coordinated Approach," *Principal,* vol. 79, no. 1 (September 1999): 6–9.

Maslow, Abraham. *Toward a Psychology of Being.* New York: D. Van Nostrand Co., 1968.

McCluskey, Alan. "Emotional Intelligence in Schools," 28 February 1997. Available: Connected Web site [Internet, WWW], Address: *http://www.connected.org/learn/school.html.*

McConnaughey, Janet. "Growth of Dead Brain Cells Excites Scientists," *Albuquerque Journal* (6 November 2000).

McCown, Karen Stone, Anabel L. Jensen, Joshua M. Freedman and Marsha C. Rideout. *Self Science: The Emotional Intelligence Curriculum.* San Mateo, Calif.: Six Seconds Publishing, 1998.

McDonald, Irene M. "Expanding the Lens: Student Perceptions of School Violence," in *Systemic Violence: How Schools Hurt Children,* Epp, Juanita Ross and Ailsa M. Watkinson, eds. London: Falmer Press, 1996.

McGinn, Daniel. "The Big Score," *Newsweek* (6 September 1999): 47–51.

McGinnis, Alan Loy. *Bringing Out the Best in People.* Minneapolis: Augsburg Publishing House, 1985.

McKenzie, Ginger Kelley. "Multiple Intelligences Put into Practice," *The National Montessori Reporter 99,* vol. XXIII, no. 3 (fall 1999): 3–5.

McLaughlin, Catherine Kellison. *The Do's and Don'ts of Parent Involvement: How to Build a Positive School-Home Partnership.* Torrance, Calif.: Innerchoice Publishing, 1993.

McQueen, Anjetta. "The Fight to Find, Keep Teachers," *Albuquerque Journal* (4 July 2000).

———. "School Violence Stereotypes Spurring Student Crackdown," *Albuquerque Journal* (12 April 2000).

Miller, Alice. *For Your Own Good: Hidden Cruelty in Child-Rearing and the Roots of Violence.* New York: Farrar, Straus & Giroux, 1984.

Miller, John (Jack) P. "Making Connections through Holistic Learning," *Educational Leadership,* vol. 56, no. 4 (December 1998/January 1999): 46–48.
Million, June. "Creative PR Could Keep You Out of Court," *Communicator,* Newsletter of the National Association of Elementary School Principals, vol. 23, no. 3 (November 1999): 5–7.
———. "A Win-Win Situation—Teaming Up with Your High School," *Communicator,* Newsletter of the National Association of Elementary School Principals. vol. 23, no. 4 (December 1999): 5–7.
Mizell, Hayes. "Choosing a Path: Making School Equity at the Middle Level a Reality," *Schools in the Middle,* vol. 8, no. 6 (April 1999): 18–20.
Mohai, Caroline E. "Peer Leaders in Drug Abuse Prevention," *ERIC Digest* (December 1991). Available: ERIC Web site, U.S. Department of Education, [Internet, WWW], Address: *http://www.ed.gov/databases/ERIC_Digests/ed341892.html.*
Monaghan, J. H., J. O. Robinson and J. A. Dodge. "The Children's Life Events Inventory," *Journal of Psychosomatic Research,* vol. 23, no. 1 (1979): 63–68.
Murphy, Brian. "Back to School Around the World: The Three R's vs. Poverty, Disease, Violence and More," Associated Press release appearing on AOL's "Life" News (5 September 2000). Available: [Internet, WWW], Closest address: *http://www.aol.com.*
Murray, Mary Elizabeth. "Moral Development and Moral Education: An Overview." Available: University of Illinois at Chicago Web site, [Internet, WWW], Address: *http://www.uic.edu/~Inucci/MoralEd/overview.html.*
Nagourney, Eric. "Vital Signs: Behavior: Stopping School Trouble Before It Starts" (14 November 2000). Available: *The New York Times* Web site, [Internet, WWW], Address: *http:// partners.nytimes.com/2000/11/14/science/14SCHO.html.*
Naisbitt, John. *Megatrends.* New York: Warner Books, 1982.
Nebgen, Mary K. and Kate McPherson. "Enriching Learning Through Service: A Tale of Three Districts," *Educational Leadership,* vol. 48, no. 3 (November 1990): 90–93.
Nechas, Eileen Nechas and Denise Foley. "Virtual Violence May Cause Real-Life Aggression," *Albuquerque Journal* (6 March 2001).
Nelsen, Jane. *Positive Discipline.* New York: Ballantine Books, 1987.
Nelson, Kristen. "Measuring the Intangibles," *Classroom Leadership,* an ASCD Newsletter for K-12 Classroom Teachers, vol. 3, no. 5 (February 2000): 1, 8.
Neville, Helen and Diane Clark Johnson. *Temperament Tools.* Seattle: Parenting Press, Inc., 1998.
Nunley, Kathie. "In Defense of the Oral Defense," *Classroom Leadership,* an ASCD Newsletter for K-12 Classroom Teachers, vol. 3, no. 5 (February 2000): 6.
Ohanian, Susan. "An Antisocial Idea" (6 March 2000). Available: *The Nation* Web site, [Internet, WWW], Address: *http://past.thenation.com/issue/000306/0306ohanian.shtml.*
———. "Silence Ain't Golden: Spread the Word" (26 September 2000). Available: Interversity Web site, [Internet, WWW], Address: *http://206.68.56.30/ events/resisting_conf/texts/Ohanian1000.php.*
Oládélé, Folásadé. "Passing Down the Spirit," *Educational Leadership,* vol. 56, no. 4 (December 1998/January 1999): 62–65.
Olweus, Dan. *Bullying at School.* Oxford, England: Blackwell Publishers, 1993.
O'Neill, John. "Building Schools as Communities: A Conservation with James Comer," *Educational Leadership,* vol. 54, no. 9 (May 1997): 6–10.
Osborn, D. Keith and Janie Dyson Osborn. *Discipline and Classroom Management.* Athens, Ga.: Education Associates, 1977.
Ostrander, Sheila, and Lynn Schroeder, with Nancy Ostrander. *Superlearning.* New York: Delacorte Press, 1979.
Owings, William A. and Susan Magliaro. "Grade Retention: A History of Failure," *Educational Leadership.* vol. 56, no. 1 (September 1998). Available: ASCD Web site, [Internet, WWW], Address: *http://www.ascd.org/pubs/el/sep98/owings.html.*
Palmer, Parker J. "Evoking the Spirit in Public Education," *Educational Leadership.* vol. 56, no. 4 (December 1998/January 1999): 6–11.

Perkins, David. "The Many Faces of Constructivism," *Educational Leadership,* vol. 57, no. 3 (November 1999): 6–11.
Perry, Bruce D. "Post-Traumatic Stress Disorders in Children and Adolescents," originally published in *Current Opinions in Pediatrics,* vol. 11, no. 4 (August 1999). Available: The Child Trauma Academy of Baylor College of Medicine Web site, [Internet, WWW], Address: *http://www.bcm.tmc.edu/civitas/PTSD_opin6.htm.*
Peters, Thomas J. and Robert H. Waterman Jr. *In Search of Excellence: Lessons from America's Best-Run Companies.* New York: Warner Books, 1982.
Peters, Tom. *Thriving on Chaos.* New York: Alfred A. Knopf, 1987.
Peterson, Kent D. and Terrence E. Deal. "How Leaders Influence the Culture of Schools," *Educational Leadership,* vol. 56, no. 1 (September 1998). Available: Association for Supervision and Curriculum Development Web site, [Internet, WWW], Address: *http://www.ascd.org/safeschools/el9809/petersoninfluence.html.*
Phillips, Vicki. *Empowering Discipline.* Carmel Valley, Calif.: Personal Development Publishing, 1998.
Piaget, Jean. *The Moral Judgment of the Child.* New York: Free Press Paperbacks (Simon & Schuster, Inc.), 1997.
Pickle, Paula. "Neurodevelopmental Therapy/Attachment Therapy: An Integrated Approach." Available: The Attachment Center at Evergreen, Inc. Web site, [Internet, WWW], Address: *http://www.attachmentcenter.org/neurodevelopmental.htm.*
Pipher, Mary. *Reviving Ophelia.* New York: Ballantine Books, 1994.
Pohan, Cathy A. and Norma J. Bailey. "Including Gays in Multiculturism," *The Education Digest* (January 1998): 52–56.
Pollack, Judy and Kimberly Hartman. "The ABCs of Middle Level Teacher Training," *Schools in the Middle,* vol. 8, no. 7 (May/June 1999). Available: [Internet, WWW], Address: *http://nassp.org/publications/schools_in_the_middle/pollack.htm.*
Popyk, Lisa. "Blood in the School Yard," *The Post* (7 November 1998). Available: The Cincinnati Post Web site, [Internet, WWW], Address: *http://www.cincypost.com/news/1kill110798.html.*
Promislow, Sharon. *Making the Brain Body Connection.* West Vancouver, Can.: Kinetic Publishing Corporation, 1999.
Prosser, J. "School Culture," *Research Matters,* The School Improvement Network's Bulletin, Institute of Education, University of London, no. 9 (autumn 1998).
Pulliam, John D. and James Van Patten. *History of Education in America,* 6th ed. Englewood Cliffs, N.J.: Prentice-Hall, Inc., 1995.
Purkey, William Watson. "Creating Safe Schools Through Invitational Education," *ERIC Clearinghouse on Counseling and Student Services* (1999).
Purkey, William Watson and David Strahan, "School Transformation Through Invitational Education," *Research in the Schools,* vol. 2, no. 2 (1995): 1–6.
Quarles, Chester L. *Staying Safe at School.* Thousand Oaks, Calif.: Corwin Press, Inc., 1993.
Racosky, Richard J. *dreams + action = Reality.* Boulder, Colo.: ActionGraphics Publishing, 1996.
Rardin, Sue. "Getting Tough on the Tough Teach," *Trust,* vol. 2, no. 4 (fall 1999): 12–17.
Recer, Paul. "Brain Regenerates Thinking Cells, Princeton Study Says," *Albuquerque Journal* (15 October 1999).
Redenbach, Sandi. *Autobiography of a Dropout: Dear Diary.* Davis, Calif.: Esteem Seminar Programs and Publications, 1996.
Reif, Sandra. *Reaching and Teaching Children with ADD/ADHD,* resource handbook to accompany training. Bellevue, Wash.: Bureau of Education and Research, 1999.
Remboldt, Carole. *Violence in Schools: The Enabling Factor.* Minneapolis: Johnson Institute-QVS, Inc., 1994.
Renchler, Ron. "Poverty and Learning," *ERIC Digest,* no. 83 (May 1993). Available: ERIC Web site, U.S. Department of Education, [Internet, WWW], Address: *http://www.ed.gov/databases/ERIC_Digests/ed357433.html.*

Rettig, Michael A. "Seven Steps to Schoolwide Safety," *Principal,* vol. 79, no. 1 (September 1999): 10–13.
Revelle, William, and Debra A. Loftus. "The Implications of Arousal Effects for the Study of Affect and Memory," *The Handbook of Emotion and Memory: Research and Theory.* Sven-Ake Christianson, ed. Hillsdale, N.J.: Lawrence Erlbaum Associates, Publishers, 1992.
Riak, Jordan. *Plain Talk About Spanking.* Alamo, Calif.: PTAVE (Parents and Teachers Against Violence in Education), 1996.
Ribas, William B. "Tips for Reaching Parents," *Educational Leadership,* vol. 56, no. 1, (September 1998). Available: Association of Supervision and Curriculum Development Web site, [Internet, WWW], Address: *http://www.ascd.org/pubs/el/sep98/ribas.html.*
Rogers, Carl R. *Client-Centered Therapy.* Boston: Houghton Mifflin Company, 1951.
Rogers, Carl, and H. Jerome Frieberg. *Freedom to Learn.* New York: Macmillan College Publishing Co., Inc., 1994.
Rogers, Spence. *Teaching Tips: 105 Ways to Increase Motivation and Learning.* Evergreen, Colo.: Peak Learning Systems, Inc., 1999.
Rogers, Spence and Lisa Renard. "Relationship-Driven Teaching," *Educational Leadership,* vol. 57, no. 1 (September 1999): 35–37.
Rogers, Wendy Stainton. "Promoting, Permitting and Preventing Bullying," *Bullying: A Practical Guide to Coping for Schools,* 2d ed., Michele Elliott, ed. London: Pitman Publishing, 1997.
Romain, Trevor. *Bullies Are a Pain in the Brain.* Minneapolis: Free Spirit Publishing, 1997.
Rothenberg, Dianne. "Supporting Girls in Early Adolescence," *ERIC Digest* (September 1995). Available: ERIC Web site, U.S. Department of Education, [Internet, WWW], Address: *http://www.ed.gov/databases/ERIC_Digests/ed386331.html.*
Sadker, David. "Gender Equity," *Educational Leadership,* vol. 56, no. 7 (April 1999): 22–26.
Satir, Virginia. *The New Peoplemaking.* Mountain View, Calif.: Science and Behavior Books, Inc., 1988.
Satir, Virginia, John Banmen, Jane Gerber and Maria Gomori. *The Satir Model: Family Therapy and Beyond.* Palo Alto, Calif.: Science and Behavior Books, Inc., 1991.
Schacter, Robert, and Carol Spearin McCauley. *When Your Child Is Afraid.* New York: Simon & Schuster, 1988.
Schaef, Anne Wilson. *When Society Becomes an Addict.* San Francisco: Harper & Row, Publishers, 1987.
Schaps, Eric and Daniel Solomon. "Schools and Classrooms as Caring Communities," *Educational Leadership,* vol. 48, no. 5 (February 1991): 38–42.
Shick, Lyndall. *Understanding Temperament: Strategies for Creating Family Harmony.* Seattle: Parenting Press, 1998.
Schilling, Diane, ed. *50 Activities for Teaching Emotional Intelligence, Level II: Middle School.* Torrance, Calif.: Innerchoice Publishing, 1996.
Schultz, Edward W., and Charles M. Heuchert. *Child Stress and the School Experience.* New York: Human Sciences Press, Inc., 1983.
Schwarz, Eitan D. and Bruce D. Perry. "The Post-Traumatic Response in Children and Adolescents," originally published in *Psychiatric Clinics of North America,* vol. 17, no. 2 (1994): 311–326. Available: The Child Trauma Academy of Baylor College of Medicine Web site, [Internet, WWW], Address: *http://www.bcm.tmc.edu/civitas/ptsdChildAdoles.htm.*
Selby, Mike. *Self Worth Now!* Sedona, Ariz.: Allisone Press, 2000.
Seligman, Martin E. P. *Learned Optimism.* New York: Alfred A. Knopf, 1991.
Senge, Peter M. *The Fifth Discipline: The Art and Practice of The Learning Organization.* New York: Doubleday, 1990.
Shakeshaft, Charol, Laurie Mandel, Yolanda M. Johnson, Janice Sawyer, Mary Ann Hergenrother and Ellen Barber. "Boys Call Me Cow," *Educational Leadership,* vol. 55, no. 2 (October 1997). Available: Association for Supervision and Curriculum

Development Web site, [Internet, WWW], Address: *http://www.ascd.org/safeschools/el9710/shakeshaftcow.html.*

Shapiro, Lawrence E. *How to Raise a Child with a High EQ.* New York: HarperCollins Publishers, Inc., 1997.

Sheldon, Carolyn. *EQ in School Counseling.* Torrance, Calif.: Innerchoice Publishing, 1996.

Shortt, Thomas T. and Yvonne V. Thayer. "Block Scheduling Can Enhance School Climate," *Educational Leadership,* vol. 56, no. 4 (December 1998/January 1999): 76–81.

Siccone, Frank and Lilia López. *Educating the Heart: Lessons to Build Respect and Responsibility.* Boston: Allyn and Bacon, 2000.

Siebert, Al. "How to Develop Survivor Resiliency," (1999). Available: Thrivenet Web site, [Internet, WWW], Address: *http://www.thrivenet.com/articles/excelnt.html.*

Siegfried, Tom. "Teen Behavior Linked to Brain," *Albuquerque Journal* (4 September 2000).

Silver, Harvey, Richard Strong and Matthew Perini. "Integrating Learning Styles and Multiple Intelligences," *Educational Leadership,* vol. 55, no. 1 (November 1997): 22–27.

Simpson, Elizabeth Leonie. "The Person in Community: The Need to Belong," *Feeling, Valuing, and the Art of Growing: Insights into the Affective,* Louise M. Berman and Jessie A. Roderick, eds. Washington, D.C.: Association for Supervision and Curriculum Development, 1977.

Sizer, Theodore. *Horace's Hope.* Boston: Houghton-Mifflin Co., 1996.

Skromme, Arnold B. *The Cause and Cure of Dropouts.* Moline, Ill.: The Self-Confidence Press, 1998.

Slavin, Robert E. "Cooperative Learning and Student Achievement," *Educational Leadership.* vol. 46, no. 2 (October 1988): 31–33.

Sousa, David A. *How the Brain Learns.* Reston, Va.: The National Association of Secondary School Principals, 1995.

Southworth, Natalie. "Experts Report Girls as Aggressive as Boys, but in Verbal Ways," *The Globe and Mail,* Toronto (23 October 1999).

Steinberg, John. "The Fourth Time They Say 'Yes,'" *Strategier,* no. 352 (1998). Available: John Steinberg's Web site, [Internet, WWW], Address: *http://www.steinberg.se/english.html#anchor245039.*

———. "A History of Affective Education," *EQ Today* (19 March 1999). Available: 6seconds Web site, [Internet, WWW], Address: *http://www.6seconds.org/jrn/jpca.html.*

Stephenson, Peter and David Smith. "Why Some Schools Don't Have Bullies," *Bullying: A Practical Guide to Coping for Schools,* 2d ed., Michele Elliott, ed. London: Pitman Publishing, 1997.

Sternberg, Robert J. "Allowing for Thinking Styles," *Educational Leadership,* vol. 52, no. 3 (November 1994): 36–40.

Stiger, Susan. "Fractured Lives: The Silent Victims of Family Violence," *Sage Magazine.* vol. XI, no. 4 (April 2000).

Stoll, Louise. "Enhancing Schools' Capacity for Learning." Paper presented at Innovations for Effective Schooling Conference, Auckland, New Zealand (August 1999).

Strauss, Susan with Pamela Espeland. *Sexual Harassment and Teens.* Minneapolis: Free Spirit Publishing, 1992.

Subby, Robert. *Lost in the Shuffle.* Deerfield Beach, Fla.: Health Communications, Inc., 1987.

Sugar, Debra. "Social Skills Instruction in Albuquerque Public Schools: An Intervention Proposal." Research paper submitted to New Mexico Highlands University School of Social Work, spring 1999.

Suhor, Charles. "Spirituality—Letting It Grow in the Classroom," *Educational Leadership,* vol. 56, no. 4 (December 1998/January 1999): 12–17.

Summar, Polly. "Troubled Students Hard to Identify, Counselors Say," *Albuquerque Journal* (24 January 2000).

Summers, Karen and Angelique von Halle. "From the Classroom to the Staff Room: Helping Staff Model Prosocial Behaviors," *Committee for Children Prevention Update* (spring 1999): 6–7.

Sunbeck, Deborah. *Infinity Walk*. Torrance, Calif.: Jalmar Press, 1996.

Sylwester, Robert. "How Emotions Affect Learning," *Educational Leadership*, vol. 52, no. 2 (October 1994). Available ASCD Web site, [Internet, WWW], Address: *http://www. www.ascd.org/pdi/brain/read4_2.html.*

———. "How Our Brain Determines What's Important," *A Celebration of Neurons* (chapter 4). Available: ASCD Web site, [Internet, WWW], Address: *http://www.ascd.org/ pdi/brain/read4_1.html.*

Tanner, Lindsey. "Psychiatric Drug Use Up for Children," *Albuquerque Journal* (28 February 2000)

———. "Reducing TV Lowers Aggression in Kids," *Albuquerque Journal* (15 January 2001).

Thornton, Claire. "Needed: Responsive Teachers," *Momentum*, vol. 29, no. 2 (April/May 1998): 77–79.

Toffler, Alvin. *The Third Wave*. New York: William Morrow & Co., Inc., 1980.

Tomlinson, Carol Ann. *The Differentiated Classroom: Responding to the Needs of All Learners*. Alexandria, Va.: Association for Supervision and Curriculum Development, 1999.

Valiant, Robert. "Growing Brain Connections: A Modest Proposal," *Schools in the Middle*, vol. 7, no. 4 (March/April 1998).

Waddell, Debby and Alex Thomas. "Disaster: Helping Children Cope," *Communiqué*, Newsletter of the National Association of School Psychologists, special edition (spring 1999): 12–15.

Waldman, Jackie. *Teens with the Courage to Give*. Berkeley, Calif.: Conari Press, 2000.

Walker, Dean. "School Violence Prevention," *ERIC Digest*, no. 94 (March 1995). Available: ERIC Web site, U.S. Department of Education, [Internet, WWW], Address: *http://www.ed.gov/databases/ERIC_Digests/ed379786.html.*

Wallach, Lorraine B. "Violence and Young Children's Development," *ERIC Digest* (June 1994). Available: ERIC Web site, U.S. Department of Education, [Internet, WWW], Address: *http://www.ed.gov/databases/ERIC_Digests/ed369578.html.*

Wardle, Francis. "Children of Mixed Race—No Longer Invisible," *Educational Leadership*, vol. 57, no. 4 (December 1999/January 2000): 68–71.

Wegscheider-Cruse, Sharon. *Choicemaking*. Deerfield Beach, Fla.: Health Communications, Inc., 1985.

Welbes, John. "Men Are Rare in Elementary Classrooms," *St. Paul Pioneer Press* (27 May 2000).

Wesley, Donald C. "Believing in our Students," *Educational Leadership*, vol. 56, no. 4 (December 1998/January 1999): 42–45.

Wheatley, Margaret J. *Leadership and the New Science*. San Francisco: Berrett-Koehler Publishers, Inc., 1994.

White, Noel, Tina Blythe and Howard Gardner. "Multiple Intelligence Theory: Creating the Thoughtful Classroom," in *Multiple Intelligence: A Collection*, Fogarty, Robin and James Bellanca, eds. Arlington Heights: IRI/SkyLight Training and Publishing, Inc., 1995.

Whitfield, Charles L. *Healing the Child Within*. Deerfield Beach, Fla.: Health Communications, Inc., 1987.

Williams, Linda Verlee. *Teaching for the Two-Sided Mind: A Guide to Right Brain/Left Brain Education*. New York: Simon & Schuster, 1983.

Williams, Mary Sue, and Sherry Shellenberger. *How Does Your Engine Run?* Albuquerque, N.Mex.: TherapyWorks, Inc., 1996.

Williams, Wendy M. "Preventing Violence in School: What Can Principals Do?" *NASSP Bulletin* (December 1998). Available: National Association of Secondary School

Principals Web site, [Internet, WWW], Address: *http://nassp.org/publications/bulletin/dec98bul.htm.*
Wilson, Jim. "Caution: Brain Work Ahead," *Popular Mechanics.* vol. 177, no. 3 (March 2000): 72–75,133.
Winfield, Linda. "Developing Resilience in Urban Youth," *NCREL Monograph* (1994). Available: *NCREL* (North Central Regional Educational Laboratory, Oak Brook, IL) Web site, [Internet, WWW], Address: *http://www.ncrel.org/sdrs/areas/issues/educatrs/leadrshp/leOwin.htm.*
Wise, B.J. "'Vaccinating' Children Against Violence," *Principal,* vol. 79, no. 1 (September 1999): 14–20.
Wright, Esther. *The Heart and Wisdom of Teaching.* San Francisco: Teaching from the Heart, 1997.
———. *Why I Teach.* Rocklin, Calif.: Prima Publishing, 1999.
X, Malcolm (as told to Alex Haley). *The Autobiography of Malcolm X.* New York: Ballantine Books, 1964.
Zand, Janet. "Hyperactivity," excerpted from *Smart Medicine for a Healthier Child* (1994). Available: *Health World* Web site, [Internet, WWW], Address: *http://healthy.net/asp/templates/article.asp?PageType=article&ID=1589.*
Zielbauer, Paul. "Discipline Figures Prompt Call to Improve School Behavior" (7 July 2000). Available: *The New York Times* Web site, [Internet, WWW], Address: *http://www.nytimes.com/library/national/regional/070700ct-students-edu.html.*

Index

A

B

C

D

F

G

S

U

About the Author

Jane Bluestein, Ph.D., is a dynamic and entertaining speaker who has worked with thousands of educators, counselors, health-care professionals, parents, child-care workers and other community members worldwide. She specializes in programs and resources geared to provide practical and meaningful information, training and hope in areas related to relationship building, effective instruction and guidance, and personal development. She is a former classroom teacher, crisis-intervention counselor and teacher-training program coordinator, and is the award-winning author of *21st Century Discipline; Being a Successful Teacher; Parents in a Pressure Cooker; Parents, Teens and Boundaries; The Parent's Little Book of Lists: DOs and DON'Ts of Effective Parenting; Mentors, Masters and Mrs. MacGregor: Stories of Teachers Making a Difference;* and *Daily Riches: A Journal of Gratitude and Awareness.* She heads Instructional Support Services, Inc., a consulting and resource firm in Albuquerque, New Mexico.

To contact Dr. Bluestein:

Jane Bluestein, Ph.D.
President
Instructional Support Services, Inc.
1925 Juan Tabo N.E., Suite B-249
Albuquerque, New Mexico 87112
phone: 505-323-9044 or 800-688-1960
fax: 505-323-9045
e-mail: *jblue@janebluestein.com*
Web site: *www.janebluestein.com*

From the Author

This award-winning collection of inspiring stories pays tribute to teachers, mentors and other special people who have made a positive and profound impact on our lives.

Code #3375 • Paperback • $11.95
Code #3367 • Hardcover • $22.00

Author Jane Bluestein looks at 20 aspects of boundary setting and clearly explains when to set boundaries and how to express and maintain them.

Code #2794 • Paperback • $8.95

More from Jane Bluestein, Ph.D.

Code #5122 • Paperback • $10.95

The Parent's Little Book of Lists is a handy reference with practical, kid-tested ideas to help parents deal with everything from monsters in the closet to unsolicited criticism of parenting abilities.

For a complete listing or to order direct: Telephone (800) 441-5569 • Online www.hcibooks.com
Prices do not include shipping and handling. Your response code is BKS.